THE
MIDNIGHT
SKEDADDLE

TIMOTHY THOMPSON

For all of those special people who have stood
by my side throughout the challenges in my life.

CONTENTS

CHAPTER 1

LOVE OUR COLTS

They rummaged through the pantheon: Johnny U, Lenny Moore, Raymond Berry, John Mackey, Don Shinnick, Bobby Boyd, et al. Colts demigods. The mission—select a hero, pay worship. And while his buddies perused the usual suspects, the 10-year-old bucked the crowd: He went with Jimmy Orr. Jersey #28. Steady, crafty, cagey; #8 all-time in yards per catch (19.8), C-clamps for hands; no stick'um, no gloves, no drops while safeties committed felonious assault. Little Timmy put Jimmy up on his pedestal. Christmas morning, 1965; the lad squints at the 8mm home movie floodlights, proudly holding aloft two gems: a Hutch facsimile Baltimore Colts jersey and helmet and an autographed photo of Orr. Mom had sewn two pairs of felt 2s and 8s on the jersey, front and back. Orr had inscribed "To Tim, Jim Orr" on the hokey, posed promo photo. The trifecta—quite a Christmas haul.

A month earlier, November '65, his dad—a lucky season-ticket-holder along with Mom—somehow scored two ducats, endzone temp seats in the open end of the horseshoe, where most of the Cro-Magnons sat slugging Jim Beam minis. A birthday present for the kid, his first trip to the World's Largest Outdoor Insane Asylum. Dad had passed up his regular comfy seat in Section 13 to sit with the birthday boy in endzone purgatory. Such is a father's love.

Billy Wilder cooked up the script for Colts-Eagles that day. In the first half, Orr ran a fly pattern down the right sideline, hounded by Al Nelson. Unitas gave it a heave, Orr looked skyward at the goal line and lunged in vain as Nelson dropped down on him like a Steinway pushed off a balcony. Orr came up hobbled, his right arm a limp wet noodle. Doubtful that 25cc of cortisone and KT tape could bring him back.

But Orr came back—and then some: The Baltimore *Evening Sun* picks up the action:

> When Orr left the arena clutching his right shoulder and blood dripping from his hand before the first half ended, with

the score knotted at 17-17, thousands figured they were seeing the last of him for the day. Many, the Colts' medical corps included, feared he could be out for the season. Jimmy was rushed to Union Memorial Hospital where X-rays on his shoulder proved negative. He hustled back to the Stadium, had his badly cut hand taped, pulled on his armor and headed back to the field, where the Hosses had managed to gain a slim 27-24 edge. Greeted by a tremendous ovation and a signal from Shula, Orr raced directly to the huddle. Unitas and Lenny Moore team up on a 47-yard gainer, then Johnny U. unleashed one to Orr, which Jimmy took on the run with defender Al Nelson clinging to his shoulder, THAT shoulder, which harbored pain diagnosed as of a pointer variety. Having shot down the Eagles, Orr retired again, with his arm hanging limply at his side.

Jimmy caught the ball in "Orrsville"—a patch of cinders, right corner of the endzone at the stadium's closed end, smack dab against the Orioles dugout. The kid sang to his mates the next day like Homer with Achilles. Headlines confirmed the heroics: **Orr Injured, Hospitalized for X-Rays and Returns to Catch Touchdown Pass from Unitas to Wrap Up Victory.** Orr had hoofed it down the street to Union Memorial, got his bum wing examined in the ER, threw his jersey on and headed back to work. Unitas found him in Orrsville. The

epilogue: Dad let Junior stay up past his bedtime on Monday—a school night—to catch the guest on the local TV show, *Corralin' the Colts*: Jimmy Orr.

Sometimes, the tumblers click into place. Love is a many-splendored thing.

. . .

Tom Matte, an old-school grind-it-out for the Baltimore Colts, used to snicker when folks claimed that the Dallas Cowboys were "America's Team." *Pshaw*. Matte said the Colts had an army of fans all over the country, groupies everywhere, and some PR hack down in Irving, TX, wouldn't change that. Ernie Accorsi, who eventually became the Colts PR director, then general manager, headed out the door in 1984 during the Bob Irsay Slapstick Hour, moving on to turn the Cleveland Browns and New York Giants into winners. He grew up in Hershey, PA: Eagles' territory, went against the grain and fell in love with the Colts:

I grew up in Hershey, PA. From 1951 to 1967, the Eagles trained there. They lived in the town, so you saw them all the time. In my teens, I never rooted for the local teams. I was kinda a Rams fan; they trained there one September. But in '53, my dad took me to a game in Baltimore against the Rams. We sat in the upper deck, but there was still construction going on [at Memorial Stadium]. The announcer said, "The people in the upper deck—because of the fog, if you can't see the field, you can move down to the lower deck." That's how small the crowd was. Except for '59, all the way through '65 or '66, they [the Colts] opened the preseason in Hershey against the Eagles. I didn't like the Eagles. When they beat the Eagles, 10-0, I was hooked. And I just became a Colts fan. Hershey's not that far from Baltimore. Then in '55, they have this great draft. [Alan] Ameche runs for a touchdown the first time he touches the ball. So, here they come [to Hershey], in '56. I paid my $2.50, and I'm sitting there, and Weeb [Ewbank] takes [QB George] Shaw out after one quarter. I'm 14 years old, and I'm screaming at the bench, "Why you takin' him out?!" So, Unitas comes in. I've never heard of him in my life. The guy sitting beside me, he's from Baltimore, and he says, "Will you calm down, kid? This guy threw seven touchdown passes Tuesday night in an intrasquad game—four for one team, three for the other." Well, I saw his first touchdown pass; it became love for that Colts uniform. The Colts win, and the rest is history.

Anyone boning up on the evolution of the NFL can pick the brain of Upton Bell. His daddy was Bert Bell Sr., the NFL commissioner from 1946-1959, who ran the show when the league got bigger britches and started challenging baseball as top dog. Upton Bell did OK for himself: He worked his way up the totem to become the Colts

director of player personnel for five years until he got the Patriots GM job in 1971. It was his idea to change Boston to *New England* Patriots. He's a cornucopia of NFL tidbits. The title of his autobiography hints at his grizzled career—*Present at the Creation*. Few have lived a suitcase life in NFL society like Upton Bell. Back then, Baltimore was the NFL sweet spot:

I've always believed that certain things are a state of mind. And if you ask me to describe what was football's Camelot, I would say it was Baltimore. It was almost the perfect place. Yes, you had the New York football Giants and the [1958] sudden-death game, and the Giants defense being on the front pages of the *New York Times*. But I always said Baltimore was the Camelot of football because it was between New York, Philadelphia and Washington. In some ways, it was the town that nobody cared about. Yet, that combination of the blue-collar worker and football was unique. Even though, later on, people like Johnny Unitas, Gino Marchetti, Lenny Moore, big Jim Parker and all those guys became mythical characters, the working class of Baltimore saw them as *their* working-class partners. There was a relationship there that I've never seen before. There was something about pro football that brought out, not the rich, but the working class of America. Baltimore had that feel that I recognized immediately when I came from Philadelphia and started working in the ticket office. I lived in a neighborhood near Memorial Stadium. And Baltimore was truly a collection of neighborhoods. People who lived in Towson and the suburbs—even though they came to the games and sat in the mezzanine—that wasn't the Colts. The Colts were working-class, we-love-you-Baltimore. Yes, there were times when there was a separation between the African-American and white communities; but never, as they say, on Sunday.

Before Kevin Cowherd left the newsroom to churn out entertaining books—six fictional baseball tales for youngsters (with Cal Ripken along for the ride), a half-dozen non-fiction books and a novel titled *The Gym*—he wrote a column for the Baltimore *Evening Sun*. Showed up in Baltimore in 1981 and caught Bob Irsay's act. The Charm City provincials impressed him. "I think it [the love affair with the Colts] all goes back to that '58 championship game [Colts 23, Giants 17, sudden death]," Cowherd observed. "I sensed that when I got here. Football was king. The Orioles were right behind them, but this was a football town. They were football fans, first and foremost. But I always thought the Colts had a special place in their hearts."

When the bird carrying the Colts touched down at Friendship Airport after the '58 title game in New York, the scene was like the last transport out of Saigon in 1975. A hurly-burly, Baltimoreans cutting loose after decades of putdowns by Philly and the Big

Apple. Former Baltimore *Morning Sun* columnist Michael Olesker paid homage to the occasion 65 years later for jmoreliving.com:

At a place we once called Friendship Airport [now BWI], the Colts' plane was scheduled to land at 7:50 that evening [December 28, 1958]. By 6 o'clock, more than a thousand fans were there, waiting for their team. The original thousand became 10,000, and then 20,000, which became 30,000. They were splayed all over the airport, as if waiting to cradle the incoming plane. When the airport garages overflowed and the long road into the airport backed up, people parked their cars along the highway and walked the rest of the way. In the next day's *News-Post*, reporter Alexander Gifford wrote, "It was a mob, a happy bunch of semi-lunatics carrying signs, carrying babies, and some of them just carrying on." The thousands who were there that night were joined by thousands more watching it on live television. They saw fans climbing onto the roofs of two Colts buses. They saw a love affair in its grandest hour.

Former Colts center Bill Curry was a wee lad in '58, but he did play in two Super Bowls for the Baltimore Colts and worked in the loony bin called Memorial Stadium for five seasons; he also logged a couple of years with Lombardi up in Green Bay. And he seconded Upton Bell—Baltimore worshipped the Colts. "It was a love affair," Curry remembered. "It didn't matter if the guy was a polished businessman from downtown with his beautiful wife by his side or if he was a Dundalk dockworker sitting next to him, buying beers. Same deal. Or a construction guy. It didn't matter. The love just flowed. And it was different from Green Bay. I was in both places. At Green Bay, I was just a kid; I was playing special teams, and I wasn't really part of the cadre that was adored by the public. Although everybody was courteous and nice—it was lovely. But it was not the same in the stadium."

After they wooed Irsay out of Baltimore, Indianapolis finally came out with a two-part documentary about the franchise, *Colts: The Complete History*. Part One covered the Baltimore years, 1953-1983. It unleashed Hall of Famer Art Donovan spinning anecdotes. Once Donovan left the Bronx and eventually wound up in Baltimore, Fatso spent the rest of his life there playing local hero. "It [Baltimore] was a blue-collar town, you know," Donovan stated in *The Complete History*. "Everybody liked to mingle with the football players. We were the king of the hill. Many and many a time, [teammate] Ordell Braase and I talk about this, and we say, 'You know how lucky we are that we played in Baltimore?' 'Cause if we had played in some other city, we'd all be gone—except maybe Detroit, some place like that. Here, we're still big fish in a small pond. And if anybody ever tells you they don't like to be recognized, they're either a goddam liar or a fool. Period. That's the way I look at it."

The Sports Legends Museum downtown was a curiosity before it got shuttered, a nice bookend to go with the Babe Ruth Museum nearby. Mike Gibbons was the former executive director of both. "The Colts were almost a religion," Gibbons remarked in Barry Levinson's 30-for-30 documentary, *The Band That Wouldn't Die*. "Every Sunday [a Colts game] was like going to church for a lot of Baltimoreans. And I think that we really did come to worship at the altar of Johnny Unitas. And I think that the further we got more involved, the further we went along with that, the more fanatical we became."

Baltimore's love for the horseshoe fascinated NFL professor Upton Bell. He explored that bond in his autobiography, *Present at the Creation*:

There has never been a relationship between a town and a team quite like the one between Baltimore and the Colts. I didn't know that until I got there in the late summer of 1961, but it didn't take long to understand the difference. There are certainly cities that love their teams, especially when they're winning, but there's a difference between a city and a *town* [emphasis mine], and the latter is what Baltimore was when the Colts were in their glory days. Not only was it a town that was nothing like Philadelphia, it was a town with an inferiority complex … which made it even less like Philadelphia. Trapped along the Northeast corridor between Boston, New York, Philadelphia and Washington, D.C., Baltimore was like a little brother always looking for attention but seldom receiving it until the Colts began to dominate pro football.

The 85-cent phone call to Pittsburgh that nabbed Johnny Unitas was what started it. And even Johnny U, who claimed he only got sentimental over kids and puppies, was struck by this nexus. "There was something special here; it was the closeness between players and fans," Unitas affirmed in a 1996 article in the *Los Angeles Times*. "The people went out and sold 25,000 [season] tickets to get the Colts in the first place. There were Colt Corrals, social clubs, set up to help promote the team. There was nothing but sellouts. On a Sunday when the Colts were in town, you could shoot a cannon down the middle of Baltimore Street and not hit anyone because they were either at the game or inside, listening to it."

For 10 years, the sergeant-at-arms and chief headhunter on defense was middle linebacker Mike Curtis—Mad Dog. So far, he's been jobbed out of the Hall of Fame. Ordinarily, he locked his feelings in a strong box, but Baltimore was different. Writer Michael Olesker wrote a piece for jmoreliving.com right after Curtis died in 2020 (Hey, Goodell, the autopsy: CTE). Olesker recollected a chat he had with Curtis a few years back. "We were talking one night in some neighborhood bar,

in the wilderness years after the Colts had been stolen away, when Curtis started reminiscing about the fans here who turned that team into a kind of secular religion," Olesker wrote. "'We were connected at the hip with these people,' he said. The muscles in his jaw clenched, but his tone had an unaccustomed tenderness. 'It felt like we were attached to this town at our very core. You understand what I'm saying? It felt like we were attached at our souls.'"

Tom Matte was the lunch-pail halfback for the Colts for a decade, and like many of the old Colts, stuck around in Baltimore for good after he retired. Lions defensive lineman Alex Karras pinned a nickname on him—Garbage Can—because Matte was a bruiser. Matte always marveled at the good vibes the Colts had in Baltimore. "The thing that I always look back on is the tradition that we had here, the tradition of winning, the camaraderie among the ballplayers and the fans," he remarked in a WMAR-TV special about the Colts' move to Indy in 1984, *The Long Goodbye*. "And this was the greatest love affair, I'm tellin' you. We [Colts players] used to go to those Colt Corrals, and we saw [superfan] Loudy [Loudenslager] out there. We'd go to those bars, have a couple beers with the people, sit down and talk football to 'em. We didn't expect anything back. The only thing we wanted them to do is fill that stadium because we had the craziest fans in the world. They were the most loving; they were the most dedicated. Other teams *hated* to come in here because our fans were so great.

Let me tell ya, if the people think the fans don't affect the ballgame, they're crazy. We'd hear it on the field. We'd get pumped up on that field when the fans went crazy. And we've lost that love affair."

That, we'll get to down the road.

. . .

An average NFL salary these days rivals the GDP of Liechtenstein, but back in the 1960s, the average was about $9,000 to $25,000, enough to put you in a tidy rowhome somewhere in town. Ballplayers couldn't spend off-seasons pumping iron in the weight room and playing in pro-am golf tournaments. They needed some green to tide them over until training camp in July. One year, Johnny Unitas spent a summer running a screed over wet concrete for a local cement company. The Golden Arm—working construction to help pay the bills. Take another Hall of Famer, Gino Marchetti. Before he found paydirt in fast-food burgers, Gino was a blue-collar guy, off-season. "My off-season occupation goes from working in a factory; I was a bartender," Marchetti recalled in the Indy Colts documentary, *Colts: The Complete History, 1953-1983*. "I worked at Sparrows Point [for Beth Steel] as an ironworker, and I set bowling pins one year at my cousin's bowling alley."

The Colts players weren't the only BMOCs in town during the '50s, '60s and '70s. No fan came close to Hurst "Loudy" Loudenslager for sheer mania, but Len Burrier was onstage every home game at Memorial Stadium, whipping up the crowd from the upper deck, first-base side, spelling out C-O-L-T-S with all four limbs. Popular sportswriter John Steadman came up with a nickname for Burrier: The Big Wheel. That's how folks knew him around town:

A lot of fans liked it [the C-O-L-T-S cheer] because they didn't have anything like that [at least not in the upper deck]. I had a friend who lived right next to the stadium, and he says, "I can't believe it. It's usually quiet here on Sundays until they have a football game. Now I can't even hear the television, it's so loud up there." People would encourage me to do the cheer. When I went to a bar, they said, "Hey, get on *this* bus. Go down there [to the game] on our bus." Then, I'd do the cheer on the bus, of course, while having a couple brewskis. When you'd go through the [Memorial Stadium] concourse on the ground level, you'd have to walk up the ramp to get to the upper deck. Walkin' up there, I felt like I was running for office: "Hey, Wheel! How you doin'?" That made me feel good.

Baltimore long played the half-pint while New York and Philadelphia loomed to the north and D.C. 30 minutes south. But it's always been a unique amalgam of quaint neighborhoods. Most Colts got tucked into those neighborhoods and became familiar faces. Take the aforementioned Jimmy Orr groupie—All-Pro safety Bobby Boyd lived in a semi-detached up the block. Sensing that the wound was still raw years after the Colts left Baltimore, Troy Lowman produced a documentary, *The Ghosts of 33rd Street*, to help folks get some closure and move on. The old Colts were just regular guys with extraordinary talents. "When they came to town," Lowman reminisced, "even more than the Orioles, the city had a love for the Colts that made them part of the community. Back then, the players didn't have real big salaries, so you would see these guys in bars and restaurants. They opened up their own businesses—car dealerships, bars, restaurants—so you saw them around town. They were part of the community, all year 'round. Not like today. You would see Unitas, Matte, Lenny Moore and the rest of them around town. They were just like your neighbors or your friends. So, on a Sunday, you went out and cheered for your friends."

His dad was a feisty conservative radio talk-show host for WCBM who also did Orioles games on the radio for eight seasons, so his son, Tom Marr IV, had a great view of Baltimore sports from the sofa as he grew up. His house was only two blocks removed from Memorial Stadium. Marr's a reservoir of factoids about the old Colts. "The Colts were a neighborhood team, full of neighborhood guys," he recalled. "The Colts trained at Memorial Stadium; that's where they had their practices. After practice, they would go into that community. A couple of them owned bars on Greenmount Avenue [a stone's-throw away], and a couple of them lived in places like Northwood and Waverly. They were

ingrained in the community. And because they needed jobs in the off-season, a lot of these guys owned liquor stores and insurance companies. They would play basketball at schools and against fraternal organizations like the VFW. These guys were your neighbors. They didn't live in giant mansions in gated communities. They lived next door to you."

Colts owner Carroll Rosenbloom promised Bert Bell Sr.'s widow that he would take care of her two boys, Bert Jr. and Upton. He brought Upton Bell in on the ground floor, and he quickly took the elevator up. Bell lived in a rowhome within spitting distance of Memorial Stadium. "Everyone loved the Colts because nearly everyone knew a Colt," Bell mused in his autobiography, *Present at the Creation*. "The players weren't royalty, like the Giants were becoming in New York and the whole league would become in a couple of decades. They lived in the same neighborhoods as their fans and many had second jobs because pro football wasn't yet a full-time occupation for everyone involved. Unitas once wielded both a football and an acetylene torch with equal flair, and the fans loved him for it, although it would be the former that made him one of those rarest of celebrities. All you had to say was 'Unitas' and everyone knew who you were talking about."

They were big shots in Baltimore, but the Colts never looked down their noses at the commoners, bellying up to the local bar after practice or tossing the pigskin around with neighborhood urchins. A perfect fit for a hardscrabble town. "The Colts quite literally owned the town, and their players were among the first to use their names to score points in business," intoned the narrator of *Colts: The Complete History, 1953-1983.* "The Colts of the late '50s were rich in star quality, yet they had a working-class humility that matched the blue-collar fabric of Baltimore. The players lived in the same rowhouse neighborhoods and drank at the same corner bars as the fans that cheered for them each Sunday."

An annual pilgrimage for Mom, Dad and the brood every summer was the 45-minute junket in the jalopy out to Western Maryland College, in Westminster, MD, to catch an afternoon with Shula and the Hosses at training camp. Informal and folksy—a chance to hobnob with and ogle the football gods. Nothing cordoned off, no cops with walkie-talkies shooing you away; a picnic basket, a Polaroid camera, an autograph pad and a lawn chair and you were good to go. William Gildea grew up in Baltimore during the glory days and published a memoir about that time, *When the Colts Belonged to Baltimore.* Those yearly treks out to Westminster were special meet-and-greets:

> During training camp at Western Maryland College [now McDaniel College] in Westminster, fans could engage the players easily on the campus pathways or as they trudged back from practice, carrying their helmets and shoulder pads. The field was set in a hollow, so the walk

back to the locker room entailed climbing a slope where many of the fans had sat watching practice. Hot and sweaty as they were, the players almost uniformly paused to sign autographs, and some would collapse on the grass to talk at length with perfect strangers who'd come to see them.

They've beaten the old cliché about Memorial Stadium to death over the years, i.e., the world's largest outdoor insane asylum, but the joint did rattle enemy nerves. The stadium was where the volk got to rub elbows. Steve Sabol devoted decades chronicling the gladiators for NFL Films. He took note of the cross-section of humanity on 33rd Street. "When I think about the Baltimore Colts fans," he remarked in *There Used to Be a Ballpark,* "that's what I remember: I remember a wonderful cross-section of blue-collar workers and corporate executives, young people, old people, all joined as one, cheering for the Colts and havin' a ball."

Most modern ballparks get squeezed between downtown concrete monoliths; Memorial Stadium sat in a real neighborhood—rowhouses next door and two high schools across the street. Enemy batters at the dish would have to squint at a curveball stuck against the white facades of the rowhouses beyond centerfield. The surrounding Waverly neighborhood was mute except when spectators converged at the park before kickoff, during the game when they bellowed and after the game as they shuffled to their cars.

Memorial was in a homespun locale—one of the reasons sticks-in-the-mud would later oppose a new stadium. Professor Charles C. Euchner taught writing at Harvard and Yale and poli-sci at Holy Cross. He also wrote an intriguing book about the tug of war cities have to woo sports teams, *Playing the Field: Why Sports Teams Move and Cities Fight to Keep Them*. He pulled out some fond memories over the phone of his days as a student at Johns Hopkins, only a holler away from Memorial Stadium:

> When I was in Baltimore in graduate school, we used to walk down 33rd Street, past Memorial Stadium, and we would listen to the radios on all of the porches as we walked by there. Even if those people on the porches didn't go to a single game all year, they were still a part of it. That's one of the great powers of sport—it's like having somebody to keep company with throughout the years. I remember when [legendary Dodgers broadcaster] Vin Scully retired, I decided to get the MLB TV network because I just wanted to listen to Vin Scully before I couldn't hear his voice anymore. And I'm glad I did. It was such a treat to have that old, familiar voice in my life, one last time.

Those in Baltimore recall kicking back on a summer's night and listening to Chuck Thompson call a game like he was relaxing in a hammock.

Baltimoreans have one hangup they can't let go of: being the stepchild who gets the hand-me-downs from big brother. The Tanner Boyle syndrome—the flaxen-headed runt who threw down against the entire Yankees outfit in *Bad News Bears*. And winning NFL championships, Super Bowls and three World Series has put nary a dent in it. They still imagine New York and D.C. snickering behind their backs. Thus the animus and despair when they lost the Colts in '84. Snatching the Browns from Cleveland eased the pain. Former Baltimore *Evening Sun* columnist and author Kevin Cowherd noticed it after he unpacked his bags in 1981. "When I first got here, the sense of Baltimore having a chip on its shoulder was overwhelming. You could sense it everywhere. So, whenever they [Baltimore] knocked off a team from New York, Philly or D.C., no matter what the sport was, they rejoiced. There was a sense of being the underdog, this blue-collar mentality in Baltimore: 'We're hard workers; we roll up our sleeves; that's how we win. We don't do anything flashy; we're not gimmicky.' That all contributed to this underdog mentality. I sensed it right away."

Now retired and living in Seattle, Wayne Lynch worked at WMAR-TV in Baltimore during the Irsay era, first as a reporter and news anchor, then got bumped up to executive news producer and managing editor. Having immigrated to Baltimore from Columbus, Ohio, Lynch could analyze the town without the built-in hangups. Lynch labeled the town "provincial," the standard take on Baltimore. Technically, it refers to the regions—provinces—outside the big city. In reality, it's about ATTITUDE, i.e., "This is the way it's done here, pal." Lynch saw Baltimore's ingrained inferiority complex driving the ATTITUDE:

Baltimore is a little town nestled between New York and [Washington] D.C. and is trying not to be a fair-haired, red-headed stepchild. It was always sort of looked at as this wharf town, mob town, crab town, and there was an insecurity about it. And because there was no NBA or NHL franchise [the Bullets moved to D.C. in 1973], there were two teams, and they were much beloved. Although I will say there was disaffection with the fans because of Irsay, simply because he was trying to cheat on Baltimore. He was not faithful to Baltimore. And when you're unfaithful, you start looking for a new paramour. That alienated a lot of people. And because Baltimore is so provincial, they took it personally.

The whole town needed some sessions on the therapist's couch, a dynamite welterweight up against heavyweights New York and Philly. Which explains Baltimore spazzing out like V-E Day after the sudden-death win over the Giants in '58. Bruce Cunningham was the Baltimore Ravens PA announcer from 1999-2019, a guy who knows his hometown. "The Colts made Baltimore big-league," he stated in Troy Lowman's documentary about the Baltimore Colts, *The Ghosts of 33rd Street*. "They predated the Orioles. And I think there was an early identification from the very beginning. Because Baltimore's always had this giant chip on its shoulder. Always has, always will. And all of a sudden [after the '58 championship game], we're big-league too. We can look you in the eye, New York. I think that had a lot to do with the way we worshipped the Colts."

Baltimoreans sometimes annoy when they call a sink a "zink" and a spigot a "spicket" and tell you to turn the "warter" off. But this is also a town of grinders. West-Coast offenses and the Pistol ain't in their repertoire. That's why the no-frills, old-school Colts was a perfect fit. "The team was shaped and molded in the image of the town—gritty, blue-collar, no-nonsense, no flash. Just workmanlike," Baltimore Colts documentarian Troy Loman professed. "The team's mentality fit the town's image perfectly. You'd go to Memorial Stadium sometime in the late '50s, 1960s, and you were a visiting team, you were going into a lion's den. The Colts had 50,000 of their best friends watching them."

After he thumbed his nose at Irsay and the town in '83, John Elway got heckled like a Redcoat in Boston when he came to town his rookie season. The decibel level had him rattled for a half. Colts fans saw the kid as a surfer boy, a prima donna. Steve Rosenbloom was hip to the Baltimore mindset. Son of legendary Colts owner Carroll Rosenbloom and eventual president of the Colts until C.R. traded them, straight up, for the L.A. Rams, he had spent most of his young life in Baltimore, learning the ropes from his dad:

> I spent a lot of time out of town, getting my education. I was away at school outside of Baltimore [Georgetown University] for a couple of years, and everybody I knew there came from all over. They all had the same thinking: "Steve, why do you live in Baltimore?" But a lot of people got the image of Baltimore coming in on a train, looking out from either window. That just added to it. And a lot of people in Baltimore were frustrated by that image. Any major-league sports team—like the Orioles—when you get to that level, and they play in Baltimore, it was a big boost for the city: "Maybe there is something in Baltimore. Why would Carroll [Rosenbloom] put his team in Baltimore?" There were other cities all over the country. But he was from Baltimore; he was born there.

· · ·

Unleash 60,000 throats, cowbells and air horns in unison, visiting teams in Baltimore couldn't hear themselves think. This was Sunday-afternoon mass at Memorial Stadium. Hall of Famer Gino Marchetti always marveled at the pick-me-up he got when the PA man boomed out the names of Colts players during pregame intros as the cheers rained down. And the Colts fight song on the turntable always lights up old-timers. "I love football probably more than anything else," Gino told veteran broadcaster Vince Bagli for his book, *Sundays at 2:00 With the Baltimore Colts*. "To me, running on that field, hearing that Baltimore Colts song—greatest song in the NFL—gave me such a thrill. I heard it for 15 years; from the first day I heard it to the last, it jumped me up a little bit. Our team was close-knit, and we had a city that we loved. I'd come in and find a note in my locker: 'Appear at such and such a place Wednesday night at 7:30.' And you went. I really felt that by the time I ended my career in Baltimore, I had met every fan in that stadium, all 57,000 of them. We had become their college football team."

In an essay for a tribute to Memorial Stadium titled *House of Magic, 1922-1991: 70 Years of Thrills and Excitement on 33rd Street*, Baltimore sportswriter John Steadman described the tornado that whipped around the ballpark:

> On Sunday afternoons in autumn and winter you can still hear the echo. A gauntlet of musicians, attired in blue and white uniforms, the proud band of the Baltimore Colts, formed a human tunnel from the dugout to the goal line. Their team was about to be introduced. And then came the deafening roar, exploding from human throats, and reverberating around this massive arena made of concrete and mortar but filled more with heart and soul. The love affair with the Baltimore Colts was real.

Loud. Boisterous. Profound. The sound waves flowing from the seats in Memorial Stadium shocked the opposition and rattled windows in neighborhood houses. The Colts were soon to kick off. The noise never abated more than a decibel or two.

If the Colts won the toss, forget about deferring. Unitas would fasten his chinstrap after the kickoff and start piling up the acreage. The offense during the pregame rollcall often got top billing. Center Bill Curry was the first to run the gauntlet:

If we won the coin toss in those days, we always took the ball, which meant that the offensive unit would be introduced. As the center, I was the first one to be introduced to the crowd. We'd be warming up, then be called back into the locker room. The feelings built on the team. There was an expectation of what we were gonna receive from the crowd. I didn't think about any of this while I was going through it; I just reveled in it. Here we are, in the locker room, and Freddie Miller, our defensive captain, gives an impassioned, go-get-'em, knock-their-teeth-out kind of speech. Then, he turns to our offensive captain, who was always standing in the same place—John Unitas. He has the same posture: his legs are crossed, he's leaning against the door, and he's got a kind of quizzical expression on his face. Freddie

Miler would ask him, "Johnny, do you have anything to say?" The pep talk was always the same: "Talk's cheap. Let's go play." We marched down this long tunnel, through the dugout and onto the field, which we called "Astrodirt." You could just feel the intensity. And then the PA guy would say, "On offense, at center, #50, from Georgia Tech, Bill Curry." And I would run out to the 50-yard line to polite applause, peel over to our bench and set up the huddle. Eventually, you had 10 guys, huddled up. And then you'd hear, "And from the University of Louisville, #19 …" And that would be the last thing you could hear. The eruption was the loudest sound I have ever heard.

Former Baltimore *Morning Sun* columnist and author Michael Olesker was a citizen of Colts Nation. One of the lucky few, he and his family were regulars at Memorial Stadium during the glory days. It was a tent revival with Rev. Johnny U. "I went to the Colts games from the time I was in high school," Olesker recounted. "We had season tickets. So, it was the passion—if they lost, you were sick all week. I remember vividly Hyman Pressman, who was city comptroller. One week, the Bears were in town, and they were standing up instead of sitting on the bench. The people in the first couple of rows couldn't see over them. And Hyman Pressman jumped down onto the field and confronted [Bears head coach George] Halas, telling him to sit down. I mean, it was that kind of lunacy. We knew to hate [Green Bay Packers head coach Vince] Lombardi, to hate Halas."

Then, in one night in March 1984, POOF—the glory, the passion, the legacy, the legal papers, the helmets, shoulder pads, jocks, doo dads—got thrown into moving vans and split. At the end of the rainbow, 577 miles and 8 hrs. and 36 mins. by auto to the west, was Indianapolis. To the victor went the spoils; to the cuckold, a decade in the NFL wilderness. University professor and author of *Playing the Game: Why Sports Teams Move and Cities Fight to Keep Them*, Charles Euchner, found a parallel to Baltimore's long sojourn in purgatory:

> There was an event that took place this weekend [August 2024] that made me really sad. It made me think of *this* situation [a city's affection for its sports team]. This radio station in New York, 88 on your AM dial, WCBS, all-news format since 1967, went off the air, and they were replaced by ESPN. And for those of us who grew up in New York, it had an emotional hold. You drive around; you listen to the news; you get familiar with the same old voices; you look forward to hearing from them; you get to know their personalities. They're kind of invisible, and you don't know them personally, but you develop this bond with them that is kind of a slow burn. But it's still a burn. For the whole weekend, they [WCBS] did this historical perspective—WCBS, New York and the Tri-State area. And it was incredibly touching. So, yesterday, I turned on the car radio to listen to ESPN for the first time on that call station, and I just couldn't listen to it. It was loud, it was noisy, it was stupid. I knew I would miss that news-radio station, but I didn't know that I would miss it so soon or so intensely. And it's because it was like an old friend.

Same goes for Baltimore. The morning the town woke up and found out the Colts were gone, Colts flag station WCBM (AM) played glorious snippets from the era that Robert Irsay had just tossed in the dumpster.

CHAPTER 2

THE GODFATHER

Carroll Rosenbloom was a lot of things to a lot of people, but one thing he was to everybody was the guy who put oomph in Baltimore's ego. Any history of The Move is a cheap shortcut without covering the Carroll Rosenbloom era of the Baltimore Colts. No Rosenbloom, no Colts; ergo, no Unitas, no sudden death in '58, no Outdoor Insane Asylum, no wedding quiz in *Diner*, no guy from Skokie hauling ass to Indy. What remained would have been the O's, steamed crabs, duckpin bowling, minor-league hockey and creamed chipped beef.

The edifice on 33rd Street was always the political football for the two Colts owners and the city; it was Carroll Rosenbloom—not Robert Irsay—who uttered the first discouraging words about Memorial Stadium during a 1965 harangue, seven years before Irsay hit town. The gripes by Rosenbloom and Irsay about the Old Gray Lady on 33rd piled up over 19 years and drove both of them out of town.

. . .

A hater to be named later always insisted that the Baltimore Colts franchise dropped from the sky into Carroll Rosenbloom's lap. Not so. Baltimore had a team called the Colts in the old All-American Football Conference that folded in 1949. When the AAFC and the NFL merged in 1950, the Colts gave it a go and bombed. With creditors on his heels, Colts owner Abe Watner sold the whole caboodle—players, uniforms, the works—back to the league. Folks in Baltimore raised a stink, forcing NFL Commissioner Bert Bell Sr. to look around for a replacement—a bunch of misfits down in Dallas, the Texans. Bell figured, *There's my out. Those bums were 1-11 last season, playing their "home" games in Hershey and Akron, and Dallas wants no part of 'em. We need somebody with deep pockets to buy the team and send them up to Baltimore.* Aha! The perfect guy—the kid he coached at Penn. Carroll Rosenbloom. Made buku bucks selling shirts and overalls … and a *Baltimore* guy, to boot.

So, Bert Bell Sr. pitched the idea and finally got Carroll Rosenbloom to bite. C.R.

was a hard-sell; he wasn't keen on running a ballclub. But Bell swung him around, and Rosenbloom pulled $13,000 out of his money belt and became the principal owner of the Baltimore Colts. A 1962 feature article on Rosenbloom in the *Morning Sun* details how Bert Bell Sr. badgered C.R. until he gave in:

> "Mousetrapped" is the word Mr. Rosenbloom uses to describe how he got into the football act. Mr. Bell, then NFL commissioner, told him he was Baltimore's last hope for regaining a franchise. This was something of an exaggeration, but the former coach's [Bell's] persuasive powers won out. Against the advice of friends and associates, Mr. Rosenbloom agreed to buy a 51 per cent share of the club's stock. At his first meeting with the other owners in his home at 1 Slade Avenue, he appeared in shirtsleeves and spoke with matching informality. He stated at the outset he wanted a championship team, and in contrast to the aspirin-rationing [frugal days of the old club], promised anything that money could buy to get it. In a classic luncheon speech in November 1953, he said: "We promise no miracles. But whatever it takes in money and hard work, Baltimore will have a championship team."

They got that in a mere six years up in Yankee Stadium when Bob Wolff shouted, "Unitas gives to Ameche; the Colts are the World Champions! Ameche scores!" Rosenbloom got knocked around by a few dyspeptic sorts in the Baltimore press. Like most in gilded society, he had an XL ego and wouldn't tolerate being second-best. You produced for C.R., you got rewarded; you choked, you got the axe. *Sports Illustrated* ran a big feature story on Rosenbloom in December 1965 titled *The Pleasure of Dying on Sunday*:

> As far as Rosenbloom is concerned, the greatest investment he ever made was buying the Colt franchise. Originally, he resisted. He was a football fan, but he had no desire to take over a team in Baltimore, where fans had a brief but bitter memory of once having had a club in the NFL [1950]. However, Rosenbloom's former backfield coach at Penn, Bert Bell, who was by then commissioner of the NFL, hounded him. Bell, who also happened to be a summer neighbor on the Jersey shore, issued veiled announcements to the press that Rosenbloom would take over in Baltimore. Finally, Rosenbloom relented. When he moved in at Baltimore, he asked the fans, who can be vociferous, to give him five years to produce a winner. It took him six.

For numbers crunchers, here is how Carroll Rosenbloom stacks up against other legendary NFL owners. Patriots owner Robert Kraft, who rode on the Brady-Belichick gravy train for two decades: 324-176, a 64.8 win/loss %; Jerry Jones of the faux "America's Team," the Cowboys: 319-261, 58%; Al

Davis of the Raiders, the guy who forced the green light for team moves: 409-310, 56%; and Carroll Rosenbloom, who turned the Colts and the L.A. Rams into winners: 226-116, 66%--better than the big names who preceded him. Subtract his first five years in Baltimore while they stockpiled the ordnance and the Colts went 136-54-5, a 71.5 win/loss percentage, best in the NFL from 1958-1971. Rosenbloom spun straw into gold.

There was no silver spoon in Rosenbloom's mouth. His father, a Polish Jew, made good money manufacturing work clothes, but the house was bursting at the seams with nine kids. Later on, when he was flush with cash, C.R. worked on Baltimore's self-esteem with that ballclub of his. What he eventually got for that up-by-the-bootstraps crusade was the raspberry from fans and cheap digs from reporters. All I did was win, he used to say, and this is the thanks I get.

JJ Stankevitz is the team writer for the Indianapolis Colts on Colts.com. He also produced a commendable four-episode podcast on Bob Irsay's skedaddle called "The Move." While doing his homework, Stankevitz came to appreciate Carroll Rosenbloom's impact on Baltimore:

> What I came to understand about it was that by creating the Colts, he [Rosenbloom] gave Baltimore something not just to be proud of, but to measure itself against New York, Boston, Philadelphia or these other big East-Coast cities that had the Yankees, the Red Sox, the [football] Giants, the Eagles and these big teams that were already established. But Baltimore, being a city without a professional sports team, kind of needed something like that. When Rosenbloom took the Dallas Texans and made them the Colts and built them with Johnny Unitas and these other superstars— Lenny Moore, Alan Ameche, Artie Donovan and those guys—it gave Baltimore something to be really proud of, in a way that the city had never had before. And that created these deep bonds between residents and the Colts that were so important to the fabric of the city and for civic pride.

Rosenbloom took a hammer and chisel and created the Colts' culture. Don't dare screw up, but business-casual is OK. Successful. Friendly. Classy. Respectable. "There was a kind of Colt Way, sort of like a 'Patriot Way.' You had to be upstanding; you had to be a team player; you had to be diligent and honest," reflected Troy Lowman, producer of an excellent Baltimore Colts retrospective, *The Ghosts of 33rd Street*. "What Rosenbloom did was he assembled the right people, and the leaders of the team drove that culture—[Johnny] Unitas, [Tom] Matte, Lenny Moore. They had a culture there. And more than doing anything else, Rosenbloom just set it up so that it could succeed. I call him the perfect CEO/owner. He put the coaches and players in place, gave them all the support they needed, cultivated a winning culture, involved the fans, and I think that's why everybody loved the Colts so much. He's a big part of the Colts' success, in my opinion."

He also wasn't a cardboard cutout, a rich stiff. He was always good copy for the local press. Former Colts personnel director, New England Patriots GM and NFL aficionado Upton Bell remembered seeing Rosenbloom at the 1960 College All-Star Game in Chicago [Colts vs. College Stars]. "I saw Carroll at the walk-through at Soldier Field the night before the game," Bell explained in his autobiography, *Present at the Creation*. "He showed up with a couple of knockout women. I looked at him and started thinking this wasn't [Steelers owner Art] Rooney or [N.Y. Giants] Wellington Mara's NFL anymore. This was a colorful, interesting man surrounded by celebrities and beautiful women. There was nobody like Rosenbloom then. He was so smooth. The world was changing from black and white to color, and so was the world of pro football."

Rosenbloom didn't march to a different drummer; he WAS the drummer. "He has never tried to run the Colts the way he would a business and says there is no similarity between the two," the *Morning Sun* observed in a feature on C.R. in October 1962. "Nor has he run it the way most other professional football teams are run. In the beginning, he told the fans of Baltimore that this was their team, and he promised them a championship if they would support it. He told team members at his first meeting with them that if the club did well, they would do well and share in the rewards. He made good on both counts."

Rosenbloom didn't give you pump fakes and empty talk; you knew where you stood with the guy. Can-do people got bonuses; those who flunked out or did him dirty got farmed out. And nothing tickled him more than when his ballplayers came through. In December 1965, Rosenbloom talked to *Sports Illustrated* for a piece titled *The Pleasure of Dying on Sunday*. "After the first year in football, I found that of all the things I've ever done, this is the thing," Rosenbloom told the reporter. "There is nothing more rewarding. You have everything wrapped up in one bundle. You meet much nicer people than you do in business. You meet the public, and you must learn to look out for them. There's no place where your word is more your bond than in sports. You'd never find 14 men who deal as fairly with one another as the 14 owners in the National Football League, particularly after some of the things that have gone on in business or on Wall Street. You play a part in the lives of young men, and you help them grow. And then every Sunday you have the great pleasure of dying."

A funny way to describe what Rosenbloom went through up in the press box during every game. The man was a chain-smoking wreck for three hours. And most of them were W's. "He [Rosenbloom] has always tried to surround himself with the best people he can find," began a paragraph in a 1962 article about C.R. in the *Morning Sun*, "and says, 'There's only one way I can run anything, and that's to have a high-class organization. As far as running the team itself, that's [head coach] Weeb Ewbank's business. We will discuss important matters and I may make suggestions, but in the final analysis, he decides who plays and who he keeps on the squad. A coach lives to win. Naturally, he's going to do the best he can.'" Ewbank won two NFL championships; the next to run the show was Don Shula, another Van Gogh that Rosenbloom spotted at a yard sale.

C.R. loved his players and vice versa. When Carroll Rosenbloom swapped the Colts for the Rams with Robert Irsay in July 1972, irate Baltimore fans ripped him like he was Benedict Arnold. Defenders stepped forward to shoot down the hecklers. Running back Tom Matte spent 11 years with Rosenbloom and was never shy about speaking his mind. He said this in the *Evening Sun* on July 11, 1972, right after the swap:

Most outspoken of these [Colts] is Tom Matte, the durable running back who has put in 11 solid years for the Colts. Going into what will probably be his final season as a pro, Matte feels Carroll Rosenbloom has been given a raw deal by Baltimore fans and critics. "The man deserves better than what he's getting from this town," Matte said yesterday. "I don't have one thing against the new owners [Irsay] at all and I'm sure they're very capable men, but you don't find men like Carroll Rosenbloom very often. People in Baltimore don't know what it's like to have a loser," Matte went on. "When was the last time the Colts

had a losing team? I think it was 1956, wasn't it? Fans don't realize what an integral part of a successful football team that management plays. We've always gone first-class on the Colts, and we've also had a team which had the potential to win a championship."

Right on all counts. Not about Irsay, whom he hadn't had the pleasure yet.

Center Bill Curry played in two Super Bowls during his five-year stint with the Colts in a long football career as player and college coach. He played for Lombardi and Shula and coached at Alabama, so he can spot royalty. Curry saw Rosenbloom as a hybrid, a combination benefactor/leg-breaker:

First of all, to me, how Rosenbloom did it was brilliant. He did what were, for him, little things, but what it meant to the team was huge. He had the capacity to make you feel as if he were doing this just for *you*. He didn't say that, but you had that sense. I had a small salary with the Green Bay Packers, and the first time I talked to him [Rosenbloom], he almost doubled it. I thought, *My gosh. How does this guy do business like this? This is wonderful.* That's for openers. He won the respect and the love of his players the old-fashioned way—he rewarded you. Now, when I got hurt during the exhibition season, he did the other part of Carroll Rosenbloom. People warned me, "Don't ever cross Carroll. If he loves you, he's gonna be great to you, but if you mess with him, and you dishonor the love he's given you, you're gonna regret it the rest of your life." When I got hurt, he walked over to my locker one day and made note of the fact that I wasn't playing, and it would be a real good idea if I got back on the field real soon. It wasn't tactful. As soon as I could, I got back on that field. It was a reward relationship, a message.

Colts (and later, Rams) employees from the boiler room up to the executive offices saw Rosenbloom as a benevolent despot. "Yes, Rosenbloom has a coliseum full of style," Thomas Boswell of the *Washington Post* wrote .in December 1978. "However, he also has an endearing, down-to-earth charm that those who oppose him never see. When Rosenbloom shows up at the Rams' practice every Thursday, he leaves a wake of smiles behind him. 'He's just an old dear,' said a young team secretary. 'Everybody loves C.R.' Of all the NFL bosses, Rosenbloom, who owned his hometown Baltimore Colts from 1953 to 1972 when he pulled his famous 'owners' swap with the Rams, is one of the most personally involved."

When Carroll Rosenbloom drowned in the ocean off the Florida coast in April 1979, testimonials came flying in. Sports columnist Ken Denlinger of the *Washington Post* served up one of many print eulogies:

The temptation is to call Carroll Rosenbloom the largest paradox who ever changed the face of sport. And he probably would not object, given his distaste for even being tied for first [like the infamous Colts-Rams dead heat in 1967]. If his Baltimore Colts did not create the "family" concept now so widely misused, they were the first to make it work. Of all the "manias," every town suddenly in love with a suddenly successful team, Coltsmania in the late '50s was the earliest. And yet Rosenbloom tried to strong-arm Baltimoreans into buying preseason tickets in order to renew regular-season tickets [more about that later]. Rosenbloom was lavish with his players, regularly assuring their orderly transition from football to business either with loans, gifts or credit. For years, his players enjoyed a unique NFL treat—a daily buffet lunch. And yet his Colts spawned the most active NFL union leaders, Ordell Braase, John Mackey and Bill Curry. He was enormously shrewd and enormously sentimental, a man who swapped franchises, even up, his Colts for the Los Angeles Rams in 1972, but who instead of firing a non-productive but loyal aide would find him a job somewhere else, often for more money or more authority.

The man with the supposedly gargantuan ego never tried to sponge credit from his troops. One of the few people on the planet who can claim employment with both the Baltimore Colts and the Baltimore Ravens is

John Ziemann. Currently the president of the Marching Ravens band, Ziemann joined up in 1962 as a percussionist and became a jack-of-all-trades with the Colts marching band and staved off extinction as "The Band That Wouldn't Die" when Irsay bolted out of Baltimore. "One thing I admired about Carroll," Ziemann explained, "he didn't step in and say, 'Look at me.' He let his team take the credit, his office take the credit. He made sure [GM] Don Kellett got the credit. He was there, but he was that man behind the curtain, and he was very proud. I just think it was a hurt for this man [to get blasted by some of the fans and press], and some of the fans went the wrong way. The average guy down at Bethlehem Steel, trying to grab every buck that he could to buy season tickets—all of a sudden, you're adding more to it? 'Hey, I got a family to support. I scrape all year to buy season tickets, and now you're adding more.' And this is what some reporters and politicians preyed on." The carpers didn't factor the pittance the Colts made from preseason crowds of a few thousand straggling in to chug Natty Bohs; and the Orioles had a lock on concession sales.

Rosenbloom could be a real shapeshifter. "He was a complex man," wrote famous *Los Angeles Times* sports columnist Jim Murray. "He had the fierce eyes of a Tartar on horseback, the pugnacious jaw of an Irish cop, and the build of a light-heavyweight prizefighter. He was a vain man. He would comb his thinning locks like a Julius Caesar. He was a 'Gimme the damn ball' halfback in football

and pitcher in baseball. He was aggressive. He loved contention. If there were two ways to do a thing, he chose the way with the most controversy. He was thick-skinned. Or pretended to be. He would seize on the most miniscule detrimental writing as a frontal attack, probably on the theory that massive retaliation for pinpricks would forestall a broadsword assault later."

Like most of us, Rosenbloom was a product of the times. He was in his early 20s when the Depression hit. Wise old salts advise not to be too hard on anyone who slogged through the Depression. "Rosenbloom is one of those men forged on the anvil of the Depression, who would be insulted to be called complex," Thomas Boswell of the *Post* explained in 1978. "He likes clean and simple goals; he looks for direct, comprehensible motives. 'I believe you should come out and say what the hell's on your mind. When you disagree with a man, don't just sit there and eat those differences. The kids today have a much better life just because they don't have so many restraints. I feel comfortable with young people because I can deal with anyone who will talk straight.'"

Come at Rosenbloom from an angle or play games with him, you got serious blowback. Rosenbloom fulfilled a promise to Bert Bell Sr.'s widow and ushered her two boys, Bert Jr. and Upton, into the Baltimore Colts family. Forever grateful, Upton Bell still couldn't get a handle on C.R.:

That's like asking, "Who was Citizen Kane?" Everybody in that movie had a different impression of Citizen Kane. I would say, when you think of Carroll Rosenbloom, think of Rosebud [Kane's sled in the movie]. In trying to explain him, and my relationship with him, Bert Bell stopped Carroll Rosenbloom when he and Marty Brill at Penn were being recruited to go to Notre Dame. Marty Brill went, and my father [Bert Bell Sr.] talked Carroll Rosenbloom into staying: "Listen, you're a local guy from this area—Baltimore—don't leave. Your future is here." So, Rosenbloom stayed. And when my father died [in 1959], the only person who offered me a job was Carroll Rosenbloom. So, when I look at him, I have to say, "Who the hell else [would hire me] but Carroll Rosenbloom, who remembered his great friendship with my father?" He's the only one who said, "Upton, come down here. You've got a job here." And that was true for both of the Bell boys. And so, I have strong feelings for a man who didn't forget.

. . .

It bears repeating that Carroll Rosenbloom was a Baltimore guy, never mind his scorn for Memorial Stadium. C.R. graduated from City College in 1927—when the school was at the corner of Howard and Centre Streets, downtown—moved on to Penn, studied psychology and business and was a two-year letterman at halfback (1927-1928). He got tight with Bert Bell Sr., his backfield coach. Their lives would collide again when NFL

Commissioner Bert Bell Sr. ran a full-court press on C.R. and talked him into dropping $13,000 on the Colts for a majority share. In between those bookend encounters with Bell, like his old man, Rosenbloom gave garment production a shot. As the *Morning Sun* chronicled in a feature on him in 1962, Rosenbloom used his smarts to make millions:

He had no special interests before college and no boyhood business ventures which might have foretold his eventual success in this field. He started to work for the Brill street car company after graduating, but was called home by his father who wanted his sons at least to try the family business. These were Depression years and times in business were tough, he says. His father put him to work cleaning lavatories in his Paca Street building at $3.50 a week. He did this for almost a year. "I had it easy in college," he says, "and this was quite a contrast." Then early in 1933, his father sent him to Roanoke [Va.] to shut down one of his plants where overalls were made [Blue Ridge Overalls]. After looking it over, the young man decided to buy it and try to put it on its feet. He borrowed some money from his mother and raised the rest in Virginia by loans. Over the years in which he ran the business, annual sales rose from $160,000 to $60,000,000.

Rosenbloom took a company barely in the black and turned it into a gold mine. Then he began investing his millions here and there, and the money piled up. The $13,000 that he forked over to buy into the Colts was loose change. The franchise was his alone when he bought out the minority owners for $250,000 and dropped $1.5 million into the teams' bank account. It was now call or fold. "That's how much I was willing to lose," Rosenbloom would later say.

. . .

These days, you can work your thumbs for 30 seconds on a cellphone and put money down with FanDuel on a jai alai match in Spain. But sports betting in the dark ages meant back alleys and greasy bookies and crossing your fingers nobody got busted. This much we know about Carroll Rosenbloom: the guy was hooked—golf tournament, boxing match, whiffleball, shuffleboard, you name it. If it had some action, C.R. was in. That stayed pretty much hush-hush until January 1963 when an NFL gambling scandal blew wide open.

An *Associated Press* story in the Baltimore *Morning Sun* dragged Rosenbloom out of the shadows: "Miami, Fla., Jan. 17 [1963] (*AP*)— The *Miami Herald* said today that the owner of the Baltimore Colts of the National Football League has been questioned about betting on his team, in the current NFL investigation of gambling rumors. The newspaper said owner Carroll Rosenbloom denied he bet. Rosenbloom's lawyer, Jerome Doyle of New York, told the *Herald* that the Colts' owner had been questioned about betting. 'Under oath, he denied it categorically,' Doyle said, according

to the *Herald*, emphasizing the denial covered 'any professional football games.'"

This one wasn't going under the rug. Unearthing solid evidence would cook him on the griddle. "Golden Boy" Paul Hornung of the Packers, the 1961 NFL MVP, and All-Pro defensive lineman Alex Karras of the Lions got slapped with one-year suspensions in 1963 for betting on NFL games and consorting with bookies, and Rosenbloom was now in the crosshairs. Two sets of incriminating loose lips were to blame. The *Morning Sun* provided details: "Miami, Fla., March 12 [1963] (*AP*)—A three-year-old deposition charging that Carroll D. Rosenbloom, owner of the Baltimore Colts, made a big bet against the Colts in a 1953 game was revealed in Federal Court today by Rosenbloom's own lawyer. The attorney, Jerome Doyle, of New York City, said the charge was a lie and was made for the sole purpose of assassinating Rosenbloom's reputation. The deposition, by Michael J. McLaney of Miami Beach, stated that he joined Rosenbloom in a $55,000 bet against the Colts in a game with the Pittsburgh Steelers. Doyle then told Judge George C. Young that the Colts did NOT [emphasis mine] play the Steelers in 1953."

The story smelled the closer you got. First off, given his chain-smoking freakouts in the press box, Carroll Rosenbloom would swallow strychnine before he bet on the Colts to go down. Number two, better get your facts straight before you take aim at Rosey. But a shady character from the numbers racket, Mike McLaney, took him on and was light on evidence. "Sam Benton, a Miami Beach private investigator, testified that he personally obtained information contained in the depositions and handed it over to [NFL Commissioner Pete] Rozelle during an investigation into alleged gambling activities in the league," the *Morning Sun* reported. So, McLaney was either legit or lying through his teeth.

C.R.'s solicitor sure earned his retainer. Defense turned to offense. A 1960 deposition by McLaney got pulled from the files to make Rosenbloom squirm. "In his opening statement, Doyle [Rosenbloom's lawyer] said that McLaney filed the 1960 suit 'to use as an umbrella under which he would attack the good name of Rosenbloom,'" the *Morning* Sun reported. "'Rosenbloom has had to fight this in silence,' Doyle said, 'but now he refuses to succumb and pay tribute.' They started out betting on golf matches, McLaney said, then branched out to pro football games, and Rosenbloom also bet on college football games. Speaking of the alleged bet on the 1953 game [Colts-49ers, when Rosenbloom supposedly bet against the Colts], McLaney said, 'Rosenbloom decided to leave several of his best players at home, but the Colts won the game and we lost the bet.' The Colts played the 49ers twice in 1953 and lost both games, 38-21 and 45-14. They did not play the Steelers" [another alleged bet in '53].

Sniffing around Mike McLaney's background, they discovered he operated a casino in Cuba, pre-Castro, probably hip-deep in the mob. Given his status, Rosenbloom getting within five miles of such scoundrels ran a red

flag up the mast. So, Rosenbloom and Doyle fed a statement to the press: "My attorneys advise me that this was a proceeding requesting the court to punish Michael McLaney and his associates for criminal contempt … This man has circulated false allegations for a long time. I firmly believe the untruthfulness of these charges will be proven."

McLaney said he dragged this skeleton out because he was suing C.R. over a business dispute. "This McLaney vs. Rosenbloom fight began back in 1960," the *Morning Sun* stated. "At that time, the case against Rosenbloom was dismissed, but in that trial certain depositions were filed concerning him that the judge deemed irrelevant to the particular case and also condemnatory to his character." No kidding. Proving a bigshot NFL owner bet on his own games would deep-six his career. "These statements had to do with Rosenbloom's allegedly having bet on pro football games, some of them involving the Colts," *Morning Sun* sports columnist Bob Maisel revealed. "The National Football League constitution specifically states that if it is proved that an owner has bet, he must sell his stock within 30 days." The parties observed radio silence while Rozelle dug into it.

McLaney had the bucket of hot tar; would Rozelle provide the feathers? Popular *Morning Sun* columnist Bob Maisel had his doubts:

> Rosenbloom's council [sic] pointed out that it just so happened that the only time the Colts and Steelers played was not in 1953 [as alleged], but in 1957,

not in Pittsburgh but Baltimore and that the Steelers, not the Colts, won it. So he [Rosenbloom's lawyer] concluded, "They have the wrong year, the wrong city and the wrong team winning." This certainly can't strengthen the effect of the affidavits, even though later statements listed the game as being against San Francisco [and McLaney got that wrong too]. Nevertheless, it's a sticky mess and Rozelle is holding it in his lap. He'll have to do something with it eventually, although he is not exactly proceeding with anything resembling speed.

Mid-July 1963, the NFL poobah issued his verdict. "Carroll Rosenbloom, the millionaire sportsman who owns the Baltimore Colts, was absolved yesterday of all charges that he had bet on National Football League games eight to ten years ago," the *New York Times* reported. "'No proof whatever has been uncovered that he ever bet on a National Football League game since becoming an owner in the league,' said Pete Rozelle, the league commissioner. The commissioner said he came to the conclusion that the charges against Rosenbloom were unfounded after the league's investigative staff had 'conducted extensive inquiries into Mr. Rosenbloom's alleged gambling activities.'" Who knows. Maybe "extensive inquiry" was corporate doublespeak for "We turned over a rock or two and called it quits." Regardless, Rozelle released C.R. on his own recognizance.

No doubt Rozelle shut the door on this mess when McLaney and his buddies started backpedaling like free safeties. This from the *Morning Sun* on July 17, 1963:

Rozelle's report said that the three accusers later repudiated or withdrew their charges in new affidavits given the commissioner. The commissioner made public quotes from the affidavit of one of the original accusers, Robert McGarvey, a former Philadelphia detective who lived in Fort Lauderdale, Fla. last winter. McGarvey's affidavit read in part: "I did all the betting on football games with usually small losses. Rosenbloom to my knowledge never bet on a pro game. I thought Rosenbloom would seek me out and offer me a job or something, but again, failure. I therefore repudiate my affidavit which I gave to you and feel sorry about the whole mess." Rozelle said Rosenbloom had delivered to him an affidavit stating he never bet on an NFL game after becoming an owner in the league in 1953. "He, Rosenbloom, freely admitted that he has bet substantial sums on activities other than professional football, principally golf games," Rozelle's report read.

Golf games, the Soap Box Derby, canal jumping in Holland, the White House Easter Egg Roll, wherever there was action, Carroll Rosenbloom had some money to lay down.

Carroll Rosenbloom scooped up Bert Bell Sr.'s two boys and gave them jobs with the ballclub. Upton Bell climbed the corporate ladder: training camp gopher, assistant equipment manager, ticket office assistant, scout, personnel director. His talent and C.R.'s recommendation got him the GM job up in New England. His resumé covers the evolution of the NFL as American Colossus. "We can get to the part that sunk him [Rosenbloom], and I've never figured this out—the gambling," Bell asserted. "Because he didn't need to. He didn't need the money. So, what was it? Some people have a hangup over sex, alcohol and drugs. What was it—when he *knew* what a problem it could be. That's the big 'why' I'll never figure out. And I don't think anybody else ever did. There was no reason for it. If my father [NFL Commissioner Bert Bell Sr.] had known—and he was very sharp—if he had known that Carroll was doing this type of gambling [on football games], as much as he loved him, he'd have fired him, thrown him out of the league."

One guy who ordinarily would have grabbed a shovel to dig Rosenbloom's grave was Baltimore *News American* sports columnist John Steadman. Strange, that Steadman was such a softie with Rosey now in harm's way. "Legal proceedings accusing Rosenbloom of betting on games, coming out of charges that have since been withdrawn, had him [Rosenbloom] fighting what had all the signs of a blackmail job," Steadman wrote on June 26, 1963, a couple of weeks before Pete Rozelle went public with the vindication. "Commissioner Pete Rozelle still hasn't absolved him of the complaints, but that is expected momentarily because, to date, there

has been no evidence turned up. Rosenbloom has never at any time appeared perturbed about the talk because he always insisted he had nothing to be worried about." A rare ceasefire during Steadman's hellfire-and-fury campaign against the Colts owner.

Upton Bell had it on good authority that Rosenbloom wagered on pro football—Colts head coach Weeb Ewbank. With Rosenbloom, Bell stated, "You're talking about a mythological character, at least in the sporting and business worlds. So what is rumor, and what isn't? But enough people that I know—including Weeb Ewbank, who worked for and liked him—said, 'Everybody knows that Carroll bets on the games.' Why would Weeb Ewbank take a chance and say that?" Hard to imagine a coat-and-tie man like Weeb Ewbank spinning a lie about the guy who signed his checks.

Upton Bell's brother Bert Jr. also weighed in on this one. He made the rounds in the NFL, just like his younger brother, working for two commissioners—his dad and Pete Rozelle—and for Carroll Rosenbloom, as business manager of the Colts from 1961-1966. Ergo, Junior saw C.R. in action at headquarters. "Years later [after Bert Jr. had moved on] Bert told a Baltimore reporter named John Eisenberg that he'd walked in on Carroll that last season he worked for the team [1966] as Carroll was on the phone making a bet," Upton Bell explained in his book, *Present at the Creation*. "Bert knew how vigilant our father [former NFL Commissioner Bert Bell Sr.] had been against gambling on games, so that bothered him, but he told Eisenberg there was something more that kept gnawing at him. 'People thought I left because someone else was promoted to GM, but I could never have worked as a GM under Carroll,' Bert told Eisenberg. 'I knew there would come a day when he would have asked me to do something illegal.'" Bert Jr. provided no specifics about C.R. trying to corrupt the lad, just the extracurriculars, the clandestine gambling. Steadman said it repeatedly and Bert Jr. implied it, but no amount of snooping uncovered proof of Rosenbloom trying to contaminate the troops.

But that never stopped John Steadman from going for Rosey's jugular. Recall Alan Ameche's plunge to paydirt in the '58 championship game. It was set up by a cheeky pass by Unitas to Mutscheller on the right sideline. So reporters wondered, *You're on the one, it's sudden death; why not trot out the field-goal unit and play it safe? Why risk the pass to Mutscheller?* "Had Unitas, on instructions from Rosenbloom, tried to beat the point spread of three and a half by going for the touchdown?" Steadman speculates in his book, *From Colts to Ravens*. "Rosenbloom had a reputation—but no hard proof was available—of being a bettor and was often in the company of known gamblers. But suggestions, mere gossip, that the owner had tried to influence the outcome were exceedingly unfair to the team and completely unfounded." A slick little two-step by Steady. Play the innocent and bring some slander disguised as curious speculation in through the back door, fling it at Rosenbloom, then cry don't shoot the

messenger. Just floating the rumor conveys guilt: "Psst. You didn't hear it from me, but…" The old accidently-on-purpose.

Steadman let fly again in *From Colts to Ravens*. "Rosenbloom admitted he had never seen the old Colts [from their All-American Football Conference days] play, so this was a new experience; he really was a rookie owner feeling his way [in 1953]," Steadman observed. "He wanted to win and in the second game of the season, with the Colts leading the Detroit Lions, he visited the locker room [at halftime] and said there would be an extra $300 for each player if they won. The obvious question: Was he betting? I don't know. At the time, he didn't realize such offers were against league rules." All crimes and misdemeanors were "obvious" to Steadman if Rosenbloom was the culprit. Everybody in the Colts circle knew that Carroll Rosenbloom would stick some extra green in your pocket if you came through in the clutch, be they ballplayers, secretaries, execs or the custodial staff. The numbers racket had nothing to do with it. C.R. rewarded the reliable and the loyal.

But the rumor about the '58 Colts-Giants game was a real bed bug. The website sportscollectorsdigest.com published an article in 2009 titled "The $3-Million Bet on the 1958 NFL Championship" which resurrected the old scuttlebutt. The opener is a mouthful: "It's a massive understatement to say that Mike McLaney was a colorful gambler and casino operator with a resumé that could have been crafted by Damon Runyon, including a link to mobster Meyer Lansky and a history of trying to overthrow or even assassinate a certain pesky communist dictator in Cuba, and you have some of the ingredients of the story."

Then we get to Rosenbloom. The writer, Tom Bartsch, introduces us to former PGA tour pro Al Besselink, who claimed he was best friends with McLaney. Besselink tells Bartsch that he has the skinny on a $3-million bet that McLaney put down on the 1958 NFL championship game:

> "I know all about it," Besselink said when asked about McLaney's shadowy role in "The Greatest Game Ever Played." Besselink was in Los Angeles to watch the game on television with another golfing buddy, then 49ers quarterback John Brodie. "Mike bet $3 million on the game, divided between himself, his friend and partner Louis Chesler and Colts owner Carroll Rosenbloom." The trio had given between 3½ and 5½ points for the privilege of betting on the favored Colts, and Besselink noted that his friend had given him a piece of the bet for free, amount undisclosed. Bessie, as he was known, told Brodie that he had a bet on the game, and they watched it head into overtime. Brodie told him he was out of luck, since a tie score would likely mean that the winning team would probably end up kicking a field goal to win, not enough the cover the spread. After the Giants were stopped in the first drive of overtime,

Unitas began the march down the field that helped install the young quarterback into the land of lore and legend. But once the Colts reached the eight-yard line, a field goal loomed. At second and goal, Unitas elected to pass, completing the heart-stopping toss to end Jim Mutscheller, who was brought down on the one-yard line. "Brodie couldn't believe that pass," laughed Besselink, who simply recited his line that the Colts would not kick a field goal. On third down, Unitas handed it to Ameche, who plunged in for the score, and the rest, as they say, is history.

Unitas was hit with the pass-to-Mutscheller query a zillion times over the years, including right after the game. It should have gotten a decent burial the first time he answered it. "Even at the end of that championship game," Bob Carter wrote on espn.com, "he [Unitas] dismissed Ewbank's instructions to keep the ball on the ground. 'We don't want an interception here,' the coach reminded him during a timeout. Two plays later, inside the 10, Unitas passed to Jim Mutscheller down to the one. Asked about the risk of an interception, Unitas said, 'If I saw a danger of that, I would have thrown the ball out of bounds. When you know what you're doing, you're not intercepted.'" And when you don't know what you're talking about, you peddle tripe about Unitas getting word that Boss Man said can the field goal and go for six. Anyone who ever huddled up with Johnny U knew enough to keep his yap shut because no one waved a play in his face, not even Shula. When in doubt, go to Occam's razor: The pass to Mutscheller was ho-hum for The Golden Arm, and the Colts kickers were about as reliable as sunshine in London. Steve Myra was 4-10 in 1958, and the long-range man, Bert Rechichar, was 1-4. You'd have a better chance with Charlie Brown and Lucy.

A parting word on the '58 title game came in Tom Callahan's biography of Unitas, *Johnny U*, proof that Unitas was a galaxy removed from point spreads that day but doesn't absolve Rosenbloom from laying one down:

> By the same formula [for the winners' share that game], the Colts quietly split another $50,000: $25,000 from their TV-radio sponsor, the National Brewing Company, and $25,000 from an unnamed "friend of the team," who everybody knew was owner Carroll Rosenbloom's gambling pal Lou Chesler [the same guy mentioned in "The $3-Million Bet on the 1958 NFL Championship"]. The Colts had been three-and-a-half-point favorites. John Steadman wrote, "When reporters asked Unitas why he went for the touchdown instead of the field goal, he made a joke about having placed a bet. Later, he told me, 'I didn't even know what the points were! I didn't even know how the points worked!' Unitas said Bert Bell read him the riot act [that was Steadman's phrase; John's was, "I got my ass handed to me"].

Nobody who knew Unitas thought otherwise, but Rosenbloom will forever wander around the yardarm, looking for absolution.

. . .

Carroll Rosenbloom was a swashbuckler, great with the commoners but positively candescent with the business lunch crowd. A middle-aged Jay Gatsby. Very few CEOs could pull off suave and hip like Rosenbloom. Tom Marr IV's dad, Tom III, covered the Colts and moonlighted on Orioles games on WCBM during the 1960s and '70s. They lived only two blocks from Memorial Stadium and saw and heard all the hubbub on game days. Tom IV recalled seeing Rosenbloom's glitterati promenade by the house now and again:

> My dad, who was a sports and newscaster in Baltimore at the time, covered the Colts for CBS radio. And he got to know Rosenbloom a little bit. Rosenbloom always made room for my grandfather whenever my father would bring him to a game. Carroll Rosenbloom would set my grandfather up in a special seat in the press box; he thought he was a good-luck charm. Rosenbloom was an interesting cat. I think he loved being owner of the Baltimore Colts. But I remember being a kid and getting the feeling that he didn't want to be in Baltimore anymore. There was that "Don't Tampa With Our Colts" in '72 [to be covered in due time]. There were a lot of celebrities that would come to Baltimore

Colt games. I have a newspaper clipping from the Baltimore *Sun* about Bob Hope and his wife in the press box, sitting with my mother for a routine game against Philadelphia in October of 1969. So, you would see a lot of celebrities during the late '60s-early '70s walking up and down our block [Windemere Avenue], just to get to the game.

Rosenbloom was pals with *Washington Post* editor Ben Bradlee; both had invites to the White House from the Kennedy boys. *Morning Sun* sports editor Bob Maisel included this bit of name-dropping in his September 11, 1961, column:

New Haven, Conn., September 10: About 10 minutes before the start of today's Colts-Giants game here, a veteran New York writer slid up to the Baltimore press section and said, "I've talked with three or four scouts around the league, and they tell me John Unitas doesn't look good at all. They think there must be something wrong with him. What do you think?" Just then, Carroll Rosenbloom edged into his seat and said, "Those Kennedys will kill you. I've already played 18 holes of golf today and been water skiing." Rosenbloom had just flown in with a party on the presidential plane from Hyannis Port [the Kennedy family home], and he heard the remark about Unitas. "He didn't look too good last week,"

he said, "but let's wait and see how he looks today."

It was the old man, Joe Kennedy, who threw together Carroll Rosenbloom and a five-time matrimonial strikeout victim, Violet Frances Irwin (alias Georgia Hayes), in 1957 at a Kennedy bash in Palm Beach. Reportedly, she could sing a passable tune in ballrooms and at state fairs, and here she was, hobnobbing with high society and getting Rosenbloom all googly-eyed. Georgia was a scaled-down Mamie Van Doren, and for the next eight years—still hitched to Velma Rosenbloom—Carroll took his blond trophy along for the ride. They had two children already in tow when Velma split in 1966; Carroll and Georgia then beat a path to the altar.

In a 1979 *Los Angeles Times* feature on Georgia Rosenbloom-Frontiere, "From Showgirl to Sports Boss, Georgia is on Many Minds," it was obvious Rosenbloom was weak-kneed for her. "'He was cuckoo for Georgia,' said a longtime family friend. 'If she sat down on the arm of another guy's chair,' a family attorney recalls, 'he was bristling. If she wanted to go swimming with someone, he got very upset and made a face.' But he couldn't keep from smiling when Georgia entertained after-dinner guests at their Bel-Air mansion, as she still does. 'She played to him 100 percent,' said comedian Jonathan Winters, a frequent visitor. 'Georgia would get up and sing to his eyes. He was like a little boy when she did that.'"

Upton Bell was busy earning points as a young go-getter with the Colts, so when

Rosenbloom put an errand on his plate, he did it, no questions asked. That included playing chauffeur for the paramour. "Whenever Rosenbloom called, I was ready for action, whether it was taking stuff to the White House for his friend Jack Kennedy, like footballs and sneakers for touch football games on the lawn, or driving his future wife, Georgia Hayes, to New York [where C.R. lived] or wherever," Bell recalled in his autobiography, *Present at the Creation*. "Carroll also had a present wife at the time whom I'd known most of my life, and that made it kind of uncomfortable for me. They told me Georgia was a singer that Carroll was friends with, but I never heard her sing. I was twenty-three, twenty-four years old. She was thirty-two, thirty-three. Carroll was in his fifties. I figured out what was happening but it wasn't any of my business. I worked for the Colts and Carroll Rosenbloom, but I knew it wasn't in that order."

Georgia Hayes-Rosenbloom-Frontiere had C.R. wrapped around her pinky, and that only mattered when his thoughts began drifting to L.A. Rosenbloom got peeved enough with Baltimore, eyeballed the palm trees out there, and no doubt the blond at his hip gave him a nudge. Dowdy Baltimore, it's been real.

Upton Bell called the man an enigma. Throw you a change-up when you expected the heater and bust you inside when you were thinking low and away. "A fascinating man, quietly mysterious, he moved in an incredible sphere of excitement, couched in duality that made him a different individual to different observers," popular sports columnist

Melvin Durslag recounted in his April 1979 obituary for Rosenbloom in the *San Francisco Examiner*. "To adversaries, he was ruthless. To those within his social orbit, he was witty and warm. To coaches and executives, he was hard, often callous. To little people in the office, kind and thoughtful. Some players snarled bitterly of betrayals by him. Others testified to deeds of his that helped them in delicate predicaments. At times, rival owners, incensed by his transgressions, took solemn oaths they never again would speak to Carroll. Some swore revenge, whatever the price. But it usually developed they returned to the nest, yielding to the horsepower of his unusual charm."

On a whim, Carroll Rosenbloom could pull arrogance, resentment, sarcasm, narcissism and pure spite out of the hopper and wallop you with them; likewise, he could do a quick U and wow you with honesty, integrity, gratitude, loyalty and kindness. And plenty of charm. There were eulogies galore when C.R. died in April 1979, many penned by reporters who covered the L.A. Rams. Mike Waldner of the *Daily Breeze* (Hermosa Beach, CA) was one:

People who worked for the Rams can tell you of his good deeds. He'd give tickets to a widow so she could take her son to a game. He'd purchase textbooks for a student. He'd help a down and out ex-player. He also had an impish side. One time [Rams head coach Chuck] Knox, concerned because his hair was beginning to show his age, found a remedy in a bottle. After the dye had darkened his hair, C.R. pointed it out to a couple of reporters. He knew they'd needle Knox. That's what he wanted. He just sat back and enjoyed the little scene. It's the other half of the scene that's locked in memory right now—Carroll Rosenbloom looking around the magazine he was pretending to read. There was a great big happy smile on his face.

John Hall of the *Los Angeles Times* also described the split personality of Carroll Rosenbloom. "The little things, it always seems, are those you remember most about a big man. The bigger the man, often, the softer the touch. Among his many faces, Carroll Rosenbloom could be the softest. When the news broke that the owner of the Rams had drowned in Florida, my first thought was that our last conversation had been a pleasant one. I was glad the words had been warm and friendly and the last thing I'd written about him had been flattering. And isn't that silly? What difference does any of it make? We went through the good and the bad—as he did with just about everybody he ever touched—and the good came out better than the bad. He was hard and he was so easy. He was tough and he was so sentimental. He had a fierce temper and he was so kind. He was an ugly brawler and he was such a gentleman and so charming."

You never knew which side would come your way. That was part of his makeup and part of the strategy. Former Baltimore Colts personnel director and New England Patriots GM Upton Bell spent decades trying to get a handle on C.R.:

Many of those powerful, influential people have various sides to them. A lot of them have a soft side that maybe you can't see. In the case of Rosenbloom, Carroll was very emotional—emotional about the game, emotional about my father [former NFL Commissioner Bert Bell Sr.], emotional about many things. I remember when we played Cleveland and shut them out [in the 1968 NFL championship game]. We had had some pretty good [NFL] drafts, and I was a part of that. I was down on the field before the game, and Carroll was down there. He was always nervous before a game. He had a lot of hangers-on with him down on the field. We were talking about the game and football, and he said—and I never thought of him as religious at all—"You know, somewhere up there, your father is looking down on you today, and I can hear him say how proud he is of you." That wasn't the Rosenbloom you would see, publicly.

•   •   •

The list is the length of your arm how many players Carroll Rosenbloom helped set up in business. He knew what many of them didn't—the peanuts they made as pros wouldn't carry them down the block after their careers ended. Players lined up outside Rosey's door for advice and (fingers crossed) a loan. "Rosenbloom has helped any number of his players into business on their own, and three of them, Alan Ameche, Joe Campanella and Gino Marchetti, are on their way to becoming multimillionaires with a chain of drive-ins and hamburger stands," Robert Boyle wrote in *Sports Illustrated* in December 1965. "According to one ordinarily cynical Wall Street man, Rosenbloom's character is best summed by his interest in his players. 'I think that Carroll Rosenbloom would be heartbroken if any of his old players ever came to him for a handout,' the man says. 'Carroll is not in the football business to make money. He is in it for two reasons: 1) to win; and 2) to help his players direct their incomes so that they are well-established in business before they are has-beens. He doesn't look upon the Colts as hired athletes. To him they are adopted sons.'"

Rosenbloom split for L.A. when former stellar Baltimore Colts running back Lydell Mitchell arrived in '72, but plenty of Rosenbloom's guys were still around. "I always heard good things about him," Mitchell stated. "He was just a good man. Back in those days, guys didn't make the kind of money they make now. But everything is relative. You made more money than the average person on the street, no doubt about it. But he [Rosenbloom] took care of his players—made sure they had an all-year job or helped them get into a business, things like that. And those are the things I remember about the Rosenblooms [Carroll and his son, Steve]. We think about all those guys—[Art] Donovan, [Gino] Marchetti, Lenny Moore had his place [the Sportsmen's Lounge], Jim Parker had his place [a package-goods store in West Baltimore], and on and on. These guys had something that they were into because they didn't make that much money on the field, but he [Rosenbloom] kinda got them ready for life after football. And I think that's what he brought to the table, and people respected him. And it worked."

Short of betraying the man, if Rosenbloom considered you part of his extended family, he'd always come to the rescue. Ernie Accorsi toiled in the NFL universe for almost 40 years, and if New York had any sense, he'd be in the Hall of Fame. He worked as the Baltimore Colts PR director from 1970-1975 and has a warehouse of stories about Rosenbloom:

I remember, it was a Sunday morning; it was during the offseason. John Steadman [Baltimore *News American*, longtime Rosenbloom enemy] had written a pretty rough column about him [Rosenbloom]. So, he called me at home. My wife was having extreme stomach pains and cramps, to the point where I was at the brink of going to the emergency room. And he calls, and he starts giving it to me pretty good [about Steadman]: "It's your job [as PR man], and you're supposed to be dealing with the press. And you couldn't talk him out of it." You weren't talking John Steadman out of *anything*. He really gave it to me. I said, "Mr. Rosenbloom, I don't wanna interrupt you, but right now, my wife is in a lot of pain. I don't know what it is, an appendicitis attack or what. But I have to take her to the emergency room." He flipped in a second. "Don't move," he said. "Doctor Friedman will be at your house within 15 minutes." This is Sunday morning. Doctors didn't make house calls. And there was Dr. Friedman, knocking at the door, at Courthouse Square apartments, in *less* than 15 minutes. He ended up giving her something to calm her down. He didn't send her to the emergency room. I would've had to take her to emergency, without the doctor. But *that's* Carroll Rosenbloom.

Bill Curry snapped the ball to Johnny Unitas and Earl Morrall from 1967-1972, all three of them working for Carroll Rosenbloom during a splendid run that included an NFL championship and two Super Bowls. Rosenbloom engineers the swap, Colts for Rams, Robert Irsay takes over, and GM Joe Thomas puts the old guard on Amtrack. Curry got shipped to Houston. Rosenbloom picked up the phone not long after and dialed Curry's number. "The fact that they had to release me after that year [1971], I understood completely," Curry admitted. "And he [Rosenbloom] called me, personally. He said, 'Bill, I want you to understand one thing about you and me. If you ever need *anything*—money, advice, attorneys, anything—call me, and you

will have it.' I think that anybody that produced for him, once he decided you were a loyal employee, a loyal person, he would move heaven and earth to try and help you."

Unitas also hit the road (San Diego) when Joe Thomas arrived, but Johnny U and Rosenbloom went way back together, to 1956, when Colts GM Don Kellett paid A.T.&T less than a buck for the phone call that got him from Pittsburgh. The *Honolulu Star Advertiser* asked him about C.R. right after he died in '79. "Unitas said Rosenbloom, the former Colts' owner who drowned while swimming in the surf near his Florida home, always listened to players' problems. 'I could go talk to him anytime I had any problems, the door was always open, he was always ready to help,' said Unitas, who now operates a restaurant in Baltimore [The Golden Arm]. 'He was always ready to help anyone on the Baltimore Colts... he never turned anyone down that I knew of,' Unitas said."

Four months after Rosenbloom died, *Morning Sun* columnist Alan Goldstein wrote about the man's humanity:

A family. It is the way the late Carroll Rosenbloom always thought of his football teams, be it in Baltimore or Los Angeles. He was the "godfather" and the players, scouts, trainers, ball boys, yes, even the management types, were his special children to spoil with praise, affection and lavish gifts. "Carroll Rosenbloom was a strong owner in what happened to the team," recalled ex-Colt tackle Bob Vogel. "He was always physically there. He wasn't an absentee owner. He offered a lot of warmth and love. He understood that football is 90 percent emotion and that if you have a happy player, he can perform miracles. I know of no situation in which his business interests overran his sense of importance of the player." When Vogel's father was dying of cancer, "C.R.," as he was known by his players, offered to arrange the best medical care possible. "That went beyond the call of duty," Vogel said. A similar story was told by Los Angeles Ram scout Bill Phillips, who developed a cancerous growth on his lungs a few years ago and needed emergency surgery. They said he had only six months to live. "The first voice I heard coming out of the anesthetic was Rosenbloom's," said Phillips, who made a remarkable recovery. "I was in the recovery room when C.R. called and said, 'Don't worry, you're going to lick it. Get better and have some fun.'" Rosenbloom sent Phillips and his family on an extended Hawaiian vacation, set up a college trust fund for the scout's daughter and guaranteed his wife a lifetime pension. "Yes, I got better," Phillips said, "but it was Rosenbloom who wouldn't let me give up. I tried every treatment, and he paid all the bills."

Much of this benevolence was conveniently discarded when the buzzards came calling.

The Ameche-Marchetti venture is probably the exemplar of player-makes-good. Baltimoreans during the '60s stopped off at two burger joints—Ameche's and Gino's—before heading home. Both men got rich, then sold their creations and retired as millionaires. But Rosenbloom's advice and loan got them started and pointed in the right direction. Dave Anderson, of the *New York Times*, wrote about it in his eulogy for Carroll Rosenbloom:

Perhaps Rosenbloom's favorite team was the 1958-59 Colts who ruled the NFL with Johnny Unitas at quarterback. Around that time three of his players—Gino Marchetti, Alan Ameche and Joe Campanella—asked him for a loan to open a hamburger stand in Baltimore.

"How much do you need?" he asked.

"We figure about $100,000," Marchetti said.

"You got it," Rosenbloom said.

"But suppose we blow it?" Marchetti asked.

"Then you blow it," he replied.

As it developed, the "Gino's" fast-food chain prospered, so did the players, and Carroll Rosenbloom got his money back.

C.R. was the man who got Marchetti thinking about life after football in the first place. In 1984, Gino told *Morning Sun* writer

Alan Goldstein about the phone call he got the summer after the '58 sudden-death game up in New York. "'We [Marchetti and Ameche] were the two luckiest Italians in the world,' Marchetti says. 'We started with nothing, both of us, but we owe it all to Carroll Rosenbloom,' the late Colts owner. 'The year we won our first championship [1958], I was in San Francisco with my wife, Flo, and I got a call from Carroll. He said he wanted to see me right away. I didn't know what to think. I figured maybe he had me involved in a trade. But all of a sudden Rosenbloom started screaming at me, "Listen, you dumb hillbilly, what are you going to do with your life after football?" Honestly, I'd never given it much thought. I'd spent the summers working for my father at the gas station in Antioch [CA]. But Rosenbloom said, "Look, Gino, you've really got a chance now to strike it rich in Baltimore. The people there love you. Why don't you make your fortune, then go back to Antioch and do as you please." Fortunately, I listened to the man.'"

The godfather groomed his son Steve ever so slowly to take over the franchise once he handed off and retired. The lad learned the business, from locker room go-fer to team president in 1971:

> My father would talk to them [the players], and he was very convincing. That was just his way. He could be tough, or he could be much softer. These were basically his children. He did it out of love for them. He knew how hard it

was to play football, so he always tried to get them to prepare for life after football. I don't know, so I can't tell you how much money he put out there to help these players get started. You don't just go out and buy a business with a smile. You have to pay for it. He was a great businessman. So, he was risking it [his money], but how else were they gonna get started? To him, this was his family, and it was nobody else's business what he did. That tells you what kind of guy he was. The players trusted him, and he lent them the seed money. He would step in, make sure they could make a buck or two, and I'm sure there were 20 to 50 other guys [besides notables like Marchetti, Ameche, Jim Parker and Art Donovan] that I wasn't privy to. But what he did for Gino and the others was not abnormal: "You guys can do something here. Make it happen."

When things didn't work out for Bill Curry in Houston, it looked like he was put out to pasture. Then the phone rang. "I was sitting at home with my beautiful wife and children [in 1974], and I didn't have a job—first time in many years," Curry reminisced. "The phone rang, and it was Mr. Rosenbloom. He said, 'Bill, I'm putting [Rams GM] Don Klosterman on the phone with you, and we would like you to think about coming out here and being a part of the Rams. We would value your skills here.' Well, I had torn my knee all to pieces the previous year, and we didn't know if I had a career anymore in the NFL. By golly, I had gotten it to where I could play a little. And he [Rosenbloom] brought me to the Rams, and we spent an incredible year on a great team. We were one play from going to the Super Bowl [a 14-10 loss at Minnesota in the NFC championship game]. And he treated me as if I were a member of his family. And we [Curry and his wife] will never forget that."

Offensive tackle Jim Parker fought to keep Johnny U off his backside for 11 seasons and made the NFL Hall of Fame in 1973 (as did Marchetti, Moore, Unitas and Donovan). The liquor store he owned for decades in Baltimore might have been just a pipedream, but for Carroll Rosenbloom. "Former offensive tackle Jim Parker credited Rosenbloom with helping start his tavern in Baltimore 13 years ago," a *UPI* story in the *Honolulu Star Advertiser* stated in 1979. "'He set me up in business. I wouldn't be in business if it weren't for him,' Parker said. 'I played for him 11 years. He was a perfect gentleman and a perfect owner,' Parker said. 'He was always a man of his word. If he promised you something, you could always depend on it.'"

Unitas went belly-up in three years with the first shot he took in the business world. Bowling alleys—tenpins. Colt Lanes, a swell family hangout in the '60s that never got momentum: dark paneling, foam walls painted royal blue and white, thick carpets with the team logo and a huge horseshoe out front. Rosenbloom and Baltimore investor George Banks III each had to swallow $162,500 of Johnny U's loan package. Rosenbloom shrugged it off as bad luck.

Rosenbloom's hot and cold moods got played up in the papers, but not his altruism. "If you were in trouble, and you got through to him—particularly the players—he was a sucker for anything the players wanted," Upton Bell analyzed. "But if something hit him, emotionally, he would take care of it and you. And he wouldn't publicize it. So, it's really fascinating, confounding—interesting—that a guy that had so many different facets about himself could be angry as hell at you for something—and in some cases, never forgot it—and in the next moment would say, 'What do you need?' There were many personalities there."

Many of Rosenbloom's intimates, like Ernie Accorsi, savored having a Gibraltar like that around, somebody who would swoop in and pull you out of the fire:

First of all, what he did with Ameche and Marchetti—there were no [loan] papers signed. That was a handshake deal: Pay me back when you can. And with the money they made, those guys paid back every penny. And he did the same thing with Unitas, did the same thing with [Art] Donovan [the Valley Country Club in Baltimore County]. I remember one time we had a receiver on the taxi squad named Paul Maliska [who later died in a tragic bus accident in 1997]. I don't think he ever played in a game. We had practice at Memorial

Stadium, and he [Rosenbloom] would come in Saturdays a lot of the times. Rosenbloom knew who he was. Nicest kid. He wasn't gonna play in the NFL. So, he's walking off the field, kinda hanging his head, and I'm standing there with Rosenbloom. And he [Rosenbloom] said, "Paul, come over here," put his arm around him, and he said, "You're a fine young man. You're gonna be a success, no matter what you do in your life. You're smart, and it may not be in the National Football League, but you're gonna be successful." Now, it struck me as being something I don't think Maliska wanted to hear, but I didn't say anything because it was almost like a death knell to him. About 10 minutes later, Rosenbloom said, "You know, I probably shouldn't have said it that way. Will you go in and tell Paul that I didn't mean that he wouldn't make this team? I think he's got a good chance. I was trying to pay him a compliment. But make sure he doesn't leave here discouraged." Now, Paul Maliska wasn't gonna be able to do anything for him [Rosenbloom] in his life. I think he spent the season on our practice squad, and that was it. But there's an example, right there.

Harry Hulmes was another guy who kept climbing at Colts headquarters. He became the business manager of the Colts in 1958, then PR director, which earned him the GM job in 1967. The Colts went 11-2-1 and 13-1 his first two years (minus the playoffs in '68). Losing Super Bowl III to the Jets got him demoted to assistant GM to Don Klosterman. In 1969, Hulmes got hired as assistant GM of the New Orleans Saints and had an orphaned house in Baltimore. Hulmes told the *Los Angeles Times* in 1972, "When I left him [Rosenbloom], Carroll asked me if I'd got rid of my (Baltimore) house yet. I told him no. He said: 'If nobody meets your offer, let me know. I'll buy it.' I thought that was generous, but I never intended to call on him until he telephoned me six or eight weeks later in New Orleans. He wanted to know if I was settled, and I told him we had a house we couldn't put a deposit on because we hadn't sold in Baltimore yet. 'How much is the deposit?' he asked. 'I'll have the check there in the morning.' No strings, no interest, no [bank] note— and I'm not even working for him anymore. That's Carroll."

And never a peep from Rosenbloom about any of this. Ted Williams and the Jimmy Fund, same thing. No doubt *United Press International* got this tidbit in December 1970 from the two colleges, certainly not from Rosenbloom: "WICHITA, Kan., Dec. 8 (*UPI*)— Carroll Rosenbloom, owner of the Baltimore Colts, has donated a total of $100,000 to memorial funds of Marshall and Wichita State universities, the schools announced today. Rosenbloom earmarked $50,000 for each of the schools, which lost most of their football teams and coaching staffs in crashes of chartered airliners this fall. Dr. Clark Ahlberg, president of Wichita State, said Rosenbloom telephoned him last week to discuss the tragedy and to learn 'the extent of our needs and of our cooperative efforts with Marshall. He indicated if he decided to do something, the gift would be significant. At that time, I had no idea his decision would be of the magnitude it is,' Ahlberg said."

More of the same. This, from the November 20, 1964, *Evening Sun*:

"Let me know what you need," said Carroll Rosenbloom. There are 50 boys in colleges this year partly because of that offer by the owner of the Baltimore Colts. None is an athlete. Or if he is, it had nothing to do with his being given the amount of money he lacked to go to the college of his choice. Neither did scholarship. The program is for the "real needy." "It was one cold day in 1958 when Carroll broached the idea," recalls Paul Menton, sports editor of the *Evening Sun*. "We were standing on the field, watching the Colts get ready for the [1958] National Football League championship game against the Giants in New York. Carroll said he would like the Colts to set up a foundation to assist Maryland boys who really needed help to go to college." It was done with the sports editors of this city's three daily newspapers (Menton, Robert Maisel and John Steadman), the Colts' lawyer and Rosenbloom as the trustees. But Rosenbloom won't allow his name used on Colts Foundation stationery.

All this boundless charity Rosenbloom wanted kept hush-hush. Breathe a word of it and he'd light you up. Ernie Accorsi, a veteran NFL executive who helped turn the Cleveland Browns and New York Giants into playoff powers after he ditched Irsay, was told mum's the word about Rosenbloom's noble deeds:

A lot of the things he [Rosenbloom] did, like picking up a hospital bill for somebody, we never knew because he didn't say anything to anybody. When he was at Penn, he was there with a guy named Marty Brill. He ended up being maybe an All-America at Notre Dame [in 1930]. That was his best friend. Brill was transferring to Notre Dame, and Carroll wanted to transfer with him. Whether Notre Dame didn't want him, or his father wouldn't let him, I don't remember. In the early '70s, when I was working for him [Rosenbloom], Brill had come upon hard times. And I don't know how much money Carroll gave him, but he gave him a pretty good chunk. He bailed him out. I found out about it, I think, from Eddie [Rosenbloom, business manager]. He [Rosenbloom] pulled me to the side in the press box in Miami. He said, "Come here. Do you know about this [helping Brill]?" I said, "Yes, sir." He said, "I do NOT want this in the newspaper. And if it gets in, I'm gonna hold you responsible [as PR director]." Now, that's a little different from picking up a hospital bill because at that time, Marty Brill was still famous. But he [Rosenbloom] didn't want anybody to know about it. And it never did get in the paper. He didn't *want* it in the paper. But that was him. And how many times he did stuff like that—I will say this: I always felt, no matter what, no matter what kind of tough situation I was in—medically or whatever—that he would have bailed me out. He would have come and helped me to get out of it. And I was a nobody. You couldn't get much lower than me then [in the Colts organization]. Everybody was higher than me. But I felt that way about him.

Rosenbloom sometimes drove the troops like Patton storming out of Normandy, but he was just as hard on himself. Do-as-I-say and as-I-do. A 1962 *Morning Sun* feature on Rosenbloom pointed out that the buck stopped with him. No excuses, no ducking: "He has also shown that he can be tough and demanding. In the middle of one poor season, he threatened to fine everybody on the team $100 for insipid play. The fine was not imposed, but he did once fine himself. The standard penalty for lateness at a squad meeting was $100. When fog delayed the takeoff of his plane from New York and he arrived late at a meeting, he levied a $100 personal fine on himself and paid another $100 for every member on the team. Such penalties all go to Kernan Hospital."

Another Colts groundling turned exec was Upton Bell: training camp attendant on up to personnel director in 1966. He blanched when Carroll Rosenbloom pinned the choker label on Don Shula after the Colts swooned against the Browns in the 1964 NFL championship and the Jets in Super Bowl III. So he vented in his book, *Present at the Creation*: "By the end of the 1969 season, his [Shula's] seventh-straight winning season but a disappointment to us all, the tension between him and Rosenbloom was clear. To understand what that meant, you need to understand that as good as he could be to you, Rosenbloom could treat you just as cruelly. You only needed to read a sentence from [San Diego Chargers owner] Gene Klein's autobiography to understand what Shula was facing. Klein owned the Chargers, and in his book *First Down and a Billion*, he said, 'He always gave you the feeling that, if you crossed him, he was capable of slitting your throat, then donating your blood to the Red Cross blood drive.' That was true. If you ended up on the wrong side of Carroll, he would not only cut you loose, he'd cut you to ribbons if he could. I think Rosenbloom never got over his anger from losing that Super Bowl. I knew that day he'd never get over it and he didn't. He held it against Shula and it blinded him to what a great coach he had. I knew something bad was going to happen in Baltimore soon." Shula got one more year of rope for the noose (1969), and in 1970 he got an offer he couldn't refuse down in Miami, escaped the evil eye, and turned the Dolphins into a dynasty.

If Roger Goodell and the suits up in New York had any sense of history, they'd get Ernie

Accorsi and Carroll Rosenbloom into the Hall of Fame posthaste. First Accorsi. Look at his body of work. He held the Colts together with bubble gum and baling wire despite Bob Irsay and henchman Michael Chernoff making a bloody hash of things. And he was smart enough to fly the cuckoo's nest and head to Cleveland, whereupon he snagged Bernie Kosar in the draft and got the Browns in the playoffs five of the seven years he was there. Then he spent nine years as asst. GM under George Young, then as Giants GM, four of them playoff runs. He's the guy who got Eli Manning. Those who have done plenty of laps in the NFL will tell you that Ernie Accorsi belongs in the Hall.

Accorsi tells the story about the time Carroll Rosenbloom gave him an errand up in New York: Hop in a car and make the rounds, delivering these game tickets. When Accorsi stubbed his toe on this one, the uh-oh had him up half the night:

It's game day. Eddie Rosenbloom, who was kinda the consigliere, his [Rosenbloom's] uncle/business manager told me, "You're in deep trouble. You screwed up. You got all the wrong addresses. You delivered the tickets to the wrong people." The truth of the matter is I made a mistake or two, but it wasn't a disaster, like it was explained to me. I said, "Am I gonna get fired?" He said, "I don't know." I'm on pins and needles. He [Rosenbloom] was sitting right next to me [during the game]. We hung on for dear life

to beat Joe Namath and the Jets, 29-22 [1970]. Didn't say a word to me. Next morning, I'm in my office, still on thin ice, and his secretary calls and says, "Mr. Rosenbloom wants to see you." I said, "Oh, shit." I went down, and he didn't say a word about the mistake I made. So, I said, "Mr. Rosenbloom, I can't take it anymore. I don't know what mistakes I made. I apologize for screwing up those deliveries." "What deliveries?" I said, "I guess I took some tickets to the wrong place." And he said, "Did Eddie Rosenbloom tell you that? He had no business getting that excited. You're doin' a nice job." And I left there. Now—the point is, he didn't forget about it. The point was made by him. Scared the living shit outta me, OK? He would do that, but at the end, no matter what the circumstances were, he would lift you up. He just had that knack. And I just loved the guy.

Like most, Jim Murray of the *L.A. Times* saw Rosenbloom as the enigma wrapped inside a riddle. Thin-skinned, impulsive, occasionally vindictive, then a 180 in the wink of an eye. "Like many trigger-tempered people," Murray observed, "he was capable of great forgiveness. When he was blackballed by an elitist country club in Los Angeles [allegedly for being Jewish], he forbade aides to quit in protest, recognizing that the rejection was not based on anti-Semitism so much as on vengeance from burned business competitors.

'Besides, he might want to move the club to Anaheim,' a member quipped [which he did]."

One thing C.R. wasn't was duplicitous. His word was 24-karat. And his players knew it. "There was a lot of trust between Carroll Rosenbloom and all of the players. And they knew it," insisted Steve Rosenbloom, Carroll's son and former president of the Baltimore Colts. "It's shocking these days how some teams are run and how they treat their players. The players see you, and they learn to trust you, which takes time. My father was very good at that. So, here's an example of trust. My father was in [contract] negotiations with Gino [Marchetti]. What my father did was just sign the bottom line on the contract, and he said, 'Gino, fill it [the salary] in yourself.' So, there was trust there. Gino was a standup guy; he wasn't gonna make the amount more than Johnny U's salary. My father and the players had that kind of trust in each other."

Given the mood swings, opinions on him ran the gamut. Upton Bell, who spent over a decade with the Colts before taking the GM job in New England, saw the hot and cold of the man. "Rosenbloom knew your strengths, but he also knew your weaknesses," Bell asserted. "And when he found your weaknesses—if he didn't like you, you were a dead-man-walking. You could love him; you could hate him; you could fear him. He had all of those abilities, depending upon his mood. There are many things he entrusted me to, and there are many things that I didn't necessarily like because I knew the other side. But

you have to go back to the original of anything and say, 'No matter what his relationship was with coaches, with Shula, with his son, with Baltimore, with the league itself, with gambling, if you go back to the original—who gave me the opportunity [to work in the NFL]? It was Carroll Rosenbloom.'"

Some folks with amnesia in Baltimore still badmouth Rosenbloom more than 50 years later. They see him as a suntanned NYC/L.A. mogul even though he had Baltimore at his core. Nobody need remind Ernie Accorsi of that:

To repeat what I have said, I loved the man. But that doesn't mean he wasn't tough. You can hear that from the old [Green Bay] Packers. They loved Vince Lombardi; that doesn't mean he wasn't tough. First of all, he [Rosenbloom] was a native [Baltimorean]. When I knew him, he didn't live much of his life in Baltimore. He had a New York apartment, and he lived in Golden Beach, Florida. He moved around. But he *was* a Baltimorean. For cryin' out loud, he went to high school [the original City College] which was at the corner of Centre and Howard Streets [downtown]. The only thing between our office [Colts headquarters] was a parking lot about 55 yards away. So, no matter how cosmopolitan he had become, his heart and soul were in Baltimore. There's a great line that Arnold Palmer used when he went back to his first high school reunion at Latrobe [PA]. He said, "Your hometown is *not* where you're from; it's who you *are*." You can't remove that from your soul. Carroll was a Baltimorean. That's what he cared about.

For shear body of work, how is it possible to freeze out Carroll Rosenbloom from the Hall of Fame? He's the NFL's version of The Guess Who. Rosenbloom and the Colts helped the NFL end baseball's reign as first fiddle. A 2018 article in talkoffametwo.com titled "State Your Case: Does Rosenbloom's Vision and Success Make Him HOF Worthy?" likewise wonders about the slight all these years:

Until the advent of Robert Kraft's New England Patriots, Carroll Rosenbloom was the winningest owner in NFL history. He created a franchise that didn't exist in Baltimore and turned it into a three-time world champion and four-time NFL champion, then made one of the savviest "trades" in NFL history [the Colts-Rams swap] to take over the Los Angeles Rams and continued the winning tradition he'd established after he agreed to buy the defunct Dallas Texans for $13,000 and turned them into what became Johnny Unitas's Colts. With the exception of Bud Adams, who helped start the AFL along with Lamar Hunt, Rosenbloom is the last of the NFL's founding fathers not to have gained entry into the Pro Football Hall of Fame. One has to wonder why.

With a straight face you can say Rosenbloom doesn't belong with these guys? Jerry Jones, Charles Bidwill, Al Davis, Wellington Mara, George Preston Marshall, George Halas. Halas, a no-brainer; Bidwill (bootlegger, gambler, Al Capone associate), Davis (Rozelle's chief pain in the ass) and Marshall (Jim Crow lover). Some ugly bonafides in that bunch. What's the knock on Rosenbloom: the gambling, butting heads with Rozelle now and again, the big swap in '72?

The blogger who penned "State Your Case: Does Rosenbloom's Vision and Success Make Him HOF Worthy" was on to something: "Rosenbloom's teams went 226-116-8, a winning percentage of .660, which was the best in history until [Robert] Kraft's 24 years of ownership of the Patriots left him with a .696 winning percentage [which has dipped, post-Brady, to .648]. The Patriots have won five Super Bowls [actually, six] and are 5-4 in Super Bowl games [sic, 6-5]. Rosenbloom's Colts and Rams won three NFL championships [1958, 1959, 1968] and were 1-1 in Super Bowls. Many have argued that the first test for a Hall of Fame candidate is to ask the question, 'Can you write the history of the NFL without him?' If one accepts that as a reasonable measuring stick, Carroll Rosenbloom measures up. Between creating the Colts, forcing the hiring of Rozelle [yes, he lobbied for Pete], swapping franchises to take over the Rams and envisioning the use of stadiums as major revenue drivers, Carroll Rosenbloom left an impact on the NFL like few other owners." Don't forget C.R.'s role as point man for the AFL-NFL merger and how he wheeled-and-dealed to get those whopping TV contracts that made everybody rich. And yet, no gold jacket for Rosenbloom. T'aint right.

For Ernie Accorsi, it's academic. "Absolutely, he [Rosenbloom] should be in it [the HOF]," Accorsi stressed. "Number one, Bert [Bell Sr.] had to beg him to take that franchise. He didn't wanna do it. He was a businessman, and there was no glamor to it at that point [1953]. Carroll Rosenbloom had a lot to do with there being a team there [in Baltimore]. That's number one. Then, look at who he hired; look at the coaches somebody hires when you talk about qualifications. He hires Weeb Ewbank [who won two NFL championships], and that wasn't easy because [Cleveland Browns head coach] Paul Brown wouldn't speak to Weeb after that [leaving the Browns]. He hires a 33-year-old Don Shula. Then he hires the perfect person—it was Joe Altobelli after [Earl] Weaver [of the Orioles]—to succeed Shula, the Easy Rider [Don McCafferty]. And he wins the Super Bowl. He goes to L.A., when everybody's hiring [Mike] McCormack and all these other people, and hires Chuck Knox, who's the most successful of all those coaches that were hired during that period. He's won championships [four], and those back-to-back championships in '58 and '59 helped to make the NFL what it is today."

Consider this discourse titled "Roanoke's Denim King" from theroanoker.com in January 2021: "Rosenbloom never had a money-losing season with the Colts, and by the end of the decade [1950s], his Colts were considered the NFL's premier franchise. Rosenbloom eventually sold [traded] the Colts and became owner of the Los Angeles Rams in 1972. In a span of nearly three decades as an NFL team owner, C.R. helped create the players' union, had been the first owner to suggest merging the NFL and the AFL, lobbied for mega coliseums, and along with Rozelle realized television contracts were key to the game's popularity and profitability. Rosenbloom's drive and, at times, abrasive personality often put him in conflict with Rozelle and other team owners, but his mark on the modern-day NFL is unquestioned."

Big deal. So he occasionally rankled the honchos, Rozelle, Papa Bear Halas, Wellington Mara, George Preston Marshall, et al. The problem could be Rosey got blackballed. If so, what a frivolous sham. Meat-and-potatoes NFL brethren like Ernie Accorsi know better:

I believe this, and I always will: I know our team [the Colts] was out of gas in '71. But I will tell you, we might've had a down year, but had he [Rosenbloom] stayed in Baltimore, we would've won. We wouldn't have had all those years of not winning [with Bob Irsay]. He would have willed it. We would've gotten the right people in there, and he would've won. The other thing is, late in his career, he took over the NFL Management Council during the labor strife [between players and owners].

He and [Pete] Rozelle had feuds at times, but Rozelle respected him. So, he had a lot of influence in the league, even then. Certainly, he was a leader. He facilitated the [AFL-NFL] merger in 1969. They hit a roadblock [about which teams would move to the AFC]; they were gonna have to start pulling slips of paper out of a hat. He was able to get that done. If you're gonna blame lousy owners for losing, then you gotta give Rosenbloom credit for winning. He built a winning organization and kept it intact. I don't know what you have to do as an owner to get in there [the HOF], but if you're gonna put owners in there, he *absolutely* belongs in the Hall of Fame. I couldn't feel stronger about it.

Carroll Rosenbloom and Ernie Accorsi into the HOF as a tag team. Who will second?

CHAPTER 3

MEMORIAL MAUSOLEUM

I f you bought Orioles tickets out front at the W-2 window at old Memorial Stadium, did a loop towards centerfield and 36th Street, then turned back for a look at the open end of the horseshoe, the place looked decked out for Easter: powder-blue box seats, Kelly green preferred reserve, canary yellow mezzanine and hot pink upper-reserve chairbacks. Real eclectic. With sublime memories. Old-timers can rattle off yarns to beat the band about mythic deeds and better times. They called her the Old Gray Lady of 33rd Street.

But for those who rented the place, it was a slag heap, a shanty. Two options were suggested: 1) Pump in millions for a makeover; or 2) Level it and start over. The Colts and Orioles preferred the latter.

The old dame wasn't always picked on. When Memorial Stadium opened in 1954, it drew a few oohs and aahs. John Steadman, sports editor of the *News American*, tracked the evolution on 33rd, from Venable Stadium to Baltimore Stadium to Municipal Stadium to version 4.0, Memorial Stadium. His eulogy

of sorts in the *Morning Sun* came when the Orioles moved downtown to Oriole Park/ Camden Yards in 1992: "Closing the gates to Memorial Stadium signifies an end to a majestic edifice and a glorious era that has produced a treasury of momentous memories, all shaped to your own individual perception and joys of recall. It becomes a deeply personal experience, this shutting down the old to make way for the new ... Yes, it was an arena of historic athletic achievement. Memorial Stadium and its predecessor, Municipal Stadium, represent a vital fabric in the growth and stature of Baltimore. It embellished the quality of life within the realm of fun and games, and provided some golden nuggets of history that deserve to endure in perpetuity."

"Edifice": why, yes; "arena of historic athletic achievement": of course, the house of champions, the Colts and Orioles; "majestic": now, wait just a minute. But it was the Baltimore town square. "This stadium, this field, really represents the soul of the city of Baltimore," former Baltimore Colts defensive lineman Joe Ehrmann affirmed in an NFL Films documentary, *There Used to Be a Ball-park*. "This was the one place of common ground. And I think, unlike stadiums today, here everybody had to wait in the same line for the same urinal. You bought from the same hotdog vendor. Stadiums today, they're very class-centric. You've got skyboxes, club seats, and then you go down to the endzone. So, it [Memorial Stadium] was common ground. And I think with the history of this stadium, both with the Colts and the Orioles, it created a venue for civic pride. The Colts and the Orioles provided the common ground for both CEOs and cabbies to have something to talk about—black and white, rich and poor. And this was the context where all people came together."

Upton Bell, son of former NFL Commissioner Bert Bell Sr., got hired straight out of college as Colts assistant equipment manager, paid his dues for 11 years, then landed the GM job with the Patriots. He knew the Gray Lady well. "It was an incredible place for its time," he said. "I've never been in a stadium where the noise level—for players coming out of the dugout for the introductions—was so loud. There was nothing like it, even in stadiums today. That concentrated noise from those fans and the way the stadium was configured—not the field, but the stadium itself—I've never heard noise like that ever again. Even the players, who were hardened by many things in life, they'll tell you, that feeling they got when they ran out of the dugout was like no other."

Tom Marr IV's dad covered the old Colts for CBS radio, and the family lived two blocks away from the stadium. The old man's kid piled up the memories. "Memorial Stadium was the Championship Stadium, where the Orioles had won the '66 and '70 World Series, where the Colts won the '59 [NFL] championship game," Marr IV declared. "That was Baltimore's Town Hall. We did *every-thing* there. It was in the center of the city [on the outskirts]. It was where we bought our Christmas tree, where we saw fireworks on the Fourth of July. It's where every spring, there was a gigantic flea market that took up the entire eastside parking lot. Pelé played there in 1972 [for Santos FC of Brazil]. The ice-skating rink they set up in winter—it was huge. I did short-track speedskating there. It was a social meeting place. It was the epicenter of Baltimore, the one thing people could look at with pride."

When many in Baltimore wanted to take a wrecking ball to the place after the Colts left in 1984, the *Washington Post* disagreed:

Baltimore set out in the early 1950s to build a municipal stadium for football and baseball, and came up with an appropriately funny-looking brick-pile. But over the years, familiarity has softened its ugliness, the concrete edges have been rounded by the passage of millions of bodies, the Orioles have become a civic institution, and Memorial Stadium has become a genuine ballpark. And since they didn't follow the current practice of making a desert and calling it a parking lot, it is located in a genuine neighborhood. More than 2 million people went there last year to watch baseball games.

Lydell Mitchell was a first-rate halfback for the Colts during the Irsay era (1972-1978, Pro Bowl three times). He ran and caught passes all over that patch of dirt that passed for turf. What a quirky place to call home. "Memorial Stadium was a combination field—baseball, football," Mitchell stated. "They couldn't sod the infield until the baseball season was over [often in mid-October]. It was a tough field to play on, but we loved that field. It was an advantage for us. You'd get those other teams on that infield, and they didn't know how to react to it. I didn't much like the dirt either; it would an incentive for us, though. We'd be in the huddle and say, 'Come on, man, let's get a couple first downs, so we can get the hell off this field, off this dirt.' But it was like the town itself—they embraced us, and we embraced that field."

YouTube can take you back to the 1970 AFC championship game, Colts vs. Raiders: "Duel in the Dust." The field was nothing but 100 yards of loam, fit for tractor pulls. But 60,000 fanatics would thunder down on the visitors. It was Cooper Rollow of the *Chicago Tribune* who coined the phrase "world's largest outdoor insane asylum" back in 1965, and it's been repeated a million times since. George Halas and the Bears were in Baltimore the first Sunday in December 1965, and a number of

Colts were out of action. So Rollow typed his lead: "'We're hurting on defense.' That's the word from Baltimore, where the stampeding Colts are preparing to play host to the Chicago Bears Sunday in Memorial Stadium, the world's largest outdoor insane asylum." He could've made a few bucks with a copyright.

John Steadman gave Cooper Rollow a nod in his 1991 *Morning Sun* requiem for Memorial Stadium, "This Old House":

Memorial Stadium represented to the Colts and their followers what Cooper Rollow, a sportswriter for the *Chicago Tribune*, referred to as the "world's largest outdoor insane asylum." There was Unitas setting records and passing to [Lenny] Moore, [Raymond] Berry, Jim Mutscheller and later Jimmy Orr. And, of course, near-crazed fanatics screaming and stomping and a real live Colt mascot circling the field after every home-team score. The Baltimore Colts became a way of life. Too bad that a team, founded in 1947 and with 35 years of tradition, was torn away during the middle of a lamentable March night in 1984. It was smuggled off to a place known as Indianapolis, where owner Bob Irsay sought greener financial pastures.

Steadman was spouting the company line about Irsay. But he was right about the magic of the place. Steve Sabol of NFL Films bounced into town for big games, and he marveled at the karma of Memorial Stadium.

"Baltimore was one of the first places where people talked about a homefield advantage," Sabol observed in his documentary, *There Used to Be a Ballpark*. "In the years from 1957 through 1971, the Colts had the highest home winning percentage. And the crowd support was a big part of that. What you saw expressed in Baltimore was a genuine love between the fans and the team. It's a bond that, despite the loss of the Colts [before the Ravens came], and now the loss of the stadium, will be felt in this community forever."

Baltimore Colts Hall of Famer Gino Marchetti talked often over the years about the crowd that jacked up the gladiators. "At Memorial Stadium, when you came out of the tunnel, they had the [Colts] band and the cheerleaders lined up as you ran out," Marchetti recalled in the documentary, *There Used to Be a Ballpark*. "And they played that Colts fight song, and it really pumped me up. I ran out there 13, 14 years, I don't know how many times. But the enthusiasm—if I felt bad, soon as I got out there, and I heard the crowd, I heard the band, it picked me up. It put me where I should be."

Back in 1962, John Ziemann earned a slot on the Colt band's percussion line; he helped keep the band going, even after Bob Irsay shoved off to Indy. His impressions are similar to most Baltimoreans over 50:

> First of all, I saw my first football game there in 1956, the same year John Unitas started. Just coming up that ramp and seeing that beautiful green field [before football cleats stripped it away]. You gotta realize there was not only baseball and football. In the summer, they had the Ice Capades there. The circus used to set up in there. So many events. Easter Sunday, they would have sunrise services in there. So, she wasn't just a place for baseball and football. She was everything to us. When she was revamped in 1953, she became the epitome of a first-class stadium. She was also a memorial to the men and women who gave their lives [in combat]. But with age, it took its toll. It broke my heart when the wrecking ball took her down, but it was *time*. We had to move forward. I saw a lot when the [Colts] band traveled around to other stadiums during the 11 years we didn't have a team. I saw other stadiums, new stadiums, going to see the Giants and their stadium [in New Jersey]. And I said to myself, *My God, what have we done?!* To see all this modernization, and we needed to move forward. In Baltimore, we didn't. And we came close to losing the Orioles over it.

Ziemann used the pronoun "she;" but of course, the Old Gray Lady. But emotions got in the way once the great stadium row got cooking. Gwinn Owens of the *Evening Sun* in 1985 was squeamish about this talk of razing her: "Right now it is fashionable to bad-mouth Memorial Stadium as a second-rate home for either football or baseball. There is no question that compared with the newer domed palaces and the latest outdoor stadiums, the Baltimore bowl is primitive. And yet, as one who spent his childhood going to baseball games in little Oriole Park [torched on July 4, 1944] and football games in that rickety wooden Municipal Stadium, Memorial Stadium seemed to me, when it was completed in 1954, to be a magnificent edifice. Since then I have spent many happy hours there as an Oriole fan and, for five years, as a Colt season-ticket holder."

Oriole Park was 2x6 kindling compared to concrete gargantuan Memorial Stadium. The latter became a lot more than just a ballpark. Lenny Moore, who got a taste of Jim Crow when he first got to Baltimore, saw Memorial Stadium as a rare spot where all that melted away for a few hours. "In the community of Baltimore, a lot of things changed," Moore reflected in the NFL Films documentary, *There Used to Be a Ballpark*. "And I think a lot of that was due to what took place right here in the stadium. It was a meeting place because here in Baltimore, things weren't the best when I came here. There was sort of a divide—blacks over here, whites over there. In this stadium, I think, was a catalyst for bringing people together."

When the beefs about Memorial Stadium started flying, someone always summoned *feelings* instead of logic. Emotional baggage (and fecklessness) brought on the 19 years of hemming and hawing about what to do with the place. But splendid Colts defensive lineman Joe Ehrmann earned the conch shell for a final testimonial: "This is where Unitas and Moore played," Ehrmann stated in *There Used to Be a Ballpark*. "And that's pretty cool. I think there's a thing called a theology of place. Being a minister, there is sacred ground. And it comes from an old Hebrew prophet—Jacob—who had a dream where these angels ascended and descended. And wherever God works out His business, and people work out their business with God, is a sacred place. And as a minister, one of the things I do is funerals. And I can't tell you the number of funerals I've done where either the Colts fight song has been played by a lone bagpipe, or they played the tape of the Colts fighting song. When you tell the story of Baltimore, woven all through the fabric of this [20th] century will be the story of Memorial Stadium and the Baltimore Colts."

. . .

So much for heartstrings and cotton candy. For almost two decades antagonists griped, moaned, groaned, bickered, squabbled, quarreled, wrangled, squabbled, sparred, dilly-dallied, dawdled and twiddled thumbs while the stadium grew warts and wrinkles. Two owners got fed up and left town. The Great Stadium Debate helped push them out.

Writers from D.C. and elsewhere added to the badmouthing: "There is uproar in Baltimore because Carroll Rosenbloom is telling city officials, with appropriate gestures, that he has had it up to here in their town," prominent *Washington Post* columnist Shirley Povich wrote in January 1972. Talk about Tampa was also whirling at the time. "Rosenbloom has vowed to take the Colts, his football team, elsewhere after only one more season in Baltimore's *miserable* [emphasis mine] stadium, an archaic structure designed to promote lumbago with its acre of backless seats."

Baltimore scribes did some piling on. "So much for what is good about Memorial Stadium," declared *Evening Sun* writer Gwinn Owens after presenting some pithy merits. "What is *bad*, I'm afraid, far outweighs the good: The most serious problem is fundamental and not changeable. The upper deck was designed for benches originally, a short-sighted capitulation to second-rate standards. The best part of the deck now has regular chairs, but jammed in so short a place as to force one's knees against the person in front. For a tall person it is miserable. The higher and outer seats have narrow benches with [metal] backs, not even designed to fit the human shape." The first 15 rows of those pink upper-deck chairbacks shortened your femur, and the backs on the benches in general admission and the bleachers were just slabs of aluminum siding.

The complaint department was open for business. "The decision to install mostly bench-type seats—decried by one contractor-fan as 'a tin-cup move'—has come back to haunt the stadium's owners, the city," the *Morning Sun* reported in November 1972. "Failure to provide better parking facilities offers another example of short-sighted economy [stinginess]. The decision to use concrete supports [those nasty poles] rather than cantilevered decking [like they have at Dodgers Stadium], while cheaper and putting seating closer to the field, has meant many obstructed seats. And, because of the supports, it is now difficult to substantially improve the seating capacity without expensive work. Because of these obstacles and others, Memorial Stadium's critics insist that despite its relative newness, it is 'an old, new stadium.'"

Colts PR director Ernie Accorsi brought on a college kid, Pete Ward, as an unpaid intern, then hired him full-time when he graduated from UVa. That gave Ward a good four years to size up Memorial Stadium:

Personally, it had a sentimental place in my heart because it was this iconic venue that I had seen so many times while watching football and baseball as a child. I thought it was beautiful inside and historic. It was just a holy place. That's how I viewed it. But it was outdated. It was not maintained well. I remember one particularly rainy day; I think it was our final home game of the '82 season. We played Miami and got killed in the mud and rain. I remember the press box leaking like a sieve. The locker room was a dungeon. I think the Orioles received preference, in terms of the locker room, and that certainly did not sit well with Mr. Irsay. There were no suites or luxury boxes. That wasn't a big factor back then; not too many stadiums had those. I think [Robert Irsay's son] Jim Irsay put it very well: If he had gotten a $12-million check or $12 million in improvements to the stadium, the team would probably still be in Baltimore. Memorial Stadium just felt "historic" in a lot of ways. In the early '80s, it felt like you were back in 1958. If you were a football fanatic and a football historian, that was wonderful. But if you were a fan, maybe not so much.

Try as he might, author William Gildea couldn't avoid damning the place with faint praise in his book, *When the Colts Belonged to Baltimore*: "It was the homely girl of stadiums. I'd watched it being built; games went on even as the second deck went up. During a Friday-night high school football game, Calvert Hall versus Patterson, I walked up the steps of the first deck and stood in dim light under a freshly poured section. To me a second deck meant that we at last had a big-league stadium, so that when I stopped beneath a light bulb and noticed the huge concrete pillars that would obscure hundreds of lower-deck views I thought they were sensational." Those stuck behind those fat stanchions over the decades would call that nuts.

As the stadium went up, the penny-pinching began. In December 1997, the *Morning Sun* described how the mindset was hardly major-league:

At the time of its final grand opening in 1954, the stadium had cost a miniscule $6.1 million—the state will spend that much on the light rail station at the Ravens stadium—and it achieved

its primary purpose: It had lured major-league baseball to town. But nearly every corner was cut. It was the first stadium built without a roof over the upper deck. Most fans sat on wooden benches without backs. There was a chronic shortage of parking and bathrooms. And the upper deck was held aloft with concrete columns that were cheap to build, but were as wide as a linebacker and spoiled the view from one out of every 10 seats.

That's not all that bugged fans in the lower deck. Down at field-level on both sides of the horseshoe, Colts fans had to peer around a line of fat behinds to catch any of the action. "For football," *Evening Sun* writer Gwinn Owens noted in 1985, "Memorial Stadium is worse. For visibility (but not comfort) upper deck seats are pretty good in any location, but the lower deck seats have a fundamental flaw. On the sidelines between the 30-yard lines, the squads and coaches of each team usually stand. Therefore the spectators in the first few rows have to stand in order to see. This means the people behind them have to stand, and so on right up to the top. In the course of a game the knee exercise is exhausting."

Colts owner Carroll Rosenbloom had a laundry list of gripes handy to unload on anyone willing to listen. C.R.'s son, Steve, was there to hear all of it. "Well, it [the stadium] was a disappointment, and it was outmoded when it was finished. You're building a stadium in an era when—how are you gonna sell tickets to people who have to sit behind a pole [pillar]? It pretty much sucked, but it was finished for us to get in there by 1953 [Rosenbloom's first year]. By the time you got to the '70s, there were teams building nice stadiums. So, my father said, 'The fans need a new house.' If you go to a friend's house, and it's messy with food sitting on the counter, wrappers on the floor, that's about how he [his father] thought about the stadium. And I agreed."

Seems the architects scaled down and went with Sakrete and rebar instead of steel. The *Morning Sun* lambasted the old girl in a 1997 article, "Only Glories Were on Field":

> It was big by baseball standards. Its use of cheap, reinforced concrete was unusual in a country accustomed to steel stadiums. News reports at the time attributed the decision to a desire to save money; concrete didn't have to be painted. The government was also still rationing steel in the late 1940s, a vestige of the war. The architects built the lower seating bowl on columns that poked through the lower deck and were capped with concrete—just in case an upper deck would someday have to be added [which it was]. Many "caps" are still visible in the exposed, northern reaches of the lower deck.

Then there was the terracotta that posed as a football field once the Orioles went on vacation until April. The guys in pads called it Astrodirt. "Memorial Stadium's playing field said everything about life: It was altogether imperfect," William Gildea declared in his testimonial to the Colts, *When the Colts Belonged to Baltimore*. "Part of the endzone in the stadium's cramped closed end stretched onto a cinder track. That endzone's right portion was called 'Orrsville' for Jimmy Orr, who made acrobatic touchdown catches there. The early games each season were played on the dirt of the baseball infield. After baseball season, sod was put down, but it was squishy soft for a couple of weeks, and after that, daily practices ate away just about all the grass so that by late November and December the field was shorn to bare earth." Carroll Rosenbloom kept peppering city bureaucrats to OK a practice field somewhere, but he got the usual hot air.

Besides his decades-long stint in the Colts band, the Maryland Stadium Authority recruited John Ziemann to inventory everything at Memorial Stadium before it got leveled. The good stuff went to the Babe Ruth Museum and the rest went on the auction block. He got a really good look at her:

> First of all, she was leaning. They had meters on her and saw she was starting to sink. You gotta realize it wasn't built as a solid stadium. They had a stadium there in 1920, then in 1948, they started tearing down one section of the stadium and building what we knew as the under-deck of Memorial, tearing down the old deck of the old stadium and building the upper deck. Finally, after 1949, they had the whole lower deck of Memorial

Stadium built. They were gonna do an upper deck, but they stopped because we lost the Colts [1950], and the minor-league Orioles had to move in there because their stadium burned down in 1944. It was basically slapped up. I don't know construction, but I think the right thing to do was tear the whole thing down, excavate it and start building the upper deck. But they had the football and baseball teams there—the old Colts—and they built it in sections. So, originally, it wasn't built right.

Despite the candy-colored seats and the fresh look off the assembly line, the grousing started right after the ribbon-cutting. "From an architectural and economic perspective, the facility was nothing to brag about," the *Morning Sun* documented in "Only Glories Were on Field." "Its two tenants [the Colts and Orioles] were grumbling about the accommodations and threatening to move barely a decade after Vice President Richard Nixon threw out the first pitch [in 1954]. The reasons were obvious. Public spending on stadiums was a new and not very popular idea in the 1940s, making money scarce. Baltimore was on a leading edge of a post-World War II wave of such construction, so there were few models to follow. 'In the 1950s, I think it was an adequate stadium, not a great one. None of the stadiums built in the 1950s and '60s were great stadiums,' said Bruce Genther, a stadium historian and model-builder from Laurel [MD] who has researched the 33rd Street structure. 'We didn't know any different. It was certainly better than what was there before,' Genther said."

And buried under the stadium was something out of *The Curse of Oak Island*. When they were looking to strip her down for parts, "They found kerosene tanks still buried in the back of the stadium parking lot, full of kerosene," John Ziemann revealed. "They also had asbestos through the whole stadium. And she was leaning. People don't realize there was an underground spring under that stadium. They would have gigantic sump pumps on her all the time. When they had the groups come in to do the excavation, I had to go down to the pilings holding up the stadium to get information for the people tearing it down. I was there with one of the guys, down in a hole, and I said, 'Hey, look. You're gonna hit water.' And he looked at me like, *Yeah. Why don't you just go away*. So, I left. I went about my business. And I get a call an hour later to come over to [section] W-7. I come over, and he's down in the hole, looking up at me, and he says, 'Guess what I'm standing in?' 'You're standing knee-deep in water.' And he says, 'Yeah. We hit water.'"

Jon Scott got to Baltimore in 1979 and was the Colts equipment manager for years. He was part of Bob Irsay's cadre that skipped town in 1984. He looked past all the mystique about Memorial Stadium and wasn't impressed:

Pretty rundown. Certainly, there were a lot of great teams that played there. Of course, you're sharing it with a baseball team, so from September into October, you gotta deal with the infield. But that was the case with a lot of teams back then. Just the locker room itself—and we only went down there to play games [because they had the practice complex in Owings Mills]. We didn't practice down there; we would move down the night before. So, we were almost like visitors ourselves. The bathrooms [in the Colts locker room] were in poor shape. You'd go in there, and there was always water on the floor. In the bathroom, you'd go in a stall to take a leak, and you look over, and there's guys reaching down to pull up their football pants so they don't get wet. It wasn't really funny—this is the NFL, and this is what you have to deal with? In other stadiums, the locker rooms weren't great. But we actually used the visitors' locker room [at Memorial Stadium]; we didn't use the Orioles' locker room. The Orioles—their lockers were nicer, so we had lockers like we saw on the road.

The old double standard in treatment, Colts and Orioles, always stuck in Rosenbloom's craw. That got tossed on the pile of general grievances that pushed C.R. out to L.A.

The conundrum was simple: She was a swell dame in her day, but a makeover wouldn't cut it. "It was a very simple, logical step to conclude that that stadium could not sustain a major-league franchise," assessed Wayne Lynch, former managing editor of the news department at WMAR-TV in Baltimore. "It had already done it for 30 years; it ain't gonna do it for 10 more, sports fans. I don't blame the Baltimore fans for loving 33rd Street [the stadium]. Think about that—the whole front of the stadium was dedicated to the [war] veterans. That's a feeling that reaches out to every guy that came back from the wars in the '40s and '50s. And there they are, immortalized. I know the love of that stadium."

JJ Stankevitz is the current Indy Colts internet scribe, but he also did some research for his four-episode podcast, "The Move." He sees Memorial Stadium as '50s drab in a bell-bottom world:

I think they [complaints about Memorial Stadium] were extremely legitimate because the NFL back then, they were in the early stages of, like, Joe Robbie [Dolphins owner] putting in premium seating [luxury suites] in Miami and realizing you could keep all this revenue, and that became a major source of new revenue to create financial stability for a lot of teams. This is before NFL TV contracts exploded. Everyone I talked to who was around Memorial Stadium all told me that there was no way it could have supported premium seating. It wasn't built for that. When it was built, there was no concept of skyboxes or club seats. It also wasn't built so that you could add them on with a snap of your fingers. To me, they were extremely legitimate complaints, and a lot of other teams around the league started to build new stadiums—including several domed stadiums—that did support what teams envisioned for the next iteration of their franchise. When Baltimore and the state of Maryland killed the "Baltodome" project [explained later], it sort of felt like that was the beginning of the end for the Colts in Baltimore.

 ❋ ❋ ❋

Catch a Colts clip from the late '70s on YouTube, and you're bound to see Len Burrier—aka The Big Wheel—in the upper deck, leading the C-O-L-T-S cheer. Loving the Colts didn't mean he was a fan of the mausoleum. "I think it was like 40% of what a major-league stadium should be," The Wheel opined. "When the [CFL Baltimore] Stallions came [1994], [owner] Jim Speros put money into the stadium. He cleaned it up a little bit. But people would sit in seats [in the lower deck] with urine dripping on them [from upstairs bathrooms]. They would tell me, 'Man, I can't sit there. It's got people peeing upstairs coming down through the floor.' It was not in good condition."

While the who shot John about the stadium was raging in 1972, the *Morning Sun* published a treatise on its sordid construction history, mentioning a 1969 study by a New York designer:

A 1969 study by a New York architect estimated that it would cost $20 million [about $77 million in today's money] to make Memorial Stadium a modern facility. The study noted that about a fifth of the seats at the stadium had obstructed views and that over half were without backs. It listed for $20 million the following alterations: an intermediate deck and an extended grandstand to add to its capacity significantly—a desirable move for football, more concession stands and toilets; complete chair seats and wider spacing between seats; new press facilities and team offices; new locker rooms, artificial turf, endzone stands, new lighting and a pedestrian overpass to improve access. The study said a dome over the field "in a temperature climate such as Baltimore enjoys" is not economical.

You don't have to twist Upton Bell's arm on that account. He got his NFL start in Baltimore and worked there for 11 years:

By 1970-71, to me, it [Memorial Stadium] had outlived its usefulness, so it was time to get one [a new stadium]. And it wasn't like he [Carroll Rosenbloom] didn't have a successful franchise. You had a franchise coming off a Super Bowl [January 1971]. Ironically, my team [when he was GM of the Patriots] came in and beat them in the last game of the year [1971], which cost them the chance to be in first place, going into the playoffs. I remember coming back [to Baltimore] for that game in December of 1971 and saying to myself as I left the press box, *You know what? This is a very old place.* So, he [Rosenbloom] started complaining then, and I don't blame him. But the time he left [for L.A.], if I didn't get a new stadium, I would have considered moving. If people weren't moving to help one of the most successful franchises in the NFL— to help them get a new stadium—then I would privately say to myself, *Where can I take this?*

The proles in nearby Waverly developed a crush on the ballpark. "Everybody loved 33rd Street [the stadium]," former WMAR-TV news director Wayne Lynch stated. "That's provincial Baltimore. That's our neighborhood stadium. It's right down the road, right across from City [College]. They [Baltimoreans] were not able to visualize that you can't build a huge [new] stadium there and expect people to come. It needs to be near major highways. And it was not any major fault of theirs; they just didn't see the future. But they [politicians] wanted to keep little old 33rd Street happy. And I get that. The neighborhood drove that stadium. People loved to walk there; they could come down Loch Raven [Blvd.]; they could come down the Alameda; they could come up York Road. It was a Sunday afternoon after church for a 2:00 game. It was a neighborhood event, and they didn't want to lose that fabric to rich people who had suites."

Stuffy sorts on the *Washington Post* editorial board stuck their noses into the debate when numbers started getting bandied about. "Some see in the list of proposed changes, with their immense price tag, a none-too-subtle hint that the old stadium isn't worth saving. Indeed, the report says, 'It would be misleading to say that all problems associated with Memorial Stadium have resolution within the context of the existing facility.' So maybe they *should* do away with Memorial Stadium—just change the name to Memorial Ballpark, keep the context of the existing facility and play ball." Baltimoreans said, worry about RFK Stadium and stay out of it.

Colts running back Lydell Mitchell toiled at Memorial for six seasons and thought its run was over:

If you were to compare it to today, it was just second-class. It was an old stadium, and there wasn't much you could do to improve upon it. They tried to renovate here and there, put a façade on it to try to make it look nice, but it wasn't gonna happen. It was an old stadium, and sometimes, you run your course. And I think that stadium had run its course. Obviously, you hated to see the Colts move, but the fact is that something needed to be done. And I guess everybody wasn't on the same page. It was time to make some decisions on a better facility because you'd seen them go up around you, all over the place [Three Rivers Stadium, Riverfront

Stadium, Veterans Stadium]. And you had to make some changes.

Sometimes, brutal honesty is the best policy. John Ziemann met his future wife at the ballpark, but that didn't change his opinion. "It [Memorial Stadium] was a dump," Ziemann lamented. "I hate to say that. I saw it first-hand before many others saw it, all the way to the end [demolition]. Just coming into Memorial Stadium [for the demolition prep], it had the feel of an old stadium. There had been a lot of patchwork done behind the scenes that people didn't see. You saw the beautiful grass field; it was a great place to watch a baseball game, except for the 'obstructed views.' But they didn't see the people that worked behind the scenes who worked so hard to keep it up. Like I've always said, it [refurbishing Memorial Stadium] was like putting a miniskirt on a 95-year-old woman. It doesn't work."

But Michael Olesker, former *Morning Sun* columnist and author of *The Colts' Baltimore:* *A City and Its Love Affair in the 1950s*, says au contraire:

There was a narrative that we liked. The narrative was, this [Memorial Stadium] was the world's largest outdoor insane asylum. It was the place where you showed up, and the same people sat next to you, year after year. The same crowd would gather out front before every game by the [memorial] plaque, some looking for tickets, so there was a narrative that we enjoyed—you gotta be there. We knew, once we got there, they weren't the best seats, it wasn't the best ballpark, but it was *ours*. This was where our history was, and we loved our history. So, we accepted what flaws there were. The only people who were arguing for a new stadium were those who were going to make more money on it.

But those guys and the baby-kissers were the ones calling the shots.

CHAPTER 4

CR HUNTS THE WHITE WHALE

Long before Bob Irsay blustered into town, Baltimore Colts owner Carroll Rosenbloom got the party started. This little nugget popped up in the August 29, 1965, *Morning Sun*: "Atlanta, Aug. 28—Does Baltimore need a new stadium? Carroll Rosenbloom, owner of the Colts, thinks so, and furthermore, he is willing to build it. 'Sure, Baltimore should have a new stadium. We want the best for our city, don't we? Our present stadium doesn't match up with all the new ones being put up around the country. We're the best and we should have the best, and I would be willing to build it,' he added."

No hot diggity dogs from the mayor and nobody on the Baltimore City Park Board grabbed a cab for Colts headquarters on Howard Street to pow-wow. Instead, the godfather went public and got crickets. Over the next 19 years, the script went about the same: Colts owner hollers about Memorial Stadium; folks seem too busy to care; owner doubles

down; officials tell him, we'll take it under advisement; owner warns of greener pastures elsewhere; politicos start to fret, form a committee; owner peddles his team to every Tom, Dick and Tampa; city coughs up dough for a feasibility study; owner huffs and puffs some more; hizzoner and lackeys sit down with owner; promises made, promises broken; owner gets price quote from Ace Moving and Storage.

The Colts were a premier NFL franchise in the '50s and '60s, along with Green Bay. Former WMAR-TV sports anchor Scott Garceau hailed from Titletown when he arrived in Baltimore in 1980. Memorial Stadium was on his beat:

It was obviously subpar. The locker rooms were very small, and I think towards the end of the Colts' run in Baltimore, skyboxes were starting to show up around the NFL. That was a new revenue stream. There was none of that in Baltimore. The inner workings of the stadium were old. I remember— it might have been an opening game, early '80s when I was here, getting on the elevator after the game to go down to the locker rooms. The elevator was packed because fans would get on the same elevator, and it was a hot day. And it got stuck. There was a pregnant lady on it. And I'm not claustrophobic, but we were stuck in there long enough that I was starting to feel like the walls were closing in. Eventually, they popped it open. But things like that happened a lot more than they should have at that place. It needed repairs in a lot of different areas.

Which is why Rosenbloom was willing to pull out his billfold to build a new stadium. First, he went to the papers. "Financing is no problem," Rosenbloom told the *Morning Sun*. "I can get that done. The only thing I would insist on is that the present stadium be pulled down." Two reasons to implode: 1) Rosenbloom thought the place was a crawlspace; and 2) He didn't want the AFL to drop a team in Baltimore, lease Memorial Stadium and park on his turf. Cameron Snyder, the reporter who heard C.R.'s beefs, knew the stadium was behind the times. "The Baltimore stadium is relatively new," Snyder noted. "The reborn Colts used it in their first season back in the National Football League in 1953. It wasn't completed until the 1954 baseball

season when the Orioles entered the American League. But compared to other sports edifices which have sprung up around the country since 1953, Memorial Stadium is as antiquated as high-button shoes."

Snyder reckoned Rosenbloom's chances of building that new stadium were about the same as James Brown singing an aria. "Although Rosenbloom's heart and pocketbook are in the right place, he is just whistling in the dark about the stadium. His plan to put in escalators was turned down many years ago. So what chance has he for a new stadium, even built by him?" Bupkis, according to city and county planners.

Carroll Rosenbloom didn't joke around about business. He wasn't griping just to get some ink. That was apparent to *Morning Sun* sports editor Bob Maisel:

When Carroll Rosenbloom was first quoted as saying he was interested in building a domed stadium in Baltimore, I thought he had probably planted the story to see what reaction it would receive in the city. I really didn't think it was possible for private capital to finance a project of this magnitude because it probably couldn't be made to pay for itself. After all, you're talking about a lot of money. The Houston Astrodome cost something in the neighborhood of $33,000,000 and they are still spending to iron out some of the kinks. If the man is kidding about building a new stadium he has carried the joke a long way.

He is dead serious about this thing, and whether or not it ever becomes a reality, he has done, and is continuing to do, considerable research on it.

Not a soul at City Hall was on top of this, however. Rosenbloom got the standard brush-off. "One thing that burns me up is the complaints about me asking for money from the city," C.R. told Maisel. "I don't know where that idea came from. I'm not asking the city for a cent. One thing I would like, though, is a little encouragement." There would be precious little of that as Rosenbloom pressed his case.

Rosenbloom thought the stadium was an Ozzie-and-Harriet relic. Time to join the '70s. "I just don't think that Baltimore can sit smugly by with new stadiums going up all over the country, and with a beautiful one with excellent parking 40 miles down the road in Washington, and another going up, possibly with a roof over it, just up the road in Philadelphia," C.R. emphasized to Bob Maisel. "How long can we expect people to battle a parking problem, then sit in the open on wooden benches with no backs, while they have domes and theater chair seats all around us? What I mean is we can't just stand still."

But stand still they did. And those rickety temporary endzone seats they threw up after baseball was another issue. Rosenbloom's son, Steve, was by his side for the whole ordeal and shakes his head. "What we had—our attendance—the number, 60,238, that was *after* the Orioles finished playing, and we could put

temporary stands [in the endzone] to fill it up to that," he stressed. "We would be playing our first few football games, and the field was a pile of crap. The players would get down in their stances, and you'd see 'em, picking up pieces of sod, getting it out of the way. The whole infield was there, so it wasn't a good situation. And in those days [the late '60s, early '70s], the Orioles were good, so their season was normally extended [by the playoffs], so we were losing that attendance. But it was a piece of crap anyway. It was an old house, and you found the first flaw when you stepped on the property."

The grumbling didn't end there. In October 1965, the *Morning Sun* ran this headline: **COLTS' OWNER PUSHING NEW STADIUM PLAN—Rosenbloom Will Put Architect to Work on Project Soon.** You thought I was bluffing, Rosey was saying. "While the Colt players and coaches were savoring their 38-to-7 victory over the Washington Redskins yesterday, owner Carroll Rosenbloom took another bite into his freshly baked pie, a new stadium for Baltimore," Cameron Snyder reported. "Carroll said after Sunday's game, 'I'm calling in an architect this week to get our stadium project moving.' Rosenbloom has said before that the present Baltimore stadium is outmoded and that he is willing to build a new stadium. However, if he does, he wants the old stadium torn down. Rosenbloom was one of the original NFL owners who was ready to sit down and talk with AFL owners. He feels both leagues are here to stay and that common problems can be solved commonly. But he apparently feels the AFL should stick in its own territory and not come tramping into areas already cultivated by the older NFL."

First off, this was four years before the AFL and NFL tied the knot, which shows real prescience on Rosenbloom's part. Second, the man was just protecting his turf. Besides, both Rosenbloom and son Steve thought renovating Memorial Stadium was just tossing money away. "That [renovating] sort of sucks because I've done renovations and built houses, some years back," Steve Rosenbloom explained. "And this is what you find: The house might have a great location, so you want to build a new one there, but there's a house already there. So, the first thought is, *Let's renovate it because we can save this house and spend less money*. Well, the reality of that—if you get into the real-estate angle—is that's not usually true. You have a vacant house there, great property, great location. OK, that makes sense, but to renovate it? They come into the house; they have to do something with these walls; you have to do something with the roof. Then you open up a wall, and you find a problem. So, the first thing you ask is, 'Do you agree that the house should go?' They could say yes or no, thinking that it's open season if you say, 'Let's renovate.' They're billing you for 10 years. So, it's probably cheaper to knock down the house that was there and build from the ground up."

And none of this was on the city's dime. Instead of greasing the skids, Baltimore bureaucrats stayed mute while Rosenbloom got busy. Meanwhile, the citizenry took notice. C. Newton Weaver sent this letter to the *Morning Sun* in January 1966: "Sir: With George P. Mahoney, former racing commission chairman, proposing that the owners of the three major race courses unify and conduct their meets at a new plant, and with Colts' owner Carroll Rosenbloom offering to build a new stadium, the time is ripe for the State to grab this plum by constructing a prodigious domed park suitable for all sports, if architecturally possible."

Somebody else also perked up when Rosenbloom verbalized—Orioles owner Jerry Hoffberger. By March 1966, he and Rosenbloom were on the outs, but Jerry saw Rosenbloom taking the lead on this one and wanted in. Bob Maisel discussed this in the *Morning Sun*:

> Several times in the last year, Carroll Rosenbloom has been quoted as saying he is definitely interested in building a new dome-type stadium in the Baltimore area. He said he would like to have the Orioles go into the venture with him, and Jerry Hoffberger has expressed interest. Even though Rosenbloom has gone so far as to experiment with architectural plans, there are a lot of people who will tell you he has never been serious about actually constructing such a stadium. Is Hoffberger interested, and does he think Rosenbloom is actually serious about eventually wanting to build a new stadium? "Yes, I'm interested," answered

the Oriole owner, "and I certainly do believe that Rosenbloom is serious about it. I've never had reason to believe he is not serious. And, if he is serious, we could hardly afford not to be interested."

Maisel opined that a new downtown stadium was a keen idea. But then the Baltimore Park Board stuck their noses into it and stopped forward progress. They wanted to patch up the old place. "The Park Board announced yesterday that it is planning extensive modernization of Memorial Stadium, while expressing interest in talk of a brand-new stadium at another location to replace the old one," the *Morning Sun* revealed. "One board member, Charles H. Rosenbaum, believes that Memorial Stadium is 'outdated to have seats without backs.' While the present arena is 'a good stadium,' Mr. Rosenbaum said, 'it has to be updated.' Most, if not all board members, agree with him.'"

Given that last line, C.R. was done for. All in favor of lipstick on a pig, say Aye. Former Colts PR director and GM Ernie Accorsi is with Rosenbloom on this one. "It [Memorial Stadium] was almost too far gone to restore," he stated. "It was just cold and dreary. The locker room was not very good at all. I went through it again in Cleveland [when he was GM there]—same thing. The fans don't care about this, but the press box was such a disjointed mess. I loved the place too much to call it a dump, but it was almost unrestorable. From an emotional standpoint, like Cleveland, I loved it. I think it was a tough place

to play. But we're not even talking about the turf. The turf was unplayable. You look at the tape of the [1971 AFC] championship game against the Raiders [aka "Duel in the Dust"], it was *dirt*. We tried to paint the endzone for NBC, and we were painting dirt."

Then, Baltimore County got into the act. "A 'modern stadium and coliseum' should be built in Baltimore County to replace the city's 'inadequate and obsolete' Memorial Stadium, a county councilman said yesterday," the *Morning Sun* declared in October 1967. "Councilman Frank C. Barrett called on Dale Anderson, the county executive, to open discussions with the Colts and Orioles about 'a modern stadium for Baltimore County to be situated on a large tract of land.' 'I think now is the time to consider the possibilities of providing a stadium in Baltimore County to house professional football and baseball.'" Barrett then invited Rosenbloom and Hoffberger to talk it over with county functionaries. Like most grandiose notions back then, it got shelved.

Beyond lip service, the Baltimore City Park Board could throw up some nifty roadblocks for Rosenbloom. "The city's director of recreation and parks voiced strong opposition yesterday to any plans to build a new municipal stadium," the *Morning Sun* informed us late in 1967. "Douglas S. Tawney, the director, said that the Parks Board and its staff are in agreement 'that it would be a complete disservice to the public of Baltimore and would be a startling unbusiness-like stance to have the city become involved in a new stadium structure elsewhere in the city of Baltimore and abandon the present structure, in which approximately $8,000,000 has been invested.' Instead of replacing Memorial Stadium, Mr. Tawney said, the city should embark on a scaled-down version of the programs of additions and renovations suggested by Mayor D'Alesandro."

Bad enough the mayor wanted money dumped into a gimpy has-been; the Park Board wanted only some rouge and lip gloss. Rosenbloom wanted no part of either. "You have the state [of Maryland] that usually can't get out of its own way; if you're from the government, you're not here to help," former Colts president Steve Rosenbloom grumbled. "That's kind of foolish [renovating Memorial Stadium]. The thing was from '52-'53, around there. It's already an old stadium. There were so many things wrong with it, and it's like, 'Do I knock down this house and build a new one?' It's the basic question. But they were only thinking, *Well, we'll go further with your money by renovating*. No. They could have done it by selling bonds and raising money while it was still palatable to most NFL cities. But we never got any enlightened help."

The savants at City Hall listed eight ways to waste taxpayer money. Among them:

- "Parking facilities for twice as many cars as the 5,000 that can currently be accommodated near the stadium."

- "Installation of chairback seats to replace as many as possible of the bench seats, and extension of the upper deck on both sides of the stadium's north end."

- "Redesigning the huge circular columns which help support the existing upper decks and interfere with the view from hundreds of lower-deck seats."

- "Improved field lighting, to meet American League (Baseball) standards."

- "Additional space for offices, commissaries, storage, meeting rooms and restaurants."

Putting wrinkle cream on a prune—what's the point?

Former *Evening Sun* columnist and author Kevin Cowherd was sympathetic:

I think of all the things you can look at, the stadium was the biggest obstacle. He [Rosenbloom] was *so* down on that stadium. There weren't enough restrooms. The seats were horrible; there were seats with no backs, seats with obstructed views. The bathrooms were antiquated; women were always complaining about the lack of bathroom facilities. To me, that was the driving force—that stadium. He kept trying to make something happen. The city was not responsive to this, plus he had other pressures and that girlfriend [Georgia Hayes] who didn't want to be here [in Baltimore]. He was so frustrated. He was getting no help from the city; city officials eventually weren't returning his calls. Yeah, he was done with it. Memorial Stadium was antiquated back *then*, in the early '70s. I got here in '81; I remember thinking, *I can't believe they play in this place.*

There was always that brick wall Rosenbloom tried to sledgehammer his way through. The local papers kept parroting the pols and rarely gave him a chance to rebut. "The Department of Recreation and Parks says the city should renovate Memorial Stadium instead of building a new one," ran a *Morning Sun* editorial in December 1967. "It should. The city taxpayer has a lot of money invested in the Stadium. It could be renovated for a fraction of the cost of a new stadium. [Baltimore City comptroller] Hyman Pressman estimates, roughly, $10 million. New stadiums cost from double to quadruple that." The *Sun* offered up three ways to raise the money: 1) The following should pay higher rentals: the ballclubs, the concessionaires, the parking lot and local TV; 2) Issue some revenue bonds for the entire Baltimore-Metro area; 3) Slap a bigger tax on tickets since everybody loves new taxes.

Vito Stellino covered the Colts for the *Morning Sun* during the Irsay era. Having spent many afternoons stuck in the pantry disguised as a press box, he had a simple solution. "The stadium was kind of jerry-built," he said. "The parking was a problem. They had those big stone pillars [holding the upper deck]. It needed to be replaced. It was totally

inadequate for a major-league stadium. But because both the Colts were winning, people put up with it. There was no question that it had to be replaced."

The opinion down on the field echoed that up in the press box. "I think people who spend their money want to come to better facilities where, if you go to the bathroom, you want toilets that work," ex-Colts running back Lydell Mitchell stated. "You want to go get decent things to eat, things like that. You just want everything run smoothly. Sooner or later, you have to make a change. Just like anything else, it [the stadium] got old; it got antiquated. Sooner or later, you have to make a change. Just like any building—you keep adding on, doing this and that. Sometimes, you're better off just tearing the damn thing down and rebuilding. Sometimes, it's cheaper that way."

Not according to the apparatchiks downtown. It didn't take Rosenbloom long to get the gist. So, he pushed a little harder. "Carroll Rosenbloom, owner of the Colts, today said the football team will not play in Baltimore next season unless there are definite commitments to renovate Memorial Stadium," the Baltimore *Evening Sun* reported in May 1969. "'We'll play in Washington or Philadelphia, if necessary. I can't allow my fans to have to use those filthy facilities any more,' he said. 'Those filthy restrooms need to be cleaned up, the concessions should be given to someone else,' and there should be comfortable seats, he said." Filthy—turning it up a notch. On top of that, Rosenbloom was fed up with his team practicing and playing on adobe. "[Comptroller Hyman] Pressman refused to speculate why Rosenbloom has failed to renew the lease," the article furthered. "City Hall sources claimed that the failure to renew is being used as a lever to force the city to pay a high percentage of the cost of putting in synthetic grass. The grass, which is now used in the Houston Astrodome, would allow the Colts to practice more often in the stadium. It costs $650,000."

The tremors weren't just local. Outsiders were tuning in. The *New York Times*, for instance: "BALTIMORE, May 20 [1969] (*AP*)—Carroll Rosenbloom, owner of the Baltimore Colts, threatened today to build his own stadium and meanwhile play home games in other cities next season unless Baltimore commits itself to improve Memorial Stadium. The National Football League club owner said he wanted the restrooms cleaned, the food and drink concessionaire changed, more comfortable seats installed and a synthetic playing turf."

Now in a lather, Rosenbloom let it rip: "Rosenbloom also had caustic comments about the Baltimore Orioles, who play baseball in Memorial Stadium," the *Times* continued. "He noted that the Colts paid the city $78,000 last year for eight games and an attendance of 436,878 while the Orioles paid only $38,000 for 65 games and an attendance of 739,534. 'This is one hell of a situation for a major-league football team,' stormed Rosenbloom. 'First we have to practice at Western Maryland College [training camp], then we

have to find some high school nice enough to let us practice.'"

Rosenbloom had dragged Jerry Hoffberger into the scrap. He poked the bear a second time. "He [Rosenbloom] said he was ready to help pay a share of improving the municipal stadium, but said, 'I don't think the brewery [i.e., Hoffberger] will cooperate in cost sharing.' The majority stockholder in the Orioles is the National Brewing Company. 'The brewery says when we can play and when we can put in extra seats for the football season.'"

The feud between Rosenbloom and Hoffberger kicked off a few years earlier, so this was nothing new. The Colts always resented the double standard: We're tired of getting table scraps. As the PR man for Rosenbloom and eventual Colts GM, Ernie Accorsi recognized the origin of it:

Look, when you tried to attract two teams [the Colts and the Orioles] to Baltimore—the Colts in '53—they were a vagabond team nobody wanted. I mean, Bert Bell had to *talk* Carroll into taking it. They had to take that wagon around town to sell season tickets. To get a major-league baseball team was a different animal. You had to come up with a helluva lease to get approval. [Bill] Veeck had tried to move the [St. Louis] Browns to Baltimore and got turned down. So, they [the Orioles] had levers to get a great lease. That didn't happen out of any prejudice; that was a much bigger jewel for the city and Mayor [Thomas]

D'Alesandro to attract than the Colts. But the Colts turned out to be THE franchise in the '60s until the '70s. At the time [the mid-1950s], the Colts were just a vagabond franchise.

More proof that Baltimore wanted to patch up Memorial Stadium on the cheap came when the mayor lopped off $13 million in suggested improvements and crossed his arms. "Earlier this year [1969], Praeger-Kavanagh-Waterbury, the New York firm which is preparing a report on improvements to the stadium, submitted a preliminary report which called for spending about $18 million on an ambitious renovation and improvement program," the *Morning Sun* indicated. "However, Mayor D'Alesandro asked the consultants to scale their proposals down to $5 million. The scaled-down proposals were presented in draft form to city officials last Friday, and the Park Board asked the consultants yesterday to print them in a final report." Rosenbloom still kept working the angles. "Joseph Rash, the Park Board chairman, said yesterday that Carroll Rosenbloom, the owner of the Colts, has agreed to advance the city money— interest free—to make the improvements he wants, and then to take the repayment for the advance in the form of reduced rentals." The Park Board dropped that into file 13.

Then the Park Board chairman lived up to his name. The board hemmed and hawed about approving the Colts' home schedule for 1970, largely for effect. "The Colts don't belong to Rosenbloom," Joseph Rash

proclaimed. "They belong to the fans of Baltimore. But I feel by approving the dates that it'll be easier to straighten out the problems." The-Colts-Are-Ours brigade would prove to be just as wrong as the flat-earthers.

Rosenbloom kept at it, pulling another ploy out of the bag and getting spun around by a starched suit. He tried the I-was-only-joking approach. "Carroll Rosenbloom said today he was only being facetious yesterday when he said he might move to Washington or Philadelphia," the *Evening Sun* divulged in May 1969. "However, the team owner said he was very serious in his demand for Memorial Stadium improvements. 'And I am quite willing to pay for them with my own money,' he added in an interview. Then he gave the ballpark another swift boot:

> Memorial Stadium, opened in 1953, "was fine until other cities started building newer stadiums," he said. "I just feel that we're being derelict to our fans if we don't provide them with improvements." Several times Mr. Rosenbloom has been quoted as saying he would like to build his own stadium, and he said that is still on his mind. "The only thing is that when I first mentioned it, people acted like I was some kind of traitor," Mr. Rosenbloom said. "I don't know why I would be. If I go into it and lose my money, nobody can be mad except my son, Steve."

Around the bend came John Steadman. Half the time, he wrote about quirky hometown characters but reserved Carroll Rosenbloom for public floggings. In his *News American* column, Steadman wisecracked that Baltimore could now heave a sigh of relief that the despot was staying put. Next came his specialty: mounting the pulpit. "Rosenbloom should know better than to get caught up in anything that even remotely suggests a switch out of Baltimore. It was this city which put Carroll Rosenbloom in the football business. It made a celebrity out of him. And that's no kidding. Baltimore was so good to Rosenbloom that it put down $300,000 in advance ticket sales for the Colts' franchise to come here in 1953. He never had to go to the bank for operating funds. The money was there and waiting."

Steadman got it bass-ackwards, as usual. First—the $13,000 that Rosenbloom put down on the Colts was pocket change. Second—Bert Bell Sr. applied a full-nelson on C.R. to get him to say yes. Third—Rosey dropped a mil-plus of his own into the Colts' bank account for seed money. Says son Steve Rosenbloom: "Football was a gamble back in the early days. So, my father finally relented to Bert's pressure. And he told me, 'Steve, I put a million dollars in the bank, and if it doesn't work out, that's it.'" But for Steadman, reason and Rosenbloom lived in two different hemispheres.

Steadman ended the tent show with more finger-wagging:

> Baltimore only needs one stadium and
> if improvements are continued on the

one we now have it should be more than adequate for years to come. The City of Baltimore has been good to Rosenbloom and the Colts—in a way that they could never repay all the generous things done for them. Threats, even kidding, are bad. The public doesn't want to hear it. Controversy between the Colts and Orioles makes for a deplorable state of affairs. It shouldn't be allowed to happen.

Actually, the guy who went all-in, rolled the dice and brought the town a winner didn't want to hear it. Fifteen minutes with son Steve would have cleared out most of the debris in Steadman's head: "The fans bought the franchise for him, Baltimore made him a millionaire, Baltimore made him famous," etc. etc. etc.

June 1969 again saw Rosenbloom out on the campaign trail, lobbying to build his own stadium. Then this occurred to him: "What would be wrong about a stadium in the Towson area [a suburb of Baltimore]?" he wondered aloud to the *Morning Sun*. "I have the ground and the money. The Park Board brought in an outfit to look over the Stadium, and it suggested that in order to bring the present stadium up to par with the newer parks, it would take $25,000,000. That is way too much money. I know the city can't afford anything like that, and I know I wouldn't want the taxpayers to suffer such a load." He followed with another dig at Jerry Hoffberger and the Birds. "All I want to do is build my own stadium. I don't know why they (the

City) have to pay baseball to play there (at the stadium) and make football pay to play there (the Orioles share the concessions at the Stadium which nearly pays the rent)."

The Baltimore County executive's reply to Rosenbloom—fat chance. "Earlier this month Dale Anderson, Baltimore County executive, said he would 'absolutely not' favor any kind of tax incentive to induce the Colts to resettle in Baltimore County," the *Morning Sun* divulged. *News American* sports editor and caped avenger John Steadman thought, *Serves him right*. "Zoning for turning spacious farms into commercial use [a new stadium] would have been virtually impossible," Steadman chronicled in his book, *From Colts to Ravens*. "The neighbors were ready to marshal an all-out fight to resist any intrusion on this magnificent natural setting. Dale Anderson, a strong, outspoken leader, the chief executive of Baltimore County, wanted nothing to do with any such plan. He made [Baltimore] Mayor William Donald Schaefer happy when he said, 'The Colts belong to Baltimore. They are important to the city. We don't want them because they are Baltimore's property and always have been. I love to go to Memorial Stadium to watch them play.'"

Whenever Steadman took aim at Rosenbloom, a little unpacking was in order: 1) Rosenbloom was like all owners—harrumphing that the Colts were "Baltimore's team" and that he should grovel aggravated him; and 2) Towson back in '69 wasn't something out of Wordsworth; the town actually had office buildings, stores and real people, not cow

pastures. The hunch is, the two honchos—Anderson and Schaefer—devised sticking it to Rosenbloom over brandy and prime rib.

The ill will between Hoffberger and Rosenbloom was forever mucking up the works. They couldn't see eye-to-eye if their noses were glued together. Witness the gulf about the stadium. Doug Brown of the *Evening Sun* pointed out in July 1969: "The problem is that the improvements which the Orioles consider important are deemed unnecessary by the Colts, and vice versa. The Colts, for instance, want artificial turf and a larger seating capacity. The Orioles don't need those things, but they'd like more benches converted into chairback seats, which the Colts don't want."

A stadium resolution stalled every time Hoffberger and Rosenbloom opened their mouths. Doug Brown explains: "The Orioles' priority list does not coincide with the Colts' or the city's, however. In the $6-million Stadium improvement plan, city comptroller Hyman Pressman lists artificial turf, a Colt locker room, a better football press box and folding football stands as the four most needed improvements. No. 5 is the Orioles' request for more chairback seats." This was castor oil down Hoffberger's throat. He sarcastically veered off-script: "Hoffberger said he hasn't had any recent discussions with Rosenbloom. 'I haven't spoken to him—except to inquire about his health—for some time.' When his listeners tittered, knowing that Hoffberger and Rosenbloom aren't exactly chummy and thinking there was an acid note in Jerry's voice, he added, 'Seriously, I heard he had been ill and called him on the phone.'" Wry smile from Jer.

John Steadman pulled out his blackjack and told Hoffberger to step aside. This brow-beating took place in his July 27, 1969, column in the *News American*:

> Rosenbloom and Hoffberger have a personal vendetta. This should not interfere with the Colts' and Orioles' dealings with the City of Baltimore. Petty complaining that the Orioles are shown partiality doesn't hold up under scrutiny. The Colts do not share in concession rights at Memorial Stadium, but the Orioles do. This was part of the agreement when the Orioles came here in 1954 as the transplanted St. Louis Browns. The Orioles installed the concession stands and food preparing equipment at a cost of around $300,000. The Colts paid not a cent of this. The Orioles' share in concession monies in 1968 at Colts' football games came to somewhere near $30,000—hardly a windfall. The Colts do get to keep all profit from the sale of game programs but this, too, isn't a major item.

Do the math: 15 seasons x $30,000= $450,000—and that doesn't include what Hoffberger raked in from Orioles games over the same stretch. And only a scam would involve a baseball team pocketing the proceeds from *football* programs. No wonder

Rosenbloom was on steady boil re: Hoffberger and the Orioles.

Was Steadman out of town when he missed Rosenbloom's incessant beefs about the stadium? And he was way off about the Park Board: "Rosenbloom has inferred the Colts get stepchild treatment from the City; that the Orioles are No. 1 and receive preferential treatment," Steadman intoned. "It has appeared to us that the Park Board has made every effort to make the Stadium comfortable for both tenants. Hoffberger and the Orioles have made their position clear on the Stadium matter. To further explain the situation and not specifically state the Colts' position, it would be helpful if Rosenbloom took the witness stand. Then the public will be able to see both sides of the issue and all concerned can get on with the work that needs to be done."

Rosenbloom's many depositions about the stadium also slipped him by. Other reporters of a more objective bent saw the double standard that Steadman missed. In his chronicle of the Browns' move to Baltimore, *Glory for Sale*, Jon Morgan mentions the bad blood between Rosenbloom and Hoffberger:

> Rosenbloom was selling every ticket he could print, and it irked him that his capacity was limited by the baseball team. When the Orioles' season ended, the city added 5,000 temporary stadium seats. But this addition was delayed if the Orioles went into postseason play, leaving some Colts season-ticket holders with no seats at all for early-season

games. The city's leases with the two teams also favored the Orioles, reflecting the greater priority on acquiring a major-league baseball team in 1954 than a football team in a fledgling league. The Orioles had control over stadium concessions and parking—even during football games. Rosenbloom had all the money he wanted and little use for the hassle. Memorial Stadium just wouldn't do. So he started dealing.

First, he turned the knob to the right: "Colts owner Carroll Rosenbloom today said if his team stays in Baltimore, a new Memorial Stadium contract 'of at least 10 years' would have to be settled 'within the next two to three weeks,'" reported the *Evening Sun* in October 1969. "Mr. Rosenbloom recently exercised an option which extends a former contract until 1972. Asked when he emerged from the meeting [with Baltimore Mayor Thomas D'Alesandro] if the Colts would stay in Baltimore for some time to come, Mr. Rosenbloom replied, after some hesitation, 'I would hope so.'"

A pause and some waffling: ominous. A rock-solid "absolutely" would have calmed the waters. A chat with *Morning Sun* sports editor Bob Maisel didn't help matters. "Convinced that there will be no major overhaul of Memorial Stadium in the near future, Carroll Rosenbloom last night said that he will go ahead with plans to build a Colt practice field, office and dressing room facilities in Baltimore County," Maisel wrote. "The

Colts will continue to play their home games in the Stadium, but that's the only time they will use it once the new complex is finished." Rosenbloom told Maisel he could lend the city $1.5 mil to pretty up the stadium and get it back in reduced rent. The mayor said no dice to the loan *and* a 10-year lease. "Look," Rosey told Maisel, "please make it understood I have no quarrel with the city. I know they don't have the money, and that many things take priority over Stadium improvements. If they can't see their way through to do it even if we advance the money, I can understand. But I own some property in the county [Baltimore] and have options on some more, and I think the time has come for the Colts to go ahead with plans. What I intend to do is build a practice field, office, dressing room, weight room, everything we need, and then we'll only need the Stadium for the day of the game." Super idea! But that also got chucked, and in '72, Rosenbloom traded the Colts to Robert Irsay—who pulled the plans out of the dumper and built his *own* complex.

Maisel got Hoffberger on the phone for his input. "What Rosenbloom has told you agrees with what I know of the situation. We were asked to extend the lease 10 years, and I'd be willing to do it to get a new scoreboard. But I believe the city just has so many things to do, and the Stadium is so far down on the priority list that the money simply isn't available. There is greater need for the money in other areas, even on the basis of paying back any loans that we might advance them."

Somewhere down near Tierra del Fuego on the priority list was the mausoleum on 33rd Street.

The Rosenblooms saw the Baltimore Park Board as a collection of stiffs. Steve Rosenbloom said they knew the score:

> If you go to a meeting and expect that there's something to talk about, and they make you think they're gonna help and they don't, it doesn't take too many meetings to figure out that you're just getting lip service. It's like you have a broken-down place that you're renting, and the landlord says, "Yeah, I'll fix some things, and it'll only cost you $2,000 a month more. Just sign a lease for 10 years." So, to arrive at an answer of "F-you" is pretty easy to come to. They can't walk you down some golden sidewalk with promises that'll never come. You know those people after you talk to them a little bit, and you might think that's what you'll get, but it only takes another couple meetings to know that they have *no* intention of resolving anything. And I've never figured that out. It would have been a big boost to the stadium Park Board. They would've looked great to the people in Baltimore. There wouldn't have been any of this nonsense going on. And in participating in helping to build a new stadium that fans would be proud to go to—it would have been a win-win.

CHAPTER 5

VOICE FROM THE PULPIT

How it all started, nobody knows for sure. But somewhere along the line Carroll Rosenbloom and John Steadman went to DEFCON 3 on each other and never dropped it down. Since Steadman had his keyboard and Rosenbloom in his sights, the war was a one-way blitzkrieg; all Rosey could do was bob and weave.

The truly nasty stuff started in the summer of '69, when Rosenbloom proposed that Colts season-ticket holders do likewise for preseason games, to Steadman a J.P. Morgan move. The chief moral arbiter and sports editor of the Baltimore *News American* contracted a severe case of indignation. Steadman nailed Rosenbloom with a bolo punch a full year before the proposal:

> Only because there's a need for it, we take pleasure in announcing the formation of the S.P.C.S.... It stands for Society for Prevention of Cruelty to Spectators. Professional sports have gone so far in taking advantage of the paying customer

that sooner or later the spectator is going to have to rise up and hold a demonstration, float a petition or stage a protest march. The Baltimore Colts, citing an example of what would be an unfair practice, would like to put on an exhibition game in Baltimore and tie it into the season ticket package. So, whether you wanted it or not, you would have to buy the meaningless practice game. What the Better Business Bureau of Baltimore would say about such blackjack tactics would be interesting. In other cities in the National Football League, such a holdup of the cash customer has been successfully accomplished. Jesse James isn't dead. You, the public, have brought pro football to the place of eminence it holds today, but the only thanks you get is a raise [sic] in ticket prices.

It was best to duck and cover when Steadman turned molehills into mountains. Rosenbloom's preseason ticket proposal was football's firebombing of Dresden. And what of it, anyway? Most NFL teams already had it. Rosenbloom so admitted in a letter to Colts fans: "For 1970, at least 20 of the 26 teams in professional football will include an average of two preseason games on their season tickets. No team could or would continue this policy if their season ticketholders did not approve. We believe that fans in Baltimore are no different."

Oh, but they were. Steadman could use that column six days a week to cudgel Rosenbloom black and blue. Rosenbloom commandeered Colts PR director Ernie Accorsi to dig him out of this mess:

I think I know what the cornerstone of it is [Rosenbloom's problems with Steadman and the press]. I think a lot of it was the preseason games. When we went to the AFC [in 1970], almost the entire American Football League had the preseason games on the [regular-season] package. That was the season-ticket package—you bought 10 games. When we went over there [to the AFC], we're competing against teams that already had that plan. It's before my time, but there was a famous game in '59 [Colts vs. Giants], after the championship the year before, when we played a preseason game against the Giants, and, like, 5,000 people showed up. So, that was the end of that. When I got there—all preseason games on the road. And the interesting thing about it was Carroll

never did it [officially tied preseason tickets to the regular-season package]. Before I got there [in 1970], he said he was gonna do it, and Steadman hammered him on that. What happened was, we decided to play preseason games at home in '71 without the package—Dallas, Kansas City and the Bears. If we were ever gonna draw, those would be the teams. We hired an advertising firm to pump up the preseason games, and it was disaster—I think we drew like 17,000, 12,000. Awful. But we never did it [with Rosenbloom]. Next year, boom—Joe Thomas [and Irsay] put it right on the package.

Steadman admitted as much (again) in a follow-up. "We remember when the Los Angeles Rams first employed this vice-like device to extract money from season ticketholders by making them take exhibition games, too. They were hoping they wouldn't get much flak, and they didn't. But even the Rams were wondering if they would get away with it. The other teams, seeing what Los Angeles was doing, decided to get in the act. The practice spread [to 20 of 26 teams] but only because there was no great cry from those being abused. In Baltimore, the case was different." Different like root beer and Natty Boh. Baltimore was Boston after the Stamp Act, Steadman playing Samuel Adams.

. . .

John Steadman was the heavyweight of Baltimore sports columnists. Folks flipping through the *New American* went right to Steadman before checking on world affairs. For almost 70 years he cranked out columns in the *News American*, the *Evening Sun* and later the *Morning Sun*. He was the Ripken of Baltimore football—attending every Colts or Ravens game from 1947 to December 10, 2000, 719-straight. In 2000, his cronies put him in the National Sportscasters and Sportswriters Association Hall of Fame. Six months after he passed, the Associated Press sports editors posthumously honored the man with the Red Smith Award, the big enchilada.

Steadman sermonized about good guys and bad guys, Dick Tracy vs. Flattop Jones Sr. But Carroll Rosenbloom got hellfire and damnation. If the stadium squabble had Rosenbloom half out the door, Steadman hip bumps finished him off. Beatdowns of Rosenbloom didn't require evidence, just elbows and uppercuts: Believe it 'cause I said so. Case in point: "Working on a newspaper had an appeal all its own and I signed a contract with the publisher [of the *News American*], Fred I. Archibald, without even looking at the financial terms," Steadman wrote in his book, *From Colts to Ravens*. "I told him, 'Pay me what you want.' I was going from the Colts [as former PR director] but would still be in the press box watching them play. Friends were surprised I made such a move. What they didn't know was that when you work for a team, at least one owned by Rosenbloom, too often

you were expected to compromise yourself. It wasn't quite the fun and games the public believed it to be." For those waiting for proof, don't bother.

The stars of Barry Levinson's 30-for-30 *The Band That Wouldn't Die* are the Colts Band and John Ziemann; he and some colleagues saved the band for reincarnation as the Marching Ravens. To Ziemann, the preseason ticket debacle put the Steadman-Rosenbloom feud into overdrive:

The NFL was progressing. After the '58 championship game, it just took off like a rocket. Football became America's Game. All of a sudden—it wasn't mandatory—but a lot of teams were making preseason games mandatory [on the ticket package]. Baltimore did not. We had three preseason games—three home games—and at that time, Rosenbloom didn't do it. But in order to stay financially above water, you needed that revenue. Finally, the Colts tried to make it part of the ticket package. Regarding the press and [city comptroller] Hyman Pressman, they went after Carroll Rosenbloom. Rosenbloom saw what was coming. He was a savvy, intelligent businessman who saw where the NFL was going: "We have to do this." The stadium was falling apart, and the people in Baltimore wanted to stay in the '50s and early '60s. If you wanted a major-league team, you had to be a major-league city.

Cartoonist Mike Ricigliano arrived in Baltimore from Buffalo during the Irsay era, landing a job with the *News American*. Steadman spotted a good recruit:

John Steadman found me right away. He found the art department and realized very quickly that I loved football. I was a football-first guy too because I had come from Buffalo. I'm a New Yorker; I'm a born-in-Brooklyn guy. But I went to school [college] in Buffalo, met my wife in Buffalo and lived there, worked for the paper there. But John would come in to my art department, and once he realized that I loved football, he would tell me stories about the Colts almost every night. He loved to tell stories, and the Colts were such a true bunch of characters that he had a very receptive audience in me. And I love John; he was just a great and unique individual. Everything I learned about the Colts was from John Steadman.

If you went to a Colts game in the '70s, you saw a big guy in the upper deck, first-base side, pantomiming the C-O-L-T-S cheer. Len Burrier. It was John Steadman who came up with the nickname that stuck. "I went with a bus that left a bar [the second week in October, Colts vs. Bills]," Burrier recalled. "I can see myself right now: We were in the upper deck, on the left side if you're looking at home plate, and it was hot and kinda boring. I said, 'Man, this team's gotta get a little

better.' For what reason, I don't know, but I got up and started using my body to get the fans cheering. It caught on. John Steadman, he saw me doing that, and at the time, I had a tire store up in Perry Hall. So, he [Steadman] said, 'Oh, he's got a tire store and is big and sells tires and wheels, so we'll call him "The Big Wheel."'"

Steadman had a sonorous voice, William F. Buckley down an octave. Almost like a Bible-thumper just getting started. "It was like God speaking to you," Mike Ricigliano affirmed. "He had quite a presence when he spoke to you, and he had that eloquence about him. As eloquent as he sounded, he enjoyed goofy stories and me as this cartoonist dude. He had other people on his staff—like Barry Levine—who were disheveled, and John just liked characters. He wrote about them all the time. We [Ricig's wife and he] had been at parties where he would tell stories, and the audience would be captivated. He was a very good spokesperson for, I guess, all things right. I didn't always agree with John, but I think he had a very strong moral code about things. And he stuck to it and was very opinionated. You listened when he spoke."

Columnists have carte blanche with opinions. That's their domain. But Steadman also loved to toss in some preachifying. Here he is thundering from the pulpit about Rosenbloom and Robert Irsay in March 1984:

How the Baltimore Colts went from being a spectacularly successful franchise—on the field and off—to what could be a terminal case is poignantly explained by a succession of dollar signs … $$$$$$$$$$$$$$$$$. The Colts played in their own garden of greed—thanks to the machinations of Robert Irsay and Carroll Rosenbloom, who put their insatiable desires for money ahead of a public confidence they blatantly damaged and betrayed. During the Rosenbloom regime, in an effort to portray an image of white-helmeted righteousness, he guaranteed that good things be spoken and written about him by paying off some reporters who sold their souls and journalistic integrity for gifts, tips on the stock market and outright financial payoffs. Too bad. Rosenbloom owned the Colts from 1953 through 1971, when they enjoyed three world championships and were a vehicle for providing untold millions of dollars. He only put up $13,500 when the franchise was granted, which is the second-best deal to the one Peter Stuyvesant pulled on the Indians when he gave $24 worth of trinkets for Manhattan Island.

Where to begin: 1) Rosenbloom got dragged into the NFL by Bert Bell Sr. and the odds were lousy of making a killing; 2) Steadman never ponied up any evidence of Rosenbloom payola to reporters despite mentioning it 527 times; and 3) Notice the hypocrisy—clapping the "spectacularly successful franchise" on the back while ignoring the guy who made it happen.

And Steadman would pound the same point over and over until it was corn meal. Take this barrage in April 1971, most of it balderdash:

> Since Baltimore put the Colts in business and made them the successful and affluent organization they are today, it's only right and proper that they stay here. They shouldn't leave Memorial Stadium. Governor Marvin Mandel feels this way. So does Mayor Thomas D'Alesandro. And, likewise, Bill Boucher, director of the Greater Baltimore Committee plus thousands of the Colts' season ticket buyers. The Colts belong in Baltimore. Had it not been for Baltimore building a Stadium it would have been impossible for the team to come here. And if it wouldn't have been for the public putting up $300,000, after the sale of 15,000 season tickets in a six-week period in 1952, the Colts never would have made it.

Why, Steady, why? First: The stadium was a hovel, and he knew it. Second, you wanna reach the majors, you need a ballpark, Rosenbloom or no. Third, the Colts' ticket drive in '53 wasn't a GoFundMe: The town had to sell 15,000 season tickets or fuhgeddaboudit. Rosenbloom bought his minority share for the $13,000 he kept in his shoe. That $300,000 Steadman kept yammering about went into the Colts' coffers. It was Rosenbloom who took a gamble on a football team in a middling league, not Baltimore.

Try this on for size; Steadman in the *News American*, July 6, 1971:

It should be of vital concern to the Baltimore Colts—not the players or coaches, but management—that they have seriously jeopardized their popularity with the public. Why? The answer is basic. It's there for all to see. When the fans are disregarded and looked upon for what can be extracted from them, they sooner or later get to wondering where they stand and the part they play. The Colts are the Super Bowl champions [Super Bowl V], which is the highest position of prestige a team can enjoy. Unfortunately for them, they have lost some favor with a series of blundering policy moves that have an adverse public reaction. The Colts have no one to blame but themselves. They have inflicted self-harm by their own mistakes. One week, they were talking about building a private stadium. The next week, there was a story the franchise was for sale. Don't ever forget that this was a team *the public put in business by the purchase of over $300,000 worth of tickets in 1953* [emphasis mine].

When Steadman wasn't thumping Rosenbloom with nunchucks, he occasionally took to grandstanding. Like hogging some of the credit for Baltimore getting the Dallas Texans in '53:

The record shows that this reporter campaigned for the successful return of pro football to this city. One sports official told us we were wasting our time—that Baltimore would never get a franchise. Our interest in the team, from the outset, *has been stronger and more avid than those of other reporters* [emphasis mine]. In fact, the other daily newspaper sports editors [the *Morning* and *Evening Sun*] were not identified with pro football 20 years ago and thus, through no fault of their own, weren't even on the scene to see the remarkable way the Colts' franchise was put together. The same goes for all the radio-TV reporters. They were someplace else—not here living the story of how much the public put Baltimore in pro football. And, furthermore, not a single member of the Colts' present front office was here to observe how the team was first financed and then an owner, general manager and coach selected by the late commissioner, Bert Bell.

Bet that thrilled sports editors Bob Maisel and Bill Tanton. And he loved doubling down to pound it into your skull. To wit, August 8, 1971: "This newspaper [the *News American*] is proud to be able to say it is the one that campaigned relentlessly to put Baltimore in the big leagues of football and baseball. The late Rodger H. Pippen [former sports editor of the paper] led the fight for baseball, and the record shows this reporter was instrumental in the return of football." "This reporter" was Steadman eschewing the pronoun "I."

But Steadman had plenty of oomph in Baltimore. Veteran NFL exec Upton Bell worked for the Colts for 11 years and paid tribute to Steadman in his NFL autobiography, *Present at the Creation*:

> Over my years in Baltimore [1960-1971] I got to know well the leading sports columnist in town, a former Colts PR man named John Steadman. Steadman was the most influential voice in the media, although in those days it was called the press. He wrote a column six days a week for 30 years, first at the *News-Post* and then the *News American*, which were the biggest newspapers in town for decades, back when people trudged home at night after a long day of hard labor at Bethlehem Steel or the Domino Sugar refinery near the Inner Harbor and picked up the evening paper. Late in his career, long after he'd engaged in a vicious battle with Rosenbloom over the owner's insistence that season ticket holders be forced to buy exhibition game tickets they had no interest in, John jumped over to the *Sun*, a morning paper that eventually became the lone newspaper survivor in town. Nobody loved the Colts more than Steadman, who went so far as to sit alone in the stands at an empty Memorial Stadium in 1984 after Robert Irsay, the owner of the Colts, had abandoned Baltimore for Indianapolis. It was the

Sunday they would have played their first game that season.

Rosenbloom aside, John Steadman knew his sports and where to find human interest stories. Baltimore had a slew of eccentrics—City Councilman Mimi DiPietro, Comptroller Rhymin' Hyman Pressman, duckpin bowler Toots Barger; even Mayor William Donald Schaefer was good for a chuckle now and again. Steadman would find folks on the fringes and celebrate them. He even amazed as soothsayer regarding the '58 championship game. William Gildea's eulogy for Steadman in the January 2, 2001, *Washington Post* tells the tale:

> On the morning of December 27, 1958, John Steadman, who died yesterday from cancer at 73, took the elevator to the fifth-floor newsroom of Baltimore's old *News-Post*. No one was there. He was the youngest sports editor in America and had been writing his column for less than a year. But he knew about the Colts. He had been the team's publicist, and before that he had covered the team as a reporter for the paper. He tapped out his column and left it behind with a prediction of the score, to be placed under a big block heading entitled "Expert Opinions." He picked the Colts, of course. He said it would be 23-17. The man in the composing room knew sports, too, and wanted to save the columnist an embarrassment. "We can't print this," the man

downstairs said. But Steadman's assistant replied: "John's gone. We have to run it. We don't have any choice." So, on the morning of the championship game, the first pick under "Expert Opinions" read: John F. Steadman, sports editor—Colts 23, Giants 17. Steadman was right that time—and for most of his writing life.

His cronies respected him; some even revered him. In June 1975, this blip appeared in the *Atlanta Daily World*: "CANTON, Ohio—John Steadman, veteran sports editor of the Baltimore *News American*, has been named the winner of the seventh annual Dick McCann Memorial Award. The award, given for long distinguished reporting in the field of pro football, is presented by the Pro Football Writers of America, whose 1975 president is Larry Fox of the *New York News*. His story on the 1959 Colts-New York Giants NFL championship game was voted the 'outstanding sports story of the year' and this marked the only time a writer from Maryland won that award." No doubt about it—Steadman was a heavyweight. And Rosenbloom cringed when he was on the warpath.

. . .

It was Carroll Rosenbloom and GM Don Kellett who turned a Dallas Texans clown show into the premier franchise in the NFL. But in November 1966, Kellett retired. Rosenbloom found his successor around the corner: Joe Campanella, who played for the Colts and joined Gino Marchetti and Alan Ameche

in the burger business (likewise as GM of the Rustler steakhouse chain). Kellett said he would groom Campy until he checked out on February 1, 1967. Two weeks after Kellett headed to Florida to work on his suntan and canasta game, Campanella was playing handball with Colts head coach Don Shula. Calamity. Tragedy. "Joe Campanella, recently named general manager of the Baltimore Colts, died yesterday afternoon at the Maryland General Hospital after collapsing with a heart attack during a handball game with coach Don Shula," the *Morning Sun* reported on February 16, 1967. "Campanella, just 36 years old, was pronounced dead at 6:50, just one hour after he was brought into the hospital's emergency room."

Besides losing one of the Colts family, Rosenbloom was in a pickle. First, he loses the architect of the championships, then his protégé. The *Morning Sun's* Bob Maisel said as much:

> I suppose if you were to name the three most important men in the development of the Colts as a team and one of the solidest franchises in the league, they would be Carroll Rosenbloom, Don Kellett and John Unitas, and you can arrange them in your own order. You don't build a franchise from almost nothing to the stature the Colts enjoy without sound ownership, management, and organization in the front office, or without a top quarterback and leader on the field. Rosenbloom and Kellett

took care of the front office organization, and who has ever done more for a ballclub on the field than Unitas, the man Kellett was responsible for bringing to Baltimore with that now-famous 85-cent phone call to Pittsburgh.

Bill Tanton of the *Evening Sun* concurred:

It's a whole new ballgame now, as the popular saying goes. Baltimore is synonymous with sports. We are big league, and no man had a bigger role in the rise of sports in Baltimore than Don Kellett, who died this week at 61 [November 1971]. The Colts, you see, made it first. They were the first to win nationwide acclaim for the NFL championships they won in 1958 and 1959. They put us on the map, so to speak, and Don Kellett made the Colts. Colt owner Carroll Rosenbloom never made a smarter move in his life than he did when he brought Kellett here from Philadelphia in 1953 to run the Colts. Kellett, in a city where pro football had failed only a few years before, made following the Colts a quasi-religious experience.

A little backslapping for Rosenbloom and a furrowed brow from Steadman.

They found a GM in-house: Harry Hulmes, another guy who earned brownie points working his way up—business manager, PR director, assistant GM. Hulmes's first year on the job was a novelty: The Colts went 11-1-2, lost the head-to-head with the L.A. Rams and got jobbed out of the playoffs. Harry Hulmes gets the nod. Which summons one theory on why Steadman slammed Rosenbloom every chance he got. Steve Rosenbloom on the theory:

We picked Joe Campanella for GM, and he was playing handball with Shula, had a heart attack and boom. That was it. Wonderful guy and still very young. So, John [Steadman] must have thought, *Oh, well, I should've been offered the job then* [after Kellett retired]. But he obviously wasn't thinking clearly. Carroll knew him well [Steadman worked PR for the Colts before moving to the *News-Post*], and he had an opportunity to hire him, but didn't. That's what torqued up in his [Steadman's] brain, and when Joe Campanella died, he probably figured, *Oh, I'll get it now*. And he didn't. When you're passed over twice, maybe you can read the tea leaves. But that's not what happened. And he just—I think that's when the marbles started to go in different directions. And he was convinced that it was all Carroll's fault that he didn't get the job. So, he got a promotion [at the *News American*] and got his own column. That's like putting a gun in somebody's hand.

If the Campanella and Hulmes hires poisoned his spleen, Steadman didn't vent in his book, *From Colts to Ravens*. Just the opposite:

It was Rosenbloom's decision, and a popular one, to elevate Harry Hulmes, who had joined the Colts when I left in early 1958 to accept the position as sports editor of the Baltimore *News-Post,* later to be called the *Baltimore News American.* Hulmes was smart, honorable, and dedicated. If any man never had an enemy, it was Harry. He had graduated from the University of Pennsylvania, as had Rosenbloom and Kellett, and everything about him was first rate, including a vast knowledge of all sports, a meticulous approach to the job, a sense of fairness, and complete integrity. He was almost too good for his own good.

It's possible that last sentence was a sideways dig at Rosenbloom. And Rosenbloom got no kudos for the choice.

Steadman turned the preseason ticket imbroglio of '69 into Armageddon. Looking for extra revenue with player salaries on the rise, Rosenbloom joined 20 other teams and slapped preseason tickets onto the regular-season package. You'd have thought the Brits had invaded North Point again. Steadman almost had an aneurysm. Upton Bell was Colts personnel director when the whole thing blew up. "The problem with the Rosenbloom-Steadman thing became *such* an issue and such an item all the way through that it's hard to define what was myth and what was the truth," Bell emphasized. "Their relationship became strained when Steadman—and I think he was right

at the time, but it became too personal— he went after Rosenbloom when he tried to force the preseason games on the fans, which today they all do. For Steadman, that was the wrong thing to do. Right or wrong, that's when their relationship really began to sour. To the point at the end where Rosenbloom, after he had sold [traded] the team to Irsay, came to Oakland [for a 1972 Colts preseason game] and physically confronted Steadman in the press box."

During this one-man crusade Steadman was like Dempsey flogging Jess Willard with no standing eight-count. Steadman went to town on August 21, 1969:

You would think, instead of adding on practice games that you must buy, that if Rosenbloom wanted to bring other teams to Baltimore so he could present them with a check [for showing up] that he would do it out of his own pocket and throw in the game as a free bonus to regular season customers. Why should you, the ticket buyer, the consumer, be faced with such an extra expense? If the Colts' owner wants to play an exhibition here on the basis that you can take it or leave it, buy it or disregard it, that's something else. But when the only way you can protect your right to buy season tickets is to buy exhibition games, then the Golden Goose who laid the Golden Egg is having his neck put in a vise. Such a practice is despicable and unbecoming any American enterprise.

We don't care if it is in the commercial interests of the great exhibition that's known as professional football. Too bad the desire for the almighty dollar is so all-consuming and insatiable. The name of this game is "shame."

If need be, Steadman would die on the hill for this one. Not satisfied with one beatdown, Steadman kept swinging. And the proles in town loved it. "Public reaction to the Baltimore Colts' decision to play two exhibition games here next year on a 'must buy' basis is being met with bitterness, disgust and resentment," Steadman railed on August 25, 1969. "Ticket holders are writing and calling this newspaper to register their complaints. They also should be telling Carroll D. Rosenbloom, owner of the Colts, what they think. He's the man who can change it." Steadman ended with a succession of buzz-off comments from fans, e.g., Danny Eckman of Baltimore: "Carroll Rosenbloom has, in effect, sold out Colt fans, twice in the same year. First, the club goes into the American League [the AFC] and then the fans have to pay for exhibition games or take a cab. What kind of individual is this who 'sells-out' the same people who helped make him a winner? Call a cab, Carroll, I'm one ticket buyer who ain't buying."

The mantra—the fans made C.R. a winner—was a chronic Steadman talking point. Rosenbloom's son, Steve, claims the constant Steadman fusillades were about vengeance. "I felt very badly about the attacks from Steadman that were nonstop and the effect that that would have on everybody in our organization, all the fans and on and on. It was almost 100% negative stuff, most of it untrue, and it was an assault and an insult. I liked John; I knew him. But when this started, I had to scratch my head: Why is he doing this? Then I realized—and he wouldn't admit to this—but it all came down to how it affected him when we didn't pick him as our GM when the opportunity arose [the death of Joe Campanella]. So, it was all about John, and it was like his problem that he complained about through his columns."

On 8/28/1969, Steadman strung together 12 inches of what-ifs condemning the preseason ticket plan:

Suppose other businesses decided to operate on the basis that to buy one product you first had to agree to purchase other goods or services:

- A restaurant meal means you must buy two bowls of clam broth before dinner whether you like clam broth or not.

- A service station says a lubrication and oil change must be made before it'll fill your car with gas.

- A hardware store will only let you buy a hammer if you first order a pound of nails and a can of turpentine.

- A drugstore won't sell a toothbrush unless you buy hair tonic and razor blades.

- A theater allows you to buy seats to a hit show but only if you take tickets for two previews.

- A grocery store will let you have a pound of butter if you agree to take a dozen apples and three artichokes.

This bit went on until you could scream. For the time being, Rosenbloom stuck to the plan despite the daily mortar fire.

Steadman had his share of wingmen during the ticket skirmish. Thirty minutes south of Baltimore was Kenneth Denlinger of the *Washington Post*:

A fan buys his season ticket realizing that a player like [Joe] Namath might be hurt and possibly be sidelined for the year. It is outrageous also to make that buyer spend an additional $30 or so and then keep even a healthy Namath or Unitas or Morrall on the bench because the coach wants to test someone else. Making exhibition tickets mandatory for regular-season ticket holders is likely to become more and more fashionable, since a number of other businesses also are successful with that practice. If you want to stock our good brand, many stores are told, you must also stock the inferior. The shopkeeper has little recourse; the NFL customer does, although too many Baltimore-like protests might make an owner who does not get exactly what he wants threaten

to move the team to a more appreciative location.

Denlinger foresaw the likes of Al Davis and Bob Irsay.

Bill Tanton of the *Evening Sun* forgot about Steadman calling him a schlemiel a while back and provided backup:

The Colt season ticket buyers have had that gun at their heads for almost a week now and their reaction is as expected: They don't like it even a little bit, and who can blame them? Never have I seen Colt fans in the uproar they are in now over being forced to buy tickets for two exhibition games to be played here next summer [1970]. They will have to buy the ducats—at regular prices—if they want to hang on to their season tickets. The mail and the phone calls continue to pour in and everywhere the fans congregate they continue to voice their displeasure. In today's mail is a poem from one plaintiff. It's entitled "Ode to Rosen's Bloom." The closing quartet reads thus: *Goodbye, Carroll, you've overplayed your hand; But no doubt some suckers will still fill the stand; Rosen's bloom, like all others, will in time fade; Left in the lurch are the fans who paid.*

The Manson family murders, the cover photo for *Abbey Road*, British troops swooping into Belfast to quell The Troubles and Woodstock up at Max Yasgur's farm were the big stories in August 1969. Baltimore was in a lather over preseason tickets. Baltimore City Comptroller Hyman Pressman, long a Rosenbloom nemesis, threatened to block the Colts from playing those two preseason games in Memorial Stadium. "[The Colts'] lease gives them the right to dates during the regular season," Pressman told the *Morning Sun* in early September 1969. "They would need approval to play earlier games. It is actually like a change in the contract. Besides that, the Orioles might have something to say about it [guaranteed to piss off C.R.]. The city could say we won't approve the right to play or we will only approve it if you (the Colts) act fairly to the fans." Rosenbloom countered: Don't you guys and local businesses get money when we rent that joint?

Go ahead and strap Rosey to a pillory, but three-fourths of the NFL already had the preseason mandate. Steve Rosenbloom got a tongue-lashing himself when he griped about the lousy preseason attendance at Memorial Stadium. "I understood clearly that the fans didn't want to be charged for those things [preseason tickets], but we had to go on the road all the time to get a payday. And we had to reciprocate to the other teams. That's how everybody else did it. It [attaching preseason games to the regular-season package] was a new thing sweeping through the NFL, and a lot of people with other teams weren't happy, but they said, 'What the hell; I'm gonna support them.' Nobody was gouged for it, but they figured they didn't want to pay for a nothing game. But he [his father] chastised

me for lashing out at the fans about the preseason game. But it was so disappointing. I was shocked, actually."

Steadman was bonkers for a month about it, rolling out crazy stuff about violations of the Sherman Antitrust Act and claiming Rosenbloom's promise to donate some of the proceeds to charity was a P.T. Barnum con. The Colts were getting nada from concessions and parking, only a few dozen people showed up for preseason games, no luxury boxes for extra gravy at the mausoleum, and his NFL buddies already had the policy. To hell with what he told the *Morning Sun* seven years earlier: "His policies on ticket sales also suggest a feeling of responsibility toward fans. Season book purchasers are never allowed to buy out the stadium, so that fans who cannot afford season tickets have at least a chance to pick up singles. *Exhibition game tickets are not packaged with regular game tickets, a device used by some clubs* [emphasis mine]. 'This would bring in extra money,' Rosenbloom says, 'but I'd feel like a bum doing it.'" Stuck between a rock and a hardhead (Steadman).

After getting smacked around for a few weeks, Rosenbloom backed down. He made the preseason tickets optional—just let us know and we'll offer them up to anybody. He sent out a letter to the fans, trying to patch things up: "Dear Fans: The Colts [sic] recent announcement of the addition of two preseason games to the 1970 season ticket package has unfortunately been misinterpreted and misunderstood … The desires of our fans have always been our first consideration. We believe our stewardship of the Colt franchise, as we begin our 17th year, proves this. We felt, and still do, that our fans wish to see their team in live action as often as possible. When all arrangements have been made and opponents and plans for these games are announced, any holder of season tickets who wishes to give up his right to these preseason games may simply notify us and we will, with pleasure, dispose of these preseason tickets through other channels." Cue a wry smile from Steadman.

During the holidays of '64, Steadman ratted out Rosenbloom for some Christmas bonuses. The *L.A. Times* provided the details on December 29:

> Officials of the Buffalo Bills and Baltimore Colts denied reports Monday that their players were rewarded with incentive bonuses for victories. Both American and National Football League rules prohibit bonuses for winning a game or title. The Baltimore *News American*, in a story written by sports editor John Steadman, said owner Carroll Rosenbloom of the Colts distributed $100,000 among his players "as a reward" for winning the NFL's Western Division title. The Colts lost the championship playoff to the Cleveland Browns 27-0 Sunday. "This means," Steadman wrote, "that each man collected $2,500 in unofficial money from the Colts' organization." General manager Don Kellett of the Colts said the report was "absolutely

untrue." Steadman said several Colts confirmed they received the extra compensation. The Colts will receive about $5,000 anyway for their losing effort in the championship game.

Bonus checks at year's end go with the sugar cookies. You have to wonder if Steadman wouldn't have squealed had it not been Rosenbloom. No other reporter even bothered to mention it. In fact, the *Evening Sun* even seemed to be in the Christmas spirit: "The Colts coaches plan to leave for California Saturday [for the Pro Bowl]. Their first meeting with the Western Division players is scheduled Sunday. Before they depart, they will check the mailman eagerly each day for the Christmas bonus which owner Carroll Rosenbloom always has given them."

All fuss and feathers. "It was pretty common knowledge that when the Colts won the '58 championship game, their share was like $4,200 a player [actually $4,718]," former Colts PR director and GM Ernie Accorsi attested. "Jerry Hoffberger, who was on great terms with Rosenbloom then and owned the National Brewing Company [and the Orioles], who was our chief sponsor, matched that offer for each player."

More samples from the Steadman Gatling gun:

1. *From Colts to Ravens*: Allegation—Rosenbloom wasn't keen on his Colts band going to Cleveland for the 1964 NFL title game. A brouhaha ensued. "Finally, with pressure

applied, the Colts Band was allowed to travel to Cleveland, to enter the stadium to watch but not to play a note or even sound a toot or tap their drums. The musical instruments, according to instructions, were to be placed in their carrying cases, piled on the ground, and guarded by the police so they couldn't be used. And Rosenbloom was just as happy they weren't going to be playing."

2. *From Colts to Ravens*: Allegation—An NFL-sanctioned Colts game was scheduled a few days before a Navy game at the stadium, a breach of Baltimore Park Board policy. The press jumped on Rosenbloom. C.R. had a tête-á-tête with editors Paul Menton and Jesse Linthicum of the *Evening* and *Morning Sun* to smooth things over. Steadman dragged out the payola business—again.

"Later Rosenbloom and Menton had a meeting, became good friends, and agreed upon a regular payoff of money that would go to Menton and Linthicum. They would be paid to keep their criticisms, if they had any, to themselves. The public had no idea what was going on. Neither did many of the rival newspapermen and other reporters who worked at *The Sun*. Rosenbloom had defused any potential knocks from two of the city's sports editors by getting Menton and Linthicum to sell themselves for a price. In that era, it was not unusual for sports editors to be 'on the take,' an earlier version of the practice disc jockeys had of accepting money to play certain records. Then it was called payola. The practice among Baltimore sportswriters went out with the changing of the guard when Bill Tanton replaced Menton and Bob Maisel succeeded Linthicum."

3. Play It Again, Sam, 12/26/1983: "Unfortunately, the media, in some instances trying to court favor with these miserable power brokers [NFL owners], sells its soul. We know some sportswriters who actually thought an owner (who's now deceased) [C.R. died four years earlier] was going to make them wealthy by providing tips on the stock market and making other extravagant offers. In turn, he was gifted with what is known as a favorable press."

Steadman couldn't see past his nose regarding Rosenbloom. The Colts band allegation in '64 was half wrong. John Zieman was a drummer in '64, then he became the music librarian, property manager, percussion instructor, PR director and finally president of the Baltimore Colts Marching Band. These days, he's the president of the Marching Ravens and a walking warehouse of memories. According to Ziemann, the Browns didn't have a marching band, so they booked Florida A&M for halftime. Owner Art Modell nixed allowing the enemy band [the Colts] to take the field. Imagine Ravens fans at M&T Bank firing rotten tomatoes at the Steelers band. Modell's roadblock got Steadman riled; he even called Commissioner Pete Rozelle for some muscle.

A compromise ensued: The Colts band would make the trip, march around the field once and sit up in the stands, instruments packed away. No tunes, no halftime. Ziemann says Rosenbloom gladly paid for transportation and the hotel. Those are the facts, which Steadman often conveniently avoided when he hammered Rosenbloom. The Colts band was super PR for Rosenbloom; implying he wanted to keep them home was bilgewater.

Steadman's payola charge is just more green cheese. Menton and Linthicum of the *Sun* were six feet under by the time Steadman fingered them and couldn't be deposed by séance. No one else has stepped forward over the years to corroborate. Former Colts personnel director and NFL authority Upton Bell spent years with Steadman and questions the bribery charge. "I don't think he paid them [reporters and editors]," Bell stated. "There were certain people at the *Sun-papers*—Paul Menton; Bob Maisel, the morning [sports] editor—and I wouldn't say he paid them. Before games, Maisel was always out on the field—why wouldn't he try to get a scoop from Carroll [Rosenbloom]? He [Rosenbloom] had developed such a hatred for Steadman and the *News American* that he was gonna feed everything he could to the *Sun*. I don't know about any payments, but I know he hated Steadman, and, therefore, he was gonna favor the *Sun*."

Michael Olesker might know if anybody does. Steadman hired him fresh out of college and loved the kid. Olesker eventually got his own column in the *Morning Sun* and wrote

a book, *The Colts' Baltimore: A City and Its Love Affair in the 1950s.* "I never heard anything about that, and John [Steadman] and I were very close," Olesker admitted. "He never breathed a word of that [the payola] to me. John brought me into the business, brought me in as an intern for two summers and made sure the paper hired me when I graduated college. His family told me he considered me the son he never had. I gave the eulogy at his funeral. And he never said anything to me about that."

Ernie Accorsi—Colts PR director, with a direct line to Rosenbloom. Ditto. "I don't ever remember anything like that coming up," he said. "And I can tell you, I was in a lot of meetings with him [Rosenbloom] when the media was souring on him, in '70 and '71, and never once did I hear him say, 'You know, we're paying this guy to be more favorable to us.' I never heard that. It would surprise me. He [Steadman] posed as a complete loyalist to other writers, other newspapermen. And I'm not copping a plea here—I never heard that."

Steve Rosenbloom just shakes his head at another hand grenade:

We had three regular sportswriters that stayed with us at training camp [in Westminster, MD], all through the years. And we knew them personally and well. I started working in '56 with the equipment manager, and I don't ever remember seeing John [Steadman] at training camp. It's crazy. I was very friendly with all three of them. So, one of them would've said something about that: "Steve, this rumor [about bribes] is going around." They would've obviously known about it. They didn't want to embarrass themselves and say, "Oh, this terrible thing your father is doing." They obviously didn't believe it either. They never asked me about it, and they asked me all kinds of things. They weren't shy about it. It's even crazy that the paper [*News American*] would let this go on because you might as well be a *National Enquirer* at the grocery store. But maybe they were thinking short-term: We're selling papers. Like my father told me, "Steve, it's tough to go to war with somebody that buys their ink by the barrel." I think he felt, *I'm not getting in a pissing contest with a skunk.*

Rosenbloom gave détente one last college try at a local golf tournament in 1970. Ernie Accorsi was part of a noteworthy foursome—Rosenbloom, Colts GM Don Klosterman, Steadman and himself. One last shot to make nice with Steady:

The 1970 press golf tournament party: We always had this big outing—golf tournament, dinner afterwards, a raffle and all this stuff. I think it was Carroll's last attempt to make peace. [Don] Klosterman, Steadman, Carroll and I were the foursome. Nobody knew that I had played high school and freshman [college] golf. So, Klosterman and I are

partners, and Rosenbloom and Steadman are partners. Steadman ran in a long, curling, downhill putt, and Carroll ran over to him and put his arm around him. So, everything was going fairly well. However, I was about even-par after eight holes, and we were significantly ahead, me and Klosterman. And Klosterman said to me, "Uh, I'm not asking you to shave points, but you're playing *too* well." So, I started not hitting the ball like I had been; I'm tanking, OK? So now, it's over, and this part Steadman told me. There was a blind raffle drawing, and all of a sudden, Steadman wins the raffle. And Steadman told me—and this is on the heels of this golf foursome, which was a very peaceful, great day—"I'll tell you two things, Ernie: I think it [the raffle] was fixed, and I never got the money [door prize]. There are no horseshoes on those helmets." I think it meant more to him [Rosenbloom] than he would probably have ever admitted because he was a businessman, and that deal [trading the Colts for the Rams] was probably too good to turn down, considering all the misfortune and battles he had about the [Memorial Stadium] lease. But he was a good person at heart.

Looks like Steadman jump-started the hatred and Rosenbloom reciprocated. "One of the problems is, when you become bitter about a situation—and there was bitterness on both sides between him [Rosenbloom] and Steadman—you don't see clearly," Upton Bell mused. "To me, if you have the evidence [against Rosenbloom], then you present it if you make an accusation. But there's no question that Carroll, in his hatred for Steadman, favored the *Morning* and *Evening Sun* and would maybe shower them with gifts and shit like that, but I think Rosenbloom was too smart to write a check or make a payoff, where he could be exposed. He was very shrewd, so I have my doubts about it [the payola]."

Another Steadman potshot was the Bugle Boys story in *From Colts to Ravens*:

> There had been an earlier crisis that had nothing to do with the Colts Band. It concerned the barring of the Baltimore Bugle Boys from Memorial Stadium. They were a group of fans from East Baltimore who enjoyed making noise at the Colts games by blowing bugles. There was a time when the Colts were hard put to sell tickets, and they would have been elated for the Baltimore Bugle Boys to be there. But now there was opposition from management [i.e., Rosenbloom, of course]. They considered them annoyances. It made for a week-long controversy that gained so much attention that a visiting publicity director, Art Johnson of the 49ers, went to a hockshop on Baltimore Street and bought a World War II army bugle that he presented to me. A photographer took a picture to document

the occasion. I took to playing it—not blowing it—at appropriate moments in the press box. It was a show of support for the Bugle Boys.

Unpeel the onion, and this is probably what went down. The Bugle Boys made a racket in the stands; bystanders took to wearing ear plugs; somebody complained to management; Rosenbloom shut it down; Steadman played homer in the press box, blowing that infernal bugle during games. The unwritten rule in the press box was don't cheer and goad out-of-town reporters. While taking a sarcastic jab at Bob Irsay in 1975 for also cheering in the press box, *Evening Sun* sportswriter Phil Jackman also bounced one off Steadman:

Dear Bob, the red-faced owner:

I very definitely would beef to Poobah Pete [Rozelle] about the shoddy treatment you and your cronies received in the Buffalo press box the other day just because you did a little cheering. I agree for a guy who put up $19 million to belong to the club, you should get no less than 30 minutes on the public address system, just like Ray Kroc did when he purchased the San Diego Padres. This is a time-honored thing, this no cheering in the press box, which has never really taken hold. Here in B'more we used to have a gent who showed with a bugle to blow the "Charge" and that was mild compared to Washington.

Certainly not all of Steadman's gibes at Rosenbloom were all smoke and no gun. Rumor long had it that Rosenbloom knew about a looming NFL TV deal, bamboozled the four minority owners into selling him their shares and got a wheelbarrow of money for it. Crafty, maybe, but a moral referee like Steadman would roll down thunder like he did in *From Colts to Ravens*:

> Within a matter of days after [Colts minority owner Zanvyl] Krieger capitulated and sold to Rosenbloom, the league signed a massive television deal with CBS—the first one that called for enormous income for all teams. Krieger believed Rosenbloom had advance information of the pending contract and, as an attorney and businessman, knew this to be a violation of the legal relationship between a majority owner and his minority partners. But instead of bringing suit, Krieger called [GM Don] Kellett and told him that he had changed his mind and wasn't going to sell. "I reminded Don," said Krieger, "that when I agreed to let Carroll have my percentage of ownership that he had told me I could 'come back in' any time I wanted. So I was electing to exercise that option. Kellett told me he would talk to Carroll. He called back and said, 'Carroll doesn't ever remember making any such promise.'" Krieger had a case but didn't pursue it, realizing again what he already knew—that Rosenbloom's word

was suspect. In the years that ensued, Krieger, usually extremely charitable, never kept it a secret that Rosenbloom had maneuvered him out of the ownership picture and continued to express a low personal regard for the man.

Steadman wasn't a regular beat reporter, he rarely caught practices, and he ditched training camp. For being a bleeding ulcer, Rosenbloom tossed him off the team plane. Steadman described the slight in *From Colts to Ravens*:

> As Rosenbloom's fury increased, and when I supported [head coach Don] Shula's right to leave without the Dolphins having to give up a draft choice [for tampering], he decided I should no longer have the same opportunity as other reporters to travel on the team charter for road trips. Traveling with the team was a tremendous convenience for reporters from the *Sunpapers* and *News American* and also the Baltimore radio and TV stations. It's the way a team should be covered, enabling the reporters and the public to learn from a close-up perspective the stories that are developing. Club officials and players also were instructed not to talk to me but they did, especially Dick Szymanski [player personnel], [GM] Harry Hulmes and [PR director] Ernie Accorsi.

The flipside would be: a) You never show for training camp or practices, so maybe you're a freeloader; b) No law says we have to let haters on our plane; and c) You're a sermonizing pain in the ass. So there.

. . .

Rosenbloom endured all this caterwauling by Steadman ON TOP OF the Memorial Stadium migraine. By 1971, Rosenbloom was 64 years old and woozy. One day, his son Steve dropped by his place in Florida and caught his dad at a weak moment:

> I was going to Florida to sign a player [as Colts president], and my father was down in Florida. So, I came down to talk to the player's agent, then I went to my father's place. When I came in, I saw he had a pile of *News-Posts* [*News Americans*] there. I asked him about it, and he tried to pretend that it [the *News American* articles] didn't bother him. I told him, "You've gotta take another approach to this [the Steadman problem]. Maybe it'll die down. I can talk to John Steadman if you want." Because I liked John Steadman. We had gotten along great. I tried to get my father to relax a bit about it and told him maybe we could find a way to cut through to John to stop this nonsense. But in reality, it had ramped up to a point where it wasn't gonna stop. And he [his father] said, "Steve, it's nice of you to point out these things, but frankly, this isn't happening to *you*. It's happening to *me*."

The preseason ticket crusade was vintage Steadman, but this next story by Michael Olesker sounds like something dreamed up by Edgar Allan Poe:

> His [Rosenbloom's] first unhappiness was when he made it mandatory that if you wanted season tickets, you had to buy preseason tickets as well. I was a sportswriter working for John Steadman. John wrote columns blasting this. By 1970, I was doing investigative reporting, and we had a meeting in [executive editor] Tom White's office. It was Tom, John Steadman, [reporter] Lou Azreal, a couple other guys and me. Not just on the basis of the preseason tickets, but John and Rosenbloom were bumping heads at this point. He thought Rosenbloom *was trying to get him killed* [my emphasis]. I don't know that it was legitimate, but that's how John felt. I remember that John wanted to do [write] something; Tom White said no. I remember John standing there, in the drama of the moment. John said to Tom, "I'm begging you—I'm BEGGING you— I'M BEGGING YOU"—to run something about Rosenbloom. I don't know if it [the article] was that Rosenbloom was trying to kill him, but he was genuinely scared. He felt that his phone had been tapped. And it's ironic because in the beginning, he [Steadman] worked for Rosenbloom as the PR guy, and he liked him. When he first got the job

as sports editor [of the *News American*] in January of '58, he was writing stuff that made it sound like he and Rosenbloom still had a great relationship. But that soured.

Curdled is more like it. But—bumping the guy off?! With C.R. asking Ernie Accorsi to get him to chill out, not freak out? "I took him [Steadman] to dinner every Saturday night," former Colts PR man Accorsi attested. "Rosenbloom wanted me to do that. We gave him gifts for Christmas and all kinds of stuff. But he was no longer being treated like he was part of the [Colts] media family, but I never heard of anything that dangerous [threatening Steadman's life]."

Steve Rosenbloom on rubbing out Steadman: "If my father knew that [about Steadman's fear], and he gave any credence to it, he would have sent somebody to talk to John about it, to calm him down. People like my father are not gonna sacrifice everything—their reputation and life—to kill a mentally-challenged sportswriter. It's ridiculous."

A guy gets the job as PR director for the ballclub he's loved most of his life. And before he signs a contract and his W-2, the boss hits him with an offbeat request. That was Ernie Accorsi in 1970:

Understand that the roots and foundation of the problem [the Rosenbloom-Steadman feud] occurred before I got there. But in my interview with Carroll over the phone, he said, "You gotta take care of the Steadman problem for me." I almost didn't take the job because of that. I was a newspaper guy. I had a major beat in the *Philadelphia Inquirer* for three years. I knew that [taming reporters] was *impossible*. The Eagles had a problem with Joe McGinness [who wrote *The Selling of the President 1968* and *Fatal Vision*], and they did everything they could to go after McGinness. There was *no* way they were gonna win that battle. So, I knew that [taming Steadman] was unwinnable. And I didn't know John Steadman. You think I was gonna take him to dinner and change his mind? No way in the world. But the genesis of everything—I don't know. I know about the preseason games. But I know it was tough, and I know it *got* to Rosenbloom. Rosenbloom had a long meeting with his lawyer, Jacques Schlenger. Top lawyer in Baltimore, and Schlenger was smart. He said, "There's nothing you can do. You can't win with the press, Carroll. You cannot win that battle." [Maryland Governor] Spiro Agnew didn't win. But I know it got to Carroll.

That was all-too-apparent to Rosenbloom's son. "You know, how much pounding can you take?" Steve Rosenbloom lamented. "And you really aren't equipped to fight back. They [Rosenbloom's critics] would love that. You'd be egging them on and hurting yourself even more. It didn't work out because it *couldn't* work out. I felt badly and thought maybe

John [Steadman] would listen to me for a second or two. But my father said, 'That's it. No turning back. Steve, all I've done here [in Baltimore] is win. What else do they want?' He said, 'I'm getting too old for this.' And rightly so—I had to agree with him. I mean, these fans were stalwart and with us *all the way*, and then when my father gets written about and some of them believe that stuff, that hurt him as well. It seemed like the fans were turning on him. At that point he [his father] was silently available for somebody to come in and talk to him about buying the Colts."

The turncoats doing the backbiting didn't know that the man was looking for an easy exit out of Baltimore. "Rosenbloom had also soured on the area, as the *New York Times* reported in July of 1972, and he felt the Colts were underappreciated," recounted Judy Battista in October 2022 for nfl.com. "He wasn't happy with Baltimore Memorial Stadium, and he was hurt by criticism from the local press, particularly from a columnist named John Steadman, who had also called Colts games on the radio. Steadman regularly criticized Rosenbloom, for whom he had once worked, in his column. Their relationship was so fractured that Rosenbloom's family has long wondered if Steadman helped to keep Rosenbloom from being elected to the Pro Football Hall of Fame, despite his team's success."

Even the locals couldn't duck the ugly truth. In a feature on Steadman's devotion to Baltimore football in the *Morning Sun* in December 1999, the Rosenbloom-Steadman war got three paragraphs:

In the early 1970s, Steadman drew Rosenbloom's ire after writing that fans shouldn't be charged full prices for exhibitions, a position he still advocates. Rosenbloom made it difficult for him to cover games, and according to Steadman, even tried to get him fired. "I had a lot of trouble getting him a credential," [Colts PR director Ernie] Accorsi recalled. "In those days, everyone flew on the team charter and stayed in the team hotel. I couldn't make him any reservations. He had to do everything on his own. And he never flinched, never complained." Steadman's opinion of Rosenbloom—"an evil man"—is even lower than his assessment of [Robert] Irsay, whom he described as "a drunk who was not responsible for himself." When Irsay took the Colts to Indianapolis on March 28, 1984, Steadman thought Baltimore would get a team back within a year. The Colts' departure created a 245-game void, including preseason and postseason.

It's no mystery who fired the first shot in this row. And every shot thereafter, leading to Rosenbloom kicking him off the team plane.

Colts and Ravens band president John Ziemann liked both guys, but he winced at how C.R. got ripped:

First of all, we're only human, and all this [criticism] was playing nationally. And I think it hurt Carroll [Rosenbloom].

Imagine at a cocktail party: "Hey, Carroll, what's goin' on in Baltimore? Can't you hold your own in Baltimore?" I think that started it. These owners have big egos. He [Rosenbloom] did a lot for the city. He brought championships, but he had to make money. He wasn't running the Colts as a charity. And I think when the press started on him, people started taking sides. People started writing letters [to the editor] against Carroll, against the Colts, and wanted things to stay the same, but financially, they couldn't. I saw this, and I was only a young guy. The poison pen of the press had a lot of people fired up.

Which left Carroll Rosenbloom to conclude: Time for a Colts yard sale, then hit the road.

CHAPTER 6

BOTOX OR BULLDOZER

Baltimore considered stoning Carroll Rosenbloom for two sins: the pre-season ticket gimmick and the AFL-NFL merger in 1970. The town flipped out when they discovered that Rosenbloom had hijacked the Colts to the American Football Conference. The *New York Times* provided the background in May 1969:

> Carroll Rosenbloom of the Colts and Art Modell of the Browns were the foresighted NFL owners who retained the least animosity for the AFL and always had believed in the concept of total merger of all 26 pro teams. Art Rooney and his son, Dan, who run the Steelers, were willing to go along. This principle of forget-the-past-and-embrace-the-future is what Rozelle had been preaching to the NFL owners for weeks but to little effect. Pro football is going to thrive in the 1970s regardless of who plays whom. There will be some money for the Colts, Browns and Steelers. The figure was undisclosed but may be around $2 million for each club. This was agreed upon early in the talks for whichever NFL teams moved as a means of making up the probable losses in comparable gate receipts until new and larger stadiums go up at Boston, Buffalo, Cincinnati and Kansas City [all AFL teams].

The pragmatists knew it had to be done. Steve Rosenbloom explains:

> We [the NFL] had no choice. Somebody up there [in New York] had to get the ownership to sit down, take this seriously: "Are we gonna have a merger or not? Are we gonna keep spending money and let them [the AFL] pound and pound on us? The result will be a lesser league in the end. We're gunning for the same draft choices; this ain't gonna work." So, it was a very crucial time. You looked around at the ownership in

the AFL in those days; there was lots of money there. So, they had all the ammunition they needed. They just had to wait us out. And it could end up eating *all* the teams. It could've ruined the NFL. My father knew the real solution was to take this problem and work it out. And when you do that—and it's fair—maybe neither side is happy with it. Eventually, everybody at the NFL meeting came to an agreement that the merger was the way to go.

Simple enough. You had 16 NFL teams, 10 AFL, 26 total. To balance it out—NFC and AFC—three NFL teams had to decamp to the AFC: Browns, Steelers, Colts. Leaving the NFL old guard to join the junior circuit guaranteed a cash shortfall. Plus, plenty of fans would pitch a fit. "The pro football establishment was trumpeting the virtues of the realignment yesterday but many of the National Football League fans who buy tickets were shocked and unhappy over the moves," the *New York Times* stated. "The fans in Baltimore and Cleveland were especially disturbed at moving to the 13-team American Conference. The Pittsburgh fans, who have never had a winner in the NFL [as of '69], took the news a bit more calmly."

WTF? was Baltimore's reaction. Some wanted Rosenbloom's head on a spike. Son Steve was hip:

To them [Colts fans], there was no excuse: "How did we go to sleep and

wake up in the AFC? This is a fucking nightmare." And you know Baltimoreans. When they get upset, or they make a pledge, that's a serious thing for most Baltimoreans. They don't do it lightly. They felt like their girlfriend or wife had been replaced by somebody else because she left them. It's not the same thing. These people [the fans] were serious. It's not like they go to the game and have a party afterwards. They go to the game, and they're dedicated: "We are gonna win. We are the Colts." But then it's not the same girlfriend anymore, no matter how you dress it up. So, what they do— they get frustrated; they get angry. "How did this happen? We didn't tell you to do that [move to the AFC]." And we knew all of that, and we did it anyway because it was for the greater good.

Longtime *Morning Sun* columnist and former rabid Colts fan Michael Olesker sides with the critics. "That was a big blow because it was emotional," he admitted. "Every year, you knew they were gonna play Detroit twice, Chicago twice, Green Bay and the 49ers twice. You knew you were gonna see, standing on the sidelines, hollering, George Halas [Bears coach] and Vince Lombardi [Packers]. You knew the players on each of those teams, and that was part of the passion. Suddenly, we were playing teams from Kansas City. Who the *hell* are the Kansas City Chiefs? Who are these people from Oakland? It took a lot of passion out of coming to the ballpark. It wasn't the same kind of family feud. Suddenly: 'What do you mean we're not playing them [traditional NFL rivals] anymore. Why are you taking this history away from us?' And it was a corporate move. Baltimore is a working-class town, and it felt as if the bigshots were taking away our history, without any approval from us. Yeah, that was a big deal."

It was like NFL moguls pulled a fast one behind their backs. Ernie Accorsi saw how the merger got people riled:

I think the biggest thing that hit that city in '70 was going to the AFC. Baltimore was a traditional, historical city that had built up sports hate—hate for the Bears, hate for the Packers—and every year, those teams came in here and played. All these rivalries. And I don't diminish that because all you have to do is look at the colleges, Ohio State-Michigan or Penn State-Pitt. You can't get a ticket. Then, all of a sudden, four teams came in there [to Memorial Stadium]— white helmets, white shirts, white pants, a team with a little fish on its helmet, the other one with a buffalo on it. There was only one team that they had any animosity towards, and it was the Jets [because of Super Bowl III]. So, I think the jump to the AFC was a huge factor in the eyes of a lot of people. I'm speaking as a fan, too. Eventually, those teams became very competitive, but in my eyes, we're going to a minor league. And I know our coaches also lost something, not that they worked any less. I remember walking out of the Denver stadium before it got redone, and [coach John] Sandusky saying to me, "God, these places are dumps." They had an attitude that it was minor-league. I think that hurt a lot. And I know other people felt the same way.

Fans in Cleveland were morose. Fans in Baltimore foamed at the mouth. "I think they [Colts fans] took it harder than in most places because it was a great fanbase, but it was like you're playing in some weird universe," former Baltimore Colts president Steve Rosenbloom observed. "I can see that mentality. They had the Colts Corrals; they knew who owned the team; they knew all the coaches who had been there; they supported everybody. And then boom. These guys didn't pay attention to the lowly AFL. And now that's what they're seeing. 'That's not what I'm paying for. I was paying to see the Packers, the 49ers, the NFL teams,' the names they all knew. It was like giving in and surrendering [to the AFL]. Those fans didn't want to surrender. And they didn't want to play these strange teams. 'Well, we're beating them,' we'd say. 'So what? They're AFL teams. We're gonna beat them anyway,' they'd say. That mentality was put in a blender, and what did you get? They had to let it work out over time." That was well into the Irsay years when bigger problems were on the plate.

Leading the Rosenbloom naysayer brigade was Mr. Everyman, the *News American's* John

Steadman. He called the AFC move money-grubbing. And the story took hold, as was pointed out in the *New York Times*:

> In Baltimore, which has some of the most fanatical fans in the NFL, the main reaction seemed to be speculation that the owner, Carroll Rosenbloom, was influenced by the money involved. It was reported that each of the three teams to move would receive compensation in excess of $2 million. One compensation for the Colts fans was that they are now in the same division with the Jets, who upset the Colts in the Super Bowl. The clubs will meet twice a year. Rosenbloom has a great desire to meet the Jets again and get even for what happened in the Super Bowl. "One of the things, as far as we're concerned," Rosenbloom said, "is that Baltimore has a natural rivalry now and for what we think will be a long time with the Jets. They beat us, and this is the only way we can get back."

That "rivalry" lasted all of two years. It was Don Shula and the Dolphins who became Baltimore's Most Wanted: Shula vs. Rosenbloom.

But when the Colts met the Jets up at Shea right after the Super Bowl, revenge was on the menu. Upton Bell noted the occasion in his book, *Present at the Creation*: "The fact Carroll was paid $3 million spread over the next five years to move didn't hurt, but the real motivation was that he saw us [the Colts] in a division with the Dolphins, Patriots and Bills and knew that all but guaranteed a playoff spot. He also saw [Joe] Namath and the Jets, who upset us in Super Bowl III, twice a year and he wanted to crush them. Ernie Accorsi told me he sat next to Carroll the first time we played them in 1970. We led 26-5 in the third quarter and were tearing Namath apart. We intercepted him six times, but he hit us deep a couple times late and we had to hold on to win, 29-22. Ernie told me after we intercepted Namath the last time in the endzone to end the game, Carroll uttered a sound like he'd never heard before. He hated the Jets."

Rosenbloom was a pragmatic guy; the merger and move to the AFC were just smart business. But Steve Rosenbloom witnessed all the backlash:

> My father wasn't a problem-maker; he was a problem-solver. And he read the tea leaves. That was very important. Maybe you're putting up a brand-new building [i.e., the AFL-NFL merger], and people are complaining that it doesn't look good. And you say, "Wait. Wait for the finished product." And it turns out to be an astounding building. The merger was things finally coming together. But how did it get there; how does it come together? This thing [the discontent over the move to the AFC] was a collusion of the fans and their loyalty and the reality. No, they weren't consulted; if they had been, they would have told us not to do it. But they didn't see what we saw. We

really had no choice; we had to come out of this fucking merger shit. We were battling each other [AFL vs. NFL]. And isn't the proof in the pudding? Look at the NFL now.

. . .

The Orioles and Colts went a few rounds in 1970 when Monday Night Football went with the Colts-Chiefs game in early September. The Orioles' super-duper lease forbade any stadium event inside a 36-hour window of an O's game—field prep and whatnot. Both landed a few body shots, but eventually TV won out and the Colts got their MNF game. During the contretemps, Rosenbloom popped Jerry Hoffberger a good one while he chatted with Bill Tanton of the *Evening Sun*. C.R. had gone to court over the MNF squabble, so Tanton asked him about it:

> "It's not a suit against anyone," Rosenbloom said. "We're just asking the court how they interpret the contract. We want to know what our rights are, and we want to know if we are entitled to the same rights as the Orioles and their owner, Mr. (Jerold) Hoffberger." Does Rosenbloom think Hoffberger has been given preferential treatment? "Hoffberger is a political animal," Rosenbloom said. "He owns a big beer business in Baltimore and it is to his advantage to be very active politically. He has the mayor (Thomas A. D'Alesandro) in his back pocket—and that's all right. I'd

rather have the mayor in Hoffberger's pocket than in the Mafia's."

And he wasn't finished. Tanton let him rattle on:

> Rosenbloom believes that he has been consistently beaten down by the politicians here [in Baltimore]. "A long time ago we wanted to put Astroturf in the Stadium so there would never again be a schedule conflict like this," Carroll said, "and we even offered to pay for it ourselves, interest-free, and let the city pay back the principal. We even wanted to construct our own office building in the open space at the Stadium where the band sits, but we were not allowed to do these things. Hoffberger did not want Astroturf, but if we had it now the date conflict would not even be an issue. Astroturf is coming whether Hoffberger wants it or not. Now we still have no place to practice. McDonogh [a private school] will not have us anymore, and we're going this year to a place (Baltimore U.) that I understand is worse. Imagine—the Baltimore Colts are the only major football team with no place to practice."

Rosenbloom had dropped a bunker-buster on Hoffberger's head. He meant it, of course, but the reverb provoked a lengthy oops from Rosenbloom. He put his mea culpa in the *Morning Sun*: "Bill Tanton has printed a column in today's *Evening Sun* containing excerpts from a conversation between us. I am human and obviously became too excited while talking to Tanton. This caused me to say things that should not have been said. I apologize profusely to Mayor Thomas D'Alesandro, for my remarks about him were unfair and inaccurate. My sincere apologies also go to others involved, and particularly to my fellow citizens of Baltimore for my intemperate remarks. If I can make amends I will certainly do so. I will comment no further on the Stadium matter [the MNF conflict] until it is resolved."

No mention of Hoffberger's name anywhere. By 1970, those two were Hamilton and Burr. When Rosenbloom swapped the Colts for the Rams in 1972, the *New York Times* reprised his feuds with Steadman and Hoffberger: "He [Rosenbloom] felt the achievements of the Colts, the Super Bowl champions of 1971, were not fully appreciated by the fans, especially when it came to preseason games. Three such games there last summer [1971] averaged only 16,000 in attendance. Rosenbloom was stung by press criticism, especially from John Steadman, the sports editor of the *News American*. He feuded with the city over Municipal [sic] Stadium, whose facilities he once described as 'filthy,' and with Jerold Hoffberger, whose Orioles, the baseball team, are the prime tenants in the stadium."

For a guy like John Ziemann, lifelong Baltimorean, former Colts fan and a member of the Colts/Ravens marching band since

1962, some of the press commentary was over-the-top:

As for the press and everybody going after him [Rosenbloom], it was uncalled for in my book. You gotta realize, all these owners have egos. If they owned a regular corporation, they might know them, but when you buy a sports team, then they're really noted around the country. If John Ziemann owns a banking corporation, no big deal. But when John Ziemann buys a big football team, then they know him on another level. So, you're human and you have an ego. And to go after them [the owners]—and I'm not saying they shouldn't be criticized—there's a time and a place to do it. You should hear *their* side of the story instead of nailing them in the papers. Get the truth before you go out there. Some press was kind to C.R.; other ones—no. And it eventually cost us to lose C.R. as an owner, and we got Mr. Irsay, and that led to the team leaving.

This was around the time that Colts PR chief Ernie Accorsi brought out a peace pipe for a communal smoke—Rosenbloom and Baltimore scribes. Rosenbloom told him to set it up:

I'm pretty sure it was 1970. He [Rosenbloom] told me, "I want you to arrange for a luncheon. I want all the media there. I wanna talk to them. Whatever they wanna eat—steak, crabcakes—I don't care. And make sure the big guns are there." Oh, I was nervous about this. So, he got up, and he said, "Why don't you love the Colts anymore?" Well, that was an invitation to get hammered. I'm sure Steadman was there, but I don't remember him talking. The only guy I remember talking was a tough guy, but not a lead columnist [at that point], Phil Jackman. He got up, and he said, "Here's why." He had a couple different things—exhibition games, threatening to move the team—blah, blah, blah. And Carroll didn't dismiss him or anything like that, but nothing good came out of it. But that was the last, desperate attempt he took to win over the media.

This Hail Mary took place on November 16, 1970, smack in the middle of the season, and Cameron C. Snyder of the *Morning Sun* was there: "Carroll Rosenbloom's press luncheon to find out why the Colts have lost public favor was submerged yesterday by his declaration the team would build its own stadium. The owner of the Colts, piqued by some criticism of the organization, particularly the management end, wanted to know what had caused the swing from 'love our Colts' and what should be done to improve the image."

He got peppered with questions about the mausoleum and his oblique remarks about moving. But then Rosenbloom had his say:

About the Colts' public image, Rosenbloom said: "This is one of the best

franchises in football, and without strong ownership and management, you can't have good franchises. The first requirement, as far as we are concerned, is having a winner. We have been lucky in that, and we have worked for that. I'm a puzzled man. Is it something we haven't or have done? Frankly, perhaps our heads have gotten too big. We don't know what we have done. This franchise is as valuable to everyone here as it is to [his son] Steve and myself." He also said that in a year or two he would turn the club over to Steve. "Owners, like players, get old and have to go."

True enough. Steve Rosenbloom grabbed the reins a year later and a year after that, Rosenbloom declared, Gotta go. He was off to L.A. and Bob Irsay stumbled into town.

. . .

By late '70-early '71 Rosenbloom was eyeballing the exits. His relations with the press and the town were on life support. Colts fans thought the preseason ticket and AFC stunts were double-crosses. By one of their own, no less. Reporters like John Steadman protested every time he sneezed. Newspaper columnist Michael Olesker understood the zeitgeist:

One of the first things [that got Rosenbloom in trouble] was the exhibition games. It's funny: [former Colt] Jim Mutscheller told me once that Rosenbloom would send them out every winter to hustle tickets, to give speeches and try to sell season tickets. He said you could get 50-yard-line seats for $3 in the early days. Then it went to $6, to $7. You know, to Baltimoreans, it was *money*. Anytime the tickets went up, that pissed us off because we saw ourselves as being *so* loyal to the team that it was like going to your mother's house for Sunday dinner, and she's charging you. "Wait a minute, Mr. Rosenbloom. We'll give you the $6, but we're *family*. We fill the ballpark, and it's not enough?! You wanna raise prices again?" The exhibition games were meaningless, so to make that mandatory—we were getting pissed off. The relationship was what it was: It was blood. We had been told, over and over, that we were the best fans in America, and we adored the team, and we put pro football on the map. We had been told that the '58 [NFL championship] game was the greatest game ever played, and we felt that we were special. This [raising prices] was saying: Not really. You may *think* that it's a love affair, but it's also a business. It was a harsh reminder: It is a business, and they're in it to make money. We had an almost childlike approach, which is what sports fans do. We go to the ballpark and put the cares of the day behind us.

Naïveté brought Baltimoreans a world of hurt: 1) by convincing them the Colts were theirs and would never leave; and 2)

by breaking their hearts when they woke up one morning and found out they were gone.

Old Baltimore hardheads wouldn't bury the preseason ticket commotion. "That's the sad part of it [the ticket debacle]," John Ziemann professed. "It's like who struck who, who started it, back and forth. It got to be vicious in the newspapers. And Steadman, [city comptroller Hyman] Pressman and the fans thought, *The Colts will never move. They're here. C'mon, Rosenbloom, bring it on. Knock the block off my shoulder.* 'We're just gonna go after him, take him down. We're gonna make sure we get the preseason tickets off there and keep the prices where they are. There's nothing wrong with Memorial Stadium. The Colts will never move. No way!' Well, they figured wrong."

The wheel was spinning inside Rosenbloom's head. How long do I put up with getting knocked around? All son Steve could do was comfort his old man:

I can only imagine how much it hurt him. I wasn't the one being attacked, but I tried to understand it and see if there was a way to help him. I saw it slipping away. It started with Steadman bombarding him, day after day, and it went up the chain. We were getting some feedback from fans that wasn't too complimentary. There were several Baltimore Colts teams [in 1947 and 1950] that failed. So, he brings the team back, and it was *his* money—not the city's, not the state's—that brought the team back. He's taking the risk; he didn't ask for applause. He wanted the same thing the fans wanted—to win. With the quest for a new stadium, he realized, as other ones were sprouting up around the country, he said, "We need a better house for our fans. They can't sit in this dumpy stadium anymore." And he tried everything he could to get this done, and nobody stood up to help. The politicians said, "Oh, yeah, that sounds like a great idea. We'll help. We'll get it done. Rah, hurrah." All of a sudden, they disappear. I assume they got some negative feedback from Baltimoreans: "We're not gonna vote for you if you pass this [appropriations] bill." So, it came down to money, not foresight. What was best for Baltimore? To have a new stadium was a pretty damn good deal. And that's all he wanted.

With Steadman unloading haymakers on Rosenbloom, two members of the cavalry straggled in—the sports editors of the *Morning* and *Evening Sun*. Maybe Bob Maisel remembered Steadman smearing Jesse Linthicum, his former boss, with the payola malarky. He wrote this in September 1971:

It is becoming progressively more popular around town to knock the Colts and the Rosenblooms. Want to pick up some support for your political future? Knock the Colts. Want to make points with the gang at the office, earn prestige and popularity at the local bar? Get on your soapbox and let Carroll Rosenbloom have both barrels. This isn't meant to talk you out of it, to say that you aren't entitled to your opinion, or even to say that you are wrong. But it is also time for the application of some logic, especially in regards to Stadium improvements.

Bill Tanton of the *Evening Sun* was right on his heels:

It's weird, this business about the Rosenblooms. Everywhere you go in and around Baltimore people are talking about the Colt owner, Carroll Rosenbloom, and his son, the team's first-year president, Steve. Talking about them? Condemning them would be more like it. With the Colt season opening this weekend, the people are talking not so much about the team as they are about the owners and their dislike for them, and frankly, the thing really puzzles me. I don't claim for a moment that everything they do is right, but neither are they always wrong either. To me, there are some other things about the Rosenblooms that are much more important that I never hear anyone say. I never hear anyone give them even the faintest praise for being the ones who produced the World Championship team we have in Baltimore [1971]. They did, you know. Nobody can say they have been cheap with their employees, either. They have the highest payroll in the league, their players averaging $31,300 in salary [$23,000 was the league average]. People complain about the increase in ticket prices. What's new? We complain about the price of everything, and that is human nature and our prerogative. But why blame the Rosenblooms? Their average ticket price is fifteenth in a 26-team league, which places them around the middle—and to see the National Football League champions live.

The Maisel-Tanton tag team might have been payback for Steadman kicking around two in the family.

. . .

With Rosenbloom airing his gripes to the press, an architect named Barton offered his two cents about Memorial Stadium, and *Evening Sun* writer Lou Panos in November 1970 sought out Rosenbloom and Hoffberger for their take:

> Lost in the shuffle over Colt Boss Carroll Rosenbloom's plans for a new stadium is the fact that the Orioles aren't too happy with the present setup, either. Bird Boss Jerry Hoffberger sums up his criticism of the 33rd Street bowl, on which his lease has two years to run, in a couple of words: "It leaks." What about the Barton plan, the one devised by the Baltimore-born architect and developer with the support of the Metropolitan Jaycees? Details are still to be unveiled, but it's said to provide for renovation and enlargement of the present stadium, for expansion of parking facilities and for a feature which would help solve the shortage of downtown parking spaces. Before the Colts game last weekend, Citizen Rosenbloom said he hadn't seen the plan but didn't think it would interest him. What would? "Our own stadium." Couldn't the 33rd Street place be made suitable? "No. There's no way football and baseball can live together in Baltimore." End of interview.

Rosenbloom didn't give a hoot that the Metro Jaycees recommended renovating Memorial Mausoleum, and Hoffberger seconded. But John Steadman, with no skin (i.e., cash) in the game, felt the two owners should stay put. "Allen Bazensky, president of the Metropolitan Council of Jaycee Chapters, and Joseph Heacock Jr., who heads the organization's Stadium Renovation Committee, want the Stadium to be improved," Steadman intoned in November 1970. "They both point out, and rightly so, it was Baltimore City, not any of the counties, which built the Stadium in the first place and made it possible for the Colts and Orioles to be there. The Colts and Orioles have a responsibility to Baltimore. It's hoped they realize it. They can cut and run if they want to, but it would be a case of turning their back on the city that made them."

The problem (as always) was the city's lollygagging. By 1970, the city would barely give Rosenbloom the time of day and many thought the stadium should be boarded up. Steadman forever sounded off that Rosenbloom owed the city eternal fealty, which was tommyrot. I'll scratch your back, you scratch mine is the most effective arrangement between owner and city, but all Rosenbloom got was speechifying.

And it wasn't just Rosenbloom who wanted out of 33rd Street. His PR director, Ernie Accorsi, also wanted to bounce. "All of a sudden, all these new stadiums are sprouting up [e.g., Three Rivers in Pittsburgh, Riverfront in Cincinnati, the Astrodome, Veterans in Philly, the Kingdome in Seattle]," Accorsi reflected. "So, Carroll wasn't one to be left behind. It [Memorial Stadium] was nostalgic and romantic, but we needed a new stadium. Not to remodel that one—we needed a new stadium. I don't know how the Orioles felt, but no one with the Colts wanted to renovate the stadium. They wanted a new stadium."

The author of *Glory for Sale: Fans, Dollars and the New NFL*, Jon Morgan, agreed with C.R.:

Team owner Carroll Rosenbloom had long groused publicly and privately about Memorial Stadium. The fans were flocking to Colts games, but the place barely handled 60,000. And it suited baseball much better than it did football. The upper deck did not circle the stadium; instead, it ended at the 50-yard line, so half of the best seats were missing. Plans to expand to capacity usually involved adding more endzone, not upper-deck, seating. And the stadium's location was awful. Traffic would tie up the streets for hours; and on game days, neighborhood residents would become prisoners of their own homes. A provision of the city charter prohibited spectator sporting events from starting on a Sunday before 2 PM. This blue law, which dated back at least to the stadium's opening, meant the Colts were the only NFL team in the nation that didn't observe the traditional 1 PM starting time. Rosenbloom complained, but area religious leaders vigorously defended the law as a way to allow parishioners to get in and out of church before the onslaught of fans [likewise so some of them could get to the game].

(A sidebar about the Cotton Mather blue laws: Maryland rescinded the 1 PM prohibition in March 1984—just as Irsay was about to pack up for Indy.)

Looking around for a place he could park a stadium, Rosenbloom happened into James Rouse, of the Rouse Company, who built Baltimore's Harborplace and aimed to turn Columbia, MD, into a Shangri-La. They got to talking about Rosey buying some land and building something nice. "Mr. Rosenbloom, long unhappy with the present stadium in Baltimore City, has been looking for a piece of land in the metropolitan area on which to build a complex that would include a stadium, practice area and offices," the *Morning Sun* reported in December 1970. "'The area has great accessibility to both Baltimore City and the surrounding counties,' a source said. 'And Rosenbloom is very much interested in it. In fact, this is his first choice.'"

Over Jack Kent Cooke's dead body. Given Columbia's proximity to Washington, D.C. (Redskins territory)—25 miles—co-owners Edward Bennett Williams and Cooke would point howitzers due northeast before they even broke ground. "Edward Bennett Williams, the lawyer and president of the Washington Redskins, reportedly has said he would not permit the Colts to move into a proposed Columbia stadium location, and that if the Colts wanted to build a stadium, let them build it in Towson [MD]," the *Morning Sun* clarified in January 1972. Not a problem since Towson is 14 miles north of Baltimore. Columbia was no-man's land.

Fed up to here with lip service, in February 1971 Rosenbloom told Baltimore City to stow the stadium lease. No more haggling. *Morning Sun* sports editor Bob Maisel noted, "Ever since the Colts announced last week that they would not renew their Stadium lease, everybody has his own personal opinion of the situation. Put yourself in Carroll Rosenbloom's place, and ask how many improvements have been made in the Stadium in the last five years. Obviously, very few have been made. The Stadium is not as good as it was five years ago [1966], and it figures to go down even more in the next five. In the meantime, Washington has a far more modern facility,

Philadelphia is building one, and Pittsburgh just opened a magnificent dual sport stadium last season. The competition is closing in on all sides."

The Orioles' beefs about the stadium never got much air time, primarily because: 1) They had a sweet lease and just a few gripes; and 2) Rosenbloom had the bullhorn and wouldn't give it up. So, when Rosenbloom lobbied to shut down the Baltimore Park Board, Steadman ran to his typewriter. This went in his April 5, 1971, column: "Jerry Hoffberger, chairman of the board of directors, and [GM Frank] Cashen represented the Orioles at the meeting regarding the Stadium. The Orioles made no requests for any specific improvements. This is understandable because they made no threat to leave Baltimore. The Colts, it's reported, are asking that direction of the Stadium be taken away from the Board of Parks and Recreation. The State of Maryland is going to try to put up $8 million for bringing about Stadium improvements. Governor [Marvin] Mandel may have to act before the day is out if he's going to bring it off before this current meeting of the Legislature. Whether the $8 million would be a loan to the city or if the State would take over operation of the Stadium remains to be seen." The result was the usual—not seen, not heard, not done.

The Park Board focused on crossword puzzles and ordering takeout. Steadman thought they were Baltimore's Joint Chiefs of Staff. He harrumphed at Rosenbloom's condemnation in the April 6, 1971, *News American*:

There's shock and dismay that the Baltimore Colts, one of the tenants of Memorial Stadium, are asking control of the facility be taken away from the Department of Recreation and Parks. Since the first Stadium was erected in 1924, the control of the outdoor athletic plant has been under jurisdiction of the Park Board. The Park Board, long comprised of outstanding citizens, has never done anything to willfully hurt Baltimore. It functions as a volunteer, dedicated unit, serving entirely without pay and in the best interests of the community. They have a record for integrity and make their decisions without prejudice. Some of their judgments, down through the years, have only rarely been open to question, especially when you don't agree with them. But to want to dump the Park Board and say it has not done a good job is beyond comprehension. Their devotion to duty says otherwise.

He also added that the stadium was a swell place for a ballgame, the city blessed Rosenbloom just building it, and the Colts should be grateful, all of it Park Board talking points.

Steadman didn't bother to query Steve Rosenbloom, who by March 1971 was president of the ballclub:

They [the Park Board] were the source that we had to talk to. As far as I know, they controlled the stadium. So, you hoped to do it [negotiate] through that channel. We didn't know at first that these were unreasonable people, and they weren't thinking this through. It eventually became a sore spot, and I knew my father was disturbed, shortly after we started going to those meetings [with the Park Board]. You're just hearing these politicians talk about nothing. And time was not an asset for us: *They aren't gonna do anything.* But to his credit, he [his father] hung in there, hoping that things would change. We got lip service, and that was about it. We thought we were talking to people who knew the value of having an NFL team there and what it brings to the city. So, an agreement would have been good for the city, good for the state and good for the team. Finally, that's when my father did go talk to [developer James] Rouse. It was just an impossible time to get something done in the Baltimore area. Unless you like to hear yourself talk, what we said was falling on deaf ears. We knew we either find a place and build our own stadium— but that's very costly. And if you already know you don't have support from the city or the state, that was nonsensical. Then, we were looking around, and he asked me, "What about Tampa [Fla.]?" I said, "That wouldn't be bad there."

The Tampa lark was right around the corner.

. . .

With Carroll Rosenbloom stirring up a fuss, Colts fans got amnesia, forgetting what he had done for the town—championships, pride, bragging rights—and turned on him. Bad enough that in July 1971 Jack Chevalier of the *Evening Sun* said he should give the fans a litmus test:

> Before Carroll Rosenbloom takes a definite move toward selling the Colts and purchasing another football team, such as the Los Angeles Rams, he is going to give the fans of Baltimore a fair and thorough trial. The owner wants to know if the love affair between the city and the Colts is really over. If Steve Rosenbloom were not in the picture, I'm convinced his father would sell the team as soon as possible. The owner is tired of fighting for Stadium improvements and searching for a better training camp and practice field. He is weary of criticism from fans and the press … At first glance, it seems unfair that Baltimore football lovers, who have supported the Colts so loyally since 1953, should have to undergo a fidelity test. But the Rosenblooms say they've received hate mail and obscene phone calls—unforgivable disturbances that would sour anybody on any city.

> The fans don't have to express any further interest in the Colts. Every time they buy a ticket, they display their "love," if such a precious term can be given commercial connotations. Certainly, the crowds that pack the Stadium shouldn't have to display their admiration any more than they have. They pay their way in and they cheer. The "love affair" started in 1953 when the same fans put up over $300,000 in the purchase of season tickets for a promised franchise that had neither coach [true], general manager [false] nor owner [false again]. The Colts' front office says it has received "hate mail" and obscene telephone calls. This, of course, is disturbing, but they ought to see the kind of letters sportswriters get or read some of John Unitas's mail from his harsh critics. The fans who have supported the Colts should not be placed on trial. You don't ever make fools out of your customers. Asking them to express "love" for the management, after they buy tickets, is doing that. They display "love" by showing up. It's tragic that greed, selfishness and ego have carried the Colts' management into a situation that has caused the public to rebel.

John Steadman had been inciting the natives with the usual bromides about $300,000 for season tickets to bail out the multi-millionaire and sermons about greed and ego. He fired back at Chevalier two days later:

Steadman was out over his skis again. First, Rosenbloom never brought up a loyalty test; Chevalier did. Second, two negatives don't make a positive. Downplaying C.R.'s hate mail and crank calls by saying reporters and

Johnny U got them just as bad didn't help his case. Better off saying you hate the guy and moving on.

But Steadman was definitely on to something that came out of L.A. On July 12, 1971, Steadman echoed news first revealed by Melvin Durslag of the *San Francisco Chronicle*: Rosenbloom was ready to trade up for the L.A. Rams:

> The stories over the weekend, apart from how the fans feel about management, caused still a different kind of stir. Melvin Durslag, columnist for the Hearst Headline Service, wrote that a scheme was being put together where the Colts would be involved in a trade of properties with the Los Angeles Rams, after a buyer was found for the Colts. The details are complex, far above the heads of we working stiffs, but it has been talked about. Whether it can be put together is another question. Durslag didn't say it was going to happen tomorrow but that it was being discussed as a future possibility. Durslag is regarded as one of America's most competent reporters and is certainly the No. 1 sportswriter in the nation. He doesn't get a story off the ceiling.

Exactly one year later, it was a done deal.

• • •

There was this riddle that had long stumped folks: Why did Colts fans prefer twiddling thumbs over a preseason game? In early September 1971, Bill Tanton of the *Evening Sun* examined that puzzler:

> In Oakland, even though both the Raiders and the Colts had been practicing only a few days and everyone knew they couldn't be sharp, there was a sellout crowd of 53,519 on hand. The following week in Kansas City there were 38,341, the largest crowd ever to see an exhibition game in that city. In Denver the Colts drew 42,499, another record, and last week in Miami, well, that was something else. They had to put in extra seats in the Orange Bowl to accommodate the crowd of 76,712, the largest ever to see the Dolphins play anywhere, at home or on the road. And then there is Baltimore. Nearly all the teams in pro football are playing exhibition games at home, but when the Colts announced last year [1970] that they wanted to play a couple of them in the Stadium this summer, there was a hue and cry like you never heard. Colt owner Carroll Rosenbloom was called everything but a bandit. The Colts were accused of "jamming these games down their fans' throats." Some even said the whole thing was immoral.

Attendance at preseason games was downright embarrassing. Outdoor insane asylum my eye. John Steadman of the *News American* started the preseason ticket rebellion and cited some figures: 28,471 attended a 1956

Colts-Redskins preseason affair; 6,218 dared show their faces for the same matchup in 1960. The point: Who gives a tinker's curse about exhibition games? We'd rather count cracks in the sidewalk. Catch you after Labor Day. Steadman had trouble explaining it in August 1971:

> When it came to the real thing, official league games, Baltimore has fought to buy tickets. The Colts have been supported like no team in the history of this city. For 51 straight games, they put up the sold-out sign—not a ticket available. Over 50,000 season tickets have been paid for months in advance of the season and this has been happening annually for nine straight years. Baltimore, for a lot of reasons, shows apathy to exhibitions. Fans don't mind making a sizable investment in season tickets, like $49 per seat, but they want the choice to accept or reject exhibitions. To the credit of Carroll Rosenbloom, he did not make exhibition tickets mandatory. Baltimore started off giving fair support to exhibitions but interest dwindled. The fans loved the Colts—always will—but not in exhibitions. Norman Polovoy, director of the Consumer's Protective Bureau of the State of Maryland, was flooded with protests when there was a chance that Baltimore might be saddled with the same type of pressure tactics, known as a "tie-in" purchase. Harry McGuirk, a Maryland state senator from Baltimore's

6th district, was prepared to start proceedings in the State Legislature if such a thing happened here. Fortunately, it didn't.

The Rosenblooms blew a fuse on August 8, 1971, when the Chiefs hit town to play the Colts and a few stragglers wandered in. "BALTIMORE, Aug. 8—The size of the crowd, and certainly not the game, was the news last night as the Baltimore Colts, pro football's champions, played the first preseason game in their home stadium in 10 years," William Wallace of the *New York Times* detailed. "The crowd was 16,771, which is likely to be the smallest of the year in the National Football League unless the Colts draw fewer fans in two future exhibitions."

Rosenbloom only had several ways to make cash: tickets, game programs, TV and radio rights. While other owners around the league were raking in preseason bucks, Rosenbloom looked around and saw 40,000 empty seats. He fumed and then let fly. The *Times* was at the game:

> The Colts fans do not support exhibitions and never have. The last preseason game here in 1961 drew 10,208 and the one the year before 6,218. But the Colts have had 51 regular-season sellouts over the last nine years and sell 50,000 season tickets. There were no excuses last night, perfect weather and a good attraction. Carroll Rosenbloom, the owner, was embittered. "Did you see what the

Rams drew in Los Angeles on Friday night?" he asked. "Eighty thousand. To support today's payrolls," said Rosenbloom, "you must play preseason games at home before big crowds rather than on the road as we used to." The Colts a year ago proposed to make mandatory for season ticket buyers the purchase of tickets to three preseason games. The hue and cry was such that Rosenbloom abandoned the idea.

Bad enough the Park Board was blowing him off; fans wanted Rosenbloom's effigy burned and writers like Steadman kept flogging him. Now the reincarnation of preseason bombs. Even mild-mannered Steve Rosenbloom flipped his lid: "The football fans of Baltimore, who packed Memorial Stadium for 51 consecutive home sellouts, were criticized by president Steve Rosenbloom of the Colts for not supporting an exhibition game," the *Morning Sun* reported. "'This makes you start to wonder if the image of the Baltimore fan is really a myth,' Rosenbloom said after a crowd of 16,771 turned out to see the Kansas City Chiefs beat the Colts 10-7 Saturday night. 'When a world championship team is not supported in its own city,' the 27-year-old executive said, 'it's time to review the situation.'"

Then Steve R. really cranked it:

"We're going to take a beating from this game," Rosenbloom said, "because we promised Kansas City a decent check, and they'll get it." Rosenbloom said after

expenses there was not much left from a gross gate of about $100,000, and added: "I was embarrassed to talk to the Kansas City people. How come we draw everywhere else we play, but not here? But we can't continue going to other people's parks. We've got to reciprocate. We've been a road team since 1961, but the other teams can't play at home all the time. If we started to lose, we wouldn't even be a good draw, and other teams wouldn't want us. As far as I'm concerned, we have 16,771 loyal fans—not the 50 million who claim to be. The people at the game Saturday night were the real Colt fans."

That bit of vitriol in town registered 3.5 on the Richter.

It wasn't the Godfather this time moping to the press. Steve Rosenbloom wasn't acerbic like the old man. Even Steadman liked him. The *Los Angeles Times* did a piece on L.A. Rams melodrama when C.R. died in 1979 and wife Georgia dumped son Steve out on the curb. Just about everybody likes the guy: "Steve Rosenbloom, during his days as the Ram executive vice president, was popular among players, reporters, team owners and executives. 'Steve wasn't like what you'd envision an owner's son to be,' said former Ram quarterback Pat Haden. 'There was a lot of depth to Steve. He could talk about anything. He was intelligent, had a quiet confidence and was retrospective. All the players liked and respected him. What I remember most about Steve is one time in Philadelphia, I believe, our bus driver got lost and Steve made him get out of the seat and he drove the bus. Steve did a little bit of everything.'"

Steve Rosenbloom picked a bad time to lose his cool; Bob Maisel of the *Morning Sun* was lurking and had his steno pad out. Decades later he explained:

I was deeply disappointed that there wasn't much more of a showing [attendance]. I was aware of what they [the fans] thought of it: "We don't want to pay for an extra [preseason] game." And I understand that. But it was my emotion, and I said, "Maybe the fans that supposedly support us so much is a myth." I regretted it, and my father got on Maisel for printing it. I put out some ads [for preseason games], but my dad said, "The ads aren't gonna get anybody there." I said, "I can't sit idly by and not throw some reasons out there to go to the games." We did whatever we could do. But there wasn't that much interest in it in Baltimore, and it had a bad smell to it. So, Bob [Maisel] stopped me on the way in [to the locker room], and it was all emotion. And I spit it out, and as soon as I did, I wished I could've squashed it. I regret it. I wish I did not say it. But this guy [himself]] sounding off about the fans—maybe it was an awakening for me. The fans supported us all those years, from '53 on, and they were the 12th man [with their cheering].

But they certainly didn't support us during the preseason games.

The baker's dozen who showed up for the K.C. game was one more thing for Rosenbloom to chew on while he worked the angles for a Colts-Rams swap. Phil Jackman of the *Evening Sun* analyzed the Rosenbloom vs. Charm City showdown in August 1971: "Several months ago, Rosenbloom called the media together in an attempt to ascertain why he, his fellow front-office types and his well-muscled employees [the players] had fallen from favor in the eyes of the public [the infamous press luncheon at the Chesapeake Restaurant]. In so many words it was explained fans didn't like being hauled into the American [Football] Conference, they blanched at pro football's sellout to TV, and constantly-rising ticket prices didn't do much to foster love, either."

Regarding the jump to the AFC, Jackman concedes, no whining: Somebody had to do it. "Besides," Jackman notes, "the Colts are scooping up $3 million for the maneuver, and without $600,000 worth of help every year for the next five [the payout], season ticket prices would be that much higher."

Bottom line for Jackman: Blame both sides.

He [Rosenbloom] blames the fans, the fans blame him, and sitting in the middle going to make up the most grandiose payroll in the game, are the players. Rosenbloom isn't like Bob Short [owner of the Washington Senators]; he has to pay the bills. If he can't do it with local exhibitions, you can't knock him for cutting corners and maybe winning fewer games, or charging $20 per pew for a regular season game. At the same time, his taking the position that these trial runs [preseason games] are a bonus to the fans is an insult to their intelligence. The worst thing a man can do in a fight is not respect the enemy, something both the club and the fans have been guilty of for too long.

Next up were the Chicago Bears, and Cooper Rollow of the *Chicago Tribune*, inventor of "world's largest outdoor insane asylum," didn't expect much: "BALTIMORE, Aug. 13 [1971]—The Chicago Bears carry their exhibition banner into the world's largest outdoor insane asylum tomorrow night. But many of the inmates will be missing when the Bears battle the Colts in Baltimore Memorial Stadium. The House That Unitas Built, which for more than a decade has quivered under the vocal harassment of thousands upon thousands of raving lunatics each time the beloved Colts take on a hated enemy, has become a rather sedate place of late."

Blame Rosenbloom for some of this, but the press also got fans in a lather. "There was an erosion [of fan support]," lamented Steve Rosenbloom. "It was in the air. I was signing some players at that point, and there was always a buzz around: 'They're not being fair to the players.' I heard stuff from fans. After

I don't know how many years of these articles by [John] Steadman, there was one common theme: The Colts are tainted; their ownership is tainted. They loved the players, but when it came to reaching into their pockets for their wallets—but ticket prices in those days were normal. In reality, maybe what I said to Bob Maisel was true: The support had become a myth."

When a new stadium lease came up, Rosenbloom said, Stop right there. "Carroll Rosenbloom, the owner of the Baltimore Colts, said yesterday that the Colts have halted negotiations with the city over a new lease agreement for the use of Memorial Stadium," the *Morning Sun* revealed in September 1971. "Mr. Rosenbloom said he was upset over reports that the Colts had demanded a number of improvements in stadium facilities with the city—in addition to requiring the city build the team a practice field—in a proposed lease to the Park Board. 'I don't want anything from the city,' he said. 'I had absolutely nothing to do with the plan.' The Colt owner said he had 'never asked nor have I ever wanted to use public funds to fix up Memorial Stadium.'"

The state was willing to pony up $7 million for a stadium spruce-up—if the Colts and the Birds signed new leases. Then they'd get to work: 1) installing Astroturf; 2) building an office complex for the Colts at the stadium, better locker rooms and facilities; 3) modernizing the concession stands and restrooms; 4) constructing two more upper-deck sections and adding two more escalators and one elevator; and 5) buying a 47-acre lot in

Baltimore County to build a practice field (the most daring of the five). Rosenbloom had talked himself silly about fixing up the mausoleum, so there it was: What is it about what I'm saying you don't understand? Steve Rosenbloom was likewise perplexed:

> There was a lot of stuff out there, and the quest for a [new] stadium] couldn't be magnified enough. The people who want to hate Carroll Rosenbloom and think it's his fault: "This is what we're left with? Irsay?" That kind of thing. That was bad enough. But the worst thing, for me, was all this stuff going on was affecting my father. And he's the guy that brought the Colts back in 1953. He's the guy that said, "We are planning on having a championship-caliber team by '58." And that happened. It was a storybook romance from the start. But then, there was an abandonment all around, and I keep coming back to Steadman because all the fans and everybody else could read this almost daily. So, what do they start thinking? "Well, it's the evil Carroll Rosenbloom." And nothing could be further from the truth. I was concerned about my father because he spent years making the Colts a prominent team. And now, he's being accused of all kinds of things. Here's a guy who gave his heart and soul to the Colts, as well as the fans. People began to believe the big lies because they were reading them almost every day: "Oh, yeah, it's Carroll's fault."

Most Americans in the '60s and '70s split their time with newspapers and TV for their news. Those days are ancient history. Back then John Steadman had a big fan club, and he sure gave it to Rosenbloom.

Rosenbloom was also at loggerheads with Jerry Hoffberger and the Orioles. The Orioles sweetheart lease always bugged him and now Hoffberger was saying no to a new one. "The Colt owner said that three times in recent years he has tried to finance improvements to Memorial Stadium with his own money without success," the *Morning Sun* indicated in September 1971. "The first time, he said the Park Board and the Mayor asked the Colts to put up $6 million to repair the stadium. The second time, they asked the Colts for $3 million. Both times, the stadium's other major tenant, the Baltimore Orioles, rejected improvement plans, Mr. Rosenbloom said. 'The Orioles never stopped throwing roadblocks in our way,' he added."

Rosenbloom and Hoffberger had a turf war going on. But they used to be two rich swells before the friendship went off a cliff. And it stayed ugly. "He [Rosenbloom] and Hoffberger had a falling out," recalled Ernie Accorsi, once Rosenbloom's PR director. "If I'm not mistaken, in the '58 championship game, the player's share was around $4,000 [$4,718]. I think he [Hoffberger] matched that, gave it to the players. That's how close they were. But they had a falling out, and it cost us to lose [HOF announcer] Chuck Thompson. We didn't have Chuck Thompson anymore; we had Ted Moore as our play-by-play announcer. When Carroll left, and [GM] Joe Thomas came in, I got Chuck Thompson back because he worked for Hoffberger; he basically worked for the brewery [National Brewing Co.]. Yeah, there was animosity, but a lot of it was based on stuff like the [Memorial Stadium] lease."

Steve Rosenbloom tells the story of how his dad and Hoffberger started a cold war over malt liquor:

That's what started it off. My father was in town [in Baltimore], and the Beatles were gonna be on the *Ed Sullivan Show* [February 1964]. This [Beatlemania] was all new stuff, and we were curious about it. So, my father said, "You wanna come over tonight? Jerry [Hoffberger] and I are gonna watch the *Ed Sulllivan Show*." He said, "Tell Dan [his brother], and you guys come over." I came over from D.C. [Georgetown University]. So, we went over, and we had a beer or two. Jerry—who my brother, my father and I liked very much—was interested in what kind of beers we liked to drink [because he owned National Brewing]. That's when malt liquor first hit the market. People loved it; kids loved it; there's more alcohol in it. We told Jerry, "This is what young people are drinking these days." We had a discussion about it, and I knew Jerry was interested because he made National Boh [bohemian beer], so he knew what he was doing. My brother and I almost

simultaneously told him, "Malt liquor is all the rage." My father was a good friend of Jerry's, and he picked up on what we were saying. They had a conversation one day, and my father suggested, "Why don't you use our logo [a horse and a horseshoe] on the can and call it 'Colt 45' [malt liquor]?" National Bohemian was a sponsor of the Colts and the Orioles, so all that was good. So, they ironed out some kind of deal—probably a few cents a can for my father for using the Colts' logo. Everything was fine until the profits got bigger and bigger, and Jerry stopped paying that and ended the agreement. At the end of all this, my father told me that he didn't want to talk to Jerry anymore. It was a big disappointment to him. That was a sad day for my father. The damage was done. If you do that to a person like Carroll Rosenbloom—you only get one chance. Lie to me, screw me, I don't talk to you anymore. Colt 45 hit the market and took off, so a few cents a bottle became a nice payday. And Jerry just stopped paying it. I don't know what Jerry's side of the story was, but you hate to see two good friends break up over something like that. I thought the world of Jerry Hoffberger. But apparently, the deal was off the table now that it was making good money. They definitely had an agreement based on mutual trust. To my father, this was treason. If your good friend is going to screw you like that—something my father wouldn't do—that's a treasonous act by a friend. If I promise something and renege on it, you wouldn't trust me. What he [Hoffberger] did was a sin of friendship. If you have a close friend, you watch his back, and he watches your back. And apparently, my father was betrayed. It was a shot in the gut.

. . .

Before the Big Swap came about, there was Tampa. The rumor that C.R. was bummed with Baltimore floated down the coast. Hearts were aflutter and phones started ringing. John Steadman got wind of it, and his column on September 6, 1971, was about two months ahead of the game. The chatter was that Tampa was a player. Steadman went to default mode—the bloody $300,000: "You, the Baltimore public, put the Colts in business by financing the team's return in 1953. The franchise was awarded to Baltimore, the city, before any ownership appeared. So, technically and legally, according to Harry Kaufman, of the Baltimore Park Board, the Colts could not be moved elsewhere. Will it come to this? The Baltimore team is different than any other in the National Football League since it was originally financed by the public through the sale of $300,000 worth of season tickets."

Showing Steadman the paperwork wouldn't stop the prattling. Rosenbloom wrote a check for $13,000, put a million pesos of his own in the Colt coffers and took a flying leap. Forget

the $300,000. Had NFL commish Bert Bell Sr.'s pushing, pulling and prodding of Rosenbloom to buy not worked, then no team. There was no stampede of fat cats willing to chance it. So, Steadman's you-the-fan routine was just currying favor with John Q. Public and spouse. For example: "So much controversy has been created by the Colts in so many areas that the performance of the team has been overshadowed, almost relegated to a different role entirely. The Colts have done some important things right—like winning on the field. But they have bungled in other aspects of the operation. There are all kinds of examples. It almost appears they have a vendetta with the fans, but of course, this isn't true."

Steadman liked tossing out red meat—Rosenbloom ordered the Ameche TD in '58 to cover the spread; he has a vendetta with the fans—then halfway taking it back, knowing the damage was done. But Steady was on point about Tampa putting out feelers. "We were going down there to talk to them about getting a [preseason] game down there [late 1971]," Steve Rosenbloom admitted. "Tampa seemed to be as eager as we were. They wanted a team; they didn't have one. It's a double area [Tampa and St. Petersburg]. The weather's nice, so I don't know if my father put the word out, or Tampa got word that the Colts might be up for sale. Tampa was definitely a willing participant, and so were we. We had to find someplace; we couldn't live at home anymore."

Not everybody smeared Rosenbloom. James H. Bready of the *Morning Sun* understood his plight:

The causes of the present mess, while complicated, boil down to this. Carroll Rosenbloom, who owns the franchise, wanted to move. He envisioned a new football stadium for the Colts and various tenants, a stadium reachable from Baltimore's and Washington's beltways. He worked out a deal last spring with James W. Rouse for all the land necessary for stadium, parking, practice field, office. When this plan became known, the Greater Baltimore Committee, the Governor and the Mayor prevailed upon Mr. Rosenbloom to go from his home in Florida to Annapolis [MD] for a protracted, cards-face-up discussion. On one side, the potential damage to Mr. Rosenbloom's original home, was made clear. On the other, these aspects of Memorial Stadium which are most dissatisfying to the Colts were listed. As a result, the Colts reluctantly agreed to call off their planned move to Howard County [Columbia]. The Governor committed himself to finding $7 million for improvements and, a few days later, the General Assembly authorized the outlay. The city pledged itself, as stadium owner, to expedite the agreed-on construction.

Nifty so far. Then, complications. You know how squirrely politicians get in election years. Some naysayers started chirping about the $7-million deal, local pols got rattled, and they backed off. Not to mention

Rosenbloom and Hoffberger wouldn't get conned into signing long-term leases *before* Memorial Stadium got a facelift. James H. Bready had this refreshing revelation: "Persons present at the Annapolis sessions and participants in talks since then agree on one key point again and again: *The Colts have been in the right* [emphasis mine]. Their specific desires are, again and again, merited and overdue. It is the city, rather, which has offered something and then been unable to follow through; it is this or that public figure who, misreading the situation or descending to personal vilification, has deliberately given offense." Sportswriters included.

The governor's flip-flop was a page-one story. The *Morning Sun* ran the headline, **Mandel Sides with Colts**: "Annapolis—Governor [Marvin] Mandel charged yesterday that city officials had mishandled the Baltimore Colts' stadium lease affair and declared that the Colts 'have been taking an unfair beating.' The Colts 'have done everything they said they would do. The city hasn't done what it said it would do,' the governor said. Steve Rosenbloom, the president of the corporation which runs the football club, flatly iterated yesterday his assertion that the Colts will never resume negotiations with the city." Imagine the buzz in City Hall when this story made the rounds. We just lost the governor—holy moly.

One argument for putting rouge and lipstick on Memorial Stadium was it would buy time to put up a new ballpark. James H. Bready pushed this in the *Morning Sun* in September 1971:

There is more in this than the average fan may have allowed for. The improvements planned in the Annapolis talks amount, it was agreed, only to a patch-up job. They would give Memorial Stadium only about 10 more years' usefulness. Ten years is roughly the minimum time it will take to plan and build the next generation's Baltimore stadium. The need for a better stadium, holding more people and giving them a better view of the game and defending them and the players against Baltimore's weather, is beyond dispute on the management level. And for the redoubtable financial task of putting up a new stadium, the continuing presence of two big-league rent payers [Colts, Orioles] is once more all-essential.

"Two big-league rent payers" looked more like a crapshoot, now that Rosenbloom wasn't holding anything back. *Morning Sun* sports editor Bob Maisel got him on the phone in November 1971 as C.R. contemplated an exit:

> Carroll Rosenbloom has been saying the same thing for the last six months or so. His position hasn't changed, nor is it likely to change. Occasionally, however, news comes from a Park Board or other meeting and there is a new crisis with accompanying headlines, denials, etc. The thing that occasioned the latest outburst was news from a Park Board meeting that it had voted to build a $1-million practice facility, with the Colts putting up the money and getting it back in rental [reductions] after signing a long-term lease. The Colts declined, although this originally was one of the things they sought. Why? "Our position is the same as I've told you for months, the same as you've written a number of times," said Carroll Rosenbloom by phone from his Miami home yesterday. "We aren't interested in negotiating with the city anymore. As I told you before, I'm just tired of being the bad guy, no matter what happens in Baltimore. When we offered to put up money for Stadium improvements, Rosenbloom and the Colts were ogres, forcing their will on the people. If the city offers to build a practice field, or do something to the Stadium that will benefit the Colts, we are squandering the taxpayers' money. If we want to build our own stadium, we're bad. No matter what we do, we're wrong."

That last line was directed at John Steadman: Yeah, *you*, pal. A coterie of rational types in Baltimore defended Rosenbloom. In yet another exegesis on Memorial Mausoleum in August 1984, *Morning Sun* writer Barry Rascovar itemized particulars in the 1971 stadium lease that got flushed:

- Installation of artificial turf at Memorial Stadium

- Construction of team offices for the Colts at the stadium

- Construction of two more locker rooms and refurbishing of the existing ones

- Construction of at least two more upper-deck sections, rollout sideline seats and two more escalators

- Expanded football press facilities to include a lounge, food facilities and a private elevator

- Modernized and increased concessions, restrooms and first-aid rooms

Rascovar wrote:

A stadium restaurant had also been under discussion. All this was to be done with a $7-million state bond. The $1-million practice field was to be icing on the cake. But like every other plan to satisfy the Colts, it ran into political opposition. This time it was the late Harry D. Kaufman, a Park Board member, who insisted the lease would be "a rape and raid on the taxpayer's body."

Rosenbloom had had enough of this burlesque show and contracted wanderlust. Ordinarily, the party line would be pro forma for William Boucher III, executive director of the Greater Baltimore Committee. But this time he sided with Rosenbloom: "The Colts have done everything the city has asked," he told the *Evening Sun* in November 1971. "They are totally justified at being annoyed by the city's inaction on the one hand and bum rap by the public on the other."

Fixing to rub Rosenbloom's nose in it, City Comptroller Hyman Pressman nixed the practice field posthaste. "As to the city building the practice field, Mr. Boucher said that the original proposal—put forth by F. Pierce Linaweaver, the city's director of the Department of Public Works—called for the Colts to build the field at their expense on city property near the Loch Raven Reservoir," the *Morning Sun* related. "But, Mr. Boucher said, Hyman A. Pressman, the city comptroller, would not go along with the plan." Rymin' Hyman would resurface in '74 to kill the new stadium plan altogether.

Suits, pols and assorted ninnies convinced Carroll Rosenbloom to scram. Steve Rosenbloom and his dad had hit a dead end:

The problems started out when the Park Board was stonewalling and being stupid. If you have a major-league team—which you had with the Orioles—what's wrong with having *two* major-league teams? It makes Baltimore look so much better. How could they sacrifice *that*? The Park Board is responsible, ultimately, for us leaving. There was not one attempt to fix the problem, just hollow words. That's all we got. My father said that he would contribute [money] when no other teams were doing that.

He knew how important it was to have a nice place for the fans to come to. "You should knock the whole thing down," which eventually happened, then build a new one if you want it there. I don't get that shortsighted, selfish, political attitude. When a small-time politician is lording over some rich guy, they feel powerful. When he [Hyman Pressman] knew he could stonewall us, he did—the whole time. The people that are responsible for this mess aren't alive anymore— Hymie [Pressman], Steadman, etc. It's a bad cast of characters. Why would they shoot themselves in the foot, anyway?

With rumors flitting about, fans got jittery, so they drummed up a little PR. "An all-out campaign was launched yesterday to 'save the Colts for Baltimore' through public-support petitions and efforts to renew negotiations for a long-term Memorial Stadium lease agreement between the local National Football League club and government officials," the *Morning Sun* announced in November 1971. "Longtime rumors of a shift by the Colts elsewhere prompted yesterday's announcement of the formation of a 'Committee to Save the Colts for Baltimore.' [GBC Executive Director William] Boucher said that fans at Monday night's game here [Baltimore] against the Los Angeles Rams will be asked—by their signatures on a petition—to exhort the Colts to remain 'in a rebuilt and modernized Memorial Stadium ... as an important economic and social force' in the community."

Boucher hopped on the city soapbox to elaborate:

"We believe that the Baltimore Colts should remain in Baltimore and should receive the support they deserve. We have the means to rebuild and modernize Memorial Stadium and to make it attractive for the Colts and the Orioles and their fans ... A fourth purpose of the [Save the Colts] committee is to correct the injustice which has been done to the Colt organization and, in particular, Carroll and Steve Rosenbloom, by the unfortunate and uninformed debate over the lease several months ago concerning this matter. We want to make it clear that the Colts have done everything requested of them. They have kept their side of the bargain but they have been given a 'bum rap' in the minds of some of the public."

Steadman's bushy eyebrows twitched hearing that. Of course he couldn't resist a rejoinder—*News American*, November 23, 1971: "The interest in the Colts' staying here is evidenced by the telegram sent today by W.H. Edwards and H.E. Pollock Jr. to [Baltimore] Mayor William Donald Schaefer. In his wire, he said: 'The sales and marketing executives of Baltimore urgently request you to take personal charge of the efforts to keep the Colts in Baltimore. Baltimore must speak with one voice. Therefore, it is urgent that you prevent threatening, belligerent, antagonistic statements from other city officials which can only damage our ability to keep the world champion Colts playing in Memorial Stadium. We offer our assistance to you as a member of the "save the Colts committee." Urge immediate action.'" This will be Steadman's future M.O. when the Colts threatened to bolt: Mayday! Mayday! All hands on deck!

An *Evening Sun* editorial on November 23, 1971, reminded everyone of the dangers of ignoring history:

> Money matters in professional football, as in all organized sports nowadays. The fiction that baseball or basketball or any of them is still at bottom a game rather than a business has been effectually punctured, these last two decades, particularly by owners who move their franchises to whatever city looks to be a more profitable scene of combat. It is often overlooked that Baltimore's Colts and Orioles were brought here from other cities that were left, to a degree, bereft. Fellow-owners are usually understanding, and the city that loses out is told to be patient and maybe it will be allowed back in in one of a given league's expansions. Baltimore, bilked by the American League in a 1902 baseball deal, had to wait 51 years before it got back in.

Steadman beseeched the powerful: "It is heartening to see public officials, men like Governor Mandel, Mayor Schaefer, Comptroller Pressman, and members of the Congress and Senate, alert and perceptive enough to want to keep the Colts in Baltimore. To think otherwise would not be in the public interest. The Colts are synonymous with Baltimore. This city made them what they are today with deep affection and total financial support. It's a love affair that will never end."

Toss Hyman Pressman overboard and peruse Memorial Stadium attendance figures to check out all that love Steadman always trumpeted. Recall the gamble that Carroll Rosenbloom took. The biggest crowd the Colts had in 1953 was 34,031 against the Redskins. The other five games were just north of 20,000 in a ballpark that held a little over 50,000. OK, give 'em a mulligan. Two years later—1955—the Redskins game got 51,587; but the Colts got 36,167 for the Bears, 40,030 for the Lions, 34,411 for the Packers, 41,146 for the Rams and 33,485 for the Niners. Scalpers took a licking. A year later, nothing to yahoo about: Bears—45,221; Lions—42,622; Packers—40,086; Rams—40,321; 49ers—37,227; and Redskins—32,944. And that was the year they got Unitas. No immediate lovefest, it appears. Not at first, anyway. By 1957 the Hosses were in the trophy hunt and the joint got crowded. It wasn't until Rosenbloom hired Don Kellett as GM and Weeb Ewbank as head coach, Kellett gave Bell Telephone 85¢ to call Johhny Unitas, and the wins started coming that Baltimoreans got that love affair going.

Mossback Hyman A. Pressman got a well-deserved slap on the wrist by the *Evening Sun*:

Notwithstanding [the ominous news about the Colts], it can't happen here, cries Hyman A. Pressman. The veteran comptroller and veteran filer of lawsuits puts his trust in a theory that the franchise belongs to a city, not to shareholders and officers and directors. He relies also on Congress and seeming promises from pro football's commissioner. They'll never take it away, he proclaims. Mr. Pressman does seem to want the Colts to stay in Baltimore, and if his effort somehow accomplishes that end, the fans will be grateful. But a strategy of negativism hasn't worked, within recent years, in Milwaukee, Seattle and Washington [baseball teams that moved], among others. To persuade the Colt management that Baltimoreans really support the team, and want it to go on calling this city home, will require something more affirmative, and more tangible and visible, than so far put forward.

Governor Marvin Mandel wasn't a doom-and-gloomer. In late November 1971, he told reporters that he thought the situation was looking better and planned to arrange a meeting with city brokers and Rosenbloom to resolve the mess. "I think some progress has been made," he told the *Associated Press*, "but I think it will take a lot more." Rosenbloom wasn't so upbeat. "Rosenbloom has made no secret of the fact that he is disgruntled over poor crowds at three exhibition games this year in Baltimore, over the conditions at Memorial Stadium and over the reluctance of the city to make improvements to the stadium," the *AP* reported. "He has raised the possibility of asking for permission to move the club to Tampa, which is actively wooing the Colts."

Tampa pulled out all the stops and Baltimore freaked.

CHAPTER 7

DON'T TAMPA WITH OUR COLTS

Tampa staged its own version of Fort Sumter. Sports editor Frank Klein of the *Tampa Times* explained in early December 1971:

Kyle Griffin told his *Memphis Commercial Appeal* [newspaper] audience the other day, "The idea is for the Colts to make their 'summer home' in Tampa, training there for next season [1972] and playing three of their preseason games. The projection is that when this proves profitable to all, the Colts will come on down permanently. Tampa's plan is a simple one: an attractive stadium rental, full houses of more than 50,000 at all the games, the use of the University of South Florida's playing fields with housing in an off-campus dormitory. It has been warmly received because: 1) on urging of special groups, fans in Baltimore have stayed away from preseason games

because they are included on the season-ticket package [sic—false]; 2) the stadium there is dominated by baseball's Orioles; and 3) the Tampa invitation is genuine." So, we've won the battle with Memphis [an early suitor for the Colts]. The real one's with Baltimore, of course.

The declaration of war was unofficial, but obvious: Tampa had thrown down the gauntlet to Charm City. That got the attention of John Steadman: "The Colts are going to Tampa for three days of practice and then on Saturday will fly across Florida to await their [1972 AFC] championship game with the Miami Dolphins in the Orange Bowl. Tampa has been romancing the Colts, hopeful that the team will divorce Baltimore and move there permanently after its contract for use of Memorial Stadium runs out with Baltimore City next year. This is just the beginning… but an appropriate time for the new suitors to start in trying to show the Colts that Tampa offers them a better future than Baltimore, which has been home to pro football from 1947 to 1950 and from 1953 until the present."

Steadman was spooked:

Here's the game plan: Tampa hopes to do so much for the Colts during their visit this week and next summer they will find it irresistible for them not to want to come there and stay. Tampa's approach in the past has been to get an expansion team from the National Football League. It has turned out exceptional crowds for exhibitions played there with hope the NFL would look upon it with favor. But now Tampa believes it can woo the Colts to leave Baltimore. It is pulling out all stops. The Colts this week will be given a sampling of the hospitality that awaits them if they'll make a promise for the future or even show a desire they like the place.

Tampa would even stoop to rabbit-punching. Near Christmas 1971, Tom McEwen of the *Tampa Tribune* sneered at Baltimore calling itself the "City of Champions" (1970 World Series champs, 1971 Super Bowl champs, 1971 NBA finalist): "How incredibly ironic it is that the current (December) issue of *The Nation's Business* carries the story it does on pages 70-72. It's titled 'Winning is a Many-Splendored Thing.' It's subtitled 'What does it mean to a city to have professional

sports teams that come out on top? Look at Baltimore, "City of Champions."'" And so on. And the irony, with Tampa so much in the Colts' future, people who believe in Santa Claus won't believe this. But we are, for the moment as a summer-long training site and for the three preseason games, that normally would have been played in Baltimore. That city, by campaign, has displayed it is disinterested in the preseason games, and has in other ways given management to believe the Colts are held as sports stepchildren [to the Orioles]."

Some petty one-upmanship ensued—airport crowds, mine's-bigger-than-yours, etc. John Steadman got sucked into it. Welcome-home crowds at Baltimore's Friendship (BWI) Airport became verboten because the natives often got a little too restless. A no-show policy when the Colts returned from Miami in January 1971 was in play. But Steadman couldn't ignore the dig by McEwen down in Tampa. His retort on November 29, 1971: "That 10 or 10,000 or even 100,000 turned out to welcome the Baltimore Colts when they arrived in Tampa was not unexpected. They should have had more, considering that Tampa is trying to romance the Colts out of Baltimore and every face in the crowd is supposed to mean something. Like instant love. The Colts don't draw those throngs to Friendship Airport when they come home from games because a mob scene creates a safety problem and airport officials are afraid of a stampede or else the good folks being run over by planes on the runway."

What followed was some middle-school repartee. Steadman kept at it:

You can get anything you want in Tampa from a good cigar to a cold beer. Rick Casares, the former Chicago Bears' fullback, has a saloon there that serves an honest drink. And in nearby Ybor City they have some outstanding restaurants. The players will enjoy their Tampa visit. No doubt about it. A third-string guard will be greeted on the street like he's John Unitas or Jim Thorpe. Tampa is all worked up by the Colts' visit there. They hope to get them to desert Baltimore and come set up ticket offices in Tampa. The crowd count at the airport is window-dressing, the kind you might want to have impress you, if you go in for this kind of display. If the Colts' management is going to be enthralled with crowds at the airport, it can be arranged for a million Baltimore residents to move out to Friendship Airport and greet them.

McEwen of the *Tampa Trib* found his inner child: "It is our pleasure and compliment, said Carroll Rosenbloom, that you wish to call us the Tampa Colts. 'Please do. You honor us,' said the owner of that football team yesterday, swept up too in the enthusiasm over the Colts that seems to be everywhere hereabouts … Even the Baltimore writers, who'd like to view the hiy'alling, good smiles and total hospitality with suspicion, are being hard-pressed to find anything wrong. One put it beautifully in his post-airport reception dispatch back to Baltimore, saying the great crowd greeted the Colts with 'love in their eyes and larceny in their hearts.' NOT bad. Though he should have said grand larceny, for the intentions are surely not petty. We're after the whole shebang."

Naturally, Rosenbloom's brief Tampa flirtation was easy pickings for Steadman's superego. He lays it out in *From Colts to Ravens*:

Rosenbloom ultimately realized the new stadium he wanted in Baltimore wasn't going to be forthcoming. There was no hue and cry on the part of fans for another place to play; it is the owners who demand better facilities, paid for, of course, by the public. Rosenbloom had stopped speaking to Jerry Hoffberger, the National Brewing Co. president who bought the Orioles, and attempted to feud with him over petty issues. Hoffberger continued to run his brewery interests and ignored the Rosenbloom insults. In short, Carroll didn't believe he was getting the full attention, or adulation, he deserved. That's when he threatened to take the Colts to Tampa. A survey of other NFL owners indicated this wouldn't happen, and [NFL Commissioner Pete] Rozelle was on record with Congress that all present franchises would remain in their current locations.

Attention? Adulation? That's not what pushed Rosenbloom into the arms of Tampa.

• • •

Hoping to wow Rosenbloom, more than 12,000 oglers showed up to watch a humdrum 30-minute kicking drill at Tampa Stadium in January 1972, prompting this dig in the *Tampa Tribune*: "It was almost as many as the 16,000 which attended one of Baltimore's preseason games this year in Baltimore." Baltimore had a case of the blues. Folks did show up at Friendship to welcome home the Colts after they got drubbed by the Dolphins, 21-0. Happy to see their boys, but full of piss and vinegar about Rosenbloom. The *Evening Sun* queried a few. "And there were fans critical of Carroll Rosenbloom, blaming the Colt owner for trying to leave the city. One said, 'You can go to hell, Rosenbloom, but leave the Colts here.' Jerry DeFord, 19, of the 3600 block Kenton Avenue, was pessimistic that his appearance would have much effect on whether the Colts moved or not. Others reflected his despair. 'Yeah, I think they're gonna go,' Mr. DeFord said. 'They play for money more than for the crowds. It doesn't matter where they play, as long as they get their money.'"

With Tampa on the warpath, John Steadman put two lanterns in the church tower: "Chamber of Commerce, City Council members and the Tampa Sports Authority have united with business and civic groups to push hard for the Colts," Steady observed in early January 1972. "Selling out the exhibitions is practically guaranteed. Tampa will attempt to pull off what it admits is 'grand larceny' [alluding to the *Tampa Trib's* Tom McEwen]— stealing the Colts from Baltimore, where the franchise was born, named, nurtured and raised to the immense success it has become. Baltimore will allow Tampa to enjoy watching the exhibitions with the Colts, but the team belongs here and this is where it should stay, even if it takes a Federal investigation and intervention." Call Washington, bring in Melvin Purvis, but do SOMETHING.

Al Davis of the Raiders was in Tampa, mouthing off, as usual. Chief Tampa Colts instigator Tom McEwen caught up with him:

Al Davis characteristically hedged not one whit on speaking out on the prospects [of the Colts moving] here yesterday, and I believe you'll begin to smile as you read on. "You can say," Al Davis began to say, that Al Davis, former coach, former commissioner of the American Football League, and now owner of the Oakland Raiders, said these things: "That Carroll Rosenbloom has made a tremendous contribution to football, and so have the Colts. I would be agreeable to anything Carroll Rosenbloom decides to do regardless of what it is. I honestly believe that whatever Carroll Rosenbloom decides to do will be in the best interests of the 26 [sic, 25] other owners and football in general." Pretty strong, EH? There's more. "Carroll Rosenbloom would have the 100 percent backing of the Oakland Raiders in whatever he decides, without qualification, and I feel the NFL would act favorably on whatever he recommends."

Not so fast. Pete Rozelle went on *Face the Nation* and told everybody there would be no forthcoming franchise moves.

The *Tampa Tribune* kept running big fat ads for the three-game preseason package that summer: $21 for the three games with the header, **The BALTIMORE COLTS will be the TAMPA COLTS for Two Months next Summer!** Frank Klein, sports editor of the *Tampa Times*, had at least one foot in reality:

What Carroll Rosenbloom wanted from the Tampa Sports Authority, to play three summer games and make more than he has any right to expect in Baltimore, wasn't just the mini-rental of 8% of the gate. He wanted some leverage—some clout—to use back in Baltimore where he's going to have to renegotiate his own stadium rental shortly. What Carroll wanted, Carroll got—the parking money and 5% of the concessions. That's what Carroll wants in Baltimore, but doesn't have just now. So Carroll's got what he wants, more than the mere low, low rental granted three weeks ago, probably the best deal of any pro football operator who uses a facility where the prime tenant is the baseball club. The idea is to make Carroll so happy this summer, with 45,000 or more guaranteed for each game at $7, that someday

he'll move his franchise to Tampa. It depends on whether Carroll gets whatever he wants in Baltimore and this little swap of parking revenue and a concessions share for $7,000 a game is going to do it, but don't tell anyone in Baltimore.

It didn't dawn on Steadman that his preseason-sucks mantra helped push Rosenbloom down to Tampa. It was always open season on C.R.:

Rosenbloom's troubles in Baltimore began when he attempted to force season ticket holders to purchase tickets to preseason games. It mattered not that the same individuals he was trying to exploit made it possible for him to enter pro football in 1953. They thought of it, but he didn't. The individual game turnouts [for the 1971 preseason games] were 16,771, 17,593 and 22,291. It annoyed Rosenbloom that the fans refused to bow to his demands and he threatened the city by talking of going elsewhere. That's when he held hands with Tampa and even took the team out of its regular Westminster training camp and deposited it in the Florida city. This was interpreted as being Baltimore's punishment for not buying preseason tickets, even though the audience clearly had demonstrated its disinterest.

Two things (among others) were pushing Rosenbloom out of town: 1) the delusion that

Baltimore owned the Colts and they weren't going anywhere; and 2) dissing preseason games—while other cities were all-in—was a major hit to the wallet. "Carroll Rosenbloom, the owner of the Baltimore Colts, was reported yesterday as ready to move the team out of Baltimore after the 1972 season," the *New York Times* announced in January 1972. "Rosenbloom, who has been conducting a feud with Baltimore city officials in recent years over Memorial Stadium's facilities and his club's financial arrangement, has been further angered by the city's poor response to exhibition games. The club averaged only 15,000 fans [sic, 18,885] for three preseason games last year."

A fed-up Rosenbloom groused to the papers again. "If they allow me to build a stadium, it won't be as elaborate as the plans I had five or six years ago, but it will have ample parking and be accessible to all our fans," he told the *Morning Sun* in January 1972. Then he unloaded on the Camden Yards stadium plan and deadweight local politicians:

> "I don't know much about the plan, only what I have heard. I don't feel it is practical, but I can't say anything about it. I just can't see anything like that happening in Baltimore. They can't agree on an East-West expressway or on how to use the $7 million the state gave them for improving the stadium." Mr. Rosenbloom will not talk to city officials because "every time I come out the bad guy. They say they are going to do this

and that, and I say OK and then they make it appear that I was forcing them to do the things they said they would do. They would like people to think I'm playing games with them. Well, I'm not. They think they can give me something. I don't want anything from them, and I never have. I don't want something for nothing. I have in the past offered to loan the city $6 million for improvements for the stadium, but they turned it down."

The man was looking for the exit ramp.

Rosenbloom had to ask himself: How many times do I get the runaround before I clear out? He first started squawking about the stadium in 1965, and a year later hit this dead-end: "In the autumn of 1966, then [Baltimore City] Mayor Theodore McKeldin talked with Carroll Rosenbloom, then owner of the Baltimore Colts, about a $45-million domed stadium just south of the Civic Center," the *Evening Sun* revealed in January 1985. "The talks fizzled and Rosenbloom, already dreaming of leaving Baltimore, suggested Towson as a site for the stadium on land he claimed he had optioned. He never revealed the location of the land and the plan evaporated when Rosenbloom swapped football teams with a man named Robert Irsay."

Rosenbloom had a laundry list of legit gripes about Baltimore, but John Steadman was aghast. "Why the man who owns the Baltimore Colts would want to take them away to another green pasture makes for one of the most baffling cases in the history of the National Football League, which admittedly has become spoiled with success," he wrote in mid-January 1972. "The owner is the only one who apparently wants the Colts out of Baltimore. And it's the opinion of this reporter that he'll have a change of heart, that the Colts will stay and go on winning games and making more money. If the Colts were to leave, it would seriously hurt the city and also professional football. Baltimore has done much to make the National Football League what it is today—proud, prosperous and prestigious." This was Steadman trying to talk himself into not worrying.

We know that Carroll Rosenbloom wasn't the shy, retiring type. In early '72, the *Morning Sun* asked him if he had bones to pick. "'Every time the city has said it would do something to improve the stadium, the Orioles have stopped it. We are paying the city $250,000 in rent and the Orioles are getting a half million for using the stadium. Are we tenants, too?' Mr. Rosenbloom also blames some of the media for the bad-guy label he and his organization have received and now feels he cannot get a fair shake in Baltimore."

While on the subject of labels, Steadman slapped another one on Rosenbloom on January 11, 1972:

> Over a month ago, Bert Bell Jr., who writes a weekly football column for this newspaper [the *News American*], outlined what he believed was almost a prearranged plan to get the Colts out of Baltimore. He cited that a bizarre feud with city officials, the Park Board specifically, the Baltimore Orioles and the press would lead up to the Colts' owner trying to say that he had been wronged. Bell contended it sounded almost like a plot, kind of a smokescreen, to get out of town and head for Tampa. Some of the points Bell made are unfolding. You couldn't say the Colts have tipped their hands. It's more like showing exactly what they have in mind. But the only force that's suggesting the Colts or their present ownership will possibly leave is, oddly enough, the present ownership. Bell's story and predictions are looking stronger all the time. Amazing in a lot of ways.

More like bats-in-the-belfry crazy. Steadman searched in the brambles and found a conspiracy. Bert Bell Jr. had a strange way of showing gratitude to the man who welcomed him and his brother Upton into the Colts family when no one else bothered. Rosenbloom didn't need stunts to justify a boogaloo out of town. The stadium, turncoat fans and the John Steadman Lecture Series were reasons enough.

Rosenbloom's Tampa dalliance was going national. Columnist Robert Markus of the *Chicago Tribune* described the basics in January 1972:

> The citizens of Baltimore may be forgiven a few un-Christian thoughts about the

state of Florida. Not content with stealing the Colts' head coach, Don Shula, two years ago, Florida now appears ready to shanghai the whole football club. It was no surprise when Owner Carroll Rosenbloom announced the Colts would train henceforth in Tampa and next year play all three of their "home" exhibition games in the Gulf Coast city. After all, there were more fans waiting to greet the Colts at the Tampa airport when the team arrived to train for the AFC championship game than there were at any of the three home exhibitions the Colts played last fall at Memorial Stadium. Now Rosenbloom has declared that after 1972 the Colts will no longer play ANY games in Memorial Stadium. This does not necessarily presage a permanent move to Tampa, but that has to be considered the most likely possibility.

Then Markus went rogue. He took on one of his own—Steadman. "It was about the same time [1970] that the Colts announced they were tacking three exhibition games onto their season ticket package. The screams of outrage were so loud that Rosenbloom backed down and made purchase of tickets for the exhibition games voluntary. The same evening paper [i.e., the *News American*] then urged fans to boycott these games, to prove what point, I couldn't say. Seldom has a newspaper campaign been so successful. It may have succeeded in driving the Colts right out of the state of Maryland, and I trust that the sports editor who led the valiant fight will enjoy covering the Washington Redskins beginning in 1973." Oof.

The piling on in Baltimore was a given. *Evening Sun* sports editor Bill Tanton fired his volley after Steadman:

It's been clear to me for a long time that Carroll Rosenbloom wants out of Baltimore. In November Governor Mandel came to Miami for the Colt-Dolphin game, even flew home with us on the Colt plane. "My purpose in being here," said the governor, "is to see what I can do to help keep the Colts in Baltimore." A little later I asked Rosenbloom if he was impressed with the governor's efforts to settle Carroll's difficulties with the city. "It's too late," Rosenbloom said with a shrug. "He should have done this six months ago." Clearly the Colt owner was unimpressed. No doubt about it, Rosenbloom has Baltimore blocked out. He wants to leave, and after the events of the last few weeks, it seems to me that he'd better leave. If he thought the people were going to panic and crawl on their hands and knees to him when he started romancing Tampa, he was wrong. That technique has backfired on him. The people here are completely sour on Rosenbloom now, and how could they feel otherwise. They are calling this office to register their disgust with Rosenbloom and to say that they are canceling their season tickets.

Tanton got in one final shot, calling Rosenbloom a "petulant child." Which reminds of Kramer scolding Jerry Seinfeld for refusing to thank a guy a fourth time for playoff hockey tickets to snag some tickets that night: "You stubborn, stupid, silly man!" Rosenbloom was too savvy to fall for name-calling.

Baltimore fans played follow the leader. A William F. Hug sent this diatribe in to the *Morning Sun* after Tanton scolded Rosenbloom: "SIR: All this talk by Carroll Rosenbloom of leaving Baltimore for greener playing fields is sickening. Let him go! Baltimore has many more pressing problems to care about: how to have a first-rate school system; how to get children home from school safely; how to save kids from the dead-end street of drug addiction; how to improve living conditions. Poor Mr. Rosenbloom. His athletes suffer the indignity of less than first-rate dressing room and practice field. His fans have to contend with congestion nine Sundays a year. Well, there are tens of thousands of Baltimoreans who contend with congestion 365 days a year, and tens of thousands of kids whose local practice field is a vacant lot covered with stones." But the Colts weren't the peewee-league Overlea Raiders. Maybe that last bridge had been burned, after all.

Many in Baltimore wanted Carroll Rosenbloom to scram, and he was looking to oblige. Up in New York, Poobah Pete Rozelle hadn't chimed in yet. Baltimore scribes queried him at the '72 Super Bowl in New Orleans. "Commissioner Pete Rozelle, of the National Football League, said yesterday at a Super Bowl press conference, 'I do not think the Colts will be moved,'" the *Morning Sun* reported. "He reiterated this comment several times during this question-and-answer session, adding or subtracting the words 'franchise area'... He pointed out that despite his feelings a franchise can be moved if 20 of 26 franchise owners vote for the switch. Squelching the move-to-Tampa rumor, Mr. Rozelle said, 'No, the league has not looked into Tampa [as a possible site for a franchise].'"

The folks in Tampa put the welcome wagon in park. Chief provocateur Tom McEwen of the *Tampa Tribune* conveyed Rozelle's prediction and tossed in a Steadman vignette:

NEW ORLEANS—Pro football commissioner Pete Rozelle said it loud and clear for 300 reporters to hear here yesterday: "I do not think the Baltimore Colts will move from their franchise area." He said it three times, in fact, under repeated questioning, largely from anxious Baltimore writers... Speculation, growing and growing, has been that if the arrangement [with Tampa] is a good one (full houses and good training and smiling faces), Rosenbloom will ask permission for the name change—to Tampa Colts, and the permanent shift. He would lease the stadium and enlarge it. Is he bluffing? went a question to Rozelle. "I don't know. I just do not feel they will move." Now the sharpest critic of the Colts from Baltimore, *Herald-American* [sic] sports editor John

Steadman, asked how pro football could allow such a shift after 51 straight regular season sellouts in Baltimore. Rozelle again said he believed one of the two alternatives would be resolved, meaning a new stadium out of Baltimore town, or vast improvement to the old place and a making-up between Rosenbloom and his detractors there.

Steady loved the Colts so much, McEwen revealed that Steadman had sent a telegram to all the other NFL owners, questioning the ethics of a Colts' move to Tampa, considering what that team and town had done for the league.

Ole bushy brows was sure a sly dog. In front of Rozelle at the press conference, Steadman went on offense—the Colts' record 51 straight home sellouts, packed houses for a decade. That was to push his case with Rozelle. The braggadocio over the years—51-straight, 51-straight. Then one day, while whaling on Rosenbloom, Steadman pulled a sudden U: "Although it was reported the Colts once sold 50,000 season tickets, this was a fabrication to try to make it appear the demand was better than it was," Steadman wrote in December 1979. "The string of a reported 51 straight sellout games was another fraudulent 'con' act. The highest actual [season-] ticket count ever reached here was 48,000. The rest was a lie. But when exhibition games were added to the package, after the team had gone into decline, resentment replaced enthusiasm." He doubled down in an essay he wrote for *The House*

of Magic: 70 Years of Thrills and Excitement on 33rd Street: "Frequent sellouts were reported [during the Colts' glory years] but nothing like the 51 straight the Colts tried to convey. Still, getting a ticket, at any time, was a difficult assignment." Steadman liked to butter it on both sides, depending on the occasion.

Ernie Accorsi fell in love with the Colts as a teenager, got jobs at the *Morning Sun* and the Philadelphia *Inquirer*, worked PR at Penn State, then landed the head PR job with the Colts in 1970. He doesn't doubt for a minute that the Colts sold out 51-straight. "As far as sellouts in the '60s," he proclaimed, "when I was at the *Sun*, I tried to buy tickets to Colts games. I couldn't buy 'em. So, if there weren't sellouts, they sure didn't have any tickets at the ticket office. When I worked in Philadelphia [at the *Inquirer*], I came back in the '60s and tried to get tickets. You *couldn't* get tickets. OK?"

• • •

The folks in Tampa figured it ain't over 'til Rosenbloom says so. Commissioner Rozelle didn't think a move was in the offing; getting 20 of 26 owners to vote yay for Tampa was a moonshot. But Tampa kept at it—the you-can't-fault-a-guy-for-trying maxim. In late January 1972, the *Tampa Tribune* proclaimed: "They're almost at the cutoff point on Colt Corral memberships. Only 18 left. The cutoff point is 390. Corral membership is achieved through purchase of a block of 50 season tickets for the three Baltimore Colts preseason games in Tampa Stadium—Washington Redskins, Aug. 5; Pittsburgh Steelers,

Aug. 26; and Detroit Lions, Sept. 4. The season ticket sale has passed 31,000. That goal is 45,000. Tampa promoters told the Colts the 45,000 would be pledged prior to the National Football League meetings in Honolulu in mid-March."

The flirting continued. The *New York Times* ran a story in late February 1972: The Colts would run a "one-day training camp for 25 rookies and a handful of seasoned players" down in Tampa, Johnny U included. This was on top of prepping for the AFC championship game in the same spot. Hmm. "In addition, there are those accusing Carroll Rosenbloom, the team's owner, of waving Tampa like a club at Baltimore city officials who have been so sluggish about improving the Colts' real home, the obsolete Memorial Stadium," the *Times* elaborated, that adjective *obsolete* just hanging there like a stalactite. "Although the evidence is thin, Rosenbloom has done little to dispel the accusation. The stadium outlook in Baltimore, however, has improved since a new mayor, William Donald Schaefer, came into office last month." Having Hizzoner in the game would definitely up Baltimore's odds.

Baltimoreans were slapping stickers saying "Don't Tampa with Our Colts" on their car bumpers, fidgety about the Rosenbloom-Tampa courtship. They weren't the only ones ripping Tampa for meddling. The *Tampa Tribune* printed a syndicated article by Arthur Daley of the *New York Times* which denounced folks there for poking around in someone else's backyard:

TAMPA—While Baltimore Colt football fans nervously wait to see if the other shoe would really drop, Tampa's pushy pigskin promoters unashamedly hope that it will. They even are ready to clutch it in tender embrace, cleats and all, in the event that the Maryland metropolis fails to keep a tight grip on its franchise ... Enter the McEwen Marauders [led by *Tampa Trib* sports editor Tom McEwen], a restless group of raiders out of Florida's Golden Triangle with Tampa, Clearwater and St. Pete at the three corners. It contains more than two million sports-hungry people and Tom McEwen, the hard-driving local sports editor, is trying to feed them a franchise in the American Basketball Association and, if he can swing it, a franchise in the National Football League. This would be the Colts.

Daley saw frazzled Baltimore reporters during the Super Bowl hypefest and tried to tone down the angst:

Remembered during the Super Bowl week were the harried looks on the faces of everyone with a Baltimore background. The Tampa pressure already had started to mount to a considerable degree and many a Baltimore correspondent ignored the preliminaries to the main war and concentrated his reporting on the guerrilla tactics from McEwen's Marauders on the Colt flanks. Neutral observers have to feel, however, that the brazen bid of the Tampa people will be blunted by crass practicality. Realism demands that Baltimore—and this also involves the state of Maryland—must arrive at some acceptable arrangement. Hey, whatever happened to Rosenbloom's angry threats to build his own stadium in a Baltimore suburb? No matter. Although it would be unthinkable for the Colts to leave Baltimore, a lot of unthinkable things have taken place in recent years in the greedy grab bag that sports have become.

John Steadman was likewise biting his nails, so he switched to default, i.e., creaming Carroll. "Rosenbloom, who frequently worked in devious ways, played to the speculation that Tampa might be trying to woo the Colts by saying the team would be leaving Western Maryland College, after 21 years, to train at the University of South Florida," Steadman theorized in *From Colts to Ravens*. "Tampa, simultaneously, agreed to host three exhibitions. This pleased both Rosenbloom and Baltimore, too, because Colts' fans didn't want to patronize games in the heat of summer when they would much prefer to be enjoying the breezes of Ocean City, Deep Creek Lake, or some getaway on the Chesapeake Bay." Once the Colts left, they could do all that and more.

Baltimore was jumpy, skittish, crabby, but not balled up in the fetal position. One Tampa transplant from Baltimore gave McEwen the what-for:

Firstly, I'm from Baltimore and I have lived in Tampa for a year. I've always been an ardent Colt fan, and some of the former greats are close personal friends. But it galls me to see a city like Tampa being duped into believing they can get the Colts. If you sportswriters and all those interested in sports would try to figure out how much Joe Doaks [the average fan] makes a week and can pay out to baseball, football, basketball, hockey and all other sports events, you would realize how far the average person can spend. I could go on and on and maybe get a big laugh from you, but somebody has to say something. Read John Steadman's columns and learn a little about sports journalism. You have a lot to learn.

Sgnd: Mike Martin, Tampa

Sports editor Bill Tanton of the *Evening Sun* was a little uptight like the rest but boxed Steadman's ears once the Colts-Rams swap talk got serious: "It looks very much, then, as if we are going to have new Colt ownership if and when the sale and tax ramifications of the swap are worked out. To a lot of Baltimore fans, this would be fine. Keep the Colts but get rid of Rosenbloom has, indeed, been a popular theme in recent years. Carroll is not well-liked or appreciated in his old hometown, which is unfortunate. Rosenbloom puts an outstanding team on the field every year. His players are the best paid in the National

Football League. His tickets are moderately priced. And no Baltimore fan has ever had to buy a ticket for an exhibition game. The new owner, whoever that might be, will find that a tough act to follow." Translated: Be careful what you wish for.

The chairman of the Tampa Sports Authority figured if all else fails, turn bootlicker. He wrote a beseeching letter to Rosenbloom late in March 1972:

Dear Carroll:

As always, we follow the progress of the Colts, the City of Baltimore, [MD] Governor Mandel and any other developments in the Maryland area. We learned with mixed emotions of a plan to build a $100-million to $190-million facility in Baltimore. We believe the Baltimore Colts deserve the finest facilities and hope that someday you will have it. However, very honestly, we were hoping the situation would be such that you would have no choice but to move to our spectacular and growing area. The Tampa Sports Authority officially requested that I extend to you and the Colts their offer to make Tampa your home in the years no facility may be available to you in Baltimore, with no commitment from you to make this your permanent home, and at the same financial arrangements for which we contracted for the three preseason games (this summer) … Again let me thank you

on behalf of the Sports Authority and the City of Tampa for your continued interest in our community.

J. Leonard Levy, Chairman,
Tampa Sports Authority

Tom McEwen of the *Tampa Trib* kept reprising his role as town smartass. He chuckled at the proposed dome in downtown Baltimore: "All this developed when last week a sort of Can-We-Build-A-Big-New-Multi-Purpose-Stadium committee of Maryland's energetic Gov. Mandell [sic] came back with the vague sort of 'Yes We Can For Something Between $100 million and $194 million.' With the 'between' they could build 19 Tampa Stadiums. But the Mandell Group, businessfolk mostly, said it would be 1975 before it could be finished. Nine'll get you 10 it'll be one or two more years longer since it's contemplated for a downtown slum section where a railroad must be put underground." Mr. Wiseguy couldn't spell the governor's name, mistook the Inner Harbor for the Warsaw Ghetto and later called Memorial Stadium "Municipal Stadium."

After Rosenbloom played his hand and traded even-up, Colts for Rams, McEwen wiped the egg off his face and stated the obvious. "What happened was that Carroll Rosenbloom got himself that offer he couldn't refuse, and when he did, Tampa's longshot at the Colts forever went to no-shot," he wrote in mid-July 1972. "Then came the great out— the chance to trade the Colts for the Los

Angeles Rams and get himself and his wife Georgia and his bright-lights general manager and wife, the Don Klostermans, back home to L.A. and all the glitter that is there. All the glitter plus the Warner Brothers Studio in which he has a bunch of money, and all the potential of the Rams. But most of all, Rosenbloom could get out of Baltimore and the press and some of the fans he thought ungrateful, away from the Baltimore Orioles and that stadium they control, and away from the gloom of that city and [to?] the sunshine of California." *And* since he loves stringing the article *and* in serpentine flourishes, *and* Tom McEwen could now stick his nose somewhere else *and* cover a ballgame now *and* again *and* donate 12 column inches to something else.

Leonard Levy, Rosenbloom's yes-man and chairman of the Tampa Sports Authority, also gave us nothing new. "It proves that Rosenbloom was honest with us when he said he wanted to get out of Baltimore," he told the *Tampa Tribune* in July 1972. "And I still feel that if Rosenbloom had the means of moving the Colts to Tampa without upsetting the apple cart, he would have done so. This was the only means he had of getting out of Baltimore." Levy was obviously unaware that Rosenbloom had been cooking up the Colts-Rams trade for about a year before Tampa became a flight of fancy. The Steal-the-Colts campaign went bust, but Tampa got the machinery humming again. Four years later—1976—they got the Buccaneers.

CHAPTER 8

EENIE, MEENIE, MINEY, MOE

John Steadman still had the jitters after Tampa. Everybody pivoted back to the mausoleum on 33rd. It mattered not that Rosenbloom told Baltimore we ain't interested. The gabfest continued. Steadman filibustered on the issue. Like this column in January 1972:

> Putting the operation of a new stadium under the jurisdiction of Maryland and not Baltimore City remains a distinct possibility as the mayor, governor and owner of the Baltimore Colts hopefully get ready to go into a course-of-action huddle. There's a $7 million appropriation waiting to be used for a face-lifting on the present Memorial Stadium, but nothing has been done because the tenants, the Colts and Orioles, and the landlord, the city of Baltimore, have been unable to agree on a positive approach … It's likely that some of the $7 million will be used for immediate improvements of Memorial Stadium with a State-owned facility coming later. Since the Orioles, Colts and the Park Board weren't able to decide on a priority plan, the governor and mayor should do what they think is in the best interests for all concerned, with the public paramount, and get on with the rehabilitation and/or rebuilding.

Three of the Big Four—Carroll Rosenbloom, Mayor Schaefer and Governor Mandel—huddled up in Annapolis in January 1972 to talk specifics. Maybe they were getting somewhere. They decided that if Mayor Schaefer spotted a decent site, they could throw up a new football-only stadium, maybe using private funds. If they could pull it off, the Colts would probably stay in Baltimore.

Rosenbloom wouldn't budge on one thing, though: "Mr. Rosenbloom made it clear that any new home for the Colts would not be shared with the Orioles," the *Morning Sun* emphasized. "'I think a multi-purpose stadium hurts both teams,' he stated. The friction between him and Jerold C. Hoffberger, owner of the Orioles, was not affected by the new spirit of optimism and cooperation kindled at the meeting. Asked if he would talk over plans with Mr. Hoffberger, he said, 'I don't see the necessity for a meeting.'"

And one more thing: "He [Rosenbloom] ruled out modernization of Memorial Stadium as not 'worthwhile,' and added: 'Eventually it would be outmoded. In just a number of years, as I said six or seven years ago, we have had new stadia built all around us ... Baltimore too should have a new, clean home. I think Baltimore, the sports fans of Baltimore, deserve the best. The money that could be spent on Memorial Stadium could be put to better use.'" And after the '72 season, Rosenbloom wouldn't play there if you tied a bow around it.

Steadman saw the Colts conundrum going one of two ways: 1) Rosenbloom gets the new ballpark and stays put; or 2) Things go south and Rosenbloom boogies. So, things being delicate, now's not the time to rough the guy up. Instead, Steady went with honey instead of vinegar:

> Because of the controversy, Rosenbloom is probably asking himself if he should leave Baltimore and turn the Colts back to the community. This has never been suggested. Rosenbloom *has been good for the Colts, and Baltimore, in turn, has reacted with outstanding support* [emphasis mine]. There's no reason the relationship can't continue without Rosenbloom

offering to sell or, worse yet, transfer the team to Tampa. Baltimore's Memorial Stadium isn't as bad as it has been described. It rates with the Orange Bowl in Miami and is better, in fact, than the Cotton Bowl in Dallas or the Sugar Bowl in New Orleans. After Sunday's Super Bowl, two Baltimore men, Herb Gough and Walter Novak, expressed shock that Memorial Stadium here has been put down in such a negative way ... They are right. Memorial Stadium might not be the last word in design, but it is far from the worst. In fact, it puts some of the others to shame.

You get no traction comparing Memorial to a dump like the Cotton Bowl. Besides, most people already thought the Gray Lady should be put in mothballs.

Steadman got to talking with a Baltimore insurance man, John Donahue, who heard a rumor that one of the schools across the street from Memorial Stadium—Eastern High (for girls) or City College (for boys)—would be phased out when new schools were built. A light bulb went on:

> There's an interesting and appealing idea advanced about a new stadium for Baltimore. The suggestion is shaped, presented and volunteered by John Donahue, prominent Baltimore insurance executive, former athlete, coach and official, who believes serious thought should be given to utilizing property at

either Eastern High School or City College, along with the present Memorial Stadium site. Donahue says that buildings at City and Eastern could be razed, streets altered and the combined properties united with the existing Stadium site, which would make the entire facility either doubled or tripled in size. He knows there would be problems, some opposition, which always occurs, but believes it would be the most progressive and realistic step Baltimore could take … Baltimore is going to have to make a Stadium decision. That's why Donahue's proposal has merit and why he has mentioned it.

What's more, they shut down Eastern in 1986 anyway and Johns Hopkins rehabbed it into offices. But Donahue's proposal went to Dante's first ring, Limbo, where all good ideas got discarded.

But the plan for a multiplex downtown was picking up speed. And for now, Rosenbloom was onboard. "[MD] Governor Mandel and Mayor Schaefer announced yesterday that a study is underway into the feasibility of building a privately-financed four-sport stadium complex in Baltimore," the *Morning Sun* reported the first week in February 1972. "Carroll Rosenbloom, owner of the Colts, met with the Governor and the Mayor yesterday and said afterward: 'If it can be done, the Colts are perfectly willing to do our part.' And Jerold C. Hoffberger, owner of the Orioles, said: 'I'm all in favor [of the study]. I took

a schematic drawing of a project over to the Governor the other day. If we need two stadiums [for the Colts and Orioles], that's OK with me. I think we ought to get together and look out for our city.'"

Carroll Rosenbloom and Jerry Hoffberger on the same page? "Human sacrifice! Dogs and cats, living together! Mass hysteria!" But with all the heavy hitters involved, maybe this one had half a chance. The Greater Baltimore Committee cut a check for $25,000 and hired a team of three architectural, planning and economic consulting companies for a preliminary "feasibility study" for a multisport stadium at the Camden railroad yards (the current site of Oriole Park at Camden Yards). Mandel and Schaefer calmed down some of the worry warts by stressing that private bucks would fund this colossus, not taxpayer dollars. By this time Rosenbloom was working out the kinks in the Colts-Rams swap, so who knows if his support here was playacting. Hoffberger was likewise keen on the plan. "Miami—Oriole owner Jerold C. Hoffberger yesterday endorsed broad longrange plans under study for a new downtown stadium complex in the Camden Yards back home," the *Morning Sun* indicated. "'A number of guys on this ballclub one day may be playing in a magnificent new stadium in Baltimore,' he told the Oriole players, manager Earl Weaver and his coaches during his annual spring-training chat with the ballclub. 'I am pleased with what Governor Mandel, Mayor Schaefer and the Greater Baltimore Committee is [sic] doing,' Hoffberger commented later. 'I feel reasonably certain that, with a lot of work and a little bit of luck, that magnificent new stadium can become a reality.'"

Although *Evening Sun* sports columnist Jack Chevalier admitted in early March 1972, "Personally, I love watching baseball at Memorial Stadium … The park is much prettier than some of the new saucers, like Washington's Robert F. Kennedy Stadium," he wandered over to reality:

Building a new stadium along the Beltway or Interstate 83 would be taking the easy way out. It would be turning our backs on Baltimore City. It would be a sociological copout. Downtown is the area that needs another transfusion. Now that the $200-million Charles Center is a beautiful reality and the $400-million Inner Harbor redevelopment project is on the way, a dual-purpose stadium in the Camden Station area seems the next logical step. "We must find a way to make our cities work," said William Boucher, chairman of the Greater Baltimore Committee, last night. "Population in metropolitan areas is growing all around the country. If we abandon our cities, we are abandoning the nation … Think of what it would mean to have 15,000 people on the streets of downtown Baltimore before and after 80 Oriole games," he mused. "Think of 60,000 Colt fans downtown 10 times a year." In this debate, it doesn't matter what sportswriters think. Oriole owner Jerry

Hoffberger and Colt boss Carroll Rosenbloom pay the rent and control the athletes, and they want a new playground. Surprisingly, they are working together. All we can do is hope they find a solution within the city limits.

His documentary about the Baltimore Colts, *The Ghosts of 33rd Street*, brought Troy Lowman some insight about Baltimore's Manhattan Project. "Memorial Stadium was pretty iconic, but it wasn't Wrigley Field or Fenway Park," he stated. "This is hard for me because when I grew up, *everything* was Memorial Stadium. So, I'm really partial to the place. But if you're looking at cold, hard facts, it was hard to get to—stuck in a residential area—which is OK, but the parking was difficult, and the sightlines weren't good. You could have renovated the stadium in a way that kept it there for a few decades. But ultimately, there was just a pull to go downtown. Eventually, that's what would have happened. It was all about keeping the franchise *in* the city. There were plans for new stadiums downtown in the early '70s that never came to fruition because they just got killed by local government. The funding just got cut."

Marvin Mandel picked up the pom-poms. "As representatives of Baltimore's four professional sports teams and Mayor Schaefer nodded in approval yesterday, Governor Mandel announced his expectation that a multi-purpose sports complex will be built and operating in downtown Baltimore by 1975," the

Morning Sun detailed in late March 1972. "He also disclosed that his administration will submit to the General Assembly as quickly as possible legislation to set up a quasi-public authority with powers to carry out the necessary planning and to float revenue bonds to finance the project, which will be constructed on a 27.5-acre site now occupied by Camden Station and its adjoining yards." Baltimore got good news from the consultants: "… such a complex could help revitalize the entire downtown area, and that the city would benefit not only by an increase in its tax base but by an influx of millions in 'outside money' that would be spent by sports fans."

Then came sticker shock. The estimate for this palace: from $107 million to $219 million. Mandel's eyelids fluttered at the cost. As for Rosenbloom, he said he was still hanging around. "The $25,000 report was rushed to completion after Carroll Rosenbloom, Colts' owner, said he would refuse to renew the Colts' lease with the city at Memorial Stadium when his lease expires at the end of 1972," the *Morning Sun* clarified. "He is dissatisfied with stadium conditions and has been feuding with Jerold C. Hoffberger, Orioles' owner, over each team's prerogatives. Mr. Rosenbloom said he is enthusiastic about the possibilities of constructing the sports complex, and indicated he would be willing to remain in Memorial Stadium on a year-by-year basis until the new facilities are completed."

There's this one nagging question only the Godfather could answer: If the downtown stadium project had gotten to the finish line, would Rosenbloom have nixed the big swap or was it a sure thing by March 1972? Not the wiser, Mandel, Schaefer, et al. kept forging ahead. The consultants came up with five different ways to build the sports complex: "For example," the *Morning Sun* described, "the consultants estimated that it would cost more than $194 million to construct separate, domed stadiums, an adjacent arena to house indoor sports and underground parking for 4,500 cars. A single, roofed stadium that would seat 70,000 for football and 55,000 for baseball and would include a 20,000-seat arena and 4,500 parking spaces could be built for less than $100 million."

Eyes rolled when those numbers came out. Consider: $100 million in 1972 (the lowball number) translates to $759,978,469 in fiscal 2025. The Disneyland plan of two domes, an indoor arena and parking ($194 mil) would cost you about a billion-five nowadays. Whereupon, a horde of grandstanders ran for cover.

How to fund this leviathan came next. "It is obvious that when Governor Mandel talks about handling the multi-million-dollar proposal without involving public money, he is banking on the railroad, the Colts and the Orioles to put up a major share of the cash," the *Morning Sun* stipulated. Wait until Jerold and C.R. get a load of this.

They needed some VIPs from the business/political world to supervise the project. Mandel dashed over to the Statehouse to push through a bill authorizing a five-member committee to finance and build the

Camden Yards complex. Maybe some suits could maneuver around the two owners jawing at each other. The *Morning Sun* noted in late March 1972, "The Colts' owner, Carroll Rosenbloom, and the Orioles' owner, Mr. Hoffberger, have had a simmering feud over their dual use of Memorial Stadium, a feud that has had the two men pointedly refuse to even be seen talking to each other in public."

The committee did a little homework. "Planners of Baltimore's project consulted with some of the architects who had designed the New Orleans Superdome, and from those conversations the original estimates emerged: At a cost of as low as $78 million, the Baltimore facility could accommodate 70,000 fans for football, 55,000 for baseball, and 20,000 as an arena," Jon Morgan detailed in *Glory for Sale*. "Two potential sites were eyed: the land under Memorial Stadium and an industrial area west of the city's Inner Harbor. The latter, a 27-acre site owned by the Chesapeake & Ohio railroad, was known for its most prominent feature. The Camden Station was the birthplace of the nation's railroad industry, a spot where the once-mighty Port of Baltimore fed cargo to rail cars for the steam-powered trip into the American heartland." Nobody was talking up leveling the mausoleum, so it was Camden or bust.

"Fell through" covers just about every proposal, project or longshot that got rolled out in the '70s and early '80s: hit a brick wall, got booed offstage or got shelved to collect dust. Bob Maisel of the *Morning Sun* summarized the futility in April 1972:

Carroll Rosenbloom had said a year ago that he would not play in Memorial Stadium after his lease expires at the end of 1972, unless it had been substantially improved, or unless a new stadium was in the works. He offered to help finance repairs, and when that *didn't materialize* [emphasis mine], he said he would build his own stadium outside the city. Governor Mandel talked him out of it and earmarked state funds for improvements on Memorial Stadium. That also *fell through* [emphasis mine] and Rosenbloom again talked of building his own. At the same time Tampa came into the picture. That's when the Governor took the bull by the horns and pushed the complex at Camden Yards. Had this *fallen through* [emphasis mine], Rosenbloom probably wouldn't have had time to build his own stadium and where would that have left the Colts?

Some local vote-chasers manned the torpedoes. One from Baltimore City seemed bent on destruction: "I hope this bill will not be taking advantage of the free tax status [of the Camden Yards site] so that the taxpayers will have to pay [to subsidize a proposed hotel and shopping center through a tax break]," state Senator Harry J. McGuirk told the *Morning Sun*. Another senator from Baltimore County didn't mince words: "Other city senators questioned the bill, and Senator Jervis S. Finney (R., 4th Baltimore County), Republican co-minority leader, called the sports complex 'the greatest boondoggle we've seen in our political lives. It's an insult to the Senate to suggest that a facility like this will be financed out of revenue bonds. It can't be done. It's ridiculous.'" The nattering nabobs of negativism were just getting started.

By June 1972, Carroll Rosenbloom had fine-tuned the terms for the Colts-Rams swap with Robert Irsay. Legal eagles translated it to lawyerese in the contracts. Rosenbloom played it cute with reporters who asked him about it. This alarm bell got rung in the *Morning Sun* in June 1972: "Asked about a rumored $18-million sale [of the Colts] to Robert Irsay, president of a heating and air conditioning company bearing his name … Rosenbloom said, 'To answer your question pure and simple, the Colts have not been sold. That doesn't mean they won't be sold. Yes, I have talked with Mr. Irsay (of Skokie, Ill., a Chicago suburb) but only as a member of a group (seeking the franchise). Many people are talking of buying or selling franchises at this time. I think the Los Angeles Ram situation has caused the interest.'" Left out was the fait accompli—the Colts-Rams deal was about to go down.

By late June 1972 the jig was up. The whole town knew what Rosenbloom was up to, but that didn't sidetrack the stadium project. "Plans for the proposed new stadium somewhere in Baltimore will proceed as scheduled despite Carroll Rosenbloom's seemingly imminent departure for Los Angeles as the new owner of the Rams," the *Morning Sun* indicated. "'So long as the Colts remain

in Baltimore, I don't think it will affect our plans,' said H. Grant Hathaway, one of the five members of the Maryland Sports Authority. 'We would want to talk to the new owners, but the first thing we want to do now is talk to Rosenbloom.'"

The *Chicago Tribune* prematurely pushed out half a load of nonsense by Cooper Rollow. "EUGENE, Ore., June 29 [1972]—The Los Angeles Rams have been sold to Robert Irsay of Skokie, Ill., the *Tribune* learned today. The National Football League has scheduled an official announcement of the transaction for next Thursday. Irsay, head of a heating and air conditioning firm in the Chicago suburb, huddled with Commissioner Pete Rozelle of the NFL in New York yesterday, at which time the deal was closed. An informed source told the *Tribune* that the original plan—which called for Irsay to buy the Rams, then trade franchises with owner Carroll Rosenbloom of the Baltimore Colts—*had been abandoned* [emphasis mine]. 'Too many owners were against it,' the source said. 'Switching the Baltimore and Los Angeles franchises could have opened up a whole herd of complications for pro football, both from the tax standpoint and from other government agencies.'"

Rollow's source was near the bull's eye, so Cooper gets a pass. Irsay also fed him a line. "It soon became apparent that the *Tribune* story was anything but a 'smoke screen' and Irsay admitted earlier this week that the original intent had been to pull out of the unprecedented 'franchise trade' described in last Saturday's *Tribune*," Rollow wrote. "As difficulties arose with that maneuver, most of them stemming from the incredibly complicated tax situation, he indicated he would settle for the Rams. 'We are interested in the Rams,' Irsay had replied when asked about the status of negotiations. 'We are not even thinking about the Colts now.'" And he said it with a straight face.

NFL.com posted an article in 2022 by Judy Battista titled "The Colts' and Rams' Really Big Deal." The swap business started with Dan Reeves. "The roots of the pact were actually planted a few years earlier, in 1968, when Dan Reeves, who was the owner of the Rams at the time, suggested to Rosenbloom, who was then the owner of the Colts, that Rosenbloom take over the Rams, as *Sports Illustrated* reported in 1972. Reeves and Rosenbloom were old friends, and they spoke on the field before their teams played a game late in that 1968 season [December 15 in L.A.]. Reeves was already ill with the cancer that would take his life three years later, and he told Rosenbloom that day that he did not think his family would keep the team after he died."

Tom Marr IV, son of former Baltimore radio legend Tom Marr and a Colts aficionado, thinks Rosenbloom was a perfect fit for L.A.:

It's something that I've thought about for a long time, especially after the move [in 1984]. It's an Occam's Razor kind of thing [i.e., the simplest explanation is usually the best]. As powerful as Pete Rozelle was at that time, and the fact that they had just stabilized that league

[after the AFL-NFL merger], that he was the one that committed the Colts to go to the AFC, he *had* to have known that Carroll Rosenbloom was unhappy in Baltimore. It wasn't the NFL it is today, but it still had the bones; it still had its lawyers, its vision and its plan. Robert Irsay would never have fit in in Southern California. I've always thought that the NFL brokered this deal. Look at how Cleveland got its team back [1999]. Al Lerner is considered a hero in Cleveland for bringing the Browns back. But Al Lerner was the guy that actually brokered the deal that moved the Browns to Baltimore. He's the lawyer that did all of that. Now, all of a sudden, he owns the expansion team that goes to Cleveland. So, yeah, I think the NFL was knee-deep in this weird and unprecedented trade to get Robert Irsay as the owner of the Baltimore Colts.

Reeves gave Rosey a slick out. Swinging the rest was right up Rosenbloom's alley. "Mr. [Dan] Reeves had cancer; he was the owner of the Rams," the late Colts owner Jim Irsay stated in episode 1 of the podcast, "The Move." "He told Carroll Rosenbloom, he said, 'Carroll, I know you want to get to L.A. I just wanna let you know that I have cancer, and I don't have much time.' So, Carroll took that in and was a pretty good mover and shaker, and so basically kinda cultivated a deal, you know, talking it over with [Pete] Rozelle and his other owner friends."

Tampa was roadblocked, and Rosenbloom was finished with Baltimore. Reeves put a wild plan in his lap. JJ Stankevitz, who produced the four-episode podcast, "The Move," explains:

As I researched it, Carroll Rosenbloom wanted to get out of Baltimore. This was pretty well-established in archival newspapers and news coverage at the time. He wanted out of Memorial Stadium, and I think he would have stayed in Baltimore, but it didn't seem like the city of Baltimore and Maryland were willing to work with him: "Hey, we'll give you a new stadium; we'll work with you on these things." That's why you saw him kind of turn his eye to, "How can I get out of Baltimore?" So, as a native son, he had a lot of love for Baltimore, but as I understood it, he didn't even live in Baltimore towards the end of his tenure there. I think he saw what a lot of other people saw, which was that Memorial Stadium was not going to be a viable venue for an NFL franchise to succeed in and to make revenue out of. So, he began to poke around and try to find his way out, and ultimately found it with the Rams and [owner] Dan Reeves. The thing that I found so fascinating is that, when I went into it, I presumed that Robert Irsay took over, then he immediately started trying to move the team, but it [the stadium conflict] predated Irsay.

Rosenbloom could now boil it down. "By then, early 1971, a romance that should still have been blooming was fast fading," William Gildea explains in *When the Colts Belonged to Baltimore*. "Rosenbloom fell out with fans, who balked at buying exhibition-game tickets with their season [ticket] books, with city officials, who wouldn't make the old stadium right for him, with John Steadman of the *News-Post* [*American*], who criticized an owner he saw as increasingly greedy and threatening the pleasures and rights of the fans. Rosenbloom devised an ingenious plan."

Son Steve was now president of the Colts while Rosenbloom was concocting the Colts-Rams deal. He saw firsthand how it played out: "The Steadman thing [the feud between C.R. and Steadman]—if you're on the receiving end by yourself, and you can't turn to your partner or friends for help because it doesn't affect them—that was tough enough. My father asked me, 'What else can I do? What do they want? Everybody is getting upset, and all I've done here is win. No. I'm not putting up with that. I don't have that much time left. We may be leaving.' I don't think in his heart he really wanted to leave Baltimore. I mean, he had a whole history there. And I didn't want to leave Baltimore. But L.A. had a nice shine on it, so, 'What do I do? Sit here and get shot at every day, or do I pursue another avenue, another team, or start over in Tampa?'" Nuts to Baltimore and Tampa; L.A. glittered 2,600 miles away. Simple elimination.

The excuse to leave came on a platter. Former Baltimore Colts scout, personnel director,

Patriots GM and NFL inside man Upton Bell thinks Rosenbloom had valid gripes:

You had a witch's brew—the Steadman thing, Baltimore and the governor not coming through and be willing to build a stadium. If they all had come to him, he would have had no excuse to leave. He would then have a really bad reputation: "This guy took off on us like any other carpetbagger. He came here and took advantage of us, won the world championships, and the minute something happens, he runs out." But they all played a role in it. The city wasn't gonna do anything for him; the state wasn't gonna do anything for him. Unlike today, I don't think he was asking for a lot. Now, owners are so rich, they build their *own* stadiums. But we're talking about 50 years removed from what it was [during Rosenbloom's era]. Basically, Baltimore gave Rosenbloom every reason to say, "I'm leaving." If it had been done differently, he [Rosenbloom] would've really been the bad guy if he had said, "I still wanna go to L.A."

It was tough sledding for the Godfather. "Carroll Rosenbloom knew that he was playing in a baseball stadium, that he wasn't drawing enough revenue, and that it wasn't gonna change," Jim Irsay explained in episode 1 of "The Move" podcast. "And the city wasn't gonna help—or the state. So, he kinda got out of there, thinking, *Wow. Somehow, I got*

someone to take this problem. Which was the stadium problem because [Dolphins owner] Joe Robbie was *years* away from coming up with the concept of club seats and seat licenses for the Dolphins."

Things got a little bumpy when Irsay's two partners bailed. Judy Battista explains in nfl.com's "The Colts' and Rams' Really Big Deal":

The deal hit a snag: [Willard "Bud"] Keland and [Clem] Ryan were short of money. [Joe] Thomas, then, came up with Irsay—who having first worked for his father's heating and air conditioning business, had begun his own company based in Skokie, Illinois—to make up the difference. Irsay didn't know Rosenbloom, and he didn't know Thomas, Ryan or Keland well, either. They met in a coffee shop in a New York hotel. The others asked Irsay if he had $5 million to clinch the deal. When, ultimately, Keland and Ryan dropped out, Irsay was left with the entire $19-million tab. It was the largest amount ever paid for any professional sports team, topping the $16 million Leonard Tose had paid for the Philadelphia Eagles in 1969.

The $15-million that Irsay took out to buy the Rams was a sack of potatoes he had to hump around for 12 years in Baltimore.

The *Morning Sun* posted the big story on July 14, 1972, and got new Colts owner Bob Irsay on the record: "A 20-year sport dynasty ended yesterday as Robert Irsay, of Skokie, Ill., took over the Baltimore Colts. Irsay and his partner, Willard Keland [who later dropped out], succeed Carroll Rosenbloom, who was in Los Angeles yesterday to assume control of the Rams. Irsay, president of the country's largest heating and air-conditioning contracting firm, cleared up a number of questions concerning the Colts: 'I bought the Colts to play in Baltimore,' he said. 'I have no thought of taking them elsewhere. We have a great team in a great sports town where they have sellouts. Why move?'" It wasn't rhetorical 12 years later.

Finances aside, the swap was straight-up—yours for mine. "It was like a real-estate deal," Steve Rosenbloom explained. "That's all it was. Somebody's got a house over here, and he doesn't want to sell it and have to pay taxes. So, he calls up a friend of his: 'I hear you're looking for a house. Let's swap houses. I'm gonna give you mine; you're gonna give me yours.' Then, it's a simple transaction with no taxes involved. That's the way I saw it. This [the team swap] was the same thing. I didn't look it up, but I remembered that you could do that. So—what's the difference? I'm trading you my asset for your asset. There weren't any rules or regulations *against* it. It was that simple—a real-estate exchange."

More particulars from the *New York Times*: "The ownerships of the Baltimore and Los Angeles franchises of the National Football League were traded yesterday in a deal that had no precedent in major professional team sports. The players and coaches were not affected and their affiliations will remain the same, but the exchange permitted Carroll Rosenbloom, the longtime owner of the Colts, to leave Baltimore and also to save $4.4 million in capital gains taxes." His lawyer probably cooked that up. Even-steven so we keep the IRS out of it.

Steadman spewed fire, brimstone and the usual pablum on July 13, 1972:

Officials of the state and city governments are interested in establishing a close working relationship with the men controlling the destinies of the Colts, the same as they attempted to assist the administration of Carroll Rosenbloom, who was put in the football business by the loyalty and generosity of the fans who raised over $300,000 with the sale of season tickets before a team ever came here. This was the only time in the history of professional sports that Mr. and Mrs. John Q. Public ever bankrolled a franchise. Rosenbloom should be eternally grateful to the great fans of the area for bringing him fame and millions of dollars in profit these last 19 years … One Colts official told ex-player Alex Hawkins, "We're at war with our fans" and he still hasn't recovered from the shock. The alienation of the public, the most loyal football following in the world, was regrettable. It was caused by greed and ego. Baltimore has been a tremendous force in putting pro football where it is today, and the fans of the city and state deserved respect and gratitude.

Steadman failed to inform Mr. and Mrs. John Q. Public: 1) that Rosenbloom had millions in the bank when Bert Bell Sr. shanghaied him into buying the team; 2) that Steadman's shock-and-awe on Rosenbloom helped start that "war with the fans"; and 3) that the Colts were a business, not the Salvation Army. C.R. didn't move the team; he traded himself to the Rams.

Also lost in *The Colts' Move for Dummies* was the huge gamble that Robert Irsay took to buy the club. His son, Jim Irsay, mentioned it in "The Move," episode 1. "He [his father] called my mom, and she had to cosign. At least in his purchase for the Rams, he started off by making $4.5 million because he got that *with* the Colts [the difference in the two teams' values]. So, now, you're into $14.5 million for the Baltimore Colts. So, he was a riverboat gambler. Him and I had been a great father-and-son team. He just— if you go to Wharton's business school or Harvard business school, or whatever, the first thing they're gonna talk about is 'diversity.' And, so, you don't usually put all your eggs in one basket. But he did, and off we went. But, again, $5 million—everything he had—he owed basically $10 million. So, he owed double what he paid for it. You can't do that now."

Irsay wanted NFL club membership, and he was willing to put wife Harriet up for collateral to get it. Indianapolis Colts writer and producer of "The Move" podcast JJ Stankevitz recognized that big gamble:

He [Irsay] was desperate to own *any* professional sports franchise. Jim Irsay told me they were looking into buying the Montreal Expos in the 1960s. When an opportunity came along to get a piece of the Rams, then trade them for the Colts, he was brought on to be an investor, along with two other businessmen. And when those guys pulled out, he said, "All right, I'll do whatever it takes to take advantage of this opportunity." He basically signed every last dollar away to get the team, every single dollar of his family's money. And the NFL did not have limits then on how much debt you could take on to purchase a team, which allowed him to purchase the Rams. He was essentially starting out $14.5 million in debt. And I was told by a couple of people that Carroll Rosenbloom told him, "Yeah, you'll probably get a new stadium." So, if he bought the team in debt, thinking that he would get a new stadium—a stadium with skyboxes where you could generate money—he could begin making money again. And that gets ripped away from you in two years? I can't imagine that was a very stable environment for someone.

Nobody ever closed the case on Rosenbloom's alleged new-stadium promise. But

Bob Irsay was hip-deep in debt when he got the Colts.

Who knows when Rosenbloom hit the breaking point and decided to bail. "My father had half a dozen reasons that he could point to for leaving," Steve Rosenbloom admitted. "How could you be treated so badly by the city, then you get lied to, and these weasels back out? And you're going around, you're trying to work things out and all that stuff. It was a whirlwind. And I guess it's like a marriage: If this shit is going on with your marriage, and then it gets to the point that you bring it up, and they say they're sorry—maybe it's too late."

Steadman never solicited comment from Colts players about Rosenbloom other than the rare backbiter. Why? They loved the guy. Headline, *Evening Sun*, July 11, 1972: **Matte Backs Owner**. Matte was a workhorse for 11 years and hated BS. He was asked by Larry Harris for his thoughts about Rosenbloom:

"That man deserves better than what he's getting from this town. I don't have one thing against the new owners at all, and I'm sure they're very capable men, but you don't find men like Carroll Rosenbloom very often. People in Baltimore don't know what it's like to have a loser. When was the last time the Colts had a losing team? I think it was 1956, wasn't it? [Correct] Fans don't realize what an integral part of a successful football team that management plays. We've always gone first-class on the Colts, and we've also had a team which had the potential to win a championship. I think it's a pretty general consensus around the league that Carroll Rosenbloom is the top owner in football. It's only been in the last couple of years that the people in Baltimore have turned on Rosenbloom. Before that, they loved him, and the shift in attitude has hurt him personally very much. Our team will be lacking when he goes. You could always talk with him if you had a grievance. He's always taken time out for his people's personal problems. I don't think I'm exaggerating when I say he's been an inspiration to many of us."

Steadman was unavailable for comment.

The Swap has inspired some intriguing what-ifs. Ben Lamers addressed a few on stampedeblue.com: "What If Carroll Rosenbloom Had Kept the Colts?" "The short-term answer is likely that the cleaning house under Irsay and General Manager Joe Thomas [the Great Purge] doesn't happen. Rosenbloom finished his career as owner with a .660-win percentage, so it's likely that the Colts would continue to succeed in the AFC. But let's step away from the field and focus on *where* the Colts would be playing had Rosenbloom kept the team. Yes, it appears that Rosenbloom was dissatisfied with the city, but all historical information indicates that Rosenbloom loved the Colts in Baltimore. Because of this, I would find it extremely unlikely that he would pick up and move the Colts." Mere spitballing, but handing over the Colts to son Steve one day *was* the plan, making an exodus hard to imagine.

Steadman outdid himself for sheer melodrama as Rosenbloom headed west:

> Bert Bell Jr., son of the commissioner of the National Football League before P.R., which stands for Pete Rozelle and Public Relations, said Rosenbloom had a ploy to leave Baltimore. Bell, who once worked for Rosenbloom before resigning for reasons of personal integrity, said the ex-Colt owner wanted to make it appear Baltimore was against him when, in fact, it was the other way around. Bell believed Rosenbloom's feuding with the press, public and politicians was part of a master scheme to cut and run ... It's a city that's been violated before although the British weren't to make it in 1814, and one of the natives, Francis Scott Key, became the first country singer, even more celebrated than Hank Williams, when he wrote a ballad about the dawn's early light and the flag still flying.

Bert Bell Jr., Francis Scott Key, Hank Williams? The scribe doth protest too much, methinks.

Steve Rosenbloom worked with both Bells, Upton and Bert Jr., so Bert has him flummoxed. "He, sort of out of the blue, went over to the Steadman camp," he lamented. "And nobody could understand that. Now, I love Bert and Upton. Upton wasn't like that. I never figured out what it was. I saw Bert after that in Atlantic City, and he was always a nice and generous person. Some background here: When Bert Bell [Sr.] died, my father brought both Uppy and Bert into the Colts organization. He didn't need a thank-you; he was glad to do it. And everyone got along in that organization. I don't know what stirred up Bert; I never knew. And when I saw him, I didn't ask him. That was history. So, I wondered, *How can Bert swallow this crap that Steadman is doing?* I don't know if Steadman talked him into feeling somewhat rejected or something. I have no idea."

Players offered quick rebuttals. "I played for him for 11 years, and I wouldn't want to play for anybody else," Hall of Famer Jim Parker told the *Evening Sun*. "He's always been a fair man. I've never met a man who worked for Carroll Rosenbloom who didn't like him." Parker never traded notes with John Steadman, who made his two years doing PR for the Colts seem like ratfucking for Dick Nixon.

Opinions vary on whether Rosenbloom would have stayed put had Baltimore delivered a new stadium. Steadman would still be dogging him and fans would be on his case. Plus, the preseason-ticket fiasco—although he nixed the idea—was like a festering sore. Former Colts president Steve Rosenbloom isn't sure how his dad would've played it:

> A new stadium would have been a monumental thing if they were actually gonna do that. Except you had the thing with Steadman and the fans believing

all of that crap, going along with that and forgetting all the years, starting in '53, with my father bringing the Colts back. That's the only reason they had the team; the commissioner [Bert Bell Sr.] was pushing my father because he knew he was from Baltimore. Castles don't get built in a day; that takes years of work. And he [his father] was ready to pull up stakes. He was tired of all the crap. The question [whether Rosenbloom would have stayed with a new stadium] is easy to answer but hard to find a conclusion. After all this pain in knowing your fans hated you now for some reason, and they've forgotten about history and what he sacrificed to bring the team to Baltimore—he could have lost his shirt on that. But he loved Baltimore. I can tell you, if they were actually willing to build a new stadium, I think he would have waited to see what the reality was. And if somebody then got Steadman to shut up—because that drained my father. You spend all those years building something, building a winner, and he gave the fans that. Then he gets the "Don't let the door hit you on the way out." He was deeply hurt by that. I would be; anyone would be if you did all that and brought a winner to Baltimore. That was the unanswered thing: how the fans feel, and are they gonna be booing Carroll all the time. If it was my team, I would have said, "Screw you," on the way out. That would be that.

A few writers took a stab at speculation. In August 1984, Barry Rascovar of the *Morning Sun* scolded Baltimore City for blowing it: "How differently things might have turned out had the city offered an attractive lease to the late Colts owner, Carroll Rosenbloom. For $7 million, the Colts would have had a modernized stadium. All of Robert Irsay's complaints would have been taken care of in 1972. We might have had a contented new owner who would still be here today."

Rosenbloom loved tinsel, bright lights and blonds, so maybe the West Coast was too glamorous for him to pass up. "The [Colts-Rams] trade was a good fit for Rosenbloom," Judy Battista wrote in "The Colts' and Rams' Really Big Deal." "When he owned the Colts, Rosenbloom would leave his home in either New York or Miami to go to Baltimore on a Friday and watch practice. He would usually return to his New York home after the game on Sunday. In Los Angeles, Rosenbloom had the beach, the city and the team all in one place. His life was mostly easier, although leaving behind the players and staff, some of whom Rosenbloom had hoped to bring to Los Angeles with him, was difficult."

Upton Bell lived and breathed the NFL, and he can't fault Rosenbloom for checking out. "I definitely think if the Kennedys were still in the [Baltimore-D.C.] area, if he could still do his deals in L.A., even if he wanted to go, the powers-that-be in Baltimore gave him an excuse [to leave]," Upton explained. "I can remember those early [season] games when we had to play on a baseball field with dust flying up. I said, 'This is bullshit. The Colts are the big draw in town.' The Orioles finally won a World Series [in 1966], but way before that, we'd practice at Memorial Stadium; it's not like today when you have your own practice field. We practiced on the dirt infield during the week, then we played games there on Sunday. I know that pissed off Rosenbloom a lot, way before the city wouldn't get involved."

Steadman didn't bother, but Bill Tanton of the *Evening Sun* gave Steve Rosenbloom a forum in August 1972:

"What do people expect?" Steve asked. "All my father did was run the most successful team in football for all those years. When he became the owner in 1953 people thought he'd lose money. He put a million and a half in a bank in New York—and he expected to lose it. When Dad took over the Colts, he was introduced at a banquet by [announcer] Bailey Goss. Bailey said, 'It's a good thing this man is in the shirt business because he's going to lose his.' He promised the fans a championship in five years, and he gave them two championships, in 1958 and 1959. But for all the team's success, there was criticism in the press, and the politicians were negative. Now the new owner is going to have to start playing exhibitions here. He'll have to do the same things we were accused of trying to put over on the public. It just has to be. That's pro football today."

Ernie Accorsi is the rare bird who worked for both Carroll Rosenbloom and Bob Irsay. He's not sure C.R. was a lock to move: "I know this—I don't think he [Rosenbloom] wanted to leave. His first year in L.A. was '72. We played the Raiders in the first exhibition game in '72. And he came up [from L.A.] and visited on the field, pregame, and shook hands with a lot of the players. And [Rams GM Don] Klosterman, who had originally hired me, came up into the press area, and Rosenbloom sat up there too. He [Klosterman] said that Carroll had tears in his eyes when he was out on the field. He said something about 'those horseshoes. I'll never forget those horseshoes.' So, I don't think he really wanted to leave. I think if they had made it easier for him to stay, he would have."

Rosey did stop by in Oakland. The *New York Times* ran a feature on the new Rams owner on 8/20/1972 and had him scolding Baltimore fans. "'He seems to be a guy who cares,' one Ram player observed this week as Rosenbloom popped up again at a morning workout. The night before, Rosey, the inveterate jock, had flown to Oakland to watch his first love, the Colts, lose to the Raiders. At the Colts' hotel, Rosenbloom was greeted with a shout from Tom Matte. 'Hey, boss, did you buy us back?' There was considerable applause ... In Baltimore, when fans became sated with Colt success (six division, four league titles and one Super Bowl victory), Rosenbloom decided to get out. 'It was like giving up family,' he said, 'but to many people there the Colts had become like the old Yankees in New York—taken for granted.'"

Ernie Accorsi was there for Rosenbloom's Oakland impromptu:

> The opening preseason game of the '72 season, we played Oakland. I was standing on the field. Carroll came up for that game with Steve [Rosenbloom] and [Don] Klosterman. He was standing on the field, and you could see he was glassy-eyed from the nostalgia. And I told Klosterman, "He doesn't look like Carroll. He's not saying much." He said, "When he walked out for the first day of [Rams] training camp [in 1972], he stopped, and he grabbed my arm and said, 'I'm not sure I can go much farther. There are no horseshoes on those helmets.'" I think it meant more to him than he would probably ever have admitted because he was a businessman, and that deal was probably too good to turn down, considering all the misfortune and battles he had about the [Memorial Stadium] lease. But he was a good person at heart.

Upton Bell thinks Baltimore played its hand like a mark. "Well, I think it's very simple, but in other ways complex. The simple thing was if you called Carroll Rosenbloom's bluff [about moving], and you said, 'OK, give us some time here. We're gonna do a public referendum. We're gonna figure out a way to come up with the money. Would you entertain the idea of a public/private partnership to get you your new stadium?' If you did that, you could have called his bluff. And they never called his bluff. There's no question, politically, that they weren't willing to go that far, and as a result, they lost their team. I could never tell you if it was for sure that Carroll would've stayed. I think he would have, but we'll never know that."

The man who covered Bob Irsay's Colts for the *Morning Sun* was Vito Stellino. In 1992, he observed the 20th anniversary of the Big Swap and how both Baltimore and L.A. got burned:

> It's difficult to judge which move had more impact on the NFL—Rosenbloom's move to Los Angeles or Irsay's arrival in Baltimore. What Irsay did in Baltimore is well-documented. In the four years before he bought the team, the Colts went to two Super Bowls and the AFC title game. They also had become a part of the fabric of the city of Baltimore, as Barry Levinson captured in his movie, *Diner*, after they won back-to-back titles in 1958 and 1959 and helped fuel the pro football boom. It took Irsay just 12 years to destroy all that and move the team to Indianapolis. Not that the team has changed much since the move. The Colts are still looking for their first playoff victory in the 20 years he has owned the club. Meanwhile, Rosenbloom's arrival in Los Angeles also had dire consequences for the

league. He made a deal to leave the Los Angeles Coliseum for Anaheim, Calif., before he drowned at his Florida winter home in 1979.

Not everybody in Baltimore wanted Rosenbloom dropped down the Shot Tower. B.J. Small, the Colts ticket manager for a decade, sent this in to the *Morning Sun* in 1996, when Maryland forked over $220 million to build M&T Bank Stadium: "Carroll Rosenbloom asked for Memorial Stadium improvements that would have cost 'peanuts' compared with the cost of the baseball stadium and the planned football stadium. Time will surely prove the waste of so much money and point up the clear foresight of Mr. Rosenbloom. And why he left Baltimore to be saddled with Robert Irsay, who ran a good thing into the ground."

Most Baltimoreans have been force-fed fed the company line: Rosenbloom was a fat-cat Hollywood wannabe who sold out his hometown and handed his team over to a bipolar drunk. It's had a long shelf life. Upton Bell's take is more nuanced:

I think Carroll probably would have stayed [in Baltimore] under better circumstances. But I also think that he had movie interests in L.A. and enjoyed it out there, and he wanted the glamor of the West Coast too. I think that was part of it. Again, you have to get back to this: He was a complex man of many different feelings, moods and moves. If Baltimore hadn't given him an excuse, he probably would've stayed, but Baltimore gave him an excuse to say, "I've had enough of this place. I hate Steadman. The city is fucking me," all of these other things, "so I'm going to the West Coast." If he had gotten the new stadium, Steadman had died or gone away, he would have had a difficult time leaving, saying, "See you later, Baltimore. I'm going out to Disneyland." But it [Baltimore's conduct] made it easy. It gave him an excuse to go. And he loved it out there [in L.A.], let's face it.

Mulling this over the years, Steve Rosenbloom thinks his dad would have said no thanks. "They [Baltimore officials] could have signed all the papers they wanted. What's that worth at the end of the day if they change their minds? But if they were willing to start right away, draw up plans and work with people in the [Colts] organization, and we gave them a little time to put things together, selling bonds, showing that they were serious, he still might have been finished with Baltimore. The way he was treated by everybody, it hit him deep inside because he considered the fans part of the Colts family. Those were the fans he loved, and it [the criticism] was like having one of your kids disavow you. So, it was very personal to him because the Colts were *about* the fans. They had a giant role to play. When they told him, 'You're just no good anymore,' that goes to the bone. He wasn't as pissed off as he was pissed *on*."

Bob Maisel of the *Morning Sun* saw the swap as a win-win but took a swipe at John Steadman:

So, the long-awaited change in ownership of the Colts and Rams is finally fact, with Carroll Rosenbloom leaving Baltimore to take over in Los Angeles, newcomer Robert Irsay assuming the reins in Baltimore as principal owner. First indications are that it will be a beneficial change for everybody concerned. Not that there is any inclination here to find excessive fault with the Rosenbloom era in Baltimore. Some seem to hold opinion that he committed some grievous crime in making a profit out of the Colts. I've never considered a poverty oath one of the prerequisites to successful ownership. So long as they run a sound organization, surround themselves with capable people, don't try to force things on you that aren't common practice everywhere else [e.g., mandatory preseason tickets], and win, they won't get much of an argument from me. All these things Rosenbloom did, and his era in Colt history will not be an easy act to follow.

A couple of blocks away downtown was Steadman and his Underwood. Ten days after the swap he took out his steno pad as Bubba Smith badmouthed the ex-boss. Bubba charged Rosenbloom with welshing on a promise:

What had Bubba Smith concerned is that the story of his [contract] holdout with the Baltimore Colts has been distorted. It's not money … it's something else. The basis for the dispute is a promise made to him that was not fulfilled. He was assured, he says, by the previous management that business opportunities outside of football would be made available. Nothing happened. And now he wants the new organization to stand behind the things that were told him three and a half years ago and repeated frequently since then … Smith's case is different. It would be a legal question for a court to decide if the new Colts' owner, Bob Irsay, would be compelled to back up the promise Smith says was given to him by the former owner, Carroll Rosenbloom. "Mr. Rosenbloom gave me his word," insisted Smith. "I know what was said to me. He said I would be in business, and he told my mother and me that. It's been like a merry-go-round. I had faith in Mr. Rosenbloom. I think he's a good person. When I went to see Mr. Rosenbloom last year, he said I would be in business when the season was over."

Steadman never devoted one drop of ink to the army of players Rosey helped set up in business. But Bubba got 12 inches of copy. And the big guy had credibility issues. He wrote a book, *Big Bubba*, and in it he claimed Super Bowl III was fixed, which sent heads spinning. Tom Matte offered this salvo in

Vince Bagli's book, *Sundays at 2:00 With the Baltimore Colts*:

> "Of all the things that have happened in my life, one of the all-time upsetting things to me was when Bubba Smith wrote in a book that we threw the game to the Jets. To this day, that upsets not just me but a lot of other guys. Bubba was one of those guys you had to kick in the butt, and then he'd go for maybe two plays and rest anyway. He wrote something about if [head coach Don] Shula had played him differently in that game, he could have done the job. Listen, he never touched the quarterback [Joe Namath] the whole game. Why didn't he do the job he was supposed to, and maybe we would have gotten the ball. He did nothing all day. And yet he has the audacity to say we threw the game. Why did he write that? I don't know. It's just outrageous."

And Steadman never called Bubba's mom to confirm, which was obligatory. He seemed content to forward Bubba's gripe and wash his hands.

Hiking the ball to QBs Morrall and Unitas that day was Bill Curry. "My response to that is, I love Bubba as a teammate and as a little brother, but he's wrong about that," stated Curry, who played for the Colts from 1967-1972. "That [throwing ballgames] was not in our DNA, not any of us. Earl [Morrall] had come to us in a trade right before the season. Unitas didn't play a snap that whole year [only a cameo in Super Bowl III]. We wouldn't have been anywhere close to the Super Bowl if it weren't for Earl Morrall. I don't know where Bubba got that idea. I never wanted to talk with him about it, and I didn't."

The *Los Angeles Times* ran a big feature on Rosenbloom in late November 1972, "Godfather to the Rams." Hall of Famer John Mackey loved the guy:

> "This man gives you no excuses to lose," says [former Colts tight end John] Mackey, "just reasons to win. For one thing he always travels with the team. That way any kind of trouble comes up, he handles it, right now. He doesn't wait for a report so he can handle it next winter. We went into Green Bay one year for a preseason game," Mackey remembers, "and couldn't find a restaurant open. It was Sunday, and Wisconsin closes on Sunday. Most teams would have survived on hotdogs and candy bars, and the next day they'd have told themselves, that's why we lost. But Carroll went to work as soon as he heard about it, and opened up a downtown restaurant. Then he got the chef down there, the owner, waitresses, the works. Within two hours after we landed in Green Bay, we were sitting down to a hot meal." This kind of thing has persuaded Mackey that football is a game "won in the front office." Ram All-Pro Merlin Olsen, an 11-year veteran, says flatly: "Carroll is

the finest pro football owner I've ever been around."

Steadman wouldn't touch such praise with surgical gloves.

Welshing on a promise was out of character for a man who saw the Colts as one big family. "Once the team started to blossom, my father was more and more involved," Steve Rosenbloom asserted. "The Colts were more important to him than the other businesses he had. He spent a lot of time in New York because that's where business was done, but that was a short hop to Baltimore. He was invested completely in the whole Colts operation. He was a very smart guy. He was very convincing when he talked to you. He loved the players, and they loved him. [Hall of Fame wide receiver] Raymond Berry called me one day, and we had a conversation. It was always interesting because he came from a different angle. And he told me, 'Steve, the reason we won is because of your father.' They [the players] had an owner who was a standup guy. He always supported his players."

Similar odes to Rosenbloom abound. In his 1986 roast of Bob Irsay in *Sports Illustrated*, "Now You See Him, Now You Don't," E.M. Swift contrasts the Irsay and Rosenbloom regimes:

Under Rosenbloom, the Colts had been like family. "There were no individualists," recalls [Tom] Matte. "Carroll wouldn't allow it." It was part of the Colts' secret of success. Veterans like Matte, Unitas, John Mackey and Raymond Berry actually had a say in who was cut and who wasn't. The coaching staff would listen to them. Curfews weren't enforced by the coaches; they were enforced by the team leaders. And Friday nights were team nights, when the players would go out and, instead of watching film, would do no more than drink beer and joke and develop that special bonding that a lot of great teams have. "Everybody lived here in town and made appearances for free. We were part of the community," recalls Matte. "That was the tradition. It made us a team."

Stories of Rosenbloom's benevolence have piled up over the years. Former Colts GM Harry Hulmes shared one with the *Los Angeles Times*. "Hulmes, the executive who moved from Baltimore's front office to New Orleans's, recalls one such personal problem. 'When I left him [Rosenbloom],' says Hulmes, 'Carroll asked me if I'd got rid of my (Baltimore) house yet. I told him no. He said: "If nobody meets your offer, let me know. I'll buy it." I thought that was generous, but I never intended to call him until he telephoned me six or eight weeks later in New Orleans. He wanted to know if I was settled, and I told him we had a house we couldn't put a deposit on because we hadn't sold in Baltimore yet. "How much is the deposit?" he asked. I told him $10,000. "I'll have the check there in the morning," he said. No strings, no interest, no note—and

I'm not even working for him anymore. That's Carroll.'"

Robert Irsay was now in hock for about $14.5 million and was clueless about running a ballclub. But that wasn't his only burden. "The [Colts-Rams] deal closed in the summer of 1972, and Rosenbloom's family flew to meet him in Los Angeles," Judy Battista explains in "The Colts' and Rams' Really Big Deal." "There had been a lot of churn in Robert Irsay's life then. He had sold his company and assumed control of the Colts. His daughter, Roberta, had been killed in a car accident the year before. But there was optimism for the Colts. He vowed that the Colts would remain in Baltimore, and that he and the city would work together to build a new stadium."

Funny. Rosenbloom had the same line.

CHAPTER 9

REIGN MAN

Bob Irsay minced into his first press conference in Baltimore like he was getting grilled by Joe McCarthy. Certainly not the blustering cyclone most people remember. Bashful Bob kept it low-key and standard-issue. He had 'em all disarmed and buffaloed. *Evening Sun* sports editor Bill Tanton bought the aw-shucks routine: "And then you get the owner who is, more than anything else, a fan at heart. That's Robert Irsay, the new owner of the Colts. The fan-type owner is fairly common these days. A guy makes millions in some business—in Irsay's case it happens to be heating, air conditioning and ventilating—and, at middle age, he decides to have some fun … He seems a decent sort, and you can't underestimate a man who can take $800 from his wife and turn it into enough to spend $19 million to get into pro football."

John Steadman, of the *News American*, later blistered the NFL for not vetting Irsay, but he likewise skipped the background check:

Measuring Robert Irsay off what he said and sounded led to one impression. He is the newest rookie owner in the National Football League and a plain-spoken sort of sport, which is kind of a refreshing change-of-pace in a world that puts a phony premium on deception and the cacophony of rhetoric … Irsay is in air conditioning and heating but, pleasantly enough, didn't come across like a torrent of hot air. His sincerity, without embellishments, was impressive. He's strictly a fan with only superficial knowledge of the game, yet said he wants to please the Baltimore public and not hurt the fans. Relationships deteriorated between the Colts' front office and the city, but now Irsay comes in to make a new start. There's hardly a way he can be as successful as the outgoing regime—thanks to discovering John Unitas for an 85-cent phone call—but there's something to be said for freshman enthusiasm as long as it's pure and honest.

He was right on two counts: 1) Irsay was in HVAC; and 2) He didn't know diddly about football.

In fact, all three sports editors at the Baltimore dailies got hoodwinked. Bob Maisel of the *Morning Sun*: "They asked him all the toughies—whether the Colts were in Baltimore to stay, whether he'd consider putting exhibition games on the season-ticket package and make them mandatory, whether he'd refuse to play in the old stadium, things like that. In all of his answers, the words, 'At the present time,' were invariably there, but when you stop to think about it, they'd have to be. He isn't that familiar with all of the people and the angles to put his hand on the Bible in speaking of things he doesn't know that much about. Even so he left a critical audience feeling he means what he says, and that his answers were all sincere and true."

They all bought what Irsay said wholesale. No picking up the phone to ask around. On September 17, 1972, *Sun Magazine* ran a two-page spread on Robert Irsay that reeked of press-release fluff: "He has a firm handshake and you soon gather, from talking to his friends and associates, that his word is bond. He's honest, they say. For a millionaire, they say, he's a helluva guy. He can be tough, they say, but he prefers getting things done with a minimum of fuss, and usually does. He likes to play, they say, but he gets

his work done first." They also say wait 'til you meet his alter ego.

Maybe Irsay convinced himself he'd be a hands-off owner: "I plan to be active and, of course, will be a factor in major decisions that are made, but basically the football team is being run by its coach, Don McCafferty, and by vice-president and general manager Joe Thomas, one of the finest football men I could have obtained. I won't be an interfering owner." No more interfering than Crohn's disease. As for McCafferty, he lasted five games with Irsay, refused to bench Unitas when Joe Thomas so ordained and got canned.

Eventually, the truth trickled out. All it took was a little shoe leather. E.M. Swift corrected some misinformation in a 1986 feature in *Sports Illustrated*, "Now You See Him, Now You Don't":

In the [Baltimore Colts] media guide he [Irsay] claimed, and still claims, to have graduated from the University of Illinois (where he supposedly was an Illini football teammate of former Colt Alex Agase) with a degree in mechanical engineering. Of his [WWII] war record Irsay told the *Sun*, "I was wounded once pretty badly in the leg, in New Guinea, hit by a grenade" and in 1975, he told the Chicago *Sun-Times* that he "came out as first-lieutenant." He spoke of the tragic death of his only daughter, Roberta, who in 1971 at age 14 suffered fatal injuries in an auto accident on Interstate 294 outside Chicago. He told the *Sun*: "They caught the kids who ran her car off the road. They were on drugs when it happened. They got 10 to 20 years, but the way things are today, they'll probably be out in five." It was an astounding collection of half-truths and prevarications. His daughter had, indeed, been killed in an accident, but according to state police records, there was no evidence of another car having run her vehicle off the road, no arrests were made, and the car in which Roberta was a passenger had, in fact, gone over a guardrail, slid down an embankment and struck a car on another expressway.

Compassion mandated that you feel for the guy. But why all the unnecessary embroidery? His statements about college and the war—total hokum. "Nor did Irsay graduate, as his biography contends," E.M. Smith corrected. "According to an Illinois spokesman, he attended school for the fall semester of 1940, the spring and fall semesters of 1941 and the summer session of 1942, leaving without a degree. He enlisted in the Marines on Oct. 23, 1942, and was discharged on April 3, 1943, as a sergeant—not a lieutenant—without having served overseas. No medals, no decorations. A Marine spokesman could provide no further details. Irsay couldn't either."

Irsay told some other lulus: that his real dad was actually his stepdad, that his grandfather raised him, that they were poor. "We weren't poor by any stretch of the imagination,"

Ronald Irsay, Bob's younger brother, told E.M. Swift. "Why would my grandfather raise him, and my mom and dad raise me? We lived in a very nice home in West Rogers Park. We weren't wealthy, but my dad owned several buildings in Chicago and at one time was one of the largest tin knockers (sheet-metal contractors) in the city. I don't know how else to say this, but my brother tried to run my father out of business. Bob actually worked to try to destroy his own father. Oh, he's a real sweetheart, all right."

Baltimore reporters dug up not a lick of this until Irsay had his luggage out on the bed for Indy. Psychologists call bull-shooting blitzkriegs like these *pseudologia fantastica* (i.e., maybe the guy can't help himself). Obviously, Rozelle and the NFL gave Irsay an olé into the league, happy that they had a stand-in for Rosenbloom.

After the sweet nothings to Baltimore reporters at the first presser, Irsay made a hash of his first team meeting. In 2017 Ryan Mavity picked up the story in "'Ghost to the Post' Still Haunts Colts":

Irsay didn't exactly endear himself to the veteran-laden team at his first training camp in August 1972. Veteran running back Tom Matte said, "He came into the team meeting, 'My name is Bob Irsay, and I'm the new owner of the Baltimore Colts.' And I looked at Unitas and Unitas looked at me, and we almost threw up. It was actually terrible. As you can imagine, I'm not very fond of this guy."

"He came in, we were told we were going to have a meeting, and Irsay was going to talk to the team," receiver Sam Havrilak recalled. "We were used to a good 20-minute speech by Carroll Rosenbloom. Irsay came in, was very unsure of himself, had never owned a team before, hadn't been in that situation, and didn't know what to say or do. He only spoke for about five minutes, if that. Then he told everyone that his secret ambition was to receive a snap from center. So we went outside and Bill Curry, who was our center, centered the ball to him. I believe he jammed his finger when he did it."

Maybe the blarney was because he was smashed half the time. His own son, Jim, saw every day how the bottle made him loopy. "We were a father-and-son team," Jim Irsay stated in Clark Judge's article, "Colts' Irsay: 'No Way' I Would Have Dealt Elway 40 Years Ago." "But he wasn't blessed to be in the business. And then the alcoholism affected him a lot because he was like Jekyll and Hyde a lot of ways. He really was a bright, brilliant, sensitive man … actually kind of shy. But when he drank, it was like an opposite thing would happen. It was tough. I just tried to support him the best I could … I could advise him some, and he would listen sometimes. But in the end, he did what he wanted to do, and I couldn't stop him many times. There were so many outrageous things that happened in those years, especially with coaches getting

fired. Of course, you're sitting there with John (Elway), and there's absolutely no way you trade him. It's just unfortunate."

Miles of buffoonery lie down the road before the Elway farce. But a man with a brilliant business mind succumbing to booze is central to the Colts' nosedive and eventual move. Robert Irsay wasn't a bumpkin; he made the Robert Irsay Company one of the biggest HVAC companies in the world. Put Irsay on the wagon for good and history takes a dramatic turn.

Irsay had his admirers in the business world. Gene Bednarz, a VP for an HVAC subsidiary of the Robert Irsay Company, spoke of Irsay's savvy with E.M. Swift of *Sports Illustrated*. "He had great charisma. By 1960 we were a force to be reckoned with. Bob was a gambler and very innovative. He was the first guy to build a big new plant out in the suburbs. We were the first company to bid on jobs on the basis on rough outline specifications, rather than finished plans, a practice that today is commonplace. He hired a lot of young superintendents and paid them over scale, and he had good rapport with his workers. This, as I say, was in the early years, the formative years, before he was rich. Before he realized that money gave him power." Then he fell into a dry martini and drowned.

The Baltimore press, a sardonic lot, jumped all over Irsay's boozing. "He had some deep problems," stated Vito Stellino, a man who has covered the wide world of sports—the Colts' move, 40 straight Super Bowls, six World Series and the first Ali-Frazier fight

(March 1971). "He was obviously an alcoholic. The joke was, you had to get him by noon, or else he was totally out of it. And there was all this stuff about him going in the press box and calling plays [which he did]. He was just not equipped to be a good NFL owner. Carroll Rosenbloom virtually picked him. He [Rosenbloom] wanted to buy the Rams and didn't want to pay the estate tax. So, he found a guy like Irsay who would agree to buy the Rams and trade franchises. Nobody trades a team in L.A. for a team in Baltimore, although in those days, there wasn't the same emphasis on markets. But, obviously, a team in L.A. is worth more than a team in Baltimore. It started with Rosenbloom wanting to go to L.A."

Tragic, that too much grog brought down a great franchise. What Rosenbloom built up, Irsay knocked down. All-Pro Colts running back Lydell Mitchell extends his sympathies to Irsay. "Mr. Irsay also had a problem where he had a sickness: He was an alcoholic. Certainly, that didn't help the situation. And I respect that—that's how I put it. He did have a sickness. He had to deal with it, and we had to deal with it as well." All onboard had to deal with it.

Lydell's teammate, Bert Jones, eschewed sympathy. The *Evening Sun* ran a feature on Irsay in mid-February 1984 and solicited comment from the Ruston Rifle. "'He [Irsay] is an embarrassment to the city of Baltimore,' says Bert Jones, the former Colt quarterback who once considered himself on friendly terms with his boss. 'In my opinion, he is a rough person who drinks way, way too much and

who does not know what the truth is anymore. You can't get the same answer from him twice.'"

January 15, 1997, was the day that Robert Irsay died. Eulogies made papers all over the country. In Baltimore, sports radio host Nestor Aparicio got John Steadman to reflect on Irsay's life. Steadman dove right in:

I don't know whether it came from how he [Irsay] was fortified and the stuff he was puttin' into his system, but he was always jumpin' around. You could never pin him down. When he'd cough, he'd say, "Oh, that's the malaria, the yellow jaundice I picked up in New Guinea [during World War II] with the Marines." Well, shucks, he was never west of the Mississippi River. The Marines, in 1943, dismissed him with a discharge that was less than honorable. He is a [psychological] study, but it's a sad study because I think when he was stone-cold sober, he wasn't that bad of an individual. He didn't get up every day and say, "I'm gonna get Nestor Aparicio," or "I'm gonna do him in today." That was not in his mindset. It really wasn't. He just wandered through life, and the trip was a lot more enjoyable for him if he was putting something into his system. He was a heavy drinker—usually vodka— and he became totally out of control. He would say anything, promise anything.

Steadman also let Irsay have it in *From Colts to Ravens*. "It can be said without the slightest hesitation that the Colt years during the Bob Irsay regime were the most difficult. Turbulence was the order of every day, or so it seemed. It wasn't that he planned it. The reporters found they were covering Irsay more than the team, but the spectacles he created left them little choice … Newspapers and wire services were too often going around in circles trying to determine the validity of Irsay's statements or describing his latest caper. His face was usually flushed and it was no secret he liked to drink."

In 1986, Irsay's wife, Harriet, confided to E.M. Swift of *Sports Illustrated* about what Lydell Mitchell calls the "sickness." "He's got a drinking problem, but he won't admit it. It started slowly, but in the last five years he really started to go downhill. I don't know why he behaves the way he does. Maybe he had a bad childhood." Not according to his brother and mother—upper-middle-class all the way.

One reporter who caught Irsay's act in Baltimore is Michael Olesker, who worked at the *Morning Sun* and for years had his own column. He was also around during the Carroll Rosenbloom years. "He [Rosenbloom] sold out the town. He took this wonderful franchise, but L.A. was much more glamorous than Baltimore, and he knew this guy [Irsay] was a drunk. He knew he was inflicting Irsay on Baltimore, and he didn't care because he wanted to go where the bright lights were. He gave us this one-man plague. Harry Hughes was governor part of that time, and he told me, 'I knew, if I had to talk to Irsay, I had to

do it before 10:00 in the morning because after that, he was drunk.'"

You wonder whether Rosenbloom knew Irsay was a lush. Rosey's son, Steve, said the two men rarely talked and let their lawyers do the work. Bill Curry was the Colts starting center for five years. Irsay and GM Joe Thomas shipped him down to Houston right away in the Great Purge. He feels Irsay butchered the transition:

I'm sure Irsay did his best, but he did things in front of the team that were not in accord with what we thought was the dignity of an NFL owner. I'm not saying it was intentional; I think it was more personality. Now that I'm sitting here, focusing on it, how in the world do you follow Carroll Rosenbloom? The answer is you can't. I wanted him to succeed. There was nobody there that wanted to ridicule or dislike him in any way. We understood this is business; this is not just a lark. All the players understood that. I don't think the fans did. He was in an element that he had to learn to understand, and I think that was difficult for him. Where he lost *us* is when he fired Don McCafferty, who at the time had the best record in the National Football League. So, I think Irsay had a tough way to start, and I've always had empathy for him.

. . .

About the Great White Dome at Camden Yards—where do we come up with $110 mil to pay for it? "The critical problems now facing the [Maryland] sports authority is money," the *Morning Sun* pondered in August 1972. "As projected, the stadium complex will require tens of millions of public dollars. Such financial burdens were not the [MD] General Assembly's original intent. As passed last March after a hasty 'preliminary feasibility' study, the bill was hailed as providing downtown Baltimore with a modern sports center at no expense to the city or state. The 27.5-acre site is planned to house a 70,000-capacity domed stadium, a 4,500-car garage and a possible arena for winter sports. An office-retailing-hotel complex would fill the rest of the land."

In Xanadu did Kubla Khan
A stately pleasure-dome decree:
Where Alph, the sacred river, ran
Through caverns measureless to man
Down to a sunless sea.

Coleridge would have told Baltimore to spend the dough on museums and libraries. But Executive Director Don McPhail and his four allies of the Maryland Sports Complex Authority held a photo-op in August 1972 amid trumpet fanfare. McPhail dove into the big stuff. "More significant were announcements that: A) The Colts and Orioles have agreed to share the facility; and B) The Authority intends to build a domed stadium," Jack Chevalier of the *Evening Sun* revealed. "With the football and baseball clubs willing to live together, you can forget all those wild

estimates of $200 million for separate stadia. The Camden Station project may not even cost half that. Now there's no sense building, say, a $65-million stadium if it won't attract new customers, enhance the city's image and stimulate business in the downtown area. That's why the Authority is talking seriously about a domed stadium. It would be the first in the East—a legitimate tourist attraction and more than just another ballpark."

A few domes sprang up in the '70s—the Astrodome (1965), the Superdome (1975), the Pontiac Silverdome (1975), the Kingdome (1976). Somehow, they got it done. But did Baltimore have the moxie?

The number-crunchers had their doubts. "Two knowledgeable securities experts doubt that the authority can finance the sports complex solely by revenue bonds," the *Morning Sun* reported in an August 1972 article, "The Stadium: Who Will Pay?" "'Without seeing any figures,' remarks James J. Cavanaugh, general partner of Alex Brown & Sons, 'sports complexes of this magnitude have not been financed by tax-free revenue bonds.' Adds Richard Mulligan, senior vice president of Robert Garrett and Sons, Inc., 'It is hard to conceive of a pay-as-you-go proposition in this project without government support or some kind of taxes. There is no precedent I know of for revenue bonding of sports stadia of this size and cost.'"

A modest tutorial on revenue bonds is in order because some bankers stated that they wouldn't get you all the way home on a $100-million dome:

Municipal bonds (or "munis" for short) are debt securities issued by states, cities, counties and other government entities to fund day-to-day obligations and to finance capital projects such as building schools, highways or sewer systems [or a stadium]. By purchasing municipal bonds, you are in effect *lending money to the bond issuer* [emphasis mine] in exchange for a promise of regular interest payments, usually semi-annually, and the return of the original investment, or "principal." A municipal bond's maturity date (the date when the issuer of the bond repays the principal) may be years in the future.

So, let's say you fork over $5,000 to the state for a 10-year muni paying 5% interest to help fund the dome. Basically, you've become a loan shark who expects to get about $250 a year in interest, then the original $5,000 in 10 years. Hold on tight to that bond, and you cash in. The state gets the stadium; you get a new washer and dryer with the interest you pocketed. Here's why those capitalists rolled their eyes at the Baltodome plan in the *Morning Sun*:

Almost all cities with new downtown sports centers have been faced with large deficits. Cincinnati's $44-million Riverfront Stadium is losing $1 million [almost $8 million in today's money] annually after two years of operation. In Philadelphia, taxpayers have and will continue to pay $2 million yearly for the $38-million Veterans Stadium completed in early 1971. The $52-million Three Rivers Stadium in Pittsburgh, completed two years ago, has annually lost $900,000. This figure does not include Allegheny County's expenditure of $5 million to clear the stadium site and the federal government's $2.4 million contribution for road and parking improvements.

Baltimore pols took turns with the conch shell. Taxing the little people for a downtown palace irked several windbags. "Such prospects have particularly angered Harry Kaufman, Park Board member, and City Comptroller Hyman Pressman," the *Morning Sun* informed. "'I think it is very wrong for taxpayers to subsidize high profitmaking private companies like the Orioles and the Colts,' Mr. Kaufman states. 'This is exactly what the taxpayer will do with this stadium plan.' The solution, he claims, is to modernize Memorial Stadium 'at a fraction of the new stadium's cost.' Built in 1954 for $6.5 million, Memorial Stadium has been steadily in the black and has $387,000 left in its debt service after this year. Mr. Pressman adds that he is 'apprehensive' of the Camden sports complex. 'If it could be done without public subsidy, I'm for it,' he remarks, 'but I find the whole scheme hard to believe.'"

Steve Rosenbloom said that dealing with the Park Board was like eating soup with a fork. In the middle of August '72, the *Morning*

Sun published an editorial—**Needed: Straight Talk about a Stadium:**

When Governor Mandel and Mayor Schaefer began to talk glowingly last winter about a new stadium complex for downtown Baltimore, their motives were clear: Colt owner Carroll Rosenbloom was threatening to move his football franchise because he didn't want to share the same playing field with the baseball Orioles. Now Mr. Rosenbloom has been traded to Los Angeles; the new Colt owner and the Orioles' Jerold Hoffberger plan to stay in Baltimore, even if it means sharing old Memorial Stadium, which has sat for all of 14 years [sic, 18] out on 33rd Street. It would seem, then, that the original impulse for constructing a new, costly sports palace has dissolved. But the Maryland Sports Complex Authority, created by the General Assembly to go ahead with the project, appears inalterably committed, despite very real evidence that the taxpayers may wind up paying for such private benefits ... Yet reliable and respected business and finance experts, using a consultant's estimate of building a new stadium, contend it cannot be done without huge, annual infusions of tax dollars.

Were other cities that took the plunge rogue kamikazes? Or maybe they had factored in other items—tourist money, hotel and restaurant revenue, more patrons from the 'burbs, a city status upgrade, fan amenities. And since when did most stadiums operate in the black anyway? To stay in the bigs, a city needed a fancy park or team owners might look elsewhere. Cincinnati, Pittsburgh and Philadelphia all built cereal bowls, the teams stayed put and no city went bankrupt. They took a plunge, and it all worked out.

Baltimore politicians, however, kept throwing up barricades when the Orioles and Colts demanded a classier joint. Baltimore City Comptroller Rhymin' Hyman Pressman took pride in gumming up the works. Former Colts PR director and general manager Ernie Accorsi saw how this drove Rosenbloom batty. "He [Rosenbloom] wasn't very positive about Hyman Pressman," Accorsi admitted. "He felt he was a roadblock. If you read the history of the Brooklyn Dodgers' move [to L.A.], it [Baltimore's situation] wasn't a heckuva lot different than [New York City Parks Commissioner Robert] Moses and [Dodgers owner Walter] O'Malley. In the books I read, O'Malley was willing to build a stadium right where the Brooklyn arena [Barclays Center] is now, where the Nets play. He was willing to build a stadium. I don't think Rosenbloom was willing to build one himself. It's just that Hyman Pressman was, to him [Rosenbloom], an obstacle. That's how he looked at it. Pressman wasn't working towards trying to get a new stadium. That's what Rosenbloom wanted." Pressman hugged Memorial Stadium with all his might and wouldn't let go.

Tom Marr IV has spent more than three decades investigating shady stunts in the home improvement business and learned about local politics through his old man, radio commentator Tom Marr. He remembers the clout Hyman Pressman had:

People want to say [former Baltimore mayor and Maryland governor] William Donald Schaefer was the most popular politician in Maryland history. They may be right; he was certainly the most popular Baltimore mayor. But look at how [Hyman] Pressman did in his elections. A lot of people think that after this disaster with the Colts, they would've kicked him out of office. No. He was a beloved politician in the state of Maryland and the city of Baltimore. And he took his duty as the protector of the people's money *very* seriously. In the last four elections he had, he won by a landslide—even *after* the Colts left. The Colts left in 1984; Hyman Pressman did not leave as comptroller until 1991. So, he kept getting elected, even after Question P [a controversial ballot issue] and eminent domain and all that. So, yeah, he led the charge on that: "This [Memorial Stadium] is your stadium, a perfectly good stadium. Why should the city of Baltimore pay any more money? We're already leveraging for urban renewal, building Harborplace, the Charles Center; we're taking back the neighborhoods and revamping Fells Point." All of this was going on.

• • •

Bob Irsay was clueless running a ballclub, so GM Joe Thomas was the day-to-day führer. Thomas wielded a scythe and kicked off the Great Purge not long after settling in. First to go was Hall of Fame tight end John Mackey, as reported in the *Morning Sun* on 9/14/1972: "Joe Thomas, general manager of the Colts, yesterday announced that tight end John Mackey, who quit the team Monday, had been placed on irrevocable waivers and was available to any of the other 25 National Football League clubs at the price of $100." Mackey had flip-flopped on retiring, yes then no. Not into gamesmanship, Thomas waived bye-bye and the Chargers claimed him, whereupon Mackey started only four games, caught four passes, then called it quits.

The Garbage Man was next. Tom Matte was a grinder and personified the Rosenbloom Colts, but for Thomas that was past-tense. When Matte demanded that the Colts put him on waivers (like Mackey), he got a quick nope from Thomas and was demoted to the band squad. In late January 1973, San Diego got Matte for an 8th-round draft pick; Matte said nothin' doin' and retired.

Then Thomas committed a sacrilege. "John Unitas, who made the Baltimore Colt franchise successful and was largely responsible for the growth of professional football, has been traded to the San Diego Chargers for 'future considerations,'" the *Morning Sun* revealed in late January 1973. "So the greatest quarterback of pro football history, so named by the *Associated Press* several years ago, will wind up his brilliant career on the West Coast where the sunshine and warmth should be beneficial to his 40-year-old bones, particularly to the right elbow."

Granted, Unitas at 40 was The Babe on the Boston Braves: old, slow, nothing left in the tank. West Coast sunshine did nothing for The Golden Arm: four starts, seven interceptions, 34-76 through the air. No way to go out. Joe Thomas was as warm as a snow cone in his press release: "Vice president and general manager Joe Thomas announced that the Baltimore Colts today traded quarterback John Unitas to the San Diego Chargers for future consideration … The Chargers will assume only his standard player contract and the Colts will of course meet all future obligations accrued by John Unitas during his playing career with the Colts. *The Colts' organization wishes John Unitas the best of success* [emphasis mine]." Unitas's lifetime job with the Colts that Rosenbloom had promised? Not bloody likely, Irsay decided.

Tossing out demigods with the leftovers appalled Steve Rosenbloom. "The fans were married to the team," he stressed. "And Irsay comes in, and he unceremoniously trades Johnny Unitas to San Diego. This is like taking the biggest war hero and sending him to Siberia. Johnny Unitas was untouchable with the fans. He was a symbol, an icon, in life and in death. And he has a big statue there [at M&T Bank Stadium]. So, you can just

imagine, when Irsay did that, what that did to the fans." The grievances were piling up.

Fans were riled up at Irsay's purge of the generals. One guy, Malcolm Marcus, was the assistant principal at P.S. 137 and a big Colts fan. Bill Tanton of the *Evening Sun* asked him about the mass sackings:

"These things that have been happening lately. They leave me with a sinking feeling. Unitas and Matte forced out. [Head coach] Don McCafferty fired. [Interim head coach] John Sandusky fired, plus [assistant coaches] Bobby Boyd, Dick Bielski. I'm just afraid that the general manager [Thomas] and the new owner are so out of touch with this city that they're losing us, and that eventually we're going to lose the franchise. You can't clean house the way they have and keep the affection of the fans. The new people are so impersonal. I think what bothers me is that the Colts are now an organization without a heart, and right now I don't care if I see the Colts play another game. I never thought I would call up the newspaper and say a thing like that."

And then Marcus gave John Steadman and the Rosenbloom haters a kick in the pants:

"We had an owner here all those years, Carroll Rosenbloom, who ran a beautiful organization. He had heart. He hired a man like [GM] Don Kellett to run the organization for him. They don't make them like Don Kellett anymore. And they hired great coaches like Weeb Ewbank and Don Shula. Those men built up a love for the Colts. Baltimore was always a second-rate town until they came along, and we had a second-rate complex until the Colts became the World Champions. And then we drove Rosenbloom out of town. That's why I say we are getting what we deserve. As time passes, the public will come to appreciate what Carroll Rosenbloom did for this town. An era is gone."

And mind, this was only about four months into the Irsay era. Irsay was just getting warmed up.

Bill Tanton added this subtle dig at Steadman: "Carroll Rosenbloom lived on Golden Beach near Miami in his latter years as Colt owner, but he was a totally different sort of personality. Everyone knew Carroll ran the organization, not Don Klosterman or Harry Hulmes or other people who served as his general managers. And Carroll was a smoothie. He knew how to be on the scene one day a week and whisper a word here, wink an eye there, or jab somebody playfully in the ribs in the locker room before a game and get an important message across. He knew how to make his players feel wanted, even loved. This area of management-player relations remains a total mystery to Irsay-Thomas, and, what is most discouraging, promises to remain so."

Slashing, thrashing Colts safety Rick Volk survived the original Joe Thomas clearance sale, but he surveyed the damage. "I used to wonder how a guy like Carroll Rosenbloom could ever tell any of us he was trading or cutting us," Volk stated in the book, *Sundays at 2:00 With the Baltimore Colts*. "If we couldn't play anymore, I think he would bring us back into the organization to coach or teach the younger players. Thomas got rid of a lot of players the fans loved—Tom Matte, John Mackey, Johnny U, Bill Curry—the heart of the team. He drafted young players and just threw them in there to play. When the fans lost all their heroes, the players everybody looked up to, and the people who replaced them on the field were guys they never heard of, who couldn't play as well as the ones who were let go, the fans began to boo for the first time in the team's history. The product was not a good product, and the fans could see that."

Vito Stellino had the thorny task of covering Irsay's misadventures and his shoddy football team for the *Morning Sun*. He advises not to exclude Joe Thomas from blame. "Joe Thomas was involved, too [in the Colts' mess]. Don't forget about him. He got rid of some of the old favorites. Now, granted, they were getting old, but that alienated people, too. Actually, Thomas probably found Irsay [for the Colts-Rams trade] more than Irsay did. So, you have to include Thomas in the whole scope of things. He alienated everybody, to begin with."

Longtime Colts and Baltimore Ravens band director John Ziemann deplored the Irsay-Thomas shredding machine:

First of all, when Joe [Thomas] came in, he saw that the team was aging, and he got his axe out and started swinging. You don't do that in Baltimore. Johnny Unitas was promised by Carroll Rosenbloom that he would have a job when he retired. Other Colts were promised jobs. [John] Steadman did a radio show on WBAL about this, and Bob [Irsay] said, "Oh, yeah, they'll all have jobs." Less than six months later, they were all gone. And that was Joe Thomas. Thomas had the foresight to know, that to move forward, we had to get younger players. But he did it the wrong way. And that's what lost a lot of fans. Look, I'm a nobody, and if I can figure it out, why couldn't they? But Thomas wanted to make a name for himself, move fast, and he knew we had to rebuild, and rebuild fast. But you don't get rid of the heroes of Baltimore and send them out to San Diego.

By '72, the Colts were a squad of varicose veins. The slows were setting in, and it was time for new blood. Superb draft pick Lydell Mitchell out of Penn State thought the Colts in '72 were like Joe Louis when he fought Marciano:

I'll take John Mackey first. He was the head of our Players' Association, so there was some obvious contention [with Irsay] there. That's why they wanted to get rid of John. But with John Unitas—who, to this day, I still think is one of the greatest quarterbacks who ever played football—very knowledgeable, and I had the opportunity to play with him on a couple of occasions. The man just had a brilliant mind. But by '72, John Unitas couldn't play football anymore. I'm just gonna be frank about it. He just couldn't play. We all wish we could play forever, but it's not gonna happen. When I got here, the team was old. And back then, you let teams grow old together because you didn't pay 'em a lot of money. Consequently, you played for a team, and that's the team you usually stayed with for 10, 12 years. In this case here [the Colts], they got old together and couldn't compete any longer. I remember my dear friend Franco [Harris] got drafted, and he said, "Man, I'm going to this lousy team, the Steelers; you're going to the Colts," who just won the Super Bowl [a year earlier]. But the opposite happened: I went to an old team; he went to a young team on the rise. Look—they just couldn't play any longer. So, whether you liked the purge—or whatever you wanna call it—it needed to be done. Today, you don't see that happening, where teams grow old together. And we could not compete any longer with the team we had then. Other than doing it [releasing older players], I don't know what else you could do.

Joe Thomas told Ken Denlinger of the *Washington Post* in December 1976 that a housecleaning was long overdue. "Thomas defends his rash and at the time unpopular actions against the Colts of Carroll Rosenbloom was necessary because the team was going swiftly downhill even while winning championships. Those championships, Thomas notes, came after the NFL-AFL merger, and against little competition except the Dolphins he [Thomas] had built … 'We could have fooled around at .500, maybe a little better, for a number of years,' he said. 'But I thought why not clean 'em out and bring in good, young players, let those guys get kicked around awhile but also grow together. I have a franchise to protect.'"

Thomas was classic good news-bad news, hacking out the dead weight while showing old heroes the door. Savvy but callous. As Colts GM, Ernie Accorsi was a sponge soaking up Thomas's football wisdom:

There was no free agency back then, but you could play out your option. If your contract was over, we had an option year on you, so you could play, but you had to play out your option year. So, after your option year, with no free agency, you just couldn't play until you resigned. When Joe took over, we had 17 unsigned players going into their option year. And he took over about two weeks before training camp [1972]. So, we're in Tampa, and he's going over all these records. It was a small organization, and he confided to me because I think he trusted me. He said, "I got

17 guys I gotta sign." He saw 17 players in one day. He had an office right down the hall in the dormitory, and the players, one by one, would come out of there—[Sam] Havrilak, [Jim] O'Brien, all these guys would come by—and they said, "He asked me what I wanted; I told him; he said OK. I should've asked for more." Everyone of 'em thought, *I got it so easy; I should've asked for more.* Now, these were down-the-line kind of players, but he just wanted to get the damn thing done. That was Joe. He was always in a hurry to get it done. I think that was just part of his personality. I never saw a side of him that said, "Screw him. The hell with him." I just think it was his nature.

Joe Thomas assembled the Sack Pack—the defensive front four that helped the Colts win three straight division titles, 1975-77. Defensive tackle Joe Ehrmann lauds how Thomas handled the atrophy. "Joe Thomas was doing a terrific job of assembling players through trades and the draft," he told Baltimore sportscaster Vince Bagli for his book, *Sundays at 2:00 With the Baltimore Colts.* "He had taken apart a team that was coming apart from age and injuries anyhow, and made it a winner in a short time. Thomas was always good and nice and kind to me. I liked him a lot."

But Thomas handled the problem with a weed whacker instead of tweezers. Consider what Joe did with loyal Colts NFL and Super Bowl champion, center Bill Curry:

The [1972] Pro Bowl was in Dallas, and I was in the Pro Bowl. When I got there, with all of the stuff that had been going on [with Irsay in Baltimore], I was interviewed. I had had a recent meeting with [NFL Commissioner Pete] Rozelle, and it had been very cordial. I said so to the reporter. I saw the newspaper when it came out; it said, "Curry Rips Rozelle." Then you read the article, and the headline-writer had done his own number on the thing. I did not rip Rozelle. I wouldn't have dared in those circumstances. And Thomas apparently told others the story that he got to Dallas, saw the newspaper and said, "Well, that's it for Curry. We're gonna get rid of him." Then he called me, and he said, "Do you know where I sent you?" And he laughed hysterically. I said, "No. Why don't you tell me." He said, "I'm sending you to Houston" [a team with an abysmal record]. I said, "Wherever you send me, I will go." He said, "What did you say? Did you say you wouldn't go?!" I said, "No, Joe. I said I will go anywhere that you send me. Thank you. I think you said Houston Oilers. Just tell 'em to give me a call." There was something about Joe that created dissension.

But most of the young bucks Joe brought onboard were with him on this. Linebacker Stan White confirmed in *Sundays at 2:00 With the Baltimore Colts*: "I think Joe Thomas was glad in a way. He wanted to remake the team in his own way. He might have been able to transition it, but he felt it was just as good, if not better, to tear it apart and start over. He did what he had to do. The guys he let go just couldn't play anymore. They had seen their best days. They had gone to the Super Bowl in 1969, and it seemed like they had all reached that stage of life where other things were more important. Joe rebuilt the team."

No doubt, Joe Thomas knew his stuff. He evaluated talent for Shula and the Dolphins built a dynasty, the last perfect team in NFL history (1972). Pick his brain for advice, but remember to add some finesse. "When Joe Thomas was there, it was very clear. I liked working with Joe," Thomas protégé Ernie Accorsi proclaimed. "Look, to this day, he's the greatest evaluator of talent I've ever been around. When you study what he did with the drafts—now, he got off the track now and again and violated some of his theories—I built the Giants on most of his theories: quarterback, pass rush, big-time receiver, protect the quarterback. He was a great evaluator of talent. He was a good guy to work for. When he looked at my salary when I got there [in 1977], I think I was making like $14,500 [as asst. GM]. He said, 'My God! You're workin' for nothing.' He jacked up all our salaries. So, working with Joe—I don't connect him with Irsay. We worked for Joe."

Lifelong Baltimorean and former popular *Morning Sun* columnist Michael Olesker agrees with most people: Joe Thomas had a big football brain but no tact:

We revered the old guard, especially Unitas. Joe Thomas was a *really* smart football guy, but he had the personality of a corporate accountant. He did not show Unitas the respect that he deserved. I mean, Unitas was a *god* here, and what they should have done was say, "We *need* you in the front office," where he would have been fine. Instead, they benched him. Look—they *had* to clear house. Those guys had grown too old. They needed the changes, and Joe Thomas would have been the right guy. But he had *no* sensitivity for the moment, at all. Then, with Irsay doing the stuff that he did—sending in plays, firing coaches and all the rest of the bluster—and openly, ostentatiously shopping the team around, that is why people stopped going [to the games]. And Irsay only got worse as we headed into the '80s, and the team was awful.

Steadman also paid him a compliment, something in short supply during the Irsay era: "He [Thomas] is honest, determined and decent," Steadman stated in his *News American* column in July 1972. "No back-slapper or beaming personality boy, Thomas has been a success in two areas of football—as a coach and talent scout. His hand has been vital in the establishment of the Minnesota Vikings and Miami Dolphins. It's generally agreed his perceptive ability to know a football player when he sees one is the equal of any man."

Nobody sat on the fence about Thomas. Phil Jackman, of the *Evening Sun*, had a satchel a nicknames for the Irsay crew—Bob, the red-faced owner for Irsay; Joe Promise for the GM; Teddy Trite for head coach Ted Marchibroda—and he ripped into Thomas in 1977: "**Joe Promise**—Seeing as how you shipped a bill for $140 to Colt coaches for coffee consumed during the season, how much did you come up with out of the can buried in the backyard for that trip to Europe looking for a placekicker a couple of years ago? It turns out your little niceties are coming back to haunt you, like kicking Marchibroda's kid off a charter flight ... And how 'bout the Monday night of the Houston game when you sold tickets to the seats the guest band occupied, and fans had to stand around on the banking near the scoreboard until the kids did their number at halftime and took off for home? Yikes, what class."

Bill Curry can't disagree. "Joe Thomas had an awful lot to do with the mood in the locker room and the way the team was treated—his being the general manager, in charge of trades and that sort of thing. When John Unitas is waked up by [reporter] Larry Harris at 8:00 on a Saturday morning to be told that he's been traded to the San Diego Chargers, that is gonna be a big story, and it has been ever since. That kind of thing also reflected on Irsay."

It all depended on whose yard you were standing in. To Lydell Mitchell, Thomas got a raw deal in the press:

Let me tell you this: As things change, some things never change. I got along quite well with Joe Thomas. We had a lot of respect for each other. But I remember him telling me one time, way back in '72, '73, that in order to have a good football team, you gotta have an outstanding offensive and defensive line. After that, you can start plugging in. But if you don't have those things going for you, you got nothing. I don't care how great the quarterback or the running back is, if you have no one that can block for him, you know what? You're not going anywhere. So, that's how he used to build a team—from the lines, out. And that hasn't changed to this day. So—he had a brilliant mind. He did some good things down in Miami as a scout. Then he had an opportunity to be a general manager with the Colts, and he embraced it. He wasn't always personable, but he was all-business. He wasn't vastly understood, and probably, he got a bum rap. Baltimore thought, *I welcome the players in my living room; they're part of my family.* And with those guys he got rid of, he got a bum rap, right from the beginning because he had to be the one to deliver the bad news: "Hey, guys, it ain't working. You can't play any longer." That's how it was with him, but I think he was a great general manager.

Type-A personalities can drive the rest of us up a tree. Sometimes they barrel past feelings or sentiment. Thomas's assistant GM, Ernie Accorsi, thinks that label is pushing it:

I don't think he was a callous human being. It was his personality to be impatient. I don't know if it came from his heart condition at a young age [he died in 1983 of a heart attack at age 61] or being passed over so many times for jobs. He felt, "Let's do it *now.*" I would go to him sometimes and say, "Joe, slow down here." I could talk to him. When he fired [offensive coordinator] George Young [1974], what happened was, [Howard] Schnellenberger tried to win the game and put Bert Jones back in a preseason game against the Falcons. And their defensive line was a monster. Fortunately, Bert didn't get hurt, but Joe went nuts in the press box. And he called me the next day and said, "I'm gonna fire George Young." I said, "Can you call a timeout here? He's an institution in this town. You don't need this." He had already gone through the Unitas thing. I said, "Don't fire him. He was the [1971] Super Bowl offensive line coach." He said, "Well, let me think about it." So, he called me back [Labor Day weekend], and said, "Don't dare say a word, or I'll fire you too." I had three kids. What the hell am I gonna do? Take him on? He said, "I'm firing him. And if you say one word…" And I said, "OK, OK." I asked him, "Well, who the hell is gonna coach the offensive line?" He said, "Dick

Szymanski." Dick Szymanski had never coached in his life. I called Sizzy, and he said, "Whaddaya want? I'm havin' a cookout." I said, "You ain't havin' a cookout. You're gonna get a call from Joe Thomas in about 30 seconds. You're the new offensive line coach." The point is, that was his personality. He didn't want to waste any time; he wanted to get something done, and he wanted it done right away.

. . .

The headline in the *Morning Sun* near Thanksgiving 1972 read: **Stadium Drama Arrives for a Long Baltimore Run**. The *Sun* ran a two-part analysis of the Great Stadium Debate and offered this for starters: "From the experiences of other cities that have faced the same problem over the last decade, Baltimore appears to be headed for a long-running, controversial and expensive project. It already is controversial. And, in the eyes of some, it has become expensive with an initial outlay of $300,000 in public money by officials who swore it would not cost taxpayers 'one red cent.' All the problems in providing modern stadium facilities for the big-time, big-business sports teams of today—and other events, from Billy Graham to Barnum and Bailey—are well-known by now."

The state recently coughed up $150,000 for consultants' studies, and some vigilant taxpayers filed a suit to block the use of $300,000 because they said it violated a '72 law that prohibited state funds from being used to build a

new stadium. The mentality back then was let the fat cats build their own mansions. "The attitude [of the fans] then was, they own the teams; let them build a stadium," observed longtime NFL insider Upton Bell. "It's not like today, when football is a national mania. No matter whether the teams are good or not—doesn't make any difference. In that case [Baltimore in the '70s], I can imagine politicians saying, 'You know what? Rosenbloom's got plenty of money. They're doing well in the NFL. Let *them* take care of it.' I understand part of that, but on the other hand, they [Baltimore politicians] weren't very far-reaching or far-thinking in understanding what was going on. Let's face it: Look at what happened to the town [after the move] when they lost the Colts for 11 years. Look at that. They were back to being nobodies."

Evening Sun columnist Kevin Cowherd was in town, watching all the posturing and mayhem. Maybe Mayor Schaefer was right: Baltimore didn't have the coin to pay for this behemoth. "It's hard for me to say, and I'll tell you why. Again, Schaefer kept insisting they didn't have the money to do this. Until that point [the move], they kept insisting, 'We don't have the money. We can't do it.' I think these teams are just holding up the fans and the cities these days: 'We want a new stadium.' Should taxpayers pay for this? I don't know. If the schools are decrepit—and Baltimore's schools were bad back then—were city leaders justified in saying, 'Hey, we can't do this now'?"

Michael Olesker of the *Morning Sun* didn't have to think about it—No can do:

My perspective was, I'm writing a news column. I went into impoverished neighborhoods every day and saw how people were living. I went to the police districts and the courthouses every day. I went into the schools and City Hall, and I saw how the city was broke. I saw the lines outside the methadone clinics for heroin addicts, and the thought of $170 million to build a playground was exactly the *opposite* of what I felt should be done. Now, if the owners wanted to put up their money—and they didn't— that was a different story. But the city was broke, and we were being blackmailed. There were ways to do this thing. They did it in a better way *later* [in the 1990s], but Irsay had just turned people off. He was just a bull in a china shop. Look—this was going on all over America: If you wanna keep your ballclub, you're gonna have to pay the price for it. But my job was to say, "Yeah, but we got a price on all these other things too." And I just couldn't get past that.

An interested bystander out in Indianapolis saw how Maryland's wallet was being squeezed. "I didn't dive into this as much as I could have, but I do wonder how much the economic situation in the state of Maryland played a role in the government's state legislators saying, 'We're not gonna allocate tax dollars to a new football or baseball stadium,'" speculated JJ Stankevitz, Indianapolis Colts writer and producer of the podcast,

"The Move." "Given that the state was losing business; they were losing residents; Baltimore was struggling as a city. I do wonder if it wasn't just the politicians who didn't want it, but the residents didn't want it either: 'We don't want to allocate our hard-earned money to a football stadium when they have a totally fine place to play.'"

Frontline capitalists told the stadium authority that relying only on private money was a non-starter. Governor Mandel broke out in a sweat. "When bond specialists in Baltimore's banking community frowned on a preliminary consultant's report this summer [1972] that a $110-million complex could be built without public funds, official optimism shrank noticeably," the *Morning Sun* reported in November 1972. "Since then, the Governor and other spokesmen have scaled down their conception of a stadium complex. Six weeks ago, Governor Mandel estimated its cost at about $70 million … 'Maybe it's not feasible, but let's find first what can be done before we prejudge it,' the Governor said in an interview recently."

Real political courage comes in thimblefuls, not gallons. So, the moment a politician starts backing up, he's headed for the door. Forget a launch date; it was looking more and more like the project would get scrapped. Mayor Schaefer heard what the bankers said: a $70-million stadium needed $7 million a year in revenue, just to break even. That didn't deter Hizzoner: "I want to bring more people downtown," he told the *Sun*, "and you only do that by having something they want to see. If the stadium would not bring people downtown, I would lose interest in it." The real danger was blue-collar Baltimore losing interest and a collective knee-jerk from the mighty ministers.

Part Two of the *Morning Sun's* stadium-debate analysis came the next day. After running inventory on some of Memorial Stadium's flaws—splinters in the benches; long queues at the bathrooms; overrated, overpriced food; those damn pillars in the way; the parking nightmare—they got down to the nub of it. Some boneheaded moves back during construction in '54 got them into this pickle:

> The decision to install mostly bench-type seats—decried by one contractor-fan as "a tin cup" move—has come back to haunt the stadium's owners, the city. Failure to provide better parking facilities offers another example of short-sighted economy. The decision to use concrete supports rather than cantilevered decking, while cheaper and putting seating closer to the field, has meant many obstructed seats. And, because of the supports, it is now difficult to substantially improve the seating capacity without expensive work. Because of these obstacles and others, Memorial Stadium's critics insist that despite its relative newness, it is "an old, new stadium."

Jerry Hoffberger of the Orioles and Robert Irsay of the Colts wanted no part in renovations. "Unlike other owners, neither man

has threatened to move their team if a new stadium is not built," the *Sun* indicated. "But professional teams are big businesses, and one sure indication of this is that the Colts and Orioles are now talking about short-term leases at Memorial Stadium until deliberations on a new stadium are completed." They weren't *about* to lock in.

The troglodytes either thought the stadium was fine and dandy or needed a spit-shine. Everyone else preferred the wrecking ball. "It was a dump," admitted John Ziemann, president of the Marching Ravens band. "I hate to say that. I saw it first-hand before many others saw it, all the way to the end [demolition]. Just coming into Memorial Stadium [to prep for the demolition], it had the feel of an old stadium. There had been a lot of patchwork done behind the scenes that people didn't see. You saw the beautiful grass field; it was a great place to watch a baseball game, except for the 'obstructed views.' But they didn't see the people that worked behind the scenes, who worked so hard to keep it up. Like I've always said, it [refurbishing the stadium] was like putting a miniskirt on a 95-year-old woman. It doesn't work."

John Steadman was done with nostalgia. During a 1974 spat with City Comptroller Hyman Pressman about Question P—prohibiting city public funds to pay for a new stadium—Steadman admits he did a 180 on the issue:

> Unfortunately, the illustrious city comptroller, Hyman Pressman, has told some

of his friends this reporter made an attack on him in regard to challenging his stand regarding the Memorial Stadium issue. This is totally erroneous. Pressman also says this writer changed his mind regarding Memorial Stadium. He's right. The view expressed early in the game was that a new park should be built on the present location and that little-used Eastern High School should be torn down and the real estate combined with the acreage at the stadium for a magnificent, modern sports facility. The plan, which had been the idea of John Donahue, was rejected by officials appointed to prepare for a feasibility study. So, after efforts to help erect a new stadium on the present site failed, we revised our thinking. Wherever they want to build it, we're for it. Just let it happen.

Steadman was in. His crony at the *Morning Sun*, Bob Maisel, was still waffling. "The point is, major-league franchises are invaluable to an area. They need adequate facilities. The city doesn't have the money, but Memorial Stadium needs improvements. I would think the state also has a stake in this issue. For instance, it's a state authority which is going to build the dome in New Orleans. I don't know the answer, but there has to be one. The time is long overdue when all parties concerned, state, city, Colts, Orioles, everybody should lock themselves in a room, cooperate, give and take, until a concrete plan emerges."

Tom Marr IV, who had a few cameos in the Troy Lowman documentary, *The Ghosts of 33rd Street*, justifies the stink about Memorial Stadium. "Irsay and Rosenbloom were very justified because it [the stadium] really did not fit anymore. The stadium did not fit; the sightlines did not fit. So, as any business owner will tell you, we needed to do something. That's been the ongoing discussion between cities, fanbases and teams. Just look at Oakland. It's terrible what happened there. But from a business perspective, I'm looking at all these stadiums being built [in the 1970s], I'm seeing the landscape change with what they can do with these stadiums, and I'd want a new stadium too. And I wouldn't want to pay for it because I'm already paying into Memorial Stadium now."

You needed somebody who had been around, seen a bunch of stadiums, good and bad, to give his take on the one at 33rd. Rick Venturi was a Colts assistant coach in Baltimore and Indy, with stints in New Orleans, Cleveland and St. Louis. He says Memorial Stadium was damaged goods by the '70s:

> In terms of playing in the stadium, it was old, but it was so historic for me. Yes, the locker rooms were awful, but they were awful in Cleveland's Municipal Stadium when I went there. But times were changing. They foresaw it. It was gonna be a league of luxury boxes. The new stadiums were gonna be totally different, based on a lot of other things that were involved. Every single place that

I left [Cleveland, St. Louis, Baltimore], it was all about the stadium—including [owner Art] Modell, who was thriving in Cleveland. But he just couldn't get the stadium deal. Like Bob [Irsay], he just couldn't get it. If people really want to know, [Saints owner Tom] Benson would've kept that team in San Antonio after [Hurricane] Katrina if the NFL hadn't stepped in because he was fighting with New Orleans to make it [the Superdome] better.

Charles Euchner wrote a book about cities going hammer and tong at each other: *Playing the Field: Why Sports Teams Move and Cities Fight to Keep Them*. The professor thinks Baltimore was better off looking at the big picture and playing Irsay's game: "A lot of this has to do with timing. It probably would have been fairly cheap for Baltimore, relatively cheap—cheaper than it ended up being—for them to basically give Irsay everything he wanted. The costs of doing business with teams has just exploded. It's gotten so expensive. So, at the time, building a new stadium for the Colts—and I understand about inflation—would have cost $40 or $50 million. I know at that time [mid-'80s], it cost $60 million to build the Humphrey Dome in Minneapolis, and it was done under-budget. The point being that the money seems just out of control, but what's happened in sports is it's just exploded in value, for all kinds of reasons. And so, they [Baltimore] probably could have had a new stadium for far less than they eventually spent."

The money angle had them all twisted in knots. They needed public money to build the thing, but one mention of new taxes and it's off with their heads. A *Morning Sun* editorial in March 1973 went over the same ground and *still* didn't come up with an answer: "The central issue is the consultants' finding that none of the three alternative designs can be financed in the way that the Governor and his spokesmen have said that the complex would be financed: without a penny's worth of taxpayers' money. The prospective revenue from the proposed stadium and attendant construction falls millions of dollars short of the amount needed to float revenue bonds. The dream of a strictly self-supporting combination of stadium, convention hall and parking garage has been dashed, and with it the legislation which empowered the Maryland Sports Complex Authority to finance its own operations with revenue bonds that in no way would involve the faith and credit or taxing power of the state, city or other political subdivisions." Fix the potholes, rehab the schools, hire more cops, build a light rail, hand out free Clark bars—just don't raise our taxes, or you're through.

Progress was like the Western Front during WWI—a stalemate. In May 1973, the Maryland Sports Complex Authority regurgitated old news: Baltimore should build a new stadium downtown and phase out Memorial Stadium. The new joint could be up and running by late 1976. There were caveats: 1)

A domed stadium would be bully, but what about the extra bucks for indoor lighting, air conditioning and the roof ?; 2) Egads, we'll have to raise taxes somewhere to make up the extra; 3) Start first with the 4,500-car parking garage, then work your way up; parking is where the big money is; and 4) Try staging dog racing inside for a few extra bucks. No joke.

Baltimoreans wanted to smash the plan with crab mallets. "Baltimore taxpayers got in their innings on the stadium question last night at a hearing held by the Maryland Sports Complex Authority," the *Morning Sun* informed in late March 1973. "The speakers were unanimously in favor of keeping the sports facility on 33rd Street and against construction of a new stadium downtown on the Camden Yards site." The economists who wrote the report and sat back to watch the squabble offered three choices to resolve this tiff: 1) Renovate Memorial Stadium and build a garage around it, which they said was the wrong way to go; 2) Renovate the stadium and add a downtown convention center ($91.7 million); or 3) Build the Camden dome and a convention center ($114 million). The two killjoys, Hyman Pressman and Harry Kaufman of the Park Board, showed up with thumbs down. "Who needs it?" Pressman wondered. "We have a beautiful stadium on 33rd Street." Kaufman complained, "They told us the Civic Center would help the downtown and the hotels and the convention business. Has it? Three hotels have closed since it was built."

Fans in other cities didn't riot when preseason- and regular-season tickets were slapped together; other cities had built concrete mixing bowls for their ballclubs with no insurrection; but Baltimore fans got misty-eyed looking at the stadium façade out front: "Time Will Not Dim the Glory of Their Deeds." They couldn't let go of the old gal. "The people of Baltimore DID NOT want to give up Memorial Stadium," Tom Marr IV professed. "If the Colts hadn't left, I don't know if [Oriole Park at] Camden Yards goes through. It goes back to [Hyman] Pressman. He *can't* be seen as a villain in this because he was doing what his constituency was reflecting back to him." The loud ones living around the ballpark, especially.

Don't ask commoners to pull out their wallets for playpens. "Much of the population is not sports fans," remarked longtime Baltimore sportscaster Scott Garceau. "When you ask them, 'If you get to vote on it, would you like to contribute money so Bob Irsay can make *more* money?' Even if it's a good owner, like [Ravens owner] Steve Bisciotti, and you're working over at Sparrows Point, and they ask you if you want to take some of your money and give billionaire Steve Bisciotti a new stadium to make even more money, you say no way. They just voted one of those down in Kansas City. It doesn't surprise me that something like that would be voted down because I would think history would demonstrate more times than not that, when it goes to a general ballot, a lot of people aren't sports fans, and they don't want any money diverted to sports teams and owners who already make a pretty good profit."

The heavies pushing the new stadium had two big worries: how to scrape together enough cash and what to do with the mausoleum if they abandoned it. So they cooked up another committee. "The mayor [William Donald Schaefer] has offered a few tentative proposals for the site, but he has been more specific—and emphatic—in promising what won't replace the 19-year-old stadium," the *Evening Sun* detailed in late May 1973. "Much in line with results of a neighborhood survey by the Memorial Stadium Task Force, he [Schaefer] has repeatedly said that low-income housing wouldn't be considered for the 31-acre site. He has also discounted the possibility of a shopping center-commercial complex on the assumption that it would irreparably damage the already not-so-healthy businesses along Greenmount Avenue."

The sports authority hit the pause button in late February 1974, about two years after getting jazzed up about a dome in Camden. "The Maryland Sports Complex Authority will not proceed with its plans—this year—to build a $114-million stadium-convention center in downtown Baltimore, authority spokesmen said yesterday," the *Morning Sun* reported. "Citing Governor Mandel's refusal to support a bill in the General Assembly that would require $60 million in state-backed, general-obligation bonds for the sports complex, and blaming the Baltimore teachers' strike, the gasoline shortage, and a 'poisonous' post-Watergate political atmosphere, William Boucher III, the project's chief advocate, said that yesterday's decision represented a one-year setback."

Another year blown. Mandel nixed state-backed revenue bonds, so there was a $60-million hole. What's more, they wanted 20- to 30-year signed leases from the Colts and Orioles BEFORE anything got built or renovated. So, here's all they had—a slick consultants' study about a pie in the sky; hot air; no action; and the same problem leering at them. "The sports complex, which grew more grandiose as the plans developed over the past few years, seems to have collapsed partially of its own weight," the *Morning Sun* observed. "When the consultants unveiled their proposal last March [1973], it included a 4,500-car parking garage, a convention facility and a 70,000-seat domed stadium. But until Monday [Feb. 26, 1974], the financing plan was never made clear. 'We considered full state funding, we looked at a lot of the alternatives, but because of either policy or regulations, we weren't able to swing it,' Mr. Boucher said."

Right after Memorial Day 1974, Baltimore found out the sports authority had been busy the last three months—playing Crazy Eights and ordering takeout. Not a speck of work was done. "The Maryland Sports Complex Authority has been 'in limbo' since February [1974], when Governor Mandel refused to support the use of state-backed bonds to finance the project, the executive director said today," the *Evening Sun* revealed in late May 1974. "Moreover, spokesmen for the Colts and the Orioles said that there haven't been any negotiations on a long-term contract for the use of the proposed complex since January. Nonetheless, Mr. [executive director Don]

McPhail insisted that the project is still 'very much alive … there's no indication that the Governor or Mayor have had cold feet.'"

The consultants' study collected mold and mildew.

. . .

Over at the ballyard, Colts owner Bob Irsay was doing his schtick. The Roman-candle routines were great entertainment and meat for reporters. Philadelphia 1974 was a real hoot. E.M. Swift covered the inferno in his 1986 *Sports Illustrated* article, "Now You See Him, Now You Don't":

> Irsay's first great public explosion came in the third game of the 1974 season, in Philadelphia. Marty Domres was the Colts quarterback, a player Irsay had once humiliated in front of his teammates by shouting, "Nice game, Marty. Too bad most of the passes you completed were to the wrong team." In the third quarter, Irsay, prowling the sideline, tugged on [head coach Howard] Schnellenberger's arm and said he should replace Domres with Bert Jones. Schnellenberger declined, adding—and here history becomes a little fuzzy—either that Irsay should mind his own business or that Irsay should attempt an anatomical impossibility while minding his own business. Whatever, Irsay took offense. "He just wanted to be part of the team …" recalls Mike Curtis. "He really wanted us to like him. That's why

> he was down on the field to begin with. And Howard was no diplomat. It was just bad luck."

> Irsay, apparently inebriated, according to several team sources, stormed into the dressing room after the game—the team's third straight defeat—and announced to the players that Schnellenberger was fired and that [Joe] Thomas would be their new coach. The team almost lynched him. In the coach's office, Schnellenberger asked Ernie Accorsi, the Colts' public relations director, what the ruckus was about. "I think he just fired you," Accorsi replied. Irsay charged in and confirmed it. Then he left in his limo. Thomas, meanwhile, couldn't get into the dressing room; he was held at bay by a security guard who was under orders not to open the room to the press. "There's a guy named Thomas demanding to get in," the guard told Accorsi. Thomas was right behind him. "What's going on here?" "Irsay just fired Howard," Accorsi replied. "What?!" "That's not the worst news," Accorsi said. "He named you as head coach." "What?!"

Marty Domres provided a vanilla account in *Sundays at 2:00 With the Baltimore Colts*: "The next week I tried to play against Green Bay and didn't play very well. So Irsay was hollering for Bert [Jones] to start the third game, at Philadelphia, but I played the first half. They were ahead by something like 17-10 when I threw an interception to Joe 'Birdman' Lavendar, who ran down the sideline for a touchdown. My receiver, Ollie Smith, had slipped and Lavendar picked it off. When I came to the sidelines, Irsay was there hollering at Schnellenberger. Howard took off his headset, threw it on the ground, and said something to Irsay. Irsay stood there, flushed, holding one of those sideline cups, telling Howard he wanted Bert Jones in the game. Howard replied that I was going in. I went in for another series, we punted, the Eagles went down the field and scored, and the half ended. After the game, Irsay told Joe Thomas to fire Schnellenberger. He was gone that day."

What Schnellenberger told Irsay on the sideline when Bob tried to play coach went something like, "F-yourself. I'm the coach. I make those decisions." Former Colts great Lydell Mitchell was in the locker room for the fireworks. Here's what he remembers:

Typically, what happens is, you get in the locker room, the coach gives his little speech after the game. Obviously, no one was happy we lost. Howard went back to his dressing room, the door burst open, and here comes Robert Irsay and his two henchmen with him, his bodyguards. They came in with him, one on each side, and he [Irsay] made an announcement: "Howard Schnellenberger is no longer your coach. Joe Thomas is gonna be your coach." As soon as the door opened, that's what he said. And then, he went in the back, and you could hear these guys [Irsay and Schnellenberger] screaming and hollering. And after a little bit, you saw Howard being escorted out of the locker room by those two guys [the bodyguards]. That's how it happened.

Schnellenberger was rather tight-lipped about the whole affair until John Bansch of the *Indianapolis Star* pried him open in February 1984. First off, Howie Hoss wasn't about to cotton to some soused nabob telling him his business. "I had some dialogue with Irsay before the season and told him I was going to play Domres the first three games," Schnellenberger told Bansch. "I also told him if Domres didn't get the job done, I was going to play Bert. I said no to Irsay because he made his request in front of our team with Mike Curtis, the captain of the defense and the oldest of the established veterans, standing next to me. If I had submitted to him at that time, I would have lost control of the team."

Then he put the hammer down:

Irsay told the team he was firing Schnellenberger before he informed the coach. The owner made the announcement in the dressing room. The players responded by "almost attacking" Irsay. Schnellenberger heard the commotion, came out of his office to see what was going on and then was told he no longer had a job with Baltimore. "He [Irsay] can take a franchise down quicker than the time it takes a rock to fall from a mountain top to the earth," observed Schnellenberger between puffs on his ever-present pipe. "Once upon a time, the Colts were a proud, winning organization. The people of Indianapolis will rue the day they ever made him an offer to move his team to their city. Writers tell people about the indiscretions of the players and coaches. I wish someone would tell the world about Irsay."

Baltimore reporters were on the case.

All-Pro center Bill Curry was in his prime during the Rosenbloom '60s, but got dispatched to Houston in '72 by Irsay and Thomas. Before the Colts shipped Johnny U out to San Diego in '73, he got a demotion—benchwarmer. Curry remembers the day it happened:

> I was in the locker room one day. It was our off day, Monday or Tuesday. And Unitas was there, getting some treatment. The phone rings, and the trainer says, "It's for you, John." So, Unitas goes and takes the phone. Then he walks back about 30 seconds later. [Offensive lineman] Danny Sullivan is sitting there—and Sully is usually our comedian to make everybody lighten up—and he says, "Well, what was it, John?" Unitas's words were, "I'm down." "Whaddaya mean, you're down?" He said, "I'm benched." So, the greatest player in football got benched with a 30-second phone call—and he got traded with a 30-second phone call. And *that* was the

culture. So, imagine how the rest of us felt. It was just the kind of thing that never would have happened in the previous [Rosenbloom] administration.

After Irsay sacked Howard Schnellenberger, Joe Thomas bombed as HC. The Colts went 2-12, so Irsay hired a real coach, Ted Marchibroda, who engineered a U-turn: 10-4 and the AFC East title. "Ted Marchibroda took over as coach the next year [1975], and the team, with [Bert] Jones at quarterback, went from 2-12 to 10-4 and won the first of three straight division titles," E.M. Swift described in *Sports Illustrated*. "These were the Irsay glory years, but they were nonetheless turbulent. Before the opening game of the 1976 season, for instance, Marchibroda resigned subsequent to an Irsayian locker-room tantrum after an exhibition game loss in Detroit. Irsay dressed down the team with such malice that 16-year-old [son] Jimmy [Irsay] climbed on the team bus afterward to apologize. Curiously, Marchibroda held Thomas responsible for the tirade, and he told Irsay in a meeting aboard Irsay's yacht—nicknamed, humbly, The Mighty I—that either Thomas had to go, or he would. Irsay sided with Thomas. When the news of Marchibroda's resignation reached the players, there was such a furor that Irsay told Thomas to ask Marchibroda back. Marchibroda returned, the Colts won their division again, and after the season it was Thomas who was fired."

Son Jimmy did indeed play the adult after Irsay blew a gasket in Detroit in '76. The *New*

York Times gave space to the bus incident in a May 2021 article titled "Sins of the Father: What Jim Irsay Learned Watching His Dad Cripple the Colts":

Sitting silently in the locker room that night [in Detroit], keeping his mouth shut amid the melee, was the owner's 16-year-old son. Jimmy Irsay was used to scenes like this, his father's fury boiling over, the coaches incensed, the players appalled. But this one grew especially heated. At one point veteran tight end Ray Chester rose to his feet and began to speak, trying to keep his cool while the owner lost his. "Hit him, Ray!" his teammates shouted. "Hit him!" Chester didn't. But that doesn't mean he didn't want to. Eventually, the boss stormed out. The players boarded the bus. Marchibroda quit. A few assistants refused to return. And Jimmy sat there alone, slumped on a bench in the locker room, sobbing. "It was like your older brothers getting in a fight with your dad," he remembers. Ten minutes later he climbed aboard the bus, shaking with nerves, and wiped away the tears. He looked the players in the eye and apologized for his dad's outburst. "We're a football team," Jimmy told them. "And emotions got in the way of that tonight." It was, a coach would say years later, "a tremendous thing for a teenager to do."

Again, All-Pro Colts running back Lydell Mitchell was there, and the boys stood by Marchibroda: "Obviously, we weren't playing well the whole preseason. Coming off '75, when we had a magic year, we got into the following year with a lot of high hopes. So, Mr. Irsay was upset. Him and Ted Marchibroda got into it. An argument ensued, and before you knew it, Ted's out. And we backed our coach. The one who gets the most credit [for the player protest] is the quarterback [Bert Jones] because they are the leaders of the team. But it was all of us who felt that way, that we were going to get behind our coach because he was doing an outstanding job—Ted Marchibroda. We wanted to support him, and we won out. And we went on to do well for the rest of the season [10-4 and a playoff berth]."

If nothing else, *Evening Sun* columnist Phil Jackman was acerbic. He hatched nicknames for Thomas and Irsay: Joe Promise and Bob, the red-faced owner. He skewered both during the Marchibroda resignation impasse:

Obviously Promise thought he had another malleable assistant when he gave up a 3-9 career as a coach and hired Marchibroda, but he found out differently once he headed into his tampering act again. The typical Joe protestations—"I hired the man to do a job and I intend to let him do it"—don't even make it by the kids these days. And when Marchibroda backed an assistant [O-line coach Whitey Dovell] who was on Joe's bad list, it was time to get Bob, the red-faced owner in here to do the dirty work. Irsay was only too happy to do the Nagasaki bit on Marchibroda because he had Hiroshima'd Schnellenberger, remember, and that was great fun. Already upset that Joe had spent the off-season sending good people away ("All I see is players going out the door, none coming through it"), Ted said he wouldn't work under the conditions. Irsay and Promise ran themselves right into a box. You can't buy class!

Sowing chaos—the Irsay Way. Even a concussion didn't make defensive tackle Joe Ehrmann woozy enough to miss Irsay's harangue in Detroit: "In the 1976 preseason game when Bert Jones got hurt, I got knocked out, too, and was out cold for quite a while," he said in *Sundays at 2:00 With the Baltimore Colts.* "When I came to in the locker room, there was a giant fight going on. Irsay came in and started screaming all kinds of names at various players. It developed into a big eruption. Stools were thrown, and it got really heated. I was sitting there, still disoriented, and I started hyperventilating from the chaos that was going on between Irsay and the players."

The demon in the bottle fueled much of the bedlam. That, and Irsay's football peabrain. Lydell Mitchell eschewed details of Irsay's rant and focused on the disease: "I don't recall all of it, only that he [Irsay] was upset because of the way we were playing. When I look back on things, I understand more of what went

down because Mr. Irsay had a sickness, and it depended on what part of the day you caught him, it might be worse. So, I imagine during the game, he was doing his thing. And he never really understood football—let's put it that way. Your emotions are always different if you're drinking and you're an alcoholic. Your mood swings and stuff. So, he was going through a whole bunch of that stuff, I'm sure, stuff that a lot of us probably at the beginning didn't realize. So, he went off, and that's what happened. Ted was out."

Then the players told Irsay and Thomas: Hell, no; no coach, no practice. Irsay caved, which prompted this shot by Phil Jackman: "To hear Mr. Promise tell it after the hatchet had been removed from betwixt Ted Marchibroda's shoulder blades, the general manager was never guilty of interfering with the coach in the performance of his duty ... Which does not explain how come Marchibroda and the Grim Reaper got in such a heated shouting match last May that it ended up as a shoving contest. What was the subject of discussion, who was going to spring for lunch?"

In the land between John Steadman's ears, we find that the team boycott isn't what made Irsay fold. It was Steadman. "Unknown to anyone, I called [Commissioner Pete] Rozelle in New York and explained the situation," Steadman modestly professed in *From Colts to Ravens.* "He obviously didn't want to get involved in the internal problems of a team. It wasn't the regular role of a commissioner. But I told him it was in the best interests of the league and certainly of Baltimore that it be resolved. He realized it was important and worked quietly in his usually effective manner and achieved solution—the return of Marchibroda for the opening game of the season against the New England Patriots in Foxboro." Steadman had gone to the phone booth, put on his cape and dialed up Rozelle. Remember how he vanquished Tampa, sending out a "Thou shalt not covet" Western Union to the other owners.

Former *Indianapolis Star* sportswriter Mike Chappell has covered the Indy Colts for so long, they named their media room after him. About the Irsay stereotype—loud, irrational, bombastic, tanked, unhinged—he says: "Some of it is very accurate. Certainly about stealing the Colts out of Baltimore. He did. Just from personal knowledge, yes, he had demons. And they followed him, and they were demons that too often got the better of him. He was volatile, as far as meddling with the team. 'Meddling' is a strange word because if it's your team, you can do what the hell you want. But he was always getting rid of coaches at the drop of a hat. There were times that Jimmy [Irsay] had to intercept him at halftime of a game on Sunday because he was gonna fire the coach. And Jimmy calmed him down. Whenever there's a reputation—good or bad—there are reasons for that. And a lot of it with Bob was true."

The *Atlanta Journal* ran a feature in late April 1984 on Indy's big win in getting the Colts. One section highlighted some of Irsay's gaffes in Baltimore:

Colt fans, once among the league's most ardent, had grown vicious. It was all Robert Irsay's fault, they charged. Since Irsay, a Skokie, Ill., contractor, bought the Los Angeles Rams and traded them for the Colts in '72, Baltimore had seen precious little excellence, and more than a little bungling. To wit: Irsay hired Joe Thomas as general manager, and Thomas first benched, then traded the hallowed Johnny Unitas. Irsay fired coach Howard Schnellenberger, now the toast of college football [winning the national championship in '84], at halftime [sic]. Irsay alienated such players as Lydell Mitchell, John Dutton and Roger Carr, all of whom were dispatched. Irsay hired Frank Kush as coach, and Kush insisted upon drafting John Elway after Elway said he wouldn't play for the Colts. Soon a civic joke, Irsay began making noises about moving his franchise to Phoenix. Those players he hadn't alienated were ready to go anywhere.

Irsay wasn't qualified to ref a flag football game, but there he was, in Philly again, trying to orchestrate strategy in '81 against the Eagles: "[Mike] McCormack was the coach when Irsay began calling the plays from the coach's booth during a 38-13 loss to the Eagles on Nov. 15, 1981, one of the low points in NFL history," E.M. Swift explained in "Now You See Him, Now You Don't." "'[Irsay] couldn't have told you how many players there were on the field, never mind what plays we had,' recalls [Bert] Jones, who was shuffled in and out with [second-string QB Greg] Landry. 'All he was trying to do was embarrass the coaches and the players. When he told me to run, I threw. When he told me to throw left, I ran right.'"

Popular Baltimore TV and radio sportscaster Scott Garceau was recounting some of the lunacy during the Irsay years in Baltimore. "How about the time in Philadelphia when he put the headset on and started calling the plays?" he recalled. "He walks into the Colts coaching booth and says, 'Give me the headset. I'm gonna call the plays.' I remember we [at WMAR-TV] had shots of him with the headset kinda crooked. He's sitting in there, and the story I got was Bert [Jones] goes in the huddle and says, 'Guys, you're not gonna believe this, but the old man is up there, on the headset, calling the plays.' And Bert said, 'Here's what we're gonna do. When he calls pass, we're gonna run; when he calls run, we're gonna pass.' The word was they went 65 yards down the field and scored a touchdown, doing exactly the opposite because Bert wasn't gonna put up with the shenanigans."

This little ditty from Warner Hessler of the *Daily Press* (Newport News, Va.) illustrates the sentiment the players had for the boss: "One of the funniest stories concerning Irsay happened during the late 1970s when Ted Marchibroda was the coach and Bert Jones the quarterback. On this particular day, Jones was fumigating the city with his bad play. Irsay, in a fit of rage, marched into the coaching box in the press box, grabbed the field telephone,

and demanded to talk to Jones. While Irsay ranted and raved, Jones walked over to the trainer's bag, pulled out a pair of scissors, and cut the phone lines."

Irsay's mouth was a Vesuvius. In *From Colts to Ravens*, John Steadman described Irsay reaching new heights of audacity:

After an exhibition game in Atlanta, his second season of ownership [1973], I was using a wall telephone in the press box. I had phoned the newspaper office to make sure all the copy had cleared. Along came Irsay, who was having trouble with his equilibrium. When he saw me, it was as if he felt compelled to say something. "The gamblers got Marty," he said. I assumed he meant Marty Domres, the quarterback. Such an assertion was totally irresponsible and without any semblance of truth. Domres was a tremendous competitor who gave the game a full and honest commitment.

Probably tanked to the gills. An alarm bell went off in Steadman's head. "What Irsay said about 'the gamblers having Marty' was the worst thing that can ever be said about an athlete," Steadman explained. "And it was totally inaccurate, a drunken lie. The next afternoon, a Sunday, I reached Jim Kensil, who was Rozelle's assistant, at his Long Island home and told him of the erroneous and reckless accusation of the previous night … Talking about a player being involved with a gambler, when no such thing had occurred, was reason for banishing an owner from the league or at least suspending him. Naturally, Kensil was concerned and said he would see that Irsay was talked to and told not to invent such charges."

Longtime Baltimore Colts fan Tom Marr IV said the media declared open-season on Bob Irsay: "He [Irsay] clearly was not well-liked. He didn't make himself warm and fuzzy. Aloof, that's what he was. I know [John] Steadman hated him, and he hated Steadman. My father [radio broadcaster Tom Marr] got along famously with Carroll Rosenbloom. A lot of the Baltimore media saw through Robert Irsay once he got there. But it's Joe Thomas that really pissed people off. They [the Colts leaders] didn't explain their vision. Obviously, Irsay didn't help himself; he got drunk at every game. Irsay wasn't gregarious like Carroll Rosenbloom. So, as far as the business perspective, with their advertisers and the press, they didn't understand this guy Irsay at all."

According to Lydell Mitchell, the formula for Irsay was simple: Get some help running the business end of it and stay off the field. "He [Irsay] didn't understand football; he didn't know much about it," Lydell declared. "He was a very rich man who could afford to own a team, but he didn't know much about the game. So, he relied on other people to take care of the business aspects of it. What he should have done is let the football people—like Joe Thomas—run it and kind of stay out of the way and take care of the other things that he needed to do."

He couldn't remember names to save his hide, so everybody got "Tiger." One time Colts safety Bruce Laird pranked the boss. Ryan Mavity picks up the story in his essay, "'Ghost to the Post' Still Haunts Colts":

Safety Bruce Laird once decided to have a little fun with this trait of Irsay's by switching his nameplate with that of 5-foot-5-inch kick returner Howard Stevens, who was black, while Laird was 6-foot-2 and white. "He would come in with six, eight, 10 people. They're all probably Chicago people, come into the locker room. He really was never around except for games. He really didn't know us. He knew our numbers. He called everybody, 'Hey, Tiger' because he didn't know who we were. So, I said, 'Watch this. I'm just gonna [mess] with him.' I put tape over my cubicle and I go sit over at Howard's thing. So, he [Irsay] looks at me and goes, 'Hey, Howard, great game tonight.' I go, 'No, Bob, I'm Bruce. I was just coming over to sit in Howard's stool for a while.' Everybody is in the background, laughing their ass off."

Cartoonists went to town lampooning the guy. "When you're doing sports cartooning, there's not that many people that you can kind of pick out and use almost as a cartoon character," explained Mike Ricigliano, long an institution in Baltimore as a cartoonist, even starting out with Steadman at the *News American*. "I read a book recently by Garry

Trudeau that had Trump as a character in the 'Doonesbury' strip, and it's because he was that strong and funny personality that set him off as himself, not doing anything else. And I think Irsay was that. I could probably name five people, total, in my sports cartooning career that were like that: [Cincinnati Reds owner] Marge Schott, maybe someone like that, or [baseball star] Albert Bell. And Irsay is the best of those, from a cartooning standpoint. He just embodied all these do-it-wrong attributes that made him a guy I could plug into cartoons even if he wasn't the subject of the cartoon."

Folks who migrated in to Baltimore, like *Evening Sun* columnist Kevin Cowherd, saw the running soap opera Irsay had going: "What I sensed when I got here [in 1981] was that Irsay was mismanaging everything. He had been for a number of years shopping the team around. So, Baltimore fans and journalists knew that this guy wasn't happy here. He wasn't happy because of the same reasons [as Rosenbloom's]. The stadium was antiquated; he didn't want to deal with this anymore. Plus, he was an irrational guy. He was probably an alcoholic. And so, there was this erratic leadership, coupled with the fact that he was *so* resentful of that stadium. As with Rosenbloom, Irsay just wasn't getting what he wanted from city officials. Again, I thought Memorial Stadium was the driving force. And if they had built a new stadium for him, he probably would've stayed."

Even a guy like JJ Stankevitz, who produced a podcast for Jim Irsay and the Indy

Colts—"The Move"—knocked Irsay's scorched-earth approach:

I did think it was the way he churned through coaches and gave these chaotic press conferences, which were some of the touchpoints with the locals. You had a lot of people who came through the organization who didn't care for him who spread the word out to the community. But I think the other part of it was, "These are *our* Colts, and you're trying to move them." That was always gonna poison the relationship between him and the fans. As soon as he started looking around and because he was a Chicago businessman—and he wasn't local—I do wonder if Carroll Rosenbloom got more of a pass because he was a Baltimore guy, and he owned the team during the Unitas era. Then, here comes this businessman from Chicago who trades Johnny Unitas and then a couple of years later starts looking to move the team. It was like, "Hold on a second. Who *is* this guy? And why is he trying to mess with our Colts?" That probably had a pretty profound effect on fans and the media, who were speaking to the fans. If I had to guess, it was like, "Here comes this outsider, trying to take away our team."

It was best to duck Irsay when he was on the rampage. Longtime Colts assistant coach Rick Venturi said Fridays were a crapshoot:

"I don't know what the stereotype [of Irsay] was, but he was volatile. And if things didn't go good—and they didn't go good for a lot of time early in my career there—you were in mortal fear of your job, that's for sure. We always had a little standing joke during the offseason: Make sure you're outta here Friday at noon because if he comes in, and he's on the warpath, somebody's probably gonna go."

A 2021 *New York Times* piece about Jim Irsay—"Sins of the Father: What Jim Irsay Learned Watching His Dad Cripple the Colts"—presents a blooper reel: "It's [the Colts-Rams swap] a transaction that seems implausible today: one NFL franchise for another, no strings attached. But that's how Irsay entered the league. And once he did, it didn't take long for one of the NFL's proudest franchises to begin to flounder. The Colts won five games in Irsay's first season as owner, four in his second, just two in his third. Johnny Unitas was traded. Other franchise pillars were cut. Irsay's relationship soured, first with his players and coaches, eventually with the local press. Stars fumed over his penny-pinching—according to that [1986] *SI* story ["Now You See Him, Now You Don't"], Irsay used to insist on keeping the hot tub at the team facility turned off during the season as a means of saving money [recall owner Mrs. Phelps in *Major League*]. He was a nasty negotiator who'd toss out cheap insults during contract talks. On top of that, he drank too much. He lied. He exaggerated. He blamed. He rarely remembered players' names, instead calling them 'Tiger.' [Rick] Venturi says he'd fire someone in a state of heavy inebriation, then forget about it the next day."

The Carroll Rosenbloom crew was agog at how Irsay mucked up a good thing in short order. Marching Ravens band president John Ziemann thinks Irsay lacked the finesse to handle a football team:

> You're dealing with a man that wasn't totally there, a man that thought he was running his air-conditioning business, that had *no* right to run a professional football team. The same way he dealt with his air-conditioning business, that's how he dealt with the Baltimore Colts. In the air-conditioning business, you didn't need public relations. Here, with the Colts, you did. He should've worked with [Mayor] William Donald Schaefer; Ernie Accorsi should've been totally in charge—let Ernie run it. And sit back, knowing what the hell was going on, but staying out of the spotlight. Don't make yourself a target; but you made yourself a target, the way you acted. This is what he should have done. That way, he wouldn't be viewed the way he is in history now.

Irsay was heavy into talks with Indy when—kaboom—the *Morning Sun* put out the "Jekyll-Hyde" feature, March 4, 1984. Never a stolid sort, Irsay went bananas. The headline was enough: **Chicago's Jekyll Becomes Hyde in Baltimore**. Doubtful that he read Robert Louis Stevenson's *Strange Case* *of Dr. Jekyll and Mr. Hyde*, but he might have caught the movie version with Spencer Tracy. No doubt the bourbon came out early that Sunday:

> In Chicago, where he made his fortune as a heating and air-conditioning contractor and where he has lived almost all his life, Mr. Irsay has a good reputation as a loyal friend and man of his word, as an ingratiating salesman who loves to play host, as a generous contributor to charities and as a tough, brilliant businessman respected for the quality of his companies' work. But in Baltimore, where he has jetted in and out as the Colts' absentee owner the last 12 years, "The Mighty I" has struck a decidedly different profile—as a loud, brutish, erratic man who cannot be taken at his word, as an interfering, miserly, incompetent manager, as a man who thrives on turmoil, no matter the cost.

Robert Benjamin and Vito Stellino revealed more dirt than dazzle. Two men had worked for Irsay in Chicago. "You can go all over the map with him," former executive VP Gene Bednarz began. "He can be charming, gift-giving, extra gregarious, reward people who've been with him only a short while, and then can react irrationally to the slightest thing from people who've given him years of service." Donald Lewis, who toiled for Irsay for 22 years, warned, "He changes his mind one minute to another, with the snap of a finger. He can put on that aggressive face first thing in the morning. If there's going to be a fight, he wants to throw the first punch." An NFL executive cut to the chase: "He's pictured as a buffoon and that's really the way he acts. You'll drive yourself crazy trying to figure him out rationally."

Who knows how much nature, nurture and booze comprised the Bob Irsay the public saw. The National Institutes of Health can explain some of the buffoonery: "Heavy alcohol use directly affects brain function and alters various brain chemical (i.e., neurotransmitter) and hormonal systems known to be involved in the development of many common mental disorders (e.g., mood and anxiety disorders). Thus, it is not surprising that alcoholism can manifest itself in a broad range of psychiatric symptoms and signs ... Mood disturbances (which frequently are not severe enough to qualify as "disorders") are arguably the most common psychiatric complaint among treatment-seeking alcoholic patients, affecting upwards of 80 percent of alcoholics at some point in their drinking careers."

Not everybody saw Irsay as Shrek on meth. Irsay had some fans outside Baltimore. One of them, David Frick, was Indianapolis's chief negotiator who helped forge the Colts-Indy deal. Frick was crucial in getting that package done. There's a wide gulf between his view of Irsay and Baltimore's:

> I would say a 180-degree difference. Over the years, I've gotten to know several owners of professional sports franchises;

as a lawyer, I represented several of them. If you're an owner of an NFL franchise, you're a big deal. I think Mr. Irsay cherished being a big deal. I don't know what caused the fallout between Robert Irsay and the people in Baltimore, the political leadership, the community leadership and sportswriters. I did *not* see behavior [from Irsay] like it was rumored to be like in Baltimore. Most of my dealings were with [Colts lawyer] Mike Chernoff, but there were a few occasions when I dealt directly with Bob Irsay. I found him to be a dealmaker, searching for a deal. And I don't mean this in a critical way, but he wanted it to be known that he owned the franchise, and I respect that. The community doesn't own the franchise; the owner does. I didn't feel that he was overreaching in our negotiation process. After coming here [with the Colts], he plugged into our community very well. The Colts have been *incredibly* generous to our community. They have their players in the neighborhoods on the off-day Tuesdays, and they've done that for years. They have given *sizeable* gifts to the hospital system here, so Mr. Irsay and his son [Jim] have done a marvelous job of inculcating the right values our community cherishes and ensuring them with all of us.

One *Indianapolis Star* writer, Robin Miller took Bob Irsay to task for years but gave him his due when Irsay passed in 1997: "No player or coach ever was safe from this man with little tact and less rationale, and more often than not his knee-jerk personnel changes and post-games diatribes were fueled by alcohol. But the sobering truth about Robert Irsay's 13 years in our city is that he brought us a National Football League franchise, created many charitable contributions, helped build a dynamic Downtown and was a good citizen … But even though his playing days at Illinois and war heroism are said to be creative writing for the media guide, the fact remains that Irsay pumped a lot of vitality into Indianapolis. He gradually loosened his grip and purse strings, which enabled the Colts to finally flourish and win a place in this city's heart."

There were rare iconoclasts back in Baltimore with a kind word for Bob Irsay. "A lot of people didn't like him, but when I first met him—and I learned years ago to call everybody 'Mister'—he said, 'No, no. You can call me Bob, and you can call her [Irsay's wife] Harriet. And that's the way it's gonna be,'" extolled Len Burrier, aka The Big Wheel. "And every time I'd see him, I'd say, 'Hey, Bob. How you doin'?' And he'd shake my hand. And Harriet, at Christmas time, she would give me a box of all kinds of Colts stuff—scarves, sweaters for my wife, things like that. Which was great."

The Mick, The Babe, Irsay—they couldn't beat the sauce. ABC News ran a story in 2014 about Jim Irsay's long battle with the bottle. They chatted with Jim Thompson, the owner of an Indy pub, Daddy Jack's. "I knew his father [Bob Irsay]," Thompson recalled. "He used to come in a lot. I never saw him sober.

I'd go to shake his hand, and he'd grab my hand and pull me over the table and knock over glasses, and I was like, 'Oh, my God.' He was not really that nice of a man, to tell you the truth. Jimmy's a lot nicer than his dad. I was expecting the worst, and getting to know Jimmy kind of changed my mind on the family. And they have been very good for this community."

But then there's this—a heart not completely riddled with carbuncles. The Big Wheel, the Colts super fan who led the cheers in the upper deck, told of a trip he made to Miami, courtesy of Robert Irsay:

He [Irsay] invited [his friend] Bud Craven and myself to a Colts game in Miami [Nov. 22, 1976]. He flew us down for free and put us up in a hotel. They got a picture of me standing out in the Atlantic Ocean with a beer in my hand. [Former Colts great Art] Donovan and a couple bar owners were also down there. Bob had a boat down there [The Mighty I]. I said, "Man, I wish I could hop a ride on it." So, Harriet calls us up and says, "Hey, you guys wanna go to the game with us?" We said, "Yeah!" She says, "OK, we're gonna leave at such-and-such time, and we're at this address." I was all excited. I said, "Bud! Get ready, get ready!" We got a cab, got in the cab and told the driver, "Look. We gotta get to this address. I don't care how you get there, but do it *fast*." He said, "No problem, sir." It was right across the road. So,

we got there, got on the boat, and it was humungous. They had shrimp that big [makes a fist], steaks and anything you wanted to eat. Some of Irsay's buddies were on there. We were on the boat, schmoozing with all of them, and they had scantily-clad waitresses. It was great. We were drinking all the way to the stadium, and apparently, Irsay sent somebody out beforehand with a bunch of booze and went to the drawbridge operators: "Hey, man, we're gonna be coming through here at such-and-such time." So, we never stopped at the drawbridge; we just cruised right on to the stadium. And the stadium [the Orange Bowl] was right next to the dock. When we came out [after the game, a 17-16 Monday-night win], we found a bus that was going back our way [to the hotel]. We got back to the hotel, and me and Bud go down to the bar, and there's Donovan and a couple other old Colts players. We're sittin' around, shootin' the breeze, and pretty soon, here come Bob and Harriet through the door. He [Irsay] got up to the bar, and he says, "Harriet, you got any money?" She says, "Yeah, I got about $500." He says, "Put it on the bar. That's for these guys. They can drink till it's gone." So, yeah—they treated me well.

But there weren't nearly enough Big Wheels, Loudys and superfans to offset the bad vibes. Irsay was ramping up for a full-blown F-4 twister, headed toward Charm City.

CHAPTER 10

HANG 'IM HIGH

Robert Irsay went crackers when the *Morning Sun* put out the "Jekyll-Hyde" feature in early March 1984. The two reporters, Robert Benjamin and Vito Stellino, dug up enough facts, quotes and anecdotes to make Irsay almost look bipolar. Relations between Irsay and the press were now akin to Nixon and the *Washington Post*. The *Chicago Tribune* scored a major interview with Irsay in June 1984, almost three months after the Indy move. On friendlier turf, Irsay let it rip. The *Trib* asked him if he felt the Baltimore press "mistreated" him:

"Oh, yes. They [the two who wrote "Jekyll-Hyde"] called about 200 of my friends, just looking for something to put on me. They saw me having a drink, and they called me a drunkard. Well, then their governor is a drunk. He drinks. They went back eight years to the Philadelphia game [1981] where I called the coach [Mike McCormack] to ask him if he could alternate Bert Jones and

Greg Landry [he also called in plays from the press box]. McCormack said fine. Well, we spent three minutes alternating the quarterbacks, and we confused the defense and we scored a touchdown. We were losing, 31-6, and we wanted to try something different. The press goes back and picks those items up."

The Mighty I was mighty confused. The Philly game in '81 saw Irsay grabbing a coach's headset and sending down cockamamie plays that Bert Jones ignored. The *Sun* got it right.

Reporters are a cynical bunch, so covering Bob Irsay was easy pickings. Veteran *Evening Sun* columnist Kevin Cowherd describes the Irsay-press relationship in one word. "Troubled. That comes to mind immediately. I think he [Irsay] tried initially to be cordial to the media, and he felt he kept getting hammered by them. But the guy was *so* erratic. And we in the media sensed it. He was just tough to deal with. He was abrasive. He had vendettas; he would freeze out certain members of the media; he would make sure that certain members of the media didn't get scoops: 'Hey, we're about to sign this player; this guy's on the injured reserve list.' He would make sure certain people didn't get that. And he had some issues, and alcohol was foremost among them. It was a very tense, troubled relationship, even when I got here [in 1981]. And that had been going on for a number of years."

Irsay's infamous rant at BWI Airport in February '84 included this directed at the fourth estate: "Whaddaya hang me for? You want me here? Why d'ya hang me?" In fairness to the man, by late '72 they had him already typecast: erratic drunk, goofy moves, lousy owner. The NFL didn't vet owners in those days, so the process was a crapshoot. Charlie Euchner, author of the outstanding book, *Playing the Field: Why Sports Teams Move and Cities Fight to Keep Them*, thinks lampooning Bob Irsay was overkill:

> The media tend to turn everything into a morality tale. I'm no fan of Robert Irsay, or Jim [Irsay] for that matter, but what do you expect? They didn't buy the team to be a fan club for Baltimore. They bought the team to make money and to increase their political prestige and status. That's why they do it; that's why everybody does it. So, I don't think Irsay really stands out. It's just like when you go to a dinner. There are certain people with better table manners than others. So, maybe he didn't have good table manners, but what he was doing was

no different from what Carroll Rosenbloom, the Mara family [N.Y. Giants] or Robert Kraft [Patriots] did.

A blockbuster in sociology appeared in the September 1976 edition of *The American Journal of Sociology*. At least it was big behind the ivy walls. Harvey Molotch wrote a tome titled *The City as a Growth Machine: Toward a Political Economy of Place*, not easy beach reading. While explaining how business, politics and innovative people help drive city prosperity, Molotch explored why local newspapers generations past swayed public opinion. "The local institution which seems to take prime responsibility for the sustenance of civic resources—the metropolitan newspaper—is also the most important example of a business which has its interests anchored in the aggregate growth of the locality," Molotch began. "The local newspaper thus tends to occupy a rather unique position: Like many other local businesses, it has an interest in growth, but unlike most, its critical interest is not in the specific geographical pattern of that growth … The newspaper has no axe to grind, except the one axe which holds the community elite together: growth. It is for this reason that the newspaper tends to achieve a statesmen-like attitude in the community and is deferred to as something other than a special interest by the special interests."

Relating that ponderous prose to Bob Irsay and the Baltimore press, Molotch felt newspapers had clout because people believed what their eyes read. Just like Cronkite, Chancellor and Brinkley on TV, newspapers had street cred. In 1969, John Steadman got Baltimore fuming over mandatory preseason tickets. The press kicked Irsay down the alley and readers joined the fun. Irsay almost invited it. Scott Garceau, veteran TV and radio sportscaster, arrived in Baltimore in 1980, just when Irsay was ramping things up:

> When I got here, it was already in a pretty bad situation. Part of the issue was, he [Irsay] was an absentee owner. He was a guy who was out in Illinois all week, and for home games, he would fly in that Saturday, and he would have a small party who would usually travel with him, enjoy the game and fly back home on Sunday. I can remember [PR director and Colts GM] Ernie Accorsi at one point told him, "You know, Bob, you need to come to town a little bit more, be around, get to know some of the media." Ernie was good at what he did, and he was beloved in the market by the media. He was just a good guy. So, he [Accorsi] brings him in, and they're gonna have a press conference— a chance to talk to the owner. He comes in, and he was fumbling and stumbling. He called [head coach] Frank Kush *John* Kush. So, the reporters were all over that, and they ripped him for it. He probably should have been ripped for it because he didn't know his own head coach's name. That was the kind of deal it was. No matter how hard they tried to make

it right, it was pretty difficult to do when Robert Irsay was the guy in charge.

Former Colts standout Lydell Mitchell thinks Bob Irsay, on the whole, got a square deal with the press:

> I think some of it [the bad press] was justified. When I reflect back, I don't want to make excuses because Mr. Irsay had a sickness, and under the circumstances, he became very impulsive. So, I understand where writers were coming from. Was he irresponsible in a lot of cases? Yes. Did he say one thing and do something else? Yes. But I try to look at the whys too. And part of it is what he was going through. At that point, *no one* could control him. He was gonna have the final say, and that was that. It sounds like I sometimes make excuses for him, but I think when you make decisions, you're in play for people to ask questions about them. I know they [the press] dumped on him a lot; no question about it. And some of it was justified. But you have to be a big boy sometimes and stand up and take it. In this case, you [Irsay] made the decision to leave [Baltimore], and you have to deal with the consequences.

Meaning, stand there and take it. Acid wit Phil Jackman of the *Evening Sun* made Irsay's do-not-give-this-guy-any-scoops list. His column on 8/16/1979 was titled **White Tornado**:

On page 88 of the Colt media guide starts 2½ pages of interesting little tidbits titled "Historical highlights of professional football in Baltimore." Of course, you probably know what information follows the date December 28, 1958—"Colts defeat New York Giants, 23-17, at Yankee Stadium in 'sudden death' game for World Championship." Pushing ahead, for July 26, 1972, we get "Robert Irsay acquires Colts from Carroll Rosenbloom in exchange for Los Angeles Rams. Joe Thomas named Vice President and General Manager." This is a highlight? Sooner had ol' Joe Promise viewed us as a combination Hiroshima and Nagasaki and unloaded a couple of atom bombs on us as Bob Irsay. Initially, I viewed Irsay as sort of a lovable oaf who came into money and simply fell into bad company (Thomas). You never know who's going to draw the bed next to yours in a hospital, do you? I had my doubts about anyone getting his hands on the Los Angeles Rams and then trading them the same day, but I let it pass. I figured here was a guy who came up through the ranks (in the Marines and in business), who sort of liked the idea of getting involved with a working-class town. Whew, what a mistake! This guy appears to be a capricious, arbitrary, vindictive little despot. Boundless in his lust for power and money. Aside from these minor flaws, I guess he's a pretty nice fella.

Flying in and out of town in 24 hours while plastered gave Irsay little chance with press hounds. Laidback Bob Maisel of the *Morning Sun* would pitty-pat his targets, and January 1979 is no exception: "That brings us to Bob Irsay, who is the perfect example of absentee ownership. The only time Irsay sets foot in this town is to fly in, watch a game and get out again as soon as possible. He is a likeable guy, but there are times when he can be completely irresponsible, and that part of it has periodically hurt the Colts. He is at it again, admitting that he will meet in Los Angeles today with members of the group attempting to secure a franchise to replace the Rams, which Carroll Rosenbloom will move down the highway for the start of the 1980 season."

Soft-soaping led to Maisel advising Irsay to lay off the micromanaging. "Unless I'm wrong, Irsay would serve himself and the Colts better by staying out of the day-to-day operations of the club altogether or spending more time here to see what makes this town tick. Baltimore doesn't respond well to threats. By coming here as seldom as he does, then attempting to run the show without really knowing the circumstances, he is making some irresponsible moves, keeping things in a constant turmoil. You don't promote winning that way." Irsay ignored the advice.

A decent vetting by the NFL would have thrown up a flare once they got a peek into Irsay's background. On Nestor Aparicio's radio show the day Irsay died in 1997, John Steadman claimed that the NFL gave Irsay an E-Z Pass:

He [Irsay] created so much havoc. Any time he was around, there was extra pressure on the organization. General managers went to bed at night not knowing if they had a job the next day. If there's any blame to be put out, it should go to the National Football League for approving him. I was convinced that they never really investigated his background. I know that they took exception to a lot of things I came up with. I had heard—when he took over the club in 1972—that he had been a part owner of the Montreal Expos in the National League. At the time, John McHale was the general manager at Montreal, and I had a longtime relationship with him. McHale was a first-rate individual, and he had a heart attack, so I didn't really know anyone [with the Expos]. There was a fellow named Fanning who was his assistant; I called Fanning, and I really got nowhere with asking questions about Irsay and why he was asked to leave [the club]—a dead end. I quickly called Jim Kensil, who was [NFL commissioner] Pete Rozelle's assistant. And he said to me, "Why are you making this such a cause célèbre with you?" And I said, "Simply because we have to live with him here [in Baltimore]. If he's an improper individual and not fit to own a football club, the league should do something about it." Well, the league *didn't* do anything about it. He was absolutely bizarre.

Former *Morning Sun* columnist and author of *The Colts' Baltimore: A City and Its Love Affair in the 1950s*, Michael Olesker, never pulled punches regarding Bob Irsay or Indianapolis: "They [the press] saw him [Irsay] as a drunk. They saw him as unreliable. If you were covering the Colts, you had the best job on the sports desk, other than a columnist. So, your loyalty [to the Colts] was deep because you had been around, and you knew and treasured the history. And this guy was not only a threat to Baltimore, but he was a threat to your job. If you wrote what you knew about him, you knew that this was a guy who was very liable to go to your editor and say, 'I'm not gonna give you any stories if you don't take this guy off the beat. He's not fair to me.' Now—that doesn't mean that it would happen, but nobody who had the best job in town wanted to face that possibility. They all felt, *I'm dealing with a lunatic here*."

Former heroes were always good for a soundbite. Reliable running back Tom Matte didn't hedge when WMAR-TV interviewed him right after the move:

The guy [Irsay] has no class. You're dealing with a guy who just does *not* have class. He doesn't even know how to be a man about it. I don't know how he ever ran his business and was a success at it—it's beyond me. And you [to Johnny Unitas] remember the first speech [in 1972] when he came in. He came into our locker room at an exhibition game down in Tampa. And when he spoke, I said, "How could this man *ever* have made enough money to buy a team?" The other thing I'm really upset about is that the owners of the NFL let a guy like this come into the league. And that was the downfall [of the Colts]. It was just a continual, gradual decline of this franchise when he became the owner. It's embarrassing.

Evening Sun columnist Kevin Cowherd took a wary approach with Irsay. "We couldn't trust him," Cowherd admitted. "He withheld stuff from us. And he seemed erratic. He would make these decisions. For instance, he would say, 'We'll do a press conference this Tuesday afternoon at 1:00 PM.' Fifteen minutes ahead of time, he'd decide, 'Nah, I don't wanna do that.' And it put tremendous pressure on his media [PR] guys like Ernie Accorsi. There was so much drama around the Colts back then that all of that contributed to this very uneasy relationship between us in the media and Irsay."

Wayne Lynch worked at WMAR-TV in Baltimore for 13 years as a reporter, anchor and executive and managing news editor. The three big Baltimore dailies were the voice of the people, he says:

They [Baltimoreans] had three daily newspapers at the time [the 1970s]. That was pretty good for the East Coast. They were strongly supported, community-type newspapers that really felt the pulse of the city. They had great

reporters—and [John] Steadman was one of them, along with Bill Tanton and Phil Jackman—and they had a real cadre of people that were willing to take shots at Irsay. And they were almost *daring* Irsay to do something because I think the Colts fans wanted to vilify him in any way they could. That was their way of getting that neighborhood revenge: "You do this to me; I'll do this to you. You're not my buddy anymore. No more beers at the Swallow at the Hollow [a bar]."

Steadman of the *News American* fed the John Does sermons about crooked, money-grubbing owners. In '79, after Irsay's brief dalliance with Jacksonville, Steadman tallied the good will Irsay had lost:

It was Bob Irsay who jumped into the boiling cauldron of grease. Then the natives crowded around and proceeded to stoke the fire. The popularity of Irsay, the always-in-motion owner of the Baltimore Colts, is close to minus-zero. Again, he accomplished it all on his own. His family and friends still love him and so does God, to repeat one of Irsay's favorite reminders to himself... With his threats to move the Colts, Irsay has created animosity and trouble for himself. Owning a pro football team, a club with the prestige of the Colts, should be a pleasure, never a burden. It's strange he didn't realize what he was doing when he launched into his ill-conceived odyssey. Irsay caused the problems himself. He could hardly think of shopping the Colts around the country, telling the governor of Maryland to "go to hell," creating general consternation and then expect to be held in high esteem. It's appalling that the Baltimore Police Department, with more pressing problems, must be concerned with giving protection to the owner of the city's football team when he comes to Memorial Stadium.

Irsay got himself flogged for affronting a whole town. "You're talkin' about a press corps [in Baltimore] that was as provincial as the city they were writing about," longtime Baltimorean Tom Marr IV observed. "Just like the team, the press corps was entrenched in the city too. And they traveled and hung out with the players. You don't see that anymore. I think the grumbling you got from the press corps was what they got on the ground from the players. And I think people realized real quick that Robert Irsay was a buffoon. And then, coming out of the gate, in '72, '73, '74, they just saw the Colts collapse. And this [the Colts] was their baby, their favorite son. The press back then were fans too. They watched how everything was stripped away from the team by Robert Irsay."

Jon Scott, equipment manager for the Colts in Baltimore and Indy, thinks Irsay was just looking for validation: "We all know that Bob Irsay had issues; that goes without saying.

But deep down, I'm quite sure he wanted to keep the team in Baltimore. He was one of those guys who wants people to like him. But it seemed like whatever he was trying to do—a lot of times not the right way—the press would never back him up on anything. That was tough to see. It was all the time in the newspapers; they were just terrible. You look at the old articles, and every week, they went after Bob Irsay. I don't know if I've ever seen a press corps like that before."

Steadman loved simultaneous smackdowns on the two owners, Rosenbloom and Irsay. "Again, the underlying force is money and how much more can be extracted from the product," he wrote in early March 1984. "First Rosenbloom, sinister in his dealings, and then Irsay, totally unpredictable, have led Baltimore through a path of trauma that no city should suffer. A high-placed NFL club official said he couldn't believe that one of its franchises—Baltimore—had been subjected to the conniving leadership it has had to endure, citing Rosenbloom and Irsay as back-to-back owners who took all the city had to give but provided little in return. Rosenbloom and Irsay became famous and extremely rich, simply because of the love of a city for its football team. Then greed and avarice reared their ugly heads. Yes, the sin of selfishness."

Steadman apparently didn't do much homework, or he would've known that Rosenbloom made a mountain of money in textiles before he bought the Colts. But he had a good feel for Irsay. In late August 1979 his colleague Phil Jackman weighed in:

Finally, it appears, we know what Colt owner Bob Irsay wants out of the city, state and other selected targets of opportunity. In a few words, everything he can possibly get... folding money, change, watch bobs, credit cards, the works. More seats, better seats, more and better everything else, including field, rest rooms, locker rooms, and so on. Does any of this come as a surprise to anyone? All owners of all pro sports franchises are pretty much the same. They always want more and better and they assume it is their right. A better lease deal, a slice of the concessions, a chunk of the parking, luxury boxes for the swells. More radio and TV dough. Instead of benches, why don't we have individual seats, they ask. And, while you're at it, why not make 'em cushioned jobs, so the folks won't do too much howling when the ticket prices are jacked up and out of sight.

Steadman labeled owners looking to turn a decent profit as robber barons. "Owners of sports franchises come in assorted sizes, with various egos, financial backgrounds and ulterior motives," he wrote in December 1983. "Most of them run to a pattern. They are rotten to the core, live to con the press, deceive the public and separate the poor fan from his money. Too many of them ride in limousines and private airplanes—which the ticket-buying spectators are paying to maintain. Fans have made important figures out of some of the most decadent individuals it has been our misfortune to know." He was thinking initials C.R. and R.I.

After the move to Indy, the *Chicago Tribune* got Irsay to sit down for a confessional. One question was about the Jekyll-Hyde feature, but the indictment covered everybody in the corps:

Question—Who is "they"?

The two *Sun* newspapers in Baltimore [*Morning* and *Evening Sun*]. They were calling my friends consistently. I have a 31-year-old retarded boy who's got a brain factor of about a five-year-old and they tried to interview him, tried to break down the door in a mentally retarded institution. I mean, calling a priest to ask how much I donate. Calling the Winnetka [Ill.] police department to ask how many times I've been arrested for drunken driving. Have I murdered anybody? Have I been ticketed? I don't need people like that. We are not going to let any Baltimore reporters in my [Hoosier Dome] press box. That's my right. I told them, don't try coming in. If they want to buy a ticket, that's their privilege.

The victim here lied about: 1) who his real father was; 2) fighting overseas during WWII; 3) his daughter's tragic accident; and 4) playing ball for Bob Zuppke at Illinois. And that's just for starters. Vito Stellino, one of the reporters who wrote the March '84 Jekyll-Hyde piece, says they never tried to interview Irsay's son, and they never went down to Florida to snoop around, much less bang on any doors.

Longtime Baltimore sportscaster Scott Garceau sides with Steadman: Irsay brought all the bad press on himself: "I understand that maybe they didn't write good things about him, but he had nobody to blame but himself for that. They wrote what they saw. And I think that press corps—John Steadman and people like that, people that had been around from the beginning—treasured and knew what that franchise stood for. It was the centerpiece of the league. It was Johnny U and the Baltimore Colts, 33rd-Street sellouts, The Big Wheel and all the stuff that went with it. He [Irsay] tore that up. And I think those people [Baltimore reporters] defended that history. This was the guy that did it, and they wrote about his personal failures, his demons and everything else. If you were chronicling the team during those years, it would be pretty hard to write great things about Bob Irsay."

Pete Ward took a ride up the elevator, getting hired to work PR in 1981 and becoming the current COO of the Indianapolis Colts. To him, the steady swirl of controversy doomed Irsay:

I wasn't there in the '70s. I'm just telling you what I heard, just surmising here. Firing [head coach Howard] Schnellenberger in the middle of the [1974] season, and then trying to fire Ted [Marchibroda] during the 1976 preseason, when Jim Irsay went on the bus to apologize

for his dad; then the Jacksonville visit [thinking of moving in 1979] were *all* controversial things. And I think that the Baltimore media was a tough bunch. They would call you out on things, and I think that Mr. Irsay was sensitive to how he was framed, how he was pictured in the public. So, I think it became contentious, with a snowball effect. Something critical would be written about him, and then he would respond in kind. And it got worse over time.

Picture Irsay picking up the *News American* in late January 1984 and reading Steadman's headline: **He deserves to be spanked.** Steady compares him to a kid in juvie: "Problems beset Junior. He has been misbehaving. His difficulties concern geography [looking to move] and an inability to deal in accurate recall. He becomes confused between Phoenix, Ariz., and Baltimore. It's a blind spot. One city is in the desert and the other on the Atlantic seaboard, but he can't keep them straight. But what to do with Junior? His behavior has created problems. He turned his back on Arizona Gov. Bruce Babbitt and dashed to be with Mayor William Donald Schaefer in Baltimore [for the infamous BWI press conference]. It's a tug-o-war, and Junior likes pulling on both ends … Part of the dilemma is caused by a communications gap. Junior thinks he is misunderstood. He might be right. Deep down, Junior is not a bad boy. He just carries on in public, creates scenes and causes embarrassment."

Steadman's milquetoast counterpart at the *Morning Sun*, Bob Maisel, would slip in a polite complaint now and again. In mid-February 1984, he got positively brazen:

There aren't many times when I feel inclined to defend the job of writing about sports as an honest way to make a living, but this is one of them. Specifically, the reference is to numerous comments and letters I've received that blame the media for most of the Colts' ills, including the apparent shaky residence of the franchise in Baltimore. The charge is: "You're running Robert Irsay out of town. Get off his back. Don't be so quick to criticize. We need the Colts" … When Bob Irsay bought the Colts 12 years ago, there wasn't a media person in town who had any preconceived opinions of him. I know I respected him for putting up $19 million of his money, and was perfectly willing to let him make his own reputation as the owner who replaced Carroll Rosenbloom. He has done that, and if his image in town is not what he would like it to be, he has nobody to blame but himself. When he does something good for the town and the franchise, most of us are happy to give him credit. But I defy anybody to make his recent airport press conference [at BWI] come out smelling like a rose, or the one where he called his coach and general manager by the wrong names, or his firing a coach on the sideline, along with the constant turmoil, etc. Even if you disliked the man personally and were out to get him, the worst thing you could do to him would be to describe him accurately. He has been his own enemy.

Irsay was just asking for it. "Let's put it this way: We [the Colts organization] were famous for serving the media Maryland crabcakes in our press box," Pete Ward recalled. "I believe it was John Steadman who wrote a critical column about Mr. Irsay. This is in 1982. And the next home game, the crabcakes were gone forever, and they were replaced with hotdogs. So, it was a contentious relationship, certainly. And he mentioned it in that airport press conference: 'Why do you hang me?'"

Rick Venturi coached the Colts linebackers in '83, and he remembers an impromptu press conference, ostensibly to patch over the cracks: "Right in that last year [1983], there was a situation where we were all told Bob was gonna have a big press conference. Part of it I think was to explain the [totally botched] Elway deal, but the purpose of the press conference—he wanted us all there, wanted to look good—and it was kinda like to make peace with the Baltimore media, and in so doing, make peace with the city. But before he could almost utter a word, it got confrontational. Then, it just went the other way, from 'We're gonna make peace' to 'I'll move my goddam team wherever I wanna move my team.' This was at the [Colts] complex. I was there. Question 1, Question 2 out of the box pissed him off. And then he was explosive. Once that happened, it was putting gas on the fire."

Irsay was helpless against a sharp wit like Phil Jackman of the *Evening Sun*. In 1973, Jackman won Maryland's award at the 14th annual National Sportscasters and Sportswriters Association banquet for the third time. In October 1975, Jackman wrote one of his "Tuesday Evening Quarterback" letters to Irsay, with the Colts in an early-season funk:

Dear Bob, red-faced owner:

Now that you've had a month to bask in the Colts' glorious [preseason] victory over the Bears before all your friends in downtown Skokie, I think it's time we discussed a few things. I know this owner business is still relatively new with you, but you just gotta get back to acting the part. There were times when you showed a lot of spunk. Like when you lectured Marty Domres on his quarterbacking ("Hey, how come you don't throw passes to our guys like you throw 'em to the other team?"). And that memorable Sunday, Bloody Sunday, you fired Howie the Hoss while waiting for your limousine to arrive. For openers, you should call your general manager Joe Promise in and, with folded arms, an arched eyebrow and a foot tapping impatiently on the carpet, ask exactly when this mess is going to get straightened out. Forget that pablum he's been

feeding you about this being a team "ready to explode" and do a little exploding of your own. Intimidation, that's the name of the game. Make it both physical and mental. Instead of a charter plane to New York Saturday, pack 'em off in a bus. Bivouac somewhere on Flushing Meadow. Have 'em eat out of a sandy mess kit, shave in cold water out of a steel pot. Issue a paycheck that bounces every so often … I realize you're expensing off all your losses on your income tax, but what's the going rate for public embarrassment, Tiger?

In his "Memos to Many" in October 1978, as the Colts' season headed south, Jackman had similar advice for Irsay: "**Dear Bob (the red-faced owner):** How's it going, ol' buddy? Didn't get a chance to talk to you after Sunday's Stadium swoon but, what the heck, I see you were busy trying to air condition the coaching staff anyway. Listen, Tiger, you're just gonna have to flee the owner's box and get your tail down on the sidelines again. It's time to come out of that shell and forget what you said when you bought the ballclub back on July 13, 1972: 'I will not be an interfering owner.' These guys need your help, especially the backup quarterbacks. I mean, look at how much you did for Marty Domres's career. Incidentally, he was at the game, giggling."

Hard jabs from Steadman; hooks to the belly from Jackman. Irsay's blustering and buffoonery just egged them on. By the late '70s, Irsay's relationship with the press was kaput.

He gave 'em the business when he touched down in Indianapolis after the move. "Colts owner Robert Irsay, welcomed to Indianapolis with a key to the city from Mayor William Hudnut and loud cheers from a crowd of about 20,000 in the Hoosier Dome, said he left Baltimore because of constant 'hounding' by the news media," *Newsday* reported on April 3, 1984. "'It was not a monetary situation,' the owner of the NFL franchise told the lunch-hour crowd that streamed into the new domed stadium to greet him. 'We did talk to several other cities, and we did have better offers.' Responding to questions from the media, Irsay said, 'You people of the press were hounding my family for two years, and I wasn't about to take any more of your hounding.'"

In the end, the disease fed on itself—Irsay boo-boo prompts flak from the press, Irsay howls, and back around again. "No sportswriter was gonna write, 'We're for Bob Irsay. We think he's the savior of football in Baltimore,'" former WMAR-TV news executive Wayne Lynch stated. "Nobody was gonna write that, not the way he was behaving at the time, where he was blustering and threatening. So, no sportswriter was gonna take the positive with him; they would all take the negative. That's what everybody wanted to read. They wanted Irsay to be vilified, and the sportswriters were leading that parade, and they weren't gonna change their minds. I believe they were daring him, calling his bluff: 'You're not gonna leave just because we're criticizing you in the paper. This is an NFL franchise.' And that played into the [Baltimore] provincialism: 'Hey, we're Baltimore. Don't screw with us.'"

Colts equipment manager Jon Scott followed Irsay out to Indianapolis because he liked the job. And he wasn't fond of all of the badmouthing:

I think it [the press treatment of Irsay] was pretty cruel. Just like with Jim Irsay, there's a lot of things that he does behind the scenes—certainly his dad somewhat, as well, giving to charity—that he never wants to take credit for. Jim has done a lot of that. His father did a lot of that, as well, but they [Baltimore reporters] were bound and determined to get the Colts a different owner. I think they were just hoping that Bob Irsay would sell the team, try to make it as hard as possible on him, probably never dreaming, *Holy crap. They ARE gonna move. They HAVE moved.* Of course, it was too little, too late.

How 'bout a better-late-than-never ploy by Baltimore? What the heck.

CHAPTER 11

LET'S MAKE A DEAL

The city comptroller pulled a slick one and buried the Camden stadium project. Got agitators sweet on Memorial Stadium some clipboards so they could stroll around the city, collecting signatures. A petition: fight the evils of the downtown ballpark, save the Old Gray Lady on 33rd. They got 11,837 autographs for a November 1974 ballot initiative. "Opponents of the proposed $112-million Camden Yards sports complex yesterday presented a petition containing 11,837 signatures—enough to put the stadium issue on the city ballot this fall," the *Morning Sun* detailed in late July 1974. "Unless the signatures are challenged, voters this November will decide to amend the City Charter to *prohibit the construction of any new stadium in Baltimore that would use public funds, credit or guarantee* [emphasis mine]. Hyman A. Pressman, the city comptroller, who presented the petition to acting Mayor Walter S. Orlinsky yesterday, said he did not expect the signatures to be challenged."

Nobody guarded the city coffers closer than Hyman Pressman, and looking out for the little man wasn't just talk. That and composing lame poetry and schtick kept him in office from 1961 to 1991. But he was googly-eyed about Memorial Stadium and drove Carroll Rosenbloom up the wall. Here was Hymie at it again, stirring the waters. While others were trying to cobble together the $112 million for Camden, Pressman was working on a way to torpedo the whole thing.

Another pol brainstormed some loopholes to stymie Hymie. "Delegate John W. Douglas (D., 2nd) said that weakness in the wording of the referendum petition would allow the sports complex to be constructed even if voters approved the proposed charter amendment to ban the project," the *Morning Sun* informed in September 1974. Douglas mentioned three possible loopholes: "1. The amendment does not block the construction of a stadium financed by private funds; 2. The amendment does not prohibit the city from selling or donating land to the state which then would build the complex; 3. The amendment was so broadly written that while it might ban construction of a new stadium, it may not block the city from building a 'sports complex.'" Delegate Douglas didn't give Pressman much to fret about. All three loopholes were DOA.

Question P got put on the Baltimore City ballot in November 1974—yay or nay on the new stadium:

QUESTION P: Charter Amendment

Charter Amendment to add new Section 9 to Article 1 to proclaim that the Memorial Stadium on 33rd Street shall be a memorial in tribute to the Veterans of our nation's wars and to prohibit the construction of any stadium for professional football, professional soccer and/or professional baseball in the City of Baltimore with the use of public funds, public credit or public guarantee for the financing thereof in whole or in part.

It was a given that the citizenry around the stadium—the Waverly and Ednor Gardens neighborhoods—shouted huzzahs for Question P. They cried bloody murder when the ballpark first went up. Then it grew on them over the years, so now with Question P on the ballot, they grabbed their muskets. It was the "war memorial" business that whipped up emotions, which got a knee jerk from the local potentates. "You have to remember that the politicians have constituents," observed former WMAR-TV-Baltimore news executive Wayne Lynch. "And they voted. And

Baltimore was a Democratic town. The [Hyman] Pressmans, the [Walter] Orlinskys, the [William Donald] Schaefers, the [Barbara] Mikulskis, they depended on the neighborhood votes to keep themselves in office. So, if the neighbors on the Alameda and 33rd Street and Greenmount [Ave.] [right around Memorial Stadium] wanted that stadium to stay where it was, they were a pretty powerful constituency. So, they're [the politicians] siding with the public because they wanted to stay in office."

A feature in the *Evening Sun* in early October 1974 on the merits of publicly-funded stadiums upped the odds for Question P. The numbers didn't lie: Stadiums built with tax dollars are money pits:

Every publicly-financed stadium in America loses money; Philadelphia [Veterans Stadium] loses $1.5 million a year, Cincinnati [Riverfront Stadium] $1 million, Pittsburgh [Three Rivers Stadium] and Buffalo [Rich Stadium] $700,000 ... To finance the building of the Baltimore complex, which will likely inflate to more than $150 million (not including bonds' interest) by the time construction starts, the authority has proposed the sale of state-backed revenue bonds. It hopes to produce immediate revenues by building the parking garages first. The problem with that plan is the state and Gov. [Marvin] Mandel have pledged in legislation to use no public money to pay for a new Baltimore stadium. Revenue bonds backed by the full faith and credit of a state create additional tax burdens if the revenue does not meet the debt service. The Bay Bridge is a classic example.

Beautiful. The sports authority was pushing the bond route, but the state AND the governor said nothing doing. Back on the treadmill we go.

The *Evening Sun* also opined about renovating the mausoleum:

Where then can Baltimore head? It can emulate New York and renovate Memorial Stadium with improved parking. As the Sports Complex Authority is quick to point out, that would require $50 million in almost direct subsidy because Memorial Stadium would definitely lose a lot of money. Isn't a pre-explained deficit easier to bear than the surprise of an unplanned-for future loss? The major tenants, however, don't want to continue at 33rd Street, even though the Colts had a waiting list for season tickets until 1973. They wouldn't mind moving downtown, but would prefer a site off Route 83 north of Baltimore. That is where the Colts and Orioles draw the most fans from.

It seemed settled: Why break the bank sprucing up a place nobody wants to rent? Phil Hersh, who wrote the article, basically concluded the heck with the Colts and Orioles. Mow the lawn, light up the grill, grab a barstool instead: "One thing is perfectly clear: What is good for the Colts and Orioles is not necessarily good for Baltimore and Maryland. The city existed quite well without major-league pro sports until the last 20 years; their loss would not be equaled by the loss of faith and money that would likely result from a stadium completely financed with public money."

Maybe it was time to throw up the white flag. Back at City Hall, the Baltimore City election board stayed mum about a lawsuit to void Question P. "In the case, William H.C. Wilson, a Roland Park real estate man who filed the suit as a city taxpayer, sought to bar the scheduled November 5 vote as illegal and as one that might result in the defeat of new stadium plans," the *Morning Sun* reported on October 10, 1974. "Mr. Wilson's suit contends that the new sports complex proposed for Camden Yards would promote tourism and bring business into the city's core areas. He said he had no real estate interest in the proposed new site." Plain and simple, Mr. Wilson wanted to keep the ball teams. Two killjoys, Charles F. Rose of the stadium-huggers, and City Comptroller Hyman Pressman, said they weren't sweating the lawsuit.

John Steadman of the *News American* took a strap to Pressman:

It's unfortunate a man in the influential position of Hyman Pressman, a highly elected official of Baltimore, is leading the fight to drive major-league sports from the city he professes to hold dear to his heart. Pressman, the city comptroller, is hindering the progress of Baltimore's major-league teams, and if the Orioles and Colts leave, much of the blame will be directed at him. He will have earned such an infamous role in Baltimore's history. The public should know where to assess the responsibility if the Orioles and Colts move away. Pressman will be number one on the hit parade … The reputation of Pressman is one of impeccable honesty, a leader for causes and a man interested in doing what is best for the city. He is generally respected, but is also called a buffoon by his detractors. But in the matter of sports, Pressman is in a foreign area he knows nothing about. A difference of opinion is welcomed in all avenues of our free society, but there is also a chance a man might fight and win for the wrong side.

Steadman also took a shot at the residents near the stadium. They howled when the stadium was going up, now look at them: "Now, the stadium game has come full cycle [with Question P]. They don't want sports played anywhere else but in the present location. Ridiculous."

Then Steadman issued his proclamation:

The referendum on the ballot will designate the 33rd-Street Stadium an official memorial, thereby blocking construction of another stadium within the city limits. This is foolhardy. It's like saying the only golf that can be enjoyed in Baltimore must be held in Clifton Park or the only tennis that can be played must be staged in Druid Hill. It's the opinion of this reporter that the public will be doing a disservice to itself to vote for that kind of a proposition. Men and women with a grain of common sense realize it would tie the hands of Baltimore for all-time if such a thing happened. What it would mean is that sports teams, if they stayed here, would soon leave Memorial Stadium and Baltimore. Maybe they would move to an adjoining county but, in all probability, it would be to a far-away city.

Steadman nailed it, and the *Morning Sun* agreed: "QUESTION P: Proponents of Memorial Stadium have petitioned to a vote on a proposed charter amendment to block any use of public funds or credit to build any other stadium within Baltimore for professional football, soccer and/or baseball. The amendment would clutter the city's basic legal document with an extraneous piece of nonsense that would tie the city's hands while practically assuring that if the state put money into a new stadium, it would be built outside the city. Vote **AGAINST**."

Steadman was a pit bull on Question P. He blasted his buddy Hyman Pressman one more time and pushed for a new stadium. And bully for him. His colleagues at the *Morning* and *Evening Sun* stayed mum while Pressman and his squeaky wheels hit the streets to talk up

Question P. Not a peep from the anti-Ps. The bell tolled on November 6, 1974:

Question P:
548 of 548 precincts tallied—
Yes.................. 50, 916 (56%)
No................... 39, 527 (44%)

Say goodbye to the dome.

The governor chickened out and Question P passed, but the sports authority wasn't ready to quit. "The chairman of the Maryland Sports Complex Authority said yesterday that he will bring plans for a Baltimore stadium back to the General Assembly despite Tuesday's passage of a charter amendment barring city funds for a new stadium," the *Morning Sun* divulged in early November 1974. "'It's another fly in the ointment,' said Joseph G. Anastasi, chairman of the authority and state secretary of economic and community development. 'But the cost figures [for the sports complex] are being updated and we anticipate submitting the proposal to the legislature next year.'" Anastasi was followed by the voice of doom. "The governor has spoken," huffed Robert Embry Jr., the city's housing commissioner. "The authority will not resubmit the proposal. Referendum or no referendum, there's not going to be a stadium."

A kabuki dance, that's what it was. The dome never really had a chance. Almost a year after the Colts bolted to Indy, the *Evening Sun* put out a piece promoting a downtown stadium. Included was a summary of how the Camden project got scrapped:

Thirteen years ago this month, the Greater Baltimore Committee proposed construction of a covered, 70,000-seat, football-baseball stadium complex above the Camden Yards. Construction of the stadium, which could have required the demolition of historic Camden Station, included a 4,500-car parking garage and a 600-room hotel. The plan would have allowed the continued use of the railroad tracks beneath the elevated stadium complex. The project quickly gained momentum and enthusiastic support. The General Assembly created a sports authority. The new stadium seemed on its way. But city Comptroller Hyman A. Pressman and residents of neighborhoods around Memorial Stadium successfully mounted a charter amendment drive that banned the use of city funds for a new stadium. Then the state legislature refused to provide money for the stadium project, which had an estimated cost of more than $100 million. Another dream of a new stadium in Baltimore dissolved.

With it the Colts in '84.

John Ziemann, Colts/Ravens band president, got hired to catalogue and preserve thousands of nicknacks at Memorial Stadium before demolition. He saw the joint as way past its prime. "No new stadium—no teams. Simple," Ziemann stressed. "You don't have a factory producing Coca-Cola using the old standards when you gotta move forward and bottle new Coca-Cola. You can't stay in the old plant [Memorial Stadium]. That's progress—in sports, in manufacturing, in business. I learned that from the front office of the Ravens. I'm old-school, but I had to learn a lot of new ways [to run the marching band]. You can't stay in the past. You can learn from the past, but you have to move forward, or you aren't gonna survive. That's the same with a professional football team."

Question P now city policy, John Steadman put Governor Mandel on the spot:

Mandel was a leader in the state's original involvement in building a sports complex. He talked about revenue bonds at an earlier date, with the State of Maryland supporting them, the same as happened with the Chesapeake Bay Bridge and John F. Kennedy Highway [I-95]. The Colts and Orioles, the two tenants in Memorial Stadium, are not happy with the facility. They are on a year-to-year lease. A referendum has just been approved to tie professional sports to Memorial Stadium. No place else in the City of Baltimore can professional football, baseball or soccer be played, according to the voters. So if the Orioles and Colts want to take a hike to Seattle or New Orleans they have the right to go anytime they want, without fear of being blocked by a contract. This brings the situation right back to Mandel. He can go out of the city and build a Stadium if he believes sports are in the public

interest... Some Baltimore voters said the referendum on making Memorial Stadium the only location pro sports could be played in the city was presented in ambiguous terms. Whether it was or not, the vote is in, and Baltimore is going to have a harder fight to keep the Orioles and Colts. The political ball is now in the hands of Governor Marvin Mandel. He can either drop it or run with it. On his judgment rests the future of major-league sports in Baltimore and Maryland.

Steadman was dead-right. And Mandel choked by not bucking the voters who had whiffed on Question P. Irsay always gets most of the blame for the move, but Baltimore blew it with Question P. "Led by Hyman A. Pressman, Baltimore's penny-pinching comptroller who favored rehabbing Memorial Stadium, opponents tried to make sure the ambitious [new] stadium project was indeed dead," Jon Morgan noted in *Glory for Sale: Fans, Dollars and the New NFL*. "They collected signatures and placed on the fall ballot a cleverly worded amendment to the city's charter. Question P called for proclaiming 'the 33rd Street stadium as a memorial to war veterans and prohibiting use of city funds to construction of any other stadium.' Fueled by the same patriotism that helped build the stadium, the measure passed 56 percent to 44 percent."

Jingoism and an eat-the-rich mindset pushed Question P over the line. "You notice, if they [politicians] put public funds for a new stadium on the ballot, people will not vote for it," stated veteran sportswriter Vito Stellino, formerly of the *Morning Sun*. "Kansas City—back-to-back Super Bowl wins. They put it [public funding] on the ballot. It lost, 58 to 42 [percent]. So, these governments, they don't want to put it on the ballot. They just approve it themselves." Sure enough. "Voters turned out in large numbers for a spring election on Tuesday, soundly rejecting a proposal to extend a Jackson County sales tax to pay for a downtown Royals stadium and sorting out the makeup of school boards across the metro," the (Kansas City) *Beacon News* reported in April 2024. "Jackson County's Question 1 failed by a vote of roughly 42% to 58%, denying the Chiefs and Royals an estimated $2 billion in sales tax money that would have funded the teams' stadiums for the next 40 years. That revenue would have been used for improvements to Arrowhead Stadium and a new downtown ballpark for the Royals. Now the future of those projects is uncertain without Jackson County funding. The team was also expected to hit up city and state taxpayers for more money even if the sales tax extension passed."

Ditching the Camden stadium project makes no sense to Steve Rosenbloom:

> That was one of the first places on our [his and his father's] minds—Camden Yards. I don't know what killed it or why, but there seemed to be a loss of interest. I liked [Mayor] Schaefer; look what he did for Baltimore. But I think it was an

internal thing, that they started thinking, *Oh, let's do this.* Then they find out that they're gonna piss off some constituents who don't want it there—all those political things. They lost interest, but why would they walk away from it? Maybe their mouths were out front, too far ahead. You know, you talk to them: "Oh, yeah, you wanna do this together? That'll be great." They jump in, then they start to think about it or research it: "Oh, that's gonna cost too much. We can't do that." There were a thousand reasons. But, yeah, they lost interest. And it could've been done.

Other cities pulled it off without going to the poorhouse: Cincinnati, Pittsburgh, Houston, Philadelphia, New Orleans. The Colts' move put such a scare into Baltimore that they threw up Oriole Park at Camden Yards and M&T Bank Stadium in less than a decade. Indy even trumped Baltimore's bid with an empty Hoosier Dome. Every joint had public money behind it. But Baltimore held on tight to Memorial Stadium and got left behind.

Rosenbloom's PR man Ernie Accorsi thinks the dome debacle pushed Rosenbloom to the West Coast. "I think it [Memorial Stadium] was a problem at the end. I think he wanted a new stadium. I picked up [sportscaster] Vince Bagli once at the airport after coming home from an away game, and it's late at night. He knew the city like the back of his hand, and he directed me over to where [Oriole Park at] Camden Yards is now. This is

11:00 at night. He says, 'This is where Rosenbloom wanted the stadium.' Ironically, that's where the baseball stadium ended up. I went through it [a similar problem] twice. It wasn't unlike [Browns owner Art] Modell having the problem trying to get Municipal Stadium replaced. But I know he [Rosenbloom] wanted a new stadium. That, I can tell you."

Professor Charles Euchner wrote about cities feuding over teams, *Playing the Field*. He doesn't think Baltimore had its act together:

> What they didn't have at that time [the '70s] was a real plan. That dome downtown [the Baltodome]—that wasn't a real plan. It was all paper and renderings. And that's why people [the owners] started calling BS on this—it's like, how many pretty pictures do you expect us to look at and take seriously? If they actually had a *real* plan that had a real site and a real design, rather than just some magical dome, which was in vogue at the time—but they didn't. Nobody had a concrete plan. What they often do in this situation is, it's a game of faking the other side out. It's a game of make-believe, a game of pretend where they *pretend* that they have a real stadium concept. But if you look at these different situations in different cities, there are literally sometimes dozens of "plans" before something happens.

And right on cue: another scheme to renovate the concrete horseshoe: "Annapolis—A bill authorizing a $25 million bond issue for the renovation of Memorial Stadium was introduced yesterday in the state Senate," the *Morning Sun* disclosed in early February 1975. "The measure would confine improvements to the stadium structure for such things as new seats, escalators, expanded concession and restroom areas and for the alteration of the playing field." Senator John C. Byrnes, whose turf was around Memorial Stadium, proclaimed parking wasn't a big deal and a downtown stadium was a dumb idea: "A vastly improved Memorial Stadium is preferable to a new, super-deluxe downtown stadium." A few years back, the General Assembly set aside $7 million for stadium cosmetics, but long-term leases didn't get signed and the bill timed out. The $25-million bill this time likewise died of neglect.

*   *   *

In late March 1976, Phoenix made the news for more than high-end spas and cacti. They were eyeballing the Colts, and the owner was intrigued. "Phoenix (Ariz.) interests are in wooing the Colts and club owner Robert Irsay has been listening to the offer," detailed the *Morning Sun*. "He realizes, however, that leaving Baltimore would be a difficult job. 'My company [the Robert Irsay Co.] has a big contract in the Phoenix area with West Co Corporation, which is building Paradise Valley, a shopping center complex,' Irsay said by telephone yesterday from his office in Skokie, Ill. 'Phoenix people were in here [the Chicago area] and made an attractive offer,' Irsay added." Commissioner Rozelle wouldn't sell out Baltimore, and Irsay's chances with an owners' vote were zilch. But flirtation was worrisome.

By this time, local scribes had caught Irsay's wandering eye. Bill Tanton of the *Evening Sun* laid out some of Irsay's beefs in March 1976:

> No doubt Colt owner Bob Irsay would love to move his franchise to Phoenix or Memphis or somewhere besides Baltimore, but the league won't allow it. The NFL is stable. The last time a franchise moved was when the Cardinals went from Chicago to St. Louis 16 years ago. I can understand Irsay's irritation with things here such as the 2 PM kickoff time and the condition of Memorial Stadium. They are legitimate gripes. After all, when Irsay bought the team for $19 million, the seller, Carroll Rosenbloom, assured him the Governor and others were clearing the way for a new stadium—and at that time they were. Irsay has called Memorial Stadium "the worst in the country." If he means by that the worst in the NFL, I will agree with him. The way we allow the home of the Orioles and Colts to deteriorate is a disgrace.

The line about Rosenbloom promising Irsay a new stadium has been plagiarized to death over the years with no hard evidence. Son Steve Rosenbloom says it's hogwash, so who knows.

But there's no dispute that Irsay was brassed off about the stadium and wanted action. "Starting June 3 [1976], I'm going to be in Baltimore for three months, raising enough hell to get some of the things the Stadium needs," Irsay warned. "I might even go door-to-door explaining our situation. There are things we would like to have done to make the Stadium a better place for the fans and the team. I will give it 90 days. Then I will take another look."

The Big Wheel loved the Colts—led the C-O-L-T-S cheer in the ballpark—but had no problem with Irsay looking to move. "I think he was justified. There's no doubt in my mind. If they had done something—build a new stadium—and not just piddle around: 'Oh, we're gonna fix this leak or patch this wall.' This [the stadium] is a crap hole. Get rid of it and build something nice that these other teams and football players will wanna come here and play for the team. Nobody wanted to come here and play in this town back then unless they loved steamed crabs. Naturally, he [Irsay] had to look around beforehand, put his feelers out because he knew what was gonna happen. That's why he was happy [about the move to Indianapolis]. He made a good deal with Indianapolis, came back [to Baltimore], and [Mayor] Schaefer's giving him a hard time. So, 'See you later, pal.'"

Hyman Pressman and the stadium cult thought they were doing right but were mainly human barricades. Reporters like Scott Garceau toiled at the mausoleum year-round and knew it's time was up:

Here's the issue: There were a lot of multi-purpose stadiums back then, which isn't ideal because we remember the Colts playing on the Oriole infield and the turf coming up. From a fan's standpoint, it was an upper-deck stadium. The best seats [for football] were in the upper deck. If you were on that lower level, it was so low and flat, you might be blocked out by players standing on the sidelines. I think there were city and state officials that probably should have been moving a lot quicker than they did, that really didn't move to get a better stadium until they lost the team. Just trying to defend them a bit, they said, "Hey, the Orioles are playing there, and they're fine. They're winning championships. People are coming out. Thirty-third Street is a pretty nice spot for a stadium." I have talked with some city and state officials. They go, "It's not all on him [Irsay]. We could've done more."

Ever the contrarian, in August 1979 Phil Jackman of the *Evening Sun* bucked his peers and backed the Gray Lady:

Irsay has owned the Colts since 1972 and in all that time, he says, "the only improvement to the Stadium is a crummy little elevator." After years of blatant disregard in the upkeep of the Stadium, there has been a dramatic change the last few years and the maintenance and improvements are getting better all the time. First, they got rid of those splintery wooden benches in the upper deck, replacing them with individual chairs. The restrooms and concession stands have been improved and now they are being added to with the towers under construction outside the horseshoe. The grounds, both inside and out, are better cared for than they have been in the past and, early in the decade, someone on 33rd Street discovered paint, and it has been put to good use since. Granted, the place is no Taj Mahal, but it never was, and to pass off the improvements and work done there as "one crummy little elevator" is absurd.

Coming in from Buffalo as a migrant, cartoonist Mike Ricigliano could assess Memorial Stadium with a more objective eye. "I felt like Irsay had a number of valid issues to move the team, including the 2:00 start time and others too," Ricig explained. "I don't know if other owners would have acted the way he did, but he definitely had some legitimate gripes—the stadium itself, which was in disrepair. They had kind of kicked that can down the road. And I think there was a complacency in the government: 'Well, he's never gonna move the team, so we don't have to worry about that. We'll address the baseball issues, and we'll revisit this down the line.' I don't think they grasped the urgency of it and just how erratic the guy was, as far as making a move like that. So, I put a decent amount of blame on state and local government here [in Baltimore]."

Former Colts equipment manager Jon Scott had explored the bowels of many an NFL stadium. In his mind, Baltimore had its chances to stymie the move. "Oh, I think the complaints about Memorial Stadium were valid. You'd see other stadiums, and even though they were older, they were getting renovations, where it seemed like there were *no* big renovations to Memorial Stadium. There was always talk about it: 'Hey, we're gonna get a dome here,' prior to Jim's dad [Bob Irsay] owning the team. But it never happened. It was always promises of, 'Hey, we're gonna get this done.' But you never saw anything actually happen. You'd go to other stadiums, and the visiting locker room was better than our *home* locker room."

Steadman had fire in his belly, and in his April 1, 1976, column, he went on a rampage:

> Unfortunately, Baltimore is getting what it asked for in leadership. It elected drones into positions of high office and is now paying the price. The sports fans, who also vote, are going to awaken some morning and find they have lost the Baltimore Colts and Baltimore Orioles. It could happen… Mayor William Donald Schaefer tried every conceivable way to see that a new stadium was erected, but it turned out he was merely a voice crying in Clifton Park. City Comptroller Hyman Pressman went the other direction. He championed the cause of keeping *Memorial Dump* [emphasis mine] where it is and led the charge to put it to referendum… Someday, somehow, somewhere, Baltimore is going to awaken to the realization that it allowed negative thinkers to control its destiny. That's a decision that could haunt Baltimore for years and decades to come. If the teams leave, the allocation of blame has already been defined. No investigation will be necessary.

And relying on Pliable Pete in New York to block a move was dicey. Irsay just needed 20 of 26 owners to thumb their noses at Rozelle and vote aye.

Entrepreneur Jim Rohn said about urgency (which Baltimore didn't have), "Without a sense of urgency, desire loses its value." Three division titles from '75-'77 didn't wake up the pols to the looming threat. "The team in '75, '76, '77, they were doing pretty good [three straight division championships]," Len Burrier—The Big Wheel—observed. "And the city *still* didn't want to do anything. That upsets me. And everybody I talk to says, 'Well, Irsay was a drunk, and he was gonna move them anyhow.' I don't care. If I own a business, and I'm in a city where I have a big following, a lot of money coming in, a lot of advertising—but the stadium looks like crap, and the city won't do anything… People don't understand that. I would've built a new stadium."

Question P being a near rout—56% to 44%--with all three local papers and Reverend Steadman lined up against it is a head-scratcher. But three factors played into it: 1) the emotional ties to Memorial Dump; 2) Pressman and his lackeys making such a racket about it; and 3) the siesta taken by the anti-P camp. "It came down to building a new stadium. Moving forward to modernization," Marching Ravens president John Ziemann emphasized. "And they [the voters] voted it down. In my opinion, Question P was the death knell for losing professional sports in the city. Once they lobbied and voted for it—once that happened—it was only a matter of time that we were gonna lose professional sports. And I'm very thankful that we held on to the Orioles."

While Phoenix played coquette with Irsay, sports editor Verne Boatner of the *Arizona Republic* thought the city was being played. At the same time, Boatner saw the disarray over in Baltimore: "What has really happened is that the city of Baltimore and state of Maryland have decided not to build the Colts a new stadium," he wrote in early April 1976. "As if that weren't enough to irk Irsay and [Joe] Thomas, season ticket sales have plummeted in recent years. The Colts used to be automatic sellouts at Memorial Stadium, once running off a string of 52 straight. But last year season ticket sales dropped to 28,500, and Irsay doesn't expect them to be a lot better this year, even though the team is on the upgrade after making the playoffs."

Although it's fair to lambaste Baltimore given their ham-fisted approach to the stadium quandary, the mindset was different back then. Indy Colts writer JJ Stankevitz emphasizes that team moves were rare:

It's easy for us to say now in 2024, when franchises do move semi-regularly, that it [the assumption the Colts wouldn't move] was misguided, but back in the '70s, teams weren't just picking up and moving in the NFL. There was some legitimate belief there because you just hadn't seen it much in major professional sports. That didn't happen a whole lot back then in the two most stable sports leagues—the NFL and major-league baseball. It was almost an unconscionable thought that they would do that, in addition to the NFL having rules back then that were there to prevent teams from moving. And until Al Davis [of the Oakland Raiders] challenged them, the thought probably was that the NFL wouldn't allow them to pick up and move.

A post-mortem on the Colts' move by the *New York Times* in December 1984 confirms that cities rarely fretted over such things. "The mayors of pro football towns have not always had to confront such trauma. In times past, the National Football League expected that a franchise that had grown up in a particular city would stay in that city; the owner was expected to work out his problems with local officials. He could, of course, appeal to the league, but he would not be permitted to move unless supported by three-quarters of the other owners. And when the proposed shift was toward a smaller city, approval was unlikely; a cut in the potential television audience could lead eventually to a cut in the annual fee the networks pay the league, currently about $14 million per team."

So, Baltimore sat back on its haunches while Irsay flirted.

. . .

Joe Thomas didn't know it at the time, but his row with Ted Marchibroda during the 1976 preseason was also his noose. He wigged out at Ted in Detroit, Ted resigned and Irsay stuck by his GM until the players said, hell, no, Ted won't go and boycotted practice. That ploy boxed in Irsay, and he talked the coach back on the job. This, of course, neutered Joe Thomas. "To this day, I believe that you stand up for what's right," Colts running back Lydell Mitchell proclaimed, defending the boycott. "There's the old saying, 'If you see a good fight, jump in.' In this case here, we had a good reason to jump into the fight—to help bring Ted [Marchibroda] back, to save his job because he *was* doing an outstanding job. We got together as a team and talked about it, and that's when we said, 'Hey, we're not practicing until we get our coach back.' And we didn't."

Détente was impossible after that. Thomas got the axe at season's end. The *New York Times* told NFL Nation: "BALTIMORE, Jan. 21 [1977]—Joe Thomas, whose tactics have brought him success in rebuilding three football teams but little popularity among players

and fans, has lost a power struggle with Coach Ted Marchibroda and been dismissed as general manager of the Baltimore Colts of the National Football League. Thomas, never reluctant to discharge head coaches or cut popular players like [Johnny] Unitas, was relieved of his duties last night by two attorneys representing the Colts' owner, Robert Irsay. He had one year left on his $125,000-a-year contract and was seeking a five-year contract at nearly three times the salary."

Chances are somebody had Irsay's ear: Michael Chernoff, VP and general counsel of the Colts, a schemer who wormed his way into daily operations. Ernie Accorsi ran PR for the Colts back in '72 when Irsay took over the team. He tells a story that portends the ensuing turmoil:

> First of all, Joe Thomas ran the Colts. We didn't know what the situation was with the ownership. When we called the press conference after the sale had occurred, I was in a meeting with lawyers I didn't know and Joe, who I didn't know, thinking about how I'm gonna survive this. I don't think Irsay had arrived yet. I said, "Who do I introduce?" Irsay's lawyer [Chernoff] said, "You do the introduction. We're all outsiders." We walked out, and Joe said, "You introduce *me*." Then Irsay's lawyer came up and said, "You introduce Mr. Irsay." Now, how about that predicament? I introduced Mr. Irsay; I'm going with the owner; it was the owner's request. He [Irsay] would

come in for games, but Joe Thomas was the strongman who made all the decisions. He was making not just football decisions; he was making *all* the decisions. Irsay didn't surface as a real factor until the year after I left, in '75 [to join the NFL office], when they had the Marchibroda controversy.

Over the years, Baltimoreans embraced two myths about the Irsay era: 1) that Bob Irsay deserves all the blame for the Colts' move; and 2) that Joe Thomas was a stony-hearted Caesar who had to go. Safety Bruce Laird played on those superb '75-'77 Colts division-winners and begs to differ. "A year later [1979] Ted Marchibroda was gone, too," Laird observed in the book, *Sundays at 2:00 With the Baltimore Colts.* "Unfortunately, he didn't have a strong front office, and when Joe Thomas left, Ted and the players lost their buffer between them and Bob Irsay. Whether or not you cared for Joe, to me and the guys who came after me in the next four or five years, he was a football guy and we loved him. A straight-shooter, he let you know where you stood with him. If you were a mealy-mouthed guy, going to play one week and take two or three weeks off, Joe Thomas didn't forgive. When Marchibroda had to deal directly with the Irsay-Chernoff echelon, I don't think he was ready for that, and something was lost. Sure, we knew Bob Irsay. He'd come into the locker room with his entourage after the games, and we'd let him hang out with us. Then he was supposed to go back to Chicago and leave Joe in control.

Joe paid our checks; he was the man. The all of a sudden, we don't have Joe."

Of all the boneheaded moves that Irsay made in Baltimore, here's what former Colts great Lydell Mitchell thinks is #1: "I think the single worst thing that happened to the organization was when he [Irsay] let Joe Thomas go, fired him. Then Dick Szymanski became the general manager. He wasn't equipped for the job—didn't understand it, tried to live in the old times, how they [NFL players during the '50s and '60s] got treated—and never changed. He also had Irsay's ear, and unfortunately, that's when it started going downhill again. Szymanski tried to run things the way [GM Don] Klosterman and all those other general managers did it back when he was playing. Consequently, that's when things started coming apart."

Ernie Accorsi wants to make one thing clear: Joe Thomas was a phenomenal football mentor. "What turned out to be a doctorate at Harvard for me was, his [Thomas's] wife did not move up [to Baltimore] right away," Accorsi explained. "And we went to dinner—I'm talking about every night now—every night at the Cinnamon Tree restaurant [in Lutherville, MD]. He got the same thing: two crabcakes, French fries and a glass of Suavé Polo wine. [Colts offensive coordinator and N.Y. Giants GM] George Young was a great influence in my life, but he kept everything close to the vest. Joe didn't; he talked. He gave me a complete education on player personnel. Gave me the philosophy I used later [as GM of the Browns and Giants], then he turns around and builds that [Colts] team in two drafts."

Zip, zam, zoom—three great drafts in a row, '72, '73, '74: WR Glenn Doughty, RB Lydell Mitchell, S Bruce Laird, LB Stan White in '72; QB Bert Jones, DT Joe Ehrmann, DE Mike Barnes, DB Ray Oldham in '73; DE John Dutton, DE Fred Cook, OG Robert Pratt, WR Roger Carr, DB Doug Nettles, WR Freddie Scott in '74; throw in OG Ken Huff in 1975. The man had zero finesse, but it was Joe Thomas who created the Sack Pack, the Shake-and-Bake offense and three straight division titles. "I'm gonna tell you—" began Troy Lowman, producer of the documentary, *The Ghosts of 33rd Street*, "I might be in the minority here, but in the Irsay era, those '70s Colts teams [1975-1977] were arguably as good as most of the Colts teams in the '50s and '60s. They had some bad luck. They had the Steelers and the Raiders in front of them. One of the best teams that never went to a Super Bowl were those '75-'77 Colts. They were phenomenal teams. I look back, and I still can't believe at least one of those teams didn't go to the Super Bowl. What the Colts did was, they ran into an all-time great team. You take the Steelers out of the mix, they probably go to the Super Bowl."

Fans saw Thomas as football's Simon Legree, but Ernie Accorsi encountered a man with a beating heart:

First of all, I thought he [Thomas] was a man of his word. That means everything to me. In 1973, the last game of the season is against New England, and it's snowing. The night before, my wife developed a serious condition. The top doctors told me it could last a year. This all happened the day of the game. I called Joe, and I said, "I have a medical emergency; I'm gonna be late for the game." He said OK. We get her to the hospital, and I'm about as low as you can get. We had three kids; my parents were still in Hershey, Pennsylvania. I didn't know what the hell to do. They came down that morning, so I could go to the game. After the game, Joe said, "Well, let's talk tomorrow morning." I didn't know if I was gonna have to resign, get another job. I explained everything to him [Thomas]. Joe, who everybody thought was this cold, ruthless guy, said to me, "You do what you have to do for your family. We got an assistant here. I'll support you every way. You don't have to worry about anything. I trust you. You will do your job. I have confidence in you. You're not gonna hear me second-guess you or anyone *else* in this organization. And if they do, come to me." Thank God. I got my kids to Hershey, had great support and was able to do my job pretty well. So, I will never forget what Joe did for me. That gives you an example of the empathy he had.

● ● ●

In 1979, Carroll Rosenbloom decided to bug out of L.A.—problems with the

Coliseum—and move to Anaheim at season's end. So, L.A. was open for business. Irsay elbowed his way in. "Colt owner Robert Irsay, who says he is incensed by red tape surrounding his plan to build a training site in Baltimore County, will meet with Los Angeles officials today to discuss a possible move of the Colts next year to the West Coast," the *Morning Sun* divulged in January 1979. "Such a move, however, would likely meet with strong resistance from National Football League officials, based on recent comments from Pete Rozelle, NFL commissioner."

Irsay's wanderlust had been on hiatus for about two years ever since he had toyed with Memphis and Phoenix in '76. But he was at it again, and the *Morning Sun* stated that Rozelle was out to sideline Irsay before he got a head of steam:

> Pete Rozelle, Commissioner of the National Football League, said in Miami before the Super Bowl game that he did not believe any team should move because all 28 teams are in the black. "It's of great concern to me," he said. "Any time a team leaves an area, there is a void, and we don't like to see it. But I don't think any existing team can justify moving to L.A. They are all being adequately supported, are in the black and have financial stability. There is no reason for them to move. I think one thing that has helped make our league great is the fact that we have had such stability. We haven't had franchises floating

around." Mr. Irsay growled his reply yesterday. "Nobody can tell me I can't move my own property. A federal judge has said that no one could prevent a man from moving his franchise." He did not elaborate.

Just a little spouting off, is all.

Carroll Rosenbloom got razzed for ping-ponging between homes in New York and Florida and wandering into Baltimore only on weekends for home games. An "absentee owner" they called him. But he was a Baltimore native; Robert Irsay was a carpetbagger from Chi-Town who couldn't wait to scram, postgame. Ken Denlinger of the *Washington Post* wrote about Irsay's sales junkets in October 1979. He quoted an insider: "I don't think he (Irsay) would mind moving at all. He's an absentee owner, anyway. That plane of his can go just as easily to Memphis. And what he's doing isn't all that different from what Carroll [Rosenbloom] tried with the Colts and [Jerry] Hoffberger tried with the Orioles to get the stadium improved. I'm not saying his style is right, but he might get something that nobody else could."

In late January 1979, Irsay headed out west with some Colts execs to talk business with L.A. officials. "Los Angeles—Several members of the Los Angeles Coliseum Commission met with Colt owner Robert Irsay yesterday and came away optimistic they could move the Baltimore team to Los Angeles despite a warning from the National Football League commissioner, Pete Rozelle, that league approval would be almost impossible to obtain," reported the *Morning Sun*. "Another meeting is scheduled tomorrow when the Los Angeles group will present other proposals to Irsay, who said he is tired of the red tape he has encountered in attempting to build a sports complex to house the Colts' training facility in Owings Mills in Baltimore County."

How much of the red tape was bureaucratic foot-dragging is hard to figure. But Irsay was irked about it. "If you want to know the truth," he told the *Associated Press*, "I was just trying to draw attention to the bureaucratic mess I've run into trying to begin construction of a practice facility for my team. It's my money, but you wouldn't believe the hassle we've had trying to get this facility built."

Such was the hurly-burly inside Bob Irsay's head. L.A. was out for now. He got what he wanted from the ploy—folks scurrying in Baltimore. "The Great Colt Scare of 1979, while not dead yet, has apparently been consigned to the back burner," apprised the *Morning Sun* in late January 1979. "Owner Robert Irsay declared yesterday that the Colts would play the 1979 schedule in Baltimore and that discussions about moving the football club to the Los Angeles Coliseum for the 1980 season—when the Rams abandon the facility for Anaheim—will be continued at a later date."

Irsay ran his standard M.O. at L.A.: cordial sit-downs, smiles and I'll-think-about-its, false hopes from the played party and a U-turn back to Chicago. Pure theater, but Irsay was still miffed about the Owings Mills slow-walk. "I've never seen a shuffle like I've gotten in Maryland," Irsay told the *Sun*. "I don't think they want the Baltimore Colts in the state of Maryland. Mayor Schaefer has been fine, but the county and state don't seem to care. All I want is for the people in the county to allow me to build my training site in time for the team to use it by Sept. 1 [1979]. But now, the Los Angeles people have made me a very interesting proposal, including a training site and office complex by them, and a big cut in the concessions and parking at the Coliseum." Mention another suitor and watch Baltimore sweat—part of the game.

Irsay turned on the blender when things got too quiet and tranquil. "Los Angeles (*AP*)—A man identifying himself as Baltimore Colts owner Robert Irsay called the *Associated Press* yesterday and said he was moving his team to Los Angeles in 1980, but local officials said they have not talked to Irsay in some five months," the *Morning Sun* indicated in mid-June 1979. "'I know he hasn't talked to Kenny Hahn [a member of the Board of Supervisors and the Coliseum Commission] or myself since last January,' said Coliseum general manager Jim Hardy. 'I'm equally sure he hasn't talked to Bill Robertson [head of the Coliseum search committee], who is out of town, since that time, either.'"

Maybe he just wanted to start a fire drill. "I decided our governor of Maryland was too busy to see me," Irsay told the *AP*. "But I had a nice conversation with [CA] Gov. [Jerry] Brown. We will move here next year. We will train here and everything will be here, everything that Los Angeles promised me. Last year was the final year on our contract, and leases starting now are all on option. In 1980, we'll come to Los Angeles. They stopped construction on our new facilities in Baltimore today. I'll be in Los Angeles another day or two. I have met with the mayor [Tom Bradley] and the governor." Either this was more Irsay phantasmagoria or he was pump-faking Baltimore into a hurry-up on the Owings Mills complex.

Now the Maryland governor was peeved; he claimed that Irsay was ducking him. "The Governor doesn't want to talk and [Mayor] Schaefer has promised a lot of things that nothing ever came of," Irsay told the press. "I canceled my vacation to meet with Governor Hughes Monday the 18th [of June 1979]. He called me yesterday and said he was not available until further notice. That's three dates canceled by the Governor. I guess you elected God, not a governor." This wouldn't be the last time Irsay picked a scrap with Harry Hughes. And all this was news to the guv. "Gene Oishi, Mr. Hughes's press secretary, said the Governor has had no appointments scheduled with Mr. Irsay and has canceled none," the *Sun* revealed. "'At this point, Mr. Irsay will have to get together with our staff, and his lawyer, and see what alleged appointments were made with whom,' Mr. Oishi said. 'After that, I think he would owe the Governor an apology.'" Obviously, somebody was lying. Cast your bets, please.

John Steadman saw the red flares go up and dashed to his typewriter. In a column in the *Washington Post* in mid-June

1979, Steadman called Irsay "irrational" and claimed Pete Rozelle would thwart a Colts' move. He saw this as a fight for the sporting soul of his hometown:

The beauty of Baltimore is its diversification. It's a major city not dependent on any single business or industry. The Orioles and Colts have become a way of life and certainly aren't taken for granted... Baltimore is not about to become a ghost town for sports, even if it has become increasingly trying in this summer of 1979 to be a Baltimore Oriole and Baltimore Colts fan, where one owner [Jerry Hoffberger] is trying to sell a baseball team and can't get a buyer who suits, and the owner of the football team, meanwhile, is threatening to go to Los Angeles because the governor of Maryland, he says, broke an appointment for a meeting. Baltimore has been much too good a sports city, with a rich tradition, to have to endure this kind of treatment from owners who never lost any money on their investment and stand to make immense profit the day they decide to sell and move away, with or without their teams.

Maybe it was gamesmanship, maybe he was serious or maybe booze mucked up the wiring. Steadman discussed this during a radio interview with Nestor Aparicio in January 1997:

I don't know whether it came from how he [Irsay] was fortified and the stuff he was puttin' into his system, but he was always jumpin' around. You could never pin him down. When he'd cough, he'd say "Oh, that's the malaria, the yellow jaundice I picked up in New Guinea [during WWII] with the Marines." Well, shucks, he was never west of the Mississippi River. The Marines, in 1943, dismissed him with a discharge that was less than honorable. He is a [psychological] study, but it's a sad study because I think when he was stone-cold sober, he wasn't that bad of an individual. He didn't get up every day and say, "I'm gonna get Nestor Aparicio." Or "I'm gonna do him in today." That was not in his mindset. It really wasn't. He just wandered through life, and the trip was a lot more enjoyable for him if he was putting something into his system. He was a heavy drinker—usually vodka—and he became totally out of control. He would say anything, promise anything.

Baltimore, Schmaltimore, Irsay was looking to make tracks. "He was building a case that he knew he was going to leave," former WMAR-TV-Baltimore news director Wayne Lynch suggested. "He had made up his mind; he just hadn't put all of the ingredients together. I think he was building a case all along, and he was picking a fight so that he would appear to be a victim. He was the antithesis of what Baltimore expected from its sports teams. He was the opposite of Johnny Unitas; Alan Ameche, who started Ameche's

restaurant; Artie Donovan, who had McClellan's, over on the Alameda; and Bill Pellington, who had the restaurant [The Iron Horse] in Timonium. This was *all* Baltimore. And he was the antithesis of that. He had no loyalty to it. So, it was very easy for him to look the other way."

. . .

Florida decided to join the party. Tampa got its expansion team in 1976; Miami had the Dolphins. But Jacksonville was shopping: "Colts owner Robert Irsay today confirmed reports he is talking with representatives of Jacksonville, Fla., about moving the team to that sun coast city," reported the *Evening Sun* in early August 1979. "Regarding the latest move rumor, Irsay said, 'I have received offers, all unsolicited, from Jacksonville, Phoenix and Indianapolis. They're all about the same.' Irsay said these offers were similar to the one he received from Los Angeles city officials early this year. 'I'm very serious,' Irsay said. 'I'd say it's a good possibility of moving to Jacksonville, based on what I've been told the city can produce. Jacksonville is one of several cities I'm looking at. I love Florida. In fact, I have a home at Bal Harbour,' a city north of Miami Beach."

Irsay relished the sweet talk and had Baltimore on a roller coaster. Mayor Schaefer tried a new tack to throw Irsay off his game. "It's Mayor Schaefer's considered opinion that Baltimore 'hasn't paid enough attention' to Colt owner Bob Irsay 'while we have been busy worrying about the Orioles,'" the *Evening*

Sun announced in August 1979 while Irsay was teasing Jacksonville. "The mayor made this remark today while Irsay reportedly was in Jacksonville, where that city threw out its welcome mat in an attempt to entice the Colt owner to move his team there. 'I think we should spend more time and effort with Mr. Irsay,' said Schaefer. 'I think the business community should recognize that he has a $19-million investment in this city.'" That one went nowhere.

Vito Stellino covered the big one for the *Morning Sun*, the move in '84. He doesn't fault Irsay for shopping around. "Oh, definitely, because he still had the Memorial Stadium problem. I don't know how serious he was the entire time. He came to Jacksonville and had this huge rally [1979]. He was justified in being upset that he wasn't getting a new stadium. But had he not driven the franchise into the ground to start with, maybe they [Baltimore officials] would have been more receptive. But it's hard to say because times were so different back then. You can't blame him for shopping the team because Memorial Stadium was just not adequate. But, as usual, Irsay didn't handle it very well."

Jacksonville played jezebel when Irsay swooped down in a helicopter on August 15, 1979. "Jacksonville—Baltimore football fans will have to admit after last night's turnout of 45,000 in the Gator Bowl that Jacksonville not only loves the Colts, but wants them, too," Cameron C. Snyder wrote in the *Morning Sun*. "The demonstration, featuring free food, a rugby match, sky diving, bands,

cheerleaders and a live horse—presumably a Colt—showed a zeal unmatched in Baltimore since the sudden-death championship victory of 1958 ... Colt owner Robert Irsay was impressed by the earlier portions of the program put on by the city of Jacksonville. But when he landed by helicopter at midfield last night and the 45,000 fans rose and shouted, 'We want the Colts, we want the Colts,' time after time, he really had to feel that he was coming home."

Throw out the good excuses for staying home—'72, '73, '74 and '78—and Colts fans had gotten pretty soft and spoiled. Rosenbloom griped about apathy when he left in '72. So, while Jacksonville kissed Irsay's rump, Baltimore gave him the finger. As usual, the Baltimore press pounced on him. Phil Jackman roasted Irsay after the Jacksonville jamboree:

Forget the way he jumped in and butchered personnel situations—the early coaching muddle, the Marchibroda-Thomas showdown, contract negotiations, etc. This indictment concerns questions of business ethics and it's lengthy enough. The mayor of Jacksonville, Jake Godbold, got an indication of what a sweetheart Bob can be yesterday when the white tornado laid down his list of demands. Eyewitnesses said the man's Florida tan suddenly became as snowy as the Tiger's dome ... Meanwhile, back here we look at the rich and proud history of the franchise and ask,

"How could a guy be so completely dissatisfied when he's making money hand over fist?" Hopefully, Bob's insatiable ego was salved sufficiently with yesterday's media happening in Jax. Writers from up and down the Florida peninsula shuttled into town to view his triumphant entry, a reenactment of DeGaulle's return liberating Paris. Little do the locals down that way know that the whole thing could end up more closely resembling Bill Sherman's march to the sea.

The players were also fed up as Irsay got ready to pink-slip Ted Marchibroda and the Colts had lost 10-straight. Colts captain and QB Bert Jones fired off a salvo. "And, while the club has been losing, rumors have grown stronger that Coach Ted Marchibroda will be ousted by the strong-willed owner, Robert Irsay, who is unhappy with Jones as well," the *New York Times* reported in October 1979. "'I don't think we need any coaching change,' Jones said from Baltimore in a telephone interview. 'But when you've got a guy who owns the ball club and who doesn't act normal all the time … He's unpredictable, to say the least.' And the Colt players, Jones said, 'bear the brunt from the fans when he says the hell with Baltimore.'"

And Baltimore was on thin ice up in New York. Rozelle didn't exactly offer full-throated support: "NEW YORK (*AP*)—National Football League Commissioner Pete Rozelle lunched with Colt owner Robert Irsay and came away with the impression Irsay doesn't want to move the team. 'He (Irsay) filled me in on what happened in Jacksonville (Fla.),' Rozelle said yesterday. 'I got the impression, or feeling, that if something were done there (in Baltimore), he would be happy to stay in Baltimore.'" Then came the scowl. "The commissioner pointed an accusing finger at the state of Maryland, saying, 'I think they (state officials) should try harder to look into it (Irsay's problem).' Rozelle said he was disappointed 'that there hasn't been at least more study given.' He said that in Maryland, 'I have never seen any indication of anything being done on a really serious problem and how it might be resolved.'"

That kick in the fanny failed to get the town scrambling. Other cities that got blasé got abandoned. Houston got left high and dry in 1996: "St. Louis [2015] is not the only city that has been victimized over the decades of relocations across the leagues," noted Jack Noonan in *The Boom in Franchise Relocations: Moving Cities, No Matter the Cost*. "In 1996, the Houston Oilers owner Bud Adams moved his football franchise to Nashville when Houston government officials would not pay $245 million for a new, domed stadium. As another team left a city, the burden, again, was left to the Houston taxpayers of an approximately $50 million of outstanding bond debt, which were incurred to pay for the stadium improvements in 1987."

Lesson: The meek do not inherit the team. "You gotta look at all of this through the lens of money," observed Colts documentarian

Troy Lowman. "The money became really big, became everything. So, Irsay was a businessman. I'm in the camp that says Irsay was a drunk, and he was an awful owner. But he was NOT the only reason the Colts left. The big difference between the Rosenbloom and Irsay eras was football was just a sport in the '50s and '60s; it became big business in the '70s. And this town [Baltimore] had a hard time with that, I think. The players at that point were making a little more money. They didn't stay in town [during the offseason]. They were a little more detached. It still wasn't like it is today, but it was evolving."

Carroll Rosenbloom heard crickets from the city when he started pushing the issue, and Irsay and Baltimore talked past each other. Phil Jackman of the *Evening* Sun indicted both parties: "Owner Bob Irsay goes galavanting around the country shouting he wants to move the Colts and he's sick of what he considers a snub by the governor, and [Gov.] Harry Hughes wonders what he's upset about when it has been in the papers maybe 15 times… Folks in Annapolis are at odds with Bob Irsay. They say they're not aware of Colt complaints and wonder how they can set something up to talk out the situation. It's called a telephone, guys."

The schoolyard squabbling picked up again in late August 1979. Irsay threatened to call off a meeting with Governor Hughes after a mood hit him one day. Taunting Baltimore after the Jacksonville lovefest, Irsay told David Lamm of the *Jacksonville Times-Union*, "Colt fever in Jacksonville, Colt cold in Baltimore." "'Baltimore doesn't care. I'm proceeding 101 percent toward October 29,' when an NFL owners' meeting is scheduled in Dallas. Presumably, Irsay can call a vote of the other owners, who have the power to approve any move. Irsay believes he has 23 votes, which is two more than the required votes he would need to shift the franchise."

With Irsay's track record of fabricating and falsifying, moaning that Hughes had snubbed him multiple times was pure hot air. And telling the governor to "go to hell" from L.A. upped the animus. Gene Oishi, Hughes's press secretary, told the *Evening Sun*, "If Irsay won't come to the Governor, the Governor will come to Irsay." Irsay was asked if he would gas up the jet and head to Baltimore to meet the governor, and he fibbed, "I've been having a lot of trouble starting my airplane lately."

Irsay, Schaefer and Hughes had their Yalta at the Timonium Fairgrounds on August 29, 1979. Irsay had a message for both: Make it quick, or I'm out. The *Morning Sun* ran an editorial the next day and offered two suggestions:

1. The city and state need to make a firm commitment to improve Memorial Stadium beyond the $1 million a year currently coming from the state and $300,000 or so from the city. It's a fact that football has taken a back seat at the stadium, which was built for baseball. Maybe Mr. Irsay won't get everything he

wants—the skyboxes with automatic martini machines are out—but seating expansion and other improvements can be had.

2. Mr. Irsay must make a simultaneous commitment—one that will impress suspicious legislators—to keep the team here for, say, five years. He says he's in no "position" to do so. Fiddlesticks. He owns the franchise outright and is fond of pointing out he can do anything he wants with it if the other owners let him. Well, between now and his October 31 deadline, let him act like a statesman. The Governor, too. This is a consistently successful franchise *made so by Baltimoreans*. If his gamble falls through, Mr. Irsay ought to sell the team and butt out.

Irsay thought playing statesman was flying down to Jacksonville and having a powwow with the mayor and Chamber of Commerce hotshots. The Jax offer included: 1) a guarantee of $6 million a year over 10 years from tickets and stadium revenues; 2) renovating the Gator Bowl—40 skyboxes, a new press box and a 40-acre training facility. Jacksonville was $2 million light in what Irsay wanted, so it seemed the trip fizzled. In late September, while Irsay mulled the Jacksonville offer, Memphis and L.A. were on the docket. He told the *Evening Sun* three times in 15 minutes,

"It's not a matter of if I'm leaving [Baltimore], but where I'm going. I'll make the final decision, but I'll listen to their [the other owners'] advice on which offer appears the most profitable."

Jack Noonan wrote a doctoral thesis in 2018 at the U of Mississippi School of Law about the hopscotching of sports teams, *The Boom in Franchise Relocations: Moving Cities, No Matter the Cost*. Cities go toe-to-toe with each other to woo owners away from home: "Cities across the country are willing to compete, to recruit, and fight for professional sports franchises because they want the alleged reputational and economic benefits that teams are believed to provide to the host city. Local governments are spending obscene amounts of money to set up the best scenarios to earn a team and a status of a 'major league city.'"

Rich guys get to call the shots and make cities grovel. "The current state of professional sports allows the individual team owners to have too much power," Noonan concluded. "This unregulated power gives a type of free authorization to team owners when deciding whether to move their franchises to cities. If the league tries to stop them, the team can sue the league, and most likely win [after the Al Davis/Raiders decision] under antitrust law claiming the league is restricting their team's free trade to move cities. As a result, cities are having to submit to demands from the teams to build brand-new stadiums, mainly from the taxpayer's pocket."

Bob Irsay was running this scheme with L.A., Memphis and Baltimore late in 1979.

Charlie Euchner in *Playing the Field* mentions Oakland and Baltimore as big-time victims of these shenanigans:

> Some of the most storied franchises in sports, like the Oakland Raiders and the Baltimore Colts of the National Football League, have shifted to other cities regardless of loyalty from the hometown fans. Perhaps more important than the actual moves have been the threatened moves. By simply exploring options for playing in other cities—by playing the field, so to speak—teams have gotten all manner of largess. New stadiums are only the beginning. The willingness to threaten departure has secured for teams a variety of land deals, lower taxes, more revenues from parking and concessions, control of stadium operations, guaranteed ticket sales, renovation of stadiums with luxury seating, control over neighborhoods and transportation systems. The list goes on.

. . .

The pistons were firing in Bob Irsay's head when he saw this headline in the October 2, 1979, *Evening Sun*: **End of a Love Affair? Colt fans despise Irsay more than they did Joe Thomas.** Labeled "commentary," it was more like an alley mugging. Jim Miller and Doug Brown implied losing was only half of it: "Only five games old, the [1979] season already has become for many the most upsetting in memory. The team has lost before,

such as the poor 2-12 record in 1974, but never has a team so turned off its town and fans. But poor play is not the reason for the grumbling. The discontent can be traced directly to Colt owner Robert Irsay's threats to move the franchise to another city. The actions of the peripatetic owner, who lives in a fashionable Chicago suburb, have done more to alienate Baltimore's football fans than any loss and have angered more than former General Manager Joe Thomas ever did."

That was just for starters. When the Colts Corrals has to fan out and drum up support for a sinking ship, times were bad:

> One group of perhaps the most loyal Colt fans, the Council of Colt Corrals, hopes to blunt Irsay's effects with a series of meetings this week to combat fan apathy. "We don't like what's happening, and that's why we're having emergency meetings with other organizations this week to see if we can remedy the situation," said Bill Isaacson, chairman of the 3,000-member organizations. "What we're scared of is what we hear from the fan, who is pretty much fed up, saying let the franchise go and we'll get another one. I don't think the ordinary fans realizes that you just can't let a franchise go and pick up another one. We have to show the league office that there is fan support here. We have to put up with the tirades of the owner, but in order to keep the franchise here, we have to show that we are here. This

is like a true fan's stand." Except for a brief chorus of "Goodbye, Teddy" aimed at Coach Ted Marchibroda, the ire has been directed at Irsay. A banner was carried around the upper deck which stated: "Irsay, the Jacksonville Jackass," and the owner himself was the target of one angry fan's tossed cup of beer.

The display showed as much class as 20,000 fans standing up and mooning the man. Irsay used "Irsay sucks" and press sniper fire to justify opting out of Baltimore. Rozelle and Co. also picked up on the bad vibes, which garnered no sympathy for the town.

Some felt Irsay got what he deserved. Longtime Baltimore sportscaster Scott Garceau recalls what Johnny Unitas told him: "I got here [to Baltimore] in 1980, and I knew they [the Colts] had been slipping, but I didn't realize to what extent. And I remember I was at The Golden Arm [Unitas's restaurant] one night, and John [Unitas] was in there, and we were talking. The subject came up: Gee, John, only 34,000 at the game last Sunday. And he said, 'Let me put it this way, Scotty. If I stood at the front door [of this restaurant] every day when people came in for lunch, and I punched them in the nose as they came in, after a while there wouldn't be many people in the restaurant. Basically, that's what he [Irsay] has done to the fans.'"

Maybe it was a doomed romance from the start: pushy, demanding, incoherent, preposterous moneybags; provincial, proud, nononsense, blue-collar town. "I sometimes think that with the Baltimore fanbase, there were the really hard-cores, the Hurst [Loudy] Loudenslagers, and then there were the other ones: 'We're a hard-working town. We love the Colts; we love our radio team with Chuck [Thompson],'" former WMAR-TV news executive Wayne Lynch observed. "These are guys who worked at Sparrows Point, at Broening Highway, and they made a good wage. They were hard-working people, and it may have been difficult for them to support somebody who was always threatening to move." Quirky, the folks didn't mind, but not a soused, pug-nosed despot.

Bob Irsay had jilted the town for so long, enough was enough. "Baltimore's a very provincial town, always has been," lifelong Baltimorean Tom Marr IV observed. "It has always self-protected, has always been in D.C.'s shadow. And they're [Irsay and Co.] messing with the Baltimore Colts, messing with their favorite son. And there's rumors that they're gonna cut or trade Johnny Unitas; they're gonna purge all the Baltimore Colts that just won a Super Bowl [two seasons before]. And they were in the playoffs next year [1971]. And so, the talk around the school playgrounds reflected what their parents were telling their kids. We would see on the news how they're destroying the Colts. All of that was rolling around. It's like, 'What have we gotten ourselves into?'"

Longtime Colts assistant coach at Baltimore and Indy, Rick Venturi, says there is plenty of blame to spread around. "I think it was just a perfect storm, to tell you the truth. You can assign blame any place you want. You can say that we [the Colts organization] were responsible for not putting a great product on the field. You can blame the [Baltimore] city fathers—whether it was legislated or not—for not having the foresight to build a better place, which they only did about 10 years later [actually, 14]. You had a volatile owner, and you had a press corps that would bait him at any moment. When you asked me the original question—where were we—we were at low ebb."

Baltimoreans raise their hackles when you bring up plummeting attendance. The question is: Do Colts fans get a pass for nosediving attendance once Irsay started bungling; or, being told the team might split, should they have packed the ballpark to suggest don't dare try it? Blaming Irsay and a team below water might be the easy out. The Colts were a clown show, excluding '75-'77, but watch the snit you get if you play devil's advocate and question the apathy.

All through the late '50s to the early '70s, Colts tickets were tougher to score than Oscars. Once the Orioles finished (sometimes only after the playoffs) and they slapped together the endzone stands, sellouts were routine—the standard 60,238. Game after game, year after year, 60,238. The 51 straight sellouts, "the world's largest outdoor insane asylum"—nobody else in the NFL could match it. Strangely, though, the streak ended the year the Colts won the Super Bowl, 1970-71. The streak bit the dust in Week 2: Only 53,911 showed up for a Monday night game

against the Chiefs, the second game ever of MNF. They played the AFC Divisional and Championship games at home and were way short: about 9,000 against the Bengals and 3,500 against the Raiders. Big games versus Paul Brown and John Madden but thousands of empties. At the asylum? The '70 and '71 World Series at Memorial had the same look, TV cameras panning to clusters of orphan seats in the upper deck.

Then there was '71—with a run to the AFC championship, no less—and the empties got more regular. A tough game against the L.A. Rams at 33rd in early November drew 57,722, about 2,500-shy of capacity. To be expected, Shula and the Dolphins sold out the last week, but 58,476 showed up for the Bills the week before. Recall the benchmark: 60,238.

Then Irsay rolled into town and Amateur Hour began. That first year, 1972, 60,000 came by to boo Shula, but nary a sellout all year, crowds averaging in the mid-50s a year after reaching the AFC championship game. Something impossible through the late '50s, the '60s and early '70s—waltzing up to the window on game day to buy singles—became the norm. In 1973, after Irsay and Joe Thomas had jettisoned Unitas, Curry, Mackey, Matte and most of the old guard, more of the same: 52,293 for the Saints, 52,707 for the Oilers, 52,250 for the Bills, 52,065 to close out a putrid season.

Let's ignore the lousy crowds in '74; this was the year that Irsay gave Howard Schnellenberger the heave-ho, and Joe Thomas drew plays in the dirt: 2-12. The nadir was the 31,651 who watched the 6-7 Jets put 45 on the Colts. Average attendance for seven games—36,012, about 25,000 empty seats per game. The next year it got interesting, 1975: worst to first. The Colts started out true to form, 1-4. Then they went nuts—nine straight and the AFC East championship. Go to war, Miss Agnes. Discount the two crummy crowds before they got hot and check out the other five, keeping in mind this was a bona fide historic playoff run: 35,235 for the Browns; 52,097 for the Jets (now 5-4); 42,122 for the Chiefs (now 7-4); 59,398 (still no sellout against Shula, now 9-4); and only 48,678 in the playoff clincher against the Patriots. The magic number was always the same: 60,238. So, what gives—outhouse to penthouse and folks still stayed home?

A Whitman's sampler of attendance over the years:

1965 (10-3-1, playoffs): Oct. 10, Lions, 60,238; Oct. 24, Rams, 60,238; Nov. 21, Eagles, 60,238; Dec. 12, Packers, 60,238

1967 (11-1-2): Sept. 17 (baseball season), Falcons, 56,715; Oct. 15, Rams, 60,238; Nov. 5, Packers, 60,238; Dec. 3, Cowboys, 60,238; Dec. 10, Saints, 60,238

1970 (11-2-1, Super Bowl champs): Oct. 25, Patriots, 60,240; Nov. 15, Bills, 60,240; Nov. 29, Bears, 60,240; Dec. 19, Jets, 60,240

1973 (4-10): Oct. 8, Chargers, 55,459; Oct. 29, Dolphins, 60,000; Nov. 26, Patriots, 54,907; Dec. 3, Bills, 55,390

1976 (11-3, playoffs): Sept. 19, Bengals, 50, 374; Oct. 10, Dolphins, 58,832; Nov. 1, Oilers, 60,020; Nov. 28, Jets, 44,023; Dec. 12, Bills, 50,451

1977 (10-4, playoffs): Oct. 9, Bills, 49,247; Oct. 30, Steelers, 60,225; Nov. 20, Redskins, 57,740; Nov. 20, Jets, 50,957; Dec. 11, Lions, 45,124; Dec. 18, Patriots, 42,250

1979 (5-11): Sept. 9, Buccaneers, 36,374; Oct. 7, Jets, 32,142; Nov. 25, Dolphins, 38,016; Dec. 9, Chiefs, 25,684

1983 (7-9): Sept. 11, Broncos with Elway, 52,613; Oct. 9, Patriots, 35,618; Oct. 23, Dolphins, 32,343; Nov. 13, Steelers, 57,319; Dec. 4, Jets, 35,462; Dec. 18, last game ever, Oilers, 20,418

They got 60,238 for a full house but could park a few more skinny rears on the benches for special occasions (60,763 for the '77 Ghost to the Post game; 60,225 for the Steelers, same year). They could get 56 and change, max, before the Orioles closed up shop in October. The problem is this: why no sellouts, regular season, in '76 and '77, when the Hosses were a legit playoff team and Bert Jones was working his magic? The Colts went from doormats to dandies overnight, and they couldn't pack the joint?

Maybe fans were still getting over the havoc Irsay wrought the first three years he was in town. One Colts fan summed up the prevailing sentiment in 1979 when Irsay was looking for new digs. "Irsay should keep his mouth shut," grumbled Memorial Stadium vendor Bob Ways to the *Evening Sun*. "He ruined the attitude of the whole club, talking and running around the way he is. We haven't had any sellouts for a while, but I think this would have been a good year if he kept his mouth shut. I'm at the point where I don't care if he moves the team. Then we can get a new team. It would be great if Steve Rosenbloom came back to run it." Careful, fella; the expansion route was out if Rozelle blamed Baltimore for any of it. Such chowheaded thinking by bureaucrats and fans left Baltimore a lap behind Indy in the battle for the Colts.

But the attendance drop was about more than just Irsay's messy bed. Steve Rosenbloom talked about how the Colts' move to the AFC after the '70 merger pissed off Baltimore fans. Former PR director and Colts GM Ernie Accorsi thinks the foul mood lasted for years:

> I think the biggest thing that hit that city in '70 was going to the AFC. Baltimore was a traditional, historical city that had built up sports hate—hate for the Bears, hate for the Packers—and every year, those teams came in there and played. All these rivalries. And I don't diminish that because all you have to do is look at the colleges, Ohio State-Michigan or Penn State-Pitt. You can't get a ticket. Then, all of a sudden, four teams came in there [to Memorial Stadium]: white helmets, white shirts, white pants, a team

with a little fish on its helmet, the other one with a buffalo on it. There was only one team that they had any animosity towards, and it was the Jets. So, I think the jump to the AFC was a huge factor in the eyes of a lot of people. I'm speaking as a fan too. Eventually, those teams became very competitive, but in my eyes, we're going to a minor league. And I know our coaches also lost something, not that they worked any easier. I remember walking out of the Denver stadium before it got redone, and [coach John] Sandusky saying to me, "God, these places are dumps." They had an attitude that it was minor-league. I think that hurt a lot. And I know other people felt the same way.

There's a fair chance that almost a decade into the merger, fans were still sulking. By then, Irsay was the culprit. John Steadman addressed the lackluster crowd after the last game in '79:

> That only 25,684 spectators turned out to watch meant the Baltimore Colts were playing before the smallest home crowd in 25 years, or 176 games ago. It was Nov. 28, 1954 when the Colts met the San Francisco 49ers in Memorial Stadium that so few bothered to come… Now it's a quarter of a century later and the Colts' gate has slipped to the depths. There were 11,542 men, women and children who bought tickets

for the Colts-Kansas City Chiefs game on Sunday but decided not to use them. Outside the stadium, a man was holding up $9 tickets for $1 each and finding no takers … The combination of two losing seasons in a row, what the public believes is arch-conservative football and the travels of Bob Irsay, the club owner, around the country—who was saying the Colts were available to other cities if they would promise him a good deal—created an apathy that hasn't been known in the history of this golden memory franchise.

In short, the Irsay traveling circus was old and stale. "I think a lot of fans got tired of all the drama with Irsay," declared former *Evening Sun* columnist and author Kevin Cowherd. "When I got here in '81, and I'm watching games during the '82 season, the place [Memorial Stadium] was half empty for these games. But there was still that loyal, hardcore base. But all the drama with Irsay, all the negative press they were getting at the time—so, maybe you can blame journalists too—the city fathers made it clear that they felt Irsay was a pain in the ass. I think all of that alienated a lot of fans."

Rooting is an affair of the heart. So, when Bob Irsay monkeyed around with the team, bile bubbled up. "There is an interdependent relationship between a sports team and city that runs deep within the people of the town," Jack Noonan noted in *The Boom in Franchise Relocations*. "The relocation of a major league sports team can bring emotional distress and sense of loss to the fans of the former team. Leagues have been subjected to tremendous criticism from its fans when a team relocates."

All right, forget loyalty. Irsay's burlesque show canceled that out. "I'm not sure you have to buy a product when that product isn't good," veteran Baltimore sportscaster Scott Garceau observed. "And when the man who makes the product is getting money from that product, you decide you don't want to give him your money. I think *that* is what happened. And the product wasn't as good because the football team wasn't as good. From winning championships, suddenly you had a team that was four, five, six games under .500. Obviously, that didn't help. I remember [longtime NFL coach] Bud Carson telling me, 'When the fish stinks, it starts from the top [the head]. And everybody in the organization knows. That's the bad thing. Even the players know—that he's not in it to win it.' That was permeating through the franchise at that point."

Cut the fans some slack, says Tom Marr IV, son of Baltimore radio legend Tom Marr. "In the cosmic realm of the entire thing, the fans played their part in it. I just don't know how you can say the fans were at all to blame. This [the Colts and Memorial Stadium] was their life. This was the soul of their city. This was the soul of who they were and how they saw themselves. What could the fans have done differently? What *would* they have done differently? Memorial Stadium was a church; it was a Sunday-at-2:00 church [kickoff time for

Colts games]. It was the second church service in a very religious, Catholic city—Baltimore. Sundays at 2:00 was their second mass."

Marching Ravens president John Ziemann points an accusing finger at the man in charge:

> You had an owner who was erratic. The saying was, if you didn't get him before 10:00 in the morning, he would be drunk. You had an owner who would get on a headset and tell the coaches what players to put in. You had an owner who would go down on the field and berate the players and go in the dressing room after a loss and berate all the players. He was a man that pulled away from the community. If the players were doing an autograph session, they had to pay for their own photographs. Some of the people out here had just had enough. You had a man that pulled out from all the local charities. The only person who kept the charities going in Baltimore was the late Harriet Irsay [his wife], who was a wonderful lady. And I don't think [Colts lawyer] Mr. Chernoff or Mr. Irsay liked that too much, from what I understand.

Bob Irsay turned the proud franchise into chopped liver, so fans naturally moseyed off. Joe Nawrozki of the *News American* wrote his own retrospective right after the Colts left: "After [Bert] Jones and the zany [fun-loving Colt] 'Looney Tunes,' the Colts became

bogus. No matter what sort of logic applied, [running back] Curtis Dickey and his millions could never compare to the athletic and humane wonder of [Colts HOFer] Lenny Moore, who eventually was fired by Irsay from the Colt front office. Many loyal fans came to resent the Colts. With Irsay at the helm, the team could have been IBM or Exxon. It wouldn't have mattered. The fans were beat over the head with Irsay's threats, his iconoclastic behavior, lawyers, agents, leases and demands that they buy preseason tickets."

Even Pete Ward, current COO of the Indianapolis Colts and former Colts PR assistant in Baltimore, can't criticize the fans. "Well, fans are fans, and you can't blame them for doing what they want to do with their money. I've always said it's incumbent upon the team to make it worth the while of the fans to spend their money on the product. But to my point: The [team] dynamic had changed, and having a good team—even a division champion—wasn't enough. I still think our fans had a 'prove-it' attitude. 'Show me how good you are.' And that meant more than just winning the division."

In December 1979, right before Christmas, Irsay stepped out of character: He apologized. Steadman was willing to postpone the court-martial:

> When Robert Irsay says he's sorry for violating the trust of friendship, the apology has to be taken at face value. So why shouldn't the public be receptive to giving him another chance? It's the

sporting way, the American way and the human way. The only way. Irsay alienated the loyal followers of the Baltimore Colts, the team he has owned for seven years, by engaging in around-the-country hand-holding and other flirtations with the cities of Los Angeles, Jacksonville and Memphis. But it wasn't serious, he says. It was all a charade. He was merely "winking at a homely girl," but not about to marry her. He realizes he made a mistake in putting Baltimore in such an embarrassing situation. Himself, too. Irsay got stinging reaction from the season ticket holders, who were upset with his forays about the country and his actions in leading Los Angeles, Jacksonville and Memphis into believing the Colts were available like some cheap hobby horse … The ticket buyers demonstrated in the only way open to a disgruntled customer. They stayed away. The team Irsay owns looks the part of a last-place outfit and that's exactly where it is.

Behold: the apology, on official Colts stationery. "In view of the events of the past several months, I feel something should be said to the people of Baltimore and Maryland who have supported the Baltimore Colts for so many years. Maybe I did not do it the right way, but what I had in mind from the beginning was a better stadium for the Colts' fans. I never wanted anything else … I also want to say I have always felt there are great people in this area and great football fans … We want to stay here and we want to bring Baltimore and Maryland a championship like we have in the past. This is all that we are committed to. I also want to wish everyone a happy holiday and promise you a fresh start in 1980."

Bob gave them coal in their stockings—the Colts were slapped around the last three games and finished 7-9. There were 30,564 and 16,941 attendees with nothing better to do.

Baltimore fans weren't about to buy a lemon. "Putting spectators in the stands is as important to the Baltimore Colts as winning games," John Steadman noted after the '79 season. "It's the dual objective. Their bread of life. One only had to gaze upon all those empty Memorial Stadium seats to realize the public was not going to accept what the Colts were offering in 1979. There's no law compelling anyone to attend a bad show, which is what the Colts were in the season gone by."

While dressing down Irsay, Steadman also dragged in Carroll Rosenbloom—an oldy and goody, and the 51-straight sellouts, always boastworthy if it suited him. But his Rosenbloom dyspepsia had flared: "Although it was reported the Colts once sold 50,000 season tickets, this was a *fabrication* [emphasis mine] to try to make it appear the demand was better than it was. The string of a reported 51 sellout games was another *fraudulent 'con' act* [emphasis mine]. The highest season ticket count ever reached here was 48,000. The *rest was a lie* [my emphasis]. But when exhibition games were added to the package [by Irsay], after the team had gone into decline, resentment replaced enthusiasm." Direct from Bizzaro World, says Steve Rosenbloom, former president of the Colts and Rosenbloom's son. Steady didn't bolster his case by plugging the 51 straight to Pete Rozelle in '72 while Tampa was angling for the Colts.

Irsay gets most of the blame for fans tuning out, but other things—the AFC move, the end of the Unitas era, a slew of lousy years—were also factors. Current Indianapolis Colts COO Pete Ward just thinks the old zest was gone:

> This isn't based on scientific research, but I think the dynamics [in Baltimore] had changed. There was a new generation. There was an older generation that grew up with Johnny Unitas and that era of icons, and I think that when that team went away, it was almost like the fanaticism that existed back then just kind of died. And it was difficult to rekindle without being a Super Bowl contender. There was a period of four or five years— from '67 through '71—when the Colts were legitimate Super Bowl contenders. They may have had the best team in football in '67 and '68. Every year was a hunt for the Super Bowl trophy,

and it wasn't easy to get that feeling back unless you had a dominant team. And when Bert Jones, the Sack Pack and that group became good in the mid-'70s and emerged as a contender, they still didn't win a playoff game. It was just a different dynamic, and I just think that the fanbase was a little spoiled or emotionally exhausted when the Unitas era ended. There is a certain magic that can occur between a team and its city, but being a dominant team and a consistent contender is a big factor in that dynamic.

The *Chicago Tribune* asked Irsay about that new dynamic, the Unitas fixation, the insane asylum, the 51 straight sellouts. "They aren't the same fans," Irsay remarked. "Do you realize that those people who were 50-year-old fans back in the Unitas days are now 75 years old? They all preached John Unitas to their kids. That's all I ever heard; never anything about Bert Jones. People don't realize there are many teams in the NFL that have never been in the playoffs."

Knocking Johnny U and the golden era— always a bad play. Especially when your team was stuck in the basement. Baleful Bob, however, had bigger problems than owning a cellar-dweller: the mausoleum on 33rd Street.

CHAPTER 12

YOU CAN'T FIGHT CITY HALL

Bob Irsay and Maryland Governor Harry Hughes finally exchanged phone numbers after all the dancing around. In early October 1979, Irsay got Hughes on the blower for about five minutes, long enough for him to keep nerves jumping: "He said it's an open question as to whether he moves the team or not," Hughes told the *Evening Sun*. "The option is still open to keep the team in Baltimore, depending on whether things work out satisfactorily." Obviously, Irsay was gauging how far he could string out finagling the city.

More intrigue came a week later. "Colt owner Robert Irsay has taken the first concrete step toward trying to move the city's professional football franchise, but *if* he can move it and *where* he plans to move it are major problems," the *Evening Sun* revealed. "A National Football League spokesman yesterday confirmed that Irsay has requested that his proposal to move the franchise be placed on the agenda of the NFL owners' meeting in Dallas October 30-31 [1979]. Irsay made the request Friday in a four-hour meeting with NFL Commissioner Pete Rozelle, in which the owner said he still intends to move the club."

Maverick Raiders owner Al Davis excluded, most NFL owners were button-down tycoons who saw Bob Irsay as a loose cannon; getting 21 of the 28 to OK a move was a non-starter. One team move in two decades: the Chicago Cardinals to St. Louis in 1960, a win-win for both cities. The Bears had Chicago all to themselves, and St. Louis got itself a ballclub. "Our position is that we have historically supported the league policy of not selling, bartering or trading franchises," Cowboys president Tex Schramm told the *Evening Sun*. "I think one of the major reasons for our stability has been that we haven't done that." Then, Schramm gave Baltimore something to fret over. "However, there is another side to that. We feel it behooves a city to have modern, first-class facilities. With what we see as competition in the future—cable television and other forms of entertainment—we think it is important for the fan who attends an event to do so in comfort. At the present time, Memorial Stadium and some others in the league are falling behind in that category."

Falling behind because of cheap talk and finger-pointing. "You can't paint them [Bob and Jim Irsay] in any kind of sympathetic light," stated Troy Lowman, the producer of the Colts documentary, *The Ghosts of 33rd Street*. "Irsay was a drunk; he was mean; he was not a nice person; nobody liked him. But when it came to brass tacks and business, he was right about the [stadium] renovations. And they would not help him."

Veteran sportswriter and Irsay-era beat reporter for the *Morning Sun* Vito Stellino condemns how bureaucrats ditched plans for a new stadium and pushed renovating Memorial Stadium:

They [Baltimore officials] were naïve. The idea of renovating Memorial Stadium was ridiculous. You would have practically had to level the whole thing. Memorial Stadium was built in stages. It was originally just one deck. Then they put the upper deck on. So, renovation was not feasible. You had to build a new stadium. There was just no sense of urgency. Everybody knew the stadium was bad, but there was no sense of urgency to do something about it. Nowadays, we've gone completely the opposite way. These owners are billionaires, which they were not in that era [the '70s and '80s]. But they still now get

hundreds of millions of dollars in public funds to build new stadiums, in Jacksonville, Tennessee, Buffalo. The threat [to move] is always there, so they get sweetheart deals to stay. But the early '80s was just a different time.

Jaws in Memphis hit the floor when Irsay dumped them in media res in mid-October 1979. "John Malmo, a representative of Memphis Mayor Wyeth Chandler, said the Tennessee city's chances of getting the Colts were 'slim' after a one-hour meeting with Irsay in Chicago," the *Evening Sun* reported. "'We took a presentation to him, and we got a little more than 20 percent through it, at which point certain questions came up,' Malmo said early today from his Memphis home. 'We started discussing the questions and answers and the meeting deteriorated from there. We never even finished the presentation. He walked out of the meeting, we caught a plane and came home.'" Malmo also said Irsay was bluffing about Jacksonville, and Los Angeles knew better than to get serious with a chronic double-crosser.

Irsay now needed gendarmes in Memorial Stadium with fans out for his scalp, like Lincoln in Richmond. Current Colts COO Pete Ward assessed the treatment once Irsay started playing Let's Make a Deal. "Not kindly. I witnessed it myself, witnessed them outside of his [Irsay's] suite at the stadium on game days, chanting things to him that were not complimentary, so I think that affected him. It impacted his sentiment towards the city of Baltimore. I'll be honest with you. When I was there [1981-1984], I always felt like it was a hostile city towards the franchise. That's how I felt, and I was an administrative assistant [in PR]. So, I imagine it impacted Bob Irsay many times more than it did me."

Irsay huddled with the other owners at the Dallas meetings while Baltimore twiddled thumbs, unless you think another plan bound for the shredder was due diligence. They hired another architect. Governor Hughes and Mayor Schaefer took a look at three options proposed for Memorial Stadium and the estimates--$17.1 to $36.3 million, this flurry coming after Robert Irsay barked a little louder. Pretty drawings, but where was the money? "He [Governor Hughes] already has said it probably would be difficult to obtain state funds for the project, since the legislature last year indicated its unwillingness to pump additional state funds into the city-owned stadium," the *Evening Sun* admitted. The Baltimore two-step—two steps forward, two steps back.

Jewell Downing & Assoc./Iffland Kavanagh Waterbury P.C. was the alphabet soup firm that got paid for the plans. They came up with three options for the stadium spruce-up:

- Extend the upper deck to cover the lower deck's bleachers, left- and right-field sides, for 9,000 more seats; maybe revamp the mezzanine level to build 50 private boxes. Cost: $17.1 million.

- Extend the upper deck all the way AND add a permanent lower deck behind center field for 13,400 more seats. Cost: $21.6 million.

- Extend the upper deck ALL THE WAY AROUND to make an oval and add a permanent lower deck behind the center field fence for 20,900 more seats. Cost: $34.2 million.

The addendum hauled out the old feud. "In addition to the major seating changes, the architect said it would cost $2.1 million for other changes sought by the Colts and Orioles," the *Sun* indicated. "Both teams, for instance, expressed interest in installing a new playing surface, perhaps the 'prescription turf' similar to Miami's Orange Bowl. The Orioles sought a modified scoreboard to include more space for messages. Other proposed improvements sought by the baseball team, according to the report, include expanded offices, $236,000; renovated media facilities (also requested by the Colts), $295,000; and renovations of the Orioles' quarters, $186,000." The Birds got the better of it, as usual. Besides more seats, all the Colts could score were better digs for the scribes at war with the owner.

Smelling the fear in town, the Colts Corrals whipped up another campaign to ratchet up gusto. The *Evening Sun* described the desperation:

Members of the Corral executive board met with Mayor Schaefer yesterday afternoon at City Hall to find ways to boost public support of the Colts. In addition, the Corral has sent letters to owners of the other 27 National Football League clubs, asking the owners to reject any appeal by Mr. Irsay to move the team … "The Mayor has set up a meeting with the Council of Colt Corrals, the Quarterback Club, the Baltimore Colt Marching Band and the Greater Baltimore Committee for next Tuesday," said Bill Isaacson, the chairman of the Council of Colt Corrals, a series of local booster clubs. "At that time we will try to decide on a program to increase fan support and, most important, keep the franchise in Baltimore where it belongs. We are hoping to get away from the defeatist attitude [of some fans]. The Mayor and the city have been very responsive in trying to help out and set up a program."

Isaacson sent a three-page letter to the other NFL owners that no doubt got into Irsay's mitts. "Irresponsible and disloyal ownership and/or management should not be allowed to destroy the product that many years of loyal and devoted fan support has created … Ownership that fails to accept responsibility to the fans and community and does not personally conduct itself in an acceptable manner can destroy a franchise." Isaacson obviously missed the irony—trying to jack up fan support while bragging to owners about the "many years of loyal and devoted fan support." And Isaacson's kicking Irsay in

the pants was dubious strategy. Bob would be drinking Smirnoff a few years hence in his box at the Hoosier Dome.

John Steadman was panicky, probably sensing way before most that Irsay wasn't just running his mouth about leaving—cobble together 21 of 28 votes and he was gone. Steadman jumped all over Baltimore politicians. He made the right call, in late October 1979:

Now that the 798th plan (or is it the 897th) to improve Memorial Stadium has been revealed, there seems to be no practical alternative but to go ahead and make *some* of the things happen. It's like when you live in an old house and there's a decision to be made about either building a new one or contracting for renovations to the existing homestead. That's precisely the kind of decision Gov. Harry Hughes and Mayor William Donald Schaefer, with the approval of the state legislature, are going to have to consider. Meanwhile, they have a gun being held to their heads. If Bob Irsay, owner of the Baltimore Colts, pulls the trigger they may have a pro football team shot out from under them … Once again, the Stadium can be correlated to that old house by the side of the road. Either build a new one and expect to pay more or else ask an architect what can be done to enhance it as it now stands. That's the sum and substance of the subject Hughes, Schaefer and the legislature are going to have to attend to with dispatch.

If you wanted stadium window dressing, Baltimore was the spot. Anything more complex, forget it. But the *News American* thought the new plan had a shot:

Today—108 Orioles baseball victories and an American League championship later [in 1979]—much of the anti-city sentiment that burned through the Statehouse last winter has cooled. Today legislators are saying that maybe, just maybe, they would approve a "reasonable plan" to redevelop Memorial Stadium and retain both the Colts and the Orioles. Such a plan, with a price tag of between $17 million and $36 million, was unveiled Monday with little comment from the governor or the mayor. Instead, the two executives are trying to devise a workable plan—one state legislators will fund and one the baseball and football teams will buy … A key to winning state approval is packaging any funding plan with commitments from the professional teams, according to [Baltimore City] Council President Walter S. Orlinsky. "If there is a multi-year guarantee of both teams being present, the reaction would be extremely different. I don't think the legislature would act adverse [sic] if they could see a genuine possibility of keeping the teams." Any other predictions

about the future success or failure of the stadium proposal are not possible now. Too many questions remain. What will the expansion plan be? How much will it cost? How much will the city pay? How much is expected from the state? Will the improvements please the Colts and Orioles? And will the owners sign long-term leases?

Way too many questions to make it viable. The last question, though, was easy to cipher: Nope. No owner would put his Hancock on a long-term rental for a place that was going to rack and ruin. Besides, Rosenbloom, Hoffberger and Irsay only said 132 times to ditch stadium rehab. Why circle back every few years?

Another politician got into the act. "The state government should help pay for improvements to Memorial Stadium by floating up to $15 million in revenue bonds, Comptroller Louis L. Goldstein said yesterday," the *Morning Sun* declared in late October 1979. "Under his plan the state would guarantee the securities and use its Triple-A bond rating to keep interest costs down. According to Mr. Goldstein several bankers have said the money 'could be raised without any trouble at all' … The beauty of the bond plan, according to Mr. Goldstein, is that it 'won't cost taxpayers a red dime.' It would, however, require the approval of the General Assembly." HOWEVER was the rub, as usual. Two factors would shoot this down: 1) The Maryland General Assembly always choked like Stalin's

Five-Year Plan; and 2) Robert Irsay and Jerry Hoffberger wanted the stadium demolished for scrap.

The hardheads wouldn't change tack: It was rehab, come hell or high water. This *Morning Sun* editorial late in October 1979 proved what a rut that paper was in:

> Robert Irsay's threats to move "his" Colts to Jacksonville or Memphis—or who knows where else—hardly produce the ideal atmosphere in which to consider just what improvements ought to be undertaken to Memorial Stadium and how to finance them. But pique at having this Irsay gun thus pointed directly at the heads of city and state officials ought not to obscure the underlying facts. The stadium *does not need major modernization and expansion* [emphasis mine], for baseball as well as football. The two teams are enormous assets to the city and state, both economically and for the image and advertising they provide. They must be kept. And one of the prices is stadium improvement. So it is good to see Governor Hughes and Mayor Schaefer moving vigorously. Tentatively, they have picked the $21.5-million, middle-range package of improvements [extending the upper deck on both sides and building permanent endzone seats] from the three suggested by a consultant this week. We do not underwrite this particular figure. Indeed, the consultant warns that all his figures, whipped up in a hasty

> preliminary report, are "soft." Moreover, the Governor and Mayor have yet to agree on a method of joint financing. So, firm judgments later. For now, cheers for the Governor and Mayor moving "in principle" toward what must be done.

More than 40 years on, it's hard to figure why so many got stuck on this road. The two men who rented the joint wanted out. Sober minds said don't waste your money on rehabbing a geriatric. Stay stubborn and you'll lose the ballclub you love so much. Harvey Molotch, in his influential 1976 treatise, *The City as a Growth Machine: Toward a Political Economy of Place*, emphasized how sports teams foster a sense of "community," which touched upon the danger of losing the Colts:

> This [the community's movers and shakers] is the general outline of the coalition that actively generates the community "we feeling" (or perhaps more aptly, the "our feeling") that comes to be an influence in the politics of a given locality. It becomes manifest through a wide variety of techniques. Government funds support "boosterism" of various sorts: the Chamber of Commerce, locality-promotion ads in business journals and travel publications, city-sponsored parade floats, and stadia and other forms of support for professional sports teams carrying the locality [city] name. The athletic teams in particular are an extraordinary mechanism for instilling a spirit

of civic jingoism [extreme patriotism] regarding the "progress" of the locality. A stadium filled with thousands (joined by thousands more at home before the TV) screaming for Cleveland or Baltimore (or whatever) is a scene difficult to fashion otherwise. This enthusiasm can be drawn upon, with a glossy claim of creating a "greater Cleveland," "greater Baltimore," etc., in order to gain general acceptance for local growth-oriented programs.

"Love Our Colts" wasn't just a banner roped to a railing in the upper deck. The ballclub was part of the heartbeat of Baltimore.

Professor Charles Euchner described the heavy emotions wrapped up in the local team in *Playing the Field: Why Sports Teams Move and Cities Fight to Keep Them*:

> The emotional hold a team has on its home city stems partly from its ability to embody and enhance the city's identity. Whether on the playing field or as the object of competition with a city that hopes to lure them away, the "home" team is a symbol for the whole community. "By virtue of having a professional team, they are distinguished from dozens of other cities as 'major league' towns" [Janet Lever, *Soccer Madness*]. This identity can overwhelm all the other ways that a city's residents think about themselves; it therefore can obscure other possible emblems of civic identity, large and small. A city's identification with a sports team creates vivid symbolism of a common interest, but it also washes away other less dramatic concerns that might be more important for the community, like schools, parks, housing, and libraries.

For every person who brags about the library down the street, count 99 folks wild about the ballclub.

Having lived in Boston, Euchner knew all about the rally-'round-the-Red-Sawks mentality:

> There's something kind of unbelievable when a team does something rather amazing, and you can be with other people and get excited about it together, whether you're at the stadium or not. I remember when I lived in Boston, I lived in the Fenway, across from Fenway Park. And I remember coming home from a visit to New Hampshire for the weekend after a Red Sox game. I would roll down the window and say to somebody on the street, "What happened?" I didn't ask who won the game; I just asked, "What happened?" And they would say, "Ah! The Red Sox won in the 9th," or "They blew it again." You didn't even have to create a context. The context was already there, in a palpable but subtle way. So, there's that every day, keeping company with the team and with all the people who care about the

team. Then, there's the burst of excitement when the team does something amazing. And that excitement—you can't make it up. The excitement is real because it's unscripted. You just never know what's gonna happen. You kind of fall back in astonishment, and you want to tell somebody about it. Sometimes the buzz lasts for days. So, it [connecting with a sports team] has two sides of the coin: the "Oh, my God, I can't believe what I just saw"—but it's also got the kind of laid-back, comfortable-old-friend quality to it.

NFL Commissioner Rozelle wasn't exactly oozing support for Baltimore at the annual owners' meetings. More like straddling the fence: He would base his recommendation on feedback from Hughes and Schaefer "on what they feel they can support" regarding sprucing up Memorial Stadium. The *Evening Sun* asked Irsay about his strategy: "Mr. Irsay was asked if his sole intention in Memphis was to prod Baltimore and Maryland officials into quick approval of funds to improve Memorial Stadium, and in doing so was he not trying to 'buffalo' Memphis. 'Buffalo?' he replied. 'That's an interesting word. No, I don't think I'm trying to fool anybody on this matter, and people shouldn't get the wrong idea about me either. I don't have anything against the news media. I don't mind the press badgering on this subject. People have the wrong misconception about me on this matter.'" As was his wont, he kept a straight face while speaking with forked tongue.

Irsay had Steadman pacing the floor at night. He knew that Irsay wasn't just gaslighting, that if he saw an open road out of town, he'd take it. Steadman described the dilemma on October 28, 1979, while Irsay was huddling with Rozelle:

Now Baltimore is threatened with another loss. This city, considering its contributions to pro football during the past three decades, doesn't deserve such deplorable treatment. It's almost as if the Colts were being transported around the country in a U-Haul truck and offered to the highest bidder. Robert Irsay, the owner of the team, has gotten offers from various cities on what they might do to make him more comfortable than he is in Baltimore... What the Jacksonville leadership has told Irsay it will do for him is expand the Gator Bowl to a capacity of 72,000 and guarantee he will receive $5.5 million a year from ticket revenue and $1 million from other sources, such as scoreboard advertising, concessions and regional radio rights. The Memphis package is supposed to be even more impressive. So this is what Baltimore and Maryland must fight to overcome if they are to hold the Colts. They have been unfairly backed up against their own endzone and placed in a position of having to produce a plan for Memorial Stadium improvements or run a risk they don't want to take of losing the franchise. [Gov.] Hughes and

[Mayor] Schaefer really have no other option than to submit.

There was always the default option—not doing a bloody thing. While Jacksonville and Memphis promised the moon, Baltimore kept hemming and hawing.

Giving owners free rein to shop around invited competing cities to rumble. Jack Noonan, in his 2018, doctoral thesis, *The Boom in Franchise Relocations: Moving Cities, No Matter the Cost*, described this free-for-all:

> The attractiveness of professional sports franchises is what keeps this constant struggle going today. It is a constant game between the cities and the owners who know their franchise values. These individuals engage in "franchise free agency" by moving, or threatening to move, their teams to cities which do not have a league franchise. This game creates cities all across the country, doing whatever they can to entice a team to come to their city. Owners are aware that local officials perceive the loss of a franchise as a psychologically damaging occurrence, and they use this as a bargaining piece. This has created a sellers' market, and a team owner enhances their own franchise's profitability at the taxpayer expense.

Most cities do "whatever they can to entice a team to come to their city." Tampa, Jacksonville, Memphis, Indianapolis—they all went hog-wild to grab the Colts. It was no-holds-barred when they entered the Octagon. Most of the time, Baltimore just stood around and watched.

Baltimore officials forever circled back to the long-term lease nobody would sign: "Colt owner Robert Irsay today reaffirmed to Governor Hughes and Mayor Schaefer his willingness to sign a long-term lease at Memorial Stadium *if the state and city make substantial improvements there* [my emphasis]," stated the *Evening Sun* late in October 1979. "State officials also are expressing confidence that their plan for improving Memorial Stadium will put off any move to get NFL owners to approve a franchise shift. 'As long as the city and state are ready to improve the stadium, we don't think the NFL is eager to rock the boat,' said one source. 'It appears everything is falling into place,' said influential House of Delegates Speaker Benjamin L. Cardin, D-City 42nd." The MD General Assembly stuck two conditions on the deal: 1) The Colts and the Orioles agree to sign long-term leases—a laugh and a half; and 2) Baltimore City pony up some money for the stadium rehab—unlikely.

Baltimore and Maryland had so far flubbed every shot at resolution: consultants, plans, studies and legislation that wasted time and money. They'd soar over the first few hurdles, then catch a spike on the next and fall face-first. But with no Plan B, all they could do was muscle Bob Irsay into signing the lease. A *News American* editorial said as much:

Colts owner Robert Irsay has played the flirt with Jacksonville and Memphis in recent weeks, but back in Baltimore he has been pretty direct in putting a price tag on keeping the team in town. He has demanded costly improvements at Memorial Stadium. For a while, that price tag seemed to have left city and state officials in a state of helpless shock. Now, however, Mayor Schaefer, Governor Hughes and state legislators have found their footing and are meeting Irsay's directness with some welcomed business candor of their own. While the city cannot provide the $36 million in improvements it would take to satisfy Irsay's every whim, the city has made it clear it could, with state help, spend $22-$23 million in improvements. Gov. Hughes and legislative leaders are signaling a willingness to come to the aid of the city. Stealing a page from Irsay's playbook, city and state officials have tied a price tag of their own to the proposition. In return for improvements, they want long-term stadium leases from Irsay and, incidentally, from Orioles officials. We don't see any need for Irsay or other National Football League owners, who would have to approve Irsay's moving the Colts, to fumble around on the offer. The city, finally, has spoken in clear terms. It is demanding only what commonsense dictates. It is imperative that the momentum of financial initiatives be exploited quickly and fully.

Most of the folks involved were rubes in these matters and Irsay held all the honor cards. Conversely, this was over 40 years ago and owners had little experience in shopping around. Baltimore's problem was a lack of shot-callers who knew the game, who could warn the others, "It's either put up or shut up, guys. Let's not waste a plug nickel on the old dame; get some sharp minds in a room and lock 'em in until they find the dough for a new stadium." Otherwise, kiss the Colts goodbye.

Give the man credit—John Steadman saw the board two jumps ahead and made the right calls about Irsay. On October 30, 1979, he laid it out for everybody:

> What offers the saddest commentary of all is that Robert Irsay, owner of a pro football team, backed the mayor of Baltimore and the governor of Maryland into the same corner—where they couldn't escape—and got what he wanted. And, unfortunately, the heavy-handed tactic he used might have been the only way improvements to Memorial Stadium could have been agreed upon. Irsay, the president of the Baltimore Colts, didn't use a hammer to get the job done. He went in with a maul ... Maybe that was the only method he could have used that would have brought the desired result. He threatened to move to Jacksonville, Memphis or any old tank town if Mayor William Donald Schaefer and Gov. Harry Hughes didn't provide the monies through the state legislature to

update the Stadium. Reiterating, the pressure Irsay applied, as much as all of us resent it, brought the city and state to an awareness that things had to be done. If a new stadium wasn't going to be built, and the mayor said this wouldn't happen, the repairs had to be made to the current facility.

That's where they kept getting it wrong—junking new stadium plans and gawking again at the rundown joint on 33rd Street. And despite their complete misread, Irsay called the shots. Charlie Euchner, author of *Playing the Field: Why Sports Teams Move and Cities Fight to Keep Them*, says that city officials needed to know that the owner controlled all dialogue:

> For the most part, the sports teams controlled the tempo of negotiations because they were the pretty girl that you wanted to keep going out with. People in that situation can call the shots. They decide when they're sick of going to McDonald's and want to go to a nice restaurant: I'm leaving you. So, they controlled the timing, tempo, the pace and the terms of the negotiation all the time. Cities were always reactive, and that's just the way it always is. For the most part, cities don't take the initiative and say, "OK, what would be best for *us*? What makes sense for us within our large development strategy?" There are very few examples where a city says, "All right, we have

a goal, we have a vision, and here are our strategy and tactics. We're gonna do it all in a coordinated and intelligent way." Usually, they're just reacting, and that period when Baltimore and the Colts were doing all those short-term [lease] extensions, the city was just reacting at that point. And when you're reacting, you're gonna lose. You might get lucky with three or four rounds of reacting, but at some point, the team—which has been constantly trying different options to see which ones get more support—dictates the terms, and the city is just reacting.

Irsay was Rafael Nadal, pounding forehands and backhands into the corners and watching the suits scramble.

Case in point—after all the blustering, Irsay withdrew his proposal at the owners' meetings for a league vote on a move. He bought himself more time and wiggle room to watch how Baltimore handled stadium renovation plans. Irsay told the *Evening Sun* in late October 1979, "As of Tuesday, the Mayor and Governor have submitted to me a complete renovation program which they are contemplating passing through the legislature. Unfortunately, the legislature does not meet until January [1980], and after that they have a bond issue problem." Nobody had any clue what the hangup was. But he tossed out a carrot to string everybody along: "I do owe it to the city of Baltimore—and I've said this in every city I've been in—if Baltimore can work out everything, I would stay in Maryland." "Every city I've been in" was code: I'm driving the bus, so keep sweating.

In late January 1984, right after Irsay's goofy press conference at BWI, 24-year-old son Jim Irsay told the *Morning Sun* his dad was just joshing about moving all those times: "There has never been a point where the team was going to be sold. The team has never even come close to being moved. Maybe he does it for a bargaining ploy to see if he can get leverage to sign the stadium lease. This is business. To listen to other offers is normal. Even if you don't take them." Maybe the kid didn't know that Irsay had been only a handshake away from whisking the Colts off to Phoenix and that Indy was on-deck, waiting to whisper sweet nothings in Irsay's ear.

Racking their brains about where to get the money for a stadium fixup, Baltimore officials had a brainstorm: Let's form a committee! "A special panel of top government officials was to begin studying how to pay for Memorial Stadium improvements that Colt owner Robert Irsay said would keep the team in Baltimore," the *Evening Sun* proclaimed in early November 1979. "By late next month, the group is expected to come up with a detailed report on how the city and state governments can pick up the plan's $22-million to $23-million tab. The plan would then be used as the basis for action in the state legislature, which convenes Jan. 9 [1980]." But again they got it back-to-front, demanding that Irsay and the Orioles' Edward Bennett Williams commit to long-term leases BEFORE commencing with the rehab.

As a columnist for the *Evening Sun* at the time, Kevin Cowherd saw how the hopeless embrace of the stadium bungled the campaign. "It [Memorial Stadium] was just a dump. Many people have fond memories of it. I grew up in a tiny town in southern New York state, and I remember going to old Yankee Stadium. It seemed great, but people were saying, 'Oh, this place is a dump.' The problem was the stadium. They [Baltimore officials] were *not* going to bend to Irsay's will, and that was what drove everything. If they had said, 'Hey, Bob, we're gonna build you a new stadium here. We're gonna give you money as a loan to get things going. We'll forgive the team taxes for, oh, 10 years or so,' he probably would've stayed. Ultimately, it was the stadium."

Apparently, Carroll Rosenbloom's move to L.A. didn't put to bed the old Colts-Orioles feud. The Birds had some gripes about the new renovation plan. John Steadman described the latest standoff on 33rd in early November 1979:

No sooner is Bob Irsay tentatively satisfied than trouble shows itself on another front. The Baltimore Orioles are supposedly unhappy that too much is being done for the Colts and not enough for them. Isn't this beginning to sound like an old refrain? General manager Hank Peters of the Orioles said he felt the planned renovation of Memorial

Stadium doesn't offer enough consideration for his team. So, in a year of baseball and football controversy, when first the Orioles were headed for Washington and the Colts to Winnemucca [Nevada], the public is about to be put through the trauma of still another battle. Needlessly, too … The Baltimore Colts prompted the proposal [to renovate] when Irsay, owner of the franchise, threatened a defection to Jacksonville, Memphis and Eagles Pass, Mont. [Gov.] Hughes, with Baltimore Mayor William Donald Schaefer whispering in his ear, moved effectively to bring about the necessary preliminary action. Irsay was so happy, he was doing a dance and even a handstand. Commissioner Pete Rozelle likewise was elated. But for some reason, Peters wasn't.

The two ballclubs were asked to submit a wish list, and six items were mutual: mezzanine skyboxes; a posh restaurant; an upgraded press box; new locker rooms; prescription turf on the field; and lowering the playing field, so Colts fans wouldn't be staring at a row of behinds on the sidelines. But the nerve of the O's—whining about the Colts, who got nothing but hand-me-downs for years. The Colts and Orioles had been at it for 25 years and counting, with no rapprochement on the agenda.

Phil Jackman of the *Evening Sun*, panned the Colts' dreadful season (5-11) in '79 with an acrostic:

(*To the Tune of Mother*)

C is for the conservatism of our leader [Ted Marchibroda].

O is for the zero on the board.

L is for the licking as they bombed us.

T is for the Tiger [Irsay] and his roar.

S is for the stiffs who man the roster.

Put them all together they spell Colt Football, a sorry sight to behold indeed.

"Cat on a hot tin roof." Translation: Bob, the red-faced owner viewed the proceedings [a loss at Miami, 19-0] on the very warm day perched atop the press box roof. If it had been a clear day, he might have seen Jacksonville.

Somebody a bit more objective—an out-of-towner, for instance—saw Irsay's moves as warranted, albeit oafish. Ken Denlinger of the *Washington Post* opined from 38 miles south:

It sometimes has been called Irsay's Odyssey, although Irsay's Idiocy seems more appropriate. Still, while Robert Irsay has acted exceedingly foolish all these months—peddling his Baltimore Colts from town to town like some latter-day snake-oil pitchman—he's not a complete fool. Irsay has been pulling one of the slickest sporting bluffs in memory—pitting Baltimore against two cities panting for an NFL franchise,

Memphis and Jacksonville. And the man ultimately responsible for the decline and fall of a once-peerless football team is in a no-lose position at the moment. He is an easy man to dislike, although perhaps no more arrogant and shrewd than most owners. What he wants is to be rewarded for bad management, if not quite incompetence. Very likely, he will be … Whatever his faults, Irsay's tactics probably are no different than most owners would try under the circumstances. The Colts play in a stadium badly in need of improvement; what better way of assuring those improvements than to threaten to move? It is the most distasteful form of political arm-twisting, but highly effective. If this is the age of greed in sports, others, including [Carroll] Rosenbloom, laid solid groundwork for Irsay. Had Minnesota not promised a domed stadium, the NFL very likely would have voted to allow the Vikings to move to Los Angeles next season.

There are two ways to explain what came next: Either Robert Irsay was playing possum or his gastritis was in remission. John Steadman in December 1979 marveled at Irsay's brief good-guy phase:

> When Commissioner Pete Rozelle next sends out report cards, he will have to upgrade the mark of little Robert Irsay, who has been sitting in the back of the room and not so much as creating even a minor disturbance. Rozelle, who in his position with the National Football League is something like a school principal, ought to call in Irsay and reward him with a prize for the way he has improved his deportment … Rozelle, hoping to guide Irsay out of the problems he was creating for himself, had a talk with the Colts' owner and told him to withdraw from the spotlight and try to assume a low profile. He advised, in all sincerity, that he listen more to general manager Dick Szymanski and assistant general manager Ernie Accorsi. So Irsay took the message Rozelle gave him as a constructive measure for improving his situation and also his personal and public relations. Since then, Irsay has made a 180-degree turn. He has been an absolute angel.

So was Michael Corleone until they tried to snuff his dad.

Further proof of Orioles favoritism came as the makeover at 33rd was going nowhere. "A new baseball stadium in Camden Yards gives the city its 'best shot' at keeping the Orioles in Baltimore should the club decide it no longer wants to stay at Memorial Stadium, says Mayor Schaefer," reported the *Evening Sun* in mid-February 1980. "Although he hopes to convince [new] Orioles owner Edward Bennett Williams to keep his club at the 33rd Street facility, the Mayor said the city must be prepared to offer a site for a new stadium if the ballclub decides to move. 'My thinking is, if Mr. Williams decides he wants a new stadium, you make your best pitch [for him to stay] in Baltimore City, if you have something available,' Mr. Schaefer said."

Irsay had good cause to throw a tantrum and point his Cessna towards Jacksonville, given what he knew about the failed Camden dome project: "Mayor Schaefer was a major proponent of a grandiose plan to build a huge, $114-million sports stadium-convention center complex in Camden Yards nearly six years ago … Opponents of the downtown stadium plan, led by City Comptroller Hyman A. Pressman, succeeded in amending the City Charter [Question P, 1974] to bar the use of city funds for any sports facility other than Memorial Stadium."

· · ·

Options A, B and C in '79 to retool Memorial Stadium were typical Baltimore folderol—floats and marching bands lined up, but parade canceled. Meanwhile, the Colts were their incompetent selves: 7-9 in 1980, 2-14 in '81 and a spiffy 0-8-1 in the strike-shortened '82 season. It was the winter of their discontent.

About 2½ years of inertia ended with this headline in the *Morning Sun* on February 10, 1983: **Mayor Makes New Pitch for Stadium Funds**. Schaefer was again giving it the old college try: "Mayor Schaefer proposed yesterday that the [MD] legislature authorize $15 million worth of improvements to Memorial Stadium in exchange for the Orioles'

and Colts' signing six-year leases to use the facility. If Colts' owner Robert Irsay continues to refuse to make any long-term commitments to the city, the mayor said, he will seek a separate $7.5 million bond authorization to make only those stadium improvements desired by the Orioles, who apparently are willing to sign a six-year lease. 'Mr. Williams [Orioles owner Edward Bennett Williams] has no trouble with a guarantee to the year 1989,' Mr. Schaefer said. 'Mr. Irsay has trouble with guarantees. He has real trouble with any guarantees.'"

Irsay didn't have trouble spotting the sham of Baltimore's long-term leases. Back in October '79, Schaefer and Gov. Hughes were pumped about digging up $22 million to add a bunch of goodies to the ballyard—extra seating, mezzanine skyboxes, a new restaurant, a new press box, prescription turf, etc., etc. On one condition: Irsay and the O's had to sign long-term leases to jump-start it. Negative, they both said. First you fix up the joint, then we sign. Result: The plan got shelved.

Charles Euchner, an expert on franchise moves, could have schooled them in realpolitik: Lest you want to lose the Colts, boys, give Bob Irsay what he wants; cobble together a legit new stadium proposal or flag down a USFL team. While Mayor Schaefer was down in Annapolis, trying to sell the latest ($15-million) plan to remodel the mausoleum, two mouthpieces told Schaefer what they thought of the place. "Larry Lucchino, representing Mr. [Edward Bennett] Williams, quoted Hank Peters, the Orioles general manager, as saying the Orioles offices at the stadium are 'the worst in baseball,'" the *Morning Sun* reported in March 1983. "[General Counsel] Michael Chernoff, of the Colts front office, said the stadium is 'if not the worst, then running a very close second-to-the-worst facility in major-league football for watching a game and producing a game.'"

· · ·

The Indy Colts handing over Chris Hinton, Andre Rison, a 1990 fifth-round pick and a first- and fourth-round in '91 to trade up for big-bust QB Jeff George was second in all-time boneheaded moves to the John Elway debacle. ESPN devoted most of a 30-for-30 to it, *Elway to Marino*. How Bob Irsay nuked the Elway impasse is prima facie of how he drove the franchise into a ditch. Football execs knew that John Elway was a kid who could catapult your franchise. The Colts' 0-8-2 record in '82 guaranteed they had Elway in their mitts. Talk about Elway going to the MLB was just a ruse to jack up his price. John Steadman knew that Elway would be a baseball palooka: "His ability in football is extraordinary, in baseball only ordinary," Steady wrote in mid-April 1983, right before the NFL draft. "That's why John Elway isn't going to be wasting his time in a sport where he has little chance to excel. He's perceptive enough to realize it, regardless of what the New York Yankees say when they refer to him as a standout prospect. They're engaging in fantasy. A scout who watched Elway from high school through his first two years in college, when the Yankees signed him,

said his chances of becoming only an average major-league outfielder are minimal at best."

Over at Colts headquarters, one guy had the skinny on Elway: GM Ernie Accorsi. "I went to [Orioles GM] Hank Peters, and I said, 'They're playing this ruse that this guy [Elway] is a baseball prospect.' He's playing in a rookie league in Oneonta [N.Y.], and I said to Hank, 'Is there any way you can give me an idea of what the baseball scouts think of this guy? I'm not asking for any inside information. You're not scouting him, so can you give me any details, give me some kind of idea?' He said, 'Let me give you a call back.' Hank called me back and said, 'I got a scout— NP.' I said, 'What?!' He said, 'No prospect.'"

Steadman put out a loopy idea once Elway let it be known he'd veto playing for Frank Kush and Bob Irsay:

Do you know what it will take to bring John Elway to the Baltimore Colts? You, you and you. An avalanche of mail from *you*. Public input is important. The Chamber of Commerce might send him a brochure describing the wonders of the city and its surrounding countryside. But personal messages will be the most important ... Elway will be impressed if a cross-section of folks from the area— be they doctors, students, truck drivers, lawyers, dock workers, nurses, teachers, oyster shuckers or window washers—write to him telling of the beauty of Baltimore ... He could enjoy broiled rockfish, corn on the cob, and steamed crabs. In fact, there are so many similarities to Baltimore and the Oakland/San Francisco area that you can hardly tell one from the other. So Elway would feel right at home. If he comes here, and doesn't have a place to stay, we guarantee the *News American* would give him a chance to shower, shave and a spot to sleep in the editorial department.

In a nutshell: Irsay and Mikey, the Wannabe GM (aka lawyer Michael Chernoff) blinked when Elway played stare-down with the Colts. They handed a future Hall of Famer to Denver for lineman Chris Hinton, clipboard QB Mark Herrmann and the first-rounder in '84 (guard Ron Solt). Snookered. Steadman flipped his lid:

> What may well be the most disgraceful transaction in Colt history unfortunately has been consummated. The Denver Broncos were gifted with the coveted, multi-talented John Elway and gave little in return. It was tantamount to swapping a franchise for a used chin strap. Consider it a steal of a deal ... for Denver. As a holdup, it ranks with the infamous Brinks job. It's a professional embarrassment to the Colts. It elevates Mickey Mouse to a mental giant ... The Colts were said to be concerned over Elway's threat to sign with the New York Yankees and play baseball. However, no sooner had John's feet hit the ground in Denver than he signed a series of five

one-year contracts. So that proves how little interest he had in pursuing Yankee dollars. After taking Elway—who is thought by some scouts as the finest quarterback prospect ever to come out of college—the Colts were applauded for their choice by other teams. Astute NFL observers said they held on to their convictions. But that's all erased. The Colts caved in without making a sincere attempt to sell Elway on Baltimore.

After the Marchibroda-Joe Thomas skirmish in 1976, Bob Irsay jettisoned Thomas; thus, the Colts lost their detail guy. Into the void slithered Irsay and Michael Machiavelli (aka Chernoff, descendant of Niccolò; aka Mikey, the Wannabe GM). When Irsay butchered the Elway deal, Ernie Accorsi was the Colts GM and had no hand in the bungling. He looked around headquarters and saw disorder bordering on bedlam:

> When I came back [to the Colts in 1977] and [Dick] Szymanski was the general manager, Irsay was more active and so was his attorney, Chernoff. I will just say this: Once I went through the John Elway situation, I knew I had to leave. When they gave away what I thought was the greatest prospect I had ever scouted—and I left my office to go to the bathroom and heard Chernoff say, "No, we can't afford to pay this guy," and Irsay say, "Look, we're gonna leave here, and we're gonna do what we want"—I

knew something was gonna happen. So, when I went through that, I knew I had to leave. But I wasn't leaving after an 0-8-1 season, so I waited through the next year when we went 7-9 and were 6-4 after 10 games and 4-2 in the division. And I thought, *OK, this is about as respectable as I'm gonna get.* There was confusion. You couldn't do your job [at headquarters]. You couldn't concentrate, and I wanted to get with an organization that was stable. So, that's why I resigned. Fortunately, I got with a good owner [Art Modell in Cleveland] and a stable situation and was able to have a good run there. But it was just confusion.

Had Accorsi run the Elway stalemate, the Colts would have made the wunderkind sweat it out, knowing baseball was a bluff. Then, with Elway getting weak-kneed as the clock ticked, Accorsi would have shopped him around: "I asked the director of player personnel for the league office, 'What's the most return that anyone's ever gotten in a trade?'" Accorsi explained. "And he told me two ones [first-rounders] and two twos. I said, 'I'm gonna get three ones and two twos, or I'm not gonna trade him.' All I hear is he's the greatest prospect in the history of football—and he might have been—and I said, 'That's my price.' I wanted a high number-one because I thought [Dan] Marino would go high. I was picking Marino. He [Marino] said, 'I'd love to play in Baltimore.' So, I probably got my backup, and I would have settled for two ones."

But Irsay and the Wannabe GM pulled some subterfuge and kiboshed the plan. GM Ernie Accorsi absolutely flipped:

I found out from Jim Fassel, who was the offensive backfield and quarterbacks coach with Elway at Stanford, that Elway's father [John Sr.] and [Colts head coach Frank] Kush hated each other. I didn't know that. He said, "I don't want my son playing for Kush." He didn't want to play on the East Coast; I understand that. I told Irsay about the phone call [to Orioles GM Hank Peters]. So, I knew that eventually, he [Elway] would come. I told Irsay, "He's gonna cost us $5 million for five years, $1 million a year." Then I went to the bathroom. When I came back, he and Chernoff were talking. They would take over my office, and I heard Chernoff say, "We can't pay that kind of money, Bob." Irsay said, "Michael, let him [Accorsi] have his day. We're gonna get on a plane, and we're gonna do what we want to do." They got on a plane, and they left, and two or three days later, traded him. I found out watching the NBA playoffs [saw the news flash at the bottom of the screen]. That's how that happened. And I should have never brought up the $5 million. Maybe sooner or later, they would've done it anyway. I don't know.

Having made a hash of it, Irsay peddled some hogwash to the media. "Irsay brushed off the fact that he made the deal without telling coach Frank Kush or general manager Ernie Accorsi," the *Morning Sun* pointed out in early June 1983. "That happened, he said, because 'we left the Denver people late at night, and before I had a chance to get back to Frank and Ernie, it was done.' He left unanswered the question of why he made the deal over their heads in the first place. But he maintained, 'We've been very close.'"

Jim Irsay wasn't in the saddle to make the call about Elway in '83, but 40 years later, he offered his take on the fiasco. "When Colts' owner Robert Irsay traded John Elway to Denver in 1983, he made the move without consulting with his general manager or head coach," Clark Judge explained in "Colts' Irsay: 'No Way' I Would Have Dealt Elway 40 Years Ago." "Unfortunately for the city of Baltimore, he didn't consider consulting his son, Jim. If he had, history might have taken a dramatic right-turn for Elway and the Colts. That's because Jim Irsay, now owner of the Indianapolis Colts, said he never would have let Elway walk. Granted, hindsight is 20-20, but Irsay was adamant when he appeared on a recent 'Eye Test for Two' podcast and was asked what would've happened with Elway had he—and not his dad—owned the team four decades ago. 'There's no way I would've traded him,' he said. 'Are you kidding me?'"

Arizona Republic sports editor Ban Hurt reeled off a few of Irsay's draft gaffes in January 1984: "Irsay also meddles at the drafting table. Two years ago [1982], General Manager Ernie Accorsi and coach Frank Kush wanted Jim McMahon, the Brigham Young quarterback. Instead, Irsay picked Ohio State's Art Schlichter, last seen at the $20,000 window [because of his gambling addiction]. Last year, the Colts tapped quarterback John Elway. Accorsi and Kush were calling Elway's bluff to play baseball with the New York Yankees when Irsay traded the quarterback prodigy to Denver without consulting his coach or GM."

Trading Elway for a song and dance points out how havoc was the norm once Irsay sacked Joe Thomas and formed a tag team with his lawyer, Michael Machiavelli, to poke their noses where they didn't belong. The Colts had pros in the front office—Walt Gutowski and Marge Blatt in PR; Lenny Moore handling community relations; Fred Schubach in player personnel; and the consummate football wizard, Ernie Accorsi as GM—and instead of letting them run the show, Irsay and his shyster had to muck things up. Thereupon, a chain reaction: They debased the football team, Irsay torpedoed stadium negotiations, Colts fans burned him in effigy, the press skewered him, and Irsay strolled closer to the exits.

* * *

The years would roll on, but the song remained the same. Memorial Stadium was kaput, bureaucrats offered nothing but hot air and feasibility studies, and the cold war reigned until the Colts and Orioles signed long-term leases. But a big fat *Morning Sun* headline in early June 1983 floated false hopes again: **Colts Will Stay, Says Irsay:**

Speaking in a rambling, almost stream-of-consciousness style at his first news conference this year, Colt owner Robert Irsay said yesterday the franchise will remain in Baltimore "unless you throw us out," and made the following points:

- The Colts won't sign a lease for Memorial Stadium until Oriole owner Edward Bennett Williams signs one, and he suggested that Williams should "put your name where your mouth is."

- The real reason for the Elway deal was that he didn't want to meet Elway's contract demands, although Irsay claimed he made a good trade and suggested the critics should buy their own football team.

Mayor Schaefer attended the 45-minute session and said he will attempt to negotiate a lease with both the Colts and Orioles, following guidelines of the $15-million improvement package passed by the Maryland legislature *if the teams sign six-year leases* [emphasis mine]. Irsay also said the fact the Colts haven't moved in the past is an indication they won't move in the future. "The Colts could move tomorrow if they wanted to," he said. "They could have moved six months ago, a year ago. When Al Davis moved [to L.A. in 1982], we could have moved. We are not moving. We didn't move. We're not moving. The proof of that is I haven't moved. I'm here, aren't I? I wouldn't be here if I was going to

move, would I? I'll tell you what I could do—and don't think it hasn't crossed my mind—but I'm not going to do it. I could pull up 30 vans and be out of here Sunday, and you'd never know who was here, but I haven't done it."

Only bluffing—this time.

A con man always knows when he has a sucker on the hook. Robert Irsay, though a midwestern galoot, knew he was in the driver's seat and played Baltimore like a mark while he explored his options. Proof of that was the *Morning Sun* editorial after Irsay's "I'm here, aren't I?" claptrap:

Robert Irsay says the Colts are in Baltimore to stay. That is about the best news for local sports fans since a Maryland team won the Preakness. Even as losers on the field, as the Colts have been in recent years, they are important to the city. To football fans, they are the once and future champions of the National Football League. To businessmen they are an industry that generates hundreds of thousands of dollars of spending in the fall. To ordinary residents of the city, they are a morale booster that keeps the city in the same company with New York and Chicago and Los Angeles: major league ... For a long time there have been mystery and heated argument about Robert Irsay's attitude and intentions. His statement that he is here to stay deserves to be taken at face value. While sports fans never stop talking about the past, surely Baltimore's can now start emphasizing what is more important—the present and the future.

Where were the cynics, skeptics and doubting Thomases who rolled their eyes every time Robert Irsay fed them a bone?

Here's just a handful of Irsay promises not to move the team:

- November 1973: "We have absolutely no idea of moving the franchise. Please tell the people that. That's not even in our minds."

- On the eve of Super Bowl XI, January 1977: "I like Baltimore, and I want to stay there, but when are we going to find out something about our stadium? I'm getting offers from towns like Indianapolis to build me a new stadium and give me other inducements to move there. I don't want to, but I'd like to see some action in Baltimore."

- December 11, 1979: "We want to stay here and bring Baltimore and Maryland a championship like we have in the past. This is all that we are committed to."

- A year later: "I have visited no cities. I have talked to no people about moving the team."

- June 10, 1981: "The Colts are here to stay. Anyone who asks [about the team moving] is not a good reporter."

- May 1982 (after Al Davis and the Raiders won in court to move to L.A.): "I don't think the implication is that every team is a free agent. As for myself, I'm happy in Baltimore. I feel confident that there's a future for the Colts in Baltimore. I think we're all going to be sticking with the cities we've already got."

- The infamous press conference at BWI, January 20, 1984: "I have *not* any intention of moving the goddam team. If I do, I will tell you about it, OK?"

Baltimore Colts QB Bert Jones generally kept his mouth zipped about Irsay, but he did unload once in the *Morning Sun*: "He lied, and he cheated, and he was rude, and he was crude, and he was Bob Irsay. He doesn't have any morals. It's a sad state for the NFL to be associated with him, but beyond that, I've removed him from my mind."

In August 1983, Irsay had his spin machine gassed up. "Bob Irsay said during a visit to the Colt camp yesterday that he plans to meet with [Baltimore's] Mayor Schaefer next week and discuss signing a lease for the club at Memorial Stadium," the *Morning Sun* indicated. "Changing his previous position that he wouldn't sign a lease until Edward Bennett Williams, the owner of the Orioles, signs one, Irsay said there was a 'very good chance' he will sign in the near future even if the Orioles don't. 'I've just taken the upper hand to see if I can help my little mayor friend and see if we can sign,' the Colt owner said." No, siree, never came close.

Jump to September 1983. Schaefer and Irsay met, talked about stadium renovations and a new lease. What else was new: Schaefer said the meeting was "not conclusive." At the moment there was $15 million in state bonds sitting in the vault to refurbish Memorial Stadium; the rub—the Colts and the Orioles both had to sign six-year leases. So, if Irsay and EBW inked the leases, here's what they would get: "If the Orioles sign a six-year lease, the state's loan to the city would provide money for a new restaurant, 50 private lounges adjacent to box seats, renovated locker rooms, dugouts and working space for reporters, a new public address system and refurbished ticket booths," the *Morning Sun* listed. "If the Colts also sign, the stadium [lower-deck] horseshoe would be enclosed and 4,000 seats added. Facilities directly related to the football team also would be improved." Facilities "improved," whatever that meant. As always, the fair-haired boys in orange and black got most of the toys under the tree.

Notwithstanding the city playing favorites, Irsay was still in charge. Professor Charlie Euchner said as much in his book, *Playing the Field: Why Sports Teams Move and Cities Fight to Keep Them*. "The sports franchises had the advantage in talks with the city because they could initiate action whenever and wherever they wanted in the long process of negotiations. Even under the leadership of its most powerful mayor in the century [William Donald Schaefer], Baltimore had limited negotiating leverage. The city's most important tool, the power of eminent domain, was not only questionable legally but also risked pushing the team out of the city."

And Hizzoner was giving it his all. In *Glory for Sale: Fans, Dollars and the New NFL*, Jon Morgan pays homage to Mayor Schaefer:

Schaefer was not much of an athlete or sports fan. His attendance at a game was more ceremonial than passionate, like the Queen attending a cricket match. But he had built his political reputation on accomplishing the impossible for his city, and appeasing a millionaire team owner like Robert Irsay Jr., intent on breaking fans' hearts, had seemed like another task entirely within the realm of the possible. "Do it now" wasn't just the anthem of Schaefer's administration. It was his personal mantra. If, on one of his frequent Sunday drives through the city, he spotted a rain-soaked mattress or other bit of untidiness in an alley, he would fire off a tersely-worded "action memo" to a hapless department head first thing Monday. City workers who valued their careers and hearing knew to have the trucks dispatched by lunchtime … A confirmed bachelor, Schaefer was married to his job. His "rule by tantrum" created a near makeover of Baltimore. He oversaw the transformation of rat-infested fruit-cargo piers into the Inner Harbor, a waterfront attraction of shops and restaurants that opened in 1980 and became a symbol of the city's resurgence. Similarly, he found the money to have highways, hotels and a subway built, despite a rising conservative political tide against public spending and cities.

Countless times the "rule-by-tantrum" mayor had to bite his tongue and smile while Bob Irsay ran his game. Former longtime WMAR-TV-Baltimore news reporter Andy Barth says Schaefer made a good go of it. "I'm into conjecture, but Schaefer worked his heart out to try to keep the Colts and thought he was doing everything he could. And it was in the context of where teams had *not* jumped in the middle of the night and run away. And Schaefer thought he was making reasonable progress at getting Memorial Stadium fixed up and all that. Nobody was more broken up by the Colts leaving than Schaefer. He took it personally, and he thought that he had failed … There were all kinds of wonderful karma about Memorial Stadium, and a fresh coat of paint and new plumbing would've gone a long way. In the atmosphere of the day, people weren't accustomed to building one new stadium, let alone *two*, the way we [eventually] did, but that was apparently what you had to do."

Rumor had it in early December 1983 that the Dolphins' Joe Robbie was keen on building his own joint and moving the team out of the Orange Bowl. Already spooked at the thought of losing the Hosses, John Steadman

of the *News American* had his latest panic attack:

The latest scenario involves Miami, where managing-partner Joe Robbie is eager to move to a privately constructed stadium planned near Calder Racetrack—located within proximity to the more populated and affluent suburban area of South Florida … Miami and Orange Bowl officials are confidently telling each other the Colts can be had. It would entail inducing their owner, Robert Irsay, who has a winter home in nearby Bal Harbour, to ship the Colts and their uniforms, along with the players to put in them, by rail. Appropriately enough, on the "Orange Blossom Special." Instead of trying to placate Robbie and the Dolphins with improvements at the Orange Bowl—as Baltimore and Maryland are trying to do for the Colts and Orioles at Memorial Stadium—the policymakers in Miami are contemplating what they can do to attract, if need be, a future tenant. That's why the Colts are No. 1 on the preferred list of teams capable of filling the Orange Bowl void—if and when the Dolphins cut and run.

All for nought. They built Joe Robbie Stadium, aka Hard Rock, the Dolphins stayed put, and folks back home still wondered what to do about the scruffy joint on 33rd.

CHAPTER 13

DEM BUMS REDUX

About 190 miles north of Baltimore, there was a town that could commiserate with Colts fans. Brooklyn was still in mourning over losing the Dodgers over 25 years earlier. Ernie Accorsi explains:

I think the only thing comparable to the Colts fans' relationship with the players was Brooklyn [and the Dodgers]. I'm really a sports historian, and Brooklyn was a unique situation. And when I lived there for 30 years, I can tell you the Brooklyn natives never got over it [losing the Dodgers in 1957]. And I don't think the people my age [in their 60s, 70s and 80s] ever got over the Colts leaving. I haven't, and I worked in the league all these years and had two affiliations [the Browns and the Giants] after that. [Colts Hall of Famer] Gino Marchetti said it better than anybody I've heard. There was a story on Gino in Baltimore in *Sports Illustrated* maybe 15 years ago. And he said, "We were like a great high school team in a small town." That describes it all. I worked at some pretty rabid places. Cleveland was a pretty rabid football town. I think the only franchise in sports that compares—Green Bay, maybe. It's such a small town. But other than that, Brooklyn [with the Dodgers]. That's how I would describe the relationship Baltimore had with the Colts.

(The *SI* article by Alexander Wolff ran in 2016. Here's what Accorsi was alluding to: "Marchetti is still tethered to the Charm City [Baltimore]; he has no affection for—even finds himself rooting against—that team in Indianapolis, which relocated in 1984 and then promptly unretired his number [89] to give it to some random tight end before an uproar finally overturned the decision. Of the original Colts and their original home, he nails it six ways from Sunday: 'We were like the great high school team in a small town.'")

A city losing its major-league cachet is like getting demoted to *town* status. Baltimore's Mayor Schaefer presaged this three weeks before the Colts ran off to Indianapolis. "And then there is the most indefinable impact of all—the loss of prestige," Schaefer noted in an essay in *USA Today*. "The largest and most viable cities, it is assumed, are the ones with major league franchises. The publicity that comes with Baltimore's name being included in the NFL roster cannot begin to be attained in any other way. There is no question that when corporations consider locating or expanding in a city, they look at the access to professional sports activities as an important factor in evaluating 'quality of life.' So when an owner has the right to move a team at will, the answer most assuredly is 'no.'"

Morning Sun columnist David Steele in 2007 saw how Baltimore and Brooklyn were members of a mutual mourning society: "The best parts of the documentary [HBO's *The Ghosts of Flatbush*] took us to new territory, especially how badly [Dodgers owner Walter] O'Malley appeared to want to keep the team in town, and all the financial, political and social circumstances that got involved. It was riveting for the myth-busting alone. All of those aspects of the story would also fuel the Colts' story—which, truth be told, could use a little myth-busting itself. And it would be new, at least to the rest of the country. That's the allure of this tale. Brooklyn and its fans were absolutely brutalized by the Dodgers' move, and it did alter the history of that city, of the Dodgers' new home [L.A.], and of

sports overall. It's a fantastic story and HBO told it well. It still doesn't beat Baltimore's story. Equals it, maybe, but doesn't beat it."

Older folks can better connect the two moves. "Undoubtedly, the gut reaction when it comes to thinking about the Colts varies by age," Jess Mayhugh points out in "Colt Following," March 2014, *Baltimore* magazine. "'If you're in your 60s and 70s, there is part of your heart that is missing. You'll always feel slighted, cheated and robbed,' says WBAL-TV broadcaster Gerry Sandusky. 'The Baltimore Colts are to you what the Brooklyn Dodgers are to someone in New York.'"

. . .

Much of this from October 1957 sounds familiar in Baltimore, save the official announcement—in Baltimore, they just loaded up the vans and scooted. "NEW YORK—The Brooklyn Dodgers announced officially Tuesday that they plan to move to Los Angeles, ending a transcontinental tug-of-war for the most famous National League franchise of them all," the *Atlanta Daily World* revealed. "[Dodgers assistant GM Arthur E.] Patterson said the decision to move to Los Angeles came only after all efforts to find a new downtown Brooklyn site for a ballpark had been rejected by New York City authorities. 'He [O'Malley] made a very good bid to stay in New York until that was completely out of the picture. He's a Brooklyn man and has been for a long time.'"

Digest this summary of Walter O'Malley moving the Dodgers in '57 and see what sounds familiar to Baltimore in '84. Walter O'Malley.com put this out in an article titled "Unprecedented 10-Year Effort to Keep the Dodgers in Brooklyn":

O'Malley wanted to privately finance, design, build and maintain a new stadium for the Dodgers in Brooklyn. He was seeking assistance in assembling land, which he would pay for, in order to privately build a domed stadium at his preferred location at the intersection of Atlantic and Flatbush Avenues. On October 14, 1946, O'Malley writes a letter to renowned designer-engineer Captain Emil Praeger of Madigan & Hyland in Long Island City, NY, "Your fertile imagination should have some ideas about enlarging or replacing our present stadium (Ebbets Field)." However, after a study completed by designer Norman Bel Geddes in 1948, it was determined that *renovating Ebbets Field made neither economic nor practical sense* [emphasis mine], as parking would be lacking. O'Malley repeatedly appealed to New York City's powerful Robert Moses, who was Parks Commissioner for the City of New York … O'Malley wrote to Moses on June 18, 1953, "My problem is to get a new ballpark—one well-located and with ample parking accommodations. This is a must if we are to keep our franchise in Brooklyn." While at least 10 potential stadium sites were considered, O'Malley preferred the intersection of Atlantic and Flatbush Avenues because all modes of transportation converged there, including nine subway lines and the terminal of the Long Island Railroad. The translucent dome stadium that O'Malley envisioned led to discussing its feasibility with some of the greatest architectural designers of the 20th century … When it was evident that the only site Moses was willing to recommend was in Flushing Meadows, Queens, O'Malley had to consider leaving Brooklyn for that site and weighing that against other options. Only when acquiring land at his preferred site in Brooklyn was no longer a possibility did O'Malley consider Los Angeles as an option.

O'Malley could come up with the cash to build the stadium, but he needed the land to put it on. "During his unprecedented 10-year effort to remain in Brooklyn and to privately build a new stadium for the Dodgers to replace Ebbets Field and its limited parking for 700 cars, O'Malley stated repeatedly that he was not asking the city to build him a new stadium," "Unprecedented" continued. "He was seeking assistance in assembling land, which he would pay for, in order to privately build a new ballpark—a domed stadium—at his preferred location at the intersection of Atlantic and Flatbush Avenues in Brooklyn."

Here was Carroll Rosenbloom in August 1965, only eight years after the Dodgers bolted for L.A.: "Sure, Baltimore should have a new stadium. We want the best for our city, don't we? Our present stadium doesn't match up with all the new ones being put up around the country. We're the best, and we should have the best, and I would be willing to build it. Financing is no problem. I can get that done. The only thing I would insist on is that the present stadium be pulled down [so the AFL couldn't move in]."

"Unprecedented 10-Year Effort to Keep the Dodgers in Brooklyn" had O'Malley's communiques on file, like this internal memo on April 15, 1955: "The Brooklyn Dodgers have long been in need of a new, modern stadium. Unless a site can be found for such a stadium in Brooklyn, the Dodgers franchise will be transferred elsewhere. A plan to be discussed provides for a new stadium in Brooklyn. The Brooklyn plan provides for the elimination of the traffic hazard at Atlantic and Flatbush Avenues. It provides for a new LIRR [Long Island Railroad] depot and will permit the new passenger cars to come into Brooklyn … The Dodgers will have a new stadium, and the franchise will remain in Brooklyn."

Recall the brick wall that Rosenbloom hit while haggling with the city about the stadium: "We aren't interested in negotiating with the city anymore," he told Bob Maisel of the *Morning Sun* in '71. "As I told you before, I'm just tired of being the bad guy, no matter what happens in Baltimore. When we offered to put up money for Stadium improvements, Rosenbloom and the Colts were ogres, forcing their will on the people. If the city offers to build a practice field, or do something to the Stadium that would benefit the Colts, we are squandering the taxpayers' money. If we want to build our own stadium, we're bad. No matter what we do, we're wrong."

Then Rosenbloom split in '72, and the stadium impasse got dumped in Bob Irsay's lap. The *Washington Post* in February 1984 summarized his beef:

Robert Irsay doesn't really dislike spruced-up Baltimore; he just despises dilapidated Memorial Stadium. And that explains much of his erratic, often bizarre behavior since he traded franchises with Carroll Rosenbloom and became owner of the bedraggled Baltimore Colts 12 years ago. This once-proud franchise is one of the weakest in the National Football League, a victim of Irsay's whim and relentless drive to rid himself of the Memorial Stadium headache. "His concern is the stadium," one Colts source said recently. "He doesn't like it, never has. If they would build a new stadium, then everything would be different." But there are no plans to build the Colts and/or the baseball Orioles a new stadium with public funds. That forces Irsay to look to beckoning cities, either as a new home for the Colts or as leverage to pry a new home out of Baltimore's city government and Maryland's General Assembly.

Some mythology got passed down the line in Baltimore that made Rosenbloom and Irsay fall guys for the Colts packing up. Folks in Brooklyn did the same to Walter O'Malley. Peter Marquis described the mainstream view of O'Malley in *Complicating the Blame Game: New York Politics, Baseball Fans and the Dodgers' Move Out of Brooklyn*:

First, from the 1960s to the 1990s, there was a vivid anti-O'Malley sentiment, exemplified by one oft-reprinted joke: A man is asked, "What would you do if you were facing O'Malley, Hitler and Stalin and had only two bullets in your firearm?" The sordid answer was, "Two in O'Malley's head to make sure he's dead." O'Malley became the arch-villain, a cold-hearted, greedy, evil capitalist, contemptuous of the fanbase that had made him rich. New York-based journalists such as Dick Young, Pete Hamill or Jack Newfield regularly rehashed the tale of the selfish owner burning the loyalty of millions on the altar of the "almighty buck."

Marquis then bashed the old mythology (pay attention, Baltimore): "Thus, the 'blame O'Malley' narrative, however seductive it may be, begs some key questions: How did Dodgers fans—the fabled 'Flatbush Faithful'—let their club go so easily? Why was there only a scant mobilization and only in the last months of a decade-long relocation debate (1946-1957)? Is it true that O'Malley had his mind set on leaving many years before the move? What did New York officials do—or fail to do—to help the franchise stay in Brooklyn or the New York area? In other words, was this really the victory of greedy, corporate America over the honest, ticket-paying American fans?"

For half of the 20th century, Brooklyn and the Dodgers held hands. "Thus ended a colorful and often zany baseball era in Brooklyn," the *New York Times* wrote right after the Dodgers' move in October '57. "The Dodgers had represented Brooklyn in the National League since 1890. They had become world-famous, first because of their erratic baseball and then because of their winning teams. In their flight to the Pacific, they join the New York Giants, who are moving to San Francisco."

John Ziemann's stint with the Baltimore Colts and Ravens bands stretches back to 1962. Like Brooklyn with the Dodgers, Baltimore had a love affair with the Colts. "This was the toughness of Baltimore. We nurtured this team for five years. We got this sandlot football player named Unitas; we were picking up players from all over that nobody wanted. Now, they're playing the darlings of the league, the New York Giants [in the '58 championship game], and all the papers around the nation said, 'You're gonna get beat.' They didn't—in the biggest game in NFL history. We—the fans and the Colts—*made* the NFL. And this is something that brought pride to Baltimore. We were the champions, little old Baltimore that nobody wanted."

"Dem bums" the Brooklyn faithful called them, a term of endearment. "In deserting

Brooklyn for Los Angeles, the Dodgers will leave an aching void in the Borough of Churches," the *New York Times* noted. "Few baseball clubs have had greater identity with, and greater impact on, their communities than the Dodgers have had on Brooklyn. A mention of New York seldom evokes a chain-of-idea response of 'Giants' or 'Yankees' such as Brooklyn does of 'Dodgers.'"

Longtime *Morning Sun* columnist and loyal Baltimorean Michael Olesker can tell you what the Colts meant to Baltimore:

> The Colts were a signal that we weren't second-rate because in so many ways, we thought we were. We had New York to the north: self-important. We had Washington to the south: self-important. And who were we? We had Fort McHenry, the Orioles, who were terrible for the first five or six years of their existence, as were the Colts. So, we had no expectation of ever being anything special. Our people didn't work in television, didn't work in politics; they worked on assembly lines and kept their heads down. But we had characters; we had neighborhoods. And suddenly, we had these guys on the Colts who were living in our neighborhoods. I used to play tackle football after school at the Seton apartments, right off Liberty Heights Avenue. This is about 1957, maybe. A kid who lived in the apartments named John LaChappelle says, "Hey, did you hear who moved in? Joe Campanella and

> Jack Kahl." This was when the two of them were scrubs. And we're all going, "You're a bullshit artist" because we thought the Colts lived on Mt. Olympus. But no—they lived in *our* neighborhoods. [HOF running back] Lenny Moore moved into Northwest Baltimore, and my friend, Bob Miller, said that Lenny would come out and have a catch with the kids. You know, who *does* that nowadays?

There was Baltimore vs. Tampa, Baltimore vs. Memphis, Baltimore vs. Jacksonville. Eventually, Charm City would go in the ring with Phoenix and Indianapolis. But Brooklyn had L.A. wooing Walter O'Malley, on paper a heavyweight against a welterweight. It was an early version of the city vs. city free-for-alls to come. "New York and Los Angeles had engaged in a tug-of-war for the Dodgers since early in the year," the *New York Times* observed in October 1957. "A plan by which the city hoped to condemn a slum area in downtown Brooklyn collapsed when the cost of the overall project was estimated at $30 million." Baltimore had the same problem—fumbling in the red zone about the stadium. Both cities got jilted.

In February 1984, Indianapolis suited up to play the game. Mayor William Hudnut stayed mum about the details, but he admitted they were in the Colts round-robin with Phoenix and Baltimore. "We're working on it," Hudnut confessed. "The less I have to say about it, the better. Things are very delicate.

I have to protect the confidentiality of the negotiations. I don't want to blow the deal." Schaefer and Baltimore must have felt like getting worked over by three goombas.

. . .

As noted, Brooklyn also had a stadium problem. And like Carroll Rosenbloom and Robert Irsay, Walter O'Malley wanted out of Ebbets Field. Paul Hirsch described O'Malley's woes in a SABR journal, *The National Pastime— Endless Seasons: Baseball in Southern California*, in an article titled "Walter O'Malley Was Right":

> Walter O'Malley was also justified in considering a move from Ebbets Field. By 1957 the rightfield screen hung in tatters, the bathroom odors were stifling, and parking was available for only 700 cars. In 2003 Buzzie Bavasi [GM of the Dodgers from 1958-1968] wrote, "Ebbets Field was a great place to watch a game if you were sitting in the first 12 rows between the bases. Otherwise, we had narrow seats, narrow aisles and a lot of obstructed views." Mid-1950s attendance compared with the Dodgers' primary rivals of that time was also disturbing. From a high of 1.8 million in 1947, as the team won five more pennants and finished second three other times, Dodger attendance dwindled. When the Boston Braves moved to Milwaukee before the 1953 season, a worrisome situation grew dire... Another

element of the profitability question has to do with Walter O'Malley's vision for his franchise. He needed profits to help build a new ballpark, regardless of where it was located. A new ballpark was his best chance of continuing to compete well in a three- or even a two-team market [in N.Y.], given that fans were staying away from Ebbets Field despite the winning ways of the team on the field. If fewer games were made available to television, and ticket and concession revenues declines were not reversed, it was debatable how much longer the franchise would be viable playing at Ebbets Field.

The 51 straight sellouts the Colts strung together in the '60s meant zip once they went slapstick and fans got fed up. "When we got there in 1982, we were at low ebb," former Colts equipment manager Jon Scott remembered in episode 1 of the podcast, "The Move." "We weren't drawing flies. For a football-rich city, we weren't drawing fans. You went in the locker room, there was like a light that hung down on a cord, seriously. A couple of nails to put your clothes on. It [the stadium] was outdated. The fans still loved it, but they weren't coming. They were down. The team was really bad. So, at that point, in 1982, there was just bitterness. The franchise had hit bottom. The fans were angry. Bob [Irsay] was angry with the city; the city was angry with Bob. By 1983, it was a franchise in turmoil, to put it mildly."

The article "Unprecedented 10-Year Effort to Keep the Dodgers in Brooklyn" has this ultimatum to New York from O'Malley: "Locally, the Dodgers are on record as offering to build their own stadium with their own money at Atlantic & Flatbush Avenues if the land can be made available promptly and at commonsense figures. For over a year the Dodgers have had a standing offer to put $5 million in a new stadium to pay $500,000 annual rent plus 5% of gross admissions as a New York City amusement tax. If all efforts fail locally, the Dodgers could buy the necessary land in Los Angeles on which to build their own stadium, which would be on the tax rolls. The same program has been offered to New York City, where the Dodgers only need the help of the city in condemning the land." O'Malley got stonewalled, so he got out.

Irsay had some reasonable demands of his own and got the same as O'Malley, as the *New York Times* explained in "The Seduction of the Colts" in December 1984. When Irsay and Schaefer met, one-on-one, in February 1984, the mayor told Irsay, "I want you to tell me what you want me to do":

The response was one Schaefer had anticipated: Irsay paced the floor of the small conference room. "He has this habit of walking up and down, up and down," Schaefer says. Finally, Irsay delivered his demands. He wanted improvements made on Memorial Stadium. He wanted to sell the team's headquarters in the

Baltimore suburb of Owings Mills for a price that would give him a considerable profit. He wanted the new $15 million loan [to pay off the original loan]. "I started writing it down," Schaefer recalls. "'Loan? I can do that. Improvements? I may be able to do that.' A couple things I couldn't do. But most of these were manageable requests." In turn, the mayor says, he sought and received a promise from Irsay, one he would extract at each of his meetings with the Colts' owner: "He gave me his word that if he was ever going to take the team out of the city, he would call me first. I looked at him each time and asked him, and each time he told me he would."

Bob Irsay stood him up, of course.

Having written a book about cities dueling for teams—*Playing the Field*—Charles Euchner sees Brooklyn and Baltimore as abandoned bedfellows:

There are two immediate similarities— the kind of local neighborhood quality of the teams, and the fans would encounter the players on the street. They called Duke Snider the "Duke of Flatbush." There was that same kind of connection in Memorial Stadium. There was a blue-collar, working-class identity. Another thing was the way it [the moves] came down—at least the way it was reported or the way people perceived it—them leaving came as this great betrayal, this great shock. But if you had been following this stuff—if you had been reading the business section instead of the sports section—you might have realized that it was almost inevitable. Because they had been laying the groundwork; Irsay had been out in Indianapolis, out in Phoenix, being greeted by the welcome wagon out there, touring sites and the whole bit. So, it was no secret on one level, but the way he did it, with those Mayflower moving vans in the middle of the night, it was considered almost like, "He blindsided us." He didn't; he was just too chicken to do it in broad daylight. There was a feeling of being jilted, like your lover left you and didn't even leave a note. But a lot of that is projection. When you think about it, that's what sports is—projecting your emotions on these guys who happen to wear the same laundry [uniforms] every day. So, the fact that they [the fans] felt jilted was in many ways a projection. They thought there was a love affair going on; they thought that they were married. But that's not how the other side saw it.

Brooklyn and Baltimore went on long roller-coaster rides of highs and lows, usually assuming the owners would never up and leave. Choose your poison—naïveté, haughtiness, ignorance, arrogance—and they fostered nonchalance, and nonchalance cost them their teams. Look at the July 20, 1957, *King Courier* (Brooklyn), less than three months before the Dodgers deserted them: "The tremendous financial possibilities of pay-TV on the West Coast were largely exploded last week when the Mayor of San Francisco said it would cost between $50- and $60-million to install just for the SF area over a period of from three to four years, a tremendous undertaking with no sure financial gold mine at the end of the tedious rainbow. With the TV scheme eliminated for the present, with the strong possibility that O'Malley gets the stadium he wants where he wants it in Brooklyn, combined with the facts that the Dodgers have made more money than any other National League team in the past five years, we believe the Brooklyn Dodgers will continue to make their home in New York's largest and greatest borough." And H.M. Warner also said talkies wouldn't cut it in 1927: "Who the hell wants to hear actors talk?"

A-s-s-u-m-e. We all know the punchline. Most Dodgers fans—even newspapers—assumed the team would stay. Ditto in Baltimore. "I never thought for a minute that the team would leave or that he [Irsay] could rip the team away," confessed former Baltimore newscaster Andy Barth. "You remember Governor Mandel—his favorite expression was, 'C'mon, fellas, we'll work it out.' Whatever problems there were with the stadium and the finances, I assumed that they would work out, and the people who had grown up going to Colts and Orioles games at Memorial Stadium would keep doing it. It never occurred to me that they'd leave."

Tom Marr IV grew up worshipping on Colts Sundays at the ballpark on 33rd. He thinks the whole town deluded itself:

None of us believed that they would *ever* move the Baltimore Colts. I don't think there was a person that believed that. The league would never let it happen. How can you get rid of the Baltimore Colts, the team that put the NFL on the map? The greatest quarterback ever to play in the NFL was a Baltimore Colt. "The league's never gonna let them go to Tampa or Nashville. The league's not gonna let them go *anywhere*." And we believed that! None of us believed that it could possibly happen. And even if they tried, we would just say, "No, you can't." So, in that way, we were completely naïve because the Colts came here from the bones of the Dallas Texans [in 1953]. And the Orioles came here from the St. Louis Browns [in 1954]. That was a perfect example of a team that was going to pick up and move because another city [Baltimore] was outdoing them. We should *not* have been so naïve. We should've taken things more seriously. But almost every single fan and probably most of the elected officials did not think that the NFL was going to let that happen.

What most jilted sports cities have in common are *naïveté* and *misapprehension*—missing the obvious when it's staring you in the face. They sober up once the team is gone, but there ain't no do-overs.

In these cases, the sage usually gets ignored. Like Mr. John R. Crews, of the GOP, in the *Coney Island Times*, about two weeks before the Dodgers split for the West Coast, who pinned the blame for the stalemate with O'Malley right where it belonged: "Placing the blame for Brooklyn's expected loss of the Dodgers on the Democratic city administration, John R. Crews, Kings County GOP leader, today warned that the team's departure will become a major issue in the November [1957] elections. Crews charged that City Hall's 'procrastinations and antagonism' is forcing the team to accept the Los Angeles bid. He accused the Democrats of a half-hearted and inept approach to the matter. 'For more than a year, they've had opportunities to realistically explore the possibilities of keeping the Dodgers here. But with one notable exception, members of the Democratic Board of Estimates kept stalling, trying to cover up their own ineptitude by casting Walter O'Malley in the role of the villain,' he said." Getting nowhere with the Park Board about the stadium, Steve Rosenbloom of the Colts blasted the suits for "stonewalling" with arms crossed.

Owners being temperamental sorts, Rosenbloom and Irsay can't get a pass regarding their spats with the city. But fundamentally, their argument was spot-on. Baltimore politicians never got the hammering they deserved for the ham-handed way they managed things. Brooklyn was also afflicted with the slows, as Lincoln put it. Walter O'Malley complained and threatened, and N.Y. politicians generally paid him no mind. In *Complicating the Blame Game: New York Politics, Baseball Fans and the Dodgers' Move Out of Brooklyn*, Peter Marquis sullied New York pols for loafing on the job:

> Andy McCue, author of [Walter] O'Malley's latest biography to date, confirms [historian Henry] Fetter's interpretation that neither the team owner nor [Parks Commissioner Robert] Moses were to blame—if one wants to be fair—but rather, New York politics as a whole. To put it bluntly, the Dodgers owner would have stayed if New York politicians had let him. To make his point, McCue makes it clear that the risks O'Malley ran by leaving New York far outweighed the allure of the Californian burgeoning market... Although McCue exposes the club president's cat-and-mouse play with the press [like Irsay] on whether he considered moving to Los Angeles seriously, the historian is adamant that the most reasonable explanation for the move lies in the fact that O'Malley failed to strong-arm Moses and other New York stakeholders into accepting to provide federal money to buy land for a privately-owned stadium. McCue concludes by stressing his bewilderment at the lack of mobilization on the part of prominent Brooklyn leaders as well as regular Dodgers followers [fans].

With quarrels, there's usually blame to spread around. Upton Bell, longtime NFL executive and son of former NFL commissioner Bert Bell Sr., thinks Rosenbloom, Irsay and the city just couldn't get on the same page. "I'd probably come down in the middle because I think it takes two people to make or break a deal. In this case, Rosenbloom and Irsay—whether you like them or not—were right. But I also look at the other side and say, 'Are the politicians totally wrong?' They were misguided. In the end, they saw that in not pushing for finding a way to build a new stadium, both parties lost. And guess what? What happened, that 11 years later, they [Baltimore] began to build a new stadium? What changed in the 11 years, that they went from saying 'No' to saying 'Yes'? The answer is, they had no team."

So, what's the right adjective for the political brain freeze: naïve, ignorant, gullible, smug, unsophisticated, clueless? Generally, not knowing your ass from your elbow. Author Kevin Cowherd likes *naïve*: "I think it's like anything else. I don't think they [Baltimore politicians] took him seriously. Everybody knew he was shopping the team around, but I think they still never thought he would pull the trigger on that [moving]. Everybody thought the relationship with the Colts and the fans was *so* strong that, 'No. This guy wouldn't dare move the franchise out of here.' This is before not a whole lot of teams moved. The Dodgers left Brooklyn, and the Giants left New York, but for the most part, teams didn't move. So, I think there was a sense that, 'He's not gonna do this. He's shopping the team around, so what he's doing is, he's loading the gun, but he's not gonna pull the trigger.'"

• • •

Carroll Rosenbloom was stymied by Hyman Pressman and the Park Board; Walter O'Malley had Robert Moses, a political Godzilla. He needed just a patch of land to build the new stadium, but Moses stopped him cold. "O'Malley was a devout capitalist, and that no doubt drove him," Paul Hirsch noted in "Walter O'Malley Was Right." "Yet finances were not his only problem. To build a new stadium in Brooklyn, he needed a cooperative city government. That's where he ran up against Robert Moses. As the head of many public agencies, including the cash cow Triborough Bridge Authority, Moses was the most powerful public works administrator in New York City. By all accounts, his influence was far-reaching and abundant—and he and O'Malley did not see eye-to-eye on the Dodgers' needs. In divorce court this dichotomy might be classified as 'irreconcilable differences.' Moses's influence was such that nothing as significant as a major league stadium could be built without his cooperation and approval. O'Malley owned the Dodgers, and his primary recourse was to move the franchise."

If this sounds familiar—a bureaucrat mucking up a plan to resolve gridlock—it should. Professor Charlie Euchner studied the Dodgers Dilemma and recognized the clout of Robert Moses:

There's one nub to this whole thing, which is that Moses was just bound and determined to do something in Flushing Meadows. He was this visionary; he could visualize the whole region and how all the pieces fit together in his own mind. Brooklyn was going a little downhill at the time [the 1950s], plus that area in Flushing Meadows—which was the site of an old ash heap—was prime for large-scale development. That's what his vision was. So, he was basically willing to give the Dodgers anything they wanted, as long as they moved to Flushing Meadows. And O'Malley wanted to stay in Brooklyn. And Moses was not gonna budge on that because it was his master plan. Moses was the only person who mattered in New York. The mayor at the time, Robert Wagner, by most accounts was a pretty effective mayor. But all the power brokers in New York were nothing compared to Robert Moses. He basically controlled all the development in New York City for about four decades. There's never been anybody like him. So, if you're running into the buzzsaw that is Robert Moses, it's just not gonna happen. You either surrender, or you get out. O'Malley wasn't gonna surrender.

In Baltimore, Rosenbloom and Irsay went mano-a-mano with many politicos, but Baltimore City Comptroller Hyman Pressman was Mr. Thumbs-Down. "Mr. Pressman went after other issues [besides Memorial Stadium]," John Ziemann noted. "I think in his heart he was protecting the taxpayer, but I also think it was self-promotion. I don't know if he was pushing to be mayor someday or what. But he did major damage. People weren't listening to both sides [about the stadium conflict]. And it led to us losing a football team and getting inches away from losing the Orioles. If we had had Ernie Accorsi [as Colts GM], Steve Rosenbloom [as Colts owner] and William Donald Schaefer [as governor] running this situation, we would still have the Baltimore Colts."

All cities panting for a team follow the script: drop largesse in the owner's lap and kiss his toes if they have to. That's how Los Angeles hooked O'Malley. "Admittedly, Ebbets Field was a wretchedly outmoded baseball arena, one with hopelessly inadequate parking facilities," Arthur Daley of the *New York Times* stated right after the Dodgers moved. "But it still could ring a lively tune on the cash register, approximately a third of a million dollars a year. Yet Walter [O'Malley] was sincerely looking for a new site in Brooklyn, preferably with assistance from the civic authorities. But once Los Angeles began the siren song, The O'Malley was so beguiled that he was lost. The City of the Angels offered him more than the keys to the city. It gave him the keys to the kingdom. New York balked at [giving O'Malley] 12 acres. Los Angeles enthusiastically proffered 300 acres. This is the biggest haul since the Brink's robbery—except that it's legal."

 . . .

Had a smitten city offered Irsay a fleet of Brink's trucks, he still didn't want to be blackballed by the other owners. The *Washington Post* in early March 1984 figured Irsay had to take a delicate tack:

Irsay is known as a company man among league officials. He votes the league line on most proposals and seems to thrive on hobnobbing with fellow millionaires. But he also knows his peers don't approve of his attempts to leave Baltimore. If he pulls out, he will be cast in the same doghouse now occupied by maverick Al Davis. That is the kind of isolation Irsay doesn't want. Otherwise, what could prevent him from driving the moving van to the front door of the Colts' Owings Mills, Md., training complex and cleaning everything out for relocation to Indianapolis? That city has everything he has always wanted: a domed stadium, an attractive lease, a $15-million loan at a favorable interest rate, luxurious skyboxes. The offer even includes a $5-million training center built to his specifications. He is all but assured of immediate sellouts and no competition from any other major league sport. With a stroke of his pen, he would be rid of Memorial Stadium, of a Baltimore press corps he despises, of fans whose support has dwindled as he slowly dismantled a proud franchise.

Some realists in Baltimore understood that Indy was loading up on goodies for Irsay. "About the only thing the city fathers are not offering Irsay is a date with [actress] Joan Collins," Kevin Cowherd quipped in the *Evening Sun*. "What is happening is this: Indianapolis is ripping a page from the Vito Corleone School of Negotiating. The city is making him an offer he can't refuse. How can Irsay turn his back on all these riches? This time, it appears he might not."

O'Malley wasn't always on the up and up about his intentions. "Although [New York] Mayor [Robert] Wagner has indicated that the city might be willing to build a stadium in Flushing Meadow Park, Queens, for use by a major league team, this might not prove as attractive as Manhattan, the Bronx or Brooklyn to an out-of-town prospect," the *New York Times* noted after the move. "The Mayor was asked at his press conference yesterday whether he thought Mr. O'Malley acted in good faith in his negotiations with the city. 'I can only say that in my conversations with him, he said that he had no commitments, and I have to take the man's word,' Mr. Wagner replied."

Irsay welshed on his promise to get Mayor Schaefer on the phone when he was set to go, as the *Evening Sun* documented two days after the move:

It's not that the mayor sat back waiting for Irsay to call Wednesday. That day, he left four messages with the team owner because he wanted to discuss the loan package the city and state developed for him. No response. Even after the near-sleepless night yesterday [moving day], the mayor's office placed a call to Irsay in Chicago. Schaefer said he's certain Irsay got the message. No response. He said he's almost as certain that the man who once said, "Don Schaefer is my friend" won't return the call. Ever. "He didn't call his old friend, Don," the mayor said bitterly, "but I'm going to call him … In a way, this gets very personal to me when I thought someone would at least pick up the phone and say to me, 'I'm going.'"

In L.A. and Indianapolis, adoring crowds welcomed the emigrant ballclubs like DeGaulle's return to Paris. The *Los Angeles Times* noted, "Major league baseball bearing the famous Dodger insigne at long last came to Los Angeles late yesterday [Oct. 23, 1957]. It arrived officially at International Airport at 6:10 p.m. amid the blare of bands, the illumination of television lights, the flashes of news photographers and the hurrahs of several thousand fans when the Los Angeles Dodgers' special taxied to a stop at United Airlines' terminal." The *Evening Sun* covered the Irsay lovefest at the Dome: "The crowd at the Hoosier Dome serenaded him, cheered him and loved him. It gave Colt owner Robert J. Irsay everything he thought he couldn't get in Baltimore. Buoyed by the thundering applause of nearly 20,000 pairs of hands, Irsay marched proudly to the VIP stand at the 50-yard line, gave the thumbs-up sign and settled in yesterday for 45 minutes of unadulterated adulation. He was the man who had brought pro football to the Hoosier prairie … 'You guys, it's not your team, it's not our team, it's my family's football team,' Irsay proclaimed." Baltimore was hip.

Team moves can be complex, but pedestrian minds see one motive: $$$. So it was with commentators. "And a bitter end it was to be for those faithful Brooklyn fans who enabled the Dodgers to amass a profit of $1.8 million over a five-year span," Arthur Daley harrumphed in the *New York Times*. "That's the one ugly and inescapable fact that sets this deal apart from all other franchise transfers. Other teams were forced to move by apathy or incompetence. The only word that fits the Dodgers is greed."

It's easy to boil down such drama to good guys-bad guys especially when an owner follows human nature and chases the goodies. Robert Irsay got pilloried like O'Malley and the rest. "When Robert Irsay skulked out of Baltimore by moonlight late last month, dragging a city's dreams along with the shoulder pads and horseshoed helmets, Colt fans in that harbor city screamed he was a bad owner—a magnate gone mad. The fools expected better," Filip Bondy of the *New York Daily News* pointed out in April 1984. "When push comes to shove, there are no benevolent professional sports owners. Some may be more decent than others; some may be more willing or able to accept financial losses than others. But in the long run, they are a

carpetbagging, opportunistic bunch—and some of the worst leeches on the economies of our nation's cities."

The human monkey wrench, Comptroller Hyman A. Pressman, never fessed up about stonewalling Rosenbloom and Irsay for years. Instead, he bashed Irsay to the *Evening Sun*: "City Comptroller Hyman A. Pressman said, 'I have come to the conclusion that money is the one goal of Mr. Irsay. That is the goal that transcends everything.'" As a *comptroller*, his job was about money. "'It transcends keeping his word. It transcends keeping his good name. I find it remarkable that a man of Mayor Schaefer's disposition could exercise the amount of patience he showed.'"

Running the Colts into the ground put Bob Irsay's finances in perilous straits. He was scraping dimes together just to pay the interest on his original $14.5-million loan in '72. Attendance had cratered, the Colts had a lousy lease, he had no skyboxes to hawk, and the bank was about to call in that loan. "Everything here [in Indianapolis] is so much better," Jim Irsay told the *New York Daily News* in June 1984. "I know a lot of people may not want to believe this, but if we had remained in Baltimore the way things were going, we would have been in big financial trouble."

. . .

For the fans who get jilted, the hurt sometimes never heals. It's been almost 70 years since the Dodgers split for the West Coast, and Brooklyn still might have a psychic bruise. "The full impact of the departure of the Giants and the

Dodgers from the New York scene, leaving the city without National League baseball for the first time since 1875, will scarcely be felt until next April," predicted Shirley Povich of the *Washington Post* in mid-October 1957. "The whole thing has been too sudden. Come the start of the 1958 season and the emptiness will be real."

In 1987, the *Los Angeles Times* did a retrospective on the Dodgers' move. Right out of the gate, despair gets top billing:

NEW YORK—In Brooklyn, they don't forget so fast. It's been 30 years since the Dodgers stopped playing baseball in Ebbets Field and the lights went out in Flatbush. Thirty years since Walter O'Malley shocked the sports world and moved his beloved bums to the cash-green pastures of Southern California. Thirty long years. Time enough for the most diehard Brooklyn fan to forget. Time to get on with life and bury the past, right? "Like hell," says Vinnie Faretra, a 57-year-old truck driver from Brooklyn. "I mean, these guys, they broke my heart. They tore the guts out of this town when they left. I should forget *that*? What's the hurry?" "It's a funny thing, but I felt listless, really kind of down, and I didn't know why," says Irving Rudd, 70, the Brooklyn Dodgers' publicist who did not move with the club to Los Angeles and is now a boxing press agent in New York. "I went to my doctor and he told me there were a lot

of cases just like mine in the neighborhood. He called it Dodgeritis and said there was no known cure."

Pretty much the same epitaph in Baltimore. Baltimorean Joe D'Adamo wrote this psychoanalysis for the *St. Louis Post-Dispatch*:

The shock is numbing. The hurt will come later, with the emptiness of a barren September. Death, even if it's after a long, lingering illness, still is a shock. Even in the most pessimistic days of recent Colts' history, there was always an outside hope that a miracle would come to pass, that some sense would be made out of the pandering of a once-glorious franchise. But sadly, that wasn't to be. The Colts are gone, and they won't be forgotten. Not by the thousands for whom they were a way of life. I weep for the countless youngsters who may grow up and never know what it is like to hold an entire football team to your bosom. I weep for my grandchildren who may never know how a man like John Unitas with his talented arm and his amazing football instincts could unify a city, or how the dashing feet of a Buddy Young or a Lenny Moore could make a city forget the color of a man's skin.

A couple from Herndon, VA, devoted Colts fans, sent a letter to the *Indianapolis Star* in April 1984 and let it all out: "We feel as though we've had a death in the family. We knew it would hurt, but we didn't realize how much. A lot of us went with the deceased; our spirit is gone … Our family didn't like just any team; we loved the Baltimore Colts. We traveled to Memorial Stadium every home game. The trip took an hour and a half, but it was worth it … But they were taken away from us in their prime. It was a slow and painful death we saw coming. Hopefully, those of us left behind will soon forget the shoddy treatment received from Mr. Irsay and [lawyer] Mr. Chernoff and think of it as a blessing in disguise. My heart goes out to the Colts as a team and the people of Indianapolis, for if this can happen to us, it can happen again to anyone."

New York magazine ran a long essay in 2007 titled "Exorcising the Dodgers," how Brooklyn has tried to flush the move out if its system all these decades. Writer Sam Anderson has this quote from Michael Shapiro, who wrote a book about it, *The Last Good Season*: "When the Dodgers left, it didn't rip the heart out of the borough. That's too much. I think people said that because they couldn't quite put into words the sense of what was lost. The departure of the Dodgers denied Brooklyn, for half the year [baseball season], this common conversation—the idle chitchat you have with people on the subway or waiting for the elevator or going to the butcher. Baseball informed so much of that. 'Can you believe that [Carl] Furillo last night? [Duke] Snider's a bum! Is [Gil] Hodges gonna get a hit?' It created a relationship between strangers—you felt close to them, if only for a minute or two. What was lost was each other."

Veteran sportswriter and former *Morning Sun* Colts beat writer Vito Stellino saw the same melancholy in Baltimore after the Colts shoved off to Indy. "Well, it was just devastating. Irsay had already helped lose the fans, but you have to realize, Baltimore was a whistle-stop between Philadelphia and Washington. They didn't have much of an identity. All of a sudden, the Colts and the Orioles were two of the best teams in the two leagues. Then they lose the Colts. It was devastating. It just wasn't the same after that. They showed Redskins games [on TV] in town, but they didn't get good ratings. After a while, they just became apathetic towards the NFL. What did keep them going was their hope to get an expansion team. But the move was a psychological blow to Baltimore."

Most owners look to the ledgers, as in, it's business, nothing personal. For fans, it's a matter of the heart. "For the city of Baltimore, as a whole, the Colts leaving town represented something much larger than a few Sunday games," Jess Mayhugh noted in "Colt Following" in the March 2014 *Baltimore* magazine. "'A population becomes invested emotionally in a team because it defines that city's sense of self,' says professor David Andrews, who studies the sociology of sport at the University of Maryland. 'And when a team goes, what happens to that?' The city was surely invested in the Colts, as players were ingrained in the community, hanging out at the same bars as fans and interacting often with the Colts Corrals, which were local fan clubs. Suffice it to say, it was more than just a game. 'Let me put it this way—I was 25 minutes late for my own wedding because a Colts game went into overtime,' says [owner of Duda's Tavern Antoinette] Duda. 'I knew the players personally because they would come down to your bull roast, and they did a lot for small businesses.'"

. . .

On his way out of Brooklyn, Walter O'Malley fed the *L.A. Times* the four reasons he had to split: "1: The desire for a new ballpark to replace the aging and outmoded Ebbets Field; 2: Insufficient parking space adjacent to the ballpark; 3: Dwindling attendance; 4: A New York City amusement tax of 5% on admissions." Most in Baltimore were up to speed about Rosenbloom's and Irsay's 20 years of grousing about the stadium. In early March 1984, with Irsay still equivocating, the *Morning Sun* explained the basics:

> At a meeting [in early March] where the owners decided they would not oppose a Colts' move, Mr. Irsay outlined the reasons why he wants to leave Baltimore. Although NFL Commissioner Pete Rozelle announced that Mr. Irsay still "intends to talk further to the people in Baltimore," two different sources talked more about why he wanted to go to Indianapolis. The Midwestern city has offered him a deal to play in the new Hoosier Dome. One source said he told the owners, "We can't draw here [Baltimore]. It's hurting the league. We're not making enough money for you guys." Another source said that Mr. Irsay complained about his treatment in Baltimore. "He said he's treated poorly in Baltimore and that the press is nasty to him and is on his case for no good reason."

Irsay of course had it on heavy spin cycle there—rationalizing, playing the victim.

Fans of all shapes and sizes take an emotional pounding when the home team absconds. In *New York* magazine's "Exorcising the Dodgers," a Brooklyn rabbi talks about his blues when the Dodgers left. "Like many Dodger fans, Kushner sees O'Malley's defection as the Watergate of American sports—not just a local betrayal but evidence that the entire system was incurably corrupt. 'When the Dodgers left Brooklyn,' he said, 'I swore off professional athletics. I could no more root for a baseball team than I could root for U.S. Steel or General Motors. It's a private, profit-making corporation taking advantage of the innocent lambs who are foolish enough to be their fans.' To this day, he refuses to speak the name of the L.A. Dodgers aloud. 'It's like Voldemort,' he said. 'My kids know never to say the name in my presence.'"

Nobody could touch Hurst C. "Loudy" Loudenslager for Baltimore Colts fanaticism. Every time the Colts hopped on a plane at Friendship Airport over the decades, Loudy plugged in his portable stereo on the runway and serenaded the players with the Colts fight song—626 times before Irsay took them away. He claims he sent 3,059 birthday cards and

3,797 Christmas cards to Colts players and staff and had his wife Flo bake her renowned black walnut cake 726 times for members of the Colts family. "I've got over half of my life tied up with this club," Loudy lamented to the *Evening Sun* after they left. "I've got a lot of love tied up in this team. Just what are we going to do in the fall? It hasn't totally hit yet, but it will then. Irsay may have owned this team with his money, but I owned them with my heart."

Besides the obvious—an owner who's fed up with a stadium, fans riding the owner, reporters taking their whacks at him and local officials blowing things up—there are other complexities. Charles Euchner, author of *Playing the Game*, points out why the Dodgers' move relates to the midnight skedaddle:

> The reason it's so important—and important to the story of the Colts—is you can talk about the fundamental factors: Sports is a monopolistic industry; the teams are under-supplied, which give teams that want new stadiums the leverage to threaten to go someplace else. All that macro stuff is important, but just as important is the real kind of local-specific and time-specific stuff that is happening. If the Dodgers had been looking for a stadium 10 years later [1967], [Robert] Moses would be gone. The new mayor, John Lindsay, would have said, "Gee, that sounds great. What can we do for you?" And it probably would have happened, and the Dodgers

would have stayed in New York. Somebody else would have moved to L.A., or they would have been the next expansion city. So, the big macro-economic stuff, that obviously sets the framework for everything. It establishes the rules and parameters for people's behavior. But at the same time, it's those specific behaviors, characters and imperatives which determine how it comes down in the end.

Legendary Penn State football coach Joe Paterno once shared with his PR director, Ernie Accorsi, how losing the Dodgers was a gut punch. "Joe Paterno, who I worked for, was an usher [at Ebbets Field] in high school," Accorsi recalled. "A lot of the [Dodgers] games would start at 3:00. And he said, 'When the Dodgers left Brooklyn, I never felt the same about baseball again.' And this is a guy who is one of the great football coaches of all-time. The cities [Brooklyn and Baltimore] were similar. They had an ethnic mix—all kinds of people. And to me, they were heartbroken cities."

Though he's been in Baltimore since 1982, cartoonist Mike Ricigliano was originally a Brooklyn guy. "My friends wondered why I don't like the Dodgers or the Yankees," Ricig began. "So, I'm watching the [2024] World Series with two of my least favorite baseball teams. My dad was a Brooklyn Dodgers fan. When they left town, he said to us—we were small children at the time—'We no longer support the Dodgers in this family. We don't support the Yankees in this family, and we don't support the Giants because they were the Dodgers' foe. We will have no team to support in our family.' Then, when the Mets came along, he said, '*This* will be our team.' And they go on to lose 120 games that first year. So, we were Mets fans growing up and Dodger-haters."

The *Los Angeles Times* captured the gloom still in Brooklyn 30 years after O'Malley made a break for it: "Vinnie [Faretra, a diehard fan]—and thousands of fans like him—simply cannot let go. They are in mourning for a vanished team and a golden sports era when baseball was more than just a business. They still grieve that a club that had stars like Jackie Robinson, Pee Wee Reese, Roy Campanella, Don Newcombe and Duke Snider has deserted them forever."

Most of the analogies from fans smitten involve mourning, losing a loved one. Author and former *Morning Sun* columnist Michael Olesker speaks for all of Baltimore about the heartache:

A death in the family. I'm sure that analogy has been made before, but there was absolute *emptiness*. [Baltimore Mayor] Schaefer did everything but weep. We all did in our way, but it was inconceivable. It was like a death in the family in that we were so close for so long. But it was a family member [the Colts] who had drifted apart. But what are we gonna do now? It was embarrassing, among other things, that the country could look at us and say, "Baltimore lost its football team? What could they have done that was so monumentally stupid when every city with a team felt, *Aren't we lucky that we have pro football?*" But the game had long since become America's game, and somehow, we blew it. It was one more way for us to feel our municipal inferiority complex. It was one more way for us to feel self-conscious and small and poor. To feel bad about ourselves, that we couldn't hold on to the thing that we once loved so much.

Requiescat in pace, Brooklyn Dodgers and Baltimore Colts.

CHAPTER 14

WELCOME TO THE MAJORS

Bob Irsay probably couldn't have pulled off the Midnight Skedaddle without Al Davis. Al set the precedent, broke the ice, laid the groundwork, paved the way for all subsequent NFL team moves, moving the Oakland Raiders to Los Angeles in 1980. Davis thumbing his nose at Pete Rozelle and besting the NFL in court gave Irsay the signal to start Operation Indy. And Baltimore looked on as Oakland tried a legal desperation heave to get their team back: "SALINAS, Calif., May 16 [1983]—The City of Oakland began an unusual legal effort today that, because of the importance to a city of having a professional sports team, it may use eminent domain legal procedures to seize a privately owned sports franchise," the *New York Times* reported. "Using the same legal process that the Federal Government and state and local governments employ to seize acreage, buildings and other private property for public purposes, Oakland, in a trial that began today, is seeking to take over the Los Angeles Raiders football team, which moved from Oakland more than two years ago."

The barristers for both sides would earn their retainers on this one. Charlie Euchner in *Playing the Field: Why Sports Teams Move and Cities Fight to Keep Them* described the stakes:

The lawsuits against the Raiders were among the most significant challenges ever made to the structure of professional sports. If an early court decision, in Oakland's eminent domain suit against the Raiders, had stood, Davis would have lost control of the franchise. In another case, the Raiders and the Los Angeles Memorial Coliseum Commission charged the NFL with violations of federal antitrust law because of its attempt to block the team's move to Los Angeles. Had the NFL won that case— quite possible, given the hung jury in the first trial of the case—Davis would have been forced to keep the franchise in Oakland and pay his fellow club owners millions of dollars. Davis won both cases, however, and took the team south.

The *Fordham Urban Law Journal*, volume 13, 1985, provides as good a summary as any of what happened when Oakland lost its first go and appealed to the California Supreme Court:

On appeal, the Supreme Court of California considered whether there was sufficient factual controversy to warrant a trial on the merits over the following issues: 1) whether tangible property could be taken by eminent domain; and 2) whether the public use requirement was broad enough to encompass the taking of a sports franchise. With respect to the first issue, the court held that taking tangible property by eminent domain was authorized because neither the federal and state constitutions nor the revised California eminent domain law distinguished between real or personal property and tangible or intangible property. On the second issue, the court concluded "that the acquisition and operation of a sports franchise *may* be an appropriate municipal function." The court remanded the case to the trial court … The superior court of Monterey County, in a bifurcated trial, rendered a tentative decision in favor of the Raiders. The trial court offered five grounds for its conclusion that the City of Oakland did not have the right to take the Raiders.

Of course, Oakland appealed and eventually got rebuffed. Score one for Al Davis. And don't think that Big Bob Irsay didn't notice.

Governments grabbing property for development has been around since the Supreme Court OK'd it in 1876 (Kohl vs. United States). The spring 1986 edition of the *University of Baltimore Law Forum*—"Recent Developments: Mayor and City Council of Baltimore vs. Indianapolis Colts, Inc."—gives us the skinny on eminent domain: "The law of eminent domain authorizes a sovereign to take property for public use without the owner's consent upon making just compensation. The majority of the case law defining the parameters of this power involve a state's condemnation of tangible property to support traditional and limited public purposes such as the construction and maintenance of streets and highways. It is not disputed, however, that this power extends to encompass property of every kind and character."

Say you own a nifty house with a pool in the backyard. They just threw up a Walmart nearby and need some room for an access road and parking. Some pencil neck raps on your door one day and tells you, you have 60 days to rent a U-Haul and move out. An appraiser cuts you a check for the market value of your digs, and you don't have a legal leg to stand on. "When the Baltimore Beltway was built, there were landowners who fought the government's efforts to turn strips of the property into roadway," the *Morning Sun* explained in April 1984. "Some families had owned their tracts for more than two centuries. In at least one instance, the Beltway ran through a family's land, leaving them parcels on either side. But it was ruled that the public's need for that road was important. In such cases, private ownership must give way. But always for a price: the Constitution requires a government to pay for what it takes." Go tell the American Indians.

Here's where it gets complex. A whole city can wrap its arms around a sports team and consider the ballplayers part of the family. Their moods soar and plummet, based on the exploits of that ballclub. Local businesses feed off it and a city can puff out its chest because it's in the majors. So, when a team pulls up stakes, folks holler, "What gives?! Who gave you the right to move *our* ballclub, you rat bastard?" In his essay, "Walter O'Malley Was Right," Paul Hirsch pondered just that:

> If one views a baseball franchise as a public trust, then a case can be made that the Dodgers should have stayed in Brooklyn and taken what they could get in New York. If one views owning a franchise as a competitive, profit-driven enterprise, then moving to Los Angeles was probably the best baseball-related gift O'Malley could give his family. In this case, at that time, for this author, the offer to move to Los Angeles made too much sense for O'Malley to ignore. The situation in Brooklyn was deteriorating and looked to get only worse, at least in the short term. It would have been an act of irresponsibility towards his stockholders and his family to remain in Brooklyn.

Replace O'Malley and Brooklyn with Irsay and Baltimore, and there you have it.

What Al Davis had in Oakland was gravy compared to Irsay in Baltimore, but Davis could only squeeze so much green out of Oakland Coliseum. So he said, see ya. "The move shocked the sporting world," Jon Morgan explained in *Glory for Sale: Fans, Dollars and the New NFL*. "The Raiders had enjoyed 12 years of sellouts in Oakland despite some of the highest ticket prices in the league. Fan support seemed exceptional. And there was little financial distress. The Raiders were among the top five NFL franchises in revenue, having earned profits of $2 million in 1978 and $1.5 million in 1979. But Davis, always a maverick, cited grievances that were ahead of his time and provided a glimpse of stadium battles to come. He complained that his facility had no skyboxes and that he got none of the revenue from parking and concessions. Because he had to share the facility with a baseball team, he said, the Raiders were always forced to play their first three games of the season away from home." Funny. Carroll Rosenbloom was on the same kick 15 years earlier.

Davis aimed his bazooka at Article 4.3 of the NFL's Constitution and Bylaws. He didn't want the whole thing jettisoned but he took the official verbiage to court and won:

> Article 4.3 requires prior approval by the affirmative vote of three-fourths of

the member clubs before a club may transfer its franchise or playing site to a different city, either within or outside its existing home territory. Article 4.3 confirms that each club's primary obligation to the League and to all other member clubs is to advance the interests of the League in its home territory. This primary obligation includes, but is not limited to, maximizing fan support, including attendance, in its home territory. Article 4.3 also confirms that no club has an "entitlement" to relocate simply because it perceives an opportunity for enhanced club revenues in another location … *Relocation pursuant to Article 4.3 may be available, however, if a club's viability in its home territory is threatened by circumstances that cannot be remedied by diligent efforts of the club working, as appropriate, in conjunction with the League Office, or if compelling League interests warrant a franchise relocation* [emphasis mine].

Irsay and his lawyer Michael Machiavelli would rely on those italics when the time came to scoot.

Davis threw the flag on Article 4.3, took it to court and beat Rozelle. "That rule has always been illegal," Davis complained to Will McDonough of the *Boston Globe* in April 1984. "I told the league that as far back as 1978. But the ruling in the courts in California pertains only to my moving from Oakland to Los Angeles. It does not give anyone else in the league the right to move. In fact, the court has said that even though the rule is illegal, there could be guidelines controlling the movement of franchises as long as they were objective and fair, rather than taking a vote that could be taken on whim or caprice. I suggested the guidelines in 1978. I suggested them again last week. The league could have forced both Hess [of the Jets] and Irsay to pass a vote, but it didn't do a thing. There is no comparison to our situation and Baltimore's because the Raiders did not shop around from city to city, and the Colts got a much better deal than we did."

The future of the Colts and all sports teams played out in California courtrooms. In *The Constitutional Dimensions of Sports Franchise Takings: Lessons Learned from the Baltimore Colts*, Travis Bullock summarized the appeals court ruling in the Davis case:

In California, the City of Oakland attempted to prevent the Oakland Raiders football team from relocating to Los Angeles. After years of litigation, the Court of Appeals for California invalidated the condemnation [seizure of the team] because of its effect on interstate commerce. The court explained that although "[i]t is well established that a state may exercise eminent domain power even though by doing so it indirectly or incidentally burdens interstate commerce," the "nationwide" nature of professional football is "so completely involved in interstate commerce" that taking a franchise is impermissible … The court concluded that indefinitely barring the Raiders franchise from moving out of Oakland would "more than indirectly or incidentally regulate interstate commerce." Finally, the court weighed the local interest of preventing the Raiders from moving against the burden imposed on interstate commerce. Finding that the burden imposed outweighs the local interest, the court affirmed the lower court decision invalidating the condemnation.

And despite what sounded pretty emphatic, Baltimore would roll the bones after Irsay cleared out.

Al Davis, who started this freelancing yard sale, told Will McDonough of the *Boston Globe* he'd refuse to take the rap for future moves:

> When a US federal court in California ruled twice in the past year for Al Davis and the Raiders, [Pete] Rozelle predicted an era of "free agent franchises." Bozo Bob Irsay, former owner of the Baltimore Colts and present owner of the Indianapolis franchise in the NFL, made a prophet out of his commissioner last week [March 1984] by moving his team from Maryland to Indiana. Thank you, Al Davis. "Don't make any comparisons between the Raiders and Baltimore," not wanting to take any bows as the man who made it all possible. "There is no

analogy whatsoever between the two situations. In mine, moving the Raiders from Oakland to Los Angeles, Rozelle has kept me in the courts for four years and forced me to spend $6 million in legal and moving expenses. No one in the league did a thing to stop Baltimore. They just let Irsay go right ahead and do it. This league is really something. They could have stopped Irsay. They could have stopped [Jets owner] Leon Hess when he moved the Jets from Shea Stadium to the Meadowlands [N.J.], but the league didn't do a thing. The only one they wanted to stop was me."

That's because: 1) The wrangling between Rozelle and Davis was personal; and 2) The Colts' move was no skin off the NFL's nose. So says Charlie Euchner, who wrote a book about team moves:

> All it did was change the dynamic of the team [the Colts] with the league. But the leagues are sophisticated enough to respond and thrive, no matter what. What actually happened after that was something I never would have predicted—that L.A. went without a football team for 20 years, the second-most important market, the glamor market in the U.S. But fundamentally, what this whole business of sports franchises and moving is all about is that the leagues coordinate with their teams. Before the Al Davis thing, it was kind of a

conspiracy or partnership with the team and the league structure to get the best deal they could out of cities and get new facilities built at public expense as much as you could. And it's still that now. But in many ways, Davis was an exception, and by him winning, the league still won. The league still controls all this stuff; the league still has a lot of tools at its disposal. And so, it was kind of like losing a round in bridge, but still the usual players keep winning. And the usual players are the league and its collection of owners with their individual and collective interests. So, it [the Al Davis litigation] was a big deal because it affected that one move at that one time, and it did a lot of damage for a long time. But in a way, the league said, "So what? It's a TV sport anyway. We don't actually need people in L.A. to care. Everybody cares about football anyway; everybody's gonna watch TV." It was a big loss; the NFL wanted to win it. They didn't like what Al Davis was doing, didn't like what an independent, rogue character he was. But the NFL is such a behemoth, it almost *can't* lose. And there are so many things it does right, losing a case like that, it's like, "OK—next? We'll just get another record-setting TV deal."

· · ·

Robert Irsay wandered into a renaissance when he moved the Colts to Indianapolis.

Baltimore had gone through the same thing in the late '70s-early '80s. Now it was Indy's turn, as the *New York Times* pointed out in June 1984:

From his office on the 25th floor of the City-County Building in the heart of downtown, the Mayor of Indianapolis can look out upon his realm and see a rapidly-changing vista. It includes the 40-story American United Life Building, the tallest structure in the city; ongoing construction of several new hotels and office buildings and, far in the distance, work on a new 250-acre, $200 million park that will include the city zoo, a performing arts center and botanical gardens. The panorama appears even more impressive and breathtaking, given the city's dubious past reputation as a place once described by author John Gunther as the "dirtiest" city in America and by native son Kurt Vonnegut as one that watches a car race (the Indianapolis 500) one day of the year and sleeps the other 364. Such portrayals later helped give rise to the notion that Indianapolis was, in the words of William H. Hudnut III, the current Mayor, a "town where you flew over to get somewhere else." Other people, he said, routinely refer to it as "Naptown" or "Indian-no-place." But all that has changed, Mr. Hudnut said proudly and forcefully from behind his desk last week, as he made a sweeping gesture with his long arms toward the windows and the scenes beyond. "Indianapolis has awakened," he said. "I now like to refer to our city as Indiana-ShowPlace."

Bill Benner covered sports for the *Indianapolis Star* for 33 years and got elected into the Indiana Sportswriters and Sportscasters Hall of Fame. He can educate you about the Indy renaissance. "Our downtown—people went home at 4:30, 5:00. There was no reason to stay downtown," he recollected. "There were three restaurants; there was nothing to bring people back downtown. [Former mayor] Dick Lugar and [Indianapolis civic and business leader] Jim Morris determined that, if an arena was to be built, it should be built downtown as a place to reverse the nightly migration of workers. They built it [Market Square Arena] in 1974, right in the middle of downtown. The [Indiana] Pacers moved downtown. The building of Market Square Arena was the first domino to fall [in their plan]."

It was a huge team effort to bring off the Indy renaissance. And it wasn't done on the double. "The sudden emergence of Indianapolis is really more sudden to those outside Indianapolis," the *New York Times* revealed in April 1984. "It is a result of a 15-year urban alliance between two long-serving Republican mayors and a collection of downtown business owners who did not plan to move on. Mayor Hudnut, now in his third term, and his predecessor, Richard D. Lugar, now a Senator, presided over a city that largely merged with surrounding Marion County, which gave the city a broader base of money and talent and gave the suburbs a stake in the city."

Harvey Molotch wrote the go-to treatise on city growth in 1976, *The City as a Growth Machine*. Consider a city as an organism that needs to beef up to survive:

> The clearest indication of success at growth is a constantly rising urban-area population—a symptom of a pattern ordinarily comprising an initial expansion of basic industries followed by an expanded labor force, a rising scale of retail and wholesale commerce, more far-flung and increasingly intensive land development, higher population density, and increased levels of financial activity … I argue that the means of achieving this growth, of setting off this chain of phenomena, constitute the central issue for those serious people who care about their locality and who have the resources to make their caring felt as a political force. The city is, for those who count, a growth machine.

And that's what the shot-callers in Indy did—put fiber and vitality into the city. While Bob Irsay haggled with the hometown pols on the East Coast and Baltimore suffered from foot-dragging, Indianapolis was on the go. JJ Stankevitz, who produced a four-episode podcast about the Colts' move, described the changes there:

I think it [the advantages over Baltimore] was a very aggressive vision from local officials in Indianapolis that began in the '60s when Mayor Richard Lugar was elected. He had a vision of pushing Indianapolis forward that involved a lot of public investment into infrastructure, and growing the city with sports was a big part of that. From 1967 through the early years of Bill Hudnut's tenure, probably the first 12-13 years, Indianapolis did have a lot of success, in terms of building the convention center and Market Square Arena, which became the home of the Pacers. There was this vision, and people around the city could feel it and see it. People had a reason to go downtown again. The cherry on top of that became, "So, we've established ourselves now as a rising city in the Midwest; let's try to get even bigger; let's try to take a really big swing." And that was trying to get an NFL team. I think the forethought that Indianapolis had as a city was really unique to America back in the '60s and '70s.

At least one person in Baltimore bears no grudge against Indy—former *Evening Sun* columnist Kevin Cowherd: "Back then, Indianapolis was determined to create a major-league presence in that town. They wanted the city to be more well-known, and I think they played it the way most cities would if they were trying to lure a team. And isn't it ironic that, 12 years later, we're [Baltimore] doing the same thing, getting the Browns from Cleveland. So, I think the Indianapolis officials—Hudnut and those guys—they wanted a team. Irsay was shopping the Colts around, and everybody in the country who was plugged in knew it. I think they [Indianapolis] said, 'This is our chance to capitalize.' I can't fault them for that. Irsay would've left anyway, and I think any other city would've pulled out all the stops to lure a major-league team."

Baltimore's mayor William Donald Schaefer chugged some more Maalox when in early March '84 he found out that Jim Irsay and Frank Kush took a bird out to Indy for a tour. "Many fans and politicians had believed the move all but complete Tuesday night when Coach Frank Kush and Irsay's son, Jimmy, flew to Indianapolis under assumed names," the *Evening Sun* disclosed. "Instead of announcing a franchise move, Kush and Jimmy Irsay kept a low profile during their visit. They took a tour of the city and inspected their prospective new football home, the Hoosier Dome. They also met Mayor William H. Hudnut III, who ate lunch with the two Colt officials at a Howard Johnson's restaurant. 'We made some pleasantries,' Hudnut said. 'I said, "Welcome to the city. I hope it all works out."'"

After Market Square Arena came the big push. Former *Indianapolis Star* veteran reporter Bill Benner explains:

The second domino to fall was Jim Morris, [former deputy mayor] David Frick, [Indiana] Supreme Court Justice Ted

Boehm and a group of city leaders, who were loosely called the "City Committee," tried to determine how Indianapolis could become something more than "Naptown" or the "racetrack surrounded by cornfields"—a one-event city [the Indy 500]. They embarked upon what was called the Amateur Sports Initiative. The passing of the Indiana Sports Act of 1978 gave autonomy to all the various [athletic] federations. So, Indianapolis formed the very first sports commission in the United States, the Indiana Sports Corporation. Its charter was to attract association and amateur sports events to Indianapolis, including college and NCAA events. As part of this vision, they built the [Indiana University] natatorium, a world-class track-and-field stadium, a world-class rowing course and began to pursue various important sporting events. The first big one came in 1982 with the National Sports Festival [U.S. Olympic Festival, held between the quadrennial Olympic Games]. With that said, we attracted U.S.A. Track and Field, U.S.A. Diving, U.S.A. Gymnastics, and Indianapolis began to gain a toehold on national sports.

Baltimore had Schaefer lighting fires under fannies; Indianapolis had Hudnut. A 2016 feature on him by Craig Fehrman called "Bill Hudnut: A Man of His Word" portrays this visionary: "Indianapolis needed a mayor who wasn't afraid to be a mascot (one of Hudnut's finest moments came when he dressed as a leprechaun during the St. Patrick's Day Parade). 'Those of you who have seen Indianapolis,' Kurt Vonnegut once said, 'will understand that it is no easy thing to be an optimist there.' But being an optimist was Bill Hudnut's calling. To revive the city's sluggish downtown, he invested in sports and tourism, most famously by luring the Colts in 1984. Under Hudnut's leadership, Indianapolis established itself as a true major-league city. His ideas didn't always work, but they were inevitably ambitious. That's why he was honored with a bronze statue of 'Mayor Bill,' which sits on the busy corner of Maryland Street and Capitol Avenue."

What really sealed the deal in the Baltimore vs. Indy scrap was the Hoosier Dome, a big white bubble. The *New York Times* in July 1984 paid it proper homage:

Perhaps nothing on the horizon better symbolizes the turnabout of the last few years than the new Hoosier Dome, a 61,000-seat indoor stadium, which the Mayor can see off in the distance without moving from behind his desk. With its billowy, white-plaited, air-supported roof, the dome fairly gleams in the sunlight, looking as if it had some sort of mystical power. Perhaps it does: The dome was built to attract more convention business to the city and at little burden to local taxpayers. And on both counts it has succeeded. Completed this spring after two and a half years of construction, the dome was financed by public and private funds in the form of a 1% county food and beverage tax that will retire $47 million in bonds and $30 million from private endowments. And according to Mr. Hudnut, stadium officials have commitments for more than $280 million in new convention business between now and 1990. But the Mayor, and nearly everyone else in the Indianapolis area, knows the dome has brought something else, too. It has enabled the city to have its first professional football team. Starting this summer, the dome will become home for the Indianapolis (nee Baltimore) Colts of the National Football League, whose owner, Robert Irsay, moved them here this spring.

Harvey Molotch in *The City as a Growth Machine* claimed that growth was a city's top priority: "I aim to make the extreme statement that this organized effort to affect the outcome of growth distribution is the essence of local government as a dynamic political force. It is not the only function of government, but it is the key one and, ironically, the one most ignored."

Indianapolis already had its convention center up and running; they just glued the bubble dome to it and voilà. "Beginning in the late '70s, one of the overriding goals of the Hudnut administration was to focus on the community, reenergize people and get the area growing again," a *BizVoice* article titled

"Indianapolis and the Colts: A Deal that Changed the Landscape" explained. "'One of the elements of that was using sports as a strategy to cause the redevelopment of Indianapolis—and that centered on amateur and professional sports,' explains [David] Frick, who had been commissioned by the mayor to work on this. Hudnut recalls, 'A lightbulb idea that a bunch of us had was to build an attachment to the convention center that would expand the convention center and its capacity for business, as well as hold a football team.'"

Hudnut tabbed David Frick among others to power up the renaissance. Frick described the team mindset:

The [Indianapolis] community was going through a self-evaluation and a lot of strategic planning under Hudnut because he was elected in '75. He was going through the process of thinking about his future in a very important way. The thing that had propelled the Indianapolis community for years during World War II and the post-war was manufacturing. Manufacturing declined substantially all across the nation after the war. Buildings that once occupied huge workforces were closing down. Companies were moving to the South and overseas, and Indianapolis was in peril because our major employers were not headquartered here [in Indianapolis]. The community, as part of that process of thinking about the future, concluded that we needed to generate a whole new set of expectations and contacts. So, as part of the city's strategy of trying to generate jobs, we started to think about what we wanted to be. One was to be a center for consumer travel—meetings and headquarters for organizations. One tiny piece of that strategy was getting an NFL franchise. We were really talking about an expansion franchise. That dream was, in part, generated by a guy named Robert Welch, who had contacts with various NFL franchises—New England, the Sullivan family; the Texas people [Cowboys]; the Rooney family [Steelers]. He knew those people, and the chairman of the Indianapolis Chamber of Commerce used to work for the Cowboys. So, we had some pretty good contact within the NFL and were told that we would be a viable candidate for an expansion franchise. And Hudnut appointed a small group with Tom Moses and the Chamber of Commerce to go about getting an NFL expansion franchise. We engaged with the NFL; I talked with some of the members out there and asked the NFL to help us design a stadium. I took plans and specifications out, and they made suggestions about what would be needed for a modern stadium. They played an acute role in helping us understand what we ought to build to receive an expansion franchise.

Hudnut gambling $77 million on a stadium with no tenant was putting his head on the chopping block. "Mayor Hudnut had a vision that the city could become something bigger," Victor Prince noted in "The Mayor Who Built Indianapolis into a Sports Capital." "During his 16 years in office, he was able convince his fellow Indianapolis citizens to invest in building dozens of major projects to revitalize the downtown core of the city. Hudnut's boldest move started in 1980 when he started lobbying his town to build an indoor sports arena that could host an NFL team, even though the city did not have an NFL franchise. In a move reminiscent of the classic Kevin Costner baseball film *Field of Dreams*, Hudnut believed that 'if he built it, they will come.'"

It was all-hands-on-deck to get the dome built. "The big thing that was missing was the NFL and a stadium that could host an NFL team," veteran Indy sportswriter Bill Benner stated. "A guy named Bob Welch [Indianapolis businessman, civic and political leader] was very bullish on Indianapolis and was a wealthy real estate developer. He was fixated on Indianapolis attracting an NFL team. He was part of a cadre of city leaders who were pushing Indianapolis as a sports destination and hoping that Indianapolis would eventually grow beyond amateur sports with further inroads into professional sports. So, they embarked on this idea of building a domed stadium without a team to play in it."

Mike Chappell started covering the Indianapolis Colts in 1984 and is still at it. He saw how Hudnut put his political rep on the line with the dome, then held his breath:

If you don't get a team, what have you got? You got a beautiful stadium, and you're gonna have what—tractor pulls and concerts? So, that's why I say they took a leap of faith with the idea that they could make this work. Now, what they would've done had that not happened, I don't know. I never really talked to Bill Hudnut about that, but when you have leaders that have a vision of "what can be," then you get this massive convention center and stadium. And the Colts were the start of all this. When you talk about "Naptown," the old joke was that at 7:00, they rolled up the sidewalks, and downtown was empty. That's not the case now.

The Hoosier Dome was a team effort, and they pulled it off. So listen up, Baltimore; former Indy deputy mayor David Frick explains the gamble that paid off:

There was a process that we had to go through in order to get a community consensus on building the extension to the convention center [i.e., the Hoosier Dome]. A lot of people were involved in the consensus-building process. We knew—and this was a tough one—that if we could raise the money through a bond issue and gifts and endowments from major corporations, the project could work, financially. Now, that didn't mean it would be a success, financially— that is, we could afford the expansion

and the stadium. But it would have been an incredible gamble for Hudnut, and Bill and I spent many nights worrying about that because I was one of his key advisors. I give Hudnut a lot of credit. He was willing to risk his future. We all knew that, regardless of the project working financially, that having a big stadium and no team, it would have been a real disaster. And that's why the relationship with the NFL was so important.

Baltimoreans broke out in hives when they heard the word *taxes* to fund a stadium, but Hoosiers took it in stride—only an occasional squawk about a food and beverage levy. "This is 'Unigov' [Indianapolis's amalgam of a consolidated city-county government], with mostly one-party Republican leadership, that pushed this [funding for the Hoosier Dome] through with a food and beverage tax," sportswriter Bill Benner explained. "There was some opposition but not enough to slow it down. And they put it [the Hoosier Dome] right downtown, as they did with Market Square Arena, and they attached it to the Indiana Convention Center. That was very strategic, and it played out in an incredible way in the years to come as the NCAA [basketball] tournament grew. But the primary driver for that was the hope to get an NFL team."

Moguls in Indianapolis showed stick-to-itiveness in ciphering a way to cobble together the cash, something Baltimore could never muster. The *Los Angeles Times* in July 1984 described how they did it:

Not many cities would support the construction of a $77-million domed stadium without the guarantee of a team to play in it. But [Mayor] Hudnut had a lot going for him besides a decidedly Republican constituency. For one thing, he said, the Hoosier Dome is merely an extension of the city's convention center (to which it is attached), and he had booked more than $280 million in convention business before he persuaded the Colts to move. For another, $30 million came from the private sector—the Eli Lilly Endowment contributed $25 million, the Krannet Charitable Trust $5 million. The city then sold $47.2 million worth of municipal bonds, to be repaid by a 1% food and beverage tax. A year and a half later, Indianapolis had a domed stadium, and about seven months after that it had an NFL team.

Baltimore vs. Indianapolis in the Colts sweepstakes was like the '62 Mets against the '27 Yankees. "You've got one fanbase, one city that wants a team and will do almost whatever it takes to get it, and another city that's got a team, but says, 'I don't think I wanna give 2% [in taxes] to keep the team,'" veteran Colts beat reporter Mike Chappell stated. "And now, isn't that how almost all of these [modern] stadiums are funded? Not totally, but if I'm on the road and go to St. Louis [when they had the Rams] and get a hotel room, it's got a 'sports tax.' So, the visiting population that comes in for these games helps pay for these stadiums as well. When they come here [to Indianapolis], they pay up; when I go somewhere, I pay."

Savvy people like William H. C. Wilson in Baltimore were sadly in short supply. When Comptroller Hyman Pressman ran his scheme to kill a new stadium in Baltimore (Question P), Wilson took it to court to shut it down. As the *Morning Sun* stated in October 1974, "Mr. Wilson's suit contends that the new sports complex proposed for Camden Yards would promote tourism and bring business into the city's core areas." Not to mention probably keeping the Colts in Baltimore.

The man who kick-started the Indy renaissance, former mayor Richard Lugar, paid his successor high praise in an interview published on scholarworks.iu.edu:

I think he [Hudnut] did a great number of things that I could not have anticipated, and I was among those who applauded all the way. I think 30 major building projects occurred during his mayoralty in the downtown area ... The second thing, after all the buildings, was that Indianapolis became the amateur sports capital of the world. A lot of this was due to very strong advocacy by Bill Hudnut, including the Pan-American Games. The 1982 National Sports Festival occurred there, and likewise there were events in the velodrome and natatorium of national significance. He was also of course president of the National League of Cities. He served on the Board of Governors, I was told, for almost the entirety of his tenure as mayor; this led to his having a good comprehension of what was going on in all the cities of America and what he had to do to keep Indianapolis ahead. And then, of course, there was the tremendous event of the Baltimore Colts coming to Indianapolis in1984. Many have written—correctly—that it was very courageous of him to finance and to build the Hoosier Dome before the Colts signed up. Then to negotiate with the Irsays to get the Colts to come. That's what is still remembered vividly by anyone who is interested in football—or interested in Indianapolis as a whole.

Before they got a football team, the $77 million big white bubble was targeted for the convention trade. "Pointing out the maze of electrical circuits installed beneath the playing surface and escorting a visitor through a nearly 125,000-square-foot convention hall, he [the project manager] said the building was designed with 'shows and conventions in mind. Other stadiums just have to jury rig for trade shows and don't attract much interest,'" the *New York Times* explained. "Thomas P. Harris, director of sales for the convention center, said the amenities offered by his building have enticed numerous groups to schedule meetings in Indianapolis. He reported that nearly $275 million in advance bookings are already on file." You almost had to feel sorry for the rundown joint that Baltimore put in the ring with the Hoosier Dome.

Baltimore already knew what it was like to go big-league, and Indy wanted a piece of that dream. "What [David] Frick always told me was they were convinced beyond a shadow of a doubt—the city movers and shakers—that bringing a team here [to Indianapolis] would lift the quality of life in the community," Mike Chappell observed. "All of a sudden, you're luring surgeons, musicians and top companies because of the quality of life, with the symphony here, the Children's Museum—and the Colts and the Pacers. I just think that the NFL was that missing piece that really super-charged what they wanted to do. They realized that the NFL would put them two notches higher than Columbus [Ohio] or a city like that. They understood that, and they followed through on it."

While Baltimore kept churning out feasibility studies bound for file 13, Indy did some serious homework. They hired an outfit in California to size up its chances to land an NFL team. "As we were preparing to compete for an expansion franchise, one of the criticisms that we felt hurt our cause was our close proximity to Chicago and Cincinnati [NFL cities]," David Frick disclosed. "One of the things we wanted to do to be accepted as a major-league city was to commission a study by SRI [International] in California to answer the question: Can Indianapolis be a favorable place to locate an NFL franchise? The Eli Lilly company, a major employer and one of the top drug companies in the world, was involved in helping us along with the process. They ultimately commissioned the study. We were prepared to deliver the study when the expansion-franchise competition opened up. We also used it in our negotiations with Mr. Irsay."

David Frick, who became Indy's chief negotiator with the Colts, worked the crowd while hobnobbing with NFL bigshots at the 1982 Super Bowl in Detroit:

The owner of the Bengals and a minority investor got us into places where we could make our case in subtle ways. One of the ways was, I went to the Super Bowl in Detroit [1982] and was in the suite with all the owners. Here's this young kid [Frick], running around in the owners' suite, with them wondering, who in the hell am I? It gave us an opportunity where we could build a consensus with other NFL owners that we'd be a good place for an NFL franchise. Lamar Hunt, from Kansas City, I can tell you was very supportive of us. The Sullivan family in New England; Cincinnati was helpful; Dallas was—the president of our Chamber of Commerce worked for the family that owned the Cowboys at the time. That helped us with the NFL. They let it be known that they were not opposed to us, and I know the NFL constantly communicated back then with the various owners. Pete Rozelle and the NFL were very comfortable with a franchise being in

Indianapolis. They thought an expansion franchise would work, and when we were trying to recruit Mr. Irsay to Indianapolis, they [the NFL] were helpful in that process.

How 'bout that—Rozelle and Co. were greasing the skids while Indy and Irsay were talking contract. All this right under Baltimore's nose.

. . .

While Indianapolis had an assembly line going, Baltimore was on its lunch break. The state had $15 million lying around for stadium improvements ($7.5 million each for the Colts and Orioles), but wouldn't release a penny until the clubs signed six-year leases. Being a grinder, Mayor Schaefer kept at it, but it looked pretty bleak. "Obviously, the mayor would like [Orioles owner Edward Bennett] Williams and Irsay to complete the arrangements simultaneously. Then he could hold a celebration and get on with more important things," stated John Steadman of the *News American* in December 1983. "As it is now, he has bad dreams, tossing in his sleep—maybe screaming out the names of the teams—as he wonders what he can do to placate the tenants at Memorial Stadium. The mayor doesn't need this kind of a worry from men making millions from fun and games, and all he gets in return is a hard time." What's mind-boggling is how Indianapolis could throw up a $77-million dome with NO team to pay rent while Baltimore jib-jabbed about eyeliner and lipstick for Memorial Stadium.

Meanwhile, the clown show continued its long run in Baltimore. "Uh-oh. Colt fans know about the circus," Bernie Miklasz joshed in the *News American* in December 1983. "Each year at this time, ringmasters Bob Irsay and [Colts lawyer] Mike Chernoff stand under the spotlights and put the franchise in peril with their highwire act ... But this isn't a normal franchise. That's because Irsay and Chernoff usually manage to louse things up from their Chicago office. If Irsay isn't trading a player, Chernoff is losing one to another league because of a heavy-handed negotiating style that went out with the hula hoop."

Miklasz introduced some prominent exhibits. "Last season's [1983] Irsay/ Chernoff circus was memorable, full of chills, thrills and, most of all, spills. [Coach Frank] Kush and [GM Ernie] Accorsi had a lot of wreckage to clean up before it came time to play football in 1983. Eight days after the draft, Irsay stuck his head into the lion's mouth and traded top draft pick John Elway to Denver without bothering to inform Kush or Accorsi. A few weeks later, Chernoff got caught on the flying trapeze and let third-round pick George Achica, a defensive lineman from Southern Cal, escape to the U.S. Football League ... Irsay also left his mark on the 1982 draft, leaving instructions to pick Art Schlichter instead of Jim McMahon when the Colts were trying to decide between the two quarterbacks. Irsay didn't like McMahon's agent. And you know the rest." The rest being McMahon winning

a Super Bowl with the Bears and Schlichter doing a 10-spot at FCI Williamsburg for wire and bank fraud.

But somebody swung the Colts' fortunes around. In '82, they were 0-8-1; in '83, 7-9. There he was, quietly working his way around the amateurs to improve the club: GM Ernie Accorsi. In December 1983, the *News American* gave him his due:

> For the first time in a very long time, people around the NFL aren't laughing at the Colts. They're not laughing at the last-place finishes and the unsold seats at Memorial Stadium. They're not laughing with the [Colts receiver] Roger Carrs who demanded out of Baltimore and the John Elways who rebuffed efforts to be brought to town. The Colts' image around the league has improved so drastically that even the snickering over Irsay's comical meddling have subsided. The reason, say many of the people who compete against him every day, is Accorsi. "Ernie always has had a reputation for being a guy with a lot of energy and a lot of enthusiasm about the Colts," [N.Y.] Giants general manager George Young said. "When he got the job, I think a lot of people felt here was a guy who'd make an effort to do as many things right as possible." "Ernie's a man of principle and conviction," said 49ers owner Ed DeBartolo Jr., who almost made Accorsi his general manager before the Bill Walsh era.

"But the thing you want to remember about him is his ambition. Ernie always has impressed me as a guy who didn't just want to have a job; he wanted to *do* a job."

Accorsi joined the Colts in PR a year before Steve Rosenbloom became the team's president [March 1971] and worked with him every day. "Ernie was smart," Steve Rosenbloom stated. "He had been at Penn State [assistant PR director], and that was a good operation. Ernie paid attention, and he learned. He had a good work ethic, and he knew the ins and outs. He was very competent. You have a guy like that, you can be more comfortable. He could fill a number of positions. He went with George Young to the Giants after we left [Baltimore], and he helped make them a winner. We worked together, and I was very comfortable with him. If he didn't have the answer, he'd find it. I liked him personally, and he could fit a GM slot or any of a number of other titles in any organization. He always got the job done." He got the job done after Dick Szymanski flubbed it as GM for five years and resigned in May 1982. But Accorsi couldn't only work so much magic since Irsay and Chernoff couldn't keep their mitts off the operation.

One of Irsay's biggest boo-boos was allowing a football illiterate like Michael Chernoff to slither over from the general counsel's office to bollix daily team ops. Veteran Baltimore sportscaster Scott Garceau believes that Irsay picked some dubious company. "When I look back at him [Irsay], personally, I don't see a bad man. I see a guy that had a drinking problem and was manipulated by other people. There were other people around him that were probably in his ear that he trusted. And those weren't people here in Baltimore. One of them was his attorney, Mike Chernoff."

Mikey, the Wannabe GM was one of Irsay's Chicago buddies who couldn't tell a pigskin from a pumpkin. But Irsay invited the guy to go tag-team with him to muck up Accorsi's progress. All-Pro Colts running back Lydell Mitchell saw Chernoff as somebody who stuck his nose where it didn't belong. "You could see that the guy [Chernoff] was gaining more and more power. And obviously, that's who Mr. Irsay relied on. He was almost like his henchman. He did the dirty work. He called the shots for him [Irsay]. I think that's what it really came down to. Back in those days, when the guys wanted to communicate with Mr. Irsay, that's who they had to go through. I just know that he [Irsay] listened to Chernoff, and sometimes, it was about football matters, which didn't make sense at all."

Forty years after the fact, Jim Irsay swore he would never have traded Elway and emphasized how his dad was in a big financial hole in Baltimore. While he was at it, he took a stab at Chernoff. "My dad and I disagreed on a lot of things," Jim Irsay stated in "Colts' Irsay: 'No way' I Would Have Dealt Elway 40 Years Ago." "I loved my dad, but his lawyer, Mike Chernoff, was still alive, and he influenced him the wrong way. That was just the wrong way to go. What people don't realize is that we were stuck in that old stadium (Baltimore's Memorial Stadium), and my dad, literally, was broke. I mean, honest to God, that was a $5-million contract back then when he bought the team. He wasn't planning on owning the entire team. Back then, there were no restrictions on owners' debt. He put up $5 million and borrowed the rest, and we had 17,000 fans the last game with the Houston Oilers. It probably worked out best, maybe for John [Elway] and us."

The players and folks in Baltimore thought Michael Machiavelli (aka Chernoff) was a conniving little interloper, but Irsay made him his wingman as he peddled his ballclub to interested parties. *Evening Sun* sports editor Bill Tanton saw the damage this guy was doing: "Irsay doesn't want this to end, said one man who worked for him here [in Baltimore]. He loves the attention. He loves having mayors and governors dangle on a string, flying to Chicago to meet him. So does Chernoff. 'I detest Chernoff,' says a Baltimore man who does business with the Colts, and knows Irsay and his lawyer better than we newspaper-types do. 'Chernoff was an insignificant little lawyer with a firm in Chicago when Irsay made him his full-time counsel. Do you know what Irsay pays Chernoff? Fifty thousand dollars a year [with inflation, $153,552 in 2025]—to the penny. Power is what keeps Chernoff working for Irsay.' One element of Chernoff's power, some close to the Colts' management say, is his ability to manipulate Irsay. Irsay, I'm told, doesn't really understand his own financial liquidity. Chernoff,

a digger, does. So in a very real sense, Chernoff runs Irsay."

Before Mikey, the Wannabe GM wormed his way into the inner circle, Irsay had a lawyer with some ethics, says former Colts band director John Ziemann:

> I understand that Mr. Irsay had a young lawyer [Robert S. Fiffer, from '72 to '75], and he was smart. He more or less kept the lid on the pot. He got Bob [Irsay] active with the Colts Corrals; he had him go down to Ocean City [MD] to be with the fans when they had the convention. He had foresight and got Bob involved with the fans. He was brilliant, from what I understand. And he died. I don't think he was there that long. Then, Mr. Chernoff took over [in 1975], and he was the fly in the ointment. He made it plain he didn't like Baltimore. To get himself more control, he had to get Bob out of Baltimore. Who was the man behind the curtain? Chernoff. He was the one who gave Bob the grenade, pulled the pin and said, "Walk out there," then walked away and disappeared.

Imagine Ernie Accorsi trying to right the ship with Irsay and Chernoff in the way. "It happens all the time," Accorsi noted. "It happens in industry. Those guys [like Chernoff], they get to be the righthand man and then have more influence than you do. Now you're taking a situation where there's an absentee owner [Irsay], an owner who is not involved.

Other than the Montreal Expos [baseball team], he had no sports background either. So, it wasn't a standard, traditional NFL operation. I had a lawyer two doors down from me, Jim Bailey, who worked in the office every day. We worked 10 yards from each other. Plus, Chernoff was negotiating [contracts] with the top draft choices." Just look at the hash he made with the Elway trade.

Chernoff had no business going anywhere near footballs and shoulder pads, but he ran some greasy Chicago politics on Irsay and got tight with him. For Scott Garceau, Irsay and Chernoff were a damaging duo who further bungled the ballclub:

I think it starts at the top. Somebody gave him [Chernoff] that power, and that guy was Bob Irsay. I think he [Chernoff] had his ear. He probably was a pretty good attorney. Socially, I liked Mike. When I'd see him, he was a friendly guy, had a smile for you. That part of it was good, but at some point, he got a lot more power than he should have had with an NFL franchise. I think he abused some of that power, so it was kind of a lethal combination. You had the red-faced owner, as Phil [Jackman] called him, who was stumbling and bumbling a lot, and then you had his attorney that had his ear and was able to manipulate him. I think Chernoff liked being around the NFL; most people do. But it would be like, you don't want your attorney calling plays with the headset

on, like the owner did in Philadelphia when he was half-drunk. The attorney was doing football things that an attorney probably shouldn't be doing and an owner who was misguided, more days than not. Added up, Baltimore was in trouble with that one-two combination.

To have a guy who doesn't know a trap play from a trap door working player contracts was just more tomfoolery. The Colts had the consummate pro in Ernie Accorsi, yet Irsay had a football rube negotiating with the top-drawer players. "He [Irsay] defended the Colts' rather strange negotiating technique in which his general counsel, Michael Chernoff, deals with most of the top draft picks and Accorsi with the veterans and the low-round selections," the *Morning Sun* observed in June 1983. "Chernoff lost the team's third-round pick, George Achica, to the USFL and has failed to sign Vernon Maxwell, the second-round selection."

Like Scott Garceau, John Steadman didn't think Irsay the fiendish sort, but he too saw the Wannabe GM meddling where he didn't belong. "Is Irsay malicious?" Steady pondered in January 1984. "An emphatic no. A great deal of the problems he causes for himself and others might possibly come from the attorney he employs. Bob is listening to Michael Chernoff instead of general manager Ernie Accorsi, which makes for a sad state of football affairs. Chernoff has been quoted as saying the Baltimore press and public will not give 'Bob a break.' The truth is Irsay has received kid glove treatment because there's fear that if he gets too much criticism, even if it is deserved, it will give him reason to depart Baltimore."

Current Indy Colts COO Pete Ward hopped on board the franchise in 1981 in the PR department. He thinks labeling Michael Chernoff a villain is off-base: "I don't think he's deserving of that status. He was working for Mr. Irsay, and to say that Mike is an arch-villain is to say that Robert Irsay is a villain. There was blame to go around, and it was just the dynamic of the relationship. Like a Carroll Rosenbloom—if it wasn't Bob Irsay owning the team, the team very well could have moved anyway."

Letting Michael Chernoff sign the big boys instead of Ernie Accorsi is like hiring a plumber to write your PhD dissertation. And Accorsi didn't take too kindly to it:

> I didn't feel very good about it, but I got the general impression that I was incapable of it. The day I left there [Baltimore] in March [1984], a month later [in Cleveland], I'm trying to sign the first draft choice of the Cleveland Browns. So, [owner Art] Modell thought I was capable of signing them. So, yes, I felt, *He* [Irsay] *doesn't think that I'm capable of this*. I'm signing the third-, fourth-, fifth-round draft choices. It didn't make me feel great. It was all part of the operation. I will you tell you this: I was the general manager for a year and a half. It was during the [1982] mini-camp when he hired me. He just walked in my room

and said, "I just fired Szymanski. You're the general manager if you want it. I can't give you a raise." And I said, "Can I go home and talk to my family?" He said, "Well, you're gonna be gone too if you don't take it." I knew then, this isn't gonna be for long.

A man who worked with Accorsi was Bob Leffler, the former Colts sales director who quit a few beats after Accorsi had had enough. In a *Morning Sun* article right after the move, Leffler panned Michael Machiavelli as just a standard, bland, word-salad legal beagle:

> He described Irsay's general counsel, Michael Chernoff, as a "detail man." "The NFL has a standard one-page trademark right agreement, and he drew up one with 14 pages with a lot of whereases," he said. "He liked to put in a lot of time and words." One detail Chernoff put in a contract showed that moving was never far from his mind. When Leffler signed a contract in 1982 to produce the team's game program for the next three years, Chernoff winked and inserted a clause reading "for the games played at Memorial Stadium." "You never know what might happen," Chernoff said. Although Leffler resigned in February [1984], he would have had the contract to produce the game program for 1984—for games played at Memorial Stadium. The arrival of the moving vans in the dead of night changed that.

To get a taste of life with Irsay and his Wannabe GM, herewith is the 1978 Lydell Mitchell contract snafu, Mitchell sharing the details:

It all started after the [1976] Pro Bowl. We were in Seattle, playing in the Pro Bowl. Joe Thomas was still the general manager at that time. I saw him at the Pro Bowl, and he told me, "Hey, man, when we get back to Baltimore, come see me. We're gonna sit down and talk contract." Joe always took care of his players. If you were playing well, Joe Thomas would take care of you. Well, on the way back home, Joe Thomas got fired. Dick Szymanski became the general manager: "Oh, I'm gonna take care of you." I think I went out that year and finished second in rushing and first in pass receiving [receptions]. So, "taking care of" me didn't happen. The discrimination suit [that Mitchell filed] was that Szymanski said to me, "You're the highest-paid black on the team." But then he tried to change it: "No, I said highest-paid *back*.'" So, we were in negotiations. Szymanski tried to live in the old times: "Well, this is what they did with the players back when I played. We didn't get paid that much." Consequently, he's probably one of the worst general managers in history. So, it didn't go well.

And then, Ernie Accorsi felt the wrath of a 1960s school marm. Mitchell added another layer in *Sundays at 2:00 With the Baltimore Colts*: "Preseason came and we still hadn't negotiated. I wouldn't go to camp without a contract, so we finally had a meeting. We're sitting there with Mr. Irsay and Mike Chernoff (often referred to as Irsay's 'hatchet man') and Ernie Accorsi, and it's so ironic. Dick [Szymanski] says, 'Isn't it wonderful. Walter Payton just signed a new contract today.' He didn't say for how much, but I wasn't asking for as much as Walter got, although I'd had a better year than he did. I said, 'You know, it's really sad. Do you think Walter Payton's worth two times what I'm asking for?' I went on and on, and we broke for lunch, and when we came back, Ernie Accorsi was sitting on the floor in the hallway. Ernie and I go back all the way to Penn State. He shook his head and said, 'Lydell, I told them not to do this to you.'"

The biggest brain in the outfit, ordered to go out in the hall and twiddle thumbs. All because Accorsi was shooting straight about Lydell:

They [Szymanski and Chernoff] thought they weren't getting an objective opinion from me. The thing about Lydell and Franco [Harris of the Steelers], they were two young 18-year-old backs [at Penn State], and I was a 27-year-old PR assistant, so we all came of age together. We created a bond that I'm not sure I had with any other players in my pro career. And I felt so much emotion about Lydell, I probably wasn't completely objective. Believe me, I'm not St. Francis of Assisi, but if I'm gonna say something in front of the general manager and the chief counsel of the club about the football team, I'm giving an honest opinion, football-wise. I don't want my first cousin playing halfback; it wasn't because he [Mitchell] was a buddy, believe me. I thought he was a helluva back, and I was right. When I spoke up, I said, "You can't let this guy get away. He's part of the heart and soul of the team." And that was the end of me in there because that's something they didn't want to hear. They were building a case. And I've found in negotiations before I became a general manager that when they didn't want to sign somebody because of money, they ended up trying to build a case against him. That's what was happening here. I was a young guy; I wouldn't say I was disrespectful, but I spoke my piece, and they didn't want to hear it. It was like, "Who the hell are *you*?"

They reconvened after lunch, and Lydell found assistant GM Accorsi outside the conference room, looking crestfallen. Mitchell had to go it alone in the lion's den:

I'll never forget this. We [his agent and he] go to lunch, come back after lunch, and Ernie Accorsi is sitting outside the room at the Hunt Valley Inn. He's sitting there, just shaking his head. They [Irsay, Szymanski and Chernoff] had kicked Ernie out of the room because he wasn't going along with what they wanted to do to me. He just said, "Lydell, I'm sorry." I get back in there; Ernie doesn't come in. And Irsay says, "We'll pay you this X number of dollars if you play out your option." So, that obviously meant I wouldn't get paid this year. And if I played out my option, they're saving money because I think you only got 10% [more] of what you were already making. And I remember Mr. Irsay saying to Szymanski, "Isn't it great that the Chicago Bears just signed Walter Payton to a new contract?" So, I said, "I'm not worth one-third of what Walter Payton is getting?" That's when things kind of broke up. I walked out. Nothing got done for maybe a few days.

Accorsi, the lone voice of sanity, shown the door after lunch. "We broke up the meeting; Szymanski got on the phone; Chernoff had a little office there he used when he was in town," Accorsi recalled. "When they resumed it [the meeting], they didn't throw me out; they just didn't let me back in. I was walking back to the meeting, and Sizzy said to me, 'You can sit this one out.' Basically, we don't want you in here. And it was because they thought I was an advocate of Lydell's."

Lydell recounts the wacky ending:

I was over in Washington, D.C. Me, Franco [Harris] and Calvin Hill had the same agent, Lee Goldberg, out of Pittsburgh. Lee was in Washington. I went down and spent the night there because I was holding out of training camp. And me, Lee and Calvin Hill went to dinner at a Chinese restaurant. I get a phone call. I'm going to dinner to celebrate, and I'm going to camp the next day: "Everything's being worked out. See you in training camp tomorrow to sign a contract." So, we're going to diner to celebrate, and man, when I get my fortune cookie at the end, I'll never forget what it said: "A change in venue is best for you." We get back to the hotel, and I get a message at my room—that Mr. Irsay had changed his mind; the contract is off. So, that was the change in venue [he demanded a trade and was sent to San Diego]. With Mr. Irsay, you caught him early, maybe he says yes; later on, he says no. I understand it more today that he had a sickness. He made his mind up when he wasn't drinking, then maybe after he was, he said, "I'm gonna change my mind again." And that's what happened.

Most of the back-and-forth of the Colts' move to Indy was a Chernoff production. "He was virtually running it because Irsay was out of it [drunk] most of the time," the *Morning Sun's* former Colts beat reporter Vito Stellino stated. "I didn't really know Chernoff. He was never around. I'm not even sure I ever met the guy. But it was him who flew to Indianapolis

to arrange the deal in March [1984]. Then he flew to Baltimore to quarterback the move. He was the driving force behind all that. But again, Baltimore gave him the opportunity, and he [Irsay] took advantage of it."

In early March 1984 the *Morning Sun* ran its audacious "Jekyll-Hyde" piece on Irsay, and Chernoff got a spanking. "His [Irsay's] resignation from Zurn [Industries] came right after the Colts had won their third division title in a row [1977]," the article explained. "Those close to the franchise attribute the next six straight losing seasons to a distinct change in the franchise's management: Mr. Irsay's previous lawyer had been replaced by Michael Chernoff, and Joe Thomas, who had held the team together, had been fired. With Mr. Irsay running the club from Chicago through Mr. Chernoff, the Colts became the NFL's three-ring circus. Says a former NFL team executive: 'You could put my child and your child together and run a smoother franchise.' Adds a longtime owner: 'I sit in awe, wondering what's on his mind.'"

Usually, it was what Michael Machiavelli piped down his eustachian tube. And Chernoff's jockeying for power pushed the real pro to the sidelines. "I thought I was being bullied," GM Ernie Accorsi confessed. "I wasn't happy about it; I can tell you that. And that happened on a number of occasions. Those kinds of things happened, where I was excluded for whatever reason. It got to a point where, I don't know if they thought I was a threat, or what I was. I think the people in town, the media and so forth, respected me, and I don't think they were crazy about that." Anybody who knows Ernie Accorsi, football or otherwise, thinks the world of the man. It was simple human nature with Irsay and Mikey, the Wannabe GM: They knew Ernie was better and smarter at the game and got a case of junior high jealousy and benched him.

• • •

By January 1984, after 0-8-1 in 1982 and the Elway Blunder, Baltimore was done with the Bob Irsay Traveling Vaudeville Show. Gwinn Owens, a loyal Baltimorean, expressed the community disgust in the *Evening Sun*:

> I repeat, I am not a football fan; base-ball is my passion. I am, however, a Baltimore fan, and my enthusiasm for the Colts was energized mainly by the contribution a great football franchise made to the excitement, the image and the economy of Baltimore. Con-sequently, I am sick over the destruc-tion wrought by owner Robert Irsay over an immense civic asset. It is not just a question of turning out poor foot-ball teams—every city must go through such cycles. It is because Irsay turned one of the city's most beloved institu-tions into one regarded with contempt or, even worse, indifference … As a result of all of this, Baltimore finds itself in a Catch-22. As long as Irsay owns the Colts and doesn't modify his behavior, I doubt there will ever be the kind of turnout the team attracted under the

era of Carroll Rosenbloom's ownership. Consequently, using poor support as a reason, Irsay can claim his only salva-tion is to move the franchise. It would seem that the people of Baltimore can't win either way.

Irsay had his excuses at the ready: 1) The city stumblebums can't get a lick done about the stadium; 2) The press has me for break-fast, lunch and supper; and 3) The fans don't give a hoot. Now, if he could only parley those beefs into something sweet …

• • •

Enter Phoenix (again): "Colts owner Robert Irsay will meet with Arizona Gov. Bruce Bab-bitt in Phoenix today, a gubernatorial aide said, but no one would confirm whether they'll discuss Irsay's intermittent threats to move his NFL team from Baltimore," the *Morning Sun* indicated on January 20, 1984. "'He does have a meeting with Irsay,' the gov-ernor's press aide, Jim West, told the *Associated Press* last night. 'I can't say any more about it.'" Let's assume Babbitt and Irsay weren't getting together for a couple rounds of quarters. And keep this fact handy: The meeting was con-firmed by the guv's press aide.

On again, off again, so went the whims of the red-faced owner: "Baltimore Colts owner Robert Irsay, flashing more moves than an all-pro running back, skipped out on a meeting with Arizona Gov. Bruce Babbitt on Friday [Jan. 17, 1984] and jetted back to the city that loves to hate him," the *Arizona Republic* reported. "Irsay had been scheduled to meet with Babbitt and a handful of prominent politicians and businessmen to discuss the possibility of moving the Colts to Phoenix. Instead, apparently angered by the publicity the meeting had generated, he hopped in his private jet and flew from Las Vegas, Nev., where he had been hiding out, to Baltimore."

Having stood up Phoenix and the governor, Irsay swooped into BWI Airport, totally sauced, and delivered an all-time lulu press conference. The *Evening Sun* was there on January 20, 1984:

> A flustered and sometimes incoherent Robert Irsay has denied reports that he is negotiating a deal that could move the Colts to Phoenix. The denial, issued by the Colts owner at a bizarre press conference here last night, came only hours after numerous government and business officials in Arizona reported that Irsay was discussing a possible deal that could include at least a partial sale of the franchise and a move to Arizona. "I have not any intentions of moving the goddamn team. If I did, I will tell you about it, but I'm staying here," Irsay said last night as he stood next to Mayor William Donald Schaefer at Baltimore-Washington International Airport. "We can get this over real quick," Irsay fumed. "I haven't been to Arizona; I haven't been to Arizona. I've got three or four places where I've got working machines of my company's. I haven't been in Phoenix; I

give you my word of honor. I'm a good Catholic. Where in hell did all this come from? Don Schaefer is my friend."

In his book, *Playing the Field*, Charles Euchner mentioned Irsay's extended rant: "Since the Colts controlled the pace of negotiations, the city had to exercise care in dealing with Irsay's mercurial personal moods. The slightest misunderstanding could have undermined negotiations. The most notorious of several public outbursts by Irsay came at the press conference in January 1984 at the airport, amid rumors that the Colts were headed to Arizona. Irsay argued with reporters, delivering personal barbs and even ethnic slurs."

Irsay looked revved up on vodka tonics and malice for the Baltimore press. "As Mr. Irsay walked toward a bank of microphones, he asked, 'Where's that tall Italian guy?' He was referring to Vito Stellino, a sports reporter for *The Sun* who covers the Colts. When told that Mr. Stellino was in Tampa, Fla., to cover the Super Bowl, Mr. Irsay said, 'That's where he belongs.' *Associated Press* writer Gordon Beard tried to ask the first question, but Mr. Irsay cut him off. 'The last time I talked to you and [*News American* sports columnist John] Steadman, you were a bad man,' Mr. Irsay said."

The reporters had the goods on Irsay—flirting with Phoenix, the meeting with Gov. Babbitt that he blew off—and they asked him about it. "You answer me—where did you get the message that I was supposed to meet the [Arizona] governor at 3:15? I was flying on that plane. Now, where did you get that god-damn message? I give you my word of honor on my kid's life. I was flying today to come over here to tell you guys off that I have no deal. And when you get these goddamn fake messages, you get them all the time."

Why not go to the transcript for edification?

• • •

Transcript:

Robert Irsay Press Conference, BWI Airport, January 20, 1984

[*Robert IRSAY walks into the lobby wearing tan trench coat. Mayor SCHAEFER greets him at the door, smiling, and shakes hands with IRSAY.*]

IRSAY: [*wanders over to bank of reporters*] Where is the one guy I'm looking for? The one guy.

AP reporter Gordon **BEARD:** Here I am.

IRSAY: Not you. The one tall, dark guy [*peering around the room*].

[*Mayor SCHAEFER escorts him over to the bank of microphones.*]

IRSAY: What do you wanna talk about?

Mayor **SCHAEFER:** I don't know. They're waiting. They wanna talk with you.

REPORTER: You lookin' for [*Morning Sun* sportswriter] Vito [Stellino]? You lookin' for Vito Stellino?

IRSAY: Yeah. Where is he?

REPORTER: In Florida, covering the Super Bowl.

IRSAY: That's where he belongs. [*To the group*] What do you wanna talk about?

BEARD: The last time we were reporting, uh—

IRSAY: [*interrupts him*] The last time I talked to you and [*News American* sports editor John] Steadman, you were a *bad* man. So, I don't wanna talk to you.

Mayor **SCHAEFER:** Let me ask the first question. OK?

IRSAY: [*looking incredulous*] What is—yo—let me ask one thing. What is all this *about*?

BEARD: The last time you courted the Jacksonville people—

IRSAY: [*pointing at BEARD*] I don't wanna talk to you … Anything else?

SCHAEFER: Let me, let me, wait a minute. Let me put it in perspective.

IRSAY: Go ahead.

BEARD: Why'd you schedule a two-hour press conference—

SCHAEFER: [*addressing BEARD*]. Give me a break.

IRSAY: Let the mayor have a chance, will ya? [*pauses for quiet*] Thank you.

SCHAEFER: In the newspaper today, there's a story that said, uh, that Robert Irsay was in Arizona and that the Baltimore Colts were about to be moved. I think everyone is concerned over that. I am. I've told everyone that *you* told me if you were gonna move the team—ever gonna move the team—you would tell me first. What they're here for—

IRSAY: [*interjects*] All right. Let me—we'll get this over real fast. [*chuckles*] I haven't been in Arizona. I haven't been in Azero—Arizona. I have been in three or four places where I got working machines going, of my own companies. I haven't been in Phoenix. I give you my word of honor. I'm a good Catholic. I haven't been in Arizone—where the hell this all come from?

BEARD: Why'd the Arizona governor—

IRSAY: I don't wanna talk to you [*pointing at BEARD*].

BEARD: Why'd the governor call it off then?

Bob **SOKOLER,** channel 13 reporter [*standing to IRSAY's right, away from the other reporters*]: The governor's aide had mentioned that last night, to, uh, the media. And that's where it came from.

IRSAY: I wanna give you my word of honor. I have *not* been in Arizona, uh, for the last couple days.

SOKOLER: Did you have a meeting planned today with the governor [Bruce Babbitt]?

IRSAY: I didn't have any meetings planned. [*looking mystified*] I don't know where all this comes from. Don Schaefer's my friend.

BEARD: You say the Arizona governor's a liar?

IRSAY: [*pointing at BEARD, glaring*] I don't wanna talk to you.

BEARD: Are you calling the governor a liar?

SOKOLER: Are you staying here, sir?

BEARD: Are you calling the governor a liar?

REPORTER: Is there any thought about moving the Baltimore Colts—

IRSAY: [*interjects*] I don't know where all this comes from. Now, somebody started this. I don't know who did it. All right, uh [*chuckles*], we are negotiating. And I will do this with Don Schaefer today. Uh, closer to a lease here. Now, why would I wanna go to Arizona, OK?

SOKOLER: Did Mr. [Anthony] Nicoli come to *you*?

IRSAY: Mr. Nicoli is a friend of mine.

SOKOLER: Has he—

IRSAY: [*interjects*] He's a friend of Frank Kush's. Now, you just put this in your bag. He's a friend of Frank Kush's, not mine.

SOKOLER: Did he offer you a—

IRSAY: [*interrupts him*] I don't—he offered me whatever I want. Money. I have *not* any intention of moving the goddam team. If I did, I will tell you about it. OK?

SOKOLER: So, you're stayin' here.

IRSAY: I said, if I have any intention of moving the team, I will tell you about it.

SOKOLER: OK.

REPORTER: What per cent—

IRSAY: [*interjects*] Now I flew in, uh, 6,000 miles almost to come over here, just for *him* [*pointing over at SCHAEFER*]. For him.

REPORTER: Where you coming from?

IRSAY: I came from Vegas, San Francisco. And you can check the FAA [*pointing at the sky*]. Call the tower, where I came from.

SOKOLER: We have word that Nicoli said he had a deal with you. Is that not true?

IRSAY: Pardon me?

SOKOLER: We have word that Mr. Nicoli said he had a deal with you.

IRSAY: Let me tell you about Mr. Nicoli. He's a friend of Frank Kush's, OK? This is, you know, this is so *jerky*, so silly, that I don't even, I won't even answer your *question*.

SOKOLER: So, it's *not* true. Mr. Nicoli does *not* have a deal with you. Just putting that to bed.

IRSAY: *What* kind of deal?

SOKOLER: 49% or 51%--

BEARD: 49%.

IRSAY: [*pointing at BEARD*] I don't wanna talk to you.

REPORTER: Sir.

IRSAY: Yeah.

REPORTER: Um, Mr. Nicoli is quoted as saying today that he had a deal with you but that the deal fell through because it could not be decided who would be the majority owner.

IRSAY: [*holds up index finger to make a point*] OK—

SOKOLER: A verbal deal of 51%.

IRSAY: Let's go backwards. Let's go backwards. OK? Uh, the Northern Trust [Bank] has $25 million of my money. Sam Lizzo and Charles Sweet, who will join me at the Super Bowl, will verify this. Now, just think about this. Uh, the other— LaSalle Bank—the Netherland people, who are my friends, I'm tryin' to buy that bank. OK? Just mark all this down now. Uh, are friends of mine. I don't need the goddam money. And I don't need the aggravation, uh. I don't need this man [Schaefer] to get upset. All right? Now, we have *no* deal with Mr. Tony. Uh, Tony is a friend—*Anthony* Nicoli is a friend of Frank Kush's. Not mine. I—that's—I can't picture what all this is *about*!

SOKOLER: Was that in Chicago, two weeks ago, sir?

BEARD: [*in the background*] Why were you supposed to meet the governor of Arizona then?

IRSAY: He [Nicoli] was my guest in Chicago two weeks ago.

SOKOLER: That's supposedly when this deal was formulated. The 51%.

IRSAY: There was *no* deal formulated.

SOKOLER: No deal. OK.

REPORTER: Weren't you supposed to meet the governor of Arizona today?

IRSAY: No. Absolutely NOT!

BEARD: Why did he say that?

IRSAY: I don't wanna talk to you.

BEARD: Well, answer it. Tell everybody else.

IRSAY: I don't wanna talk to you.

BEARD: Why would the governor say that?

IRSAY: [*miffed*] Any other questions?

SOKOLER: Why would he [the governor] say that? Why *would* he say that?

IRSAY: I don't—call *him*. Call the governor. Why don't you—call Governor *Hughes*!

REPORTER: Mr. Irsay, how strongly do you feel about staying in Baltimore? Give us a good idea.

IRSAY: I'm very strong about it. I have no problems with the mayor. I have a very fine lease, all right? I—let me tell you—

SOKOLER: [*interrupts him*] Will you sign the [lease] contract for the mayor now? Will you sign the contract with the stadium for the mayor?

IRSAY: Let me tell you. I flew a couple thousand miles to be here tonight, and I don't need any of your avra—aggeration. All right? And I only came because of him [*pointing at SCHAEFER*]. Because a him. And I tell ya, I flew a *lot* of miles today. That's my plane out there. And that burned—burns a *lot* of fuel. I come over to tell *you*—I don't know what the hell this is *about*. Only because Anthony Nicoli made a statement. Now, why don't *you* make a statement [*gesturing towards the REPORTER*]?

SOKOLER: Well, I think—speaking on behalf of the media—we love the Colts, and we wanna make sure, on behalf of everyone who lives here, that it stays *here*.

IRSAY: [*incensed*] If you love the Colts, why don't you treat me right? I'm gonna send you some, uh, articles. This man here [pointing at BEARD], number one. And Steadman. And a couple others. *Hang* me all the time. Whadayya hang me for?

SOKOLER: That's a reporter for a local paper that you're referring to.

IRSAY: Nah, I'm refouring to—uh, read the papers. Whadayya hang me for?!

SOKOLER: OK.

IRSAY: You *want* me here? Why dinna you hang me? What do you hang me for?!

REPORTER: How close are you to signing a lease, Mr. Irsay?

IRSAY: Uh … I'll be here. All right? The governor and I—the mayor and I are very close to signing a lease. We have some problems with the baseball team [the Orioles], but I don't know why you're all here for.

REPORTER: Will you sign a lease before May 1?

IRSAY: [*a bit miffed*] There's no deadline, to start with, number one. Number two, I'm not running. I flew over here just to answer you guys. I don't know what the hell you're doin' here.

REPORTER: We're here, Mr. Irsay, because of a—I guess—a rumor that there was a deal.

IRSAY: All right, now I'm going to Memphis. Freddy Smith from Federal Express is my personal friend, and I'm going to visit him next week. Now, when I visit him, are you going to be back here again when I flew in here? It's *silly*.

REPORTER: Why did you come to Baltimore tonight?

IRSAY: For *him* [*pointing at Mayor SCHAEFER*].

REPORTER: Did he ask you—

IRSAY: [*interrupts him*] Because jerks like *you*—jerks like *you*—put things in the paper that I'm moving to Phoenix or to Memphis.

[*IRSAY storms off and leaves Mayor SCHAEFER alone at the bank of microphones. SCHAEFER looks a bit bemused.*]

SCHAEFER: [*with a wry smile*] Now, let me give you an impression.

[*The reporters break up in laughter.*]

SCHAEFER: First of all, I just want to tell you—he's, again, one of the most interesting men that I've ever met in my life. I never met anybody like him. I like him. I can't say that I don't 'cause I do. You never know exactly what he's going to say. But he told me—he told me—that, "If I'm going to move the team, I will tell you." And I read all this in the newspaper, and I got concerned. You heard him. He said he's not moving the team. He did not say he had a lease. I will talk with him tonight about getting a lease. And I am encouraged. I really am. I don't think he's made a deal. I think he would have told us.

[*Mayor SCHAEFER pauses and turns to the reporters.*]

I think one thing he *did* say—and I said this today to the press—he *does* feel very defensive with all of you, and I understand why he feels this way. But he has a very important asset in the city of Baltimore—a very, very important asset to the city of Baltimore. And if we could be just a little *more* gentle, maybe it would be—would work—both ways. He would be a little more gentle with you, and you'd be a little more gentle with him. That might be helpful. We're going to work hard to keep the Colts here. And I'll tell you—if they go, trying to get an expansion team is one difficult thing. So, don't think it's any easy. If the Colts go, it's tough, alright.

. . .

At the time, current Colts COO Pete Ward was working in the Colts front office. He got the word about the BWI press conference from Ernie Accorsi:

It was January 19 of 1984, and I was an administrative assistant. I was down the hall from the general manager, Ernie Accorsi. Jim Irsay was in Tampa for the Super Bowl. I was delivering a document to our general manager, and he was on the phone with Mr. Irsay. And he hung up. It was me and one other person, the director of marketing [Bob Leffler], who was a close friend to Ernie back then. And he [Accorsi] said, "We're moving to Phoenix. We're moving." And he looked at me. I was cheap labor. And he said, "I need you to help with the logistics" because that was part of my job, buses and things like that. And I went back to my office, kind of in shock, but also excited because I had been to Phoenix, and it appealed to me. I think the first thing I did was call my parents. I said, "Mom, I was just told we're moving to Phoenix. I don't know when." And then, 20 minutes later, I get called down to Ernie's office. I get paged: "Pete Ward, come to my office." I went down there, and he's on the phone *again*. And he hops on the phone with Mr. Irsay, and he [Accorsi] says, "OK. Yeah, Bob, OK. OK. OK, Bob." And he hung up the phone, and he said, "Somebody from the governor's office leaked the deal, and he's pullin' out. He wants me to call a press conference at the airport tonight." And then he looked at me, and he goes, "What the fuck is he doin'?"

As Colts GM, Ernie Accorsi had to stomach Irsay's harangue at the airport, but two weeks later, he told Irsay arrivederci. But that day he won't soon forget:

It was Super Bowl Friday, the day of the party. I did not go to the Super Bowl because of all the hysteria that was going around. He [Irsay] was in Arizona. I get a call: He's coming from Arizona to Baltimore and to call a press conference at the airport. These poor media people—they've had enough of my press conference calls. Steadman was at the Super Bowl; so was [*Morning Sun* reporter] Cameron [Snyder]. But there were enough people there. Here's what's interesting: The plane pulls up, they get off, Irsay comes in—Chernoff never got off the plane. So, Irsay walks in; he's not in great condition. And I'll never forget—[*Associated Press* reporter] Gordon Beard was a great guy and really witty. He asked a question, and Irsay said he was nothing but a troublemaker and wouldn't talk to him. So, he goes on with that press conference, and all of a sudden, he bolts. Off he goes. Here's Mayor Schaefer, facing the press, and they ask him, "Do you have any hope that this team will stay?" And he says, "I do." And they ask why,

and he says, "Because I don't think he's made a deal yet."

Sportscaster Scott Garceau wasn't there, but the spectacle was yummy fodder at the water cooler. "What happens is, they fly in on the private plane. Ernie's [Accorsi is] at the airport. E goes out to greet them at the plane. Irsay is shitfaced drunk, and Ernie is telling [Michael] Chernoff, 'You cannot take him in there.' Meaning, he cannot face that press conference because he's in no shape to get up there and talk. He knew he was drunk. And Chernoff sent him in anyway. I think Ernie's excuse was, 'He has the flu; he's not feeling good; he'll meet with them [reporters] tomorrow.' And eventually, Ernie resigns once he sees they're gonna move."

Phoenix came within a sliver of nabbing the Colts. "Baltimore Colts owner Robert Irsay and Phoenix businessman Anthony J. Nicoli came within a handshake of moving the franchise to Arizona, a newspaper official close to the negotiations said yesterday," the *Morning Sun* disclosed two days after the press conference. "'We were hoping to get a handshake agreement Friday,' said Bill Shover, director of community services for the *Arizona Republic*. Mr. Shover was one of four Arizona business leaders who were supposed to attend the meeting with Mr. Irsay and Arizona Governor Bruce Babbitt—a meeting that was canceled amid rumors that the team was about to be sold. Had Phoenix officials gotten that handshake, it would have set off a mass exodus from the Colt training complex and offices in Owings Mills [MD] this weekend, for which five Mayflower Moving and Storage vans had reportedly been reserved."

Anthony Nicoli was supposed to make it happen. He was also the guy Irsay flicked away at the press conference, snarling that Nicoli was a "friend of Frank Kush's" and nobody special. Kush was the middleman who got Irsay to call Nicoli and set up a meeting on January 5, 1984. Irsay hung out with Nicoli in Phoenix, then Irsay hopped on the plane to Chicago. Six days later, Nicoli met with Irsay and Chernoff in Chicago, hashing out some of the details of a move to Phoenix. As the *Morning Sun* documented, things got pretty heavy:

> The meetings continued January 13, when the foursome [Irsay, Chernoff, Nicoli and Nicoli's accountant] flew to Philadelphia and Baltimore. They toured the Colt complex in Owings Mills, ate lunch at a Baltimore County restaurant and flew back to Chicago that night. On January 14, the four men met to discuss a price [for Nicoli's partial ownership]. "At that point," Mr. Nicoli said, Mr. Irsay "wasn't prepared to release 100% of the club. He would entertain very seriously to sell me 49%, and as a matter of fact, on a very tempting, reasonable basis. The problem was I wasn't interested in 49%… We had set up a meeting for Tuesday after the Super Bowl," said Mr. Nicoli, who found a training site in Phoenix for the Colts. "Because things went along swiftly, I called Mr.

Irsay back and said I had everything arranged." [Arizona state senator Burton Barr said,] "At 5:20 a.m. [MST, January 17], Mr. Chernoff called and told me that Mr. Irsay had informed him that he saw the story on TV and would prefer to call off the meetings [with the governor]. I suggested that he think it over and get back to me. At about 9 a.m. I talked with Chernoff. Frankly, I couldn't understand why he wanted to cancel the meetings."

No beating around the brambles here: Irsay flat-out lied when he said he had no meeting planned with Babbitt. And he also didn't fess up about Nicoli schmoozing with him in Chicago and Baltimore. The headline of a *News American* editorial about summed up what Baltimore was thinking—**Enough is Enough**:

> Once again, the city and the fans who have loyally patronized this city's National Football League franchise for 30 years have been subjected to the whims and insults of Colt owner Robert Irsay… This lunacy has gone on long enough. We are left with only three recourses: first, to plead to the man's pride to end this public embarrassment, which reached a new and unimagined low Friday night, put his signature where his mouth is—on the lease with the city—and let the decent football professionals in his organization

run the football team. Second, if the team or a portion of it is for sale, let's hope that Baltimore financial interests could muster the cash to purchase it. And finally, it's time for NFL Commissioner Pete Rozelle to act. At what point must Rozelle recognize that his league and its reputation are tarnished badly by wanderings and meanderings such as we witnessed Friday? At what point must Rozelle put an end to this latest odyssey by brokering the lease agreement with the city? We have an answer: Right now.

As usual, Baltimore had it backwards and sideways. First, Rozelle was now hamstrung after getting whipped in court by Al Davis; he couldn't stop Irsay with an RPG. Second, according to David Frick, a big-time player in the Indy NFL campaign, Rozelle and New York weren't in Baltimore's corner anymore. Finally, no matter how many nights Schaefer kneeled by the bed and prayed, Irsay wouldn't sign a long-term lease for the slag heap at 33rd. Baltimore would throw down some cards, but it had a losing hand.

Baltimoreans had a smorgasbord of opinions. The *News American* posted some right after the shambles at BWI:

- Herman Wilkes, retired, 63: "Irsay owns the team, and he has the right to do as he pleases. I hate to see them go."

- John Shock, retired, 66: "Terrible. It can't happen. They should shoot the guy who owns them."

- Richard MacMahon, computer operator, 51: "I was a Colt fan for years, but I lost interest when Irsay took over. I think it will be a downfall for the city of Baltimore to lose them."

- Sanford H. Hudson, retired, 67: "I think the whole problem is the city. I think they spent too much time talking about renovating the stadium. We need a dome."

Bob Irsay's boy, Jim, was down in New Orleans for the Super Bowl and missed his daddy's drunken airport slobber. But it sure made an impression when he caught the video, as he explained on Barry Levinson's documentary, *The Band That Wouldn't Die*:

You could not believe that that happened. If you see it [the video] now, you would think, you would say, "It couldn't happen in this day and age. That really didn't happen. I can't believe that 14-minute press conference." My dad—believe it or not, there was a big, soft heart inside of him that got taken away as time went on—from his daughter dying, from his son being sick and dying from alcohol. It kinda made him have to be where he just couldn't allow himself any sentimental aspects anymore. I tell my kids, "You know, man, when he [his father] was a young guy, boy, he was something before time and alcoholism wore him down."

Having been smitten—twice—Phoenix was in an ornery mood. Bob Hurt of the *Arizona Republic* thought Irsay was a sly old dog running a con on several cities: "Once upon a time, he was going into the Los Angeles Coliseum. Another time, he was going to sell to New York's Donald Trump. No one bit harder on Irsay's overtures than Jacksonville, Fla., and Memphis, Tenn. In 1979, he had them bidding against each other. At Jacksonville, Irsay landed at the 50-yard line in a helicopter to be welcomed by 50,000 shouting potential customers at a rally specifically for him. There, commitments were in the bank for $11 million in tickets over a three-year period. Is there a lesson in this?" Rhetorical question, obviously.

And there was Ernie Accorsi, a brilliant football mind, stewing in Irsay's juices, mumbling to himself after that jackassery at BWI. At least John Steadman had his back. And this time, some Steadman melodrama was perfect for the occasion:

> Much of what Ernie Accorsi does is repair work. He's always trying to put something together after it has fallen apart or been shot so full of holes it's beyond recognition—like the good name of the Baltimore Colts, a team that has been in business for 35 years and earned extensive credits. Accorsi is a sincere, convincing talker, open-faced with nothing to hide. He goes through life making friends because of the kind, considerate way he treats those he meets.

He may have the most undesirable position of any general manager on earth, but he doesn't show it … The natural deduction is that Accorsi is a lover of pain, a masochist who enjoys being abused in a perverted way. His character is continually tested, but he bows his neck and continues onward—like the lead man ascending Mount Everest. He is bruised yet uncomplaining. Awards are cheap in sports. They have become so numerous there's no meaning to them. But Accorsi, off what he has been through and the way he has handled himself, qualifies as a hero who should be called to the spotlight and appropriately decorated— something akin to the Croix de Guerre or Congressional Medal of Honor.

Robert Irsay could have negated a lot of past mutilation—firing good coaches, sacking Joe Thomas, spewing incoherent rants, becoming pals with Michael Machiavelli— just by backing off, sucking down martinis in the owner's box and letting Ernie Accorsi do his thing. It's scandalous that Accorsi isn't in the NFL Hall of Fame, considering the winners he created everywhere he went. So—what does Irsay do with such talent? Tosses him out in the hallway like a kid who chewed gum in class. And all Irsay had to do was hand the ball off to Ernie and get out of the way.

Accorsi will tell you he was pretty much up to here with all the chaos and dysfunction before the calamity at BWI. But the press conference pushed him over the edge:

That was pretty much the death knell for me. If I had any second thoughts, that pretty much did it. I was embarrassed. It was kinda sad because the one thing old Colts fans and I have in common was we grew up worshipping that franchise. Listen, I loved the Cleveland Browns [when he was GM there], but I didn't grow up a Cleveland Browns fan. I grew up, from the genesis of my interest in pro football in 1953, as a Baltimore Colts fan. In every respect, I lived and died with them—died with them in '57 when they blew the [Western Conference] title, also in '64 [when the Colts lost in the championship game to the Browns]. So, the last thing in the world I wanted to do was give up my dream job. I pretty much knew before that [the press conference], but I knew for sure then that I had to leave.

So he did, on February 7, 1984: "Ernie Accorsi resigned as general manager of the Colts yesterday to 'explore new opportunities,' a decision he reached with 'regret' after several weeks of soul searching about his future," announced the *Morning Sun*. "Accorsi, 42, phoned Colt owner Bob Irsay at his Skokie (Ill.) home early yesterday morning to inform him of his decision, and made the formal announcement at a morning news conference at the Cross Keys Inn. Although one club official said there was no smoking gun or single incident that led to the decision, one source said that Accorsi became concerned when friends around the league started calling and advising him that his reputation was being damaged by the turmoil surrounding the club. They suggested that he would be better off quitting and pursuing his career with another team."

That would be Cleveland. GM Accorsi directed the Browns to five straight playoff appearances (1985-1989), losing the AFC championship twice to John Elway and the Broncos, pretty ironic considering Accorsi drafted Elway for the Colts in '83 and wanted to stick with the pick. Accorsi maneuvered the resignation with Belligerent Bob in mind:

The day we picked [to resign] was the day that Irsay had called for a meeting with [Pete] Rozelle in New York. We decided that I would *never* resign from a job without a face-to-face meeting. But I was afraid to do that because I thought before I left town, I might get fired, publicly. I told Pete [Rozelle] that I didn't want to do it this way: "If he's in your office, how about if I call Thelma [Rozelle's secretary] and ask to interrupt you, so I can speak to you? And I'll resign on the telephone." That is about as far from anything I'd normally do, but I thought it had to be done that way. And Pete said fine. And that's how we did it. So, what we did at the last minute was, I got Ron Shapiro [the famous sports agent] to call a major sports press conference at the Cross Keys Inn because I knew he had the stature that they would come. I was afraid that the minute it got out, he'd fire me, publicly. I wanted to resign before he had a chance to do that. I called Irsay from Cross Keys, told him and walked right into that room. I knew he was in Rozelle's office, so I knew I was safe. Chernoff called me later that day and said, "Would you meet me and Bob at Martin's airport tonight?" I said, "No. I'm not gonna do that. I've made my decision. There's no reason to have that meeting."

Somebody else noticed the irony of Irsay and Mikey, the Wannabe GM sending Accorsi off to sharpen pencils while they broke the Colts into pieces: Bob Leffler, the Colts marketing director. "He [Leffler] said the ultimate irony was that during the last year [1983], under Accorsi's direction, the Colt staff was showing signs of turning it around," the *Morning Sun* explained right after the move. "'Ernie had the staff unified and working hard,' he said. 'We had a skeleton crew, but they'd work half the night because Ernie would. I think we had it cranked up. We would have sold 30,000 to 35,000 season tickets in Baltimore this year. We were on our way. We had people calling for blocks of 40 tickets.'"

Of *course* the players loved Ernie; just about everybody did. "To Colt players, he wasn't just a general manager. He was a confidant, a friend—someone they could trust," the *News American* affirmed after Accorsi quit. "Ernie Accorsi got things done for the players, serving as a medium between the employee and the employer. Such was the feeling expressed by Colt players Tuesday, hours after Accorsi had resigned as the team's general manager. All agreed it was a sad day for Colt football."

Linebacker Barry Krauss called Accorsi "a good friend of mine" and spoke his mind about the man's value. "I'll tell you a story about Ernie. When he was the assistant general manager, he used to go to those little Colt Coral get-togethers. Those are just little things, but people remember those things— I know I did. The people of Baltimore knew that Ernie wasn't too good for them. He always had time for the little people, and he always had time to come to those little things and speak, if only for a couple of minutes. I'll never forget that."

Count Colts/Ravens band director John Ziemann as another big fan. "Someone who knew what he was doing—there, you just described Ernie Accorsi. He knew football, and he knew the fans. Ernie was a mentor to me. If I'm doing anything right with the Marching Ravens, one of the people I learned from is Ernie Accorsi. The way he managed the team, the way he managed the fans. He got out there and talked to people. And that's why Ernie was the ultimate GM, as far as I'm concerned—if you left him *alone*. If he had been left alone in Baltimore, he would have had the touch of gold. Look what he did with the Browns, the Giants. To me, Ernie never got the credit he deserves. So, if he had been left alone, with Steve Rosenbloom running the team and William Donald Schaefer as governor, the Colts would still be called 'Baltimore.'"

Part of the "Johnny Unitas Colts" that Irsay whined about was center Bill Curry. To him, the switch from the Rosenbloom era to Irsay was jarring. "Well, think about this for a contrast. You got Upton Bell and Ernie Accorsi [working for Rosenbloom]. You can go and talk to either one of them about anything, any time. They're in your corner. They may be able to do something about your problem, and they may not. But they're in your corner; they're trying. Then, if it's a big deal, it goes to C.R., and C.R. is gonna fix it. Imagine living in that culture and then doing a 180 to no communication, no apparent respect for the whole organization. That's what happened."

You got no argument from Tom Matte, another old-school warrior. In a January 1996 article in the *L.A. Times*, he unloaded like always on Irsay. "Hey, the management there [in Indianapolis] treats the alumni like dogmeat. There's no class at all. When I sign autographs, I don't just sign Colts; I sign *Baltimore* Colts. The only thing that franchise has done for me is forward my mail to my address. Otherwise, I've never heard from them. There was a time when they were even passing out the retired numbers to new players until Pete Rozelle put a stop to it."

Accorsi obviously looked past the bush-league bungling for as long as he could but had to split to save his rep. Steadman lauded him on his way out: "This is a testimonial to decency, honor and self-respect. He wouldn't prostitute himself any longer. Accorsi handled

the strain with the resiliency of a thoroughbred. He never cracked. Other jobs await him. And, if Robert Irsay, the owner of the club Accorsi worked for in a span of 13 seasons, ever agrees to behave in a more responsible manner, he will consider coming back. 'I told Mr. Irsay,' Accorsi said, 'that I think he's a good man.' But it's obvious that Mike Chernoff, a lawyer, and two other individuals who make up what could be called a Bermuda Triangle, have more influence with Irsay than Accorsi ever had. So it became apparent that he had to make a move, however reluctant, to get out."

A few blocks north at the *Sunpapers* building, Bob Maisel concurred: "No matter what he told us for the record, the reason Ernie Accorsi resigned as general manager to take a lesser job with the Browns was because he became convinced the job of building the Colts back into a good, winning organization couldn't be accomplished under Irsay. Accorsi loved both Baltimore and the Colts. You don't rise to the position of general manager of your favorite team in your favorite town, then quit for any other reason than that the job had become impossible."

You are the company you keep, so it goes. And Irsay palled around with Michael Machiavelli, who knew what buttons to push. "He [Chernoff] had Irsay's ear, and I didn't," lamented Accorsi. "And I think Jimmy [Irsay] had his problems with him too. Jimmy moved him out, I'm pretty sure. You know, he [Chernoff] would disturb the waters. You couldn't have a smooth operation. If I had to go to [Giants owner] Wellington Mara and say,

'Look, I want to give up two draft choices to move up and get Eli [Manning],' and John walked in, the attorney, we would have a nice conversation. If Wellington said, 'I don't want to do that,' I wouldn't have done it. But it was a straight, open, frank discussion. That couldn't happen with that operation [in Baltimore]. You try to go to Bob, and Chernoff would have the last word."

Accorsi bugged out of Baltimore to do a quick cleanup of his reputation. "Maybe Accorsi's resignation will serve the purpose of convincing Irsay his way is not working," Bob Maisel speculated. "When a good man, a capable, respected man who loves a town and a franchise, finds it necessary to leave to preserve his self-respect and get on with his life, it should provide at least a clue that something is wrong." When you know zip about football, are basking in all the transcontinental attention you're getting and are letting a $500 suit ('80s prices) give you rotten advice, you'll ignore that clue.

Accorsi started paying attention when smart people told him to bow out. "All of a sudden, I faced the Elway situation," Accorsi recounted. "I was concerned that my career was gonna be wrecked at age 41 years old. I was afraid I was not gonna overcome all of this. I talked to some real confidants. I talked to George Young, who was the best friend I ever had in the NFL. I talked to people I worked for at Penn State, administrators, and I said, 'Is my career being tarnished?' The two or three people I respected the most in sports said, 'Yes. Do you have to work for them?'

That's when I realized that if I wanted to save my career, I had to leave. I took a chance."

. . .

By late February 1984, Mayor Schaefer still thought the Colts would stick it out in Baltimore at least one more year, this despite Indy having entered the sweepstakes. After another face-to-face, Schaefer told the *Morning Sun*, "He [Irsay] didn't rule out signing the lease, but he didn't say he would sign either. My mood is better because we had a very frank discussion and he got some things off his chest, face to face." Seems Schaefer was reading coffee grounds, not tea leaves. "The mayor went out of his way to describe the meeting with Mr. Irsay, who is often portrayed as unpredictable, as quiet and constructive. 'He was not nasty to me. He was calm. He was collected. He just calmly said to me, "You were going to get me a 1 o'clock starting time. You haven't done it." I said to him point-blank, "Are you talking with other cities?" He said, "You know I am. They've made offers to me. They're fantastic." And I believe him,' Schaefer added. 'Because I know what I'd offer a football team.'" Apparently not, because Baltimore was still walking around in circles, dazed and confused.

But Schaefer was up on the high wire. Lest he insult the red-faced owner, he had to play nice and appease the man. "The mayor doesn't sway or make a foot fault," John Steadman observed. "Then the Colts would go tumbling down, like Humpty Dumpty and be beyond recovery. So the role Schaefer has created for himself is sensitive and difficult. He's working overtime at being a diplomat, and that ordinarily is not his style. Schaefer's position is somewhat analogous—but only in a football way—to that of John F. Kennedy during the Cuban missile crisis. One mistake and it could be over… The easiest thing to do would be to go public with his innermost feelings and fire verbal punches. But that only would achieve self-satisfaction, something he could savor for the moment and possibly regret. This can't happen. He's trying to arrange a contract with Irsay that will permit the Colts to remain in Baltimore and bring the haggling to an end. Then he might throw a victory party for a handful of friends and have Irsay as the guest of honor. Schaefer, most emphatically, is not about to lose his wits or, if he can help it, the Colts." One out of two would have to do.

Irsay got ripped by the *Evening Sun* in mid-February 1984 (headline: **Just Who Is This Guy Irsay?**), one more complaint in his quiver. The article included this oops from Schaefer: "As owner of the Colts, Irsay has warred with coaches and quarterbacks, linemen and sports columnists. He has shopped his team in Memphis, Tenn., Jacksonville, Fla., Indianapolis, Los Angeles and Phoenix. He has refused to pay good players competitive salaries and tried to call plays from his box at Memorial Stadium. He has made a series of demands and statements about a lease at the stadium that have no logic. 'There's really no way to negotiate with him,' says Mayor William Donald Schaefer. 'He doesn't negotiate. He just does what he wants.'"

The jig was up by late February '84; Indianapolis was sweet-talking Irsay. Tom Keating of the *Indianapolis Star* had Indy mayor Bill Hudnut dishing out candy corn for Schaefer: "I told Mayor Schaefer I knew what he was going through right now, worrying about his city losing a professional sports franchise. I went through the same thing last year when it looked like we would lose the Pacers. I wrote a guest editorial for the *USA Today* at their request, and I think they are going to run it this week alongside one written by mayor Schaefer in an attempt to sort of play us off against each other. But we remain friends, and he said he bears no ill will toward anyone in Indianapolis." A few years before, someone asked Hudnut to name the 10 best mayors in the country. He put Schaefer at #1. Once the move finally played out, though, the we're-buddies blarney would be tossed for compost.

Some in Baltimore thought Schaefer swallowed way too much pride sucking up to Irsay. "It always struck me that Schaefer, whose heart was broken by Irsay during their time trying to work it out and even after, when Irsay fucked the whole city over, Schaefer *always* referred to him as 'Mr. Irsay,'" former *Morning Sun* columnist Michael Olesker noted. "I don't know why."

Those outside Baltimore saw the awful spot Schaefer was in. "If I were the mayor of Baltimore and had Irsay sitting across a table trying to use Indianapolis, Phoenix, Memphis or Podunk as leverage for a sweetheart stadium deal, I'd go for his throat," Ken Denlinger of the *Washington Post* proclaimed. "I'd shake him till he begged for mercy. Then I would pretend to be [placekicker] Steve Myra in the final moments of regulation in the 1958 NFL title game and that Irsay's behind was the football. As Irsay was flying between the uprights of my office door, I would shout: 'And if you *don't* take the Colts somewhere else, I will dedicate every spare second to having what you already pay the city tripled.'"

Most of the time it appeared Mayor Schaefer was going solo while the rest of the town stood around and watched. "I think Mayor Schaefer, especially, he did all he could within the confines of the state and local legislatures, but the overarching theme was that legislators and government officials were willing to help, but they weren't willing to go far enough to build a new stadium because I don't think they ever thought the Colts would actually leave," JJ Stankevitz, producer of "The Move" podcast, opined. "I think that ties back into how important the Colts were to the city of Baltimore and how ingrained they were in the city. I imagine it was really hard for anyone in Baltimore to picture the Colts *actually* leaving. So, if you're not gonna leave, you're playing a game of chicken, like it's an empty threat: 'They're not actually gonna leave. We don't need to allocate all these taxpayer resources to a new stadium for a team that's not gonna pick up and leave.'"

Had they grabbed binoculars and peered 2,600 miles west, they would have noticed Al Davis in the owner's box at the L.A. Coliseum. There was your wakeup call.

Schaefer couldn't possibly handle this conundrum by himself. "The Baltimore side just was not gonna play ball [with Irsay]," former WBAL-TV-Baltimore news executive Wayne Lynch said. "Schaefer was not gonna be able to play ball with him. He should have. Look at it—he built Harborplace in the '80s, the [National] Aquarium was '81. It was on a roll. But I think the Schaefer administration to a degree took for granted that Irsay was just bluffing. He was a guy with a lot of bluster, fueled by alcohol in the opinion of most people. I mean, Phil Jackman [of the *Evening Sun*] called Irsay 'Bob, the red-faced owner.' Baltimore didn't like the guy, who was a reported alcoholic, *stealing* their wife [the team], their partner."

What the town needed was one stone-cold realist who loved the Colts and processed things like Spock: even-tempered, rational, pragmatic. Tom Marr IV is steeped in Colts and Baltimore political history: "He [Schaefer] was one of the savviest, most popular politicians this country ever created, and I think he believed Irsay," Marr stated. "That was a fatal flaw. I think he had too much faith in the league, too much faith in the cachet of the Baltimore Colts. I mean, the Oakland Raiders were something, but they weren't the Baltimore Colts."

Every time Robert Irsay went on the road, he sampled other parks and got even more peeved: "Those who know Irsay say he looks around the league and sees either old stadiums getting new looks (Cleveland Stadium has new loge boxes; Soldier Field in Chicago has been remodeled) or relatively new stadiums in every city," the *Washington Post* detailed in February 1984. "Then he looks at Memorial

Stadium, with its old facilities and inadequate parking, and he becomes upset."

After Irsay cleared out of Baltimore, the *Chicago Tribune* got Irsay to binge on complaints about the town he left. About Memorial Stadium, Irsay said, "The stadium is very old. It's worse than Soldier Field. I consider the Baltimore stadium probably the worst in the NFL. They made promises over there. Mayor Schaefer tried very hard to hold onto the team and help me. I don't think he got the support of the business people. We were paying rent of 3-4-5 hundred thousand in Baltimore, and the city of Indianapolis gives us $500,000 to play there. Now that is being treated right." Bob used a euphemism for we played them like bongos.

Steadman was scrambling to save the Hosses, but that didn't preclude the usual backhand slap to Rosenbloom. In mid-February, he wrote this:

> All the criticism dealt Robert Irsay has been earned, but now it's time to let up and permit the man breathing room. Pounding him with insults at this point isn't going to do anything productive for the city or the future of the franchise. To Irsay's credit he has taken the heat and never once tried to have a newspaperman fired—as the late Carroll Rosenbloom, who was Irsay's predecessor, attempted when he sent a stooge to see a publisher in an effort to have a reporter discharged. The ridicule of Irsay has become a popular sport but

it's evolved into overkill. If Baltimore isn't careful, it'll have a martyr on its hands … The owner has been heard to utter that sportswriters are "out to hang me," which is ridiculous. As with most of us, he brings troubles upon himself. There's no way he can act in an irascible manner and not expect to read about it in the newspapers. [Ernie] Accorsi was supposed to be able to protect him from himself but it didn't work out that way. He tried but Irsay apparently paid little attention to what Accorsi was telling him. The result: Irsay and his attorney, Michael Chernoff, came off being the All-American whipping boys.

The Rosenbloom sucker punch while telling folks to go easy on Irsay was proof that Steady was jittery.

. . .

With rumors flying, Bill Hudnut got it out in the open in late February 1984: "Mayor William H. Hudnut confirmed Saturday that negotiations are underway with Baltimore Colts owner Robert J. Irsay to bring the National Football League team to Indianapolis," the *Indianapolis Star* revealed. "It was the first admission by local officials that talks are under way. 'We're working on it,' said the mayor, who declined to go into any details of the discussions. 'The less I have to say about it, the better. Things are very delicate. I have to protect the confidentiality of the negotiations. I don't want to blow the deal.'" Smart.

Someone in Phoenix blabbed about a deal and Irsay went home in a huff.

Indy courting Irsay didn't start in February 1984; the seed was planted back in 1977 when a guy named Paul Oakes got on the phone with Irsay one day. Tom Keating of the *Indianapolis Star* told the whole story after the move:

> By now, everyone in Indianapolis who cares knows the story of the lengthy negotiations that brought the Baltimore Colts football team to this city. Only a few people, however, know how long ago Indianapolis started talking to Colts owner Robert Irsay. The first contact was made seven years ago by local insurance executive Paul Oakes… One day, Oakes heard Irsay was upset with Baltimore and was thinking about moving the Colts. Since this was in early 1977, you can see Irsay's been upset for some time. "I just took a chance and called Irsay at his office in Skokie, Ill.," Oakes said. "I made an appointment to see him and then tried to figure out what I was going to say. Right away, I called the mayor (William Hudnut) and he got ahold of Jim Morris of Lilly Endowment and Frank McKinney at American Fletcher National Bank, and the four of us flew up to Skokie. When we talked to Irsay in his office in 1977, we told him about these various plans to build a stadium in Indianapolis, and he said if we broke ground, he'd move the Colts

here. He even said he'd play his home games at Purdue or Indiana for a year if they would let him until the stadium was finished. We were pretty excited at first when we left him."

Oakes bragged about being the guy to get things rolling in his book, *How the Colts Came to Indianapolis: My Quest to Bring Professional Sports to Indianapolis, 1956-1984.* First came the rumor: "I came back to the city in 1972 to run my company's Indianapolis operation and took up where I left off," Oakes wrote. "Soon after, Mayor Bill Hudnut asked me to spearhead the movement to build a new stadium, and although very little major league talk was going on in 1977, I had heard that Robert Irsay wanted out of Baltimore… When I heard that Irsay might be willing to move the Colts, I took the initiative and prepared myself for the most important call of my lifetime. It was a phone call that would change my life, and Indianapolis, forever."

Oakes got on the phone with Irsay and gave him his spiel:

> When I dialed the telephone and the owner of the Baltimore Colts came on the line, I calmly asked him if he would be interested in moving his team to Indianapolis. Although it was the most important call of my life, it didn't seem so. I treated it like any other of thousands of calls I had made in my lifetime asking for an appointment. Mr. Irsay

made it clear he was looking to move out of Baltimore. He knew Indianapolis could be a player in his game. I made the case for Indianapolis as clearly and eloquently as I possibly could … The call went better than I could possibly have hoped, and not only did I confirm Irsay's interest in relocating the Colts to Indianapolis, but I was able to schedule an actual appointment. I could not have been more excited. But immediately, problems began to arise. When I hung up from the telephone call to Bob Irsay in 1977, I excitedly called Mayor Bill Hudnut, who was positively floored by the news. "What do we do now, Coach?" was all I could think to ask him. Hudnut paused on the phone before saying, "Let's go see him."

Hudnut, Oakes and a crew of heavies flew up to Skokie to sell Indy to the Disgruntled Owner. Oakes picks up the story in *How the Colts Came to Indianapolis*:

We arrived at his complex [in Skokie] and Mr. Irsay greeted us in his amphitheater office. His long desk was on one level and we sat in theater seats above him. He did not stop talking after I introduced our group and Mayor Hudnut explained that we were there to explore obtaining an NFL franchise for Indianapolis. He told us first off that Indianapolis was generally known to be the leading city for an expansion club. As part of a disjointed and rambling presentation, the Baltimore and state of Maryland political scene was described; [VP] Spiro Agnew was in trouble, as were the mayor and governor, including indictments and numerous failed promises of a new stadium and practice field. He was carrying a note of credit for $16 million and couldn't buy new players. Home attendance had fallen to 25,000, one of the lowest in the league, despite outstanding success on the field. The meeting lasted for two hours, and Irsay didn't stop talking for most of it. He talked almost nonstop for the first hour, then Hudnut and [bank president] McKinney made presentations. When Jim Morris discussed his role as a Vice President of Lilly Endowment, a $2-billion private foundation, Irsay became animated and exclaimed, "You guys are serious!"

At this point, it all seemed legit, but didn't Irsay ever suspect this was some reporter trying to gaslight him to see if he'd bite? The gabfest over in Skokie, the Indy bunch headed back home. "When the four of us got on the plane and headed back home," Oakes reminisced, "it was generally agreed that since the Colts were talking to other cities, Irsay was probably blowing some amount of smoke. But one thing was clear: Indianapolis was a prospective sale."

. . .

Hoosiers weren't doing the boogaloo just because Bob Irsay was looking their way. At first, most thought he was playing a shell game. In fact, Hudnut and his cronies were zipping it to avoid irritating irascible Irsay. The *Indianapolis Star* tried to keep citizens apprised:

> Robert J. Irsay, owner of the Baltimore Colts, once again is shopping his National Football League team around, and one of the cities he is mentioning is Indianapolis. Irsay, who is involved in negotiations for a new lease at Baltimore's Memorial Stadium, told Baltimore Mayor William Donald Schaefer that other cities had made "fantastic" offers for the Colts. Schaefer indicated one of those cities was Indianapolis. That apparently comes as a surprise to most of the people who have been involved in the local effort to place an NFL team in the 61,000-seat Hoosier Dome which is scheduled for completion in May [1984]. "To my knowledge, there are no negotiations going on," said Robert V. Welch, who has been pursuing an NFL franchise for the city for more than a decade. "He's been doing that in city after city. But when it gets down to the tough part, he walks off."

Two possibilities regarding Mr. Welch: 1) He was playing coy to keep reporters and regular folk off the scent; i.e., he knew the Colts and Indy were talking; or 2) Hudnut and the first team were keeping him out of the loop. One thing was certain: They needed any old football team to move into the dome. "There is the more important matter that the Dome is the crown jewel in the city administration's downtown renewal program, it is virtually complete—and it has no primary tenant," the *Indianapolis* Star indicated in late February 1984. "When it comes to low-cost housing, the city could be in a position where it would want to offer Irsay a deal he couldn't refuse. Lilly endowment provided a $25-million grant that was the seed money for building the Dome. It, too, could be getting nervous about the 'vacancy' sign hanging on the front door."

Highly doubtful, but maybe Dad was being so tight-lipped about his maneuvers, son Jim had no clue. Jimbo rolled out this mirage in the *Morning Sun* on February 16:

> The Colts are planning to play their 1984 season in Baltimore, but probably won't start selling season tickets for the games at Memorial Stadium until early March. That's the impression Jimmy Irsay, son of club owner Robert Irsay, received in a meeting with his father at the Colt complex Tuesday. "Everything is planned for here," the younger Irsay said yesterday. "I don't see any indication that we're going anywhere else." Jimmy Irsay said he's so convinced the team will play at Memorial Stadium that he didn't bother to ask his father that question Tuesday. "As far as I know, we're planning on staying

here," he said. "I assumed the whole time we'd be here. I've never felt the need to ask him if we're leaving. I hope I'd know if we were going. We plan on being here."

It's hard to work through the weeds on this one. Here's what we know: Irsay was a "handshake away" from sealing the deal with Phoenix when the story leaked, he freaked, then flew to Baltimore for that zany press conference at the airport; Indy and Irsay's chief chiseler Michael Chernoff were in the first round of negotiations; Irsay wasn't about to tip his hand to anyone, maybe not even his own boy. "During the whole period, it was touch and go, touch and go," Jim Irsay told *United Press International* in March 1985. "With my dad, we didn't know until he said we were going. He said, 'Call and get the trucks rolling,' and I don't think he knew it until he said it."

Pete Ward was just a young guy trying to hustle his way up the Colts' ladder while all this was swirling:

Honestly, I don't think any of us knew what was next—including Jim [Irsay]. With the Phoenix thing behind us, I think it was one where everyone, in the back of their minds, just assumed that we would be there in Baltimore for the upcoming [1984] season. And as each day rolled by, it became more and more obvious to me that Mr. Irsay was just trying to leverage a better deal with the city of Baltimore, not really intending to move. Because we were getting too late in the year. I was anxious about the workload that we would have ahead of us—because we had waited so long to do that—but I truly thought that that was all part of the performance to leverage a better deal with Baltimore. I just didn't think moving a team that late into the year was practical.

It could be that Irsay and the Indy team learned from the Phoenix blowup—keep everything on the down-low until you sign the papers. That's probably why even people at the Colts complex had no idea what Irsay was up to, including a coach like Rick Venturi:

Coaches have the lifespan of a fruit fly. We're basically able to live in capsules. We tend to be into our football, into the draft. But there was no question about it: There was a tension and a bit of anxiety because you knew that it [the situation] was a fluid deal. And trust me—from our standpoint, the Arizona deal looked like it was gonna be consummated. There were a lot of rumors, and you'd just look at them and say, "OK, wait until the next day," but when the Arizona thing rolled, we thought, *OK, that's reality.* I'm thinking, *We're moving to Arizona. It may not be what we want, but we gotta be ready for this.* And then, ironically, when that thing blew up at that [BWI] press conference, everything went quiet. The Indianapolis thing was kept *way* under wraps. We really didn't know about that until it happened.

By late February, Irsay was getting serious with Indianapolis but still playing footsie with Baltimore. "Mayor William Donald Schaefer said today Colt owner Robert Irsay acknowledged he is negotiating with Indianapolis officials about moving his football team there and set a new, undisclosed condition for keeping the franchise in Baltimore," the *Evening Sun* reported. "Speaking to the mayor by phone today from Chicago, Irsay said he would not reveal his intentions to move the team or keep it here, the mayor said. The mayor also said Irsay asked him 'if I could do one thing, which is almost impossible for me to do. But I said I would try.' Schaefer would not reveal Irsay's new request, but he said it had nothing to do with the pending stadium lease between the team and the city. He described the talk as a 'very fine conversation.'" Fear being a dandy motivator, Irsay was having fun playing with his puppets. All part of the grimy game.

Besides imposing some ridiculous mystery demand to Schaefer, Irsay got in some licks about the local press. Seems Mr. Mercurial got obtuse when reporters dug around in his backyard. "I had to explain to him that the press is a free press and they have a right," the mayor told the *Morning Sun* in late February 1984. "He didn't dispute that. But he said, 'I never get a good word from the *Sunpapers*. I don't deserve that.' I didn't argue with him. I said to him, 'You're a nationally

known figure.' I said, 'When you're a celebrity and a special person, you're going to get some press.' He said, 'If *your Sunpapers*, quote *your Sunpapers*, want to drive me away, just have them keep that up.' He feels it's his team. It's his money. He feels there hasn't been fan support. He said, 'I've tried to be friendly to the fans.' He said, 'I feel if I walk in there, the fans are hostile to me.'"

Hostile, he said. Hmm. Wonder why: 1) Fired good coaches—Schnellenberger, Don McCafferty; 2) Tossed the old guard—Unitas, Mackey, Matte, Bill Curry and Jerry Logan—out in the alley like Glad bags; 3) Gave the boot to Joe Thomas, the man who assembled three straight division champs; 4) Peddled his team all over Hell's half acre; 5) Turned a proud NFL franchise into the Keystone Kops; 6) Showed up soused and ornery for a press conference; lied that he wouldn't move the "goddam team"; 7) Parked out back for powwows with Indy.

Irsay grumbling about the press reprised the poundings Carroll Rosenbloom got for years. The difference is Irsay made himself a human bull's eye. Rosenbloom had a solid case; Irsay just sounded like a whiner. Irsay's complaints about the press hounding him inspired conspiracy theories and ushered in the stale material about Rosenbloom. Alan Goldstein of the *Morning Sun* indicted both in late February 1984:

Losing the Colts will be tough enough. But now Irsay is fermenting a plot to place all the blame on a negative, unloving press. It's a familiar political ploy first practiced by Carroll Rosenbloom, who placed his desertion of Baltimore on the head of sports columnist John Steadman, who aggressively blocked his plan to incorporate exhibition games into the season ticket plan. Rosenbloom conveniently avoided mentioning his franchise value was $16 million when he swapped the Colts for the Rams. Now we are hearing the same nonsense from Irsay, who can get back his original investment by simply selling 49% of the team to some innocent(s). We'll take the blame, and Irsay will take the money and run.

Out in Los Angeles, famed *Los Angeles Times* sportswriter Jim Murray heard about Irsay's bellyaching. "Irsay wants a 'change of attitude of the press toward him,'" Murray noted. "He wants the media muzzled. Irsay introduced this salubrious condition in city-franchise negotiations with Baltimore Mayor William Donald Schaefer. The notion is not altogether new. You will remember that the late Carroll Rosenbloom, then owner of the Baltimore Colts, once similarly indicted the local knight of the printed word when he said he was considering moving the team to Tampa because the sporting press had a 'vendetta' against him. Rosenbloom did much better than that. He unloaded the Baltimore Colts for the Los Angeles Rams."

But, Murray wondered, where in the Fourth Estate Handbook was there an edict about playing nice guy with hombres like Irsay:

But, of late, Irsay has taken to promenading around the country keeping various municipalities standing on tiptoe waiting to be kissed. Irsay and the Colts have produced fluttering hearts in Jacksonville, Phoenix, Memphis and now Indianapolis. Clearly, desperate measures on the part of Baltimore are called for. If only Irsay wanted something simple, like new paint or the keys to the city or free rent. But the kind of write-off he's asking for is something new in city-franchise tradeoffs, and a great many front offices, to say nothing of national politicians, are waiting to see how it succeeds. Such a condition would require us poets of the press box to change the habits of a lifetime. It would be like trying to change the instincts of a jaguar, the spots of a leopard. It would require bringing into play a whole new set of muscles and nerve endings for things like compassion, empathy, patience, tolerance—all things journalism is not. I mean, the function of journalism is to impeach, not excuse, convict, not condone.

Leading the posse was John Steadman of the *News American*, who forever pounded Carroll Rosenbloom like a meat mallet on a slab of shank. By March 13, 1984, all Steady could do was shake his head:

From Baltimore to Phoenix, Ariz., to Indianapolis and now back again to Phoenix—the cycle is complete—or what goes around comes around—qualifies as another demeaning chapter in the degrading of an NFL franchise. Remember the Baltimore Colts? They once had their individuality, even when they were the poor trash of pro football. Now they are being dragged about the country much the way you would transport a circus sideshow. This is known in some circles as pandering, or more politely, testing the market. Ostensibly, the Colts will go to the highest bidder, an act of cheap commercialism that is revolting to the once-proud legacy of the NFL. Yes, Phoenix is back in the chase for the Colts.

Come one, come all to Sotheby's. Item #1953—the Baltimore Colts. Who'll start the bidding? Ah, yes, Phoenix indeed was back on the board even after Irsay snubbed them a month before. One city not in the hunt was Oakland; they were still licking their wounds after Al Davis whisked the Raiders to L.A. But Dave Newhouse of the *Oakland Tribune* could commiserate with fans over in Baltimore:

Wonder what the folks in Baltimore are thinking? Bet they're plenty worried about their Colts. It's becoming an all-too-familiar feeling, a National Football League owner with wanderlust in his heart. One day, Robert Irsay is moving the Colts to Los Angeles, the next day Memphis, the next day Jacksonville. Then he flies off to Phoenix and arrives in Indianapolis. Robert Irsay spends more time in the air than [astronaut] Frank Borman. He hasn't met a town he wouldn't like to move his Colts to, unless it's Baltimore. In Irsay's mind, he has left Baltimore forever. But with his mind, you never know. It changes every five minutes.

Jim Murray had a point: The press is a democratic jewel, but they're also a cynical lot. Bob Irsay demonizing reporters was like a schoolkid moaning about getting detention for smoking in the bathroom. "You can't establish a relationship with a guy like that," observed former *Evening Sun* columnist Kevin Cowherd. "And so, there was the sense that he [Irsay] wasn't being forthright with us. He lied. He would withhold certain information that you needed. And then, towards the end, right before the Colts moved, things were really, really bad. You remember that [BWI] press conference? That was the absolute nadir of his era in Baltimore. I thought they [the Baltimore media] were very fair. I think, initially, with most reporters, they were willing to give the guy a break, to see what he was about. But when he lies all the time; when he obstructs your job; when he plays favorites; when he's constantly grousing about the team, the stadium and everything, people get turned off by that. The media is no different. But he was who he was. He was not a sympathetic figure."

E.M. Swift of *Sports Illustrated* generally slammed Irsay in his 1986 feature, pointing out the warts on Irsay's character. One episode involved a Baltimore radio station in 1983:

Harold Deutsch was the vice president and GM of WCBM, the radio station that carried the Colts games in Baltimore. In 1983, Deutsch and [Colts GM Ernie] Accorsi hammered out the details of a new contract that called for the station to pay the Colts $1 million over three years. Irsay thought he could get another $50,000 out of Deutsch, so he told Accorsi to ask him to come to a restaurant in Chicago so they could close the deal. "I assumed it was going to be a private lunch, but there were about 16 people there, and they were drinking and it was noisy, and so many rounds were ordered that I lost track of them," Deutsch recalls. "It was horrible. One by one people started to leave, and finally Bob and I were alone. 'Should we go over the contract now?' I asked. But he turned down talk about business just then and invited me back to his club. Asked me to spend the night. I told him I really had to get back that evening. Then he said, 'Just a minute,' and excused himself. Ten or 15 minutes later, he still hadn't returned, and after 25 minutes I became genuinely concerned for his health. So I called the captain over and suggested we might have a medical problem and suggested he take a look in the men's room. There was a smile on his face. 'You're Mr. Deutsch, aren't you?' 'Yes.' 'Mr. Irsay had another appointment, but he'd be pleased if you would stay as long as you like as his guest. Can I bring you a drink?' I got my coat, grabbed a cab and flew back to Baltimore."

In pursuit of Irsay scoops, sometimes Baltimore reporters stepped over the line. Indy's chief negotiator with the Colts was David Frick, whose daughter was in the hospital with a ruptured appendix. Getting tugged back and forth between the hospital and the negotiating table was a rough go for a while. He got a sampling of ethics all akimbo from a Baltimore reporter:

I got a taste of the Baltimore media that I found *highly* offensive. Reporters figured out that if they tracked me, that would perhaps help them locate Irsay and Chernoff. I know they tracked Irsay's plane. One of the reporters that covered the Colts who was trying to figure out where David Frick was called my wife at the hospital. The message he left was that she had to talk to the reporter about *me*. My wife got frantic; here she was with her daughter in the hospital, and this guy is calling the hospital, and she doesn't know why. She thought something bad had happened to me. So—we all tend to overreach at times. I felt that was an incredible breach by the Baltimore media.

Cartoonist Mike Ricigliano came to Baltimore from Buffalo in the early '80s when Irsay and the press were going at it. Working for the *News American*, he naturally hung out with some of the scribes. "As a cartoonist, you don't really have direct access to any of these athletes or owners. It's all second-hand stories," he said. "But I knew people, journalists in the area, who *did* have these stories and would describe them to me and document them themselves. I knew [*News American* reporter] Bernie Miklasz really well, who had all kinds of run-ins with Irsay; [*Associated Press* reporter] Gordon Beard, who I used to do a cartoon with—he had plenty of run-ins with Irsay. And, of course, John [Steadman]. None of my experiences in Buffalo as a sports cartoonist compared to the kind of soap opera story that was just ongoing in this town [Baltimore]."

Steadman shared a juicy anecdote with radio talk-show host Nestor Aparicio the day Irsay died in January 1997: "I can think of when we went to Denver and John Elway. That morning, at 11:00 at the stadium, he [Irsay] was walkin' around after trading Elway [in 1983] with a 'John Elway Fan Club' hat on. And we looked over at the owner's box; it was right alongside the press box at Denver stadium. And there he was, necking with some woman that wasn't his wife, kissin' and huggin' and all that."

Both Rosenbloom and Irsay went to war with the Baltimore press, but Irsay was easy game. Colts assistant coach Rick Venturi had a front-row seat to the combat:

It [Irsay's relationship with reporters] was adversarial, no question about it.

And I think the fact that Bob met with Jacksonville [in 1979] and that he was shopping the team created a problem. I do know that in the year that we left [1984], about a month before the actual move to Indianapolis, that thing in Arizona [negotiations with Phoenix] was hot. There were no cell phones back then, but we were told, "Don't leave town because something is really brewing. This thing [in Phoenix] is ready to hit. We could be the Arizona Colts by Monday." If Arizona State doesn't get involved [in the deal] and want too much of the pie, I think it might've been done. I think with all of that going on, and then a bad team, the press and Bob became adversarial.

Phil Jackman of the *Evening Sun* used to pepper Irsay with sarcastic digs, inventing clever nicknames for GM Joe Thomas and Irsay: Joe Promise and Bob, the red-faced owner. Asked during a WMAR-TV-Baltimore retrospective after the move, *The Long Goodbye*, if Irsay got a raw deal with the press, Jackman said no way: "No. That [excuse] is the formula for getting out of town. You pick a fight with the local media. In [famous maverick GM] Bill Veeck's hustler's handbook, it happened in Kansas City; it happened in Milwaukee. They [sports executives] have to have something that, in the fan's mind, 'They're picking on us, and we're gonna have to leave town,' and all that business. So, it's always gonna end up our [the media's] blame."

Cooper Rollow of the *Chicago Tribune* had a long sit-down with Irsay three months after the Colts' move, and Irsay blistered Baltimore, especially those loathsome reporters: "People say to me, 'Bob, don't you talk to these people [reporters]? Don't they know you?' Well, you can't talk to them. They just write what they want. They hired a force of 10 newspaper guys to go over the country and find out what I did wrong. They can't find anything." He was referring to the huge "Jekyll-Hyde" feature in early March 1984 in the *Morning Sun*. Only two guys—Robert Benjamin and Vito Stellino—wrote the piece, not a platoon, and they did the usual legwork you would expect for a big exposé. Out came some old factoids but also some new dirt. Naturally, Irsay flipped his lid when he saw it.

Irsay also had a bone to pick with the fans—no loyalty, boorish behavior. But Irsay invited the outrage by putting a clunker on the field and peddling the team. "That's why the fans became disillusioned with Irsay, the players, everything," Marching Ravens president John Ziemann declared. "Look at the record. He destroyed the team. I'll reiterate: How can people put their hard-earned money into Irsay's pocket when they could do something else with it other than Baltimore Colts tickets? Don't get me wrong—I loved my Colts, my *Baltimore* Colts. But this was wrong. That was not a pro team, playing in a stadium full of dirt and mud. It just went downhill fast and crashed and burned."

Baltimore fans weren't shrinking violets. They spat their slanderous epithets about Irsay

on command. "Every time Rovin' Robert trips out, every time he visits a foreign capital to discuss a possible move, Colt fans panic," *Evening Sun* columnist Dan Rodricks noted in late February 1984. "They do more than that. They get angry. They get surly. They get nasty. They say things you can't print in a family newspaper, things I wouldn't say even to the Ayatollah Khomeini. They sit in bars, watch the news and curse. Given the chance, most Baltimoreans probably would boo Rovin' Robert all the way back to the hayfields of Illinois."

Attendance at Memorial Stadium tanked—and this was after the Colts won three straight division titles, 1975-1977. John Steadman lamented how far down in the ditch the franchise was: "In 1982, the Colts, for the first time in their 35-year history—going back to their initial season in the defunct All-America Conference—didn't win a single game. So, in 1983, with little enthusiasm prevailing, they couldn't sell more than 24,000 season tickets. The Colts were last in the NFL in home attendance last year [1983]. Even though Irsay said the live gate wasn't important, considering the fact each team gets $14 million in network television fees, it becomes an ego as well as monetary factor to fill the stadium. [Mayor] Schaefer realizes this all too well."

Kevin Cowherd doesn't buy the argument that Baltimore fans weren't loyal to the club. "My counterargument to that is that all fans are notoriously fickle. So, if you make it a pain in the ass to get to the stadium—if you do anything to make it hard for fans—the 'love' they speak of diminishes over time. You have a team that's not doing well; you have a stadium that's beyond antiquated; you have ownership that is erratic; you have negative press all the time. You can love something, but all those factors chip away at that love."

Business was business, and Bob Irsay was cruising around for the sweetest deal while Baltimore fumed. "Was Irsay right, that he needed a better ballpark?" former influential *Sunpapers* columnist Michael Olesker wondered. "In the context of pro sports, bringing what it does, and America being in the place that it was, which is to say, the real financial and emotional blossoming of pro sports, yeah, he was right in that sense. He was part of the tidal wave that was washing over America. But in terms of real justice, if we're being adult about this, we have public schools where kids are reading textbooks from the 1940s, and that's not right. But he [Irsay] didn't make the sales pitch he should have, and that was one of the reasons people stopped going to games. Who goes around the country, dragging TV cameras with him, showing Baltimore, 'I'm not happy, and I'm looking around,' openly trying to take your beloved football team away from you? Of course they stayed home."

The beast had been unleashed. After Al Davis cleared out of Oakland and beat the NFL in court, this was how the new game was played. Author and professor Charles Euchner doesn't sweat too much about Irsay's vagabond strategy:

There's part of me that wants to vilify him because he took something valuable away from people who loved it. But on the other hand, what do you expect? An owner's gonna own; a manipulator's gonna manipulate. It's the way of the world. Morally, I think it's a shame that he was not more forthcoming and honest, but that was a tool in his toolbox. And if he doesn't do it, then somebody else was gonna move to Indianapolis or get a deal somewhere else. There have been teams that have lost opportunities because they didn't act with alacrity. It's just the nature of the beast. I don't think it was Robert Irsay himself that is the matter. It's the structure of the industry. At the end of the day, you have to say, "Well, what do you expect? What do you expect a profit-maximizing persona to do—*not* maximize profits?"

The mindset got ingrained—if an owner gets the least bit antsy, he scans the marketplace for better digs. "As a sports cartoonist, I guess my pet peeve is carpetbagger owners," Mike Ricigliano confessed. "That is the one issue as a sports cartoonist that would get my blood boiling. Irsay had that precedent with Al Davis moving the Raiders, and Irsay felt that it was his right to do this. And I guess it is his right to do it; he owns the franchise. But there are a lot of people's hearts attached to a team that he crushes when he moves a team out of that city."

The media's attitude about Irsay reflected the fans' or vice versa. "The one night at the

[BWI] airport [the infamous press conference]: 'Why are you hangin' me?' He was talking to the reporters. And the reporters represent the populace; they are the conduit between the ownership and the fans," onetime Baltimore TV news executive Wayne Lynch stated. "And they're hanging him, and so, by default, the fans are also hanging him. They want to spit at him; they want to call him names. They didn't wanna call him 'Bob, the red-faced owner'; they wanted to call him something a lot worse."

The Colts' swan song at the mausoleum had a tawdry look. Few knew at the time—maybe not even Irsay himself—that the curtain would fall and never rise again. John Steadman, who covered 719 consecutive pro games in Baltimore, was up in the press box and described the scene in *From Colts to Ravens*:

The last game of the season, in Baltimore, on December 18, 1983, was a farewell to the Colts. They played and beat the Houston Oilers, 20-10, before an assemblage of only 20,418. The conduct of some fans in the modest-sized gathering was embarrassing. Through much of the second half, building to a crescendo, there was a unified voice from the stands screaming "Irsay sucks, Irsay sucks." When the game ended, I packed up and left the press box, with the thought that no owner, not even Irsay, would be comfortable with the kind of insults he heard directed towards him.

The pact, the bond, the marriage, the love affair was beyond fixing.

Then you hear this story from Len Burrier and you wonder how it all would have played out had fans kept their tempers under the hood. "Bob [Irsay], he treated me pretty good," The Big Wheel admitted. "Harriet [Irsay's wife] would tell me to come down to the Hit and Run [Gridiron] Club every game. And I went down there one time, and [GM Dick] Szymanski said, 'Where you goin'? You can't go in there.' I said, 'Yeah, I can. Go ask Harriet Irsay.' So, he went in, and I saw her going like this [wagging her finger] at him. Then, he came out and said, 'Go ahead.' That was a treat."

In early March 1984 Paul Attner of the *Washington Post* stated the obvious: "Perhaps this time, however, Irsay has gone too far with his courtship [of Indianapolis]. Even if he stays in Baltimore, his already perilous relationship with Colts fans has been destroyed. The Colts, who once sold out game after game, sold only 24,000 season tickets last year, and that was before this latest folly. Irsay hasn't even sent out season ticket applications. It's difficult to imagine many will be returned even if they are eventually mailed. Why support a team that appears to be in Baltimore on a lend-lease basis?"

In 2014 the *Indianapolis Star* looked back 30 years to the move, and former QB Mark Herrmann described the foul mood in Baltimore at the time, thrilled to hightail it out of town:

That whole season [1983], we heard rumblings something was going to happen.

Mr. Irsay was not happy. There was not a smooth relationship between he and the city of Baltimore. The fan support was not great, by any means. It was not a fun season. I had just come from Denver [in the Elway trade], where everybody was just so rabid about the Broncos. It was such a shock to me to have to go into a half-empty stadium and not have the support from a tremendously traditional franchise that had been behind that team forever. As players, we put those distractions on the back burner, but it was always being brought up and talked about. I think a lot of those fans were living back in those Johnny Unitas days—Artie Donovan, Tom Matte, the late '50s and early '60s. We were kind of underachievers, and those guys still lived there, so it was always there, and there was always that comparison. That gave you an empty feeling: "This is our team, but we're not there to support you, really. We're kind of living in the past, and you guys aren't living up to our view of what the Colts are in our minds."

You can't call that kvetching because NFL vets like Ernie Accorsi said the same thing: A lot of Colt fans were stuck in a time warp and never cut the new guard a break. Even Irsay upbraided Baltimore fans for obsessing over the "Johnny Unitas Colts."

Much of the Colts front-office staff got abandoned in Baltimore, but Jon Scott, the equipment manager, hopped on the plane to Indy. What he saw back in Baltimore right before the exodus distressed him: "Yeah, I was really surprised by that [fans cursing at Irsay]. Certainly, that last year [1983], we were playing pretty good football. And yet, it didn't matter what we did. It was almost easier to go on the road. I was quite surprised: 'Hey, we're turning the corner here. We're lookin' pretty good.' So, to see fans do that—I think there was one game where they had this image [effigy] of Bob Irsay, a stuffed dummy. And they were putting a noose around it. Just awful things. It was shocking. Even when Jim's dad passed away [January 1997], there were people that were cheering that. A human being has passed away, and you're *cheering* that? That's sad."

Relations were too far gone for this Dan Rodricks ploy:

Why do you think Mayor William Donald Schaefer has worked so long and hard? Most of his efforts have been aimed at pampering Irsay, humoring him and making him feel like the cat's meow. Why do you think Schaefer showed up at the airport last month and stood, tight-lipped, through that embarrassing press conference? The mayor tries to show Rovin' Robert that Rovin' Robert commands respect. Baltimoreans have not picked up on this subtlety of diplomacy. Irsay goes out of town and raises questions about the future of the beloved Colts in Baltimore, and what do we do? We badmouth the guy. Is that any way to treat a lord of

Baltimore? So now, before it's too late—again—we have to do the only thing that's left. We have to love Bob Irsay.

It was another fine mess Irsay had gotten them into. Rick Venturi described the State of the Franchise when he arrived in '82:

I think it was at low ebb, really. I had just gone through a terrible experience at Northwestern [University]. When Frank Kush gave me a second chance, the chance to be in pro football, I was just thrilled. The team could've been in Guatemala, and I would've been happy as all get-out. I liked Baltimore. I enjoyed the two years there. I liked everything about the town. But in terms of our franchise, it was at low ebb, in all ways. The talent was gone: the Sack Pack, Bert [Jones]. Everything was over. Baltimore is a great sports town, but they were at war with Bob [Irsay]. There's no question about it. That wasn't a good product on the field. Thirty-third Street [Memorial Stadium] had gone from what they used to call the greatest outdoor insane asylum in the world to crowds that were diminished. The stadium was historic, but it was in bad shape. Everything about the situation was really volatile.

Colts executive Pete Ward gave it a go in Indy and is now the team's COO. The tack that Bob Irsay took while courting his suitors has him puzzled. "That certainly was part of the contentious relationship that he had with the city and state. Whether it was actually to find a home or just as leverage to get a deal done in Baltimore, only he knows for sure. It was certainly something that was controversial with our fanbase and the Baltimore media. And it all contributed to the contentious relationship. But given the stalemates [with the stadium] that occurred during his time in Baltimore, it may have been out of frustration. I never talked with him, and I don't know what his reasons were. I think it was incredibly risky because if you don't get the deal you're looking for, you're alienating a good portion of your constituents and your fans—and sponsors."

To Baltimoreans, Irsay looked like a goofy used-car salesman on TV. John Ziemann on the consensus view:

I'll go back to people using their hard-earned money to support the Baltimore Colts. How can you do that when, all of a sudden, he's in Indianapolis: "Want my team? Make me an offer." They flew him [to Jacksonville's Gator Bowl] on a helicopter, made a big thing about it. How can you support that? You don't have millionaires sitting in those seats; you have the average guy. I love the fans in Baltimore. I couldn't defend him [Irsay] when I talked to people. "How can I support this idiot when he might take the team out of here?" That's what they used to say to me. I couldn't fight that. If we filled the stadium, they were gonna move. The moving vans were in Hagerstown, Maryland, one week before the move, not telling them where to go. That's where I defend the fans about not supporting the Colts.

Still, you have to wonder if a Triple-C approach—cool, calm and collected—plus some facsimile rah-rah posing by the fans and some genuine political know-how at the Statehouse might have gotten Irsay to hit pause on a move.

Irsay hawking the Colts like a Ronco Veg-O-Matic was a villainous affront. "It was disastrous, from a PR point of view because we in the media found out that he was shopping the team everywhere," author Kevin Cowherd proclaimed. "So, he was like a hooker standing out on a street corner—Jacksonville, Phoenix, Memphis, Indy. Soap opera was exactly it. I don't think there's ever been a more dramatic exit for a team that I can think of. And by the end, people were *so* sick of this whole thing. I guess you can look back in hindsight and say, 'If the city had caved and built him a new stadium, he might still be here.'"

Ricig the cartoonist had good company: Alan Goldstein of the *Morning Sun* was done with the grifter routine:

Everyone, of course, has grown weary of Irsay's snake-oil salesman routine. Commonsense says he should take the money and run to Indianapolis or Phoenix with the promise of bigger and newer stadiums and a new media to judge him. But we know all too well that there are no standard guidelines for the unpredictable behavior of this middle-aged chameleon. "He won't move," a source says. "Why? Because he's too much of a coward. When it comes time to make a tough decision, he backs down. He did it in Memphis and Jacksonville, and now he'll do it in Indianapolis and Phoenix. He just doesn't have the guts."

Just one more kisser with egg on it on the morning of March 29, 1984.

Baltimore made two colossal mistakes that cost them: 1) They kept forgetting that Robert Irsay was a Chicago guy with no roots in the town; and 2) They basically ghosted the guy and assumed he'd stick around. "Irsay was a transplant; he wasn't from Baltimore," asserted Troy Lowman, producer of the documentary, *The Ghosts of 33rd Street*. "He didn't have any allegiance to Baltimore. So, they [Baltimore officials] should have read the room with the guy. What Baltimore basically did is, they just dismissed the guy. They should've put out the fires. And then the fans, they started burning Irsay in effigy and all that. Look, he's a human being. When you see that, you start to say, 'Fuck everybody. Forget this town.' He probably had a chip on his shoulder at the end. And there was probably a point where he wasn't gonna stay, no matter what."

A great love dies, the audience gasps. Everything about the soap opera tore up Ernie Accorsi:

I turned down a bunch of jobs for more money to stay in Baltimore. When they built the Capital Centre, I got an offer to be the vice president of both teams' PR [the Bullets and the Capitals] for a lot more money. I loved the Colts; my heart and soul were with the Colts. When Upton [Bell] went to New England [to become the GM of the Patriots], he offered me the assistant general manager's job, which I was *entirely* not qualified for after only one year in the league. But I turned it down. I just didn't want to leave the Baltimore Colts. And believe me, when I left, it was heartbreaking even though it wasn't the same Baltimore Colts anymore. It was still Baltimore. And when I left, I did *not* want to be a part of that franchise moving, no matter what the circumstances were. And that broke my heart.

Echoing what Colts marketing director Bob Leffler said, unabashed Colts fan Tom Marr IV thinks Irsay's PR was done on the cheap: "As the Colts were declining in attendance," Marr noted, "the Orioles began a boom in attendance. I don't know how you explain that [decline in attendance], other than the Colts were a front-office disaster. They were a mess. And they turned off a lot of fans. The Colts had terrible PR. They did not know how to sell themselves the way the Orioles did."

And no blame goes to Leffler for that. If it weren't for Irsay riling the public, there'd be no public relations at all. Leffler slammed Irsay's laissez-faire PR policy on the WMAR-TV special, *The Long Goodbye*:

I think I had seen it coming for quite a while. It's sort of a mentality type of a situation. They [the Irsays] really kinda wanted to go, and whatever we did here in Baltimore to try to make things happen in the marketplace [a marketing push], they didn't really want a whole lot to do with that. They had their minds made up, and I think they flirted with the idea of going for a long time. And they just got pretty far along this time [with Indianapolis], and they let it rip. But I don't think they ever really understood this market [in Baltimore] and what Colt football meant to Baltimore people. They saw it as a commodity. It's a scarce commodity that's being bandied around from city to city, but I don't think they ever really understood it as a popular, cultural entity in this marketplace.

And by mid-February 1984, Indianapolis was going like gangbusters to woo the Colts out to the prairie.

CHAPTER 15

GAS UP THE VANS

ndianapolis cranked up the vigor in late February while Baltimore stood there and chewed its fingernails. "Indianapolis officials negotiating with Baltimore Colts owner Robert Irsay have offered him a package deal that includes modest rent for the city's brand-new, domed stadium and help with Mr. Irsay's approximately $14-million debt, and a practice facility, according to an Indianapolis source close to the negotiations," disclosed the *Morning Sun* on February 27. "Under the proposed deal, Mr. Irsay would retain majority ownership of the team. 'The point we're at now is that Irsay has everything he's asked for,' the source said. 'The only question is whether Mr. Irsay's willing to move the team.'"

The tale of the tape presaged a rout: Indy vs. Baltimore, Joe Louis vs. the Bum of the Month. The Dome, the loan, the practice facility: Indianapolis whipped up a superb package. Over in Baltimore, Schaefer was still all-business, but his cronies were on sabbatical. "In an interview yesterday morning on Baltimore radio station WCBM, Mayor Schaefer

said he was 'not overly optimistic' about the prospects of keeping the Colts in town," the *Morning Sun* indicated. "In a meeting last week with Mr. Irsay, the mayor said yesterday, 'He [Mr. Irsay] gave me absolutely no assurances that he was going to stay in Baltimore.'" At least Irsay was honest for once.

The two mayors had a round of battling essays in the March 8, 1984, edition of *USA Today*. William Hudnut played happy warrior and threw down the gauntlet:

In the economic development game today, cities find themselves in very competitive situations. They are attracting and losing investment constantly. You win some, and you lose some—from this vantage point, the Baltimore Colts represent a business and a business opportunity for us. If there is nothing illegal about moving that business from Baltimore to a Memphis, a Phoenix, a Jacksonville or an Indianapolis, we should give it a try. If a deal could be worked out to everyone's satisfaction, the free-market forces would have prevailed, in typical American fashion. Should we go for it? Of course!

The exclamation point must have unnerved Mayor Schaefer. Pure can-do.

William Donald Schaefer, staring at a Panzer tank rolling his way, could only solicit sympathy: "A professional team is not an island of investment that can be cut loose at will. It is more like a large tree with a deep and integral root system that cannot be transplanted without considerable damage to the tree and its surroundings. Owners do a city an injustice by considering a sports franchise as a business investment. They may pack their bags and leave without care, but in their wake a city weeps for the loss of part of its youth, part of its spirit—and, yes, part of its pocketbook." The woe-is-me almost sounded like surrender. Almost two months after the move, Hudnut wrote a letter to Jim Irsay and scolded Baltimore for its hypocrisy. He knew his history: "Parenthetically," Hudnut told the younger Irsay, "I might observe that I didn't hear Baltimore complaining back in the early 1950s when the Dallas Texans became the Baltimore Colts or the Chicago Zephyrs became the Baltimore Bullets or the St. Louis Browns became the Baltimore Orioles!"

To his credit, John Steadman saw that the end was near and went to default—melodrama. His February 27, 1984, version of Outlined Against a Blue-Gray October Sky:

Backed against his goal line and with the clock moving, Mayor William Donald Schaefer is endeavoring to pull off a desperation play to keep the Baltimore Colts in the game. Time could be running out on a once-coveted franchise that has been here since 1953. The countdown is on. Indianapolis, with an $80-million domed stadium and nothing to put in it, is offering Colt owner Robert Irsay an opportunity to transfer the team there for what would be a financial bonanza. Free rent, a practice facility and a personal loan to Irsay are the main inducements. Schaefer can't begin to match the deal that has been thrust in front of Irsay by Indianapolis. But, typically, he's going to give it his best effort. The only strategy seemingly open to him at this late date is to guarantee Irsay sellouts for all eight home games next season.

Indy fretted not: "Sellouts? We'll show you sellouts. We've already got a season-ticket line from here to Muncie."

Charm City had no idea what it was up against. They looked like a bunch of bushers. Only after losing the Colts did it dawn on them, says JJ Stankevitz, producer of "The Move" podcast:

I do think their [Baltimore's] approach of, "Well, we don't think the Colts are gonna leave" ultimately did kind of hamstring them when it came time for like, "OK, now, it really *does* look like the Colts are gonna leave." I don't know if they were as prepared as they could have been for that moment. What was really telling was, after the Colts left, there were all these articles in the Baltimore *Sun* about, "Well, what are we gonna do to keep the Orioles?" That was the wakeup call. Then, [Oriole Park at] Camden Yards gets built seven years later—they repealed Question P [in November 1984]. Now Baltimore has a state-of-the-art stadium, and the Orioles are thriving. I do think that not being ready for the team [the Colts] to actually pick up and leave—which there were legitimate reasons to think they wouldn't—ultimately hampered their effort to keep the team because they weren't serious about it.

Weren't serious about it—that pretty much sums it up.

Baltimore had a weak hand for a host of reasons—a bunch of political paper tigers, no vision, no unity, a homely ballpark and no plan—but Indianapolis had the ultimate trump card: the Hoosier Dome. Former Colts beat reporter Vito Stellino offered one reason that Indy had the winning bid:

Because they built a stadium. It's that simple. They had a history of building things. They became a home for college sports, a hub for the NCAA. And their stadium was part of the convention center. They are not a major-league city like Baltimore. Indianapolis will never get a baseball team. They don't have the population to support one. But once they built a stadium, that made them a player. And they built it on spec; they didn't have a team. They had [William] Hudnut as mayor, so they came up with the idea of a combination convention center-stadium. It was new, and it was better than anything Irsay had. Indianapolis was not a great market, but they had a new stadium. That's how they got the team.

Realists saw how this would go down. Kevin Cowherd of the *Evening Sun* took one look at the Hoosier Dome and figured it was N/C—no contest:

Mayor William Donald Schaefer is supposed to meet again with Irsay sometime today [Feb. 27] in his ongoing battle to keep the Colts in Baltimore. But do not hold your breath here. This is a high-stakes poker game being played out between Baltimore and Indianapolis. And when Mayor Schaefer bellies up to the table and stares across at the blustering Irsay, he will not exactly be showing off a full house—or anything even close. What Mayor Schaefer has to offer is a 30-year-old stadium and the promise of some modest improvements. Think about that for a moment. If the reports are correct, Irsay gets a multi-million-dollar loan, a new stadium built expressly for football, and a new practice facility to move the Colts to Indianapolis. If they stay in Baltimore, a city he has never felt comfortable in, a city he perceives as hating him, he gets a run-down Memorial Stadium.

Indianapolis jumped into the lead when Phoenix gave up an own goal by leaking the Colts story, which infuriated Irsay. "They had this thing done in Phoenix, and it fell apart," longtime Indy Colts beat writer Mike Chappell stated. "I don't know if they [the Colts] could've mended fences and gone back to Baltimore. It was almost like Indy was there as a consolation prize. And I hate to misrepresent it, but after Phoenix didn't work, I don't know if he [Irsay] felt pressure—'Man, I've gotta do this or else.' A lot of people thought that this was gonna happen in Phoenix. So, I don't know if the fact that it fell through there, and Indy said, 'Hey, wait a minute. We're right here. We've got a stadium.' And he [Irsay] thought, *I've gotta move 'cause I've gotta move*. Going back to Baltimore really wasn't much of an option."

How many ground hog days did Baltimore have over 19 years, and they still didn't get it right. Way back in '65, when Carroll Rosenbloom started talking up a new stadium, that was when they should've gotten some smart noodles together to build a new ballpark. Exactly what Indy did, says former Colts assistant coach Rick Venturi:

In retrospect, it's very easy. They [Baltimore] had to build a new stadium because the minute another city was there with the necessary tools for a stadium, then he [Irsay] was gonna make that deal. The reason that he couldn't in Arizona was because they didn't have a [pro] stadium. They had to build one, so he would've had to play at Arizona State until they did that. But then you had Indianapolis, and they were just the opposite. Indiana is a conservative state, to say the least. But it is a progressive state, economically, that can rally all the counties for the greater good. They had a stadium ready to go because they had been promised an [NFL] expansion team. And when that went south because of the USFL feud [with the NFL], they were stuck with an empty stadium. They had this new stadium with all the amenities with it—the [training] complex, the loan, the guaranteed income for 12 years. I mean, they put together a package that was probably the greatest package ever written at that time. You can look back in retrospect and say they could have improved Memorial Stadium, but one way or another, I think they would have had to build him [Irsay] a new stadium. Which they did more than 10 years later [for the Ravens].

Nobody in Baltimore—not even Willy Don—hugged a new stadium for dear life. How the plot might have changed: The Irsays would have hung around and Indianapolis would have been forced to woo another team or wait for expansion. But Indy got a gift: Baltimore putzed around and it cost them.

The man who worked out the Colts-Indy deal with Michael Chernoff was former Indianapolis deputy mayor David Frick. He looked at his competition to the east and here's what he saw:

> Well, the stadium—that was the first thing. The Colts described to me what it was like to be in that stadium. It was a mess. They had rodents; the showers didn't work; the dressing rooms for the players were ugly. The fan amenities were not good. The second thing is, the city of Baltimore and Bob Irsay got off the tracks. There was no shortage of people who told Mr. Irsay that he had to get out of Baltimore. Carroll Rosenbloom even wanted to get out. Irsay and the local leadership in Baltimore just got off-track somehow, particularly the media; the media was vicious. Bob Irsay brought a lot of that on, but I saw it. It was obvious how much they hated Irsay, and they were not prone to be silent about it. And if you were an owner of a franchise, and you're trying to operate your business, it was gonna be hard to operate it in Baltimore.

The *Morning Sun* ran this editorial on March 2, 1984, with much envy and maybe a little jealousy: "Two jaded old cities with declining population and industrial base took stock of themselves in the late '60s. Baltimore decided to become a tourist mecca, Indianapolis a sports capital. Each did it. Indianapolis, considerably smaller than Baltimore, is healthier economically and with more downtown development in relation to what it was. Its development pattern, parallel to Baltimore's but different, is worth a look... All this was done with remarkable public-private sector cooperation promoted by two Republican mayors. The first, Richard Lugar, is now a United States senator. His successor, the Rev. William H. Hudnut III, is enjoying a third term. One of Mr. Lugar's achievements was 'Unigov,' the partial merger of Indianapolis city with Marion County. This made the mayor the chief executive of the county and gave suburbanites a voice and stake in downtown development." So, while Indy politicians peered at tomorrow, Baltimore ordered flapjacks for breakfast and read the paper.

Having no plan and being ho-hum put Baltimore laps behind Indy. Documentarian Troy Lowman thinks the pros didn't act the part:

> Irsay said, "I need you to do this, or I'm gonna leave." They [Baltimore politicians] thought he was crying wolf. I mean, he didn't do it in a very professional way, but they were well aware that he was looking at other places. This is where Schaefer and them should have stepped up and said, "Look, we're gonna give you everything you want to keep

the team here." So, they [Baltimore officials] didn't act very professional either. Or they flat-out dismissed the guy. Schaefer dropped the ball; he was ill-equipped to handle this stuff. It's like an analogy you could use with cancer. You find out you have cancer in stage one, you can fix the problem. They were trying to fix it in stage four. It was too late. These other cities were already in play, and Baltimore probably couldn't match up with the stuff they were gonna do.

Sports editor Bob Maisel in 1986 recalled the warnings Rosenbloom gave the city about the stadium: "The warning fell on deaf ears. I supported a new stadium then, and although there is no guarantee the Colts would still be in Baltimore had one been built, you've got to like the chances better than the alternative. One thing I am absolutely sure of is that Baltimore would be better off had a new stadium been built then, just as New Orleans is better off [with the Superdome]."

While Indianapolis batted around the idea until they got it right, Baltimore had plans for a dome a decade earlier and scrubbed the mission. The *Evening Sun* ran a story in March 1984 with the headline **Domes Are Doomed:**

The domed stadium idea surfaced here in 1972, when the Greater Baltimore Committee proposed one in combination with a downtown convention center. Back then, domed stadiums were planned or built in Detroit, Houston, New Orleans and Seattle. One here would be good for business, the GBC said. Then-Gov. Marvin Mandel picked up that cudgel and flailed it around the State House. But when the General Assembly heard $200-million estimates for a 70,000-seat stadium, the idea died, as all unpopular legislative ideas do, in committee. Two years later, city officials proposed a domed stadium for Camden Rail Yard. The site had all sorts of potential: It was near downtown businesses and the popular Inner Harbor. It was short-lived. The General Assembly derailed a proposal to let state taxpayers buy a $50-$100-million Crabtown complex. And angry local sports fans sidetracked the city charter; they amended it [Question P] to bar city spending in any stadium but well-weathered, wide-open Memorial Stadium uptown.

Over and over, Baltimore choked in crunch time.

While Indianapolis had the all-for-one, one-for-all vibe going and built a dome with no tenant, no problem, Baltimore had almost two decades and couldn't get it done. "Do I feel at fault? Absolutely not," Mayor Schaefer told the *Morning Sun* in October 1993. "Sure you feel bad when you lose something like that [the Colts]. Everything that happens while you're mayor is your responsibility. But I knew we did all we could do. We couldn't build him a stadium." Wrong on two counts: *Schaefer* did all he could; the other gladhanders sat this one out. And scratch "couldn't build"; more like "We *wouldn't* build him a doggone stadium."

Sensing the city was floundering, the Baltimore *News American* pitted the Hoosier Dome vs. the Mausoleum. All the old gal had going for her was "tradition":

> Outsiders probably think it's strictly no contest. What with the $78-million joint's translucent fabric roof sewing all that space-age architecture (heaven forbid a raindrop should fall on one of those lovely Colt-blue seats—a color that is coincidental, they say in Indianapolis). However, there's something to be said for the old dame on 33rd Street. Granted, she's no spring chicken. But she's got reputation on her side. And Johnny Unitas. As far as Baltimoreans are concerned, she goes back more than three decades with the Colts. And as [Jimmy] Cannon, the late sportswriter, once said, "Marlene Dietrich is still my No. 1 dream girl."

Bob Irsay didn't give a tuppence about all that rot.

. . .

Memorial Stadium got built on the cheap back in the '50s, but there was also some penny-pinching in Indianapolis. "Even the Hoosier Dome has a couple of drawbacks from the fans' standpoint," *Morning Sun* sportswriter Vito Stellino noted in March 1984. "They ran low on money, so they installed bleacher seats with backs instead of individual seats in the second deck. And the stadium is located in the middle of the downtown area where parking is going to be a problem. It's still quite an improvement over Memorial Stadium, however, and remains Indianapolis's ace-in-the-hole in the bidding war ... Indianapolis is one of the closely-knit Midwestern cities where they seem to get things done. They managed to build a domed stadium even though they didn't have a football or a baseball team. Baltimore has both and hasn't been able to accomplish that." I.e., Indy winked and Baltimore blinked.

The sports editor of the *Indianapolis News* was a shameless homer, but he understood the battle of the stadiums. "Why would Irsay want to leave Baltimore to come to Indianapolis?" Wayne Fuson asked wryly. "The reasons would fill up this page. The Hoosier Dome offers him everything he wanted but never got at Baltimore—a sweetheart of a rental agreement, a city hungry for big-league sports, a new indoor stadium with all the refinements, including skyboxes, that pro franchise owners desire these days, and a chance to become the toast of the town. In return, Indianapolis would get a team with instant recognition. The Colts are one of a handful of NFL teams that everybody knows about." That failed to register with the cavalier crowd in Baltimore.

Former Colts coach Rick Venturi figured this was a no-brainer: "Considering the shape of the franchise and totally not being able to get a stadium, how could you *pass* on

Indianapolis? Nothing to do with the city [Baltimore], but how could you pass on the deal? They gave him everything. They presented him with a palace, right down to the blue seats, which was a fluke. The low-interest loan, the 12 years of guaranteed attendance, the Colts complex, all those concepts when your cash flow was way down. Honestly, you're fine to hardline it if you're the city of Baltimore until you come up against a really good offer. And then BOOM—you're outta there."

Baltimore was doomed by its own nonchalance. "[Baltimore] City fathers have long known that the best way to please both Irsay and Orioles owner Edward Bennett Williams would be to build a new stadium," Paul Attner of the *Washington Post* pointed out in early March '84. "That Memorial Stadium still stands is akin to playing political Russian roulette with the Baltimore sports franchises." And the bullet was in the chamber.

Schaefer doggedly kept the town in play, but even he blew it by taking a new stadium off the table. "Mr. Schaefer said he can make $7.5 million worth of improvements at Memorial Stadium should Mr. Irsay sign a six-year lease, thus releasing that amount in state bonds. But those modernizations, he said, cannot compete with a new domed stadium in Indianapolis," the *Morning Sun* detailed in early March 1984. "'He [Irsay] knows I can't build a new stadium,' the mayor said. 'He hasn't asked me that in a couple of years.' He also said Baltimore cannot offer the stadium rent-free, as Indianapolis is rumored to be doing. 'We could modify the rent, or

something we could do—but no free rent. As far as I'm concerned, I'm not interested in building another stadium. That's our stadium [Memorial]. That's it.'" Irsay then nodded and started hoarding boxes for the move.

Although Colts-Indy negotiations were hush-hush, Hoosiers knew their dome was the big goody in the basket. "Both deals [Baltimore's and Indy's] are believed to be basically the same on several items," the *Indianapolis News* stated in early March. "One would be a modest stadium rental agreement. Another would be a low-interest $15-million loan. And a third would be a virtually free practice and office complex. The main difference, of course, is that Indianapolis is offering Irsay a brand-new $80 million, 61,300-seat Hoosier Dome—built primarily for football. It has everything Irsay wanted in Baltimore but couldn't get in the old Memorial Stadium, built primarily for baseball."

Why dig in your heels and refuse to add some sweets when you're behind in the game? "All things equal," *Indianapolis Star* columnist Bob Collins mused, "our new domed stadium and slightly larger seating capacity should swing him here. Baltimore's Memorial Stadium, I'm told, is in sad shape and no amount of rehabilitation could put it in condition anywhere near the Hoosier Dome. Another plus is that football fever [in Indy] is raging out of control. Baltimore sold only 24,000 season tickets last year. The Colts could sell that many here in three weeks."

Baltimore foot-dragging stretched all the way back to 1966. Carroll Rosenbloom and the mayor actually talked shop about a domed stadium downtown. That went nowhere. "In autumn of 1966, then-Mayor Theodore McKeldin talked with Carroll Rosenbloom, then-owner of the Colts, about a $45-million domed stadium just south of the Civic Center [probably at Camden Yards]," the *Evening Sun* revealed in January 1985. "The talks fizzled and Rosenbloom, already dreaming of leaving Baltimore, suggested Towson [a suburb] as a site for the stadium on land he claimed he had optioned. He never revealed the location of the land and the plan evaporated when Rosenbloom swapped football teams with a man named Robert Irsay." Baltimore County executive Dale Anderson squashed C.R.'s plan when he harrumphed that he wouldn't cut Rosenbloom any breaks if he deigned to move out there. Baltimore was the nonpareil of botched stadium campaigns.

Long floating in the ether was the rumor that Bob Irsay got jobbed out of a *promise* for a new stadium. Nobody could ever trace it back to the source, but this always stuck in Irsay's craw: You people welshed on your promise. John Steadman talked to former GM Dick Szymanski, who was fuzzy on the specifics:

Dick Szymanski, a former Colt general manager, while speculating if the team is coming or going, said he recalls that Irsay was promised a new stadium when he came here in 1972. But he's not sure if the proposal was made by then-Gov. Marvin Mandel, Schaefer or former Colt owner Carroll Rosenbloom. In all the

conversation that has ensued, Irsay has not reintroduced the thought of a new stadium. Maybe he forgot it or, possibly, it was empty conversation or wishful thinking that a structure would be built.

Irsay might've figured, why waste my breath when I plan to make tracks?

Gossip was rife about Rosenbloom filling Irsay's ear about a new stadium to goose him into a swap. Steve Rosenbloom thinks that's bunk. "This is out in left field. First of all, he [his father] didn't go around talking in people's ears. He had no reason to tell Irsay, 'Baltimore is gonna build a stadium for you.' And I assume this was the time they were negotiating [the swap]. OK, who in their right mind would believe an owner who comes up and whispers in your ear, 'You're gonna get a stadium from Baltimore'? This, from Carroll, who had already been run over six times about a new stadium and hated all the politicians there [in Baltimore] for that? Unless you're brain-dead. Say that actually happened, and it was a guy dressed up like Carroll—and you hear that, what do you do? Say, 'Thank you'? Carroll Rosenbloom didn't have anything to do with building a stadium. They wouldn't even allow him to build his *own* stadium."

The *Morning Sun* ran a retrospective in 1993: **Colts' Final Days: The Inside Story.** They asked Schaefer about the alleged promise to Irsay:

To this day, Schaefer says he feels Irsay was negotiating in good faith during the long, arduous process. The discontent arose, Schaefer said, from Irsay's belief he was promised a new stadium when he made the famous franchise swap with Carroll Rosenbloom, who wound up with the Los Angeles Rams. "He was under the impression when he bought the team there was a commitment to build a stadium," Schaefer said. "I never made a commitment to build a stadium. The last meeting we had was on the Saturday before he left. We were negotiating, and, quite frankly, we had met just about every demand he asked. That's one of the things that disturbed me. Everything he asked for, we gave him. But he wanted a new stadium, and we just could not do that."

Hurricane Bob could let fly some real stretchers, but it's doubtful he concocted the promise about a new stadium. Somebody fed him a line, but Steve Rosenbloom insists it wasn't his dad:

My father was not sneaky. He didn't whisper things in people's ears. He would tell you to your face. He was always a good negotiator. So, is that now called "conniving" and "sneaky," being a good negotiator and getting a good deal for yourself? And I'm talking about his whole life, not just the Irsay deal. When they were working on this [the swap], my father had a bunch of New York lawyers; they'd come down like a tribe, their knees on the floor, going through all these papers. So, I don't think any stone was unturned. And I would be pissed [if I were Irsay] at my attorneys: "This [promise] is a simple thing. Why didn't you research this for me?" It's amazing that this thing [the rumor] would get any traction. In the first place, he [his father] wasn't talking with Irsay much, if at all. "OK, this is the deal we have. You're taking it, or you're not." Even Irsay's people would know that Baltimore had a tough time with this piece-of-shit stadium that was outmoded when it was built. That's [promising a new stadium] the last thing he would tell anybody. He knew you couldn't rely on these lousy politicians—talk about *liars*. And Hymie [Pressman] and the Park Board stonewalled the whole time. They never meant to do anything. I think he [Pressman] liked having Carroll Rosenbloom on his puppet strings. So, my father would never have promised anything like that because the opposite was so obvious.

• • •

The mood inside the Colts complex as February turned to March was like a week of rain at the beach. *Morning Sun* sports columnist Alan Goldstein went out there for a look:

There was no "Out of Business" sign on the front door of the football complex in Owings Mills yesterday. It wasn't necessary. The Baltimore Colts, as we knew and loved them, were already in their death throes, and the skeleton crew that remains appeared to be holding a wake for an old, departed friend. "We've heard nothing," said a survivor, awaiting the latest bulletin from Indianapolis. "We're always the last to know. Season tickets?" he laughed. "Our ticket people have been sitting on their hands for weeks." Gloom and doom. Wonder why Bob Irsay didn't start the ticket sale in January and pocket the interest on the money before calling the moving vans? He probably got sound advice from sidekick Michael Chernoff not to risk a lawsuit in selling tickets under false pretenses.

Jon Scott was the Colts equipment manager at the time. He says almost everybody was uptight. "There was tension, certainly, with the fear that the Colts would leave," he admitted. "I was a single guy back then and lived in an apartment right next to the complex with several other players. Those were the guys I hung out with. I didn't associate too much with the writers, the press, whatsoever. But I knew from watching TV and hearing other neighbors talk—'Are you guys really gonna leave?'—and I didn't want to leave. I was happy to be in Baltimore. But there certainly was a lot of talk about it."

Once things ramped up between Indy and Irsay, folks at the complex started getting fidgety. Future Colts chief operating officer Pete Ward was on front-office detail and saw the change:

It wasn't that extraordinary until things kinda heated up, move-wise, and a bomb was dropped when Mr. Irsay almost struck a handshake deal with Phoenix. Then that night [January 20, 1984] was the infamous airport press conference. That, in addition to some of the things that happened in the past, like the helicopter visit to Jacksonville [in 1979], the night of the press conference and the day after, when I had to go outside of Baltimore to find a security firm to guard our facility because we were getting death threats, that's when any semblance of a relationship that we had with our fanbase was blown to hell. I guess the feeling at that time for the employees was one of insecurity and uncertainty. And then Ernie Accorsi resigned shortly after that [Feb. 7]. So, the atmosphere within the building was one of instability and uncertainty.

Hoosiers not in the loop weren't so sure themselves, given Irsay's erratic past. "Sunday afternoon, amid reports that Baltimore Colts owner Robert Irsay was negotiating to move his team to Indianapolis, Baltimore sportswriter Bob Nusgart stifled a yawn. 'The reaction in Baltimore is, "Here we go again,"' Nusgart said by phone. 'All I can says is, let Indianapolis beware of Bob Irsay. Five weeks ago, I was talking to Phoenix in almost exactly the same words. I'm afraid your city is getting conned by Irsay just like Phoenix did.'"

Morning Sun sportswriter Vito Stellino tapped a source in Indy for some inside stuff. "The first source stressed that it could all change if the unpredictable Mr. Irsay pulls out one more time as he has so often in the past. He gave a group in Phoenix the impression he was a 'handshake' away from a deal in January before he rejected that agreement. 'The only guy who really knows is Bob Irsay, and he hasn't signed anything yet,' the source said. But he added that the two sides are now at the stage where they're writing the documents to seal the agreement."

That was early March, so once the lawyers stepped in to churn out the legalese, Baltimore was in Dutch. But that didn't stop Indy from fretting. Sportswriter Bill Benner said folks out there had their doubts. "Personally, I was skeptical because I was skeptical of Bob Irsay. He came off as—how do I say this—being a bit of a crank. So, I was never sure that Irsay wasn't playing Indianapolis to get what he wanted in Baltimore. I would have to say that I, among many others, when I got the phone call at the [1984] Final Four in Seattle that the Mayflower vans were on their way, I was a bit aghast. And I would also say that Hudnut, Frick and [Jim] Morris did an incredible job of keeping those negotiations out of the public eye."

Total pros, those guys in Indy. Button-down, nose-to-the-grindstone big-leaguers. David Frick was the chief negotiator of this superb team. "This whole process was only six weeks long, so a lot got packed into those six weeks," he stated. "One of the things we were cautious about was, we did *not* want to be used in Bob Irsay getting a better deal out of Baltimore. So, we were very conscious about leverage. He had to get comfortable about whether they [the Colts] were serious about Indianapolis."

Indy popped up on Irsay's radar back in 1977, when Paul Oakes rang him up one day and finagled a sit-down between owner and Indianapolis honchos. So, moving to Indy may have been percolating in his brain for years. Those over in the Land of Pleasant Living looked on with the usual disgust. "It is all more than a bit sad now, isn't it?" *Evening Sun* columnist Kevin Cowherd mused. "Not funny, the way it used to be. Jacksonville and Phoenix, Memphis and New York, and now Indianapolis. Bob Irsay, the Daniel Boone of the NFL, keeps blazing new trails to new cities, trying to find a better home for his Colts and a sweeter deal for himself—and all Baltimore can do is watch him. That is the truly sad part of this black comedy, of course. Irsay wants out of Baltimore, sticks his tongue out at this city. Irsay peddles the Colts around like a second-hand piano and there is not a damn thing anyone can do to stop him." And after the Raiders' Al Davis skunked the NFL in court, all Pete Rozelle could do now was grab a seat in the bleachers.

Given the comfort level, Hoosiers could afford to loosen up a little. Bob Collins of the *Indianapolis Star* offered this tongue-in-cheek commentary: "According to the latest rumor,

Robert Irsay will move the Colts to Iowa City. Informed sources say he will get free use of the University of Iowa Stadium and a guarantee that he can rig the 1988 Democratic caucus. Irsay also will be given a Holstein herd. The cows apparently clinched the deal after Irsay learned milk is better for him than what he's been drinking. The report caused consternation in Vancouver, Buenos Aires, Casablanca and Tucumcari, N. Mex., where officials already had sunk millions into excavation of an old adobe Indian stadium for the Colts."

All of this was jolly good fun for Bob Irsay, what with all eyes on him. With little more left than the signing ceremony with Indy, the question was how long would Irsay string this out. Peter A. Jay of the *Morning Sun* wondered that himself:

As I write, Mr. Irsay is enjoying his moment in *The Sun*. We read about him every morning over the grapenuts. He's been trying to peddle Baltimore's Colts to a bunch of Hoosiers who don't know a cornerback from a cornpicker, and it may be that by the time this gets to you, he will have done so ... Right now, he's only having some boyish fun with the municipal psyches of Baltimore and Indianapolis. And who can blame him? Wouldn't you like to perch for a moment in that catbird seat, able to call a midnight meeting in the Peoria Hilton, demand that the mayors of Baltimore and Indianapolis and the governors of

Maryland and Indiana show up, and feel pretty darn confident that on the stroke of 12 all four would be there, shuffling their feet and with their hats in hand?

You have Indy on a string and Baltimore in desperation mode. So why hurry? Bernie Miklasz of the *News American* sensed it wasn't a bluff this time:

One thing is for sure. Irsay isn't in a hurry. He doesn't have to be or want to be. He enjoys the attention and romance that comes his way when he hangs the "For Sale" sign on the Colt horseshoe. Irsay realizes that once he signs the proposed 20-year lease and moves the Colts to Indianapolis or any other place, no longer will there be potential suitors lined up at his door each offseason. No longer will strangers say nice things to him because they want his football team. No longer will they lay large bills in front of him. And that's what scares Irsay most of all. Irsay doesn't want to take his football team to the altar. But he will. He just has a case of the jitters. Sort of like the bridegroom on the night before the wedding.

There were still some worrywarts out in the Heartland. J.R. Depp of Indianapolis was so edgy he stuck a letter in the mail to the *Indy Star*: "From where I sit, I sense that the owners of the Colts merely are trying to shuck Hoosier corn. In order to force the city of Baltimore to pay their way the Colts have threatened to move to this city. I keep seeing in my mind headlines that read, 'Colts flim-flam Indy in power play with Baltimore,' or 'Hoosier hopes rise and fall as Baltimore coddles Colts.' I just don't believe that the Colts intend ever to leave Baltimore. They are just using Indianapolis as a tool, to make the city of Baltimore bow to their demands. The Colts want free rent. They want a free training facility. They want either Baltimore or Indy to be their mommy and daddy."

Pete Ward wasn't the only one in Owings Mills who eyed the calendar. Equipment manager Jon Scott thought March was way too late to pack up. "Very few teams back then did that [moved]. The [Oakland] Raiders did, the Brooklyn Dodgers. There was always a possibility, but for that to happen—our complex in Owings Mills was a brand-new facility. Why would we move? Although our stadium could have a better atmosphere and improvements, I don't think we're gonna move. And it was starting to get late now for a team to move. So, I didn't think we would do it that late."

Mayor Schaefer had no clue either. For once in his life, Bob Irsay was keeping his yap shut. "If Mayor Schaefer knows where the Baltimore Colts will be playing this fall, he's not sharing the news," the *Morning Sun* reported in late February 1984. "After a morning phone conversation with Robert Irsay, the mayor said he still has no idea whether the Colts' owner will keep the football team in Baltimore this fall or move it to Indianapolis—or some other city. 'I don't know if he going

to stay or if he's going to leave,' Mr. Schaefer patiently told reporters. 'If I sound pessimistic, it's because I'm not as optimistic as I was two years ago.'"

Those who almost had this deal in the can—the Indy negotiators—were as tight-lipped as clams. David Frick was having regular one-on-ones with Michael Chernoff, and they were now down to proofing the verbiage in the contract. Weeks before, Mayor Hudnut gave Mayor Schaefer a courtesy call. Frick stated, "In the process, when it became obvious that Irsay was shopping the franchise, Bill [Hudnut] told Schaefer—and I was there and listened to the conversation—'We understand Irsay's looking around. We do not want to be used by him to get a better deal out of you, but if he is in fact gonna move, we are going to compete to get the franchise.' And Schaefer said that he understood, and we moved on."

Getting no help from his friends and now Indy had laid down the gauntlet. Imagine Schaefer creaking the floorboards at night. Former WMAR-TV news boss Wayne Lynch knew Schaefer was in a vice:

He had two very difficult owners. And if he gives Irsay what he wants, what's he gonna do for [Orioles owner Edward Bennett] Williams? "Hey, quid pro quo. You gave Irsay this. What are you gonna give *me*?" So, he's trying to hold the line—politically, financially, economically—and he's caught in the middle of these two beloved franchises and two rich owners who could move if they wanted to. That's a tough spot. And Schaefer was such a bleeding heart for Baltimore. He was a great advocate for the city. But if you're caught in a scissors-movement, and the scissors are slowly closing on you, you either have to be a great compromiser or be willing to take your lumps. And he had to take his lumps.

The Phoenix flameout taught everybody in Indy to keep a lid on it. "Nobody has found Robert Irsay, owner of the Colts, to find out what he is thinking," the *Indianapolis News* indicated in late February '84. "Indianapolis officials, who have been quietly negotiating with Irsay for two weeks, are afraid to say anything for fear they will upset the apparently upsettable Irsay. But nothing—repeat nothing—has been signed. Irsay has been tempted to move to places like Jacksonville, Memphis and Phoenix, too, but pulled out at the last moment for one reason or another."

David Frick and Michael Chernoff plowed their way through negotiations in about six weeks. *BizVoice*, the magazine of the Indiana Chamber of Commerce, described the manic pace:

The initial meeting between the city of Indianapolis and the Colts organization took place here [in Indianapolis] on February 11, 1984, and was between the two attorneys: Frick and the Chicago-based [Michael] Chernoff. The Colts representative made it "crystal clear that the team

was not (definitely) leaving Baltimore, but rather they were exploring other options. They were looking for a market that was a good market for NFL football, a fair lease to both sides, and they were looking for a long-term relationship," Frick shares. "I reiterated what I thought Indianapolis's interest was. We were looking for an NFL franchise that would be willing to be a community asset which would be a long-term relationship, a favorable deal for the franchise, but a fair deal for our community. This all culminated in the Colts moving to Indianapolis six weeks later. For a deal that has meant so much to our community, it's kind of ironic that it was done so quickly," Frick remarks.

Not so ironic, actually. You had powerful dynamics in play: Irsay wanted out and Indy wanted a team. Indy had a $77.5-million bubble to rent, and Irsay couldn't stand the sight of Baltimore anymore. Both sides were willing to talk themselves hoarse to get that deal done.

Bob Irsay's legal hawk Michael Machiavelli-Chernoff worked like a consummate pro during that six-week stretch with David Frick. On this particular job—maybe the biggest in his career—Chernoff was clutch. In a December 1984 article, "The Seduction of the Colts," the *New York Times* portrayed the man who sealed the Indy deal: "A 48-year-old Chicago attorney, Chernoff is a pale-faced man who speaks very deliberately, carefully weighing each word. He has been Irsay's aide for close to 10 years. Chernoff knew that his boss was tired of Baltimore's spartan, open-air Memorial Stadium and that he wanted something with a roof, an Astroturf playing field and a row of luxury skyboxes. The Hoosier Dome had them all. And there was something else: 'I couldn't help noticing,' he recalls, 'that the seats were already done in Colt-blue.'"

The *Indianapolis Star's* award-winning Colts beat reporter, Mike Chappell, sees Mike Chernoff as Irsay's steady, reliable pro who got the man's business done with no fuss, no muss. "He [Chernoff] was the great lieutenant. He was a guy that did the stuff from Irsay's end, and getting information out of him, the few times I had to try, was never easy. This is after the move; we were the good guys all of a sudden. He was almost loyal to a fault, and I thought they did a great job of keeping it [the negotiations] under wraps."

No debate here. In the most consequential job the man ever had, with the most on the line, Chernoff nailed it. The role was tailor-made for a meticulous guy like that. David Frick (Team Indy) and Chernoff (Team Irsay) got together that first time on the 11th of February and went over the basics. Frick was carrying some heavy baggage:

> Mike Chernoff came down to take a look at the stadium, post-Super Bowl. He came down, and I met him, but unfortunately, I could not spend much time with him that day, negotiating. My daughter came down with a very serious illness [ruptured appendix] and was in the intensive care unit at the hospital. So, I apologized to Mike Chernoff. I shared with him what we expected during the negotiations and promised him that we would give him a good deal, a fair deal, and we're looking for a long-term commitment through a long-term lease. We described together what we called "the pillars of the deal." As he marched down the things that he was looking for, I matched that against what we were expecting, and it fit. We didn't have any disconnects at all. We knew the framework of what the deal would look like. It worked for the Colts, and it worked for us.

There were two heavy loads on David Frick's shoulders: his daughter in bad shape in the hospital and his job, dickering with the Colts. But there was no doubt Bill Hudnut picked the right man. "As he looked skyward for the airplane carrying Indianapolis Colts executives Thursday, David R. Frick recalled Feb. 16—'a day I never want to repeat. The mayor called me that day and told me he wanted me to be the city's negotiator [with the Colts]. And that was the day Amy went to the hospital,'" the *Indianapolis Star* documented in late March 1984. "Six weeks later, Amy Frick was recovering from appendicitis and returned to school, and the father has ended countless hours of negotiations with resounding success."

Hudnut tabbed his former deputy to hash out the crucial one-on-ones with the Colts'

Chernoff because he knew Frick would make the right calls. He's the man Hudnut always turned to in a pinch. But only somebody special could handle heavy pressure from two fronts. Frick paid homage to Chernoff for being compassionate and flexible:

> The overlay is, while I was trying to do something very important for the community [of Indianapolis], I had a daughter who was in very serious physical shape. She had a ruptured appendix; it was real touch-and-go. I have an angel for a wife, and she moved into the hospital to spend time with her because I couldn't negotiate the deal and at the same time be with my family. I didn't want to fail my daughter by not being there, yet at the same time, not turn away from the [negotiation] process. And I think that this is when I developed respect for Mike Chernoff. At our first, relatively short meeting, I told him, "There's things we both want, but I got to go see my daughter. Bye." And he was very concerned and expressed his willingness to postpone any kind of meaningful conversations while I went to the hospital. So, I deeply remember Mike playing a role in that.

Part of being a great leader, supervisor, boss, manager is picking good people to do your bidding. Indy Mayor William Hudnut made a crackerjack choice in David Frick to run the negotiations. "I've always considered Bill Hudnut to be the driving force [of the Indianapolis renaissance], but I always thought David Frick was *the* guy," veteran Indy Colts beat reporter Mike Chappell professed. "I know there were other guys, but David Frick—I'm tellin' ya, he was sort of the point man, and I've always had great admiration for what he's done for this city. If there had been other people in place, other than them, this probably wouldn't have gotten done."

Frick asked Chernoff to cut him some slack while his daughter was on the mend and cut to the chase. The *New York Times* picks it up from there: "Chernoff obliged, clearly spelling out Robert Irsay's terms. He wanted a low, low rental on the stadium. He wanted a guarantee that the team's receipts for each game would be at least equal to what 40,000 paying spectators would contribute. He wanted a new training facility for his team and his coaches, complete with practice fields and offices. He wanted assistance with the physical job of packing and moving his team. The next and last demand was the toughest to satisfy: a $15-million, low-interest loan. In 1972, Irsay had borrowed $15 million from a Chicago bank for his Colt-Ram transaction. The interest was 8%, the collateral was 100% of the Colt stock, and the loan was about to come due. Irsay wanted a second loan primarily to pay off the first, and he wanted the interest rate on the new loan to stay at 8%, about 3.5% below the then-current rate." Ergo, Irsay couldn't play with his fiddle much longer; he had to score a primo deal, get the old bank off his back and boogie out of Baltimore.

Frick and Chernoff negotiated from start to finish on the QT, which impressed former *Indianapolis Star* sportswriter Bill Benner. "Much to their credit, that was the way they thought it *had* to be handled. That it could not be a public back-and-forth, it could not be a public pissing contest, it could not be a public bidding contest; that it had to be one-on-one in a room at the [prestigious] Columbia Club. It couldn't be something that they did in the newspapers. They were very smart about that."

Baltimore should have taken note: This is how two pros get it done, Frick and Chernoff in a room, haggling, bartering, stipulating, compromising, putting it all on paper. Everybody knew Frick was a champ; what we found out was Chernoff was born for this moment. And Frick said he couldn't have pulled this off without the legal talents of Michael Chernoff:

> Bob Irsay was very fortunate. He had a smart and savvy guy as his general counsel. Mike Chernoff was very loyal to Bob Irsay at a time when a lot of people were *not* very loyal to him. Mike Chernoff and I just developed a relationship during this negotiation process so that we ended up trusting one another. Mr. Irsay listened to Mike Chernoff when critical decisions had to be made. He looked to Mike Chernoff to get the best deal he could. So, Mike was instrumental in the relocation. He became an advocate for

Indianapolis because he felt that was the best thing for Bob Irsay.

Think of what a hash Bob Irsay would have made of it at the bargaining table; lucky for him he had Chernoff to hammer out the details. All he had to do is show up sober at closing and autograph the deal. While the wheelers and dealers were at it, Bob Maisel back in Baltimore was just like everybody else in town—speculating:

> Lone Ranger Robert Irsay and his Tonto, Michael Chernoff, are at it again, but don't expect a long harangue about their latest caper. They will either move the Colts before another season, or they won't, and there is nothing we can do about it. Since they will not return calls or issue a state-of-the-franchise statement, we are reduced to trying to read Irsay's mind, which is impossible. What Irsay has done now is put a hold on sending out season-ticket renewal applications. I'm a season-ticket holder and usually figure on receiving the renewal form by the end of January. When it didn't come, you had to start being suspicious.

Chernoff spoke to the press about as often as the Jets win Super Bowls, but he did share some thoughts for the magazine *BizVoice* in 2011: "I'm not saying this in a disparaging way toward any of the other cities that made offers or that we had conversations with, but it was clear that the city of Indianapolis and its representatives were dependable, and we could look to them to keep their word. That's very important, particularly when you pull up stakes and move halfway or a third of the way across the United States." That was a little dig at Baltimore—well-deserved if truth be told. However, Mikey, the Wannabe GM always held his nose regarding Baltimore, got heartburn when he went there and preferred fraternizing with moneybags in Chicago. In Indy, hammering out the deal with David Frick, he was Irsay's cleanup hitter, a Lou Gehrig of litigation; put him in the Colts complex back east and he morphed back into the GM wannabe.

You'd have to comb the town these days to hear a kind word about Indianapolis, but Baltimore filmmaker Troy Lowman can empathize: "I don't blame them. They wanted a team. The Colts were gonna go somewhere. You can't blame the place that got them. I know a lot of people in Baltimore hated Indianapolis after that [the move], but what were they supposed to do? Say, 'Don't come here'? Right now, you have a dozen cities that would steal any team in the NFL if they could. Look at poor Oakland. They've lost everything [the Raiders, the A's and the Warriors]."

That 8% loan Irsay wanted was a no-go until some bean counters found a way to finesse it down from 11%. Tom Keating of the *Indianapolis Star* described the snag at the start:

[American Fletcher National Bank board chairman Frank] McKinney said

he met with Chernoff a week ago Monday [early March] and found him to be a sharp and professional businessman. "We talked for several hours last week on Monday and Wednesday, at which time we made him a loan proposition. I also encouraged Mr. Chernoff to shop around with other banks and see if he could find a better deal, which I assume he is doing. From our viewpoint, it was a standard loan proposition, the same as we would make to any other potential customer with whom we would like to do business," McKinney said. "I don't know where that 8% interest figure came from. It's not prudent for any bank to loan money at that rate right now." That said, McKinney explained that Chernoff may be trying to negotiate income sources that would, in effect, make up the difference between a prime interest rate and an 8% rate on the loan.

Indy had the wherewithal Baltimore didn't—they scrabbled together enough cash elsewhere to drop that 11% loan to 8. Such ingenuity might have built a new stadium in B'more and changed history. The loan and the Dome cinched the deal.

Just enough news trickled out to get Hoosiers a little cocky about their chances. Bob Collins of the *Indianapolis Star* thought Baltimore now had no shot: "A man once said, 'Money isn't everything, but it's way ahead of whatever's in second place.' Still, there is no way anybody other than Irsay knows if cash in his pocket and promised renovation of an ancient stadium will soothe his ruffled feelings. If he has made up his mind to leave, that's it. No Baltimore proposal will change his mind."

Leopards can't change their spots, as the saying goes. It was far too late in the game for Baltimore to huddle up and save the day. Troy Lowman, who produced the excellent documentary, *The Ghosts of 33rd Street*, knows where to point fingers:

> I gotta blame the [Baltimore] local government; I gotta blame [Mayor] Schaefer. Schaefer was a beloved figure in Baltimore, but he had the stance that if they stayed pat, Irsay would keep squawking and not do anything about it. And he misfired. By the time he realized he was in trouble, and Irsay was looking at Phoenix and Indianapolis, it was too late. Irsay had already made up his mind. So, I have to say that Schaefer and the local government get a lion's share of the blame. In a big way, they deserved to lose the franchise because they found themselves in a landscape of big money in the big-business NFL, and they were still trying to run it like they were in the '50s.

Fellow Baltimorean Tom Marr IV sees this as the only blemish on Schaefer's lofty résumé:

> William Donald Schaefer, Hyman Pressman, [City Council President] Wally Orlinsky and some of the other politicians in Baltimore back in the 1970s really did the job of making Baltimore a renaissance city. For that, you can't give them anything else but an A [on their report card]. It was truly a remarkable turnaround for a city. The last great hurrah for the city of Baltimore was the 1970s. But the reason they can't get an A is because they have an F on their résumé for what happened to the Colts. That's the one thing during the Schaefer era that's never gonna be left out. He's the guy that lost the Colts. They should not have been naïve, but they were. They should have done more to keep the Colts here; they didn't. But at the time, the voters had decided [Question P], and that was that.

Schaefer was Baltimore's one-man hurry-up offense, working any angle to hook Irsay. The last day in February 1984, the *Morning Sun* described a man bent on finding a way: "As the uncertainty over the Colts' future continued yesterday, the mayor spent a lot of time on the telephone. For the second consecutive day, Schaefer spoke to Irsay. He plans to talk with him again today. 'The only thing he said was that he has not signed a deal.' Schaefer said he is 'still working on some things' with Irsay in an effort to keep the Colts here. He would not list what those 'things' are, saying he does not want any more details of negotiations in the press." This last-gasp business had as much chance as Brooklyn promising

Walter O'Malley free shoeshines for life if he'd just stay put. But considering Schaefer was basically going solo, he rolled the bones.

No getting around it—Baltimore blew it every time they had a shot. "This is the one thing that they [Baltimore politicians] really failed at," former rabid Colts fan Tom Marr IV admitted. "Those politicians turned the city of Baltimore around, from 1968, after the riots, to the 'All-American Charm City.' Harborplace, the urban renaissance—they did all of that. So, they weren't so myopic that they didn't have *that* vision. It's this, 'We're a perfect city as it is, and we already have a stadium that you don't have to pay for.' That's where the myopathy came from—the NFL vision that they could not see. To say that they were completely naïve, that's missing the point because they really did rebuild a city."

Why drag the pols into this, says former *Sunpapers* columnist Michael Olesker, when the blame should get dumped in one guy's lap? "I blame Irsay. The man was a lunatic. And Schaefer sucked up to him in every conceivable way. And it didn't matter. He [Schaefer] tried very hard, and if there was a reason to blame him, it would've been all over the airwaves. I didn't hear anything like that. It was Irsay, and I think that's fair. The guy was a drunk, a lunatic and a spoiled brat."

For obvious reasons, the Indy team didn't say boo about the negotiations. And to his credit, Irsay likewise put a lid on it to avoid gumming up the works. Wise move on his part, says veteran *Indianapolis Star* sportswriter Mike Chappell:

I always hated these behind-the-scenes negotiations because as a reporter, I want transparency. Most of the time, transparency is not a good thing, for the team, for the company, whatever. So, I just think it was probably totally beneficial to Indy not to let anyone else outside—Phoenix, Jacksonville, Baltimore—know, "Hey, these guys are serious." And if someone else didn't step up, Indy was right there. And there was a freakin' stadium, right there. But I think it behooved everybody to keep it quiet—which, considering how Bob Irsay was, is amazing to me that he didn't say, "You know, we got Indy, right there" because he had a hard time keeping things to himself. I just think it's beneficial when it's high stakes like this to not tip your hand and let everybody know how far you're willing to go to get this done.

Indy's shot at the Colts was riding on David Frick's shoulders, and he didn't let them down. Nobody else had to say much, with two consummate pros on the job. Within a few weeks, he and Michael Chernoff had hammered out the basics:

The basic framework [of the contract] was what we concentrated on initially: What's the real deal here? Once we reached a consensus about what the deal was, we turned the lawyers loose to turn that into paper. I mean, there were times when I would be up all night, working on the transaction. All of this got compressed into six weeks. We established the deal points, and once you get those negotiated, then you have to put the verbiage down. But the verbiage wasn't gonna kill the deal. The deal got cut, mentally, at the point where we said what we needed, and they said what they needed, and we agreed on all of the wants of each party.

Irsay got dazzled by the Hoosier Dome, but Indianapolis had to handle two big issues before the deal was done. The April 1 *Indianapolis Star* laid them out: "On the evening of Feb. 22 [1984], Mayor William H. Hudnut made his decision about the Baltimore Colts. 'Go for the gusto,' he told his friend and chief negotiator David R. Frick. Frick had just informed Hudnut that preliminary talks were positive, but Colts' owner Robert J. Irsay presented two roadblocks. 'He wants that low interest rate for $15 million [on a loan] and a guarantee on ticket sales,' Frick told Hudnut. 'I knew this city could do it,' the mayor said. 'We have no equal in the nation of business, civic and government working together for a common goal as we have here.'" Righto, compared with the dysfunctional bunch over in Baltimore, who couldn't even huddle up without first hiring a consultant.

Frick pulled out his legal pad while Chernoff sat across from him, a man who, in this one historic moment, was a crackerjack barrister. He made quite the impression on David Frick:

In making deals, you need to make sure that each party understands the words that are *not* written that you rely upon. I developed confidence in Mike that everything surrounding this deal was his imprint on why it worked for Bob Irsay. So, if the time came that Mr. Irsay was going to move, this would be a deal that Bob Irsay could live with for 20 or 30 years. He [Chernoff] was somewhat of a controversial figure; there's no doubt about it. I can't evaluate why people in Baltimore felt that way about him, but we found him to be a very honorable lawyer who was protecting his client and who lived up to his word. First of all, he's smart. Good deals get made when both parties are smart. I think I know what I'm doing, and it was clear that Michael knew as well. Secondly, I never felt Mike was pushing us to an extreme level. By that I mean, when we came down to an important point, we both would roll up our sleeves to figure out how to solve it, that it was never gonna be solved at the expense of making our overall transaction fair to both sides. And he [Chernoff] bought into that concept of "Let's be fair." No, we [Indianapolis] did *not* have the best deal; Phoenix had a better deal on the table. But the kinds of comforts that we gave Mike Chernoff and Bob Irsay were things that Phoenix did *not*.

Chernoff had Phoenix spooked while they were still in the hunt. They knew he had his grubby mitts all over the franchise. "Phoenix officials are worried that Michael Chernoff, Irsay's general counsel, may be pushing him to go to Indianapolis," the *Morning Sun* declared in late March 1984. "That city is a lot closer to Irsay's Chicago base than Phoenix, and that would make it easier for Chernoff to have a more direct hand in running the team. Chernoff likes to have a major behind-the-scenes role in operating the club. Chernoff also negotiated the Indianapolis deal with [David] Frick while Irsay dealt directly with the Phoenix officials." Witness Irsay's little Wannabe GM horning in on GM Ernie Accorsi's turf despite not knowing which way the shoulder pads went on. But the Indy deal was Chernoff's one shining moment.

. . .

Baltimore was awash in opinions about Irsay, mostly about where to string him up in a tree. Hall of Fame offensive lineman Jim Parker said if the team leaves, good riddance. "Ever since Carroll Rosenbloom sold the club [in 1972], we've been flimflammed by Irsay," he told the *Evening Sun*. "Myself and the people in my neighborhood are fed up. Let's get it over with. Pack 'em up and give 'em a one-way ticket to Indianapolis. We don't deserve this kind of ownership and an absentee landlord." Mike Ward, a CPA, thought like a capitalist: "I think Irsay has a large business in the Colts, and unfortunately pro sports everywhere have become more of a business than a game. Apparently, he has a better deal in Indy. I really don't think you can blame the man for

moving." Then there were the miscellaneous sorts. "Let them go," marketing director Jan Tennenkoon huffed. "Who cares? I'd rather see a pro basketball team here." Chip Giardina, a wine and deli merchant, stated, "I hate to see the Colts go but not to see Irsay go. He was so unpredictable. Baltimore deserves better." Sure, Baltimore deserved better, including from the bureaucrats sleeping on the job.

The dam burst in late February 1984 when an appeals court made the call about the Al Davis suit: "San Francisco—A federal appeals court, deciding that the National Football League violated antitrust laws by conspiring to block the Raiders' move from Oakland to Los Angeles, ruled yesterday that the league has no power to prevent future franchise moves—including any transfer of the Baltimore Colts," the *Morning Sun* ruefully reported. "The effect of yesterday's ruling on the possible relocation of the Colts, however, remained clouded because the 9th Circuit—in which yesterday's ruling was issued—does not include Maryland ... Although conceding that the NFL is a 'unique business organization to which it is difficult to apply antitrust rules,' the three-judge panel's majority concluded that the lower court had correctly applied federal antitrust laws. And the appellate court said the six-woman jury had sufficient evidence to decide that the NFL had conspired to restrain trade in its attempt to block the Raiders' move to Los Angeles."

Bob Irsay could now steal Frank Costanza's warning to Morty Seinfeld that he was moving to Del Boca Vista, like it or not, and fire it at Baltimore: "This is Frank Costanza. You think you can keep us out of Florida?! We're moving in, lock, stock and barrel. We're gonna be in the pool. We're gonna be in the clubhouse. We're gonna be all over that shuffleboard court! And I dare you to keep me out!"

Baltimore and Oakland were kindred spirits—they both got the bum's rush. And in a few weeks, both would be NFL orphans. "In many ways, the Raiders were for Oakland what the Colts had been for Baltimore," Mark Miller of the *News American* noted in late March 1984. "Like Baltimore, Oakland suffered for years from a poor national image. And like Baltimore, which always could point to the Colts—especially in the glory days— Oakland eventually was able to point to the powerful Raiders when outsiders tried to put the city down."

Travis Bullock in *The Constitutional Dimensions of Sports Franchise Takings: Lessons Learned from the Baltimore Colts* neatly summarized what went down when Oakland tried to pull eminent domain on the Raiders:

> In California, the City of Oakland attempted to prevent the Oakland Raiders football team from relocating to Los Angeles. After years of litigation, the Court of Appeals for California invalidated the condemnation because of its effect on interstate commerce. The court explained that although "[i]t is well established that a state may exercise eminent domain power even though by doing so it indirectly or incidentally burdens interstate commerce," the "nationwide" nature of professional football is "so completely involved in interstate commerce" that taking a franchise is impermissible. Citing a prior case, the court confirmed that each franchise was connected and interested in each other's franchise, essentially making the NFL a "joint venture of its members organized for the purpose of providing entertainment nationwide." The court concluded that indefinitely barring the Raiders franchise from moving out of Oakland would "more than indirectly or incidentally regulate interstate commerce." Finally, the court weighed the local interest of preventing the Raiders from moving against the burden imposed on interstate commerce. Finding that the burden imposed outweighs the local interest, the court affirmed the lower court decision invalidating the condemnation.

Oakland swung and missed on eminent domain. Seeing that whiff, Baltimore would waltz into the batter's box in about a month.

When you're out in a hurricane, any lamppost will do. Besides contemplating a hail Mary for the heck of it, Baltimore clung to one nugget in the Oakland case. This was spelled out in *Forbes* magazine, "Over 30 Years Ago, Maryland Tried to Seize an NFL Team":

> While it did not rule in favor of the city and sent the case back to a lower court,

the California Supreme Court did hold that "providing access to recreation to its residents in the form of spectator sports is an appropriate function of city government." Instead of determining if the seizure was even appropriate, the majority opinion ruled, "the courts have no authority to choose those items of property which they deem appropriate for condemnation." They must defer to the legislature to decide what property can be taken. That includes "any property necessary to carry out any of [a city's] powers or functions."

The CA Supreme Court kicked it back to the appellate court, which said nothing doing to Oakland. They took their licking while Baltimore looked on, thinking they were slick enough to conjure some legal mumbo-jumbo to pull a fast one in court. They'd soon find out how wrong they were.

The eminent domain lawsuit was Oakland's business alone, but Al Davis was in the middle of another one: teaming up with the L.A. Coliseum to take on the NFL. Rozelle told Davis he couldn't move the Raiders without the owners' say-so, and Davis said, just watch me. In *Glory for Sale*, Jon Morgan explained why this case was a big deal for Irsay:

Before the case went to a jury, the NFL suffered a serious blow: The judge sided with Davis on a key issue, the league's structure, and issued a direct verdict on this point. This meant the jury had to accept Davis's contention that the league was a collection of competing businesses, not a single entity. The first trial ended with a hung jury, but Davis prevailed in the second one, in May 1982. The team was allowed to move, and the rest of the NFL was ordered to pay its wayward partner [Davis] $34.65 million and to pay the LA Coliseum $14.58 million in damages … Davis's move ended a long period of franchise stability. In fact, it had been 23 years since the last team move, when the Chicago Cardinals had relocated to St. Louis [1960]. The only move before that was in 1946, when the Cleveland Rams moved to LA.

Al Davis cut the mooring line and allowed ships to head to any harbor in the country. Bob Irsay already had his spot in the queue. The *Atlanta Journal* did a lengthy piece on how Indianapolis snagged the Colts:

God apparently looks after dreamers and Hoosiers. In one of the neater ironies of our time, the very act that imperiled Indianapolis's chances of landing an expansion team—Al Davis moving his Raiders to Los Angeles—greased the chute for Indy getting not a faceless license, but a living, breathing organization, complete with uniforms and coaches and players. Feeling trapped in a time warp for fans for whom life began and ended that sudden-death day in 1958, the Colts wanted out of

Baltimore. The methods of its owner-ship might've scared off more circumspect suitors, but one beggar couldn't afford to be choosy. Indianapolis had the space. The Colts had the goods. It was a marriage made in commerce.

Mr. Iconoclast implied that Irsay had carte blanche to find greener pastures. "Al Davis is partial to the Los Angeles Raiders' silver-and-black colors, but he's wrapping himself in red, white and blue these days," Vito Stellino of the *Morning Sun* began. "Davis, the managing general partner of the Raiders, is the man who made it possible for Colt owner Robert Irsay to shop his franchise around the country. If Davis hadn't gone to court to move the Raiders from Oakland to Los Angeles without league permission, Irsay would have needed 21 votes to move his franchise. Commissioner Pete Rozelle claims that has created franchise free agency, but Davis looks at it differently. 'That's America,' he said. 'America has always been based on total competition.' Discussing Irsay's shopping spree around the country, Davis said, 'I don't particularly like what he's doing in some areas, but it's his right. He owns the team, and he's doing what is best for the team.'"

. . .

Talk picked up in Baltimore to mimic Oakland and hit Irsay with eminent domain if he pulled up stakes. The first public hint came on February 27, when the *Evening Sun* tossed this out: "One action to stop the team from moving that has been considered by [Baltimore] city officials would be to push for state legislation to take over the team by eminent domain, a legal maneuver state and local governments use to seize property for the public good. Such an effort is supported by General Assembly leaders in Annapolis. But Schaefer said today he was reluctant to support such an effort. 'I don't want to threaten anyone with eminent domain.'" Not yet, anyway.

If Schaefer had designs on eminent domain, he wouldn't tip his hand to Irsay and Michael Machiavelli. But it's not like this was a sudden brainstorm. On March 2, 1984, mayoral aide Mark Wasserman sent Schaefer a memo that got him thinking… Charlie Euchner in *Playing the Field* quoted Wasserman's memo:

"I can't help but assume that Irsay has himself so boxed in that there is almost nothing left but for him to move the franchise. Even if the Indianapolis deal were to fall through this morning, the situation here is so badly deteriorated that it would be virtually impossible to think that he would or could [remain] here. I find it hard to believe that we are going to sit back and watch him go without so much as a whimper after the mistreatment we (you) have been subjected to. For my money (what little there is), we ought to take our best shot and complicate the move any way we can. I recommend that you consider seriously seeking [Baltimore City] Council passage of a condemnation ordinance today and couple that with seeking an injunction."

The Wasserman memo implies a few things: 1) Schaefer was playing coy with the press when he dismissed the idea; 2) Wasserman assumed the idea would gum up the works but tank in the end; and 3) Baltimore had all but given up. They knew they were just spinning wheels, hoping to delay the exodus.

The Raiders' victory in court put sudden gleams in the eyes of cities across the country. Now they had a shot at stealing a team. "Indianapolis and other cities may want Mr. Davis to defeat Oakland's [eminent domain] suit, so that there can be migratory franchises for them to lure," George Will observed in the *Morning Sun*. "But if they land one, their huge capital investments (stadiums) will be at the mercy of buccaneers like Mr. Davis who are nimble at the art of getting cities to bid against one another." On the mat at the moment were Baltimore and Indianapolis (with a pinch of Phoenix thrown in).

Indy's ace negotiator David Frick stayed current with events on the West Coast:

I was deputy mayor [from 1976-1982], and I was curious at how eminent domain was being used against Al Davis by the city of Oakland. So, I was familiar with the antitrust litigation going on with Al Davis. We had a somewhat similar experience with the [Indiana] Pacers. The Pacers were struggling financially

when the NBA allowed four teams in from the old ABA, a terrible deal for those four teams. The Pacers were on their way to Sacramento. We tried to figure out how to keep them in town, and we concluded that there was no way they would voluntarily agree to be sold [to someone in Indianapolis]. There was no legal document tying them to Indianapolis. So, we didn't try to stop them through the courts. We ended up buying them out [with Herb Simon].

George Will boiled down Oakland's argument for eminent domain, something Baltimore would import when it was their turn: "Oakland argues, irrefutably, that a professional team becomes woven into the civic identity, especially in 'second-tier' cities such as Oakland. Oakland also argues that reacquisition of the Raiders would serve social, recreational and economic needs, including the usefulness of the stadium." Oakland had the legal world going point-counterpoint. It's a given that Sal's two Famous Pizza Palace shops in Dundalk and Patterson Park aren't "woven into the civic identity," no matter how good the calzones are. But a beloved ballclub is part of the beating heart of city, a public trust, an heirloom passed on from generation to generation. Sal could pack up and head for Indianapolis, a McDonald's and a Burger King could move in, and nobody would swallow a bottle of Paxils because of it. Oakland was a trailblazer, and even though they took their lumps, this kind of maneuver wasn't settled law yet. And Baltimore would be right on their heels.

Next came the shot across the bow while Frick and Chernoff were banging out the deal, as described by the *Morning Sun* on February 29, 1984:

> Maryland's attorney general is "ready to go to court on a moment's notice" to stop Colts owner Bob Irsay from moving his team out of Baltimore, Deputy Attorney General Paul F. Strain said yesterday. "We are geared up and ready," declared Mr. Strain. He added that a team of three assistant attorneys general began "investigating the possibilities" of a lawsuit "long before" word leaked out last month that the Colts' owner was considering moving the team to Phoenix … The legal theory being explored by the state and city lawyers is the same one that local governments use when they want to acquire land for highways. The land is claimed by the state through what is called "eminent domain" for the general public good. The government then pays the former owners the market value for any property that has been "condemned."

Condemning a ballclub then swiping it was a wild legal stab akin to being blindfolded and taking a cut at a Sandy Koufax curveball. Nevertheless, the news shot out to Indianapolis. "As expected, Baltimore has begun an all-out battle to keep its National Football League Colts, reported to be on the verge

of moving to Indianapolis," the *Indianapolis News* reported on February 29. "Maryland's attorney general said he's 'ready to go to court on a moment's notice' to prevent Colts owner Robert Irsay from moving the franchise from the rundown Memorial Stadium in Baltimore to the spanking new Hoosier Dome in Indianapolis." Don't think for a moment that Michael Chernoff was holed away in some basement with David Frick and missed all this.

. . .

Irsay got one step closer to dousing the lights at the Colts complex when he sent his son and Coach Kush out to Indy for a look-around. "Many fans and politicians had believed the move all but complete Tuesday night [March 7], when Coach Frank Kush and Irsay's son, Jimmy, flew to Indianapolis under assumed names," the *Morning Sun* revealed. "Instead of announcing a franchise move, Kush and Jimmy Irsay kept a low profile during their visit. They took a tour of the city and inspected their prospective new football home, the Hoosier Dome. They also met Mayor William H. Hudnut III, who ate lunch with the two Colt officials at a Howard Johnson's restaurant. 'We made some pleasantries,' Hudnut said. 'I said, "Welcome to the city. I hope it all works out."'" Jimbo and Kush didn't seem put out that Hudnut dragged them into a HoJos for a 3D burger and fries instead of Harry and Izzy's like the big guy would rate.

How the trip came about was a typical Irsay brain bobble born of too many White

Russians before noon. Jim Irsay explained what got him out to Indy in the 30-for-30 documentary, *The Band That Wouldn't Die*:

> I tried to calm him [his father] down most of the time, but sometimes you get a little testy. I know he called me up one day, and this is before the move, and he had been drinking, of course. And I said, "Now, what are we doin' here? What are you thinkin'?" And he said, "I don't know. Maybe you should get down to Indy." I go, "Really? You want me to go to Indianapolis?" "Yeah. Take Kush with you." I knew he probably would barely remember the conversation. So, I called Frank Kush. I said, "Frank, old man called. We gotta go to Indianapolis." "What?! Indianapolis! Jim, you gotta tell your mom we gotta go to Arizona [where Kush lived]. Who wants to go to Indianapolis?" So, we fly to Indianapolis. We get there; it's no secret. We're walking through the airport. The media's there all of a sudden. So, then, I call my dad the next day. And now it's in the morning, and I said, "Dad, we're here." "You're where?!" "We're in Indianapolis." What are you doin' in Indianapolis?!" I said, "You *told* us to come." "Oh, my God, OK. I'll call you back." You know, that was a tough time, and I was on the merry-go-round, part of the ride.

The two aliases these guys used were cute but pointless. The Baltimore press sniffed out the trip and spotted them at the airport. "It was not certain whether Mr. Kush and Jimmy Irsay returned to Baltimore last night," the *Morning Sun* indicated. "Two men using the names of Owens and Renfield—the two Mr. Kush and the younger Irsay used while making the Tuesday night flight—were booked on a Wednesday night plane from Indianapolis to Baltimore. But neither man was on the flight." The name Renfield might refer to R.M. Renfield, the loon who helped Count Dracula victimize Mina Harker in Bram Stoker's novel. Owens? Who knows. Maybe Jesse Owens. Point is, the attempted fake-out was for nought.

Why Kush and Jim Irsay flew out to Indy, not even the old man could figure out once he sobered up for five minutes. David Frick didn't think it worth a diary entry. "Bob Irsay asked them to fly out to Indianapolis to check things out," he said. "I don't know what that meant. As part of the process, I met with them and told them the Indianapolis story. At some point, Bob Irsay said, 'OK, come home.' So, it wasn't a negotiating session. It was just, 'Here's the stadium; we're a great place to have an NFL team.' But negotiations were always with Mike Chernoff and Bob Irsay."

The 2011 *BizVoice* magazine article, "Indianapolis and the Colts," has this snippet from Jim Irsay: "Current Colts owner Jim Irsay, who became general manager shortly after the move, summed why his father chose Indianapolis. 'It was a brand-new stadium in a town hungry for NFL football.' He also credits the 'get-it-done mentality' of Indianapolis for enabling things to move swiftly and properly at crunch time."

Mayor Bill Hudnut piled on the charm in a letter he sent to Irsay on March 9, 1984, addressed to the "President, Baltimore Football Club" in Skokie:

It was a pleasure to meet your son Jim and Frank Kush the other day when they were in town, and I have enjoyed touching base with Mike Chernoff over the past two weeks or so during the negotiations process. But I have had no direct contact with you, so I thought I would drop you this personal note to let you know how sincerely and eagerly I am hoping that you decide in the very near future to bring your franchise to Indianapolis. This is not the place to go over the details of the deal because they have been negotiated in good faith by Mike and my trusted lieutenant Dave Frick. And yet I do want to assure you that a warm welcome awaits you here and that we will do everything within our power to make the deal a super success for you as well as Indianapolis.

Going heavy on the frosting wasn't enough for Hizzoner. He sprinkled some jimmies on top: "Mayflower Moving Company, through its Chairman Johnny B. Smith, who is a suite owner in the Dome, has offered to move all your office and training facility equipment out here on a moment's notice free of charge (with the hope that Mayflower will be given the opportunity subsequently to move your personnel to Indianapolis at a reduced mass-move rate) ... So you see, Indianapolis really wants the Colts! We are convinced that with our Domed stadium, our central location, our growing market, and the enthusiastic spirit of this Community, we can be—and will be—a great NFL town and a great new home for you and your franchise. I hope you will consider our offer carefully ... act on it positively ... and come to Indianapolis! I guarantee you, you will not be disappointed." Yessir, you lay it on thick with big egos like Irsay.

. . .

While Hudnut was doing some obligatory rump-kissing with Irsay, Baltimore politicians were talking up eminent domain. Obviously, this was desperate-measures-for-desperate-times territory. The *Morning Sun* described the planned charge up the hill: "In Annapolis yesterday [Feb. 29], Delegate Dennis C. McCoy (D, Baltimore), chairman of the city House delegation, said the city favors a bill filed by two Colt fans in the legislature which would clarify the eminent domain law, giving the city authority to condemn and take the team in the public interest. The bill favored by the city does not call for any money for purchase of the team. The law does not clearly allow this now, Mr. McCoy said. A bill sponsored by Delegate Joel Chasnoff (D, Montogomery) and Delegate Gary R. Alexander (D, Prince Georges) would make the eminent domain statute apply to taking the property interest in a sports franchise." Nice try, fellas.

Try making a call out to Oakland to see how things went there.

The desperation was understandable, but the game wasn't over. "Negotiations to bring the Baltimore Colts to Indianapolis continued Tuesday with several points of contention remaining before a proposal would go to club owner Robert J. Irsay," the *Indianapolis Star* reported on February 29. "Indications were that the parties were in agreement on major portions of a proposal but that there still are some substantial sticking points. 'There are so many elements involved, and they all have to be right,' said Mayor William H. Hudnut. 'Ninety-eight percent of the elements could be right, and it's not enough. You have to have everything.'" Concrete poured, it was time to take a bull float to it.

The *Morning Sun* on March 1 figured it was time to load all the guns and fire away:

A football team like the Colts is an enormous economic asset and morale builder for a city. Unless one of the following things happens, Baltimore will soon lose its football franchise, maybe forever. 1. Robert Irsay decides to keep the franchise here for a season or for a longer, stated, contractually agreed upon period of time. 2. Mr. Irsay sells the Colts to investors committed to keeping the team here. 3. The National Football League owners vote to prevent Mr. Irsay from moving, in keeping with the NFL Constitution and traditional NFL policy. 4. Congress passes a law similar to one proposed by Senator Charles Mathias [MD] that would prevent franchise shifts except in special circumstances, such as economic hardship. 5. The city or state uses eminent domain to "take" the Colts in the public interest... We have long believed Option 4 was the best solution for all concerned. This would have dealt with the legal and business interests involved on a national scale... Option 5 is a last resort that no one would prefer, but must not be shunned, if it is all that is left.

George Pickett was no longer available to pursue Option 6.

One of those "sources close to" figured Irsay had backed himself into a corner. "But the source close to the NFL countered, 'This (threat to leave Baltimore) seems stronger than all the others,'" the *Indianapolis Star* reported. "'He's (Irsay's) got to know he's despised in Baltimore and there's nothing there for him to go back to. I think that's why his GM (general manager Ernie Accorsi) bailed out three weeks ago.'"

"Despised in Baltimore" meant folks wrapping him in duct tape and tossing him off Pier Six. "The city is consumed by anti-Irsay sentiment," the *Miami Herald* reported a week after the move. "An usher combs the cave-damp crannies of Memorial Stadium each night, looking for a dead rat to ship to the Colts' owner. A half-dozen songs fill the AM airwaves, most along the lines of Scott Carpenter's *Take Your Team and Shove It*. A Bob

Irsay dartboard hangs in the Swallow in the Hollow tavern out on York Avenue [sic, Road]. The cheers of derision break out every day, aimed at the Chicago sheet-metal mogul who finally lifted his team out of this deeply heart-feeling city of marble and sandstone and soft-shell crabs."

Andy Barth, who filed a few stories about the move for WMAR-TV-Baltimore, had some advice for Hoosiers. "I didn't know him [Irsay] personally, but I did have an experience on the day after the Colts left at midnight. The next day, I got sent out to Indianapolis to do 'live shots' and telling some of the people in Indianapolis that you were just getting to meet him. I guess I said something to the effect that we in Baltimore thought of him as the devil incarnate. But people out there said, 'Well, it doesn't seem that way to us at this point.' And I said, 'Well, it's just because you haven't gotten to know him.'"

Colts former equipment manager and current archivist Jon Scott recalls how ugly things got at Memorial Stadium towards the end. "As the games went by, we were getting fewer and fewer fans in the stands. We won our last game [20-10 vs. the Houston Oilers; attendance 20,418]. Less and less fans there, and that was really tough. And the chants about Jim's [Jim Irsay's] dad—'Irsay sucks' and all that kind of stuff going on in the stands—there were some rough times there."

A provincial, blue-collar town like Baltimore would only put up with so much buffoonery. "It's not the people of New Baltimore who have been enraged by Robert Irsay," the

Miami Herald indicated. "It's the fanatic faithful of the 1960s, the people who backed the Colts back when the Orioles drew zilch, the people who laid the sports foundation that has allowed the Orioles to blossom. When the Colts were kings, the harbor was still a harbor, and Baltimore was the rowhouse way station between Old-Family Philadelphia and the Doric columns of Washington, the southernmost NFL city. Their fans were the steelworkers from Dundalk, the dockworkers from Little Italy."

A few of those fanatics were sorry they ever badmouthed Carroll Rosenbloom out of Baltimore. "Everybody knew what Irsay was like," professed veteran sportswriter Vito Stellino. "The addiction [to alcohol] was the main problem. [Writer] Frank Deford once said, 'Anybody who spoils pro football in Baltimore could spoil the waters at Lourdes.' I just think it's almost kinda pointless to get into Irsay because everybody now knows what he was like—just totally ill-equipped to run a franchise. Except for Ernie [Accorsi], he didn't hire good people."

Colts and Ravens band president John Ziemann shared a story about a time when Irsay embarrassed him at a party, probably when Bob was blitzed:

> I only had one situation [encounter with Irsay]. It was the last game of the year, 1983. We had the so-called "holiday party." My wife, Shar, was pregnant with our youngest son, Patrick. I was talking to Jimmy and Meg Irsay. Everybody

knew the team was gonna leave. He's there [Irsay] and yells, "Where's John Ziemann?" And I thought, *Oh, my God. I hope there's another John Ziemann in this room*. I didn't want to upset my wife. "Where the hell's Ziemann?" Jimmy [Irsay] said, "You better answer him." I said, "Mr. Irsay, right here." He goes, "Ziemann, I found out something." "What's that?" He said, "I paid $19 million for a marching band." I wondered, *Where's this going?* He said, "19 million for a marching band. They're the only ones who performed this year. It sure as hell wasn't the team." Now, the whole team's there. And I thought, *How the hell am I gonna handle this one?* I said, "Mr. Irsay, I think everyone performed." "Nope! $19 million for a marching band." The players are just looking at me. Then he went on to something else. I walked over to the team, and I said, "Hey, guys." They said, "John, we understand. We understand." And Jimmy said, "I'm so sorry." I said, "Jimmy, don't worry about it." Then, Mrs. Irsay came over and apologized.

Maybe the moment Irsay got hooked on Indy was the first time he saw the Hoosier Dome. Thereafter, the guy was smitten. David Frick was up to his elbows in negotiations by that time but was there for the tour that day:

Bob Irsay had never been to Indianapolis, so as part of the process of negotiating a deal, at the same time competing with other cities, we thought it important to get him here. His counsel, Mike Chernoff, arranged for him to come down and have dinner with a small group of business leaders and Herb and Mel Simon [of the Simon Property Group, who bought the Indiana Pacers]. As part of that tour of Indianapolis, I took Mr. Irsay over to the Hoosier Dome. We were about four months away from completion, but you could see what the place was gonna look like. The idea of blue seats I take responsibility for. I visited several cities across the country that had stadiums, and I love the colored seats that Minnesota put in their stadium—blue. I held firm on blue seats. So, you had the blue seats, and the upper deck was silver bench seats. The roof was white—the Colts' colors. We orchestrated the path we'd take in [during the tour], so it would overwhelm him once he got on the floor of the stadium. He went silent on me. I remember saying, "Mr. Irsay, are you OK?" He *never* was silent. We must have spent two or three minutes, and nothing was said. Then, he said, "This is meant to be." It was at that point that I was relatively confident that we were gonna get him, that if he was gonna move from Baltimore, we had a real shot of convincing him to come to Indianapolis.

Hudnut debated Schaefer via *USA Today* essays, and in his he offered two assumptions when they built the Hoosier Dome: "First, that the Hoosier Dome would not be a free-standing facility in a cornfield somewhere, exclusively dedicated to sports, but a multi-purpose facility yoked into the Indiana Convention Center that would greatly enhance our competitive position in attracting convention business, justifiable in and of itself, so that if pro football or baseball came, they would be icing on the cake. And second, that hopefully the NFL would hope to expand in the near future, and we would be positioned favorably, with local investors in the wings ready to walk on center stage with a franchise, if the NFL awarded one to a city." The NFL put a temporary freeze on expansion after they got schooled by Al Davis in court. But lo and behold, Bob Irsay appeared over the horizon and Indy zeroed in on the Colts.

Mayor Schaefer must have turned three shades of purple when the next news flash came in on March 2, 1984: "Indianapolis—Colts general counsel Michael Chernoff and former Indianapolis Deputy Mayor David Frick finished the work on documents for the shifting of the Colts franchise yesterday and took them to Chicago for the inspection of Colts owner Robert Irsay, a source said," Vito Stellino revealed in the *Morning Sun.* "All Mr. Irsay now has to do is sign the documents in order to make a shift of the National Football League franchise from Baltimore to Indianapolis official. A source familiar with the negotiations, however, said there still might be a chance Mr. Irsay might find fault with the documents Mr. Chernoff

and Mr. Frick spent four days writing this week." There was little chance of that, given the two meticulous pros churning out the paperwork. Besides, Michael Machiavelli had been on the horn constantly with Irsay, getting OKs on all the particulars. Nah. Short of getting cold feet or a genie dropping a new dome with blue seats and luxury boxes in downtown Baltimore, the Indy deal was a lock.

Hudnut had a Pete Rose quality about him; people in Indy loved the guy while over in Baltimore they saw him as the eighth deadly sin. Former Baltimore newscaster Andy Barth just thought he was doing his job:

> With their [Indy's] leadership, I only met Hudnut. He was certainly an amiable guy, and he was acting in the interests of Indianapolis. I don't think what he did was aboveboard or honorable, but he was working for his city, and I have to say he was doing essentially what Baltimore did after the team was gone, and we tried to bring another team back here. There's just no getting around that. I don't know how he [Hudnut] felt about it. He was pleasant, composed, and he understood that I would be bringing up Baltimore's point of view, could feel aggrieved and would report that the people in Baltimore were upset and furious with him because of what he had done—the chicanery and behind-the-back negotiations. But he did what he had to do, and he did it successfully.

February 23 was when Irsay ambled into town and met Indy's heavy hitters and toured the Hoosier Dome. Probably then things started moving faster down the track. Dinner at a swank restaurant was the Indy team's chance to size up Irsay. "That was at J. Pierpont, a restaurant owned by Herb Simon [co-owner of the Pacers]. Herb and Mel [Simon] were there, I was there, other business leaders and Hudnut were there," chief negotiator David Frick recalled. "It was just a get-acquainted, Indianapolis-is-a-good-place-to-be, kind of rah-rah meeting, trying to impress Mr. Irsay. Irsay had never been to Indianapolis. We needed to impress him that we were the real thing. There was a lot of puffery going on, I'm sure."

Some of the NFL good ole boys weren't exactly ready to cotton to Irsay eloping with Indy. "Many of the league's old guard are aghast at the idea of Irsay abandoning Baltimore, a city that has supported the Colts generally well over the years," the *Chicago Tribune* disclosed. "Under Irsay's bungling stewardship, the Colts suddenly are a team with no general manager, no front office and few skilled players. Ernie Accorsi quit as a general manager Feb. 7 after declaring 'my intestines are tied up in knots' as a result of watching Irsay peddle the Colts around the country."

Ken Denlinger of the *Washington Post* saw Irsay and Walter O'Malley as bookends. "Simply put, Irsay is a simpleminded Robert Short [who took the MLB Senators to Texas], who was a bush-league Walter O'Malley. Take what the town'll give you, these athletic strip

miners whisper, and move on. For an unforgivably long time, Irsay has treated Baltimore like a ten-dollar trollop. This ought to be the final fling. The human mind can only take so much. Go. Get out of our lives, Irsay. Even if your Colts stay in Baltimore, they won't be Baltimore's team. The last link to civility, to at least the fast-fading notion of an Olde Town team, left with Ernie Accorsi less than a month ago."

On March 3, with Frick and Chernoff proofreading the contract, Irsay was still mealy-mouthing about a move. And though it wasn't a no-confidence vote for Baltimore, Commissioner Pete Rozelle started backpedaling, a bad sign. "When Mr. Rozelle was asked what his personal feelings were about the possibility of a Colt shift, he said, 'Personally, I have a lot of respect for Baltimore. I have great respect for the fans and their enthusiasm and the way they've followed the Colts, although not as well recently as before.'"

The decrepit stadium on 33rd alone was enough to push a guy out of town, but a law from the Dark Ages just added more oomph. Baltimore's blue laws, which forbade the Colts from kicking off before 2 PM on Sundays so churchgoers could have a two-fer—the Sunday service and the ballgame—was an anomaly that had to go. This meant that network programming went askew, every other game starting at 1:00 and the 4:00 games thrown for a loop. This caused three-hour migraines for Rosenbloom and Irsay seven Sundays a year. "Other than the team's awful record of late, do you know why the Baltimore Colts' home football games are never nationally televised in the 1 p.m. time slot?" the *Washington Post* queried in February 1984. "Because a Baltimore City ordinance forbids games before 2 o'clock. Why? Because churches near Memorial Stadium don't want game spectators pouring into the neighborhood early, grabbing their parishioners' parking spaces." And as if it mattered, Mayor Schaefer said he'd jump right on it and try to wheedle the state to join the rest of NFL Nation for a 1:00 kickoff.

John Steadman of the *News American* had been spot-on of late, what with his beatdowns of Memorial Stadium, his campaign for a new ballpark and his Churchillian warnings about the Colts moving. He also had it right about the two o'clock kickoff time:

> The irascible Irsay got the mayor [Schaefer] to jump through a hoop and the governor to turn cartwheels [with his threats]. Additionally, he accomplished something positive that will prove helpful to the majority. Yet for 14 years the idea got nowhere. It had to do with Baltimore changing the starting time for Sunday afternoon athletic events from 2 p.m. to 1 p.m. Every other city in America permits games to begin at 1 p.m. There may have been fear here that we would go to hell in a handbasket for violating an archaic law. That still might happen, but hopefully it won't be punishment for going to sports contests an hour earlier on Sunday. Yes, dear old Baltimore and its methodical ways. The rest

of the nation was out of step. It's commendable to have individuality, but this was flagrant abuse of the privilege.

If you could stumble out of a bar well before 2:00 and break almost every commandment before lunch, it stood to reason kickoff at the stadium could commence at 1:00.

Schaefer the pit bull said, "I haven't thrown in my hand. I haven't thrown my hands up" when he knew Indy's contract was sitting on Irsay's desk. He let out some steam in the March 3 *Morning Sun* when he revealed how he chided Irsay for sniveling about the press:

> In answer to a question from one of the [state] delegates, the mayor said he is not certain what it is that Mr. Irsay wants. He described Mr. Irsay as "an interesting man. I don't dislike him," he said, though Mr. Irsay is "up and down a lot" and difficult to talk to on occasion. "It's strange to say," the mayor said, "but I think he'd like to stay in the city. He could sign [another deal] today. He hasn't done it. I don't know why." He said Mr. Irsay complains to him considerably about the press. But the mayor said he suggested to Mr. Irsay that sports reporters are "tough" everywhere. "If he thinks he's going to have a free ride out there [in Indianapolis], he's in for a rude awakening," the mayor said.

Sage advice from the boss. But about the "I don't know why" business—was he mystified about why no owner with half his marbles would sign a long-term lease on a stadium with rats in its catacombs and junior high locker rooms?

. . .

A special owners' meeting for early March 1984 in Chicago got hyped because Irsay put the Colts' move on the agenda. Bated breath for all. But Irsay pulled a quick retreat. "Rosemont, Ill.—If Friday was D-Day for Indianapolis's entry into the National Football League, the D stood for dud," the *Indianapolis Star* reported. "Nothing happened. It was a day like the 10 or so that have come before it, filled with rumor, conjecture and all sorts of people saying 'no comment.' There was a special meeting of the NFL owners at the O'Hare Hyatt Regency here, called, according to Commissioner Pete Rozelle, at the request of Baltimore owner Robert J. Irsay, to discuss the possibility of him moving the Colts to Indianapolis—or someplace else. 'Mr. Irsay said he had not made up his mind yet on what he was going to do,' said Rozelle. 'He said that possibly he would move. He stressed he hadn't made a deal with anyone.'" More like hadn't *signed* a deal yet. The esquires on retainer had already cranked out the contract and sent it Fed Express to Irsay.

As Rozelle stated at the March 2, 1984, owners' meeting on the WMAR-TV documentary, *The Long Goodbye*, "Mr. Irsay came back in [after he left the meeting so the owners could talk] and addressed the membership, and he said he has not made up his mind about what he wants to do. He's continuing to talk with Baltimore, with Mayor Schaefer and the people in Baltimore. He acknowledged the highly-publicized discussions he's had with other cities, and he said he had *not* made up his mind. But there's a possibility he would move." The odds at this point were a good 7-5, Indy's way. David Frick has said the deal wasn't a sure thing by March 2, with only 30-40 pages typed up, but the snowball was rolling downhill.

The "Jekyll-Hyde" feature in the *Morning Sun* hit the streets on March 4, and the scat hit the fan. This was Exhibit A of Bob Irsay's bellyaching about the Baltimore press. A huge treatise, with some pros and mostly cons about the red-faced owner. All kinds of facts, anecdotes and testimony about: 1) his erratic behavior; 2) fudging the truth about the tragic death of his daughter; 3) the phony baloney about his military service; and 4) drinking like a fish.

This section about the boozing is typical:

Three sources—two in the football world and one who knew him socially in Chicago—say that Mr. Irsay stopped drinking for a while in 1982 but then resumed. One of the Colts' agents recalls Mr. Irsay, his *face red* [my emphasis] and flushed, arriving at a 1983 negotiating session in which he consumed six to eight vodkas during two hours. "He definitely was not nursing them," the agent says. "It was boom, boom, boom." Bert Jones, the former Colt quarterback who lost a contract dispute with Mr. Irsay and then was traded away, puts it bluntly: "He's a liar, a cheat, crude, with no manners, and he drinks too much."

The article's headline, **Chicago's Jekyll Becomes Hyde in Baltimore**, implied the fascinating dichotomy of the man:

> In Chicago, where he made his fortune as a heating and air-conditioning contractor and has a good reputation as a loyal friend and man of his word, as an ingratiating salesman who loves to play host, as a tough, brilliant businessman respected for the quality of his companies' work… But in Baltimore, where he has jetted in and out as the Colts' absentee owner the last 12 years, "The Mighty I" has struck a decidedly different profile—as a loud, brutish, erratic man who cannot be taken at his word, as an interfering, miserly, incompetent manager, as a man who thrives on turmoil, no matter the cost.

More of the yin and yang and mystery of Robert Irsay:

- "Football fans remember when Mr. Irsay gave a $10,000 bonus [which he never paid] to a field-goal kicker who had just cost the Colts a game and then fired him the next day; the negotiations with a Jewish agent for a Colt in which

he said, 'Don't Jew me to death on price'; his phone call to coach Mike McCormack during a game, ordering him to alternate quarterbacks on every play."

- "There was a time in 1977 when Jimmy [Irsay] and his father were in Little Italy, and Mr. Irsay lined up all the kids around and bought them free ice cream. 'That was him at his best,' the younger Mr. Irsay says. 'He wants to be loved.'"

Naturally, Irsay zoomed past the good and fixated on the bad. Had he been a volcano, upon reading "Jekyll-Hyde," Skokie would have been ankle-deep in ash.

With all the stability of a tropical depression, Irsay claimed the *Sunpapers* hired a platoon of J. Edgar Hoover's goons to dig up dirt on him. He told the *Chicago Tribune* that the *Sun* "hired a force of 10 newspaper guys to go over the country and find out what I did wrong. They can't find anything." Only about 30 column inches' worth. The *Trib* gave the *Sunpapers* a call in June for comment:

> Marty Kaiser, executive sports editor of the Baltimore *Morning Sun*, said, "That's just not true. The whole point is ludicrous. We ran a long Sunday piece on Irsay, going back and talking to people in Chicago. But the paper never, ever hired 10 people to go out and investigate him. We found that Irsay's image in Chicago is completely different than

his image in Baltimore. His image is a lot more positive in Chicago. There are people here in Baltimore who are just as glad the team is gone, even though it means losing the football team, just to get rid of him. Irsay was saying it was the newspaper's fault the team had to leave. He was after us at the end."

Two reporters did all the legwork: Robert Benjamin and Vito Stellino. This was Stellino's take on Irsay's conspiracy theory: "The story ran the first Sunday in March, right after the Friday meeting in Chicago when Irsay met with the owners on his projected move to Indianapolis. It wasn't a hatchet job. It was more favorable than he deserved. It portrayed him as a Jekyll and Hyde type and quoted his friends in Chicago as saying he is a hard worker." In a state of delirium or inebriation, Irsay accused the two reporters of heading down to Florida and trying to break down the door at a psychiatric hospital so they could interview Irsay's son. "Nobody went down there, let alone tried to break down the door," Stellino insisted. "We merely tried to reach the director of the institution by telephone. We were attempting to present a complete portrayal of Irsay."

Over forty years later, Stellino sticks to his guns about the Jekyll-Hyde piece. "His file was almost a complete lie. Almost everything in there was not accurate once you checked out his military record and some of the other stuff. If you look at the 1983 [Colts] media guide, virtually everything in the bio is made

up. Until then, nobody had really gone deeply into his background. I can understand that he was not happy to be exposed that way. Much of his bio was total fiction. I wasn't bothered by his criticism because I just considered the source. I just brushed that off. That was just typical Irsay."

No doubt there came a point when the Baltimore press would flog the man if he sneezed. Usually Irsay brought it on, but there was almost a mob mentality about it towards the end. Charles Euchner in *Playing the Field: Why Sports Teams Move and Cities Fight to Keep Them* explored the flip side of the Jekyll-Hyde article:

Around the time of Irsay's exit, Baltimore newspapers exhumed Irsay's past and found patterns of deceit that made Irsay's betrayal [of Baltimore] the inevitable denouement in a modern tragedy. Upon his arrival in Baltimore, the local media had given Irsay an enthusiastic welcome. But with each day of crisis, the reports became more deeply personal ... The whole [Jekyll-Hyde] portrait could have been pulled together in a more sympathetic way by paying more attention to the tragedies in Irsay's life— the institutionalization of a retarded son and the death of a daughter in an automobile accident. The article and its extensive detective work on Irsay's educational, military and family background, was an exercise in demonizing. When, after the move to Indianapolis,

Irsay's wife [Harriet] sued for divorce and demanded half the value of the Colts, Baltimore newspapers rejoiced as if the world was being made right again.

Hard feelings die hard if they die at all. Safe in the bosom of the new Colts faithful in Indianapolis, Irsay let fly one more shot at the press. "Colts owner Robert Irsay, welcomed to Indianapolis with a key to the city from mayor William Hudnut and loud cheers from a crowd of about 20,000 in the Hoosier Dome, said he left Baltimore because of constant 'hounding' by the news media," *Newsday* revealed in early April 1984. "'It was not a monetary situation,' the owner of the NFL franchise told the lunch-hour crowd that streamed into the new domed stadium to greet him. 'We did talk to several other cities, and we did have better offers.' Responding to questions from the media, Irsay said, 'You people of the press were hounding my family for two years, and I wasn't about to take any more of your hounding.'"

· · ·

Baltimore reporters were tripping over each other, trying to get the latest scoop. They figured a move was in the offing; they just didn't know when. As the managing editor of news for WMAR-TV in Baltimore, Wayne Lynch could only guess at how this would play out:

Obviously, we all wanted to break the story first. But back then, everybody in news expected some type of big news

conference where a move would be announced. Nobody expected these moving vans to come in. It was a total surprise to everybody. I don't think the Colts employees expected anything like that. I think they figured they would be called in and be told, "We're leaving. You're gonna get severance; you can come in tomorrow and pick up your stuff." Because that's the way business was done then, even in sports. Nobody was skulking out in the middle of the night. If they had had a news conference, it might've spurred protests. There might have been a complete upheaval by Baltimore citizens against this. It could've been extremely negative. And I don't think Irsay wanted any more confrontations, anything public. He wanted to do it without anyone knowing, and he created the unexpected. And all of the news departments were basically caught off-guard.

And Irsay sure as heck didn't want reporters tracking him down in Vegas. Veteran sportscaster Scott Garceau was on his trail sometime in February-March 1984 when he caught a real eye-opener:

Irsay disappears [after the BWI press conference in late January]. Nobody sees him after the press conference. No statements from him or the team. I get a tip that he's in Las Vegas, and if he's in Las Vegas, he's always at Caesar's Palace. So, I get a photographer, and off we go to Vegas. We literally walk into Caesar's, and it's midafternoon, maybe two o'clock, and I look over, and what do I see at a blackjack table—Bob Irsay and Mike Chernoff and two young women. They could've been working ladies, for all I knew, but it looked pretty suspicious. I knew Mrs. Irsay, and it wasn't her, and I had met Mrs. Chernoff, and it wasn't her. I tell the cameraman to go to the side and set up the shot and give me a thumbs-up when he's ready to roll. I get it, so I walk up behind the table, and I say, "Hello, Mike. Hello, Mr. Irsay." And Chernoff looks like he's seen a ghost. He literally turned white. I'm making small talk, telling them that everybody in Baltimore is looking for you guys. "Do you have anything to say?" All of a sudden, Irsay sees the camera, and he goes nuts. "What the hell?! Get that fuckin' camera outta here!" The pit boss comes over and things kinda break up. I apologize that the cameraman didn't know you're not supposed to film in a casino, and he says no problem. Then the pit boss says, "Let me tell you something. Every time he [Irsay] comes in here, there's something: The dealer gave him the wrong card; somebody did something next to him; they took his chips. It's a show every time he comes in here. But he's a good customer, so we try to take care of him." So, we showed [on TV] that he was alive, and I think the women were in the shot too.

"Looked for dirt and couldn't find a thing," protested the red-faced owner. And there was Michael Machiavelli, the button-down barrister and Wannabe GM, with a Vegas coquette on his arm. The brain trust of the Baltimore Colts. Stories like this are probably why a sardonic scribe like Phil Jackman couldn't help himself. For instance: **Dear Bob, the red-faced owner:** Now that you've had a month to bask in the Colts' glorious [exhibition game] victory over the Bears before all your friends in downtown Skokie, I think it's time we discussed a few things. I know this owner business is still relatively new with you, but you just gotta get back to acting the part. There were times when you showed a lot of spunk. Like when you lectured Marty Domres on his quarterbacking ("Hey, how come you don't throw passes to our guys like you throw 'em to the other team?") And that memorable Sunday, Bloody Sunday, when you fired Howie the Hoss [Schnellenberger] while waiting for your limousine to arrive."

David Frick and Michael Chernoff had bartered their way into a pile of legal papers ready for Irsay to sign. The *Indianapolis Star* listed the basics a few days after the move, and they were tasty:

The Capital Improvement Board signed up the Indianapolis Colts Saturday, making some big commitments but planning on some profits as well. Under the lease, the National Football League franchise will play in the Hoosier Dome for 20 years, with the team having the option to add two five-year extensions to the contract. The Colts will pay an annual rental of $250,000 to play eight regular season and two preseason games in the Dome. The rent will be $225,000 this year, however, because only one preseason game is scheduled for the Dome. For the first 12 years, the board will guarantee the Colts $7 million annually from ticket sales and, possibly, radio and television broadcast rights. The board will also help pay interest [3% of the original 11%] on a $12.5 million loan to the Colts from Merchants National Bank and will construct a $3 to $4 million training facility for the team. In addition, $500,000 in payments to the board for luxury suites will be paid to the Colts.

Yucking it up in the owner's luxury box at the Dome and not some pantry at Memorial Stadium was also part of the deal.

As they say, a day late and a stadium short. The Irsay crisis finally got Baltimore grandees to halt the mere yapping and put up something tangible. Right before midnight, unfortunately. "After days of hustling, Governor Hughes and Mayor Schaefer yesterday completed the financial package intended to keep Robert Irsay and the Colts in Baltimore—a deal that the mayor said 'may' involve city funds," the *Morning Sun* divulged on March 9, 1984. "The package is expected to include a $15-million loan at 8% interest and some form of grant or purchase to relieve Mr. Irsay of the financial burden of the Colts training facility. City and state officials have been working with business leaders for a week to fashion a financial package intended to keep Mr. Irsay from moving the football team to Indianapolis. But the private contributions may not be enough."

Hughes and Schaefer implied they would drop everything—even photo ops—to sit down with Irsay and deliver their offer on a platter, said the *Sun*:

Mayor Schaefer said he will try to reach Mr. Irsay in Chicago today to set up a meeting. Though he failed to reach the team owner by phone yesterday, he left word that the deal was nearly ready. The mayor added that he's ready to go anywhere anytime, but does not expect that meeting to take place over the weekend. "He will be here sometime next week," the mayor said of Mr. Irsay. "I expect we'll talk then." Mr. Hughes stressed the importance of a face-to-face meeting with Mr. Irsay. "I think you can do a lot better sitting down and talking with someone, as they say, eyeball-to-eyeball, rather than over the telephone," he said.

The desperation was obvious when they hinted that taxpayer bucks might be thrown into the pot. You can't really blame them for trying although this ship may have already sailed. But there was no getting around it: No amount of prestidigitation could pull a new stadium out of the hat.

Even the fans who burned him in effigy and wanted to spit on his Johnston and Murphys were in fire-alarm mode. On March 9, they tried to rally the troops, but that fizzled, according to the *Morning Sun*: "They swallowed their pride. Opened their arms, and bled from the heart last night as about 125 Colt fans gathered at the downtown Holiday Inn to do their parts in trying to persuade club owner Bob Irsay to keep his football team in Baltimore. Resembling religious revivalists asking people to go out and win souls for Christ, a half-dozen speakers urged the crowd to go home and say good things about Irsay, to say good things about the Colts and to take people to task for not believing the team can be kept here. It was the second meeting in three weeks of the Coalition to Save the Colts, an informal group of fans who hope against hope that more than cold cash will warm Irsay's heart." Given their previous and longstanding campaign of contempt for the man and the lack of a first-rate ballpark, delusional thinking was the common thread at the Holiday Inn.

This should sound familiar: Brooklyn Dodgers fans got just as desperate when Walter O'Malley was making noise about moving. Peter Marquis chronicled the exploits of the "Keep the Dodgers in Brooklyn Committee" in *Complicating the Blame Game: New York Politics, Baseball Fans and the Dodgers' Move Out of Brooklyn*:

In the fall of 1956, when the word was out that the Dodgers might leave

Brooklyn for Queens or Los Angeles, some Brooklynites mobilized, albeit tardily and in relatively small numbers: 25,000 signed the "Keep the Dodgers in Brooklyn" petition launched by borough President [John] Cashmore, including 3,500 from Brooklyn College. In comparison to the yearly attendance of one million paying customers at Ebbets Field, this understandably may have signaled to O'Malley that the "Flatbush Faithful" also had lost hope.

Maybe Dodgers and Colts fans were better served calling off the embarrassment if this was all they could muster. A *Morning Sun* ad on March 11 probably more accurately displayed true public sentiment—a big rectangle stating, "Stick it to Bob Irsay with the Bob Irsay Dartboard." This novelty for your bar or den by GMZ Enterprises in Reisterstown, MD, could be had for $10 + $2 shipping.

* * *

Governor Hughes, Mayor Schaefer and the posse flew out to Chicago on March 11 to pitch their latest offer, only to find out that Phoenix was back on the burner (again). The *Morning Sun's* Vito Stellino had a source who claimed that the Indy crowd suspected they were now third fiddle behind Phoenix and Baltimore. "He [the source] said Indianapolis officials were puzzled because Mr. Irsay seemed to be rejecting their deal and was again talking to Phoenix investors, who he believes will offer to build a domed stadium and match the rest of the Indianapolis offer, including a $15-million, low-interest loan and a $5-million practice facility." Probably just diabolical machinations by Irsay to make all parties sweat, especially Indy. No sense in letting them get too comfy, you know. But by March 11, the Indy deal was solid, printed and bull-clipped, and Irsay was just fooling around with his baton.

All suitors in these situations are willing to show off with cartwheels, backflips and back handsprings to woo the big guy. Bob Hurt of the *Arizona Republic* thought Phoenix "seems headed back toward the front burner." He cajoled his readers to stomach a lout to snare a team: "Mr. Congeniality, Irsay is not. Irsay has not endeared himself to Baltimore with his frequent threats to move. He has been known to call plays for coaches, make trades and fire assistants without consulting either coaches or his general managers … The arrival of the Colts and Irsay [to Phoenix] would loom as a mixed blessing, but you can't have one without the other. Valley citizens would stand in line to buy the Colts' franchise, but Irsay is not selling. Irsay, face it, won't be around forever, but an NFL franchise could be. Maybe, it would be worth the trouble that comes with an absentee owner." Former Baltimore Colts personnel director and Patriots GM Upton Bell upbraided Baltimore with the same logic: Irsay wouldn't be around forever, the ballclub would, so forget your silly pride and give the man what he wants. They got stuck in their feelings, dug in their heels and lost the Colts.

With all of this intrigue swirling around, John Steadman of the *News American* grabbed Johnny Unitas by the elbow and solicited comment. The Golden Arm didn't mince around: "What the man who owns them wants to do with the club is his business. It won't affect me an iota if he goes or stays, but there will be a lot of broken hearts among the fans if we lose the team. I feel sorry for the people. It's a slap in the face. He's an embarrassment to football. Not one good thing has he done for football. And not one thing to help the community. He has pushed for six or seven cities in the last six years, and it could be another four or five before he's through."

Why not work a two-for-one? Clap Rosenbloom and Irsay in irons and browbeat both. Such was Steadman's ploy in his March 4, 1984, column:

How the Baltimore Colts went from being a spectacularly successful franchise—on the field and off—to what could be termed a terminal case is poignantly explained by a succession of dollar signs … $$$$$$$$$$. The Colts played in their own garden of greed—thanks to the machinations of Robert Irsay and Carroll Rosenbloom, who put their insatiable desires for money ahead of a public confidence they blatantly damaged and betrayed. During the Rosenbloom regime, in an effort to portray an image of white-helmeted righteousness, he guaranteed that good things be spoken and written about him by paying off some reporters who sold their souls and journalistic integrity for gifts, tips on the stock market and outright financial payoffs. Too bad.

Sheesh. The payola business again. Just another bit of backstabbing to smear C.R. and Paul Menton and Jesse Linthicum of the *Evening* and *Morning Sun*. Poking around the archives and asking those in the know—journalists, friends and Colts executives—revealed no kernel of truth to it. Maybe somebody actually witnessed Rosenbloom greasing the palms of reporters to go easy on him, but he's kept his yap closed all these years. Menton, Linthicum and Rosenbloom shuffled off this mortal coil decades ago and couldn't be reached for comment.

Phoenix scurried around and slapped together its last-ditch plan to snatch the Colts. "Phoenix officials worked yesterday on what one source called an 'alternate proposal' to present to Robert Irsay in hopes of luring the Colt franchise to the Arizona city," Vito Stellino reported on March 17 in the *Morning Sun*. "Eddie Lynch, the developer who heads the committee studying a downtown domed stadium in Phoenix, confirmed that the Phoenix officials were 'communicating back and forth' with the Colt owner by phone. 'It's like any other deal,' Lynch said. 'There's give and take' … One of the sticking points was Irsay's demand that Phoenix officials guarantee the sale of 45,000 tickets a game. 'They don't think they can guarantee 45,000 tickets, but they're going to come up with an alternate

proposal,' the source said. 'If he finds it interesting, they'll keep going.'"

The Phoenix redux even had a consummate pro like Indy negotiator David Frick a little spooked:

I was at the NFL owners' meetings in Hawaii [March 1984]. Mike Chernoff and I were trying to finalize the documentation of our negotiations, so I decided to fly out there. He [Chernoff] needed to be there because Bob Irsay relied upon him. So, Mike and I spent a little time working on the documents, then he left. There was a big void. His parting words were, "I gotta go to Phoenix," so I knew it might be bad for us. I don't know the details of that meeting with Phoenix, but I do know that there was some attraction that Mr. Irsay found in the Phoenix offer. There's no doubt we didn't have [head coach] Frank Kush's support. I think Jimmy [Irsay] also favored Phoenix because he and Kush were close.

Not everybody in Phoenix was buffaloed by Irsay. Vito Stellino caught up with one guy who suggested Irsay was a tad loopy. "A Phoenix source said he doesn't think Irsay is deliberately orchestrating the delay. 'I can't tell you he's stringing Phoenix along intentionally. I think he strings himself along. He's insecure and doesn't know which way to turn. He's like a guy who can't decide between 50 colors of ice cream. I can't tell you he plans all this.'" It's also possible that Irsay had his mind made up—Indianapolis—and was lapping up all the attention he could get before he signed.

When it became obvious that Phoenix had been played again, Tom Fitzpatrick of the *Arizona Republic* lambasted Irsay and Arizona Governor Bruce Babbitt:

> Here in one corner is Irsay, the lowest of low-rent entrepreneurs, who owns a second-rate professional football team called the Baltimore Colts. In the other corner is Babbitt, the intellectual from Flagstaff, who shunned football as a youth and now is willing to seize on it as a vehicle to get enough votes to take him to the U.S. Senate. At the slightest hint that Irsay might be willing to move the Colts from Baltimore to Phoenix, all doors in Arizona are promptly thrown open to him. Babbitt immediately makes a place on his calendar to meet with him. It is as though Irsay was a man who had discovered a cure for cancer or was a winner of the Nobel Peace Prize. The entire episode is worthy of the acerbic pen of Jonathan Swift.

Fooled once, fooled twice, Phoenix jogged to the side of the track and hit the locker room. An *Arizona Republic* editorial on March 26 captured the prevailing feeling out there but butchered the inference: "Tears may be flowing somewhere in the state of Arizona over the news (?) that Robert Irsay has decided to keep the football Colts *in Baltimore* [emphasis mine]. But those who know Irsay, or have dealt with him, are dry-eyed. The man is incorrigible, boorish, undependable and unreliable. He also uses well-meaning, but naïve, communities to advance his own fortunes. Phoenix may be the most naïve of them all. It has been burned twice by the arrogant Irsay ... Presumably, this humiliation of being used—twice—has taught Arizonans a lesson. It has, hasn't it?"

As was his wont during decadent times, John Steadman took to the pulpit on March 22 to sermonize, with a quart of melodrama for good measure:

> Never in the history of sports—where the bizarre is commonplace now—has anything been so far removed from what constitutes normal behavior as the wandering proceedings of the Baltimore Colts. A sad new record has been established for incongruity. Decency has been thrown for a loss. Every man, woman and child who survives the escapade will attest to having lived in the strangest of football times. They deserve battle stars. An owner named Robert Irsay, holding the rights to a valuable franchise, turned it into a laugh-a-minute road show ... The demeaning aspect to the entire episode is that professional sports have become a business that is more like streetcorner prostitution. Money has become a god, and that's unfortunate. For the last 31 years, first

Carroll Rosenbloom and now Irsay, have made millions. Baltimore shouldn't be backed into a corner and made to put up a financial fight for the right to hold on to *what it properly considers to be its property* [emphasis mine]. But, because of an age of permissiveness, yes, even in pro football, teams are free to come and go. Is the price right?

It's likely that only Bob Irsay and Mikey, the Wannabe GM knew what his next move would be. His son Jim always maintained he didn't know beans until he got the phone call to load up the vans. So maybe the younger Irsay was on the level in late March when he told Baltimore to hang in there; maybe Pop kept the lid on so tight Jimmy wasn't the wiser. "Jimmy Irsay, son of Colt owner Robert Irsay, said yesterday there is still a 'possibility' the franchise won't be moved, and the Baltimore fans should 'keep your fingers crossed' that the franchise will remain there this year," the *Morning Sun* proclaimed. "When Jimmy Irsay was asked what he thought Baltimore could do to keep the Colts, he said it was 'hard for me to answer directly,' but suggested the city would have to 'come close to what the other cities are offering.'" Who knows if this was part of the Irsay string-along or Dad deliberately kept his boy oblivious. All this did was keep alive the fallacy that Baltimore still had a shot.

Spurned by Irsay and riled up, Verne Boatner of the *Arizona Republic* ticked off a long list of Irsay's misdemeanors and transgressions for context:

- **March 30, 1976:** "Irsay claimed a Phoenix group 'was in here and made an attractive offer.' His general manager at the time, Joe Thomas, said the Colts 'have been contacted and told Phoenix would build a stadium if we were willing to move.' Phoenix leaders denied any knowledge. Irsay just had been notified the city of Baltimore and the state of Maryland had decided not to build the Colts a new stadium."

- **June 11, 1979:** "Irsay said he 'had a beautiful deal' in Los Angeles and wanted to move the Colts there. 'I had a nice conversation with Governor Jerry Brown,' he said. 'We will move next year.' LA officials denied any contact with Irsay for five months."

- **Sept. 26, 1979:** "Irsay claimed he had a firm offer of $60 million in revenue over 10 years if he moved to Jacksonville. He also said he had offers from Memphis and Los Angeles. He was quoted as saying, 'It's not a matter of if I'm leaving, but where I'm going.'"

- **May 16, 1982:** "Commenting on the Raiders' move to LA, Irsay said, 'I don't think the implication is every team is a free agent. As for myself, I'm happy in Baltimore. I feel confident there's a future for the Colts in Baltimore. I think we're all going to be sticking with the cities we've already got.'"

- **Jan. 20, 1984:** "At a meeting with reporters at the Baltimore airport, Irsay denied he had any plans of moving. 'I'll be here,' he said. 'I don't know where the hell all this is coming from. I can't picture what this was about.'"

- **February 1984:** "Irsay began negotiations with Indianapolis. At the same time, he was talking to Memphis."

Boatner had a final thought: "Is it any wonder the Baltimore media is paranoid?"

Psychologists call this wild ping-ponging of statements—you can't make up your mind—*ambivalence*. What was with this guy? He'd been caught spoon-feeding the press a raft of lies about his past, so was it what the shrinks call *pseudologia fantastica*—pathological lying? Did the martinis loosen up his tongue? Or did he just like toying with people for sport? And the effect in Baltimore anybody could understand: Some heel keeps bemoaning to his wife about all the dames he could have if he weren't stuck with her. Finally, she's had enough, packs his suitcase and tosses it out on the front lawn: "There, Romeo. You're not worth the trouble. Go out, find somebody better and get the hell outta here."

Steadman wasn't about to stop ragging on Irsay. Only six days before the move, he shared some comments from Roger Stanton, publisher of *The Football News*. Mr. Stanton cut to the chase: "In the 12 years Mr. Irsay has run the Baltimore franchise, it has deteriorated considerably and he does not have the respect of the Baltimore fans, Baltimore city officials, the media or his fellow NFL owners. His track record there is a poor one. There is no reason to believe it would be anything else in Indianapolis—even with your beautiful, new, domed stadium … The fact he needs a loan of $15 million at a low interest rate in order to bring his franchise to Indianapolis indicates what a poor businessman he has been in the football world and out of it."

Baltimore wasn't running a fire drill to keep him, and the Indy deal was still dangling on a string. Time for the red-faced owner to pull the trigger.

CHAPTER 16

VOYAGE OF
THE MAYFLOWER

t was something out of *High Plains Drifter* redux: A stranger ambles into town to save the day: "A San Francisco developer involved in the effort to lure an NFL expansion team to Phoenix expressed interest yesterday in building a new stadium in Baltimore financed by the private sector," the *Morning Sun* proclaimed on March 23, 1984. "Samuel G. Meason said his company, Diamond Circle Properties, would arrange financing and arrange for a contractor to build a 60,000- to 80,000-seat stadium in Baltimore, if the city would donate the necessary land and the two major tenants—the Colts and the Orioles—agreed to leases of 25 years or longer."

Huzzah! Tell Irsay to hold the phone. We got ourselves a new stadium, boys; we're back in business! The *howevers* put a halt to that: 1) Indy had a pretty dome of its own, and Michael Machiavelli had already hammered out a super deal; 2) Mayor Schaefer basically said no dice to the offer: "I don't know where

that came from. I heard it this morning," he told the *Morning Sun*. "This is the worst time in the world for people to go through this new-stadium bit. We never promised Mr. Irsay a new stadium. The question of a new stadium should not be raised now, and let us get on with what we're doing." 3) Governor Hughes said he never heard of the guy (Meason); 4) Meason demanded 25-year leases from the Colts and Orioles, a real stretch; and 5) What alien spaceship dropped this guy off?

Besides, the paper-pushers in Annapolis had a bill authorizing $15 million for improvements at Memorial Stadium ($7.5 million for the Orioles, $7.5 for the Colts) if both teams signed six-year leases. On offer since the Taft presidency, Edward Bennett Williams and Bob Irsay weren't lunging to pick up a pen. Hopes got buoyed by a stranger offering to build a field of dreams, but Hizzoner put a match to that: "Even if a group of investors offered to build a multipurpose sports stadium in Baltimore, Mayor William Donald Schaefer says he is not interested," the *Evening Sun* indicated on March 23, 1984. "The mayor said last night that renewed talk about a new stadium would only cloud pending negotiations between the Colts and the Orioles. Because of those talks, he said, reports about Samuel G. Meason's interest in building a sports facility in Baltimore are 'ill-timed.'"

Strange indeed that Meason hadn't talked with any bigshots in Baltimore; he just hit up a few reporters and made his pitch. But Baltimore had blundered down the wrong path again, trying to sell the Colts and Orioles on another dubious plan to fix up the mausoleum if they first signed good-faith leases. Irsay and Williams wouldn't be played for suckers, so the ploy went nowhere (again).

Indy got one step closer to paydirt on March 27: "Colt owner Robert Irsay had phone conversations with officials from both Indianapolis and Phoenix yesterday and set up a meeting in Chicago today with David Frick, the lawyer who leads the Indianapolis negotiating team," the *Morning Sun* announced. "'Frick thinks he's going to Chicago to fine-tune the deal so they can shoot for a closing by Friday,' an Indianapolis source said yesterday. 'We've all been here before, but Frick thinks it's for real this time.'" And you could almost bet the house on David Frick's word. More evidence that the deal was done was Michael Machiavelli going with Irsay to wrap things up. Who knows why Phoenix was still hanging around: "Irsay also gave two Phoenix officials the impression yesterday that he's going

to meet with them 'in the next couple of days,' so it's difficult to predict which city has the edge because Irsay has managed to convince both Phoenix and Indianapolis officials that he is coming to their city by the end of the week," the *Morning Sun* stated. Maybe Phoenix was just Plan B if things went awry with Indy. But only Indianapolis had an actual contract, that new domed stadium and Michael Chernoff selling it hard to Irsay.

Jim Irsay's many protestations that his dad really didn't want to move ring hollow when you look at the bulk and heft of his threats over the years. But he said this on episode 1 of "The Move" podcast: "It was a different time 'cause Al Davis had just moved the Raiders to Los Angeles and took on the league and won in court. And so, when my dad—'cause he wasn't one to really want to move; people think he did—but he had no choice." That last part we can grant, considering the hatred for Irsay in Baltimore and all his badmouthing about the town and the creaky stadium on 33rd. Some folks might be right—there was no turning back.

The *Morning Sun* called it—David Frick *did* head to Chicago to finalize the Indy-Colts deal. "I do remember that we met with Bob Irsay," Frick recalled. "Nick Frenzel, the CEO of Merchants Bank, and I flew up to Chicago and met Bob Irsay at the country club for breakfast. He and Chernoff met with us and we had some discussions about terms. We listened to what he wanted, and Chernoff would tell him, 'We've already got that, Bob.' It was after that meeting that Michael Chernoff and

I excused ourselves, and we went to the airport Hyatt, got into our room, called our lawyers in, and we worked all night, getting the deal documented."

Then came a moment of panic when the press got wind of Frick's visit to Chicago. The *Indianapolis Star* stated, "[Nick] Frenzel [of Merchants Bank] said, 'We completed work on the loan agreement and had that signed and approved by Tuesday afternoon.' Frick finished the lease negotiations, flew back to Indianapolis late Tuesday night and met with [Bill] Hudnut at the mayor's home. 'When I arrived, Mike [Chernoff] was very upset because Baltimore reporters had called him to find out why I was in Chicago. No one was supposed to know, and I know my face went completely white because I thought we had blown it. I only told seven people, and I was disappointed that one of them might have said something. As it happened, someone told someone else. However, Mike then laughed about it, and I knew we were OK again.'"

Talk about irony: Jim Irsay was feeding the press we-don't-know-yets the day *before* he got the call from Pops to pack up: March 28. This was the big story in the *Morning Sun* that day:

> Jimmy Irsay, the son of Colt owner Robert Irsay, was home from the NFL meetings and at the club's Owings Mills complex yesterday, and said he thinks his father will be "talking to all three cities [Baltimore, Phoenix and Indianapolis]"

this week before making a decision 'fairly soon' on where the team will play in 1984 ... Even though he had a "long talk" with his father yesterday after returning from the league meetings in Honolulu, Jimmy Irsay said his father didn't give him any indication whether he's leaning toward Phoenix or Indianapolis, or staying in Baltimore. "You're not going to believe this, but everything is still open," Jimmy Irsay said. "He realizes he has to make a decision fairly soon, but there's nothing definite on any of the fronts. He doesn't have any definite leanings. He wants to touch base with all three cities, then step away and make the decision."

There's no evidence that Irsay the Younger was fibbing. Bob Irsay had the Indy contract in the can and was a sliver away from giving his son the go-sign but was uncharacteristically tight-lipped to the end. Jim Irsay knew only a smidgeon more than reporters dogging his heels.

. . .

The five-alarm fire at the Colts complex was called in when the Maryland Senate passed Bill 1042: "AN ACT concerning Baltimore City—Eminent Domain—Sports Franchises." Mikey, the Wannabe GM (general counsel Chernoff) freaked, got on the blower with his boss, who then called Jim Irsay to activate Operation Skedaddle. The official overview of Senate Bill 1042 read: "FOR the purpose of clarifying a class of property rights which Baltimore City may acquire by nego-tiation or condemnation, by specifically des-ignating professional sports franchises within such class of property rights; stating certain legislative findings; and making this Act an emergency measure." No trickeration here: Baltimore City was trying to snatch the Colts out of Robert Irsay's chubby fingers.

Of course, with a gaggle of lawyers con-structing this, there was a pile of WHEREASES:

- WHEREAS, the existence of a number of teams engaged in pro-fessional sports within Baltimore City has had a salutary effect on the welfare of the inhabitants of this City and contributed substantially both directly and indirectly to the economic development and gen-eral welfare of Baltimore City; and

- WHEREAS, it is in the further-ance of the public interest and pro-motes the common good that such teams continue to operate in Balti-more City and represent the City in the several leagues or associations devoted to professional sports;

Then the let-it-be-knowns:

SECTION 2: AND BE IT FURTHER ENACTED, That the Laws of Maryland read as follows: The Charter of Balti-more City/Article II—General Powers:

(2) (B) TO ACQUIRE BY PURCHASE OR CONDEMNATION ANY PROFESSIONAL SPORTS FRAN-CHISE WHICH HAS OR HAD THE TERRITORIAL RIGHTS TO REPRE-SENT BALTIMORE CITY ON OR AFTER JANUARY 1, 1983, INCLUD-ING, WITHOUT LIMITATION, (1) THE FRANCHISE RIGHT TO COM-PETE IN AN ORGANIZED LEAGUE OR ASSOCIATION; (2) THE BUSI-NESS ENTITY OWNING OR OPER-ATING SUCH FRANCHISE; (3) ALL CONTRACTUAL RIGHTS OWNED BY THE BUSINESS ENTITY WHICH ARE NECESSARY, INCIDENT, AND APPROPRIATE TO OWNERSHIP AND OPERA-TION OF SUCH FRANCHISE… AND TO SELL OR OTHERWISE DISPOSE OF SUCH FRANCHISE AND COLLATERAL RIGHTS, IN WHOLE OR PART, SUBJECT TO SUCH RESTRICTIONS AND RES-ERVATIONS AS MAY BE NECES-SARY OR APPROPRIATE.

At the end, they slipped in a we're-serious-about-this clause: "SECTION 3. AND BE IT FURTHER ENACTED, that this Act is hereby declared to be an emergency measure and necessary for the immediate preservation of the public health and safety… Approved March 29, 1984."

Whether Michael Chernoff had a look-out posted in the Maryland State House or he picked up a paper at a newsstand, he dis-covered the subterfuge and everything got rolling. The *Morning Sun* chronicled the ploy on March 28: "Legislation that would give Baltimore the power to seize ownership of the Colts slipped quietly through the state Senate yesterday on a vote of 38 to 4. Senator Thomas Bromwell (D, Baltimore County), the bill's sponsor, acknowledged he was surprised there wasn't more controversy over the measure, which expands the city's power of 'eminent domain' to include professional sports franchises."

There's no doubt a move was on the horizon, but Professor Charles Euchner says in *Playing the Field* that Bill 1042 signaled to Irsay it was time to scat:

> Before seeking the legislation, Baltimore officials had contacted David Self, the Oakland lawyer who had filed the legal action to condemn the Raiders franchise. Self privately advised Baltimore to avoid state legislative action because it would antagonize Irsay. He claimed that the city already had sufficient authority to take the team. Baltimore officials never contacted him again. Going to the general assembly did indeed alert the Colts. Rather than striking quickly and decisively, Baltimore had just given the Colts notice of an impending war. The legislative process gave Irsay enough time to arrange the team transfer. Irsay later said that he moved the club as a direct result of the legislation. The city also probably undermined its legal case by seeking special [emergency] legislation. The action

reflected the city's lack of confidence in its authority—and gave the courts room to doubt the new legislation.

And just like the stadium paralysis, snubbing the Oakland lawyer and cold-slapping Irsay were two more bloopers by the rubes in Baltimore.

Eminent domain didn't sneak past the folks in Indianapolis. The *Indianapolis Star*—probably daily reading for Michael Machiavelli—had this to say:

> It may be decision time for Robert Irsay. The owner of the Baltimore Colts might have to make up his mind if he is going to move the National Football League team in the next two days, or the decision could be made for him. In Annapolis Tuesday, the Maryland Senate passed without debate legislation that would allow the city of Baltimore to take over the Colts through its power of eminent domain if Irsay tries to move them. The bill went to the Maryland House today and is expected to go to Governor Harry R. Hughes's desk by Thursday. Thus, it would behoove Irsay to announce a move before the bill could be signed into law.

"Announce a move," hell; it was time to make a run for it. Jim Irsay explained his dad's quandary in episode 3 of "The Move" podcast: "The bottom line is they forced him to move because eminent domain means—for people who have never heard of the law—is that it means, 'We're building a new highway for the public interest. We're gonna claim your house, and it says your house is worth $200,000, so you don't have a choice. Here's $200,000; get out of your house 'cause the highway's comin' through.' They were gonna try to use that on the football team: 'OK, we're takin' the Colts because they have to stay here for the public interest.'"

David Frick's skills as a negotiator sewed up the Indy-Colts deal, but he still thinks that Baltimore fumbled on their own 20 with eminent domain:

I'm not sure it was well thought out. Obviously, they should not have done what they did in passing it with an emergency provision that ultimately cost them the franchise. The city's strategy was that they knew they didn't have a winning lawsuit; they just wanted to gum up the works and postpone the Colts from getting into Indianapolis and setting up operations. Once the Colts were here, and you had an operation going, no court was gonna force them to go back to Baltimore. Their strategy was good, but the implementation was terrible. In passing it the way they did, under emergency authorities, they caused him to move. He *couldn't* stay in Baltimore. They would've had him trapped as they fought it through the courts, like Al Davis did in California. It didn't work.

Same thing with the new stadium campaign: good strategy (save the Colts), but the hayseeds bungled the execution. The skedaddle by Irsay the night they found out about eminent domain fostered a myth that may never die—that he "stole" the team in the dark of night like a cat burglar. In reality, he couldn't risk the chance of hanging around for state police to cordon off the place. "I think it's [eminent domain] what triggered the move on such short notice," current Colts COO Pete Ward stated. "I honestly don't know if we would have made the move at all if that hadn't happened. We were kind of treading water in one place, and that's what tipped the glass over. There was still a chance to salvage things. Eminent domain was a declaration of war. So that was it. We probably would have moved regardless, and things were moving rapidly with Indianapolis. But Mr. Irsay had pulled out of deals before, so I don't know that, if not for eminent domain, he would have gone over the edge without that."

Irsay already had a juicy contract with Indy on his desk, and that's probably where he was headed. But suppose you're from L.A. and you're in New York on business. You didn't set your watch three hours forward for EST, you have a meeting at 11:00 only 10 minutes away on foot, and your watch says 7:00. No sweat. Grab some Danish, sip some java, watch a little CNBC. Then the clock on the tube stares at you: 10:00—EST. Blimey! Only an hour to shave, brush my teeth, throw on my Armani suit and scoot down the street! Not a second to dawdle, else I blow this appointment.

THAT'S what caused Irsay and Co. to scram in the wee hours, not some *Ocean's 11* nonsense. Eminent domain rang the alarm. The man wasn't a fraidy cat; Baltimore had thrown down the gauntlet, and the clock was ticking.

David Frick thinks Irsay might have been stuck in neutral until eminent domain came after him. "I think Bob Irsay did *not*, down deep, want to move, would not make the commitment to move. But when the decision was made by the political leadership to pass the bill for eminent domain, that was the key ingredient. Irsay then had to go somewhere. Mike Chernoff and I had pretty much wrapped up the deal, and we were just finalizing the paperwork."

In "The Seduction of the Colts" in the December 9, 1984, *New York Times*, Mikey, the Wannabe GM described the jolt he got when he picked up the newspaper on the 28th: "As Mike Chernoff tells it, the end came suddenly: 'Wednesday, March 28, I awakened and picked up the morning paper. Scanning the sports page, I noticed an item buried away under "Notes." In just a few sentences it mentioned that the Maryland legislature had passed an eminent domain law allowing the city to seize the Colts for public use. They were putting a gun to Mr. Irsay's head and cocking the trigger. I got to the office [in Chicago] first and then Mr. Irsay got there. He asked me if I'd seen the paper and I said, "Yes." Then he simply said to me, "Implement. We're moving to Indianapolis." I said, "Yes, sir."'"

Chernoff typically clammed up for any media other than big boys like the *New York Times* or friendly faces. *BizVoice*, the magazine of the Indiana Chamber of Commerce, got him to opine in their September/October 2011 issue: "We couldn't afford to have that bill signed by the governor. They would have then immediately condemned the Colts and taken it over and we would be out. We had no choice. You are not going to turn over something that you put your blood and money into; you prevent that from happening. We had been negotiating with the city of Baltimore toward trying to get some reasonable resolution of the problems, but now it was wrecked. They demolished it."

They torpedoed it, all right, but a little reality check here: There was no way Baltimore could storm the beachhead and make off with the Colts. Irsay would have thrown this into a courtroom and put up his dukes. The battle would have dragged on for months, appeals might have taken years, and Irsay would have declared victory and kept his ballclub. But Indianapolis would have been the patient sitting alone in the examination room, waiting for Doc to get to him. The Colts and Baltimore engaged in a mano-a-mano in court, an empty dome and irritable citizens, Indy would have had a tough go of it. Irsay was smart to split—pronto.

Former *Evening Sun* columnist, author and Baltimorean Kevin Cowherd agrees that Irsay couldn't afford to hang around:

That [eminent domain] was *the* last straw. He was gonna move. By that point, when Irsay heard the rumblings that the city might claim the team under eminent domain, that was the final bullet in the chamber. Now he has to get out right away. And that's what precipitated everything. He calls [Mayor William] Hudnut, tells him, "We're ready to do this. We gotta get out of here. This city is turning on me. They're gonna claim the team under eminent domain." Hudnut's got a buddy who works for Mayflower [CEO Johnny Smith]. Hudnut coordinates this whole thing: "We're gonna get the Mayflower vans in there, and we're gonna get you out tonight." And that's what they did.

Cooper Rollow of the *Chicago Tribune*—the inventor of the phrase "the world's largest outdoor insane asylum"—sat down with Irsay two months after the move and plied him with questions. He asked Irsay what got him pointed toward Indianapolis besides the generous stadium lease:

> The domed stadium. The terms they gave me, the $15-million loan, the fact they're paying me about a half-million dollars a year to play in the stadium. They're building my $10-million sports complex for a dollar-a-year rent. They've made a lot of commitments on many items that Baltimore never even would talk about. It was just an overall package. It was not the best package. I think Baltimore at the end did come up with a better package. The day before I moved,

the Maryland legislature passed a law on eminent domain, keeping every team in there. Fortunately, it was not signed until Friday, and we left on Wednesday [night]. I just felt it was a very bad situation when the mayor and the governor are negotiating on good terms with me and then to have the legislature pass a law like that.

Again, Baltimore bungled like bush-leaguers: slapping together a wing-dinger of a deal right before midnight; treating Memorial Stadium like a tool shed in the back yard; ignoring the advice of an eminent-domain expert who warned them not to push that button; feuding with a loose cannon instead of schmoozing him to keep the beloved team. Recall what McEnroe shouted to a Wimbledon chair umpire: "How many are you gonna *miss*?!"

In a 1993 article in the *Morning Sun* titled "Colts' Final Days: The Inside Story," Colts offensive line coach Hal Hunter explained why they had to get all the paperwork out of Maryland toot sweet: "At the 5 p.m. meeting, the coaches received final instructions from young Irsay [Jim]. 'We had to get projectors, notebooks, all the things we used, ready. Jim told me the moving company was coming in at 8:30 or 9:00, and gave me a list of how things would go. The first truck was for contracts, legal papers and anything that had to do with players or legal matters. The second truck was to be all the football equipment out of the players' lockers and equipment room.

Each truck had a priority.'" Physical location—the need to get the paperwork out of Maryland—would be crucial when this tussle went to court.

Who knows whether Phoenix lawyer Harry Cavanagh was just bitter that Phoenix got kicked to the curb or a Maryland crabcake gave him food poisoning. Quoted in the *Indianapolis Star* on March 29 when he was told that the moving vans were in Owings Mills, Cavanagh said, "I think they [the Colts] made the deal that made the most business sense. Indianapolis was willing to make more guarantees. It's like he [Irsay] is trying to decide between three Miss Americas and if he chooses Baltimore, he chooses the ugly one."

* * *

A real busybody could have tracked this maneuver and sent the alarm out to Baltimore, but Indy was clandestine enough to slip this by unnoticed. The convoy of moving vans that swooped in on the Colts complex in Owings Mills, MD, was assembled piecemeal. In the *Indianapolis Star's* 30th anniversary exposé about the Colts' move, "Remembering How Colts' Move from Baltimore Went Down," Mayflower Moving supervisor Rick Russell explained how they snatched vans from hither and yon to avoid suspicion:

> We had guys in our traffic department in Indianapolis searching for empty tractor-trailer units starting out within 100 miles of the Baltimore training facility.

We probably had 3,000 trucks then (but) they had to get there quickly. We widened the circle to 200, 300 miles before we came up with 14 empty ones that were available to handle the job. We didn't tell the drivers what they were going to be doing. We just gave them a location to head towards. They went to our Alexandria [VA] office and then gradually were sent out one at a time to the Baltimore facility in Owings Mills. I think the first tractor trailer was there in the 7 p.m. range, not long after dark [on March 28, 1984]. Then we just kind of sent them in one at a time. There wasn't room to have all 14 there. The media was onto it by 8 or 9 p.m. They started showing up, knew we were there and what we were doing. We had enough people on the scene to do the job fairly quickly.

Colts equipment manager Jon Scott lived up the hill from headquarters and got the official word from Jim Irsay to pack everything up:

> I lived at an apartment called Morningside Heights, where a lot of the players lived, and it overlooked the complex. So, I was *that* close. That was a Tuesday [when the eminent domain bill was introduced], and about 10:00 that night, I get a telephone call. I pick it up, and I recognized the voice right away. It was Jim Irsay: "Jonny, I just talked to my dad. We're movin'." It's the 27th [of

March], at night, and I go, "Oh, my gosh. When?" He said, "Tomorrow." And I go, "Oh, my gosh." Then I said, "Phoenix?" "Well…" And there's a long pause. He goes, "No, Indy." Then he told me, "Hey, you gotta keep this quiet. You can't tell any of the staff workin' with the Colts. You can't tell your friends. You gotta keep it quiet from your family." I go, "What's goin' on?" We didn't know at the time the state of Maryland, the city of Baltimore, they're tryin' to get the team through eminent domain.

News of the eminent domain broadside created a chain reaction: Michael Machiavelli-Chernoff and Bob Irsay had a quick yeah-I-know chat, Irsay grabbed the phone and called Mayor Hudnut, and Hudnut got Mayflower CEO Johnny B. Smith on the phone and told the movers to get jumping. When the caravan arrived, the Baltimore media were zooming up the driveway in dribs and drabs. Vito Stellino of the *Morning Sun* filed this report: "A fleet of moving vans arrived at the Colts complex in Owings Mills last night amid reports that a deal had been finalized to move the Colts to Indianapolis. Pinkerton security guards kept the complex gates locked to keep away reporters and photographers as police kept traffic moving in front of the facility. The vans arrived shortly after Colts general counsel Michael Chernoff flew into Baltimore on owner Robert Irsay's private plane last night after spending the day in Indianapolis meeting with David Frick, the

city's former deputy mayor and head of the negotiating team trying to lure the National Football League club there."

Stellino wasn't sure Irsay had it in him to push the button:

Not until the trucks pulled up that night. Because you never knew what Irsay was gonna do. And late March was pretty late to move a team. Is he gonna stay another year? There wasn't a point where you said, "Yeah, he's definitely moving." He was so unpredictable that you had to wait and see how it played out. I don't even know if he was hell-bent on moving. He was Irsay. You never knew what he was hell-bent on doing. I think he was still reluctant to pull the trigger. At that time, teams weren't moving, and the fact that he didn't do it a couple months earlier [to Phoenix] when we thought he was gonna move, you just couldn't predict what he would do. But at that point, it was a big topic of conversation. We were in a wait-and-see mode.

Chernoff and Frick huddled on Tuesday the 27th for a final look at the contract, and the Indy contingent was pretty sure they had it locked. Michael Machiavelli had been goosing Irsay toward Indianapolis all along, and the eminent domain sneak attack turned Irsay's raspberry cheeks crimson. There was this no-duh in the *Morning Sun* on the 29th: "Lou Panos, Governor [Harry] Hughes's press secretary, said he agreed with a television commentator who said the eminent domain legislation may have angered Mr. Irsay. 'I don't think that helped sway the decision toward Baltimore, and it might account for the surreptitious' goings on last night. 'It's just too hard to analyze what this man [Irsay] does and why he does it,' Panos said." In this case, not hard at all. There was the lawyer from Oakland who swung away at eminent domain and warned Baltimore that Irsay would blow his stack and bolt. Once again, the town bungled things.

In episode 3 of "The Move" podcast, front-office executive Pete Ward recalled when he got the word from Jim Irsay:

Late in the day [March 28], Jim [Irsay] calls me in his office and says, "My dad says we're moving tonight to Indy. Go home; get your personal life in order." I lived like five minutes away in an apartment. "But be back here by 10:00 because all the trucks are gonna arrive, and you need to bring some semblance of order to the move." And I had very few possessions and not much of a personal life, so that part was easy for me. After the Phoenix thing, I had to hire a guard company [Pinkerton] with guard dogs because we were getting death threats and bomb threats. We had them on call, and right after I was told we're moving, I called them up, so we had security there.

Linebackers coach Rick Venturi got the call about a big meeting with Jim Irsay before the move kicked off:

About midday, [offensive line coach] Hal Hunter, who was a real close friend and staff mate, stopped me in the hallway, took me aside very quietly, and said to me, "Don't go home after work tonight," which was odd in the offseason back then. He said, "Coach [Frank Kush] is coming in for a very important meeting. So, no matter what happens, just hang around here after work." We were scheduled to have a meeting with Jim [Irsay] at about 6:30. The meeting was held up a little bit till around 8:30. [PR director] Walt Gutowski was playing racquetball, and he wasn't part of the move. So, this gigantic meeting was held up by a racquetball game. We get around to the meeting about 8:30—the coaching staff, a couple key guys with Jim—and we were sitting at the conference table. In those days, before he made a presentation, Jim always cleared his throat. And he said, "Men, the deal has been done. We're moving to Indianapolis tonight. We will move with the secrecy of moving an embassy. The trucks will be here at 11:00. You will all assist in the move. You will not tell your wives, your girlfriends; you will tell no one. This will be stealth." I remember calling [Venturi's wife] Sherry, and I said, "Honey, I'm gonna be late tonight." And she said, "Well, how late is that gonna be?" And I said, "I don't know if I'll be home or not." She told me, "Well, *that's* gonna take an explanation."

This was no Operation Overlord; Irsay's call was a bolt from the blue and they scrambled. "There were no discussions [before the actual move]," Jon Scott emphasized. "I get that call [from Jim Irsay on the 27th], and I knew, *I gotta start packing up everything*. And knowing that I didn't have enough boxes, I'd go behind a grocery store and grab boxes and load up the team van I had. But no one came down [from the front office] telling me, the trainers or the film guys, 'Hey, let's have a meeting about this move.' There was never any discussion about that." Primarily because Irsay set off the bomb the moment Maryland pulled eminent domain.

Mayflower needed some extra warm bodies with strong backs to hump a whole complex into the vans. Somebody had a brainstorm: Recruit some college kids nearby. They rang up the Sigma Chi, Gamma Chi chapter at the University of Maryland and pitched their offer. Deadspin.com has a 2014 article titled "The Frat Boys Who Moved the Colts Out of Baltimore." The phone rang at Sigma Chi. "Joe Ponzo, then a junior at Maryland and a Sigma Chi brother, remembers hearing the phone ring on the second floor of the frat house on the College Park campus and taking the call from a Mayflower supervisor that got it all started. 'We had a lot of guys who worked part-time, and they said they needed a lot of people that night and they were paying $10 an hour [about $31 now],' says Ponzo. 'So I went to the lunch room and told the guys. Everybody said no. So I go back to the phone and he said he'd go to

$15. They said no again.' Ponzo says he had too much schoolwork to take on any moving job, but he bargained hard on behalf of his brothers and ultimately goaded Mayflower into upping the rate to $20 an hour—'paid in cash,' he says [almost $62 now]."

Jim Irsay called it a stealth operation, and that it was. "Even after they'd boarded the bus alongside several veteran Mayflower movers and decamped from College Park, the [frat] brothers weren't told where they were going," the deadspin.com article continued. "That level of secrecy seems unnecessary, given that this was years before cellphones and social media. But the unknown caused the youngsters' minds to race. 'We were thinking it had to be CIA or something in D.C.,' says [Duffy] Welsh, whose father, George Welsh was the longtime football coach at the University of Virginia and the U.S. Naval Academy. But the buses headed north, away from the nation's capital. It wasn't until they turned at the exit sign on the interstate for Owings Mills that it dawned on Greg Gaston, who now hosts a sports talk show middays on WHBQ-AM Memphis, what was going on. They knew where the Colts' headquarters were located."

Inside the Colts complex, human spinning tops were careening all over the joint. Jon Scott had a full plate, packing up all the equipment and keeping an eye on the college kids:

I only got a couple hours' sleep [after Jim Irsay called], got to the complex, looked to see if anyone was there at 4:00 in the morning. I just went into the equipment room, looked at all of the stuff and thought, *I can't believe this is gonna happen.* Then you get in a work mode, and you do it. I shut the door of the equipment room. I didn't know if anyone else knew, so I just started boxing things up and labeling them. That took a good portion of the day. Then I started working on the locker room. When the movers came in, they started taking the boxes into the trucks, and you had to trust those guys. I had heard that the busload of guys that came in were from D.C. I'm thinking, *Well, they're Redskins fans.* Then, I'm looking at these guys, and it's a cold night, and they've got jackets on. But then I see the words "Baltimore" and "Colts" under their shirts, and I think, *Holy crap. They're ripping me off.* I talked to the foreman: "Hey, what's goin' on?" He goes, "Hang on. Give me 10 minutes." He came back 10 minutes later, and there's a mountain of stuff on the floor. And quite frankly, I'm sure we did lose some stuff.

They were kids in a candy store with Colts booty for the picking. Until they got nabbed. "The Frat Boys Who Moved the Colts Out of Baltimore" described the timeout to hand over the goodies:

> The thievery got so bad that Mayflower management called a timeout in the middle of the night and gathered the workers in a meeting room. A company official told the crew that so long as everybody agreed to stop stealing and to pile up any illicit bounty they'd already filched in a corner of the room, Mayflower wouldn't get anybody in trouble. Mark Updegrove, a New Jersey native, recalls watching his frat brothers, having fattened themselves on stolen Colts gear, beginning to thin out as they took advantage of the amnesty deal. The regular Mayflower staffers couldn't hide their hate for the collegians. "All my guys from Sigma Chi, well, we looked like Michelin Men," Updegrove said. "I remember watching a friend of mine peel off more layers than an onion, and this one [Mayflower] lifer just started shaking his head with this look of utter disgust at all of us. 'That boy's got shoulder pads on! And he's got Coach's pants on! Look at him!'"

The import of the move socked Jim Irsay in the ribs when he saw the vans roll in. He described the moment in the 30-for-30 documentary, *The Band That Wouldn't Die*: "When those trucks were in low gear and were pulling up the hill in Owings Mills, that's the thing that I'll never forget. To hear them—that was the thing. I was like, 'My God. That is so loud. Everyone in the state of Maryland has to hear that.' You literally felt that there was an earthquake occurring, from many different standpoints. You know, it was complete chaos, and there was some feeling that there was literally gonna be state troopers with bazookas, say-ing, 'Turn those trucks around.'"

The move didn't change Irsay's status in Baltimore one scintilla—pariah then, pariah now, pariah forever—but Mayflower also became a dirty word. Charlie Euchner in *Playing the Field* lumped the two lepers together:

The scene at the Owings Mills complex became more vivid in the public mind as time passed, and it was an impor-tant influence in the city's eventual deci-sion to build a new stadium. The image of the departing moving vans became the symbol of Robert Irsay's under-handed and cowardly ways. The name *Mayflower* took on sinister overtones, because that was the moving company that did the dirty deed. Irsay's action was dubbed the "midnight move" and "midnight raid," conjuring up images of furtiveness and deceit. Irsay was reviled as a coward, a carpetbagger; his physi-cal attributes were the source of bitter local parody. Bumper stickers condensed the long and sorry episode: "Will Rog-ers Never Met Bob Irsay."

Pete Ward eventually became buddies with Jim Irsay and got promoted to Colts chief operating officer. The move was a life-changer:

It started like any other day for me, and I was convinced that we were gonna be in Baltimore for the [1984] season because it was so late in the year. We

had the draft in less than four weeks, and shortly after that, we'd have mini-camps and training camp. We had just signed a new deal with Western Mary-land College [McDaniel]. So, Jim Irsay called me into his office late in the day and said, "We're moving to Indianap-olis, and we want you to come with us." Sure enough, at 10:00 at night [March 28], the trucks started rolling in. They had their lights off because we were out on Bonita Avenue, just off Reis-terstown Road. We had 14 trucks and a bus. I was wondering what the bus was for. I thought maybe they ran out of trucks. I got on the bus, and all the packers [college kids] were there. They didn't know they had come to the Bal-timore Colts headquarters. One guy asked me if it was an embassy; they had moved embassies before in the middle of the night. "No," I said, "it's a foot-ball team." Another guy asked, "Which team is this?" I told him, "The Balti-more Colts. You're in Baltimore." So, they descended on the complex, and there was a supervisor, but because it had to be done in 10 hours—and hast-ily—they descended on all areas of the complex at once. So, there was no label-ling of boxes. I couldn't be everywhere at once; nor could Jim or our equip-ment guy [Jon Scott]. It was kind of a chaotic scene. I finally went into my office to make sure that everything was packed and labelled. That kind of contributed to the chaotic feeling when we got to Indianapolis because they dumped everything in an elementary school auditorium. We had to figure out what was what and where it was going when we should have been focused on business. So, it was playing catch-up from Day One. There were no memorable discussions at the Colts complex that night; it was all focused on the move, getting everything out, trying to get it done before daylight. The goal was to do it before a court order was signed that would halt everything.

At least one of the frat boys got a guilty conscience about helping the Colts sneak out the back door. "The utter strangeness of the job impressed itself on [Mark] Updegrove as he and his buddies broke down the Colts' trophy case, which contained baubles from the team's various NFL titles, including Weeb Ewbank's fedora and what looked like the Lombardi Trophy from Super Bowl V. 'So I'm holding these championship trophies and thinking about how great this team really was,' he said. 'Right away, it hit me that leaving town in secret in the middle of the night just wasn't right for the Colts' fans, that what Irsay was doing was the ultimate sissy move.'"

The news started cascading all over Baltimore, and a horde of fans and reporters invaded the campus. "As night headed toward morning and the thrill of being surrounded by professional football tchotchkes wore off, the move became more like any other move,"

"The Frat Boys Who Moved the Colts Out of Baltimore" recounted. "Crowds began gathering at the complex as word got around Baltimore about what was happening in Owings Mills. Fans and reporters were kept outside. [John] Ziemann, who worked for a local TV station, watched the movers while standing among the banned. He didn't see any biker gang doing the work [which was the speculation]. 'There weren't any Hell's Angels,' he says. 'I was outside and I saw the kids [students].'"

One reporter was poised to cover the chaos, *Evening Sun* columnist Kevin Cowherd:

I was at the *Evening Sun* that night. We kept getting phone calls from people who lived out near the Colts complex. And people kept saying the same thing: "Hey, there's a lot of noise going on at the Colts complex. We're hearing trucks and a lot of noise." The calls kept coming in. So, around 10:00, I was sent out there. I left with Phil Jackman [sports columnist] and a couple other people, and we went out to the Colts complex. It was an amazing sight. Along the road leading in, cars were already lined up. By this time, it was 11:00. And sure enough, the Colts complex is lit up, and you hear trucks and things thumping inside the moving vans. And we said, "Holy shit. This is it." That went on all night long. More and more people showed up. By now, media were all over the place. At some point, it starts to snow hard, and eventually, around one or two in the morning, the gates would open, and a moving van would leave. We stayed there all night, till about six in the morning when the last Mayflower van left. I just remember about 7:00 the following morning, Chris Thomas [WBAL-TV], Jackman, me and a photographer, sitting in a coffee shop, thinking, *Holy cow. The Colts are gone.* We were just in shock. And there were people in that coffee shop who had just heard the news: "The Baltimore Colts have left Baltimore." And that's all they talked about. They were in shock: "Can you believe this happened?" It was surreal.

Colts band PR director John Ziemann was out that night, checking out some prospects when he found out: "At the time, besides being in the drumline, I was also percussion instructor, plus public relations director. My wife, Sharlene, was the flagline instructor. That night, we had auditions. For some reason, going home, we did not have the radio on. We got home, and the babysitter was there. She just looked at Sharlene and me and pointed at the television. I saw Mayflower moving vans and 'Baltimore Colts,' and she didn't have to say anything. I got a call from Wayne Lynch [WMAR-TV newsroom director]. He said, 'Hate to do this to you, Z, but I gotta pull you in.' I was the last one in. He said, 'You need a light kit [equipment]. Meet [reporter] Susan White-Bowden out at the complex.'"

The sportscaster for WMAR-TV was Scott Garceau, the intrepid ace who caught Irsay, Michael Machiavelli and two tarts at a craps table in Vegas. Once the move went into overdrive, he was in for a long night:

On the night of the move, I'm doing the 6:00 and 11:00 news, and we start getting calls around 9:00, 9:30, that there's some action going on out at Owings Mills. We send crews out. Nelson Benton, longtime CBS newsman, is our news anchor. Now, we're getting pictures of those Mayflower vans, and we extend the 11:00 newscast. We can see with our eyes the moving vans and what's going on. We stay on the air. Meanwhile, the "Today" show—because we're an NBC affiliate—they want a piece from me for the morning show. The crew gets back about two in the morning. I start working on the piece for the "Today" show. I finish that up, and I leave the station, and it's daybreak. I'm running on adrenaline; it's one of the biggest stories I've covered. I go home, get a few hours' sleep, then I dig in the next day and see the shot of [Mayor] Schaefer coming down the steps [of his house] with tears in his eyes, saying the man always told me he'd call me before he did this. This town was kicked right between the legs, a gut punch—maybe a little below the gut. Man, the unthinkable has happened—we don't have a football team.

With the trucks chugging west to Indy, who knew if Governor Hughes would call out the National Guard with bazookas to stop the convoy? Mayflower execs were taking no chances. "The last truck left at about 4 a.m. on March 29," supervisor Rick Russell stated in "Remembering How Colts' Move from Baltimore Went Down." "The drivers were instructed to scatter. We didn't want to be in a caravan. We didn't want them hanging out together so as to draw attention to them. We told them to drive 100 miles or so and find a place to get some sleep, then call in the next morning, and we would give them their next instructions."

Jim Irsay was somewhere in the building after the trucks pulled out. Getting him out without an angry mob stringing him up on a lamp post took some planning. Equipment manager Jon Scott had an idea—ferry him out in his car:

Now, it's probably 2:00 in the morning, and I'm thinking, *Well, as we pull out, I'm sure there's gonna be press and everybody else. What if they see Jim Irsay?* Jim said, "I'm gonna hide down here, on the passenger's side." I had a blanket in the back, and I threw the blanket over Jim, so he wouldn't be seen if we got stopped. Sure enough, we pulled up, and press was everywhere. They were looking at me; no one was pounding on my vehicle or anything. They allowed me to pass through there, thinking it was just me, the equipment guy. We [Scott and Jim Irsay] went over to my apartment, got a few hours' sleep, then we flew out of Washington. We didn't go to Baltimore.

To avoid winding up like Mussolini and his mistress.

John Ziemann remembers the guy who was playing racquetball and held up the move. "We [the WMAR-TV crew] were out there all night in the freezing rain and snow. And it was tough. In the morning, the employees came in. When they got there, I found out they didn't have any furniture to sit in. They more or less put the phones on the floor, picked up the desks and put them in the moving vans. Just stripped it. All their [employee severance] checks were from a bank in Indianapolis. Now, you don't do that overnight. Come on. It was all done for months. The last one out was [PR director] Walter Gutowski. That night, he was working [and playing racquetball] and came out to the parking lot and saw all the coaches' lights on. He knew something was up. He went back in, saw them packing up the boxes and went in and cleaned out his desk, knowing what was coming, and went home. He came back the next morning, and he was the last one out. I remember him closing the gate, and we're standing out there in the cold. And he told us, 'Guys, it's over. Go on home. There's no use standing out here in the cold.' And that was it."

Ken Murray of the *Morning Sun* was out there, covering the story. It was like nothing he had ever seen. "It was a surreal scene," Murray stated in "30 Years on, Baltimore Better Without the Colts." "I remember feeling a numbness, not from the cold, but from the realization it was actually happening. I was standing in on history, watching the physical dismantling of one of the NFL's great franchises. A handful of people had gathered [at first], as much in curiosity as anything else. It was solemn and funeral-like."

The emigrants invited PR man Walt Gutowski to come along, but he had already decided to pull an Ernie Accorsi and ditch the operation. Patti Singer of the York *Daily Record* asked him about it:

> Even before the Colts galloped out of Baltimore and hi-hoed it to Indianapolis, one of the Colts jumped the fence. Walt Gutowski, the public relations director while the Colts played at Memorial Stadium, left his job for reasons he declined to say. The fact that a once-World Championship football team was turned into a fly-by-night organization may have had something to do with it, but Gutowski said he decided to leave the Colts before the March 29 flight. The team made him an offer to continue as PR director in Indianapolis, but he turned it down. "My gut feeling was that they were going to do it, especially after the Indianapolis deal crystalized," he said. "When you look at that deal, it was made to order, with its proximity to Chicago."

When the move came, regular staff felt like they were thrown down the basement steps. "'Part of the feeling in the office as it dragged

on was a lot of them were lulled into a false sense of security,' Gutowski said. 'They said, "It's not going to happen." They started to feel a little more secure. Then, bang, it happened overnight.' Nearly a week after the fact, what still seems to surprise Gutowski is that the entire training complex, 43,000 square feet filled with pads, helmets, cleats, weights, footballs, air pumps and a six-foot Jacuzzi could be cleared out in one night. 'I didn't think they could get it done that quick,' he said. 'They did. They had enough trucks. They made it happen.'"

Former *Evening Sun* columnist Kevin Cowherd likewise couldn't get over what went down that night. "At one point, when I was standing out there, watching this, I said to Chris Thomas [of WBAL-TV], 'This is like a Fellini movie. Here you have the snow coming down, almost blowing sideways, the gloom, the darkness, the lit-up Colts complex in the distance that we can't get near. This is like the most surreal thing that I've ever been a part of.' And to this day, it's probably the most surreal story I ever covered."

. . .

Jon Scott and Jim Irsay spent the night after the move hiding out in Scott's apartment and getting some shuteye. Precautions had been made for the flight to Indy to avoid getting bushwhacked by the masses. He got the itinerary from Junior:

> We were never told what was next. Now, it's after midnight, and I remember Jim

[Irsay] coming down, and I was close to being finished. That's when he said to me, "You and I are gonna fly out [to Indianapolis] tomorrow on my dad's plane, along with Frank Kush and Mike Chernoff. We're gonna fly to Indianapolis the next morning [the 29th]." But Jim said, "I'm gonna need to stay at your apartment [tonight] because there's too many death threats and everything else." If I'm not mistaken, Jim had sent his wife and his two young daughters down to Florida because he was afraid that something would happen. He couldn't go back to his place.

This was probably around the time that Jim Irsay called an impromptu meeting after everything was packed and ready. "Maybe it was 2-3 in the morning, and Jim called us together," assistant coach Rick Venturi recalled. "Remember, this is not a very big crew. We really moved to Indianapolis in Irsay's private plane with enough people for three station wagons. They were mom-and-pop operations, not like it is now. Jim called us all together and said, 'This is all we can do now. Just stay cool, and we will take my father's plane out to Indy. We'll fly out of Dulles [airport]; we obviously can't fly out of Baltimore. We'll go out to Indianapolis.' And the eerie part of it is that at 5:00 that evening [the 28th], that was a fully functioning complex. And by dawn, it was like an empty airplane hangar."

After the hurly-burly that long evening, Pete Ward slept like a hobo. "I fell asleep on the floor in my empty office," he reminisced in "Remembering How Colts' Move from Baltimore Went Down." "When I woke up, there were employees arriving for work. They didn't know what else to do, so they came in. It was 8:30 in the morning. I lifted my head off of the floor and here were my fellow employees staring at me. That was an emotional moment. They were all pretty broken-up about it. They had no Idea what was going on, what the future held for them. We had a company meeting and basically said who was going and who was not. I wasn't in charge of that, but that's how it went down."

The bunch that absconded had to know this was a crummy way to treat the folks who got left behind. A WMAR-TV news crew stopped assistant PR director Marge Blatt on her way out after getting jettisoned: "When you have to sneak out in the middle of the night, don't inform your employees of your intentions, I don't wanna work for people like that. I wouldn't go [to Indianapolis]—unless I were paid a million dollars—then I would have to think about it. Really. Because I think these were very poor tactics with employees. I had entered my 11th year with the Baltimore Colts, and to not inform people about what is going to happen, I think is really despicable."

As usual, Baltimore shut the barn door after the Hosses ran out. "Gov. Harry R. Hughes this afternoon signed special eminent domain legislation allowing the city to try to condemn the Colts in hopes that the team might still be kept here," the *Evening Sun* reported on March 29. "The special legislation permitting such a legal maneuver passed the House of Delegates earlier. This morning a dozen loaded moving vans rumbled out of the Colt training complex and down the highway leading to Indianapolis, leaving behind a bitter and humiliated Mayor William Donald Schaefer. Somber and dejected as he left home today, Schaefer said, 'The trucks were out there, and I think that's the final humiliation … If the Colts had to sneak out of town at night, it degrades a great city. And I hate to see a grown man cry.'"

Pushing aside Bob Irsay's gripes about the fans and the press for the moment, the blood and guts of the two deals had Baltimore besting Indy. But Indy's killer trump card had always been the Dome; Baltimore's Achilles heel Memorial Stadium: Sophia Loren vs. Ethel Mertz. "The Baltimore Colts, whose tradition was once one of the proudest in the NFL, will move to Indianapolis next season, Mayor William Hudnut announced yesterday, hours after a fleet of moving vans emptied the team's Baltimore-area offices in the middle of the night," the *Washington Post* revealed on March 30. "In Baltimore, officials had said all along that they could not match the domed stadium that Indianapolis had to offer, but they had hoped the 31-year-old tradition of the Colts would hold them." So, besides being: 1) arrogant; 2) apathetic; 3) backwards; 4) balkanized; and 5) foolish; they were also 6) naïve.

The funeral was announced in gargantuan font on the front page of the March 30 *Morning Sun*: **Baltimore's Colts are gone**. Mayor

Schaefer had a few words for Irsay and Mikey, the Wannabe GM: "I want Mr. Irsay and Mr. Chernoff to know that we don't like this. They have taken away from us a great tradition. There are some people who almost live for the Colts. They're the ones. They're the great Colt fans. I'm not the No. 1 fan. I'm the No. 1 guy who maybe's been used by somebody."

The *Morning Sun* on the 30th indicated that Schaefer and Gov. Hughes gave it one last shot a few days before Irsay cleared out. "Governor Hughes said Mr. Irsay flew into Washington's National Airport Sunday [March 25] for an unannounced meeting with Mayor Schaefer and Mr. [secretary of economic and community development Frank] De Francis at a nearby country club, and the deal that the government officials believed met all his demands was presented. But Mr. Irsay issued a 'whole list of new demands' in a telephone conversation with Mr. De Francis Tuesday night [the 27th], the economic development secretary said—and that was the last contact between the owner and government officials here." Efforts to get Irsay on the horn were for nought.

What probably happened was Irsay was already hooked on Indianapolis, tossed that stun grenade at Schaefer and Co. for cover when the press came calling, then scooted out of town. Even at City Hall right after the move, Schaefer still wouldn't uncork his infamous temper. "I take this as sort of in a way very personal," WMAR-TV broadcast in its special, *The Long Goodbye*. "For two years, I tried. I had to live through Jacksonville [1979],

Memphis [1976, 1983] and Phoenix [1984] and all the rest of these. And we worked very, very hard—sometimes quietly, sometimes with a little irritation. So, in a way, this is personal. It gets to be very personal to me when someone I thought would at least pick up the phone and say to me, 'I'm going.' But he didn't."

Pack up and leave—understood. But the one-finger salute to Schaefer on the way out was genuine scurvy. The *Evening Sun* empathized:

It's not that the mayor sat back waiting for Irsay to call that Wednesday [the 28th]. That day, he [Schaefer] left four messages with the team owner because he wanted to discuss the loan package the city and state developed for him. No response. Even after that near-sleepless night yesterday, the mayor's office placed a call to Irsay in Chicago. Schaefer said he's certain Irsay got the message. No response. He said he's almost as certain that the man who once said, "Don Schaefer is my friend" won't return the call. Ever. "He didn't call his old friend, Don," the mayor said bitterly.

Even the ones who figured Irsay would head for the exit thought his snub of Schaefer was shabby and cheap. Go you one better: Even the choir who defended the move would call it a two-bit cop out. *Morning Sun* sports editor Bob Maisel wrote, "Maybe the most distasteful part of the whole seamy act was Irsay's humiliation of William Donald Schaefer, a good man and one of the best mayors in the country, to the point of reneging on his promise to at least call to notify him when the deed was finally done. That, too, was not only typical but predictable."

Michael Machiavelli likewise deserves a hide-strapping for being half a man. Schaefer groused to reporters, "I feel very disturbed that he would let [Colts lawyer Michael] Chernoff sneak into town and not even have the common decency to pick up the phone and tell me, 'I made a deal in Indianapolis.'"

The *Miami Herald* provided analysis on April 8 and saw Schaefer as a rare hero in this saga: "For all the hate Baltimoreans hold for Robert Irsay, they hold just as much respect for mayor William Donald Schaefer. 'What hurt was the way he treated our mayor,' said Irv Hoffines, hunched over a beer at Brownie's, beneath an oil painting of John Unitas. 'He's one of the best mayors in the country.'" But Schaefer basically pulled a Lindbergh on this mission, flying solo with an occasional assist from Governors Mandel and Hughes. The odds were long no matter how much blood, sweat and inspiration he put into it.

But change your vantage point, then take another look. Mayor Schaefer kept his lip buttoned and placated the man so Irsay wouldn't melt down like Chernobyl. With all that hate in Baltimore, maybe Irsay saw Schaefer as a buddy—"my friend, Don." But when Baltimore socked him with eminent domain, he felt Schaefer had betrayed him, so guess what—forget the phone call, bub.

John Steadman 15 years later brought that up in the *Morning Sun*:

> Irsay, in all fairness, was not a malicious man. His drinking presented problems in change of personality and deportment. Schaefer, the record shows, and as those survivors from that time so well remember, tried to humor him, much as you might do with a difficult child. It was a ploy. Irsay, unpredictable as could be, believed Schaefer was the only true friend he had in Baltimore. Schaefer insisted Irsay gave his word he would not take the team away. Irsay assumed he had a staunch ally in Schaefer, but when the eminent-domain action was filed, the Colts vanished under the cover of darkness—like thieves in the night. A reprehensible act, but not as difficult for the rest of the country to accept as the 1995 Cleveland defection to Baltimore.

Irsay shipped old-school warrior Johnny Unitas out to San Diego to graze. No surprise, then, that Johnny U vented after the move. "Robert Irsay has done nothing but rape the team since he got here," Unitas told the *Evening Sun*. "He has done nothing but slap the people in the face since he got here. He took Colt football, which was the top franchise in the country, to the outhouse and it is sad. I'm sorry to see it happen, but believe me, this city is going to be a lot better off without him. I blame the league too. A man like Irsay and his background should never have been permitted to get into football. Just because he has the money shouldn't mean anything. It's [Commissioner Pete] Rozelle's problem to go back further than the money."

Heroes of the glory days echoed The Golden Arm. Talented safety Rick Volk stated, "Over the last few years, the support has dwindled down because of the owner and the organization. We'll miss what was on the field during those championship years more than anything else." Hall of Famer Lenny Moore worked for Irsay in the front office as community relations director. "Over the years, I could see from the inside that the organization was going down to nothing. It was complete decay after Mr. Irsay took over," he lamented.

Good thing Irsay's plane didn't invade Baltimore air space once word got out. They might've scrambled the Maryland Air National Guard to take it down. Baltimore fans felt like they were kicked in the stomach. "I *was* a Colts fan," former season-ticketholder Charlie Meagher told the *Evening Sun*. He was plopped on a stool at a Towson bar right next to a Robert Irsay dartboard. "But I haven't been a fan since Irsay did his act. I've only been to two games in the last seven years." Bartender Joe Aberle was tired of the abuse. "This is different from a strike or anything else. We've had this rubbed in our nose for a long time now. He [Irsay] could bring the team back, but his attendance would be nothing."

The spittle was flying in Baltimore. "Although Baltimore had feared the loss of the Colts ever since Mr. Irsay opened negotiations with Indianapolis and Phoenix several weeks ago, the sudden departure stunned the city," the *New York Times* chronicled. "'It's sickening,' said Brian Yaniger, one of the few fans who went to the suburban training center [complex] as the moving vans were being loaded early yesterday. 'It's unbelievable, the callousness of this man.' He added, 'Just because he has a couple of bucks, he can tear a whole city down on his whims.'"

A former member of the Colts Corrals likened the blow to being cuckolded. "It's like being married for 25 years, and your wife leaves you for somebody else," he said in the documentary, *The Band That Wouldn't Die.* "Occasionally, you see her on the street, like you see the Colts on TV, and you couldn't quite watch it. It hurt too much. It's not just the game; it's not just the team; it's everything involved. You're emotionally attached. And when they leave you, there's a big void there that never quite heals."

Naturally, John Steadman treated this like the Lincoln assassination. But he did have his finger on the pulse of the town in *From Colts to Ravens*:

Since that infamous midnight ride of March 28, 1984, when Irsay and the Colts suddenly vanished, Baltimore endured what seemed a bad dream. The move of the team occasioned two reactions: self-sympathy and brutal denunciation of Irsay. The city kept reminding itself of what it had lost; it was a community wronged by a reckless man who knew little about its grand football history and the fans' passionate love for a team. He simply didn't care … The Colts' loss in 1984 cut deeply into the psyche of Baltimore. It was so unprofessional for a team to up and disappear one stormy night in March. A dirty deed had been perpetrated under the cover of darkness, and it brought with it the kind of shame associated with a holdup on the street.

A plot like this could have been ripped from the pages of Sir Arthur Conan Doyle. "The shock was, 'Well, he finally did it,'" Baltimore author Kevin Cowherd admitted. "Did we think he was gonna do it? Yeah, of course. And he did it quickly, in the dead of night. There is something almost poetic about that. Here it is, during this crappy night, and here are these Mayflower vans taking this team away. It was right out of Edgar Allan Poe or Robert Louis Stevenson."

Superfan Hurst C. "Loudy" Loudenslager probably needed a grief counselor that night; the man had played the Colts fight song at the airport for the team coming and going 626 times. "I've got over half of my life tied up with this club," Loudy proclaimed to the *Evening Sun.* "I've got a lot of love tied up in this team. Just what are we going to do in the fall? It hasn't totally hit yet, but it will then. Irsay may have owned this team with his money, but I owned them with my heart."

This was one time when being maudlin wasn't a sin. "On March 28, 1984, the Colts sneaked out of Baltimore on a snowy night and left a football town in mourning,"

Jamison Hensley noted in "30 Years on, Baltimore Better Without Colts." "Grown men and women cried. People drove around the city the next morning with their headlights on as if somebody died. 'It's one of those few moments in life that you vividly remember,' said John Moag, who later lured the Cleveland Browns to Baltimore as chairman of the Maryland Stadium Authority. 'You hate to put it up with the assassination of John Kennedy, but it had that type of import here.'"

A little over a decade before he would pull the same stunt, Art Modell of the Browns was rich with foreboding and righteous indignation. "This is the legacy of the [Al Davis] Raider move," he protested to Vito Stellino of the *Morning Sun*. "Baltimore is paying for it now and others might be in the future. My only interest and concern is the welfare of the league. It is only as good as its weakest link. I'm not arguing the merits of the move. I'm concerned about the future of the league. We had no choice in this matter. I only hope the Supreme Court will hear our case [they did; they lost]. If it doesn't, only Congress can do something. It's a sad commentary that the league can't control our destiny in the future. Other teams are starting to look now." Including yours, Art, 11 years later.

John Steadman tapped into a 50-gallon drum of melodrama for the occasion. He mounted the pulpit:

Now the stroke of final indecency. Stealing away under the cover of darkness, like a common thief in the night. The Baltimore Colts, a once-proud and precious tradition, have apparently been kidnapped from their home and loved ones. It was this city that gave them birth and nurtured a franchise to the pinnacle of fame and fortune. A despicable injustice. An outrage. First torture, then rape. It could, if the dastardly deed is done, be referred to as the murder of a football team in the first degree. Yes, a foul blow, but Baltimore will be back to rise above the cutthroat tactics that have been inflicted upon it by the sheer madness of money. Every man, woman and child realizes what has happened. Greed has asserted its ugly face. You, the public, have been wronged. Deprived.

Steady had cause to vent. That team was in his heart under lock and key. But about this "thief-in-the-night" hogwash: Flush it down the loo. Along with the kidnapping claptrap. Baltimore had almost two decades to resolve the stadium problem after Carroll Rosenbloom first started complaining about it in 1965. They bolted down some cheesy metal benches, upgraded an elevator and put hand-dryers in the bathrooms. Irsay wasn't the first owner fed up with an antediluvian stadium (e.g., Walter O'Malley, Al Davis), and he wouldn't be the last. Irsay owned a business, paid rent on a slag heap, heard promises over the years about a new stadium, got no follow-through from the city, got sweet overtures from suitors, got slapped in the face with eminent domain and decided to boogie. And every time Steadman droned on about the "proud and precious tradition" of the Colts, he always patted the fans on the fanny and NOT the guy who brought glory and championships to the town—Carroll Rosenbloom. The shock, the grief, the hurt, the anger— they're all justified. But taking a dump truck and dropping a load of grief on Robert Irsay's grave is simply the wrong take on history. Baltimore needs to take its share of the blame and deal with it.

* * *

When *Morning Sun* columnist Michael Olesker heard about the skedaddle, he pondered how to capture it. Maybe a line from *The Great Gatsby*:

My first thought was, *I have to write about this*. I do remember I had some kind of line from F. Scott Fitzgerald in *The Great Gatsby*. I ran down to the Pratt Library a few blocks away and rummaged through the book. You try to come up with something when you gotta write poetry, and the clock is ticking. Writing is a craft, and you can't bleed it all over the page. It's like when I asked Raymond Berry what it was like when they ran onto the field [in the 1958 NFL championship game], there was less than two minutes left, and they were down by three. What was going through your head? And he said, "Muscle memory took over." And I think there's some of that when you sit down at the keyboard. There are muscle

memories in the brain that say, *You've been doing this a long time. Now, compose yourself*. You can't sit there and say, "Oh, I have writer's block." Just throw something down and get it on the page. Your emotions are there, but as a writer, a professional, this is what you do.

The line from *Gatsby*: "Life starts all over again when it gets crisp in the fall." And Olesker let muscle memory do the rest:

Not anymore, it doesn't. There are to be no more late autumn Sunday afternoons at Memorial Stadium. Game called on account of darkness. Robert Irsay is taking his football team to Indianapolis. Do we listen to our hearts or our heads? Our heads say: The community is better off without Irsay. Indianapolis can have him. Getting Irsay in your town is like getting food poisoning. But our hearts say: Something precious and irreplaceable has died. Not just a football team, but a symbiotic relationship between a team and a town that transcended athletics and even, once, transcended money. When the moving vans appeared in the dark of night at the Colt complex, it was a message to every city in America that has a team owned by somebody from out of town: Nothing is forever. Loyalty means nothing. Money is all.

In charge of the news on move night at WMAR-TV in Baltimore was Wayne Lynch.

For Irsay, he says, this was a shotgun wedding that he decided to annul. "Baltimore fans had a love affair with the Colts. For Irsay, it was an arranged marriage. Don't forget, those Colts [players] who first loved Baltimore were born in the '30s and '40s. It was a whole different generation of players who had to take second jobs to make a living every year. They weren't making a lot of money then. They weren't business-oriented; they were sports guys. They were football players. They didn't mind going down to work at Sparrows Point after the season was over. They loved the city because they fit into the city. They gave a lot of people a lot of pleasure, and for that, we [in Baltimore] should've been happy, but they were left a little bitter until the Ravens came back."

Michael Olesker also used the marriage metaphor for team and city in his requiem for the Baltimore Colts:

> This was a 31-year marriage that began to end a dozen years ago, maybe more. Something died when the team was shifted from the old National Football League to the American Football Conference. It was still the same Colts on the field, but who were those strange guys they were playing now, and where was Vince Lombardi and where was old George Halas prowling the enemy sidelines at Memorial Stadium the way they had for so many years? The marriage got worse. The original husband, Carroll Rosenbloom, traded away his wife for the Los Angeles Rams. The new husband, Robert Irsay, moved in with some pretty terrible habits. He was abusive. He drank and made threats and never got anybody's name right. And then the old man started sleeping around, and one of his ladies fell for his sweet talk and his football team. Now he has followed through on his threats to leave, and we watch him exit with a sense of bitter relief, except for this: The bum took the children, too.

Indy's crackerjack team, of course, did what any bereft city would do if an owner winked at it: buy some candy and flowers. And they outhustled and outslugged Baltimore for a TKO. With tongue planted firmly in cheek, Mayor William Hudnut played the gracious winner. "I am, of course, sorry for my friends in Baltimore," he told the *Evening Sun*. "I used to live in Annapolis. I think Mayor William Donald Schaefer is one of the great mayors in the country, and just as his heart breaks, so my heart breaks for many dear friends I have in Baltimore. This is a symbol of the kind of competition cities get involved in when they are competing for business assets." Jungle rules apply, gentlemen.

Hudnut was right—it is bare-knuckle time when cities compete for businesses. And instead of lambasting Indy for the solar-plexus punch, Baltimore functionaries should have done some soul-searching. David Frick, the man who packaged the Colts-Indy deal, thinks Baltimore didn't show the Colts *enough* love, and it cost them:

I don't have first-hand knowledge, but any large employer that reaches out, and you want to be a good partner, you have to spend time with the leadership of that major employer. I consider a football franchise the same way. You've *got* to get the owners to buy into the community where you live. Just being a good citizen and reaching out to your business base is something that Baltimore failed on. There are different judgments about who was at fault, but for some reason, it [a conflict resolution] didn't get done. And they [Baltimore] overplayed their hand with eminent domain, and but for their overreach and lack of love—you've gotta love your owner—I don't think the Colts would have ever come to Indy.

The *Philadelphia Inquirer* published a retrospective in late August 1984. One former Baltimorean had an ah-hah moment that eluded others. "Paul Green, a sales distributor for Coca-Cola, and another Baltimore native who landed in Indianapolis, said, 'I don't blame Irsay. That was probably the only way he could have left Baltimore. You've got to realize that people who don't protect what they've got, lose it.'"

* * *

Hoosiers welcomed the Colts like John Glenn after his tin-can ride in space. Everything but tossed roses at their feet. Equipment manager Jon Scott was wide-eyed about it: "We [Scott, Jim Irsay, Frank Kush and Michael Chernoff]

get on his dad's plane for a short flight, and when we do get there, it's just the opposite [reaction from Baltimore's]—people cheering and press everywhere. Everywhere we went to look at the different facilities, there were friendly faces, press that was being over-the-top friendly and nice to us, especially Jim. We were in an elevator, and I remember Jim saying, 'This must be like when the Beatles came over to America [in 1964].' Which I thought was pretty funny. You couldn't make this up. It was stranger than fiction."

It's always easy to be gracious in victory; no wonder Indy was all aflutter. Baltimore was the one that took its lumps and had its heart broken. Pete Ward got dubbed director of operations when they got to Indianapolis. At first, the move tugged him in two directions:

Relocating a franchise is a nasty business. You're leaving behind good people, employees. You're leaving behind loyal fans. No matter what city you're in, it's a nasty business. But when you're leaving a bad situation and going to a great situation, there's also adrenaline and a feeling of excitement. It's mixed emotions. There's a lot of adrenaline, optimism and excitement, but at the same time a feeling of dread and sadness. I still had friends back in Baltimore, fellow employees that were friends. And there were some uncomfortable discussions with some that I had a relationship with back in Baltimore because here I was, one of the villains. There were some people that expected me to refuse to go along with the villains, but that wouldn't have helped anything. And it certainly would have derailed a dream of mine that I had had since I was 11 years old, to work in pro football. So, it wasn't a tough decision for me. But I certainly felt sadness. I always think of the 10-year-old fan with the jersey. How do you explain it to that fan?

Another fellow torn-between was Colts assistant coach Rick Venturi. He had no beef with Baltimore, but what—give up a new life in Indy? Venturi explained:

I can only speak for myself, but I enjoyed Baltimore. There was nothing about me that said, "I want to leave Baltimore." But obviously, when they tell you, "You're gonna pack tonight; you're gonna go," you don't have any choice. These are decisions way above our pay grade. This is not a homer line, but I really enjoyed my two years in Baltimore. Did I wanna go to Arizona? No. That lifestyle was different. But once they said we were going to Indianapolis, I had coached four years at Purdue, coached at three Big-10 universities. My parents lived in central Illinois. So, if we were gonna go any place, in a way, I was moving back home. There was the bonus that with Indy, I had a lot of roots in that area. For me, it was an easy transition once we got there.

The Hoosier Dome still needed some drywall sealer and a few doo-dads before the Colts could move in, so they set up headquarters at empty Fall Creek Elementary School. Once the movers lugged everything off the trucks, the place resembled an episode of *Hoarders*. The *Indianapolis Star* on March 31 described the clutter:

Less than 48 hours after they left their old ones, the Indianapolis *nee* Baltimore Colts are in their new quarters. Sort of. Right now, what was the Fall Creek Elementary School resembles a warehouse. Desks, files, cartons, wastebaskets—even a potted plant—are stashed here and there along the corridors. Still more things are stacked in the various offices that have been assigned. A paper sign taped to one door identifies an erstwhile classroom as the new working space of general manager Jimmy Irsay. Another says where the player personnel department will work. Above the doors are still yellow cards in metal frames that remind that this time a year ago Mrs. Jones was teaching Grade 3 here and Miss Smith was teaching Grade 4 there. Two phones with four lines have been installed. One sits on the counter in the reception area; the other is in what once was the assistant principal's office. Neither has any chairs. Those are still in the halls.

WMAR-TV in Baltimore sent Andy Barth out to Indianapolis for a look around after the move. "I remember we went out, and I just tried to find people to talk to and get some idea of how to say, 'It ain't so,' but it was so," Barth recalled. "They were exultant, exuberant and happy as can be. They had the team. I don't think there was any regret or embarrassment on their part. They were exuberant, thrilled. And I do remember, at the end of the first day there, when we had already done our live spots, we went to a party somewhere in Indianapolis where the local people were celebrating. They were drinking. There were two drinks that were being served at that party: 'Colt shooters' and 'Colt kickers.' The people were celebrating fervently."

They got 20,000 Hoosiers and some dignitaries at the Hoosier Dome on April 2 to plant one on Bob Irsay's tuchus and get a taste of boorishness from the Irsay sampler. "The crowd at the Hoosier Dome serenaded him, cheered him and loved him. It gave Colt owner Robert J. Irsay everything he thought he couldn't get in Baltimore," the *Evening Sun* reported. "Buoyed by the thundering applause of nearly 20,000 pairs of hands, Irsay marched proudly to the VIP stand at the 50-yard line, gave the thumbs-up sign and settled in yesterday for 45 minutes of unadulterated adulation. He was the man who had brought pro football to the Hoosier prairie. He was harsh to members of the press, chastising them for the 'hounding' he claims forced him to abandon Memorial Stadium and reminding them that he alone owns the contracts of the players who wear the blue horseshoes. 'You guys, it's not your team, it's not our team, it's *my* family's football team,' Irsay proclaimed."

Here's a letter dated April 26, 1984, from Mayflower Moving Co. vice president Bryant E. Gauthier to Colts lawyer Michael Machiavelli for historical posterity:

Dear Mike [Chernoff]:

Following is the information you needed on the Colts' move. The last van left Maryland at 8:00 a.m. on Thursday, March 29, 1984. The first van arrived in Indianapolis on Friday, March 30, at 6:00 a.m., and they continued to arrive until 11:00 a.m. The convoy of ten vans left Mayflower Corporation at noon and arrived at Colts' headquarters at approximately 12:30 p.m. One van was late in arriving from Maryland (2:00) and then went straight to headquarters, arriving about 2:30 p.m.

Must dot all the i's and cross all the t's for the anal-retentive barrister, you know.

. . .

In a battle for businesses, Bill Hudnut proclaimed it'll always be a knockdown-dragout. Which seems to mean that all's fair in war—including clandestine hijinks and maybe a little debauchery. Documentarian Troy Lowman cringes at the spectacle Irsay invited with his shopping spree: "I think all these cities kinda whored themselves out because they were so desperate to get an NFL team. Some of them, even though they might be respectable businessmen and politicians, they bend over backwards for these teams. We [Baltimore] kinda did it when we got the Browns. We can't say we didn't. You're standing there, with hat in hand, saying, 'Yes, sir, we'll do whatever you want. Please come to our city' because you desperately want that team. I think it's the nature of the beast. There's no way around it."

The permanent vibe about Robert Irsay in Baltimore is simple: He sits one rung above the Brits who bombarded Fort McHenry. "In the Baltimore Colts story, I can't even call him [Irsay] the Grinch because the Grinch became nice at the end," opined Tom Marr IV, former Colts fans and son of popular radio broadcaster Tom Marr. "He is the villain A #1; he is Blofeld from James Bond; he is the bad guy. There's no gettin' around it. Just like they hate [Art] Modell in Cleveland, and we love Modell here [in Baltimore], I'm sure that they love Irsay in Indianapolis. But he is Baltimore's greatest boogeyman."

Recall that David Self, the Oakland lawyer who struck out with eminent domain, warned Baltimore not to go there. Whereupon, Baltimore cocked a loaded .45 at Irsay—and he bolted. Then they fired the darn thing after he was gone: "Mourning gave way to action in Baltimore today, as city officials began legal maneuvers aimed at forcing the Colts to remain in Memorial Stadium," the *Evening Sun* indicated on March 30, 1984. "Mayor William Donald Schaefer pledged yesterday that 'we're not going to sit still' and the City Council scheduled an emergency session for today to introduce, discuss and enact eminent domain legislation. City officials said they want to file the eminent domain suit as soon as possible because each passing hour increases the chances that Colt owner Robert J. Irsay could escape the already slim legal hold this city has on his football team." The old cliché says slim just left town.

• • •

Baltimore, which couldn't rub two wooden nickels together a decade earlier to spruce up the stadium, suddenly found 40 mil under the floorboards at City Hall. "Yesterday, according to state officials knowledgeable about the effort to keep the Colts, the city wired a $40-million offer to Robert Irsay, the team's owner," the *Morning Sun* revealed. "Such an offer of purchase is normally a prelude to an eminent domain action."

Desperation born out of denial was what this move was all about. Keep hope alive, on a wing and a prayer, go down fighting and all that rot. James H. Bready in the *Evening Sun* examined the strategy:

> The most interesting detail in the recent Colts discussions was Mayor Schaefer's assertion that, following seizure of a major league sports franchise via eminent domain, the city would sell it and Baltimore would come through with the requisite $40 million. Was the Mayor bluffing? Or kidding himself? Or are there now, in Baltimore, people of large means who have neither destined their

money for non-profit institutions nor put it into trust funds for the lifelong coddling of their children and grandchildren? If so, that would be a news story in itself... Let's hope he [Schaefer] wasn't whistling past a cemetery. Baltimore's record is not good. Still fresh in memory is that episode in the late 1970s when the Orioles, a winning team, were up for sale and Baltimore's capitalists, given plenty of time, couldn't raise a mere $12 million. Baseball is the theme of an earlier Baltimore experience: in 1953, when a major league franchise could be had, at last after 51 years, for all of $2,475,000. To raise even that much took a great civic whoop-and-holler, and many participants.

All this verbiage and politicking presumed that Irsay would blink and take the offer. He wrapped it around his cigar and smoked it. Schaefer was now stranded at Dunkirk, hoping a trawler would happen by and save him and the town. "I know one thing," Schaefer told the *Morning Sun* about an hour after a Baltimore judge blocked the Colts' move with a toothless writ. "He [Irsay] will get to understand how I feel. He will understand. Because every ounce of my energy that I can expend to pursue our legal rights, I will expend. He will understand how I feel." Always the fighter, Schaefer, but he was both Sacco and Vanzetti, waiting for a stay of execution.

Mayor Hudnut sent a windy exclamation point to Irsay, dated April 2, 1984:

Dear Bob:

Yesterday was a great day for Indianapolis, and I hope a great day for you and your family! We were so glad to welcome you to the City, and hope that you felt the warm and enthusiastic response from the crowd [at the Hoosier Dome]. Everyone wants this to be a very successful marriage between your franchise and our City, and I pledge to you all the resources at my command to make it work... Thank you for deciding on Indianapolis! We hope that every day you will feel that your decision was a wise one, and that you will never regret it. We certainly do wish you the very best of everything in your new relationship with our City.

**Sincerely yours,
William H. Hudnut III**
(cc: Michael Machiavelli)

The general ugliness in the air invited some acid reflux in Baltimore. Irsay and Chernoff naturally were on the hit list, but there was also that moving company... "Because there was no one around to heckle the Colts, many Baltimore fans took their frustration out on Mayflower," Jon Morgan explained in *Glory for Sale*. "Though the company's local franchise had not been involved in the move, company employees received telephone threats, and some company trucks and vans were stoned. Fans boycotted the line. To make amends, the company offered free service to the Colts band, which would now be marching without its team. It turned out to be a longer march (and a larger gift) than anyone expected."

Maybe Mayflower-Baltimore was a pariah for a spell, but company supervisor Rick Russell claimed folks there had short attention spans. "The day after the move out, I got calls from our agents in Baltimore," Russell stated in "Remembering How Colts' Move from Baltimore Went Down" in the *Indianapolis Star*. "'Do you know what's going to happen to my business this year? It's just going to go to hell. Nobody is going to call me.' I said, 'Hold on, you know what they say about PR. There's no such thing as bad PR. Let's follow up and talk again as the year goes by.' And we did. That year, they [the Baltimore office] had a 20% increase in his business. It didn't affect him negatively at all. The agent apologized later for giving me such a hard time about it."

Looking for kicks in '84 after the Colts left, some Baltimoreans headed up to Philly on October 14 to catch the Colts-Eagles game. Popular local cartoonist Mike Ricigliano fashioned a papier mâché effigy of the red-nosed owner. Known for his cartoon caricature of Irsay, fans got a kick out of it. Ricig on how the dummy came about:

> It was not the first papier mâché dummy I ever constructed. One of them was of [famous sports broadcaster] Howard Cosell when I lived in Buffalo that we brought to a Monday-night game. As it turned out, that dummy ended up

being part of the intro to *Monday Night Football*. I had a skill and a fondness for doing those kinds of things. When I got here [in Baltimore], I had the idea of doing one of Irsay, and I just kinda put it together like the others, with chicken wire and papier mâché and a lot of time spent on the face. The body was chicken wire and clothing. I found a light-blue suit and white buck shoes, which he was prone to wear, stuffed it with money, with the idea of taking it to a game when they [the Indy Colts] came close to town here. And the next season [1984], they were scheduled to play in Philly, so I figured that's the game I would bring him to. And, of course, that's the game that 5,000 [former] Colts fans went to, to protest the taking of the team.

During the post-mortems, Mayor William Donald Schaefer got kudos for being the little train that could (almost), but expletives were reserved for Bob Irsay and sidekick, Mikey, the Wannabe GM. "There is some comfort, now that the deed is done, in the knowledge that Maryland and Baltimore, in the persons of Governor Hughes and Mayor Schaefer, acted honorably in negotiations with people to whom that word means little or nothing," *Morning Sun* op-ed writer Peter A. Jay noted. "There's much more comfort in the knowledge that Robert Irsay and Michael Chernoff can now be eliminated, at least, from the municipal consciousness—though doubtless every setback they encounter in their new campsite in Indianapolis will be the source of a certain amount of local glee and snickering."

Schaefer gets the lion's share of the accolades for his flurry of punches before hitting the canvas. The other collection of Baltimore politicians and assorted geniuses should have paid their penance for doing next to bupkis to help him.

Meanwhile, Mike Ricigliano has that cartoon dummy of Irsay and is trying to get it past the turnstile at Veterans Stadium in '84:

Our thought really was, let's just waltz this thing into the stadium and we showcase it at the game with all our fellow [Baltimore] Colts fans and have some fun with it. But the very first gate we go to, we're turned away. So, we tried *every* gate around the stadium, and no one lets us in. And they had been walky-talkying each other, saying, "Don't let that thing in here." We ended up going into the stadium and asking management. At the time, Leonard Tose was the Eagles owner—another kind of misbehaving owner—but he wasn't there. But his daughter [Susan] was there. We made our pitch and plea to her, and she decides, "All right, I'll let you in, but it's gonna take up a seat, so you have to buy it a ticket." So, now, we're good to go. The daughter has sent security with us to our tailgate and is gonna escort us to our seats in the stadium. We got to our seats, we go to sit the Irsay dummy down with us, and security insists that Terry [his wife] sit *in* the seat that we purchased, which is on the *opposite* side of the stadium. That's dumb. First of all, when we walk this up into the stands, all the Colts fans go crazy. Secondly, they overhear this argument we're having with security; we're like, "All these seats here? He can't just sit here with *us*?" "No. You bought the ticket over there. That means you [Ricigliano] *have* to be with the dummy, but she [his wife] has to go to the seat you purchased." That's crazy. And people around us, overhearing this, not knowing us at all, start chanting, "Let her stay! Let her stay!" This chant picks up, and security, realizing this is gonna be *more* of a problem if she has to go, decides to let her stay in her seat, and we were able to stay there and watch the game.

The Colts lost, 16-7, doubling the fun.

CHAPTER 17

BAWLMER'S HAIL MARY

Two days after the move, the *Morning Sun* printed a laundry list of sweet nothings and Irsay promises to keep the team in Baltimore. Grant him one thing: He was consistent.

- **November 1973:** "We have absolutely no idea of moving the franchise. Please tell the people that. That's not even in our minds."

- **January 29, 1979:** "If we can get our [Owings Mills training] complex completed, there would be little reason to think of moving."

- **February 1979, to the Council of Colts Corrals:** "The [Chicago] Bears, with 10 or 12 million [people] to draw from, never had such enthusiastic support as you give the Colts."

- **January 20, 1981, letter to Colts season-ticket holders:** "We are the Baltimore Colts. We want to play here, and we want to give you the kind of team you can be proud of again. This is our commitment."

- **June 10, 1981, after signing two-year lease:** "The Colts are here to stay. Anyone who asks [whether the team is moving] is not a good reporter."

- **June 2, 1983, press conference:** "We are not moving. I wouldn't be here if I was going to move, would I? I'll tell you what I could do—and don't think it hasn't crossed my mind—but I'm not going to do it. I could pull up 30 vans and be out of here Sunday and you'd never know who was here, but I haven't done it."

He only needed 14 to vacate.

Dave Anderson of the *New York Times* pilloried Irsay for hypocrisy if nothing else:

At the opening of the Baltimore Colts' new suburban offices and training complex four years ago [1980], Robert Irsay addressed the small audience that had gathered in Owings Mills, Md. "This building," the Colts' owner said, "is a symbol of our dedication to bring winning football back to our fans. We want our team to match the standards set by this building." Dedication and standards—words to remember Robert Irsay by now that he has shown he understands neither. But in trying to sneak his National Football League club's belongings to Indianapolis in the dark of night in 12 moving vans, he did show what a grimy business so much of sports has become… By moving the Colts' franchise in such a murky manner, Robert Irsay almost makes Al Davis look like a silver-and-black knight. Almost. But at least Al Davis went to court… If the Colts can be moved that way, any other franchise area in any sport can wake up some morning to find itself without a team.

It would be another 25 years before he made the documentary, *The Band That Wouldn't Die*, but filmmaker Barry Levinson got something off his chest. "That place [Memorial Stadium] was the outdoor insane asylum," he told the *Morning Sun* right after the move. "He's not going to find that in Indianapolis."

The *Morning Sun* queried some of the old guard and got a Campbell's soup collection of opinions:

- **Hall of Famer Gino Marchetti:** "I think it's a shame. One of the best franchises in the NFL goes to hell. We were filling the stadium when most of the franchises were a half to three-quarters filled. Attribute it to poor management. I remember playing for Dallas [the Texans of 1952], and we heard the team was moving to Baltimore. Artie [Art Donovan] said to me, 'You are going to love it, Gino. They are the best fans in the world.'"

- **Hall of Fame Coach Weeb Ewbank:** "I hate to see it. The history that the Colts made will live. I can't think of the Indianapolis Colts. It doesn't and never will sound right. They will always be the Baltimore Colts to me. I have a lot of pleasant memories, and Lucy [Ewbank's wife] still says it was her favorite place to live."

- **Linebacker Bill Pellington:** "I really feel sorry for the Baltimore fans and the guys playing for the Colts. The guy running the Colts is so devoid of public relations that nothing is right. I'm disappointed, but I can see Indianapolis's side, too. The people there want a football team for their new dome."

- **Hall of Famer Lenny Moore:** "When we came here, everything grew together, the team, the fans, the city. Now the Colts have left a bitter taste in the mouth. It takes no crystal ball to see the problem: just one man. Yes, I'm hurting in the heart, but that hurting in the heart has been going on for a long time."

The Horse had a more nuanced take on the matter. "I find no fault in a system that allows an owner to move his team elsewhere if he wants," Alan Ameche told Bryan Burwell of the *New York Daily News*. "It is an entrepreneurship, and if he's not making money in Baltimore (Irsay was losing more than $500,000 a year), he should not be shackled to the city. I think, under the current system, he should be able to move where he can make a profit. The NFL is at fault for allowing the situation to get so bad that he would want to move. The situation in Baltimore went from a time when 20 years ago [1964] you couldn't get a ticket to the point where the Colts were only drawing 15,000 to some games. How long can that go on? If the league is so upset with the Raiders leaving Oakland, if they don't like the Colts leaving Baltimore, they should do something to prevent it from happening. Maybe they should do a better job of evaluating potential owners." John Steadman's very point: The NFL barely did a once-over of Irsay's bio and found out the hard way once they let him in the door.

Just in case people thought the band of merry jesters had put on business suits and upped their game once in Indy, there was this faux pas, courtesy of the *Associated Press* on August 31, 1984:

BALTIMORE—The hardcore football fans of Baltimore will be in shock if they tune in Sunday's televised game involving their beloved and departed Colts. Out there on the field of the Hoosier Dome in Indianapolis, wearing the familiar blue-and-white uniforms with the upturned horseshoes, will be players wearing jersey Nos. 82 and 89. In a rare move, the Indianapolis Colts have unretired the numbers worn by Hall of Famers Raymond Berry and Gino Marchetti and assigned them to journeymen tight ends. Coach Frank Kush cited a shortage of available numbers in the 80s, those now designated for wide receivers and tight ends, as the reason for the move. But former Colts players blame owner Robert Irsay, who had the once-proud franchise spirited out of Baltimore last March during the dead of night. "What he did was as close to sacrilege as you can get," said Sam Havrilak, a former running back. "He has no class whatsoever," said Tom Matte, another former running back. "It's just the kind of guy he is. He'll probably unretire No. 19 [Johnny U's #] too."

They backpedaled faster than Ali around the ring—back to retired after getting their ears blistered with outrage. What they got from Marchetti was a shrug. "My ties and my memories are with Baltimore," he told the *Morning Sun* the day after the boneheaded stunt. "What happens in Indianapolis is not important. I think if they had some class, they'd have called me or Raymond." Had Ernie Accorsi still been anywhere near this operation, MIT calculated the odds of such a blooper as "impossible."

Other than Hoosiers and the serenely rational, Irsay wasn't getting wholesale sympathy. Tim Sullivan of the *Cincinnati Enquirer* beat him with a two-by-four:

It will be Irsay's epitaph that he did his best to ruin one of football's strongest franchises and then move it out of town under cover of darkness, like a thief. National Football League franchises must be precious if a city such as Indianapolis could embrace such a sleaze. Their consolation is that he is mortal. Mine is that memories don't fit into moving vans. While pro sports franchises operate for a profit, they do so by trading heavily on a city's name and its citizens' loyalties. There have been few fans more loyal than Baltimore's. In 1979, when Johnny Unitas was inducted into the Pro Football Hall of Fame, the *Enquirer* graciously assigned me to the ceremony. I arrived in Canton to find that Colt fans had come in busloads to pay homage to football's greatest quarterback. I doubt that many of them will commute to the Hoosier Dome this year. My uncles in Brooklyn have no

allegiance to the Los Angeles Dodgers, and I doubt that Colt fans will long follow their Colts in Indianapolis. Once you've been jilted and the object of your affections takes another's name, it's not wise to pursue. Even reminiscing can hurt, but it's unavoidable.

Frank Deford had hit the bigtime writing for *Sports Illustrated*, but he still loved the royal-blue. "I grew up in Baltimore, with the Colts, and I know just how much they meant to that working-class city, forever in the lee of Washington and New York," he wrote on April 9, 1984. "The Colts were ours—even more so than the baseball team that came to town about the same time. Its very name, Orioles, belonged to another time, that of our grandfathers. The Colts were one with the city. It's really quite amazing. A man who could screw up professional football in Baltimore would foul the water at Lourdes or flatten the beer in Munich."

One of those Orioles wondered who the heck was vetting guys like Irsay. "I don't think he has any conception of the tradition and meaning of football in Baltimore and what it has meant to the city," Hall of Fame pitcher Jim Palmer observed in the *Evening Sun*. "And he hasn't conducted himself in a classy manner. It's a shame the NFL would let somebody like this type of person buy a franchise in the first place. Maybe that's why they're having the trouble they're having. He never presented himself to the town as somebody who cared, and it has shown all along. I think there were a lot of people who wanted to be Colt fans, but found it impossible as long as Irsay owned the club. It just goes to show that money does not buy class."

There were no teardrops for Cleveland when Baltimore snatched the Browns, so bashing Indy was pure hypocrisy. They observed Marquess of Queensberry Rules and won in a TKO. "This city [Indianapolis] doesn't care about Irsay's offhand remarks or his track record," the *Los Angeles Times* noted in July 1984. "It doesn't care if the Colts were 7-9 last season and 2-12 the year before. It doesn't care who brought the team, only that it is here. 'It doesn't make any difference who they are,' Tom Moses, chairman of the committee that negotiated the deal with the Colts, told the *Atlanta Journal*. 'All we know is it's an NFL team, and look out for us. Let's face it, we're all rubes. The slightest mention of glamour and we act like it's the second coming of Hedy Lamarr.'"

It was easy kicking a guy like Irsay, who walked through life with his fly open. Just about everybody piled on and ignored the fact that Irsay had to scoot to break free and start fresh. Ron Reid of the *Philadelphia Inquirer* issued the usual pablum:

> Often an embarrassment to his league, and a bad joke to football people everywhere, Irsay has pulled some of the meanest bad-taste maneuvers of any owner in any sport. He fired a coach at halftime, threatened an NFL officiating crew with a federal lawsuit and rewarded

a field-goal kicker with a $10,000 raise after three errant kicks brought the Colts a loss [note: Irsay never paid the kicker and fired him the next day]. But Irsay's shameless pandering of his club to Jacksonville, Memphis, Phoenix and other cities, while trying to force a better stadium lease out of Baltimore, probably topped his NFL offenses. The hustle ended in March, in a scene that spoke as much for the state of the NFL as for Irsay's philistine bent. The Colts loaded up their office furniture and sneaked out of Baltimore in the dead of night. It was a dreary exodus for a franchise that, in 1958, beat the Giants for the NFL championship in an overtime classic often called "The Greatest Game Ever Played."

Toss-aways like "under the cover of darkness," "in the dark of night," "like a thief in the night" got stale fast. The man got sideswiped by eminent domain and figured it was time to abscond before the courts hit the brake pedal. Irsay was a scaramouche who turned the Colts into an afternoon soap. But when Maryland pulled that eminent-domain whammy, it was time to make tracks. That "thief-in-the-night" mantra is missing the point: You can't burgle your own ballclub.

Defense Exhibit A: John Steadman playing Henry Wadsworth Longfellow, circa 1987, the *Evening Sun*:

> The Baltimore Colts had been *stolen away under the cloak of darkness* [emphasis

mine]. It was the lowest moment in National Football League history. The occasion will be marked with a ceremony tomorrow evening [March 28], when a handful of the faithful gather for a candlelight procession. The group believes the world should not soon forget, but always remember, what happened when a city that had professional football for 35 years was devastated by a monster lacking in both heart and soul. It was March 28, 1984, when a man, who didn't know a football from a pumpkin, thrust a fatal dagger into the vital organs of a city and state. The Baltimore Colts were taken away. And it quickly became America's shame.

Some Baltimoreans wouldn't let bygones be bygones. "Here's an FYI to Baltimoreans reflecting on Bob Irsay today: There's neither biblical nor federal law against speaking ill of the dead," *Morning Sun* columnist Dan Rodricks wrote on January 15, 1997, the day after Irsay died. "The point is, you can—if so inclined—speak ill of Bob Irsay without violating federal or divine law. I offer this just in case anyone was holding back malignant thoughts, though I can't imagine there are any left. It was all said years ago, wasn't it?"

Ernie Accorsi, formerly the brains of the outfit, bumped into Irsay months after the move and gave Mikey, the Wannabe GM, a parting shot. "It wasn't until the owners' meeting in Hawaii, the league meeting in March [1984], when Irsay came up to me, and he

was in fine condition when he did—it was in the morning—and he said, 'Why did you leave?' I said, 'Too much confusion, Bob, but largely because of your attorney [Chernoff].' That was the only time. He never said anything nasty to me or reacted in a negative way to me."

Indy Mayor William Hudnut knew Easterners—Baltimoreans, especially—would pound on him and the boys. In the draft of a generic letter to dignitaries dated April 5, 1984, Hudnut told everyone to duck and cover:

We never expected the eastern press in general and the Baltimore press in particular to be supportive of the move. The facts were simply that Mr. Irsay was faced with the immediate threat of condemnation of the franchise [eminent domain] in what can only be described as a completely hostile atmosphere. He has been blamed for failing to meet with Maryland officials. He decided against the meeting only after he learned of pending eminent domain legislation. He simply moved his property out of what turned into enemy territory to prevent its seizure.

Some of the crew who drove the Colts into a crevasse squawked about the reverence Baltimore had for the "Johnny Unitas Colts." Irsay griped about it in an interview with the *Chicago Trib*. Linebacker Gary Padgen, who was probably gumming a pacifier when QB Unitas was reinventing the position, groused to the *Atlanta Journal*, "Everyone wanted out of Baltimore. There was so much tension there. Everybody was saying, 'Irsay's a jerk.' I got tired of hearing it, and I hated the idea of living in the Unitas era. It was like the current team couldn't do anything right. All we heard about was the '58 team." Coach Frank Kush, who may have lost the next Unitas (John Elway) by being an old-school hard-ass, fussed about it in a July 1984 article in the *Los Angeles Times*: "There's no doubt it's [the relationship between fans and the team] a two-way street. This has been a rebirth for this team, especially the players. The response [in Indy] has been incredible, fantastic. In Baltimore, there was this undying image of (Johnny) Unitas and the '58 team. Now these guys will have a chance to build their own image." With contributions from Padgen and Kush, that image went 4-12 in 1984.

Jim Irsay seemed thunderstruck that a city that was out on a ledge with a stadium and no team was happy to see him. "It's been a tremendous outpouring," Irsay the Younger told the *Atlanta Journal*. "It's unbelievable how everybody in Indianapolis has opened their arms." Jimbo was a student of history; therefore, he should have known how giddy the townies were when the Dodgers made it to L.A., the Boston Braves went to Milwaukee, and the St. Louis Browns became the Orioles. Ju-bi-la-tion.

A flag-football game—Indy Colts vs. USP-Terre Haute prison guards—would've sold out the dome, such was the fervor in Indy. "For the first few weeks, we got between 75 and 100 calls an hour," PR assistant Gretchen Meyer gushed to the *Los Angeles Times*. "And most of them were just people calling to say, 'We're glad you're here.' It was incredible. And the television film crews would be here every morning just to shoot us answering the phones." Hoosiers had cause to celebrate their victory; they dropped Baltimore and Phoenix with haymakers.

From The Truth Hurts Dept.—Ann Flaten, of Carmel, Indiana, mailed in her thoughts to the *Indianapolis Star* on April 8, 1984:

O, yes, the people of Baltimore loved the Colts when it was easy, back in the days of Johnny Unitas and other greats. But later on, when it counted, they didn't love the Colts enough to improve Baltimore's playing facility [Memorial Stadium]. Not enough to see them through an irascible ownership. And not enough to buy tickets when the team was losing. Perhaps Irsay is no saint, but I think there are few saints in professional football, and other cities have gone through similar trials with their pro teams without turning their backs on them completely, as the people of Baltimore did to the Colts, even to the extent of singing an obscene chant at the closing game of their last season. So now, the Colts are gone from Baltimore and some Baltimoreans are glad. So be it. Indianapolis will take the Colts, warts and all, and we will love them more than they loved them in Baltimore.

Baltimore, take your medicine in one big gulp. Here is yet another broadside from Carmel, Indiana, a John Parnell, who sent this to the *Evening Sun* on April 23, 1984:

> When are the bleeding hearts of Baltimore going to realize that they have only themselves, their city fathers and the Baltimore press to blame for Robert Irsay's moving to Indianapolis? When are they going to face the fact that the Colts have been playing in one of the dumpiest stadiums in the NFL, and that for years Irsay has been trying to get the city to remodel it? What Irsay did was not new to sports. Walter O'Malley moved his Dodgers out of Brooklyn because he could not convince the city fathers that the bandbox known as Ebbets Field was no longer major-league. Irsay's midnight move from Baltimore was his way of thanking the so-called fans who "supported" and serenaded him during the last Colts home game. It was also his way of thanking the caustic Baltimore press that has derided him and his family for years, and the city fathers who were initiating legal action to prevent him from moving his team. The bleeding hearts of Baltimore deserve no less. We welcome Robert Irsay and the Colts to Indianapolis with open arms and a brand-new domed stadium.

A smorgasbord of emotions usually follows loss—depression, despair, grief, shock, denial, anger—and Baltimore fit the M.O. Baltimore writer Joe D'Adamo unveiled some of that in the *St. Louis Post-Dispatch*:

> Memories. That's all we Baltimore pro football fans have left today, memories of the way we were, as the song says. Memories, in my case, go way back to the days of the All-American Conference when the Colts wore the green and silver colors of the former Miami Seahawks and the stars were people named Bud Schwenk, Bill Hillenbrand and Racehorse Davis. The shock is numbing. The hurt will come later, with the emptiness of a barren September. Death, even if it's after a long, lingering illness, still is a shock. Even in the most pessimistic days of recent Colts history, there was always an outside hope that a miracle would come to pass, that some sense would be made out of the pandering of a once-glorious franchise. But, sadly, that wasn't meant to be. The Colts are gone, and they won't be forgotten. Not by the thousands for whom they were a way of life. I weep for the countless youngsters who may grow up and never know what it is like to hold an entire football team to your bosom. I weep for my grandchildren who may never

know how a man like John Unitas with his talented arm and his amazing football instincts could unify a city, or how the dashing feet of a Buddy Young or a Lenny Moore could make a city forget the color of a man's skin.

Donald Smith, of Westminster, MD, got something off his chest in a letter to the *Indianapolis Star*: "The Colts are dead! They have been for a long time now. The fans in Maryland have been like the loving husband or wife who refuses to accept the death of a spouse. The signs were there, but we would not acknowledge them. For the record, the Colts died when they were bought by Bob Irsay. I am tired of speculation concerning his motives. They are inexplicable to me. Who among us can explain why he would take a city prepared to open up its heart to the new owner and then tear out that heart for seemingly no reason? Who can understand anyone who would do this and then accept none of the responsibility, but instead blame the fans for their lack of loyalty (ha) and the media for attacks upon his methods?"

Sympathy for Baltimore even extended out to the West Coast. Vinny DiTrani of the *The Record* (Stockton, CA) felt that Colts fans deserved better:

Perhaps it was those horseshoes on the helmets. Maybe it was the squatty little coach with the funny first name [Weeb Ewbank]. Or the quarterback with the high-tops and that distinctive dropback action. Or the slow-footed receiver who caught everything within reach [Raymond Berry]. Maybe it was the win in the "greatest game ever played." Or that group of distinctive last names like Mutscheller, Rechichar, Kerkorian, Taliaferro and Myrha, and the marching band that followed them around the National Football League. There was something about the Baltimore Colts that lifted them above the average franchise of those pre-explosion NFL days of Weeb Ewbank, Johnny Unitas and Raymond Berry. While they may never have reached the America's Team status of the Dallas Cowboys, the Colts had a certain special presence... A middle-of-the-night slink-away to Indianapolis certainly was not the right way for the relationship between Baltimore and the Colts to end. True, the love affair had died off in recent years, ever since owner Robert Irsay started running the franchise into the yellowed turf of Memorial Stadium. But to pack up and leave *under the cover of darkness* [my emphasis]—the Colts fans deserved more than that. One Baltimore resident, interviewed on TV after the midnight slink, may have summed up the city's feeling about Irsay and his team best: "Indianapolis is the luckiest city since Hiroshima," he said.

Once several cities battle it out for a team, Neal R. Peirce of the *Pittsburgh Post-Gazette* said it's the fans who take it on the chin: "New York moves to New Jersey, Baltimore to Indianapolis, Oakland to Los Angeles, Los Angeles to Anaheim. Minnesota may soon head off for Tampa. The moves by hometown football and baseball teams are touching off constant furor. Who's to blame? First, the greedy owners with an eye on bigger bucks. Second, the mayors who themselves fuel the bidding games as they cozy up to teams they have or try to seduce new ones. Who are the victims? Fans and taxpayers. The fans build up a head of enthusiasm for a team, often support it for years before it starts winning, and then are bitterly disappointed when it steals away (in the Baltimore-Indianapolis case, by *dark of night* [my emphasis])."

At a time like this, outside scribes might turn to a Baltimore veteran for context. The *Washington Post* did a feature on John Steadman's angst after the Colts left. "The 57-year-old 'sports conscience of Baltimore,' as Pete Rozelle calls him, is at odds with a world in which heroes have agents and loyalty is a cliché. His is a story of betrayal in Baltimore. 'I used to pray for players. I used to pray for teams,' said Steadman, lead sports columnist for the Baltimore *News American*. 'I don't do that anymore. I figure they're not praying for me.'"

Recently off the therapist's sofa after climbing into the bigs with New York and D.C., getting shown up by Indianapolis was a real civic comedown. Former WMAR-TV reporter Andy Barth saw Baltimore's humiliation:

It [the move] was a terrible blow. Baltimore, which is one of the great cities in the country and the world, despite false and erroneous criticism that comes from irresponsible people, felt like a second-class city in some ways, a smokestack, working-class, gritty city. It was all of those things, but Baltimore felt somehow lesser than New York and Washington. In many ways, when the Orioles and the Colts won world championships and beat New York, we had all-stars and champions, and the Colts and the Orioles went a long way in making Baltimore feel first-class—which it is. Losing the Colts undermined that. If you were a sensible person, you realized that there are a lot of great institutions in Baltimore—Johns Hopkins University, the University of Maryland, the art museum—so there are plenty of reasons that Baltimore was still a great place to be even without the Colts. But people were set back.

Lifelong Baltimorean and Colts and Ravens band director John Ziemann thinks the town took a mammoth hit. "He [Irsay] took major pride out of the city of Baltimore. I said this many times: When we lost the team, the sun came up, commerce was moving in Baltimore, thank God nobody died, but we lost a big part of our heart. We lost our civic pride. We were stripped of it. We were embarrassed around the nation that we couldn't hold onto our football team—not because of the fans, but because of one man, who was an alcoholic. And even without the alcohol, he was a vindictive man."

There was little precedent for a team bolting before Al Davis took on the NFL and won. Prior to the Raiders absconding to L.A., you had to go back to 1960 when the Chicago Cardinals headed to St. Louis. "You gotta realize the times back then," former *Morning Sun* sportswriter Vito Stellino explained. "Franchises just didn't move in those days. All of the blame went to Irsay. There was never the blame: 'Well, why didn't you give him a new stadium?' It's hard to say. Would they [Baltimore] have handled it differently if they thought he might move? All of those things are unknowable. At that point, Irsay had ticked off fans so much that it was almost too late. That was always the feeling: Don't do anything for Irsay. Even before he moved, he was not a beloved character. It was devastating to Baltimore fans, but I don't think you can blame the fans because it was just a different time." But let's also drag in Baltimore politicians—minus Mayor Schaefer—for a good 50 lashes for being naïve, inert, arrogant and pigheaded.

Some had the wherewithal during the grieving to pine for the Rosenbloom era. Bob Maisel of the *Morning Sun* took stock of the two commanders-in-chief:

The Colts had two owners in their time here. Under Carroll Rosenbloom, they became one of the best, most successful franchises in the country. In that era,

they took part in two of the most significant games in NFL history [the 1958 championship and Super Bowl III] … Irsay's legacy? Well, he was the one who destroyed all that, then spirited the once-proud franchise out of town. Amazingly, while doing it, he gets a sweetheart deal, all sorts of other inducements, and rides into his new town a hero on a white horse. So he winds up the winner, Baltimore the loser.

When Bill Hudnut died in 2016, Michael Olesker used the occasion to rip him and Irsay on jmoreliving.com:

What Hudnut and Irsay did was set loose a modern cutthroat bullying of struggling cities by prosperous professional sports teams. Irsay wanted a new ballpark with higher ticket prices and luxury suites and profits beyond all previous counting. The city, struggling to pay its teachers and its cops and firefighters, struggling with that era's diminishing tax base, said the millions it would cost for a new ballpark made a new stadium impossible. Out in Indianapolis, William Hudnut said: Hey, Irsay, we've got a brand-new ballpark waiting for you. Enter, and never look back, and never mind the broken hearts back in Baltimore. What Hudnut and Irsay did was destroy the myth of a two-way love affair between a community and a team. They cemented the role of blackmail in the world of pro sports. You want to hold onto your ballclub you pay the Irsay price or watch the team head for the welcoming Hudnuts of the world. You think not? Ask the fans who thereafter lost teams in St. Louis and Houston and Los Angeles and Oakland. And—oh, yeah—that team out in Cleveland.

But the law of the jungle prevailed: Pony up to placate the fat cat or lose your ballclub; fork over the green for talent or step to the rear for the Yankees, Red Sox and Dodgers.

. . .

Howard Cosell—famous and infamous, both—had a 30-minute show on ABC called "Sports Beat," a chance for Cosell to impress with $20 multi-syllabics. He tackled the Colts' move one Saturday, claiming he would stay neutral and dispassionate. According to "TV Sports" columnist Ira Berkow of the *New York Times*, Cosell was anything but:

On April 7 [1984], "Sports Beat" did a segment on Irsay's move of his team, the Colts, from Baltimore to Indianapolis. The segment had the guise of an even-handed approach, the same as the one on the Raiders [and Al Davis]. That is, according to Cosell, it did not "take a position," but reported "the various conflicting viewpoints." That was not done in the Baltimore story. It was a diatribe against Irsay and how the city had been "raped"—Cosell's word—by the owner. It also quoted two men—former football players, not psychologists—on Irsay. One said, "He can't be playing with a full deck," and the other called Irsay "diabolical." There was no rebuttal from Irsay, or from supporters of his position. Bonventre [a journalist who worked on the story] says that Irsay was asked to appear on the show, but refused. Somehow, at least to give the appearance of fairness, Irsay's motivations ought to have been explored. They were not. There were only superficial references to his distaste for the Baltimore press and Memorial Stadium. This is advocacy journalism; it is expected in editorial comment, as Cosell generally gives at the end of a segment, but when it pervades the story, it becomes in effect a witness for the prosecution.

The take on Irsay outside of Indianapolis saw him as a heartless Yankee carpetbagger. But the road less traveled was that Irsay was right about the stadium and stonewalling politicians. Irsay did what any prudent businessman would do—he bailed.

In an interview with the *Chicago Tribune* in June 1984, Irsay was asked what was the "most important single reason for your decision to leave Baltimore":

The principal reason was that the team, the management, the coaches, the players never could do anything right... Our players were disgusted. Our coaches wanted to leave. The players and coaches are so happy to be out of Baltimore. I think they were just crucified like Carroll Rosenbloom was crucified when he was there. The city can't forget the 1958 Super Bowl team [sic] with Johnny Unitas. That's all we ever hear over there. Unitas, Ameche. Hell, that was 1958.

Son Jim Irsay got tired of all the piling on and defended Dad to the *Indianapolis Star*. "He's a tough but fair businessman who is good to his word—a handshake is as good as a signing to him. He comes from a tough background—the Bucktown section of Chicago and the Marines—and I think that has shaped his personality. He's had to fight for everything he's got. He's a simple man in that he appreciates the little things and family pleasures. He's a very generous man. He's been a real good father to me."

Defending Bob Irsay went against the grain, then and now, but Troy Lowman, the producer of the documentary, *The Ghosts of 33rd Street*, doesn't bash him for moving the team:

I would have been a lot more diplomatic [than Irsay], that's for sure. He didn't have an allegiance to Baltimore. So, they [Baltimore officials] should have read the room with the guy. What Baltimore basically did is, they just dismissed the guy. They should've put out the fires. And then the fans, they started burning Irsay in effigy and all that. Look, he's a

human being. When you see that, you start to say, "Fuck everybody. Forget this town." He probably had a chip on his shoulder at the end. And there was probably a point where he wasn't gonna stay, no matter what.

Baltimore reporters naturally took umbrage at Irsay hurling harpoons at them. Most of them initially gave him room to grow but lost all sympathy once they got to know him. Bob Maisel of the *Morning Sun* wrote, "Irsay will probably pin much of the rap for his defection on the Baltimore media. Baloney. Nobody in the media had any preconceived ideas about him when he came here. He made his own reputation. The only thing the media did was quote and report him accurately. Just to make sure he wasn't being bum-rapped, I periodically asked people in the organization who would level with me off-the-record if we were being unfair to him. The answer was always in the negative, with the kicker that he was even worse than being pictured."

Jim Irsay provided counterpoint in the *Indianapolis Star*, affirming that boisterous fans and cynical reporters helped make his dad's mind up. "He felt that he got some bad raps and that the situation was turning to animosity. Nobody wants to hear that. I feel he deserves better than he's gotten. This [Indianapolis] is an opportunity for a fresh start."

• • •

Thomas Bromwell, the politician who pushed eminent domain down everyone's gullet, doubled down after the move. "State Sen. Thomas L. Bromwell, D-Baltimore Co., today announced the formation of the Colt Legal Defense Fund, an incorporated group to raise funds to help finance Baltimore's legal battle to force the football team back to the city," the *Evening Sun* reported. "'I'd like to call it the "Stick It to Bob Irsay Fund," but we want to keep it as professional as we can,' Bromwell said at a City Hall press conference with mayor William Donald Schaefer. 'We're setting up a private sector fund, a support group, for efforts to bring the Colts home,' Bromwell said. He called Irsay, 'the Ayatollah Irsay,' and characterized his years in Baltimore as a 'reign of terror.'" Schaefer was probably involved in this; earlier he jumped in with both feet, promising to "fight all the way."

The stakes got higher when the squabble got dragged into court. Baltimore landed the first punch, as reported in the March 31 *Morning Sun*:

> A city judge yesterday signed a sweeping order blocking the Colts from leaving Baltimore—ordering anyone with formal ties to the team not to help transfer the franchise from the city. Baltimore Circuit Judge Robert L. Karwacki, meeting in his chambers with city lawyers who requested the order, signed an injunction that expires in 10 days. It can be extended, however, "for good cause." Baltimore's lawsuit is part of a formal proceeding—unique in Maryland history—taken by the city to acquire the

football team under eminent domain, a legal concept usually used to obtain land through condemnation for public use. The move into court followed an emergency session of the City Council, which unanimously approved a bill giving the city the right to move to seize the team. Mayor Schaefer immediately signed the measure into law.

Then, things got fuzzy. Pushback would come when the Colts stated the obvious: We ain't in Maryland no more. We're gone, lock, stock and jocks. You can't get back what you don't got. The *Morning Sun* discussed this:

> A main issue in the case is the present location of the team. Maryland courts do not have jurisdiction in a condemnation proceeding over property outside the state. For a number of reasons—including the fact that moving vans took virtually everything out of the Colts' Baltimore County training facility Thursday night—the location of the team or the franchise granted to Mr. Irsay by the National Football League is a legal mystery. "The franchise is here," declared City Solicitor Benjamin L. Brown yesterday after he emerged from Judge Karwacki's chambers in the downtown courthouse. "We've had no notice from (the league) or Irsay that the franchise has been moved."

Once the suits jumped into this, the great parsing of words began. The Colts could hold up their lease in Indy: We signed this for 20 years; that kinda means we're staying here. Baltimore could throw a feeble jab: The NFL hasn't told us a bloody thing about a move, and besides, Baltimore is still the designated site for the Colts' "home" games in '84. But Baltimore's best shot was the "public use" angle—that the Colts are a public trust designed for enjoyment, and as such, the whole community has a stake in it. "Public uses are not limited, in the modern view, to matters of mere business necessity and ordinary convenience, but may extend to matters of public health, recreation and enjoyment," the U.S. Supreme Court pronounced. "Generally speaking, anything calculated to promote the education, the recreation or the pleasure of the public is to be included within the legitimate domain of public purposes," a federal appellate court agreed. A longshot, sure, but the Hitless Wonders took the 1906 World Series, didn't they?

Thomas W.E. Joyce, in his 1985 article in the *Fordham Urban Law Journal*, "The Constitutionality of Taking a Sports Franchise by Eminent Domain and the Need for Federal Legislation to Restrict Franchise Relocation," told Irsay not so fast:

> Using only the location of tangible assets to determine the situs [site] of a sports franchise should be avoided. For example, the NFL Colts "fled Baltimore under the cloak of darkness" with eight [sic] moving vans full of equipment bound for Indianapolis in an effort to avoid Baltimore's eminent domain

jurisdiction. While the Colts apparently felt that moving tangible property alone was sufficient to change the team's situs, this action does not satisfy the other two criteria established in *Raiders* [the Al Davis case]. Baltimore was still the team's principal place of business since the team transacted no business in Indianapolis prior to the date that the condemnation petition was filed and was still the designated site for Colts home games. Moreover, as a practical matter, courts would be reluctant to allow an owner to insulate a team against valid acquisition by moving its tangible property as soon as it learned of an intended action to condemn the team.

Baltimore had a feisty, old-guard politician to provide covering fire: Representative Barbara Mikulski. She played up the "public entity" angle, as explained in the [Minneapolis] *Star Tribune*:

> Mikulski, who represents most of Baltimore's ethnic blue-collar neighborhoods that formed the heart of the Colts' support, said that it's simply not right that a team owner should be able "arbitrarily and capriciously, based on greed alone, to move." A team should provide profits for its owner, Mikulski said, but it is not a private business in the usual sense. "When a sports team is a franchise, it becomes a public entity, "she said. "It's tied up with the emotions of

the people and the pride and identity of the community. Greed or spite are not good enough reasons for moving a team."

Irsay had his nose barely above water in Baltimore and couldn't put a dent in the principal of the $15-million loan he took out in 1972. And spite certainly wasn't the reason he jumped to Indy; it was saying sayonara to bad vibes and Memorial Stadium. But the "public entity" angle was gaining some traction.

Though Baltimore gave him the brush-off after getting advice about eminent domain, David Self liked Baltimore's chances. "'We paved the way for Baltimore with our blood, sweat and tears,' said David A. Self, who represents Oakland in its case," Self told the *New York Times*. "'To the extent that Maryland respects the decisions of the California courts, Baltimore stands in an excellent position to acquire the franchise.' Whether Baltimore eventually purchases the Colts, however, may hinge more on factual technicalities than on legal theory. Of greatest import, the city's lawyers say, are the completeness and timing of the sudden move by Robert Irsay, the Colts' owner, and whether they mean that nothing is left in Baltimore to buy."

There was no pure apples-to-apples comparison between Oakland's and Baltimore's beefs. Davis moved the Raiders in-state— from Oakland to L.A. Irsay cleared out of Maryland for Indianapolis. "Even if Baltimore survives a public-use argument, it's a big fat question what happens if its action is incompatible with interstate commerce,"

NYU law school professor John J. Costonis told the *Times*. "The question of picking up and moving franchises is obviously a matter of Federal concern, but Congress hasn't told us anything about it. There are just huge gaps in the law here." And that was precisely the one shot Baltimore had.

Pete Rozelle's hands were tied after the Raiders case; short of an owners' thumbs-down, the NFL couldn't stop a move. That didn't mean Rozelle went laissez-faire on the matter. "In an exclusive interview with the *News American* today, the [NFL] commissioner expressed his personal feelings about the defection, said expansion plans must remain vague and talked about what Baltimore's rich pro football heritage represented," John Steadman revealed on March 30. "Under questioning, he admitted the move 'obviously hurts the league from the standpoint of tradition.'"

Baltimore tried the picket-fence play on Irsay, right out of *Hoosiers*. "Colts owner Robert Irsay lives in Illinois. The Baltimore Football Club, Inc., is a corporation chartered in Delaware," the *Morning Sun* explained. "The stadium is in the city, but the training facility is (was?) in Baltimore *County*. And perhaps the Mayflower vans that left the area loaded with Colts equipment in the dark of the night last Thursday carted off whatever physical property could be considered the last remnants of the Colts as a Baltimore team. But in its condemnation action, city lawyers are contending that the team is still here. For one thing, they say, the National

Football League has not told the city that the Colts are going anywhere. And Baltimore is still the designated site for the team's 'home' games."

Michael Chernoff anticipated this legal eephus pitch and raced the legal papers out of Maryland. The *Indianapolis Star* emphasized the sense of urgency:

Chernoff and a Mayflower executive, who would direct the loading of the team's materials, flew to Baltimore Wednesday evening. Reporters followed them from the airport, but the two checked into a hotel. If they had gone to the Colts' office, reporters would have learned the move was in progress. Chernoff and the executive directed the movers to load everything that could be moved. Chernoff, in addition, ordered the team's business records loaded and moved first. "What is a franchise? What is a business? Most court decisions hold it is the business records and official books. Mike wanted those moved first," [David] Frick said. "The threat of that seizure changed the picture totally. The man [Irsay] faced losing his entire investment. I believe he did the prudent thing."

Bruce Smith, executive assistant to Mayor Hudnut, told the *Morning Sun*, "The Mayflower vans are already gone from Baltimore; the bulk of the physical assets are here [in Indianapolis]. Since the team physically has left Baltimore, the court in Baltimore really lacks any further jurisdiction."

This tale of two cities eventually went to federal court, the U.S. District Court for the District of Maryland: *Maryland and City Council of Baltimore vs. Baltimore Football Club, Inc.*, Walter E. Black Jr., presiding. Black identified the three particulars: "There are three issues which the Court will address in this inquiry as to where the franchise was located. First, what is the relevant date to determine the location of the Club: the date of the filing of the condemnation proceedings (as the City proffers) or the date when the compensation is paid (as the Colts proffer) [i.e., when Baltimore wired the $40-million offer to buy the Colts]? Second, what standard is the appropriate test for determining the situs of an intangible franchise in condemnation proceedings? Third, was the franchise *in Maryland* [emphasis mine] at the time when situs must be determined?"

Indianapolis had its own homer judge to counter Judge Karwacki in Baltimore. Now there were men in robes butting heads. "INDIANAPOLIS (*AP*)—Attorneys for the Colts won a temporary restraining order yesterday blocking a court action in which Baltimore claimed rights to the National Football League franchise. The suit was filed on behalf of the 'Indianapolis Colts' against Baltimore's mayor and City Council … The temporary restraining order issued by Judge [William] Steckler is in effect until another order is issued, Mr. [Colts lawyer Alan] Becker said. 'This prevents the parties from doing anything further,' he said." This edict canceled out Karwacki's 10-day order that the Colts belonged back in Baltimore. The legal games were revving up.

Having conferred about their talking points, Irsay and mouthpiece Michael Machiavelli opined to the *Evening Sun* about eminent domain. "I negotiated with [Mayor Schaefer] for six weeks," Irsay protested. "I flew to Washington to meet with him. He flew to Chicago to see me. Then, I wake up one day and see the governor has put a bill through the legislature that is against all American freedoms." Machiavelli peddled his go-to gun metaphor: "Later, Colt attorney Michael Chernoff agreed with his boss that the legal maneuvers had hurried the moving plans along. 'Nobody likes to have a gun put to their head,' Chernoff said of the General Assembly action that paved the way for Baltimore's eminent domain suit."

Back-and-forth quibbling prevailed until this matter was settled. "There is something else that rankles: Mr. Chernoff's claim that the decision to move was sparked by a bill in the Maryland Legislature," the *New York Times* stated in "The Seduction of the Colts." "'That's a downright lie,' Schaefer says. 'That bill had been pending for a long time, and Mr. Irsay knew it was there. He never said, "Don't file it" or "Do file it." He knew it was there, and so did Chernoff.'" Yep, Irsay knew it was there. But it sat around for a spell, then they voted on it. That's when Irsay pushed the "activate" button and ordered the vans in.

Civility hung around for a while, but eventually the two mayors got into it. William

Hudnut published his autobiography in 1987, *Minister Mayor*, and took several shots at Schaefer. One was greased with a compliment, and Schaefer probably saw through the sweet talk:

> The poorest loser I've ever encountered in politics was not someone I defeated in an election, or even a Hoosier. It was Donald Schaefer, former mayor of Baltimore, one of the finest mayors in the country, who led a magnificent city to fantastic renewal. When [as mayor of Indianapolis] I stepped down as president of the National League of Cities in 1981, I was asked who, in my opinion, were the top 10 mayors in the country, and I put Mayor Schaefer at the top of the list. Consequently, I was very disappointed by his reaction to the loss of the National Football League Colts.

· · ·

Robert Irsay fessed up after the fact—Maryland put a better offer on the table. But Indy's trump card had always been that spanking new dome. The *Morning Sun* offered small solace to Baltimoreans:

> The offer that Maryland officials made to Colts owner Robert Irsay was even more lucrative than has been previously disclosed—and the financial terms apparently were more favorable than those Mr. Irsay finally accepted from Indianapolis. In an effort to keep the Colts in

Baltimore, Maryland officials offered Mr. Irsay a $15-million loan for 10 years at only 6½% interest—well below market rates and below the rate offered in Indianapolis—the state official who oversaw the negotiations said yesterday. Under the Maryland deal, Mr. Irsay also would have received $4.4 million in cash for the Colts training complex in Owings Mills—while still being guaranteed use of that facility for rent of only $1 a year. That deal was the result of an extraordinary statewide effort in which city and state officials were joined by others in Baltimore County and even Carroll County—as well as by the state's business leaders—to come up with an offer that would satisfy the unpredictable Mr. Irsay.

Unfortunately, not a dollar short, but a day (or maybe six months) late. Mayor Schaefer scrambled on the pond with the ice about to break and whipped together a beautiful, last-minute offer. But the mission was doomed for the usual reasons: 1) That dump on 33rd Street was the same old place; 2) Other than Schaefer, local pols didn't give a tinker's cuss about fixing the problem; 3) The Baltimore press would ride Irsay's keester if he stayed there; 4) Most fans wanted a pox on Irsay and his son; and 5) There was no place like Dome.

The *Morning Sun* mentioned Irsay's short list of gripes: "An aide to [Indianapolis] Mayor Hudnut, who asked not to be identified, said Mr. Irsay had told Indianapolis officials several other reasons he wanted to move: that he felt the people of Baltimore did not appreciate the team, that local politicians didn't like him and that the local press picked on him."

The breakdown of the Indy and Maryland offers:

Indianapolis

1. **Loan:** $12.5-million loan at 8% interest for 10 years

2. **Training Facility:** a new facility costing between $3- and $4-million will be built. Irsay will pay $15,000 a year rent and has an option to buy it for $4 million

3. **Tickets:** guaranteed annual broadcast and ticket receipts of $7 million for 12 years

4. **Stadium:** the Hoosier Dome, capacity 63,000, including 87 luxury suites; Irsay signed a 20-year lease

Maryland

1. **Loan:** $15-million loan at 6½% interest for 10 years

2. **Training Facility:** Irsay would get $4.4 million in cash by selling the facility to Baltimore County and would get to use it for $1 a year

3. **Tickets:** guaranteed average attendance of 43,000 per home game

4. **Stadium:** Memorial Stadium, capacity 60,240; would have to sign a six-year lease to get state money for renovations, including skyboxes

Irsay wouldn't pick up the tab at an Indy saloon without that loan. "The most important consideration in moving the Colts was money," Will McDonough of the *Boston Globe* pointed out. "Irsay took a $15-million loan in 1972 when he purchased the team. Reportedly, he was supposed to repay the bank $1 million in interest every year. Irsay paid the interest only. After 12 years he had not paid a cent of the principal. So, the bank started pressing him. He also owed the city of Baltimore and the state of Maryland $2.3 million in back taxes." Debt was threatening to swallow him whole, so he needed a reboot. Eminent domain shoved him out the door early into the waiting arms of Indianapolis.

Baltimore got its day in court in late October 1984 when the feds agreed to adjudicate its beef with the Colts: "Barring an appeal to the U.S. Supreme Court, an appellate ruling has cleared the way for the trial in Baltimore's federal court of the city's lawsuit aimed at bringing back the Colts—minus their controversial owner," the *Morning Sun* announced. "The ruling by the 7th U.S. Circuit Court of Appeals, announced yesterday by Baltimore's deputy city solicitor, Ambrose T. Hartman, denied a request by Colts owner Robert Irsay for a restraining order that would have halted the trial." No doubt Irsay's lawyers had checked the terrain and told him

Baltimore had barely a puncher's chance of winning, but he still had to sweat this one out.

The legal load for Irsay got lighter in early November 1984 when the NFL's appeal of the Raiders case got shot down by the Supreme Court. Any owner who met the simple criteria could boogie, and the league couldn't do a thing. *Busted*, thought Baltimore. Al LoCasale, Al Davis's righthand man, rejoiced. "When it [the Supreme Court] upheld the *Raiders* verdict, the Court of Appeals stated that the NFL has the opportunity to be directly involved in franchise relocations, as long as they establish reasonable standards and guidelines," he told the *Philadelphia Inquirer*. "The second part of the ruling was that, once the guidelines and standards were in place, they had to be uniformly applied in all cases." No such standards were in place when Irsay did his thing.

For those with a notion of heading out to the empty Colts complex in Owings Mills with a sledgehammer, it wasn't Irsay's, for the time being. "It should have been just as easy for that pickup-truck visitor to Owings Mills [who stalked the property] to walk the 100 yards to the building, instead of ramming the gate, and throw rocks against all the glass," the *Miami Herald* described in April 1984. "But if you walk in, you'll see that a court order seizing the property has been pasted on the smoked glass. It belongs to the people now—and their mayor [Schaefer], who offered to buy it from Irsay for $4.4 million, double its original cost, to keep the team in town."

There was plenty of commentary about eminent domain in both backyards. "Where the public has a special interest, there are special regulations for corporations," Maryland Senator Charles McC. Mathias Jr. told the *New York Daily News* in June 1984. "The president of a nuts-and-bolts company can say he's closing down tomorrow, but the president of a gas company can't because the public has an interest. I believe that professional sports franchises are a business like that. If this bill [Senate Bill 2505, prohibiting arbitrary team moves] had been law, I don't think the Colts could have moved." Jim Irsay provided rebuttal: "That's great, except for one thing—it isn't *their* team. It's my father's team. He bought it, he paid for the team, and he did it as a business investment. This is America we're living in, right? This is private ownership. If it isn't profitable in one place, you have the right to move."

The blunderbuss was a stubby firearm with a fat muzzle that wasn't much for accuracy; the Baltimore blunderbuss emphasized the blunder and was just as inaccurate. "I've always felt that Baltimore lost the franchise," Indy's chief negotiator, David Frick, told the *Morning Sun* in 1993. "Even though the negotiating process was getting firmer with Indianapolis, the real trigger mechanism for departure was eminent domain."

The myth that took hold about the Colts' move over the years had Bob Irsay whining and stealing his way to Indianapolis. The eminent-domain debacle got some play at first, but many people—Baltimoreans, especially— bought the standard Irsay-the-thief version and forgot the rest. Learning from his mistake was one Mark Wasserman, Schaefer's

chief aide, the one who wrote a memo to the mayor pushing eminent domain. "When the situation was so ridiculously deteriorated, it seemed like that was one option that ought to be thought through and maybe considered seriously," Wasserman confided to the *Morning Sun* in 1993. "My sense is that there was a lot of shifting sands. All signs pointed to a certain level of disingenuousness. It became a cat-and-mouse game. 'Should we make a move or not? If we do, what will the reaction be?' Unfortunately, we found out." Wasserman didn't clarify who was being evasive and playing word games, but he banged the drum for eminent domain while many legal scholars raised their eyebrows.

Schmoes sitting on a stool in The Horse You Came In On saloon in Baltimore figured, Hey, it's *our* team; that fat jerk's got no right to move out. Such were the thoughts of Filip Bondy of the *New York Daily News*. "The cities' frail situation could be strengthened immeasurably if some gutsy federal court justices would grant the cities of Oakland or Baltimore eminent domain over the Raiders or the Colts in pending suits. This kind of ruling would represent the most important precedent in the history of sports. No longer would an Irsay be able to hold an entire city hostage. In a refreshing turnabout, a host city would be able to threaten appropriation of a franchise at the smallest sign of discontent with an owner." Baltimore and Schaefer could only wish it were that easy.

If wishes were horses, beggars would ride, as the saying goes. Maybe they deluded themselves, but Baltimore's eminent-domain campaign was doomed from the word go. "The City of Baltimore loved their Baltimore Colts. But after a controversial ownership change [Rosenbloom for Irsay] and several bad seasons, the franchise's relationship with the city was strained," Travis Bullock observed in *The Constitutional Dimensions of Sports Franchise Takings: Lessons Learned from the Baltimore Colts*. "When negotiations to keep the team in town broke down, the city employed its last resort—eminent domain—to take ownership of the team to prevent it from leaving. The city, however, was a few days too late. The team left the city and was beyond the city's eminent domain jurisdiction. Even if the city had condemned the team while it was in Maryland, the condemnation would have been invalid under the [interstate] commerce clause."

In *Maryland and City Council of Baltimore vs. Baltimore Football Club* in 1986, Judge Walter E. Black Jr. shot down Baltimore's argument: You offered $40 million to the man as just compensation to seize the club, and he said no; nice try, fellas:

Recognizing fully that the precedents cited by both sides do not address the issue of *intangible* property [anything with no assigned value and can't be held in your hands], the Court is nonetheless persuaded that the Colts' view must prevail on this issue. It seems untenable to the Court that the mere filing of a piece of paper in a court with no

compensation being paid can restrict the owner's use of the property. The statutory scheme provided by the Maryland legislature provides a clear framework of the procedures for acquiring property through eminent domain. The general rule is that until the condemning authority [Maryland] pays compensation, no right of possession is obtained.

Clearly, Walter Black wasn't a homer, siding with Irsay even though he was born in Maryland and grew up loving Johnny U and the horseshoes. The Colts had left the barn, he stated in *M. & C. Council of Baltimore vs. B. Football Club*, so eminent domain was out: "It is, of course, axiomatic that a sovereign state's power to condemn property extends only as far as its borders and that the property to be taken must be within the state's jurisdictional boundaries. Now, of course, the Colts are no longer in Maryland, nor would they be here at the time of judgment were this case to go to trial. The inescapable conclusion is that the franchise is beyond the jurisdictional reach of Baltimore City."

Travis Bullock in *The Constitutional Dimensions of Sports Franchise Takings* listed a trio of reasons that Judge Black squashed Baltimore's ploy: "Ultimately, three factors led the [federal] court to conclude that the Colts left Maryland by March 30, 1984. First, the Colts' principle [sic] place of business was not in Maryland.' Second, the team's 'essential tangible property' including its 'certificate of membership in the NFL' were not in Maryland by

March 30. Finally, Irsay's intent as the owner of the franchise was to leave Maryland by that date." He beat that by a full day.

Judge Black threw in a few more reasons for good measure. One was that the NFL never took a stand on the move either way. Black assumed that meant Article 4.3 of the Constitution and By-Laws had been shelved for this one, i.e., that meant tacit approval. The bottom line for Black: The Colts are way over there in Indy, and you can't touch them:

> For the foregoing reasons, the Court finds that Baltimore City lacks the power to condemn the Colts' franchise. Until the City pays the owner compensation for the property taken, it has no right under Maryland law to restrict the owner from moving that property beyond the jurisdiction of the state. Even if the applicable date for determining the situs of the franchise were the date of the filing of the condemnation petition rather than the date of payment of the compensation, the Court reaches the same conclusion. The team's principal place of business and its tangible property were both outside Maryland on that date, and it is clear that the owner's intention was to relocate outside of Maryland. Under any of the workable tests for determining the situs of the franchise, the Court concludes that the Colts were "gone" on March 30, 1984.

Ballgame.

• • •

Rebuffed in court, Schaefer hopped in his car and headed down the B/W Parkway to grab a few elbows. "Mayor Schaefer and a chorus of Colts fans, among the most recent victims of what a Senate committee chairman called the 'inexcusable callousness' of sports franchise owners, laid bare their wounds here yesterday in hopes that, come kickoff time next season, their team will be back," the *Morning Sun* reported. "Formally opening the second major front in an offensive to thwart Colt owner Robert Irsay's March 29 move of the football franchise to Indianapolis, the mayor pleaded with the senators to enact a bill that could block a team's move. The bill also would give cities like Baltimore 'the right of first refusal' to match whatever offers may be luring a team to other places." The Jake LaMotta approach: Get clocked but keep on swinging.

There was little appetite at the Capitol to rumble with the 1887 Interstate Commerce Act, but they let Schaefer speak his piece. Jaded Colts fans packed the Senate panel room as a show of force. The real topper of the day, though, was a piece of paper that a Senator held up—correspondence from Michael Machiavelli, alias the Wannabe GM: "The only strenuous opposition raised to the legislation yesterday came in the form of a telegram from Michael G. Chernoff, vice president of the Colts," the *Sun* revealed. "'Please be advised that the Indianapolis Colts registered the strongest possible objection.

The Colts believe said bill to be unconstitutional and a total repudiation and violation of the basic principles upon which America was built.'" The barrister didn't include a recording of Kate Smith singing "God Bless America."

Chernoff never bothered much with Baltimore, other than hopping on Irsay's jet, catching a ballgame, smooching the behinds of the rich and powerful, then heading back to Chicago Sunday night. There were those occasional sojourns, though, when he made the rounds at headquarters to nose around and meddle, assuming his role as Wannabe GM. "You approach it one of two ways," Chernoff professed to the *Atlanta Journal*. "Either you're going to work with them or against them. In Baltimore, we apparently were unable to work with them. Here, you start with the spirit, with the people, with the open cordiality, and you'd have to say it was an excellent move." Pissed off Baltimoreans had billy clubs at the ready should Chernoff ever return.

The move brought on a run of lawyers flinging around torts and briefs. Indy's chief negotiator, David Frick, felt in his bones a lawsuit coming his way. "Frick, like everyone else, expects a flood of lawsuits in the next year or two," the *Indianapolis Star* declared on April 1, 1984. "One of the suits may be aimed at the man who did the bulk of the negotiating for Indianapolis. 'Since the Colts pulled out of Baltimore, there has been some talk of my being sued,' Frick revealed. 'A Chicago law firm made some telephone calls to various Indianapolis firms saying they wanted to file a suit against someone named Frick. One of the calls was to one of my law partners. Another call went to the firm representing the CIB [Indy's Capital Improvement Board].'"

The lawyers made hay with these legal jousting matches, most of it just huffing and puffing, but it still had David Frick worried:

> The thing that shook me up was that I've accumulated a little wealth in my life, and I had never been personally sued. But the city of Baltimore sued me, Bill Hudnut and Johnny B. Smith [the CEO of Mayflower]—sued us personally for moving the Colts to Indianapolis. They had a theory that we interfered with their contract [with Robert Irsay]. I knew that once you got that case in federal court, you would have fair judges. We did not want to be in the city court of Baltimore. All of our legal expenses ultimately got paid, but it's no fun to be sued for $100 million. Bad things happen, and that was one of the bad things on the part of the city of Baltimore.

No harm, no foul; this mess got settled in Indy's favor. Mayor Hudnut sent out this press release on March 17, 1986:

> Mayor William H. Hudnut III announced today a tentative agreement to dismiss all the suits arising out of the relocation of the Colts to Indianapolis. Under the terms of the settlement, the City of Baltimore has agreed

to dismiss its condemnation case against the Colts and the related case against the mayor, David R. Frick, John B. Smith, the Aero-Mayflower Transit Co., the Capital Improvement Board and the Colts. In return, the Colts have agreed not to pursue its various actions against the City of Baltimore and its officials for alleged violations of the Colts' civil rights. The settlement bars all sides from bringing any future lawsuits against one another related to the move of the Colts to Indianapolis.

The hatchet got buried—in the hearts of all Colts fans back in Baltimore.

The settlement package included these terms:

1. The Indianapolis Colts will pay $400,000 toward the legal fees of the City of Baltimore.

2. The Indianapolis Colts will give to the City of Baltimore memorabilia associated with the former Baltimore Colts football team.

3. The City of Baltimore will acquire the Colts' Baltimore training facility and 100 acres of land for $4.6 million.

4. The Colts agree to vote in favor of an expansion franchise for the Baltimore area if the issue comes up for an NFL vote prior to April 1, 1989.

And check this one out:

5. **The Colts agree to discuss with the owner of an expansion or relocated Baltimore-area franchise the transfer of the name and logo "Colts." The obligation ends April 1, 1989.**

The five-year window closed on April Fool's Day, 1989.

Michael Chernoff got his deserved kudos for bringing off the move, which let him return to his original role as Mikey, the Wannabe GM. Mayor Hudnut sent him a letter of thanks on April 21, 1986, for being a trooper:

Now that the litigation surrounding the move from Baltimore is behind us, I want to write you a note to thank you for everything you did to make that move possible. We are grateful for the opportunity we had in the spring of 1984 to negotiate with you, and for your resourcefulness and patience and professionalism along life's way since then. Personally, I thought the lawsuits filed by Mayor Schaefer and his colleagues in Baltimore were malicious, capricious and avaricious, and I can only hope that I would behave in a more gentlemanly manner should that particular shoe ever be on my foot.

No beef with Hudnut about Chernoff. David Frick confirmed that the man was a slew of superlatives at the negotiating table—adroit, knowledgeable, skilled, meticulous, patient, professional. He nailed that deal for Bob Irsay. But Hudnut's shoe metaphor sounded a tad like virtue signaling. He was never on the other end of it to find out. Schaefer was the guy who fought Indy almost singlehandedly and got spat on by Irsay, not Hudnut.

In his autobiography, *Minister Mayor*, Bill Hudnut shares an anecdote that further sullied Schaefer. Older folks in Baltimore knew enough to clear out when Schaefer boiled over, but apparently Hudnut thought they should be pals again after the move, no hard feelings and all that. The Schaefer brush-off story:

After the Colts left in late March, Mayor Schaefer instituted eminent domain proceedings against the Colts, and nine months later he authorized a lawsuit to be filed. All the lawsuits were finally settled out of court, but at a cost of several million dollars to the parties involved. Twice, Mayor Schaefer refused to speak to speak to me on the telephone when I called him in early 1985 to discuss this (and other related matters) with him. In March of 1985, I bumped into him at the White House, shook his hand, and made a comment to the effect that he was a pretty hard fellow to reach by phone. He retorted, "That's right," and abruptly turned on his heel and walked away.

Sportswriter John Steadman loved the good vs. evil angle. Indy was just like any city with the wherewithal to grab a ballclub—including Baltimore (e.g., the St. Louis Browns, the Dallas Texans, the Cleveland Browns). But Steady mounted the lectern to shout down the demon (12/23/1986): "It's a beautiful relationship. The mayor there, William Hudnut, a onetime minister who jumped from the pulpit to politics because, no doubt, he wanted to change the world, made the transaction with Irsay. Odd isn't it that Irsay's own mother referred to him as a 'devil on earth.' But the ex-preacher man, who holds the top office in Indianapolis city government, didn't mind making a deal with this 'devil.'"

The hypocrisy of bashing another city for wooing a team wasn't lost on everybody in Baltimore. "Baltimore has a new team, the Ravens," *Morning Sun* columnist Ken Rosenthal pointed out in January 1997. "Baltimore got that team by making like Indianapolis and finding an owner to pull an Irsay [Cleveland's Art Modell]. Baltimore lost its claim to the high moral ground. Oh, Cleveland kept the Browns' name and heritage, and the NFL guaranteed it a new team within three years, while Irsay took everything with him. But really, who cares anymore? Purple and black has replaced blue and white."

Give Steadman credit; he was an equal-opportunity moralizer. In his book, *From Colts to Ravens*, he gives Modell the business:

That the Browns, one of the most successful of all National Football League teams, looked upon by their devoted followers as a civic landmark, were defecting from their happy home of 49 profitable years, was looked on as preposterous. Not that Baltimore was any bad place to be, far from it, but rather that Cleveland football had been a bellwether of stability, the future of its franchise never in doubt. The team was a tower of respectability, and its attendance, far and away the best in the league, was a constant. And down on the field a team performing amidst a wave of fanatical enthusiasm was lifted by the spirited crowds that identified with the Browns and the subtleties of the game they knew so well. This was a city, Cleveland, trapped in all the emotional entanglements that develop after you give heart and soul to a cause. All of the same could be applied to Baltimore because it, too, once had its team, the Colts, pulled away in an earlier case of grand larceny.

Maybe it was time for the glad-handers in D.C. to stop jawing with each other and get a law on the books. "Congress needs to takes steps to protect the public interest that the current system is ignoring," Jack Noonan wrote in *The Boom in Franchise Relocations: Moving Cities, No Matter the Cost.* "This article proposes two solutions for legislative change. The first solution is to create a third-party agency to oversee professional sports franchises. The second requires making slight changes and amendments to existing law or creating new legislation altogether."

That would be those folks traipsing around the hallowed halls of the Capitol. Congress decided to explore a law that would put guard rails around owners migrating to better pastures. William Donald Schaefer went down to D.C. for some sympathy and got an audience. The (Minneapolis) *Star Tribune* hinted that something might be brewing:

> The departure of the Colts and fears that it could happen elsewhere have revived a slumbering issue in Congress: Should a professional sports team be able to move anywhere it wants, or should it have a legal commitment to its hometown? Senators and representatives from such cities as Baltimore and Oakland, which lost the Raiders two years ago, may join those from such cities as Minneapolis and St. Paul to support legislation making it tougher for teams to move. Ahead may lie a fight between politicians representing the losers and those representing the burgeoning cities of the Sunbelt— and a few others with new stadiums— that are eager for the status that comes with having a major-league team.

Congress considered three different angles to tame this animal. Thomas W.E. Joyce III in *The Constitutionality of Taking a Sports Franchise by Eminent Domain and the Need for Federal Legislation to Restrict Franchise Relocation* listed the options:

1. **Arizona Senator Dennis DeConcini's Proposal:** "Senator DeConcini has stated that he will introduce legislation 'designed to protect

sports communities from arbitrary abandonment by club owners.' The best way to accomplish this goal, according to Senator DeConcini, is to allow sports leagues to prevent member teams from moving in spite of antitrust challenges and to allow leagues to enforce rules that 'tend to promote comparable economic opportunities for member clubs.' This would give threatened cities some muscle to fight back."

2. **The Professional Football Stabilization Act:** "The Stabilization Act would make it unlawful for professional football teams to relocate if they have played home games in a municipality for six or more continuous years unless one of the following exceptions is met": a) Somebody other than the owner broke the stadium lease, and it can't be fixed in time to avoid the owner taking a hit; b) The stadium the team is using is "inadequate," i.e., a dump; c) The team goes in the red for three straight years or is in danger of going under.

3. **The Professional Sports Team Community Protection Act:** "Senator Slade Gordon of Washington has introduced a bill which would apply to 'any proposed relocation of a professional baseball, basketball, football or hockey team which

plays its home games in a community within the United States.' Under the bill, a professional sports team could not leave its community and relocate unless two criteria are met": 1) The league says the move is "necessary and appropriate"; and 2) An arbitration board has given the go-ahead.

Option 3 looked doable, but it would probably have meant curtains for Baltimore anyway. The NFL could OK a move if it thought the owner was justified. Three factors were the rationale, and Baltimore was dicey on two of them: 1) the stadium; 2) fan support; and 3) operating losses. All Irsay had to do was get an assessor to roam around Memorial Stadium and label it a slag heap and take photos of all those empty seats at ballgames to clinch it.

Joyce, in *The Constitutionality of Taking a Sports Franchise*, thought the Community Protection Act was the best route: "Legislation regulating sports team relocation is necessary since cities have provided benefits to teams and, therefore, should not be subject to the harm that accompanies unnecessary relocation. The exercise of eminent domain to take a sports franchise arguably violates the [interstate] commerce clause and, therefore, legislation to protect the interests of cities in restricting sports franchise relocation must come from Congress. Moreover, Congress is best suited to provide relief that is uniform and non-discriminatory. The Professional

Sports Team Community Protection Act would provide such relief."

The senators rolled up their sleeves and got to it.

- **On January 24, 1985, in the Senate:** Read twice and referred to the Committee on Commerce.

- **On February 4, 1985, in the Senate:** Committee on Commerce. Hearings held.

- **On February 20, 1985, in the Senate:** Committee on Commerce. Hearings concluded. Hearings printed.

For those with bated breath, don't bother. All the blather went nowhere. Died in committee. Back where we started.

Cities that get dumped are told tough luck, Charlie; to the winner go the spoils; you win some, you lose some; finders keepers, losers weepers. "No one knows just when cities began to measure municipal worth in 100-yard increments," Steve Daley observed in the *Chicago Tribune*. "Perhaps no one understands what a sports franchise means until it departs. But the Colts are gone from Baltimore, swept away by greed and incompetence and the blandishments of a Midwestern town that wanted a football team in the worst way and got its wish."

Losing the Colts was Baltimore's kick in the pants, blow to the heart and hit to the wallet. "In the hearts of the fans, a professional football team traffics not simply in dollars and cents but in legend and drama and pride in city," the *New York Times* noted in December 1984. "'There are people who almost lived for the Colts,' says Baltimore Mayor William D. Schaefer. 'They're the ones I'm sorry for.' But the dollars and cents of pro football are far from paltry. According to the Maryland Department of Economic and Community Development, the move of the Colts represents a loss to the state of $35 million a year [about $108 million in 2025], and that doesn't include the prestige that the presence of a National Football League team bestows on a growing community."

Not only does the money roll in—or out for Baltimore—cities get to puff out their chests when they hit the big-leagues. The *New York Daily News* ran a piece called "A Tale of 2 Cities," looking at what happened to Baltimore and Indy after the move:

The Colts did get a bundle from Indianapolis, yet this was a two-way street. According to an economic impact study commissioned by [Mayor Bill] Hudnut, the direct economic impact of an NFL franchise in the city would mean more than $21 million in revenue [$64,637,000 in today's dollars], plus $153,638 in increased tax revenues to the city and surrounding Marion County. By 1989, assuming a 6% annual rate of inflation, the direct economic impact will rise to more than $28 million [$86,183,000 today]. "Also, there is an incalculable indirect benefit in terms of the city's reputation," said Hudnut. "Many businesses will generate a lot more money than the Colts. RCA. General Motors. Indiana Bell. It's not the biggest business in town, but there is nothing in this town—nothing—that could have happened to this city that all of a sudden grabbed the national attention. Indianapolis is no longer a minor-league town with the Colts here."

Getting their affairs in order for the '84 season, Colts tickets were as hot as the Beatles' *Ed Sullivan* gigs. "Within a month, the team, without a season ticket plan, took out newspaper advertisements that were season ticket forms," *UPI* reported in late March 1984. "People stood for up to six hours in line on a cold, rainy night for the first of such papers to be printed. But street vendors weren't able to get to the people in line because others were running up to them and buying as many as 20 papers at a time. The Colts received more than 150,000 season ticket requests, 2½ times the capacity of the team's Hoosier Dome home."

In 2005, a couple of researchers took a look at this madness in *The Value of the Indianapolis Colts to Indiana Residents and their Willingness to Pay for a New Stadium*. Mark S. Rosentraub and David Swindell put together their PhD thesis and came up with some key findings:

1. "The annual value of the intangible benefits of the Indianapolis Colts to Indiana residents is $83.9 million [$137,548,000 in 2025]."

2. "Indiana residents are willing to pay $66.3 million each year [$108,565,000 today] to ensure that the intangible benefits of the Indianapolis Colts are retained and continue to be available to Indiana households."

3. "The intangible benefits of the Indianapolis Colts are a 'good buy' for Indiana residents."

4. "Indiana residents believe the Indianapolis Colts make a critical contribution to the state's identity."

5. "Human resource directors from Indianapolis's largest employers consider the Colts an important recruitment tool."

6. "A substantial number of Hoosiers living outside of the Indianapolis metropolitan area are willing to pay to ensure that the Colts remain in Indiana."

7. "Hoosiers support a variety of sources as preferred financing mechanisms for a new sports facility."

This is where Baltimore flubbed the whole shebang: Those folks in the Heartland get it; B'more failed to grasp the basics. That's why people kicked and screamed when Mandel and Schaefer talked up the new stadium downtown in the early '70s, voted aye for Question P in '74 and politicians dragged their feet about stadium renovations. Hoosiers figured it out—Keep up with the Joneses if you wanna keep your ballclub.

Take a family like the Fischers from way over in Montana. They flew in to Indy once a year to catch the Colts and play tourists. "'This is our Christmas gift,'" Ron Fischer told WTHR-TV in Indy in 2006. "'We love the Colts and wanted to come to Indianapolis to watch them play.' Football isn't the only draw. The Fischers' trip here includes lots of shopping and enjoying the sights. All together, they will spend about $3,000. 'There's a lot of activities and things to really enjoy; Christmastime here with the way they light up the town.'"

In their PhD dissertation, Rosentraub and Swindell asked Hoosiers, "When you tell people you are from Indiana, what do they mention to you about the state?" Here were the top three: motor sports (the Indy 500), 27.1%; the Colts, 23.8%; and the Indiana Pacers, 17.2%. They asked 24 human resource directors to rank Indy institutions as recruiting tools on a scale of 1-10. The state's universities rated a 6.6, public schools at 5.9 and the Colts at 5.1, #s 1, 2 and 3 on the list.

Indy now had a new ATM—the Colts. "Millions of fans will get a glimpse of Indianapolis during Monday night's game [against the Bengals in 2006]," WTHR-TV indicated. "But if the Colts can score a playoff game at home, the city can really cash in. 'All the additional revenue that comes from an additional home game, it's gravy. That's more money than we predicted,' said Bob Schultz of the Convention and Visitors Association. More fans equals more money. Each home game brings an estimated $4 to $5 million to the local economy. During last year's playoff showdown with the Steelers, 5,000 to 10,000 more fans traveled to Indianapolis for the game."

Rosentraub and Swindell also asked Hoosiers, "How much would your household be willing to pay to keep the Colts in Indiana?" They found out folks there are OK with ponying up some cash to keep the team: 34% in the $80-$160 per year range, 28% at $160+ per year. With no squawking and no squealing. A pollster in Baltimore back in '84 would have been clapped in the stocks merely for asking.

They call it putting on your big-boy pants, in this case, making the majors. Getting the Colts did what the Indy 500 couldn't, as explained in the *Los Angeles Times*:

Most of the world sees his [Mayor Hudnut's] city as little more than a racetrack in a cornfield. Still, Hudnut insists that Indianapolis—the 13th largest city in the country, with a population of 710,000 [1.9 million in 2024]—doesn't have a bad image. "We just have *no* image," he says. The Colts' move, in Hudnut's estimation, is a cornerstone in a bid for the bigtime. "It's had a galvanizing effect on this city," he said. "It's given us all a great lift. Everyone is excited. This means we're major-league and now the rest of the country will be paying attention to us."

The two Irsays and the players grabbed the headlines once the Colts moved in, but the real heroes were the brain trust that put the deal together: chief negotiator David Frick, first and foremost; William Hudnut; and the men in Indy's "706 Club," the group that supervised the whole affair: Frick; Otto Frenzel III, CEO of Merchants National Bank; Jim Morris, executive VP of Lilly Endowment; P.E. MacAllister, chairman of the Capital Improvement Board; and Tom Moses, chairman of Indianapolis Water Co. These heavy-hitters advised Frick along the way.

Frick knew this gambit had to work for Indy to move up in the world:

I have a pretty thick skin. I've screwed up some things in my life. Most of the time, I deserved the criticism. People can believe what they want [about the ethics of wooing Irsay]. We have a different view of the facts, but we were doing the best job we could to serve our community. And in the last 40 years, if there is one thing that made Indianapolis a successful city, it's that we got the Colts. But for that, we would still be considered a minor-league city. In the last 40 years, it's the biggest thing that ever happened to the city of Indianapolis. Had we not done it, we would still have had a good community, a good place to raise a family and have a decent job. But we would

not be viewed as we are today without the Colts coming to Indianapolis.

. . .

Skipping out of Baltimore and landing in seventh heaven was a major relief in the Colts command post. "First and foremost, I was able to reach out to my folks and my brothers and say, 'This really did happen. I'm now in Indianapolis,'" former equipment manager and current Colts archivist Jon Scott admitted. "Just going from a place where there was so much negativity with the club and going to a place where we could have a brand-new start... touring the dome—that was an equipment manager's dream. Going from an outdoor stadium that we shared with a baseball team, and now you got a place by yourself, everything brand-new. That was fun."

And the late Jim Irsay was hardly a spitting image of his old man. If he found a worthy cause, he'd wheelbarrow some money over to it. For instance, Jim Irsay was all-in on Kicking the Stigma, a promise he and his daughters made to confront the mental health crisis in Indiana. The Colts held a week-long fundraiser during Mental Health Awareness Month in May 2021 and raised $4.5 million for Kicking the Stigma Action Grants. The man had a big heart and didn't mind pulling out his fat wallet to help. Longtime Colts beat writer Mike Chappell lauds what he was about:

Jimmy took it [charitable deeds] to the highest level possible. You always want to leave a footprint when you're gone—or even while you're still here—and his generosity knew no bounds. They've got this Kicking the Stigma thing now that they are really behind. His daughters are behind it too. It's about recognizing mental health, and they've endorsed that. They've endorsed cancer research. Sometimes, we'd see an occasion when Jimmy would do something, monetarily, for a homeless shelter, a women's shelter, or whatever. But that's the tip of the iceberg. And he was quirky. He'd go to a training camp and pass out $100 bills. Sometimes, he'd tape $100 bills to a mini-football and toss them out to the fans. He was very, very connected. He believed that if you're gonna own a team here [in Indianapolis], you need to be an active part of the community. And he was; he was visible. All of that was real. He got a lot of acknowledgements for what he did, but we only saw a part of that. He believed that's what you do, and he did it for the right reasons.

While Indy whooped it up, Baltimore ran an emotional gamut. Most favored firing a V-2 rocket at Indy, but a few were ambivalent. "It's a relief, now that it's over," 46-year-old Grenville Whitman told the *Morning Sun* the day after the move. "To see the mayor of a major city and the governor of a major state in the grip of a _ _ _ _ ing sports team owner was too much to bear." Loyola College student Rick Aybar just shrugged it off inside

the Baltimore Museum of Art. "If it were the Orioles, I wouldn't be at a museum. I was into the Colts when I was 14 or 15, but now …"

The #1 Colts fanatic, Loudy Loudenslager, got run over by a roller compactor. The man who played the fight song at the airport for the departing Colts was lost when the new season started. Bill Hageman of the *Chicago Tribune* plotted his whereabouts on opening day, 1984:

While the Colts were opening their season Sunday in their new home in Indianapolis, several longtime fans showed up at empty Memorial Stadium in Baltimore. Leading the way was Hurst "Loudy" Loudenslager. A city parks board official had promised Loudenslager and his wife, Flo, they could sit in the empty stadium and pretend it was old times. But when the couple arrived, they were turned away by a security guard who mumbled the fateful words: "Sorry, no game today." "I even brought an American flag," said Loudenslager, 70, who was dressed in his "Sunday best" Colts T-shirt and blue pants. "I was going to stand up and sing the anthem, close my eyes and pretend I could see Unitas, Moore, Donovan, Marchetti and Berry running around out there. All of them, just one more time."

Current Ravens owner Steve Bisciotti thought that first autumn was like a weird dream. "It was kinda surreal, to not have a team," he confessed to Barry Levinson in *The*

Band That Wouldn't Die. "I remember thinking back then what it was like to be a city without a football team, to have watched games and have no rooting interest, have no conference, division games that mattered. It was just something that I had never experienced, and didn't know until you *did* experience it how tough it was to view the NFL as a world that you weren't really a part of."

News American sportswriter Bernie Miklasz had followed Robert Irsay's traveling circus around the country and figured Baltimore said good riddance to the man. "Baltimore people will always have that resentment toward Irsay, but Baltimore people are tough, and generally their attitude is, 'The hell with them.' People just don't care anymore," he told the *Philadelphia Inquirer* in August 1984. "Our people had been through so many near-misses for so long that they knew the move was inevitable. It was going to be Indianapolis or somewhere else. Now, apathy has set in."

Sure, their egos and emotions had been stomped on, but Baltimoreans weren't about to do a swan dive off the USF&G Building. The glass was half-full, claimed Bob Broeg of the *St. Louis Post-Dispatch*; the Birds were still in town:

Baltimore has a charming mayor. He is William Donald Schaefer, a mountain mover whose community has rebuilt downtown dramatically. Schaefer and associates dazzled baseball at the Hall of Fame induction ceremonies two years ago [1982] at Cooperstown, N.Y. They installed a giant tent on the lush lawn of the lakeside Otesaga Hotel and threw a Baltimore seafood bash. In baseball, they're eating high on the crabcakes now in Baltimore. The Orioles drew more than 2 million spectators last year for the first time and won the world championship [1983]. They drew more than 50,000 for Monday's opener with the White Sox. Presumably, they're still two-buck horse players [at Pimlico], but they don't own the Colts anymore.

Truth is, Baltimore put up a front to hide the shock and hurt—the line in "Eleanor Rigby" about wearing the face that they kept in a jar by the door. "When the Colts left, what I saw through the '80s was a whole area that felt like a widow," Baltimore documentarian Troy Lowman observed. "They didn't know who to root for, didn't really have a team. And you also had people who had kids aged 5-15 that parents had no game to take them to watch the hometown team. So, there was a whole lost generation—people born in the '70s and grew up in the '80s and '90s—who didn't have a football team. And it left a big, gaping hole for people."

Was it a blessing or a curse that the younger tribe wasn't around during the glory days? They only heard about Johnny Unitas and Lenny Moore from grandad and Uncle Silas at Thanksgiving or saw old, grainy videos on the tube. "There are some young football fans who don't know the Baltimore Colts ever existed or that one of the greatest quarterbacks in NFL history threw passes here," Jamison

Hensley observed in 2014 in "30 Years on, Baltimore Better Without Colts." "Memorial Stadium, once known as 'The World's Largest Outdoor Insane Asylum,' has been demolished and replaced with senior housing. This is what happens when the Colts have been gone for 30 years, which is as long as they played in Baltimore (1953-1983). Even Super Bowl-winning quarterback Joe Flacco was born 10 months after the Colts moved." How do you ever recapture Shula vs. Lombardi or Unitas running the two-minute drill?

The best move for older parents was to don the purple and black and not recite eye-rollers about the good ole days. "This generational rift is unique to Baltimore," Jess Mayhugh stated in the March 2014 issue of *Baltimore* magazine. "With most sports teams, you are loyal to whomever your parents (or grandparents) rooted for. Because that can't happen here, another interesting phenomenon is starting. 'I think now families are connecting again,' says Kevin Byrne [former senior VP of public and community relations] of the Ravens. 'Normally in sports, the generational love moves downward. Here, it's moving upward. Old Colts fans are being persuaded by their grandchildren to give the Ravens a chance.'"

In no way did that mean that the old guard would smile and make nice with Indy. Most of the heroes—especially Unitas, Tom Matte and Lenny Moore—had a raised middle digit ready if they called. Longtime Baltimore sportscaster Scott Garceau tells of the time the NFL Hall called to give tight end John Mackey the glad tidings:

These guys [Colts players] lost their legacy. One of the things I remembered after they left was John Mackey. The Hall of Fame called John and said they'd like to present the Hall of Fame ring at a Colts game in Indianapolis. And John said, "I'll take the ring at a crab house in Baltimore before I will at a Colts game in Indianapolis because I never played for the Indianapolis Colts." [Broadcaster] Tom [Davis] and I did a preseason game between the Colts and the Saints on the radio. It was sold out, and with about 3-4 minutes left in the first half, all of a sudden out of that dugout on the first-base side [of Memorial Stadium], here comes Artie [Donovan] with the #70 jersey on. And here comes Lenny Moore, Tom Matte. All the old Colts came out with John [Mackey], and the place went nuts. All of a sudden, you had 60,000 people on their feet, going crazy because all the favorite Colts were out there with their jerseys on, ready for the halftime ceremony when Mackey went out to the 50-yard line, and the Hall of Fame presented him with his ring. It was incredible. One of my favorite sports moments— those are *our* guys. Those are the *real* Colts.

After watching a 2007 HBO documentary about the Brooklyn Dodgers, *The Ghosts of Flatbush*, *Morning Sun* columnist David Steele had an idea:

It still doesn't beat Baltimore's story. Equals it, maybe, but doesn't beat it. And, of course, take the images and national cachet of the cities out of the picture, and the wattage of the rosters and their physical and emotional ties to their fanbases are a draw. Jackie [Robinson], Pee Wee [Reese] and Campy [Roy Campanella], meet Unitas, Lenny Moore and Artie Donovan. These aren't, say, the Seattle Seahawks, these are the Colts, one of the NFL's jewels. That makes this relevant enough for a courageous producer to take this on. Then there's this final selling point: an owner who out-O'Malleyed [Walter] O'Malley. Need a good villain? Ask the locals. To them, Bob Irsay makes O'Malley look like St. Francis of Assisi. Put it all together in documentary form, and it would be a cinematic masterpiece. So, c'mon, you budding Spielbergs, you Spike Lees-in-training, you Ken Burns wannabes with the Colts Corral membership cards still in your wallets. Your time has come. *The Ghosts of 33rd Street*. It's begging to be made.

That courageous producer is Troy Loman, and that doc. is already in the can (2020). Google it, press play and enjoy. The documentary is an hourlong ride down memory lane and a chance to put the Colts' move in cold storage. "I was always intrigued by the fact that there was no closure," Lowman stated. "There was no closure about the Colts leaving. They left an open wound, and there was no closure

for the fans of that era. Even when the Ravens came, a lot of people still didn't embrace them right away because they were Colts fans. I think it took a whole generation for it to switch over. What I wanted to do was give Colts fans some closure: This is what happened; don't forget them; if you put this in a box, it was a great time in your life. The end was beyond your control, and this is why it happened."

The Baltimore Colts were blessed with two cracking GMs, men with huge football IQs: Don Kellett and Ernie Accorsi. When presented with a what-if—what if Carroll Rosenbloom had stuck around and handed off to son Steve—Accorsi saw history changing:

> None of us could have foreseen what was gonna happen the next year [in 1972, when Robert Irsay arrived]. But if that could've been [Baltimore building a new stadium], how different it would've been. Steve [Rosenbloom] would have stayed in Baltimore. He was a Baltimore guy. It just could've been so different. What a great owner he would have been. We all loved Steve. It's just a shame it happened the way it did. That's fate; nothing you can do about it. But when he [Steve Rosenbloom] became president [of the Colts], we all assumed he was gonna take over. Obviously, Carroll— as long as he was alive and still had his fastball—he was gonna be an influence. But I think that if it was Steve's decision, that team would never have left.

The old-school icons and magnates of the '50s, '60s and '70s got washed away with the tide once the '80s rolled in. The sport pledged allegiance to the almighty dollar. The glory days of Unitas and Memorial Stadium were now only in Super-8 film canisters and stored as sweet memories. Tom Marr IV grew up on Colts football, but the cold reality of modern sports stands in stark contrast:

I don't know if there is any deeper meaning to this—you know, the old Brooklyn Dodgers and Frank Sinatra: "There used to be a ballpark." The Baltimore Colts were a product of their time, especially from 1953 to 1971. That was their golden era, and then they had the silver age with Bert Jones [1974-1977]. I guess you could say, "When you're young, when you're living through it, living through World Series and NFL championships, enjoy it because it goes away." I don't know if I want to take anything more cosmic out of it than that. When you lose your team in your 20s, you become cynical about sports. I had already lost the [Baltimore] Bullets when I was nine [1973], and when the Colts left, I knew sports was a business. And they really don't care about the fans if they're not giving them money.

But for lucky sorts who can see in the mind's eye Unitas hitting Berry on a down-and-out, Spats Moore scooting to paydirt, Mike Curtis impaling a tight end, #28 cradling one over the shoulder in Orrsville, they're worth as much as a winning Powerball ticket. And they can't steal those from you—even if they made off with your team.

CHAPTER 18

POSTPARTUM IMPRESSIONS

This is about diagnosing The Move, not the baby blues after delivery. The Latin word *parere*, a close relative to partum, can mean "to bring into being." Robert Irsay did that with the Indianapolis Colts when he hightailed it out of Baltimore. The blues came when Maryland woke up Thursday morning, March 29, 1984, and found out they were football orphans. Emotions concentered at the two poles—jubilant and dour, ecstatic and sour: Hoosiers and Baltimoreans.

John Fogerty of Creedence Clearwater Revival penned a number called "Wrote a Song for Everyone." Jim Irsay composed what we'll call "Wrote a Song to Piss 'Em Off." Kevin Cowherd of the *Evening Sun* started off his November 16, 1984, column with it. Somebody should have told Jimbo: Write on the blackboard 100 times, *I stink at songwriting.*

Daddy called me up on the telephone.
"Son, is there anybody listenin'?
Are you alone?
It's goin' down tonight around 9 p.m.

The trucks are on their way as soon
    as I say when."
Well, the trucks pulled up to Baltimore.
The people 'round there didn't want us
    no more.
So we packed up our bags and drove
    out of town.
And 12 hours later, we were Indy-bound.
Well, we had it tough a couple of years.
Just a lot of empty seats.
Lord, there was no one to cheer.
But we heard about a place that had
    a big white dome.
And it didn't take long for us to find
    a home.
Hoosier Heartland, that's where we
    do roam.
Hoosier Heartland, gettin' down in
    the Hoosier Dome.
Hoosier Heartland, and the Indy
    Colts have found their home.

Some additional rhyming couplets could have been added, like:

473

You guys drove the Colts right down
    in the muck
'Cause your daddy and Chernoff,
    they really do suck.

• • •

Even the free press got into scraps with each other. Wayne Fuson, of the *Indianapolis News*, was a smug little skunk who dragged *Evening Sun* sports editor Bill Tanton into his grimy column called "Time Out!" on April 20, 1984. Fuson was at Augusta, scarfing free grub while covering the Masters:

> Most reporters at Augusta, Ga., thought it [Indy getting the Colts] was great. One Baltimore sports editor even asked the wearer to send him a similar shirt [the Indy Colts T-shirt Fuson was flaunting]. But Bill Tanton of the Baltimore *Evening Sun* really saw red when he saw the Indianapolis Colts emblem. He taunted, accused and criticized Indianapolis, Irsay, the Colts and the wearer of the Colt shirt all week. He hasn't gotten over it yet … and probably won't for a while … Tanton is rather typical of the soreheads in Baltimore. He either has forgotten or is too young to remember that the Colts weren't conceived in Baltimore, you know. Baltimore got the franchise from Dallas. As in Texas. And how about Baltimore's beloved Orioles baseball team? Do you think they, too, were strictly from Baltimore from the start? No way. Heck,

> the Baltimore Orioles used to be the St. Louis Browns! Then there were the Baltimore Bullets of the National Basketball Association. They used to be the Zephyrs—in Chicago! So get off your high horse, Tanton.

Any Baltimore guy working the docks would have sunk a loading hook into Fuson's hindquarters and dragged him up and down Pratt Street.

John Steadman of the *News American* got jaw-to-jaw with Irsay in Indy at the Colts' '84 home opener against the Jets and recounted the pleasantries in *From Colts to Ravens*:

> I had a seat in the first row of the press box inside the dome and I was enjoying pregame practice. The punters were airing out the ball, the passers were warming up their arms, and the individual talents were on display for inspection and appreciation. Suddenly, behind me, came the sound of heavy feet pounding the steps. I looked over my left shoulder to see that it was Irsay himself. I thought maybe he was coming to gloat over the new "house" his team was playing in, compared to Memorial Stadium. He appeared to put out his hand and I got up to say hello. With that, he pulled me in close to him and said, "How does it feel to be a shit-heel?" I pushed him away and replied, "How does it feel to be devoid of common decency?" With that, he hurried back up the steps.

Tanton got steamed because Fuson was rubbing his nose in it. And there were more snide hijinks out in Indy. Getting the team from Baltimore wasn't enough. Some smart-asses had to push the issue. "In any case, Indianapolis and Baltimore aren't exactly candidates for sister cities," the *Los Angeles Times* observed in July 1984. "And this Cold War is definitely escalating. There's a new item on the racks of the many stores hawking apparel, key fobs, bumper stickers, mugs and every other imaginable form of Indianapolis Colts paraphernalia, and it's one of the biggest sellers these days. This is not just another T-shirt. It boldly proclaims, 'Home of the Indianapolis *Orioles.*'"

Likewise from the can't-leave-well-enough-alone department, this snippet from the *Ventura County* [CA] *Star* in September 1984:

> And how did they [Hoosiers] feel about the folks in Baltimore, who had felt so deeply about the loss of the team that had been there for 31 years? "Sad luck, friend," said [Hoosier Joe] Barnett. "That's the way it goes. Their loss, our gain." Ted Buehlford, another Indianapolis native, said, "We didn't care what team we got. We would have taken anybody." He was candid and not nearly as supercilious as the sign in a downtown gift shop here, which read: "First the Colts. Next the Orioles." And the shop was selling T-shirts with the inscription, "Indianapolis Orioles."

Weren't these the same humbugs who lambasted Baltimore fans for chanting obscenities to Irsay?

Freelancing owners guaranteed ugly mano-a-mano fights between cities. Only the fittest and most conniving prevailed. "Cities across the country are willing to compete, to recruit, and fight for professional sports franchises because they want the alleged reputational and economic benefits that teams are believed to provide to the host city," Jack Noonan stated in his 2018 doctoral thesis, *The Boom in Franchise Relocations: Moving Cities, No Matter the Cost.* "Local governments are spending obscene amounts of money to set up the best scenarios to earn a team and a status of a 'major-league city.'" Look at how creative Indianapolis got to bring down the interest rate from 11% to 8% on Bob Irsay's $12.5-million loan—a 1% food and beverage tax on commonfolk dining out. Baltimore countered: $15 million at 6.5%. Don't expect such a break on the condo you've been eyeing.

Teams had been flitting about long before Al Davis and Bob Irsay amscrayed in the '80s. Baseball had a raft of team moves over the decades. Just a sampler: Boston Braves to Milwaukee, 1953; St. Louis Browns to Baltimore, 1954; Dodgers and the Giants to L.A. and Frisco, 1957; Milwaukee Braves to Atlanta, 1966; Washington Senators (part two) to Texas, 1972. Lots of nomads in the NBA as well: Minneapolis Lakers to L.A., 1960; Philadelphia Warriors to San Francisco, 1962; San Diego Rockets to Houston, 1971; Baltimore Bullets to Washington, 1973; New Orleans

Jazz to Utah, 1979. You get a team and louse it up, you get cuckolded too.

Indianapolis ran circles around Baltimore to get the Colts, and they've made it stick, says Colts writer JJ Stankevitz:

> You can pretty definitively say that Indianapolis, over the last 40 years, has made good on their opportunity as an NFL city. The circumstances in which we acquired an NFL team were certainly challenging. Another city had to lose a team. And a lot of people I've talked to in Indy said, "I *did* spare a thought for Baltimore in my elation about getting the Colts." But over the last 40 years, the Colts have become just as ingrained in Indianapolis as they were for their 30 years in Baltimore. This city is so connected to its football team in a way that, [my] coming from Chicago and being a Bears fan, Indy's different because it's a smaller town. There's a certain pride that comes with the Colts here than you'll get in a lot of bigger cities. Big cities are prideful; they love their team. But in Indy, the players are in our community. All over the city, you see them everywhere, constantly doing community events, donating their time and money to the community. Peyton Manning didn't just bring Indianapolis a Super Bowl; he brought a children's hospital [Children's Hospital at Ascension St. Vincent]. The players are so deeply entrenched in the community in a way

that is so rewarding as a resident that you can feel that.

One side of the seesaw goes up, the other down. So it went with Indy and Baltimore. Hoosiers relished feeling like big shots. "They [the fans] were faithful to the fact that we had an NFL team," veteran Indianapolis sportswriter Bill Benner stated. "Being in the NFL then, as now, said to America, 'We're big-league.' And that's with no disrespect to the Indiana Pacers and the NBA. But the NFL was the golden ring, and Indianapolis put it on its finger."

To former *Morning Sun* columnist Michael Olesker, all the tumblers fell into place for Indianapolis, and Baltimore got snake-bitten:

> It was a series of one-shot deals that came out of nowhere. Who would have expected Carroll Rosenbloom to trade the team in the first place? And that's what set it off. But to have traded the team to a drunk who then demands, "I want a new ballpark," and openly shops the team around—the love affair in its heyday was *so* strong. And then the second love affair in the mid-'70s [three straight division championships] was so strong. I remember [Baltimore sportscaster] Vince Bagli saying to me that the second love affair [from 1974-1977] was as strong as the first, that the fans were just as passionate. I don't know about that, but it was certainly passionate. And it was tied in with the rebirth of

the city. So, it was inconceivable, but there it was. Once it was set into motion with the original trade [of teams] and it brought Irsay here, maybe it was inevitable. It also came at a time when the city had lost faith in itself. I remember every winter, Mayor Schaefer had to go down to Annapolis and beg—BEG—the legislators for money. We were on our knees in so many ways, we couldn't *let* ourselves believe that we could lose that football team.

From a man not prone to hyperbole or spin, this head-scratcher. "Bob [Irsay] had an attachment to Baltimore," David Frick, Indy's star negotiator, professed to the *Morning Sun* in 1993. "That decision to move came very hard for him. I watched the man in the process. While the stadium was not the quality stadium that other teams were playing in, and fan support had declined dramatically at the end, that was a longstanding franchise, and it troubled him to move it." We're left to conclude that Irsay's infernal dawdling about a move was either toying with the suitors for sport or wedding-day jitters. But nobody in Baltimore believes that Irsay ever took a shine to the town.

It's fair to say that Baltimore and Indianapolis still look askance at each other after all these years. "When Robert Irsay moved his Baltimore Colts to Indianapolis in late March 1984, it altered the economic climate and psyche of two states," *BizVoice* stated in "Indianapolis and the Colts: Deal That Changed the Landscape" in its September/October 2011 issue. "Now it's hard to imagine what Indiana would be like without an NFL team, and many in Maryland, the Baltimore area specifically, still harbor bad feelings—and getting the Ravens franchise 12 years later seems to have done little to erase that."

Considering how Baltimore got socked in the jaw, veteran *Indianapolis Star* sportswriter Mike Chappell isn't keen on preaching grow-up-and-deal-with-it to the wounded. "What I always get pushback from in Baltimore is when others tell them, 'Get over it.' Now, 'Get past it' might be the better phrase. They're never gonna 'get over it.' You're getting less of that now because you're another generation removed, and people are passing away. The younger generation over there [in Baltimore], I don't think they care. You got a team [the Ravens] with two Super Bowls, but I wanna say, don't tell somebody to 'get over it.' 'Get past it,' 'Get through it,' OK, but there's a segment that, until they pass away, that's never gonna happen."

Looking at the five stages of grief—denial, anger, bargaining, depression and acceptance—Baltimore plowed through the first four in the decades since, but that last one is a tough bugger. In *Baltimore* magazine's "Colt Following" in March 2014, moving on past the move wasn't so easy:

For the city of Baltimore, as a whole, the Colts leaving town represented something much larger than a few Sunday games. "A population becomes invested emotionally in a team because it defines that city's sense of self," says professor David Andrews, who studies the sociology of sport at the University of Maryland. "And when a team goes, what happens to that?" The city was surely invested in the Colts, as players were ingrained in the community, hanging out at the same bars as fans and interacting often with the Colts Corrals, which were local fan clubs. Suffice it to say, it was more than just a game. "Let me put it this way—I was 25 minutes late for my own wedding because a Colts game went into overtime," says [Duda's Tavern owner Antoinette] Duda. "I knew the players personally because they would come down to your bull roast, and they did a lot for small businesses."

It was Maryland state senator Thomas Bromwell's ire that pushed the eminent-domain bill across the finish line. He told the *Miami Herald* right after the move, "You can say what you want about Dallas and Washington. There's no doubt in my mind that the Colts of the 1960s and 1970s were America's Team. I don't think anyone could forget them. We sat in the rain. We sat in the cold. We put our hearts and our spirit in the Baltimore Colts. My father was a pretty tough man, but I remember him crying the day John Unitas played his last game at Memorial Stadium. That ought to be worth something instead of a reign of terror."

You don't sit out in the rain and cold inside a dome, but Hoosiers got their own love affair going right quick. Former *Evening Sun* writer Michael Janofsky examined the Colts frenzy in Indy and Baltimore's ambivalence in a July 1984 *New York Times* article:

Mr. Irsay defended his action [the move], in part, by citing the rabid enthusiasm of fans and civic officials in Indianapolis to the coming of the Colts. After season-ticket applications became available, the club received 143,000 requests. In their last season in Baltimore, the club sold 28,000 season tickets. "Even when we won the division three times, we couldn't fill the stadium," Mr. Irsay said, although they came close, playing to 79% capacity in 1975, 90% in 1976 and 92 % in 1977. By 1982, in the season shortened by the players' strike that the Colts finished with their worst record ever, 0-8-1, attendance was also at a record low. An average crowd of 26,912, or 44% of capacity, had watched the four home games. However, when the team began to improve last season [1983], finishing 7-9, attendance increased by 15,000 a game, lending credence to the theory that folks in Baltimore don't mind watching a team if it's interesting. Still, Mr. Irsay pleaded that the fans "could have supported the team better," and that by remaining in Baltimore all those years, he lost more than $20 million.

Bill Benner, formerly of the *Indianapolis Star*, rolled out an old cliché about getting too comfy: "When you think Indianapolis now, and you're sitting in Spokane, Washington, you're thinking that's the place where they do sports—and when they do 'em, they take them to another level. Never take anything for granted because it's an increasingly incredibly competitive environment. You cannot sit back and think that the Oakland Raiders will stay the Oakland Raiders, or the Oakland A's are gonna stay the Oakland A's. You can't take *anything* for granted. And I will tell you that Indianapolis, even after achieving all that it has through sports, is not taking anything for granted. It will still be creative, ingenious, and it will muster whatever resources are necessary to maintain Indy's status as a major-league city."

The Colts would put to bed all the old gibes about Indy: They turned off the lights downtown at 5:00 and went home for the night, and it's a racetrack surrounded by cornfields. In sportswriter Mike Chappell's eyes, the team gave the city a makeover:

> When the Colts came here, this city was basically the [Indiana] Pacers, which were having trouble, IU basketball and the Indy 500. The Colts just transformed the city, transformed the perception of the city. Now you're one of 32 [NFL teams]. I don't care if you're the 32nd team in value and competition, you're one of those guys. The power of the NFL is incredible, still the most popular sport in the country, so it was pretty cool that Indy joined that group. And it all goes back to [Mayor] Hudnut, [David] Frick and those other guys, having the vision to make it happen. The fact that they landed a team was the crowning moment of their vision.

The Move finally prompted the Indy Colts to create a podcast in 2024—titled "The Move," of course. JJ Stankevitz produced the four-episode history: "Like Baltimore in the '50s [with the Colts' success], it gave Indianapolis a chance to say, 'Every Sunday in the fall, we are going to have a presence on national TV,'" Stankevitz stated. "And more people started to think, *What about Indianapolis as a place to move?* Why does Indianapolis—a place people thought was a cow town in the Midwest—why do they have an NFL team? Then you start looking at it. They have all these major corporations; the cost of living is low; it's a great place to raise a family; look at all the stuff there is to do. 'Maybe we should think about moving there.' All of a sudden, you see this massive expansion in and around the city that's still going on to this day. The Colts played a part in that. I don't think you can brush it aside and say the Colts had nothing to do with that."

People started settling down in Indy in droves. In 1984, the population of the Indianapolis-Metro Area was 869,000. The line on the graph kept angling up: 921,000 in 1990; 1,063,000 in 1995; 1,225,000 in 2000; 1,495,000 in 2010; 1,807,000 in 2020;

1,903,000 in 2024. A lot of folks figured that Indy was a sweet spot to lay down roots, and the Colts factored into that. But Baltimore was no slacker either; their Metro-Area population followed the same trajectory: 1,787,000 the year of the move; 1,849,000 in 1990; 2,079,000 in 2000; 2,207,000 in 2010; 2,325,000 in 2020; 2,370,000 in 2024. But there is the uh-oh—the actual population INSIDE the city has careened down a ramp: over 900,000 in 1970; 785,000 in 1980; 735,000 in 1990; 642,000 in 2000; 585,000 in 2020. The suburbs gained bodies; the city kept losing them. A shrinking tax base makes it tough to pay the bills. Contrast that with Indianapolis proper. Its population eased up the hill over the years: 700,807 in 1980; 782,254 in 2000; 820,445 in 2010; 887,382 in 2020—baby steps the other way.

. . .

Those 87 luxury suites in the Hoosier Dome for the hoity-toity got gobbled up like Walmart merch on Black Friday. The 87 suites ranged in capacity from eight seats to 16, cost $40,000 ($123,000 in 2025 money) to $100,000 ($307,800 nowadays) and had annual renewal fees of $10,000 to $24,000. "Gloria Mills, marketing director for the Capital Improvement Board which operates the [Indiana Convention Center] and the Hoosier Dome, said the final two suites for the Hoosier Dome were rented Monday [April 2]," the *Indianapolis Star* reported. "Only 16 had remained before the announcement that the Baltimore Colts were moving here. Since Thursday [March 29] the remaining suites were rented on a first-come, first-served basis, Mrs. Mills said." Hoosier Hysteria was on the loose.

The Big Wheel, who led C-O-L-T-S cheers in the upper deck at Memorial Stadium for years, doesn't blame Bob Irsay for how things turned out. "He didn't steal the team," Len Burrier opined. "He was forced to take the team somewhere. And Indianapolis came up and said, 'Hey, we got the money, we have a new stadium. Come on down.' No qualms, ifs, ands or buts, they just did it. And Baltimore got left holding an empty bag. People here [in Baltimore] don't look at the inside of stuff. They just look at what the [TV] news says, what the paper says, stuff like that. If people get into *why* Irsay left, they might have a different idea. He [Irsay] was a drinker, but he wasn't always whacked out. I guess I felt different towards him than the rest of the people. I sort of realized that something had to happen. And it finally did."

Built into the bricks and mortar of the myth of The Skedaddle is this image of Irsay playing the burglar and making off with his team in "the dead (gloom, dark, etc.) of night" while Baltimore slept. Some folks just can't wrap their brains around Maryland forcing Irsay to scram the day it OK'd eminent domain. Nobody knew if the courts would tell Irsay to stay put while the legal war games played out. "The reason for the stealth, the reason for the immediacy, was that Baltimore was gonna try to block Bob from leaving with the legal concept of eminent domain, which essentially said that the community owned the franchise, and you couldn't move it," former Colts assistant coach Rick Venturi explained in episode 3 of "The Move." "And I guess he and his legal people felt that maybe they could do that. And so, he was gonna get outta Dodge before it [the bill] got to the [MD] House or whatever."

John Steadman, now with the *Morning Sun* in 1998 after the *News American* folded, always lumped Irsay with Ivan the Terrible and Vlad the Impaler, but granted that eminent domain gave him a shove. "From all aspects, it appeared the Colts were close to heading to Indianapolis, but it wasn't a *fait accompli* until Irsay said so. Once the eminent-domain papers were filed, Irsay signaled, 'Go.' Would the Colts have left had it not been for the state legislature's move? We'll never know." We do know one thing: Annapolis started a game of chicken and Irsay didn't blink; he just split.

Jim Irsay went to confessional with the *New York Times* in 2021 in "Sins of the Father: What Jim Irsay Learned Watching His Dad Cripple the Colts." He admitted that Dad screwed things up but couldn't ride it out in Baltimore:

> Almost 40 years later, Jim acknowledges his father's many faults: "He messed up a ton of stuff," he says, "with his volatility, his drinking, his lack of knowledge of the game"—but the son takes issue with how the Baltimore move is remembered. He believes Bob had no

choice. "People lose sight of how dire it was," Jim says now. "The stadium situation was a disaster, and it wasn't getting resolved. Some people say (former Browns owner) Art Modell was going to give my dad $25 million and allow him to pay it back. That's such bullshit! Art was on the verge of bankruptcy for godsakes! The only thing I don't like in how my dad is painted is that Maryland was going to the state legislature to pass an eminent-domain law. OK, then, what was he supposed to do? Call them up at 9 in the morning and tell them, 'I'm thinking of moving the team'? You think that'd be OK?"

Shipping the shoulder pads, helmets, jerseys, blocking sleds—the whole caboodle— to the enemy was what you get for playing nonchalant with a beloved team: You get jilted. What got Baltimore fuming was running off with the horseshoe. "Had he changed the name to something specific to the history and traditions of either Indianapolis or Indiana, and left the name Colts, the horseshoe insignia and colors and the legacy here, then all would have been good," Johns Hopkins Writing Seminars professor Greg Kane complained in "When the Colts Left Baltimore: Taking a Team is One Thing; Stealing a City's Legacy and History is Quite Another." "I think that's why there's still such bitterness and resentment against Bob Irsay and his son, Jim … It didn't help that after the Irsays got to Indy, they made public comments blaming

Baltimore fans, not their own incompetence, for the team's pathetic showing during their latter years here and during the early years in Indianapolis. They also opposed moves by other owners who wanted to bring their teams to Baltimore, claiming that frequent moves would make the league unstable." Art Modell, who harrumphed the same thing after the Colts moved, skipped off from Cleveland to Baltimore in a hypocritical about-face.

David Frick, the man who hammered out the contract with the Colts, is tired of hearing the stale myth about the move:

I gave up years ago trying to convince people that we didn't "steal" the Colts, that they didn't leave "under the cover of darkness." It's terribly unfair. A colleague of mine once said, "You're never gonna convince the world that you didn't steal the franchise under the cover of darkness. Give up." So I gave up. But the reality is, it didn't happen that way. It happened because to get all the documents done, printed out and in a position to sign them, we did all that on the 28th [of March]. [Michael] Chernoff then flew on the company plane back to Baltimore. The time frame worked; he [Chernoff] didn't get out there to Baltimore until nine or ten o'clock [to supervise the move]."

Irsay's flirtation with Indianapolis started in 1977 when Paul Oakes caught rumors that Irsay was peeved with Baltimore. He got Irsay on the phone, felt him out and set up a meet-and-greet between Irsay and Hudnut's crew. In his 2012 book, *How the Colts Came to Indianapolis*, Oakes debunks the thief-in-the-night claptrap but plays it a little too cute:

By the way, if you are standing in line at the grocery store or at a service station and you see someone wearing a Colts sweatshirt, ask him about the move from Baltimore to Indianapolis 25 years ago. The discussion will start with, "They moved in the middle of the night." And nothing could be further from the truth. Mayflower moving vans were sent to Baltimore simply to pick up Mr. Robert Irsay's personal property, since the city was about to exercise eminent domain and confiscate the helmets, pads, shoes and footballs the next morning. In fact, the very next morning the Maryland legislature did indeed try to enact eminent domain [sic, they did it the day Irsay moved], and if Irsay had waited another day, the city would have locked up all of his property. Bob Irsay simply beat the city that had divorced him to the punch.

Oakes gets credit for one thing—stating that Irsay had to shove off before eminent domain put up a roadblock. But it's drunk driving to claim that Maryland could have swooped in and impounded Irsay's bits and bobs after they passed the law. Before he could scoot, a judge MIGHT have commanded

Irsay to stick around—probably for a month of Sundays—until this got sorted out. Neither Irsay nor Indy wanted to sweat bullets and wait.

Former Baltimore Colts and New England Patriots executive and NFL wiseman Upton Bell thinks Irsay should have been more forthright; that would've put Baltimore in a bind:

> Let's say that Irsay *didn't* move them in the middle of the night, which became a mythology in itself. Let's say he confronted them [Baltimore officials] and said, "Listen, if I don't get a new stadium, I'm going to move the team." And he then, in a very orderly manner, told them, "Look, I've gotta tell ya, here's the ultimatum: If we don't get a new stadium or the *promise* of a new stadium, I'm moving the team." And then, after a while, if he had moved the team in an orderly way—not at midnight—and made a deal with Indianapolis, what excuse would they [Baltimore officials] have had then? So, everybody's to blame—except *them*, huh?

In his column in the *Morning Sun* the day after Irsay died (January 14, 1997), Ken Rosenthal shoveled no BS about Irsay's virtues, but he did indict Baltimore for losing interest in the brand and butchering the stadium problem:

> There's no need to take a revisionist view of Irsay—none of this happened

out of the goodness of his heart. Indeed, many old Colts fans are offended by the national fawning over Green Bay for the way it obsesses over the Packers. Baltimore had the same bond with its team before Irsay tore it down. The consecutive sellout streak, the world's largest insane asylum, Loudy [Loudenslager] and the Corrals and Johnny U.—that tradition should have continued forever. But the crowds dwindled under Irsay, and the Maryland General Assembly played no small role in his departure, giving Baltimore the power to take over the franchise through eminent domain. With that, Irsay felt compelled to act. The lesson Baltimore learned was that it costs far more to *replace a team* [emphasis mine] than it does to keep it. It's a lesson that cities—most recently Cleveland—continue to ignore.

Jon Scott kept his job as equipment manager after the Colts moved. He thinks like most of the crowd in Indy. "I don't think the standard version about Mr. Irsay is the correct one. People don't know the whole story. Eminent domain is rarely talked about. It's always all about the 'midnight move.' It's all about them sneaking out. Well, why *was* it that they had to go in the middle of the night? The owner was possibly gonna lose his team. A real possibility. People don't know the whole story. And if they did, they would think differently because they never knew all of this. Obviously, it [eminent domain] wasn't the way to do it. I think they thought Jim's dad would never just go ahead and make the move. But he did."

No sober melon thinks Irsay would have stayed in Baltimore, the vibes being what they were. But in "Colts' Irsay: 'No way' I Would Have Dealt Elway 40 Years Ago," Jim Irsay said it was academic after eminent domain: "A lot of people think that with my dad it was, 'Oh, he moved in the middle of the night. That's so sneaky.' That's not true at all. They were going to pass an eminent-domain law, and they were forcing his hand. I loved [Mayor] Donald Schaefer. He was a really good guy. He could've come up with $10 million and kept the Colts for 25 years. But there was just nothing in the negotiations." Until the 11th-hour desperation heave after Irsay and Indy already had the contract printed.

A husband who knows some guy is wooing his wife and she's getting weak-kneed can either mount a counter-offensive or shrug. Upton Bell thinks Baltimore should have appeased Irsay and grasped the big picture:

> I think Jim Irsay has talked about his father's own problems and understands them. Listen—over a period of years, you get new owners. Owners change; teams change. If you're farsighted, which I can't say most cities or politicians are, you realize that you're gonna have good owners and bad owners. You'll have people you don't like and people you do like. That isn't the point. The point is,

the city and the fans and what is right for the city. And I'm probably talking about something that will never happen, but that's what the lesson is for the fans and the powers-that-be: It's the TEAM, stupid. It's what that team means to the town. What does it mean to Baltimore? It's about the city and what franchises mean to a city. Always remember—it's the *team*, stupid.

The ultimate sin was Baltimore mucking around for almost 20 years instead of bearing down about a new stadium. Baltimore author Kevin Cowherd regrets the lack of prescience with disaster on the horizon:

> Stadium, stadium, stadium. Had they done that, they would've had a shot. They had to come up with the money for that stadium. The stadium was the reason he [Irsay] left. It's that simple. So, the only thing they could've done was build him a new stadium. I don't think *any* amount of renovation [to Memorial Stadium] would've satisfied Bob Irsay. He felt the place was a dump—which it was. It had great memories for a lot of people—and I don't think there was anything else they could've done. I think they needed a new stadium. Remember, the feeling was a downtown stadium would be perfect back then. Are you gonna have *another* stadium on 33rd Street? I don't think so; I don't think that would've worked.

The mechanic asks you, "You kept hearing the scraping and squealing in your brakes getting worse, and you thought everything was OK, do *nothing*?" Baltimore kept the stadium problem sitting in the inbox. And they paid for it. "The city should have woke up," filmmaker Troy Lowman declared. "They were sleeping like it was still the 1950s. The government needed to be proactive with those renovations. They should have read the room better. That's what I would've changed. I would've sat down with him [Irsay] and said, 'What do you need here?' and kicked the can down the road. But look—everything happens for a reason. They finally woke up, got the Maryland Stadium Authority and kept the Orioles [via the new ballpark]. Then they got the Ravens. It was all about the renovations of the stadium. He didn't necessarily want a new stadium. Ultimately, they would have needed a new stadium anyway. Memorial Stadium wouldn't have lasted that long. Places like Wrigley Field and Fenway Park are rare."

Current Indianapolis Colts COO Pete Ward might have had the same gig in Baltimore had they mustered the unity and creativity that Indy did. That would've been fine with him:

I think just attempting to be reasonable with the obvious needs of a pro football franchise, that being a stadium that is contemporary with the peers of the league, in terms of amenities for the fans, the team and the media, that's what they should have done. It seems like it would

have been easier with a stadium that has both baseball and football. You could take care of the same needs in one fell swoop. But I don't know everything that Mr. Irsay was asking for or what the Orioles were asking for. It may have taken a totally new stadium for either the baseball or the football team. It may have taken two. But I just thought at some point, a new stadium had to be the consideration for both franchises because Memorial Stadium was too antiquated. I don't think it could have been retrofitted to accommodate suites, club seats and that sort of thing. But as a stopgap, a [hefty] check would have been enough to keep the Colts there.

Charles Euchner, author of a fine study of feuding cities, *Playing the Game* and a topical book for 2025, *Rules of Activism*, thinks both Baltimore and Irsay kept chasing their tails:

I would have been frustrated because both sides were playing games, and I would have said if either side *really* wanted to solve the problem, they would have come up with a contract that had certain kinds of triggers, and they would have agreed in advance that if there was a dispute, there could be some kind of arbitration. But the sense that I got was that they were playing a game of chicken, and neither side wanted to veer their car over. They both had points, and they both had interests. That's what happens in politics sometimes. They're kind of going for broke. Irsay was obviously already looking elsewhere, so there was something about him that wanted to go. And the city [Baltimore] had its own problems to deal with. It was reaching its lowest point, at least in the '70s. But the problem is, one side [the owner] is always on the offensive, and the other side [the city] doesn't actually say, "OK, what do we need; what do we want; what are we willing to do?" It's all done reactively. So, when the city said, "OK, we'll do it as long as you sign a long-term lease," I'm sure on one level they were 100% sincere, but I'm also sure that at one level it would be rejected. In that situation, that's where you need a mediator. And as far as I know, nobody ever suggested that. But that's what happens when you have legitimate interests on both sides, and they come to an impasse. You have to take it beyond the immediate thing that they're stuck on and figure out a win-win solution. But that was never really a thought, and it was because they were so much on their own tracks that they weren't thinking about the overall situation and how they could win by giving a bit.

Nobody even thought about mediation, and if anybody budged an inch, it was Irsay, giving Baltimore a little more time to figure things out.

Baltimore blundering its way out of a new stadium got *Morning Sun* sports editor Bob Maisel to thinking about 1972, when he toured a hole in the ground that would become the Superdome. He asked folks down there, why go into hock for such a project:

Bill Connick, the secretary of the Superdome Commission and one of its driving forces, said, "Maybe it all started with the United Fruit Company. Our two main sources of income in this area are our port and tourism. We sort of took tourism for granted, and we weren't keeping the port up the way we should. I suppose we were also taking that for granted. Well, the United Fruit Company had been one of our main industries for maybe 100 years. They were one of the family. Then, all of a sudden, they moved. Lock, stock and barrel, they went off to a port in Texas. Just like that, they were gone, and when we analyzed the move, it was obvious why they had done it. The other port simply offered better, more modern facilities. I think it made a lot of us realize what could happen, and we decided it was time to do something constructive, something positive to make people and businesses want to stay, and to attract new ones. We didn't want to have to beg them," Connick said.

Replace United Fruit and New Orleans with Irsay and Baltimore and the song remains the same. That's the basic postmortem Baltimore did before they built Oriole Park and M&T Bank. Lesson learned the hard way.

. . .

Robert Irsay wins the debate on the whys and wherefores of trucking off to Indy. The bridge was washed out, reconciliation was hopeless, the stadium crusade was dead, and Baltimore fans wanted his scalp. But what he did to the Cadillac of football franchises was almost treason. The same Gordon Beard who got scolded by Irsay at the BWI press conference as a "bad man" wrote a eulogy for the Baltimore Colts on March 31, 1984:

The Colts not only won National Football League championships in 1958, 1959 and 1968, and the Super Bowl following the 1970 season. They won the hearts and minds of the community. They owned the city. In a simpler time, players and fans mingled at local watering holes, drinking beer together and becoming friends. General manager Don Kellett personally returned telephoned complaints. Fans by the thousands drove an hour to the summer training camp [in Westminster, MD] to watch their heroes … and bend more elbows. Memorial Stadium, once described as "the world's largest outdoor insane asylum," was the home playground for future Hall of Famers John Unitas, Art Donovan, Gino Marchetti, Raymond Berry, Jim Parker, Lenny

Moore and coach Weeb Ewbank. Many of the players settled in the area, with Marchetti and Alan Ameche launching fast-food chains that made them millionaires. Others met with lesser success in business, but they were offered no less love and respect. Then Robert Irsay arrived.

He was a football rube and a boozer. When he was sober, he didn't know a flea flicker from a flea market, and when he was sloshed, hell hath no fury. He also held onto his wallet with two hands. "If there has been any kind of consistent thread to the Bob Irsay years with the Colts, it has been that the bottom line always comes first," Vito Stellino of the *Morning Sun* explained in February 1984. "To understand the Colts has been to understand the bottom line. Fire Lenny Moore. Fire ticket manager Bill Roberts. Trade John Elway. Those moves were all public relations disasters, but they had a common theme. They saved Irsay money. He has always put saving money ahead of the won-lost column. He prides himself on being 28th and last when they rank the NFL clubs by payroll." And look at all the L's and the paltry W's—pretty rank as well.

You'll not get much carping from former Colts assistant coach Rick Venturi, not given how the Irsays treated him:

He [Irsay] was a volatile man; there's no question about that. Our franchise was very volatile. But I will say this— the Irsays personally—the old man and

Jim—over the years have been great to me. They've written a lot of paychecks for me. I have nothing but good feelings for the Irsay family. Was it volatile in Baltimore? Yes, it really was. I think Jim learned a ton about how *not* to do it, and I think Jim then became one of the great owners in the National Football League. It was a volatile time, but it was also a hard time. The team had diminished. Financially, he [Bob Irsay] was hurting. There were a million things involved, and when you have a suitor [Indianapolis] that is willing to give you *everything*, it's gonna happen.

Back to the Jekyll-Hyde theme. For every accolade about Irsay coming out of Indiana, there was an indictment in Baltimore. "You can understand the sorrow of a John Steadman, the graceful columnist [of the *News American*] who reigns as perhaps the single leading authority on the Colts," Kevin Cowherd wrote on April 5, 1984, in the *Evening Sun*. "You can understand the despair of everyone who lived in Baltimore, the fans who did nothing less than turn over a piece of their hearts to this franchise. Bob Irsay, the kind of man who could ruin Christmas Eve, ruined pro football in this town. Sent it packing in Mayflower vans in the middle of the night. And nobody seems willing to forget that, not just yet."

This plunge down the slope alone in the *Washington* Post gives you an idea of the decline Irsay wrought:

In 1968, when the Baltimore Colts were 13-1 and won the NFL championship, tickets were so hard to come by that star running back Tom Matte could only buy endzone seats for his parents. Today [May 1983], anyone with a pocketful of change can buy a choice seat at Memorial Stadium. Last year, the Colts didn't win a game, finishing the strike-shortened season with the league's worst record, 0-8-1. While an average of 26,912 turned out each week to watch their team wallow in the pits of ineptitude, not only did the city of Baltimore ponder the Colts' fall from glory, but the entire nation wondered what had befallen the franchise that produced such Hall of Famers as Johnny Unitas, Gino Marchetti and Lenny Moore. Colts' fans saw six head coaches come and go in 10 years under the leadership of owner Robert Irsay. They saw star players such as Ted Hendricks, John Dutton and Bert Jones traded in their prime, and, most recently, watched as college football's best quarterback and the Colts' No. 1 draft pick, John Elway, refused even to consider the city as a place to call home.

Apparently, Irsay took incompetence with him to Indy, along with everything else. *Indianapolis Star* sportswriter Robin Miller noted that it was business as usual in October 1991:

The bottom line is that the Colts are weak at the top. From babbling Bob, the out-of-town and out-of-touch owner, to his son, Jim, who received an NFL team as an early Christmas present back in 1984, the Irsays are the main reason this franchise may forever be stuck in the muck of mediocrity. The elder Irsay looks at football like most women do—it's a social event he really doesn't understand. A wealthy man because of the heating and cooling business, his air ducts aren't always open. In the 20 years he's owned the once-hallowed NFL club, Irsay has run off competent coaches and players with dumb decisions and a barroom temper. He's thought of as an embarrassment around the league.

Then Peyton Manning happened along in 1998 and made everybody look like a genius. His dad's Boris Yeltsin routine pointed Irsay the Younger in the right direction—the other way. "And maybe that—however unintentional—remains Bob Irsay's greatest feat as an NFL owner, perhaps his only one," the *New York Times* observed in 2021. "He molded his son into a football man, then showed him how much a meddling, controlling, impulsive boss can cripple a franchise. It has forever shaped how Jim runs his team. 'He didn't just have the keys handed to him,' [Robin] Miller [of the *Indianapolis Star*] says. 'After being a GM himself, and screwing it up, and knowing the game, he said, "You know what? I've gotta go get someone else. We're never gonna do anything if I don't." To look in the mirror and accept that? Not a lot of

guys in his shoes would be able to do that. Trust me.'"

Don Henley had some good advice in "The Heart of the Matter" for the jaded and jilted in Baltimore: There are people in your life/Who've come and gone./They let you down./You know they hurt your pride./You better put it all behind you, babe,/'Cause life goes on./You keep carryin' that anger,/It'll eat you up inside. Actually, one of their own, the *Morning Sun*'s Ken Rosenthal, advised just that in 1997, the day after Robert Irsay died: "Former Gov. William Donald Schaefer put it best yesterday: 'Now that he's dead, I don't want to say bad things about the man. It's over.' Actually, it was over a long time ago, this love affair with a team and a time unique to the city's history. If nothing else, Irsay's death brings closure. It's over. Enough anger. Enough venom. Enough of March 28, 1984."

Some people who knew him well said Bob Irsay could be a really decent guy. Catch him at the right moment, especially before the martini lunch, and you got his best. "When you get a chance to sit down with Bob Irsay, one-on-one, you find out that he's really a nice fellow, a regular guy," Phoenix lawyer Harry Cavanagh told Bill Tanton of the *Evening Sun*. When Tanton begged to differ, Cavanagh said, "I can understand your feeling. For some reason, whenever Bob Irsay gets around the media, he self-destructs. He just can't handle that pressure. But away from it, he's fine." Years of broadsides by the Baltimore press probably brought on the blustering and bombast. But to be fair to the scribes, they didn't declare war until Irsay started the chronic bumbling, then all civility was lost.

One guy who wouldn't give the Irsays a break was sportswriter Robin Miller of the *Indianapolis Star*. For years he rode both of them, but he softened the rhetoric as he got to know them. When Bob Irsay died in January 1997, Miller paid homage:

> No player or coach ever was safe from this man with little tact and less rationale, and more often than not his knee-jerk personnel changes and post-game diatribes were fueled by alcohol. But the sobering truth about Robert Irsay's 13 years in our city is that he brought us a National Football League franchise, created many charitable contributions, helped build a dynamic Downtown and was a good citizen. His mother once called him the "devil on earth," but Irsay's behavior in Indianapolis was almost angelic compared with the hell he raised in Baltimore… But even though his playing days at Illinois and war heroism are said to be creative writing for the media guide, the fact remains that Irsay pumped a lot of vitality into Indianapolis. He gradually loosened his grip and purse strings, which enabled the Colts to finally flourish and win a place in this city's heart. The cruel irony for Robert Irsay is that he lived to create a respectable NFL team and, for all intents and purposes, died before he could truly enjoy it.

• • •

Bereft of the Colts and feeling maudlin, Baltimoreans started asking, "Whatta we do now?" Answer: Go whole hog to snare an expansion team and build a new stadium. In his April 6, 1984, column, John Steadman posed as the Answer Man:

> There's no need for a meeting at City Hall or a visit to the State House in Annapolis. Why waste the valuable time of a mayor and a governor when it's all so elementary. Here it is, written in the form of a preliminary presentation and all for the cost of today's copy of the *News American*. For Baltimore to advance its sports identity, the following three proposals must be addressed posthaste:
>
> • That a blue-ribbon committee should be named to decide on the location of a new stadium, whether it's to be in the city or outside of it, a domed or open facility, and, of course, how it will be financed.
>
> • That continual legal resources be marshaled against Bob Irsay for stripping the city of its NFL franchise and every avenue be pursued to find a way to restore the franchise.
>
> • That a group of investors prepare themselves for either buying out Irsay, in the event the courts order him to return the Colts to Baltimore, or be available for getting in line to purchase

an expansion franchise when the NFL decides it is ready to act.

Commandment #2 was a waste of ink. Granted, a few legal minds wanted some wiggle room on whether eminent domain had a ghost of a chance, but the Raiders case alone made Baltimore's gambit a kamikaze attack.

Everyone but the squeaky wheels near 33rd Street was ready to chuck Memorial Stadium and go new. Damn the sentiment, full speed ahead. Gwinn Owens of the *Evening Sun* was ready to cut her loose:

> On balance, taking into account the levels of comfort that fans will inevitably expect, Memorial Stadium has to go. Furthermore, I do not hold with the skeptics who insist that no new stadium should be committed without long-term leases from team owners. Business people are unlikely to commit themselves that far in advance. Insisting on long-term leases probably means no new stadium at all. Baltimore is a big city and big sports market. A first-class stadium is not going to lack for teams to play there. The stadium itself is the lure. In condemning Memorial Stadium after 31 years of thrills there, I feel a little like the Seal Eskimo putting grandpa on an ice flow. But I do not think our major-league future is very bright so long as we try to renovate the unrenovatable.

Losing the Colts in '84 got people with long memories to give ole Question P a death blow. It had been on the books since 1974, the city ordinance prohibiting any funds to be used to build a new stadium—Hyman Pressman's contribution to The Skedaddle. A new ballot initiative was whipped up hurry-scurry to reverse it in November—Question O. One contrite citizen who voted for P 10 years before wrote to the *Morning Sun*, explaining his flip-flop:

> As one who 10 years ago supported the drive to restrict public monies to Memorial Stadium only, I wholeheartedly believe that today's and tomorrow's realities make such a Charter prohibition counterproductive to this city's best interests and welfare. In 1974, Baltimore had three major-league sports franchises [sic]. Today we have only one. What this city will or won't have in these regards, four years from now, will depend on what its voters decide on November 6 [1984]. One thing is certain, however. There will be a new stadium built in the greater Baltimore area within the next several years; if not in Baltimore city, then most likely in Baltimore, Anne Arundel of Howard County. For this city with its economic and spiritual well-being at stake to be considered as a possible site for a new stadium, it must reach first base as a result of its citizens voting "For" Question O on Election Day.

With so much on the line—a chance to kick-start the stadium campaign again—the script called for a Baltimore politician to show some sanity for once. Joe DiBlasi obliged. "It's important, says City Councilman Joseph DiBlasi, that city voters understand they are not being asked to vote for or against a new sports stadium in Baltimore," the *Morning Sun* conveyed about a week before the vote. "No, that is not what Question O on the November 6 ballot is all about. It simply asks whether voters want to repeal a 10-year-old City Charter amendment that prohibits using public funds to construct a stadium other than Memorial Stadium … Mr. DiBlasi feels that it is imperative for voters to approve the question to show the National Football League it is serious when it says it wants to attract a new football team to replace the Colts, who moved to Indianapolis."

Countering DiBlasi was a stick-in-the-mud from the same 33rd-Street syndicate that pushed Question P:

On behalf of the Waverly Improvement Association's Board of Directors and general membership, I want to express our opposition to the repeal of the City Charter amendment regarding public expenditures for Memorial Stadium only. Although Waverly residents experience many inconveniences from the influx of Stadium crowds into our neighborhood, we consider Memorial Stadium an asset and agree with Mayor Schaefer that it is a perfectly good facility.

Therefore, we urge other voters to vote "no" on Question O and support renovating Memorial Stadium, rather than spending millions of already limited public funds on a new stadium.

Dorothy Dobbin [president of the Waverly Improvement Association]

Mayor Schaefer would dig in his heels down to China if he was nettled, and the stadium commotion had him ornery. The good news for the future of football in Baltimore was that folks this time paid him no mind. Question O won the day, 91,981 to 56,175—62% of the vote. Build it and they will come.

Nothing like a crisis to get the mind percolating. Having lost the Hosses and fretting over the Birds, Baltimore threw up two new stadiums within six years—Oriole Park in '92 and M&T Bank Stadium in '98. All it took was some heartbreak and gumption. In his 2024 exploration of Maryland's stadium funding, "Fans Will Love It, But Will Taxpayers See a Return on Billions Spent on Stadium Projects?" Jon Morgan explains how they came up with all that money:

The state's building boom totals at least $1.8 billion, not including borrowing costs, and is being driven by the shifting tastes of fans and insatiable profit demands of sports. Under legislation passed in 2022, $1.2 billion in state funding has been set aside to bring the Orioles and Ravens stadiums up to modern standards and upgrade heating, air conditioning and other infrastructure. That's more than the nearly $500 million it cost to build them, not accounting for inflation, when they opened 25 and 32 years ago. Another $400 million is set aside for Pimlico. The spending on Camden Yards could actually go up even further. The law established $1.2 billion as a cap on outstanding indebtedness at any given time, divided equally between each stadium. As *bonds are paid off with lottery revenue* [emphasis mine], the Maryland Stadium Authority could, with the approval of the Board of Public Works, borrow more as long as annual principal and interest payments don't exceed $90 million, and the bond maturity dates don't extend beyond the teams' leases. That sounds wonky, but it's important and has drawn the interest of other cities. The restrictions are designed to encourage the ballclubs to exercise optional extensions in their leases to unlock more money. The hope is that regular stadium upgrades will keep the teams from threatening to move, an ordeal Baltimore has endured more than once.

M&T Bank basically got financed three ways: tax-exempt revenue bonds, the state lottery to pay off the bonds and cash from the Ravens. If the MD lottery has been around since 1973, and Irsay was jawing about a new ballpark for 11 years, why didn't somebody say

Aha! and toss the lottery into the till? Baltimore took over a decade to figure it out and still choked while Indy put up the Hoosier Dome in two years.

Look on the bright side, says sportswriter Vito Stellino—you got rid of Irsay and inherited the Ravens and Steve Bisciotti. Not a bad trade:

I don't think right from the start that Irsay was interested in moving the Colts, but as time went on, he was. Obviously, he needed a new stadium. But you have to realize, in playing the long game, it was better that he left town because without that, they [Baltimore] never get two stadiums. They would've built one of those combination [football-baseball] stadiums, like in Philly and Pittsburgh. Those have become obsolete. And in the 12 years that Baltimore didn't have a team, the Colts were just awful, so they didn't really miss much. Without the Colts moving, there's no [Oriole Park at] Camden Yards. That had a huge impact on building modern baseball stadiums. It was unfortunate that Rosenbloom stuck Baltimore with Irsay and [Joe] Thomas, but in the long run, Baltimore made out. They have a much better owner [Steve Bisciotti] than the Colts do. Jimmy Irsay was way over his head in running a franchise. In the long run, it actually worked out OK, but it was certainly traumatic when they left.

Maryland taxpayers squealed in protest years before when politicians proposed siphoning money from the front end for a new stadium. Nary a peep now when it comes out the back from busted lottery tickets. That's money ill-spent, suggests Jon Morgan in "Fans Will Love It, But Will Taxpayers See a Return on Billions Spent on Stadium Projects?" "[Dennis Coates, an economist at UMBC] just wishes the public subsidies were honestly sold to taxpayers. They [stadium projects] are costly expenditures that boost a city's quality of life and enrich team owners and players but don't pay for themselves or generate riches for their host cities. In Maryland, the lottery revenue that's paying for the projects would find its way to other priorities if the stadiums weren't there. Moreover, generous lease terms have put the Orioles and Ravens among the elite of their sports both on and off the field, despite playing in a medium-sized market. It's a big reason the Orioles sold for $1.725 billion this year [2024]. *Forbes* estimates the Ravens are worth $4.63 billion." Big money--$489 million—is paying for upgrades at M&T Bank Stadium to improve the "fan experience," i.e., more cushy frippery. A sprucing up of Oriole Park at Camden Yards will cost about $400 million over the next few years. No placards or protests this time around, unlike the early '70s when Baltimoreans ruptured their spleens over a $100-million ($720 million nowadays) domed stadium funded by revenue bonds.

· · ·

Indy fans eventually got blasé even with Peyton Manning slinging it. Near the end of a 10-6 2002 season—no playoffs—the *Chicago Tribune* took note of a drop-off in fervor:

INDIANAPOLIS—It's basketball season again, and no room left in the Hoosier Sporting Inn for football's Indianapolis Colts. Empty seats in the NFL's smallest stadium greeted the Colts in their playoff quest Sunday. After they responded with a 44-27 loss to the New York Giants, the *Indianapolis Star* labeled the performance "gutless" and "disgraceful." The paper was referring to the team, not the attendance. Colts general manager Bill Polian characterized the estimated 3,000 no-shows in the 56,127-seat RCA Dome as "worrisome," especially in light of continuing speculation over the future of the franchise in the city … "What's interesting is the TV ratings are strong locally," Polian said. "It's just that people won't buy tickets, for whatever reason. I don't know why. You don't have to sit out in the cold. There's absolutely no reason why, other than maybe people aren't fans of the Colts. In all my years in this business, I've never seen anything like it. When we were in Cleveland, they had 35,000 in the Dome for the Indiana-Purdue basketball game. They'll draw 35,000 for a regular-season college basketball game, but we can't fill it up for a [Colts] game that means everything."

With Bob Irsay gone, you couldn't blame it on chaos and calamity. Polian had missed all the fun Baltimore. So where was the blowhard who boasted, "We'll love the Colts more than you guys in Baltimore did"?

Indy went through its own scare—talk of the Colts abandoning the town for L.A. Stadium issues, what else. In 2016, WTHR-TV-Indianapolis published a story by Bob Kravitz, "How Close Did the Colts Come to Relocating to LA? Closer Than You Think": "When the St. Louis Rams relocated to Los Angeles earlier this month, the flowing thought came immediately to my mind: *That could have been the Indianapolis Colts.* Don't laugh. In the early 2000s, the Colts had a foot—maybe half a foot—out the door and were seriously contemplating a move to rich and robust Los Angeles. Just like so many franchises before them and so many franchises after them, the Colts had an eye focused on LA at a time when Indianapolis was feverishly attempting to undo a terrible lease agreement with the team. It seemed to reach critical mass in 2002, when ESPN's Chris Mortensen ran with a story that suggested the Colts were all but ready to make the move as negotiations with the city slogged along with no agreement in sight." A reprise of the old song. This time it was Indy with the willies.

The dynamics were a little different, though: Jim Irsay wasn't howling about a new stadium; he just wanted the lease tweaked. But Indy had plans in the works for a new dome anyway—Lucas Oil Stadium. Jim Irsay took a gander at the plans and was hooked.

"And then came the game-changer," Kravitz wrote. "The city solicited stadium drawings from a number of architectural, stadium-building firms. Irsay was floored. Once he could actually see the possibilities, once he could see what a new stadium might look like and what it might provide in terms of revenues, he began to soften on his stance. Soon, he began to see the situation the way the city saw it." Crisis averted, fire doused.

. . .

In Baltimore, almost everyone blamed Bob Irsay for the move. But EVERYBODY wanted Indy to hand over three things, pronto: the name, the uniform, the logo. A few could rationalize—yeah, we lost the Colts, but at least we got rid of that clown Irsay. But those horseshoes—no way in hell. John Steadman lobbied Pete Rozelle about it and got a wishy-washy response: "The Colts nickname and logo could be used by Indianapolis, but the commissioner doesn't know if that will occur. 'I can't honestly say because he (owner Robert Irsay) hasn't discussed it with me. It would just be a guess. I guess they probably would.' Rozelle, a historian of the league he oversees, was aware that a Baltimore resident, Charles Evans, named the Colts in 1947. He agreed the name 'Colts' is more indigenous to Maryland than Indianapolis."

Maryland was horse-breeding territory, the home of the Preakness. The name, the helmet, the uniform, the logo, the fight song—all Baltimore's. The Irsays had nothing to do with any of it. Indy had a few two-bit racetracks for hacks, nags and plugs bound for the glue factory. They should have followed Baltimore's lead in 1947 and 1996: Have a contest to name the team; winner gets a pair of season tickets and a John Deere tractor.

Hold it right there, protested David Frick. "They will be called the Indianapolis Colts," he told the *Indianapolis Star* on March 31, 1984. "That was non-negotiable. It was on my initial list of items I wouldn't give in on. I don't apologize for being parochial." Parochial—limited or narrow in outlook. Translated: bullheaded and wrong.

A guy like Johnny Unitas should have had some pull on this one, considering he turned the Colts into a religion. "The tradition is in Baltimore," he told the *Los Angeles Times* in 1996. "There is no reason for any of us who played for Baltimore to be with Indianapolis. They have never invited me there with a personal invitation, but if they had, I would have said, 'Thank you, but no thanks.' The Colts' name belongs in Baltimore just like the Rams' name belongs in Los Angeles. If the commissioner had any power whatsoever, he would petition the owners to vote in that fashion."

Baltimore sportscaster Scott Garceau heard a funny one from Art Modell about Jim Irsay maybe selling the name back:

> Art Modell told a story that they were at a league meeting, and he goes into the men's room. Jimmy Irsay is in there. Art says hello and says, "Jimmy, why don't we do what's right and get the Colts' name back to Baltimore." I think at this point they've announced that the name "Ravens" was the winner of the contest, but it's not a done deal. I'm not gonna have the number right, but Jimmy says something like, "I would do that for $25 million," or something like that. And Art laughed and said, "That's the day I figured out that 'Ravens' was a pretty good name."

(It's probably a good time to reveal that about nine months of requesting, urging, cajoling and almost begging Jim Irsay for an interview went for nought. The official excuse: tired of being asked what happened over 40 years ago, not interested, no dice. But the real reason was probably that Jim Irsay was battling for his life, and it took all the strength he could muster just to fight the good fight.)

Most sports junkies know the up- and downsides of Jim Irsay. The man had a big heart, but he was haunted by demons. But one thing he definitely wasn't was a Xerox of his dad. In many respects, the apple fell far from the tree. Kyle Brandt from "Good Morning Football" admired how Jim Irsay wasn't your typical cardboard cutout owner: "I've always felt that Jim Irsay was unique among owners," Brandt told *Sports Illustrated*. "He became the youngest owner at 37 years old, and he had this image of the hippie, flower child, rock star owner. I think Jim Irsay was the closest thing we had to [Marvel comics character] Tony Stark in the NFL."

And the fact that Jim Irsay grooved on old rock and roll and had flaws that the world could see made him sympathetic and human. "I also think that many owners who may even be successful in football or may even be beloved in their communities aren't relatable to fans," Brandt explained. "Because how could they be? Their lives are so different. But I think in a way, Jim Irsay was. I think it was because of his flaws, because of his demons. Jim Irsay wasn't just a suit in a suite. He'd been through some stuff, and again, that's relatable. And I think despite all he endured, parts of Jim Irsay were really, really cool."

. . .

William Donald Schaefer rolled the bones with Baltimore's various lawsuits, and when he settled with Indy in March 1986, this one got yellow highlighter: "The Colts agree to discuss with the owner of an expansion or relocated Baltimore-area franchise the transfer of the name and logo 'Colts.' The obligation ends April 1, 1989." Since Commissioner Paul Tagliabue jobbed Baltimore out of several expansion derbies, April Fool's Day '89 ended that hope.

Colts QB Mark Herrmann spent his college days at Purdue, so the move had him all giddy. But in "Remembering How Colts' Move from Baltimore Went Down," he understood the hostility about Irsay making off with the name and uni. "There's a part of me that thinks, *Yeah, move on. Get over it.* But then, families have grown up cheering for the horseshoe. To see that horseshoe move to Indianapolis, it probably would have been easier for the fans if they [the Irsays] would have changed the (Colts) mascot and left that there. That would have eased the pain a little bit. Generations grew up with the Colts. There was that relationship, that feeling that this is our team and you took our team away. As pathetic as it is for those folks to hold this venom against the city of Indianapolis, there's a part down deep that appreciates the loyalty."

Even more empathy and sympathy came from veteran *Indianapolis Star* sportswriter Mike Chappell:

One of the major burrs in the butt in Baltimore is that Irsay took the name, took the logo, took the history. I totally understand Baltimore's angst and lingering anger. But I talked to Jim Irsay about it. He said, "This is our family's business—it's part of the family." So, I understand why they did it [took the name], but it was a mistake that was not repeated when Baltimore got the Browns. The Irsays would have fought tooth and nail to keep the family business intact, logo and all. And we can argue that until hell freezes over. I know it always angers people in Baltimore that the club records include the Baltimore days. In the Colts media guide, Johnny Unitas is prominently in there, Lenny Moore and all that. It's really awkward. If I'm Jim and Bob Irsay, I'd probably do the same thing. But I think that's probably 80% of the lingering anger for people in Baltimore.

Forthwith, some of the goofiest team-name transfers in sports history, bearing in mind that only a scoundrel would hijack the name Colts to Indianapolis: 1) the Brooklyn Trolley Dodgers to L.A., which ditched streetcars after WWII; 2) the New Orleans Jazz to Utah, one of the least hip places in America; 3) the Minneapolis Lakers to L.A., 1,800 miles from Lake Superior; 4) the St. Louis Cardinals to Phoenix, where a cardinal sighting is as rare as Halley's comet. There oughta be a law.

Longtime sportswriter Vito Stellino doesn't think Indianapolis Colts rolls around in the palate: "I remember [veteran NFL exec] George Young saying, 'I just wish they would take the horseshoes off the helmets.' But in those days, teams kept their names. The Minneapolis Lakers moved to L.A., and there are no lakes in Los Angeles. They kept the Laker name. That was ridiculous. But what *really* annoys me is Indianapolis still tries to claim the legacy of the AAFC [All-American Football Conference] team in Baltimore. The team that moved had *nothing* to do with the late '40s-early '50s team [in Baltimore]. They'll talk [in Indianapolis] about Johnny Unitas. I don't know that the guy ever stepped foot in Indianapolis. They still use their records, and that's also annoying. Indianapolis is not horse country."

Professor Charles Euchner, author of *Playing the Game: Why Sports Teams Move and Cities Fight to Keep Them*, makes a sage point about brand names:

We're talking about two things: one is the brand, and the other is identity. I guess it kind of cuts both ways. When the Colts moved to Indianapolis, did it really matter that they were called the Colts, instead of the Hoosiers or something like that? What else would you call a team from Indiana? When the A's moved from Philly to K.C., then to Oakland, to Sacramento and to Las Vegas, are they really the A's anymore? Do they have *any* kind of touchstone with Connie Mack and Philadelphia anymore? So, then, it's just like carrying something forward that doesn't really have any point to it anymore. When you look at how we talk every day, we use all kinds of expressions that we don't know the origins of. I think a lot of names and brands have that kind of quality. They become logos. It doesn't make you visualize anything but what the current brand is.

Case in point: the Dodgers. Other than baseball wonks and hopeless cranks in Flatbush, who connects that brand with dodging trolleys anymore?

. . .

For John Steadman, seeing the Colts leave was like getting his wisdom teeth removed with nose pliers. His love for the Colts and his churlish hatred for Carroll Rosenbloom got played up in a September 1984 *Washington Post* article:

It was a Pat O'Brien kind of world that John Steadman lived in, with good guys and bad guys. Nothing so inspired him in those early days [of his career] as a half-baked idea called the Baltimore Colts … Steadman boosted the team and in 1955 left his sportswriting job to become assistant general manager and publicity director. Steadman, who is described by colleagues as "the least mercenary man I have ever met" and "naïve," was shaken, he says, when he saw owner Rosenbloom paying off sportswriters to win their good will. Rosenbloom's maneuverings did nothing to shake Steadman's devotion to the Colts. Throughout their halcyon years, Steadman remained a faithful and tireless booster. It was always Steadman's contention that the team belonged to Baltimore, not to the clothing manufacturer with the New York penthouse.

Steadman never passed up the chance to spin that Rosenbloom payola yarn with anyone who would bend an ear. What he *never* did was back it up with concrete evidence.

Nine years after Rosenbloom got put in the ground, Steadman was still taking potshots. In March 1987, he baited Eugene "Reds" Hubbe, the guy who used to walk the gravel path inside Memorial Stadium with the "We Love Our Colts" sign: "The pain of not having a team has been unbearable. I don't know if I can go through another evening of grief [on the anniversaries of the move]. I haven't been myself since that woeful March night of three years ago. Our property was stolen

away. The fans created the Baltimore Colts. We were the ones who brought them back, not Carroll Rosenbloom, who became a multimillionaire at our expense, or the other stiff he sold out to in 1972." For the umpteenth time, Hubbe is spouting the Steadman mantra, so let's clarify: 1) Irsay didn't "steal" anything; the club was his; 2) Bert Bell Sr. and Rosenbloom brought the Colts to Baltimore, not the fans, pal; and 3) Rosenbloom was already a multimillionaire when he bought the club; where do you think he got the cash in the first place?

A little over a year before Steadman passed in 2000, the *Morning Sun* paid tribute to the streak: 719 consecutive Baltimore Colts/Ravens football games. But avoiding the Steadman-Rosenbloom war was impossible, even in a feel-good piece:

In the early 1970s, Steadman drew Rosenbloom's ire after writing that fans shouldn't be charged full prices for exhibitions, a position he still advocates. Rosenbloom made it difficult for him to cover games, and according to Steadman, even tried to get him fired. "I had a lot of trouble getting him a credential," [Ernie] Accorsi recalled. "In those days, everyone flew on the team charter and stayed in the team hotel. I couldn't make him any reservations. He had to do everything on his own. And he never flinched, never complained." Steadman's opinion of Rosenbloom—"an evil man"—is even lower than his assessment of Irsay, whom he described as "a drunk who was not responsible for himself." When Irsay took the Colts to Indianapolis on March 28, 1984, Steadman thought Baltimore would get a team back within a year. The Colts' departure created a 245-game void, including preseason and postseason.

Given Irsay's bumbling body of work, Steadman's crucifixion of Rosenbloom was around the bend, over the top, downright malevolent. The hatred was obvious and ugly. With a thousand former players, employees and regular folk ready to line up and sing C.R.'s praises, let's reprise loan shark Tony Gazzo in *Rocky I*: "Some guys, they just hate for no reason. Capisce?"

Al Davis takes the Raiders to L.A. Rozelle takes him to court. Davis kicks his fanny. Robert Irsay bails out of Baltimore. Schaefer and Co. take him to court. Irsay triumphs. It was open season on host cities. In April 1984, Frank Deford lamented the new sports landscape:

Here's another Colt question: In what cities did the Colt franchise fail before it came to Baltimore? Answer: New York and Dallas. Imagine that, Baltimore supporting a football team when New York and Dallas couldn't! Look it up. And now, just because some egomaniacal carpetbagger named Irsay needs to cover his mistakes, the Colts leave Baltimore under cover of darkness. Of course, it's much easier now for the modern highwaymen who own sports franchises to use up cities and throw them away. Thanks to the antitrust laws, they don't have to ask for anybody's permission; all they need is a credit card to get a moving van in.

Sure, the courts turned owners loose to hopscotch around the country, looking for deals. But take a good gander in the mirror, Baltimore. No absolution for you. Not for choking in the clutch. "I think what Baltimore fans should realize is that the city itself—even some of the fans—got caught in an era that was changing rapidly, and they did not change with it," declared documentarian Troy Lowman. "That's the gist of it all. They just didn't change with the times. And that still happens today. If you don't change with the times, you could lose your team."

. . .

Owners espied luxury boxes in the early '70s as a new cash cow. They built the first one in the Astrodome in 1965; the first such boxes at the Indianapolis Motor Speedway were dubbed "Turn Two Suites." When they opened Miami's Joe Robbie Stadium in 1987, the joint had 216 suites, some with 10-year leases at $65,000 per year, easy money for Joe. When Bob Irsay first ambled through the Hoosier Dome, he gawked at the blue seats and heard ka-ching: upstairs, 104 luxury suites. Memorial Stadium had no suites, lousy bathrooms, rats and 1950s ambience.

The *Los Angeles Times* took a look in 1987 at the new refuge for NFL tycoons:

Skyboxes, the glittering private suites lining the rims of more and more stadiums and bringing in profits that, unlike ordinary ticket sales, do **NOT** [emphasis mine] have to be shared with visiting teams. Often equipped with closed-circuit television and wet bars, they lease for as much as $80,000 a year, each. And corporations are lining up to pay that price to entertain their customers at stadiums around the country, even though the new tax law terminated the deduction for the cost. With player salaries rising and television revenues leveling off—or worse—in the aftermath of the [players'] strike, skyboxes represent a sure way for the owners to keep big profits rolling in. "They are a source of great revenue, without which a club has almost no chance whatever of breaking even, much less making a profit," said [former Redskins owner Jack Kent] Cooke, who has complained that he loses money on the Redskins each year.

That said, imagine the pinch on Irsay's wallet in Baltimore with only 25,000 rumps in the seats, a nickel-and-dime TV/Radio contract, a penny-ante cut on concessions and all the bills to pay. No wonder his son said he was in rough shape and looking for extra cash. Thus, the inevitable circle-back to the stadium. "They probably should have committed to saying, 'Yeah, let's build him a new stadium,'" Indianapolis Colts writer JJ Stankevitz professed. "I think with a new stadium there's a good chance the Colts would still be in Baltimore. But that didn't happen. They didn't have the will to do that; they didn't think they needed it. And here we are today—now you got the Ravens. They're awfully successful, and they got a new stadium. The Colts are here in Indy, and they're successful. We got a new stadium [Lucas Oil Stadium]. It all worked out the way it worked out."

The kumbaya ending belies the heartache and hardship Baltimore endured to get there. They also had to take a crash course in realpolitik. "A community can't rest on its laurels and think that, because the team is here, it's *always* gonna be here," former Baltimore Mayor Kurt Schmoke admitted in the documentary, *The Ghosts of 33rd Street*. "It's just a competitive environment that has changed. It's unfortunate because I think there's a connection that a community develops with a sports team, you know, like a football team. But I don't think Baltimore will *ever* be in the situation where we believe it can't happen to us." Which is what caught them flatfooted, naïve, nonchalant and downright harebrained while Irsay traversed the country.

Suppose Irsay had left daily ops in the hands of superior football minds like GM Ernie Accorsi and Ted Marchibroda (when Ted let Bert Jones air it out); suppose they hadn't sent Bert out to get dismembered in Detroit during preseason '78, wrecking his slingshot; suppose Irsay had told Mikey, the Wannabe

GM to stay in Chicago until further ordered and write "Whereas," "Whilst," "Whereupon" and "Whereby" on the blackboard 1,000 times; and suppose the outdoor insane asylum was filled to the brim every Sunday. Irsay probably would have observed a moratorium on shopping, and Baltimore would have remained clueless and presumptuous. Given that, it's obvious now that Irsay would have pivoted back to the concrete bowl on 33rd Street and started regurgitating the old gripes, demanding action. Minus a new stadium, the town was bent on getting jilted. Veteran Baltimore sportscaster Scott Garceau opined on what Baltimore could/should have done:

> Number one would have been to find a different owner than Bob Irsay. And number two, find another way to have top-flight facilities. Right now, the Ravens have a great training facility; M&T Bank Stadium is a great facility. Camden Yards is a great facility even though it has a little age on it now. Keep your facilities up-to-date. If there are 32 teams in the league, you don't wanna have the 30th- or 32nd-ranked stadium. You don't have to have the first or second, but you gotta stay competitive because that stadium produces a revenue stream. But the biggest thing is to have a winning team. With that, you're gonna fill the seats. But the game is driven so much by shared TV revenue today that all that might not be as important in football as it was in the early '80s when the Colts

were here, certainly not in the '50s when Johnny U and the Colts were making the NFL the product that it would become.

One thing for sure happened after the Raiders and Colts moved, back-to-back: The alarm was sounded. "At least for a lot of cities, it created a sense of urgency, like, 'Yeah. It *can* happen. We can't equivocate forever. We really have to figure out what our position is and build a coalition. Or if we don't care, that's fine too, but we need to say it,'" stated Charlie Euchner, author of *Playing the Game.* "In other words, we need to be honest, and we need to act. If this really matters to us, we need to do something about it, rather than just kick the can down the road. A lot of cities felt a great amount of urgency to get something done. That's why the Orioles' stadium ended up working. If the Colts hadn't left, the path forward for the Orioles would have been different." And Baltimore did none of that for the Colts, not when they should have anyway.

Upton Bell, NFL guru, said it best: It's the *team*, stupid. According to former TV newsman Andy Barth, that's the hard lesson learned:

> I think you couldn't help but realize that teams needed and would demand nice facilities, up-to-date, clean, efficient, safe facilities, and Baltimore went ahead [after the move] and built two of them, two of the best. And success followed. Most people would say that those two new stadiums were successful, helped the city, were worth the money put

into them, that it was something that we *had* to do. It was a lesson for everybody: You can't go out there without a modern, attractive stadium and expect to recruit a team or keep a team. It's partly why the city fathers and stadium directors insist on long leases because there's always gonna be someone else building a newer one.

In '84, Baltimore got schooled by Indy and vowed never to screw up like that again.

Team owners have long known they have host cities by the short hairs and a mere wink at a suitor brings hysterics. Not a whole lot will change in the near future, says Jack Noonan in *The Boom in Franchise Relocations: Moving Cities, No Matter the Cost*:

The current state of professional sports allows the individual team owners to have too much power. The unregulated power gives a type of free authorization to team owners when deciding whether to move their franchises to cities. If the league tries to stop them, the team can sue the league, and most likely win, under antitrust law claiming the league is restricting their team's free trade to move cities. As a result, cities are having to submit to demands from the teams to build brand-new stadiums, mainly from the taxpayer's pocket.

These scares come like 17-year cicadas—an owner gets to grousing about something,

rumors fly, fans and officials get the heebie-jeebies, and it goes one way or the other, the owner playing puppet-master. Item: In 1997, even Indy got some night sweats. Robin Miller of the *Indianapolis Star* explained:

The Irsays are shipping big crates to Ohio daily. Jim Brown is helping Marshall Faulk pick out a house in Cleveland. Jim Irsay was seen dining in The Flats [in Indianapolis] the other night with the president of the Dawg Pound. Trucks are taking furniture out of the Colts' complex on West 56th Street and heading east on I-70. It's a done deal for 1998… the Cleveland Colts. You've heard it, I've heard it, and Jimmy Irsay's dealt with it every day since ESPN's Chris Mortensen guaranteed it a few months ago. No matter how many times Irsay denies it, the buzz around the country is that Indianapolis's NFL franchise is Not For Long because the city can't afford the Colts and the Pacers.

Just a bowl of applesauce, as it turned out. But the threat is always there, and the paranoia and shakes soon follow. All part of life as the host city these days.

Heck, even Kansas City got rattled in 2024—after two straight Super Bowl wins and fans pledging eternal fealty. Imagine that: The Hunt syndicate was grousing about Arrowhead. Alex Kirshner in slate.com described the ploy:

The franchise wants to facilitate the $800 million in upgrades to Arrowhead Stadium, which would help the Hunt family that owns the team make more money. The Hunts, who are worth at least several billion dollars, say they'll kick in $300 million. That leaves taxpayers to cover the other $500 million before any cost overruns. The Chiefs hope that voters will OK a 40-year extension of a three-eighths-of-a-cent sales tax in Jackson County, one that costs a resident 38 cents per every $100 they spend in the county. According to the *Kansas City Star*, taxpayers are still paying back hundreds of millions of dollars from the *last* time Kansas City's football and baseball stadiums were renovated. Chiefs president Mark Donovan told the city's NBC affiliate last week that if voters didn't extend the tax, the Chiefs "would just have to look at all our options." A reporter asked if that meant leaving the city the team has always called home, and Donovan said, "I think they would have to include leaving Kansas City." He then said the team would be "willing to accept a deal" to stick around its home city.

We've seen this in mob movies—some guy with a bent nose walks into a bar and tells the owner he must now pay for protection from other thugs. "And if you don't, fella … Say, you've got a wife and kids, right?" As old as the hills. "The Chiefs are making one of the least credible attempts in the history of stadium strong-arming," Kirshner wrote. "Not only are they not going to leave the Kansas City area; they are unlikely even to leave the site of Arrowhead Stadium, a certainly profitable venue that is already one of the envies of the football world … Can taxpayers win a game of chicken against a sports team owner who is clearly bluffing?"

The thumbs-down in K.C. left no doubt. "Jackson County voters have resoundingly voted against a sales tax extension to fund stadium projects for the Chiefs and Royals," KCTV-Channel 5 declared on April 2, 2024. "With 100% of its precincts reporting, Kansas City voted 30,791 for No and 22,399 for Yes. Jackson County voted along the same lines: No—47,561, Yes—34,207." The bluff tanked.

Power to the People.

Baltimore didn't get its second wind to scrap for a ballclub right away. First, a little grieving was in order. Charlie Euchner described the abrasions and contusions on a town's psyche when a team quits on it:

> However upsetting all these developments may be, the transfer of a sports franchise produces the most devastating effects. Psychologists have compared the loss of a sports franchise to the trauma experienced at the death of a loved one. Popular opinion holds that teams have a responsibility to the city, that sports is as much a matter of community and culture as it is industry and commerce. By their own reckonings, teams are integral

parts of their communities because, as one study puts it, they provide "a sense of continuity and unity in a discontinuous and increasingly atomized society." When teams move or threaten to move, they upset a fragile relationship—a relationship based increasingly on profit seeking but undergirded by the lore of community values.

WISH-TV in Indy interviewed a kid pockmarked with zits wearing a varsity jacket as the vans rolled in on March 29, 1984: "I've been a football fan all my life, and I'm just really excited that they're gonna be here, right in my backyard." They then stuck the mic in front of Baltimore reporter Russ Robinson, who offered the yang to that yin: "It hurts to see them go. It leaves a big hole in the community, especially the way it happened, you know, with the vans coming in in the middle of the night and being loaded up. It's a bitter disappointment." Such are the emotions after a tug of war between two cities over a ballclub.

Had The Bard witnessed The Move, he had enough material for play #39: *All's Well That Ends Well—Except in Baltimore*. It had all the elements, says veteran Colts beat reporter Mike Chappell:

A Shakespearian tragedy. You got the triumph and the tragedy. You couldn't have had two more extreme situations. You wake up on March 29, and you see this snowy scene of the Mayflower trucks pulling away. This is back when we didn't have social media. So, people wake up in Baltimore, and they say, "What do you mean, we don't have a team anymore?!" And people wake up in Indy and say, "We got the team? Hallelujah!" The shock on each end—at two extremes—that's what just jumps out at me. How one city and its surrounding community had to deal with the fact that, all of a sudden, you were no longer a part of the NFL; you just weren't. And the other city is celebrating: "We got a freakin' team! And good for us." People here weren't thumbing their noses at Baltimore at all. Baltimore wasn't in their thoughts. It wasn't like, "Sorry, Baltimore. We got the team, you lost the team." No, it was just, "This is about *us*." It just had an incredible, contrasting impact on two cities.

• • •

More moves will come down the road. That's a given. Some owner will get a crabapple stuck in his craw, and he'll thumb through the playbook: Walter O'Malley, Al Davis, Charlie Finley, Robert Irsay, et al., editors. The premise: I want what I want, and if I don't get what I want, hasta la vista. But no matter how those moves go down, odds are Bob Irsay's slapstick odyssey will trump them all. TMZ could get a ton of mileage out of it: how 'bout calling it *The Midnight Skedaddle*? Weird Al Yankovic could parody Neil Diamond's "Brother Love's Traveling Salvation Show" (original lyrics available online):

Flitting here and there like a spinning
   top,
And then he decides to Indy he'll bop.
I'm gone, Brother Bob say.
Brother Bob's Traveling Migration Show;
Pack up the players and screw
   Little Mayor
And everything goes
'Cause everyone knows Brother
   Bob's show.

And how about a tribute to the old Baltimore Colts and the folks in Indianapolis who won the club in a fair fight? It's set to the Ol' Blue Eyes tune about the Brooklyn Dodgers: "There Used to Be a Ballpark":

There Used to Be a Ballclub

And there used to be a ballclub,
   a champ in days of yore
Until a guy named Irsay became a
   drunken bore.

And the club became a clown show,
   the mayhem very clear.
Yes, there used to be a ballclub,
   right here.
And the boss, he had a lackey,
   a meddling mouthpiece malign.
With Machiavelli Chernoff they
   wrecked the club by design.
Sad fans watched in horror at
   harebrained stunts of the
   bungling puppeteer.
And there used to be a ballclub,
   right here.
Then the despot packed up his
   kingdom and loaded up the vans,
Headed west to a town called Indy
   and broke the hearts of fans.
And the folks woke up next morning,
   saw their club had disappeared
And told each other, "Screw that guy.
   We gotta persevere."
Yes, there used to be a ballclub,
   right here.

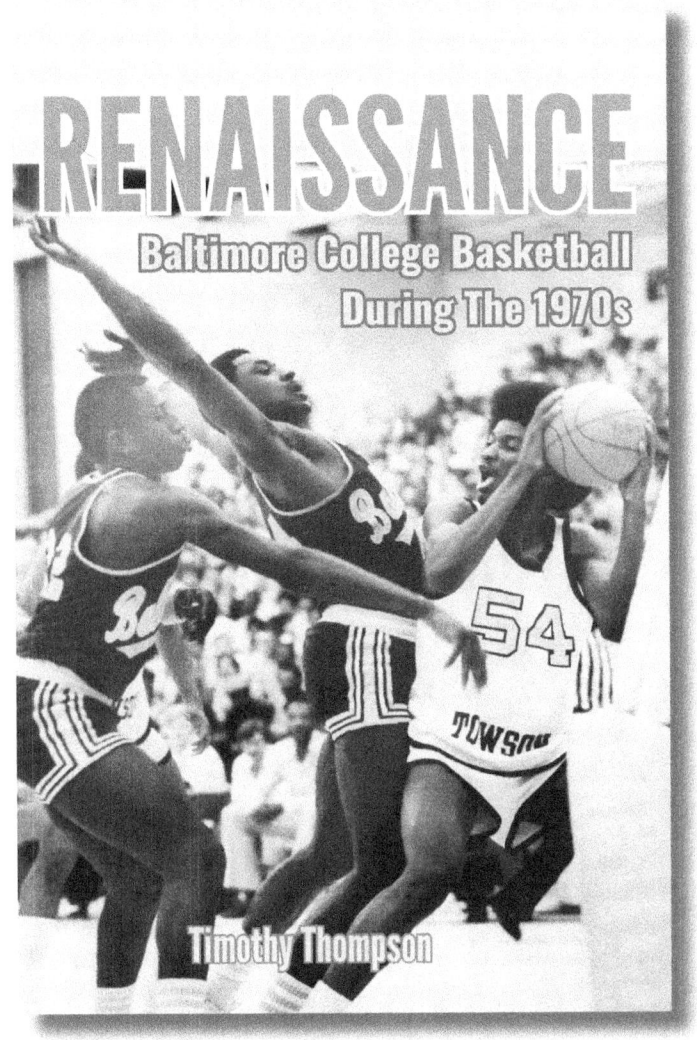

In *RENAISSANCE*, author Timothy Thompson takes us back to a golden age of Baltimore basketball—the 1970s—when many factors coalesced to turn Baltimore colleges into basketball powerhouses.

RENAISSANCE explores the perfect storm that created a magical time in Baltimore sports history, when each local school had its turn on center-stage to enjoy the glory of packed gyms, championships and life in the spotlight. No era in Baltimore basketball history—before or since—rivals the 1970s renaissance.

RENAISSANCE brings that golden age back to life.

AVAILABLE NOW ON AMAZON